THE WORKS OF SRI CHINMOY

TALKS & ESSAYS

VOLUME II

THE WORKS OF SRI CHINMOY

TALKS & ESSAYS

VOLUME II

★

MY ROSE PETALS

FIFTY FREEDOM-BOATS TO
ONE GOLDEN SHORE

LYON · OXFORD

GANAPATI PRESS

XC

© 2021 THE SRI CHINMOY CENTRE

ISBN 978-1-911319-34-4

See appendix for notice regarding this edition.

FIRST EDITION WENT TO PRESS ON 7 APRIL 2021

TALKS & ESSAYS

VOLUME II

PART 1

MY ROSE PETALS

MY ROSE PETALS

BOOK 1

1. Is death the end?

Death is not the end. Death can never be the end.

Death is the road. Life is the traveller. The soul is the guide.

When the traveller is tired and exhausted, the guide instructs the traveller to take either a short or a long rest, and then again the traveller's journey begins.

In the spiritual life, when an aspirant does not cry for a higher light, bliss and power, it is the birth of his death.

In the ordinary life, when an unaspiring man wallows in the mire of ignorance, it is the real victory of death.

What can we learn from the inner life which desires the extinction of death? The inner life tells us that life is soulfully precious, time is fruitfully precious.

Life without the aspiration of time is meaningless.

Time without the aspiration of life is useless.

Our mind thinks of death. Our heart thinks of life. Our soul thinks of Immortality. Mind and death can be transcended. Heart and life can be expanded. Soul and Immortality can be fulfilled.

When the mind and death are transcended, man will have a new home: Light, the Light of the Beyond.

When the soul and Immortality are fulfilled, man will have a new goal: Delight, the transcendental Delight.

Today man feels that death is an unavoidable necessity.

Tomorrow man will feel that Immortality is an unmistakable reality.

Unfortunately, most of us cherish wrong conceptions of death. We think death is something unusual, it is something destructive. But we have to know that right now death is something natural, normal, and to some extent, inevitable.

Lord Krishna tells Arjuna, "Oh Arjuna, certain is death for

the born and certain is birth for the dead. Therefore what is inevitable ought not be a cause for thy sorrow."

The Chāndogya Upanishad tells us something significant:

> When the hour of death approaches (that is to say, in the final hour), what should we do? We should take refuge in three sublime thoughts: we are indestructible; we can never be shaken; we are the very essence of life.

When the hour of death approaches us, if we feel that we can never be destroyed, nothing can shake us and we are the very essence of life, then where is sorrow, where is fear, where is death? No death.

Sarada Devi, the consort of Sri Ramakrishna, said something very significant. She said, "The difference between a spiritual man and an ordinary man is very simple. Easily you can know the difference between the two. An ordinary man cries and sheds bitter tears when death approaches him; whereas a spiritual man, if he is really spiritual, he will laugh and laugh when death approaches him, for to him death is fun, nothing else."

Here we have to say that a spiritual man enters into the cosmic game; he becomes a conscious instrument of the cosmic game. That is why he knows that death is not an extinction. It is only a short or long rest.

Again and again, we shall have to come back into the world. We have to work for God, here on earth. There is no escape. We have to realise the Highest here on earth. We have to fulfil the Highest on earth. God will not allow us to waste or squander the potentialities and possibilities of the soul. Impossible.

Kipling's immortal utterance runs,

> They will come back, come back again,
> As long as the red Earth rolls.
> He never wasted a leaf or a tree.
> Do you think He would squander souls?

Each incarnation is leading us towards a higher life, a better life. We are in the process of evolution. Each incarnation is a rung in the ladder of evolution. Man is progressing consciously and unconsciously. But if he makes progress in each incarnation consciously, then he is expediting his spiritual progress. His realisation will be much faster than those who are making progress unconsciously.

We know we started our journey from the mineral life, and then we entered into the plant life. Then we entered into the animal kingdom. From there we have come into the human world. But here is not the end. We have to grow into divine beings. Unless and until we have become divinised and transformed, God will not be satisfied with us. He can manifest in us and through us only when we are totally transformed and fully illumined and divinised. So when we think of our evolution, inner evolution and outer evolution, we get abundant joy. We lose nothing, nothing in the so-called death.

Jalalu'd-din Rumi most beautifully and soulfully tells us about evolution:

> A stone I died and rose again a plant,
> A plant I died and rose an animal;
> I died an animal and was born a man.
> Why should I fear? What have I lost by death?

What is death after all? Death is a sleeping child. And what is life? Life is a child that is playing, singing, dancing at every moment before the Father.

Death is the sleeping child inside the heart of the Inner Pilot. Life is inspiration. Life is aspiration. Life is realisation. Life is not the reasoning mind. Life is not the intellectual mind. Life is not a game of frustration. No.

Life is the message of divinity on earth. Life is God's conscious channel to fulfil divinity in humanity on earth.

There is much truth in what Confucius says, "We don't know life. How can we know death?"

Now I wish to say, we can know life. If we know life, realise life as God's embodiment of truth, light, peace and bliss, then we know what life truly is, and death is nothing but a rest, and a rest is necessary at the present stage of evolution.

There will come a time when rest will not be necessary at all. Only Life will reign supreme — the Life of the Beyond, the Life of the ever-transcending Beyond. This life is not and cannot be the sole monopoly of an individual. No. Each human being is to be flooded with this Life of the ever-transcending Beyond, for it is here in this Life Divine that God will manifest Himself unreservedly — here, here on earth.

2. The end of all knowledge

> *Aum.*
> *Pūrṇam adaḥ, pūrṇam idam, pūrṇāt pūrṇam udacyate.*
> *Pūrṇasya pūrṇam ādāya pūrṇam evāvaśiṣyate.*

> Infinity is that.
> Infinity is this.
> From Infinity, Infinity has come into existence.
> From Infinity, when Infinity is taken away,
> Infinity remains.

The end of all knowledge. The end of all knowledge is God-knowledge. This knowledge tells man what he can eventually be. This knowledge tells man that he can have a conscious and inseparable oneness with God.

Here at this point, the Son of God tells us, "I and my Father are one". On the strength of his highest realisation and inseparable oneness with his Father, he says, "I and my Father are one."

God-knowledge tells us that God is not only within us and not only for us, but also we are, each human being, is *of* Him. Finally, this God-knowledge tells us that each human being has to become God Himself.

Brahmāsmi... "I am the Brahman. I am God." This is what we have learned from the Vedic seers of yore. The Vedic seers realised the supreme Truth and then offered the supreme Truth to mankind. Today's man, today's unrealised, unfulfilled man is tomorrow's realised and fulfilled God.

The end of human knowledge is the beginning of the divine knowledge. The divine knowledge and human ignorance — these are two things we see in our day-to-day life. The divine knowledge is an illumining, fulfilling and immortalising power. The human ignorance is a mad elephant, a destructive power. The divine knowledge is the very birth of Immortality. Human ignorance is the song of death.

I am sure most of you are well acquainted with our Upanishads. There is an Upanishad named Kanshitaki Upanishad. Unfortunately, this Upanishad is not well known. This Upanishad offers a sublime knowledge, wisdom. It says,

> Speech is not what one should desire to
> understand.
> One should know the speaker...
> The deed is not what one should desire to

understand. One should know the doer...
Mind is not what one should desire to understand.
One should know the thinker.

Here at this point, I wish to say from the spiritual point of view, peace, light and bliss, these qualities are not what one desires to understand, but one has to know the living embodiment of peace, light, bliss and power. It is he who can bring to the fore these divine qualities — the peace, light and bliss of the sincere aspiring souls. It is he who has the capacity to inspire the seekers, and at the same time, it is he who is of considerable help to awaken the slumbering consciousness of human souls. It is he who expedites the seeker's journey.

The end of all knowledge is self-knowledge. "Know thyself", which all of you are familiar with. The Sanskrit term for it is *Ātmānam viddi*. Know thyself. How can we know ourselves? We have to know ourselves by taking help from someone who has already known himself. He is our teacher. He is our private tutor and not a school teacher. A school teacher is entitled to examine us, to pass or fail us, but this private tutor helps us to pass the examination well. He wholeheartedly teaches us, helps us to pass the examination. So a spiritual teacher is a private tutor and not a school teacher.

Self-knowledge is self-discovery, and in self-discovery we feel the conquest of our own self. Self-discovery, God-knowledge and self-conquest — these are one and the same.

The *Welsh Triad* says,

> There are three kinds of men:
> man in man, who does good for good and evil for
> evil; man in God, who does good for evil;
> and man in the devil, who does evil for good.

In our spiritual life, we have one more category: the man of God, the messenger of God, the representative of God, the channel of God, the instrument of God. This instrument of God constantly feels that he is not the doer; he is a mere instrument.

Lord Sri Krishna in the Bhagavad-Gita, the Song Celestial, tells his dearest friend and disciple, Arjuna, *Nimitta mātram bhava savyasāchin*, You just become an instrument."

So the man of God feels in the inmost recesses of his heart that he is a mere instrument. He works for God, he lives for God. He feels that God-realisation is not enough. He feels that God-manifestation here on earth is of paramount importance.

Many have realised the Highest, the transcendental Truth. There are few who cry for the perfection of humanity. There are very few who try to change the face of the world. The chosen instruments of God want to manifest God here on earth. They do not care much for earthly good or evil. They transcend the so-called good and evil. They care only for God's inner dictates. Constantly they listen to the dictates of their Inner Pilot and then on the strength of their oneness, inseparable oneness with their Inner Pilot, they offer their selfless, dedicated service to humanity. They try to offer knowledge, divine knowledge, to aspiring humanity. Again, they tell humanity that God-realisation is not their sole monopoly.

Everybody has to realise God, the transcendental Truth. Everybody is destined to realise the highest Truth, but he who cries for the inner light will naturally reach the goal sooner than the one who is still fast asleep.

The great Saviour has taught us, "No man can serve two masters." Here we have two masters: ignorance and knowledge. Now if we want to wallow in the pleasures and mires of ignorance, we are serving ignorance the master. Again, it is we who have the opportunity to serve the other master, knowledge, the light. Now if we aspire, then our master is knowledge and knowledge-light. If we want to serve our master, knowledge-light, then the message of realisation, the message of perfection can never remain a far cry.

The immortal poet, George Eliot sings, "Our deeds still travel with us from afar, and what we have been makes us what we are."

From the spiritual point of view, what do we learn from this soulful message? We come to learn that we have been victims to teeming desires and here is the result: we are still earth-bound. We are bound by the fetters of ignorance; we are caught. We want to possess the world. To our widest surprise and sorrow, we are already caught, we are already possessed.

Now again, it is we who have the capacity, potentiality, opportunity to free ourselves from the mire of ignorance. If we aspire today, tomorrow we are growing into a divine reality, and in that divine reality our realisation will loom large.

We have to know at every moment that we have to be true to ourselves. Do we want light? Do we want perfection? Or just out of curiosity do we want to have an iota of light and truth? Unless and until we are true to ourselves, true to our inner quest, we can never, never see the face of reality, fulfilment and perfection.

Most of you know that the immortal poet, Shakespeare, in *Hamlet* says,

> This above all: to thine own self be true,
> And it must follow, as the night the day,
> Thou canst not then be false to any man.

If we really want the inner light, if we really have the inner cry to see God face to face, there can be nothing either on earth or in Heaven to deny us, deny our soul's inmost quest. Each individual being has limited freedom. This freedom can be utilised either to aspire or to desire. If we desire, the teeming clouds will undoubtedly eclipse our knowledge-sun. If we aspire, God, the Inner Pilot will inspire us to run fast, faster, fastest towards the destined Goal, the Goal of the Beyond.

When we enter into the spiritual life, we come to realise that there is no end to our journey. Today we may think that this is the goal we have been crying for. But when we go deep within, we feel that today's goal is tomorrow's starting point.

God is in everything. We have to see God in everything, feel God in everything, in every human being. But that is not enough. We have to see, feel, realise; then we have to go one step further. We have to realise that there is no end to our realisation. Every moment we have to feel that on the strength of our highest realisation, we are going, we are running towards the ever-transcending Beyond.

The end of all knowledge is God-knowledge. We have to see God. This is the ultimate knowledge. Now, there are three ways to see God. One way is to see God through a window. This we can do if we concentrate daily, say, for six hours on God. But if we want to see God through an open door, then we have to meditate. We have to meditate daily for at least twelve hours. But if we want to see God face to face, as you are seeing me and I am seeing you, then we have to meditate twenty-four hours a day.

To see God constantly face to face is the beginning and blossoming of the transcendental Knowledge.

3. Perfection-Goal

Perfection is the seeker's fulfilling realisation and fulfilled manifestation. Everything else has dawned on earth save perfection, perfect Perfection.

Perfection is the tree.

Perfect Perfection is the fruit.

Man's speculation about perfection is his ignorance. Man's concentration on perfection is his knowledge. Man's meditation on perfection is his wisdom. Man's contemplation on perfection is his world-illumining, world-transforming inner eye.

> God's Message is Perfection.
> Man's message is temptation.
> God's Message is Perfection.
> Man's message is frustration.
> God's Message is Perfection.
> Man's message is destruction.

Perfection-Goal and the freedom-soul go together. He who reaches the state of freedom-soul has conquered his inner life and immortalised his outer life. He is the chosen instrument of God. He is the direct channel of God. He is the representative of God here on earth.

Cry and try.

When we cry to see the transcendental Light and when we try to perfect our outer nature, our perfection does not remain a far cry. Perfection is ours.

Exert and control.

When we exert the divine in us and control the animal in us, perfection begins to dawn within us. The flower of perfection blooms.

See and be.

When we try to see the truth with the Eye of God, not with our eyes, and when we consciously try to be the surrendered instrument of God, perfection in no time dawns. The Golden All of perfection beckons our aspiring hearts. It is true that perfection cannot be achieved overnight. Realisation cannot be achieved all at once. It takes time.

Let me tell you a story.

A young seeker once came up to a spiritual Master for initiation and was duly initiated. Then the following day he said, "Master, now that you have initiated me, you have to give me realisation. I want to see God."

The Master said, "My child, how is it possible for you to realise God in one day?"

Two days later, he said, "Oh, I want to realise God."

The Master said, "You are not ready."

A few days later, again the same question: "Master, I want to realise God." He had not completed his task. He had not launched into the spiritual path properly. Just the other day the Master had initiated him, but now he was crying for realisation without following the proper method. Without swimming in the sea of aspiration, he wanted to realise God.

On his way to the Ganges for a dip, the Master invited this particular disciple to come with him. As the two entered the water, the Master pressed the disciple's head underwater for a couple of minutes. When he released it, the Master asked, "What did you feel when I pressed your head into the water?"

"Master, I gasping for air. I was practically dying and I thought I would not survive. The moment you released me, I got my life back."

The Master said, "If you can come to that same state of consciousness and feel that without God you cannot live even for a few minutes, you will realise God. You will realise God at that moment on the strength of your highest aspiration. Your inmost inner flame has to be kindled, and then you have to cry — cry for God as a child cries for his mother. Only then is God-Realisation possible."

The disciple learned the lesson. Truly and soulfully he entered into the spiritual life and listened to all his Master's dictates. Wholeheartedly he launched into the spiritual life. He felt the necessity of freedom from the domain of desires. He felt the necessity to grow into the mounting flame of aspiration, constant aspiration. Then realisation for him was not a far cry. He did realise God.

When we use the term "Heaven", we feel Heaven is all light, delight and perfection. But where is that Heaven? It is deep within us, in the inmost recesses of our hearts. High Heaven, higher Heaven and highest Heaven are all within us.

When we offer our soulful thoughts to our brothers and sisters, we live in high Heaven.

When we offer the results of our soulful actions to mankind, we live in higher Heaven.

Finally, when we offer our soulful existence to humanity at large, unreservedly and unconditionally, we live in the highest Heaven.

We can live in the highest Heaven every day. God has given us the capacity. He has given us the potentiality. It is we who have to manifest our inner potentiality and capacity. We all are surcharged with indomitable inner courage. Unfortunately, we do not use our inner unlimited capacity. We use our outer limited capacity. We are afraid of diving deep within. Inside is the treasure. Inside is the key. We do not know where we have kept the key. We have totally forgotten. We do not know where the treasure lies.

Here at this point is the necessity of a spiritual Master who knows where the key is and where the treasure lies. He does not give something of his own to the seeker. He only brings to the fore the seeker's inner wealth. God-realisation is not his sole monopoly. Everybody has to realise God without fail. It is a matter of time. One realises God today on the strength of his highest realisation. Another realises God tomorrow on the strength of his sincere aspiration. Everybody has to realise God, at God's choice Hour. Again, the sincere seekers can expedite their journey. We can walk towards our goal. We can march towards our goal. We can run towards our goal. If we run, naturally we shall reach the goal sooner than one who is walking towards his destination.

Perfection-Goal. Perfect Perfection here on earth has to be manifested, but how? We have to start our journey with inspiration. We have to feel deep within us every day in all our activities the necessity of inspiration. No inspiration, no proper achievement. Then we have to go one step ahead. After inspiration we have to feel the momentous necessity of aspiration. Inspiration is not all. We have to aspire to reach the Golden All, to see the Golden Shores of the Beyond, the ever-transcending Beyond. This is what we expect from aspiration, the mounting flame within us.

Then, aspiration is also not enough. We have to meditate. Aspiration includes meditation. When we meditate, we have to feel that we are entering into infinity, eternity, and immortality. These are not vague terms — infinity, eternity and immortality. These are our possessions. To enter into our own divine possessions, infinity, eternity and immortality, is our birthright.

Then, when we are advanced in our meditation, when meditation starts offering its fruit to us, we enter into the realm of realisation. We realise the highest Truth in this body, here on earth. We do not have to go elsewhere to realise God. We do not have to enter into the Himalayan caves or sit on the snow-capped mountains in order to practise spirituality. No. Here on earth, in the hustle and bustle of life, we have to practise spirituality. We have to accept earth as it stands, as it is. If we are afraid of earth, if we fight shy of earth, then God-realisation will always remain a far cry. Here on earth we have to realise the highest Truth.

Then, realisation is also not enough. After realisation we have to reveal our realisation. If we do not reveal our realisation, we act like a miser; we want to hoard our treasure. No. We have to offer our realisation in the form of revelation to mankind.

Revelation is also not enough. We have to enter into the domain of manifestation. If we do not manifest what we have realised here on earth, if Mother Earth does not receive the fruit of our realisation, and if She does not have it for good, we can never be truly fulfilled. Mother Earth has to be fed with the fruits of our realisation. Here on earth the manifestation of realisation has to take place, and when manifestation takes place, perfection is bound to dawn. Perfect Perfection is nothing other than the absolute manifestation of God's Transcendental Will here on earth.

We are all seekers of the Infinite Truth. It is our bounden duty to rise high, higher, highest. Each human being has come into the world with the message of perfection. No human being on earth will remain unrealised. No human being on earth will remain unfulfilled. No human being on earth will remain imperfect.

Realisation, fulfilment and perfection — these three are brothers. Realisation is the youngest, fulfilment is the middle, and perfect Perfection is the eldest in the family. These three brothers must go together. They have to walk along the field of aspiration. They have to swim in the sea of meditation. They have to fly in the sky, the blue welkin of contemplation.

God-realisation, God-revelation and God-manifestation can

take place only when man feels that he has to transcend himself. His goal of today is not the ultimate Goal. Today's goal has to be transcended tomorrow. Today's goal is the foundation-stone. Every moment we have to transcend ourselves, and while transcending, deep within us we shall cherish the message of perfection.

Perfection is bound to loom large and important in all our activities if we feel that aspiration is the only thing we need, the only thing we are striving for.

In aspiration is the key that can ultimately open up the door of perfect Perfection.

4. How to conquer fear

Our body is limited, that is why the body has fear. Our vital is unconscious, that is why the vital has fear. Our mind is obscure, that is why the mind has fear. Our heart is not aspiring, that is why the heart has fear.

To free our body from fear, what we need is the glorious experience of our soul. To free our vital from fear, what we need is the dynamic and conscious expansion of our soul. To free our mind from fear, what we need is the transforming illumination of our soul. Finally, to free our heart from fear, what we need is the fulfilling perfection of our soul.

Man's fear does not allow him to see the face of reality, the Ultimate Reality. Man's fear does not allow him to reach the Golden Shores of the Beyond. Man's fear does not allow him to fulfil God for God's sake.

But God, the Author of all good, has boundless Compassion, Concern, and Love for mankind.

God's Compassion saves man.
God's Concern liberates man.
God's Love fulfils man.

When we unconsciously think of fear or cherish fear, fear smilingly shakes hands with us. When we consciously think of fear or cherish fear, fear triumphantly embraces us. And when we unconsciously think of our inner courage, God cries with His divine Cry, for He feels that here He has a chosen instrument of His.

Now, earth is afraid of Heaven's transcendental Light. Heaven is afraid of earth's abysmal ignorance. God says to earth, "My son, do not act like a fool. Heaven's transcendental Light is not going to blind you. Heaven's Light is not going to expose you. On the contrary, Heaven's Light is going to illumine you. Heaven's Light is going to transform you."

God says to Heaven, "Do not be a fool. Earth's abysmal ignorance cannot bind you, cannot destroy you. On the contrary, earth's ignorance will be offered to you. It is you who will transform the face of earth."

God says, "I need both of you — Heaven and earth.

"Heaven! The message of realisation you will have to give to earth.

"Earth! The message of manifestation, My divine Manifestation, you will have to offer to Heaven."

Fear comes from our deep-rooted ignorance. We do not see the light with our inner vision. We see the light with our outer, human, limited, earth-bound understanding.

Let me tell you a short story. An old man was walking along the street in the evening. There was no light. He came across a rope. He thought that this rope was nothing other than a snake. He was all fear. He cried out at the top of his voice and he ran as fast as he could, and while running he fell down and broke his leg. His friends nearby heard him shouting and screaming, so they came together with sticks. He was shouting all the time, thinking that there was a snake. When his friends came, they too thought that it was a snake. It was all dark. They started striking the rope, and while striking, unfortunately they hit one another.

Now, the shouting continued and another party came with a light. When they came with the torch, they discovered that it was just a piece of rope and not a snake. So when the light entered, they discovered that it was a rope and not a snake.

Similarly, in our human life, when light enters into our physical consciousness, all kinds of fear are bound to disappear. We are wanting in light, that is why fear, at every moment, consciously and deliberately looms large in our life of desire and in our life of aspiration.

But if we are sincere enough to go deep within and feel that inner courage belongs to us, inner courage can at any moment dawn. It is more than willing to come to the fore. To bring this inner courage to the fore is the conscious awakening of our inner being. Everyone has this inner being. Unfortunately, very few of us want to feed this inner being. We feed our body in order to strengthen ourselves. We study books to feed our minds. We do many things to energise our outer being, but we do practically nothing to feed our inner being.

It is in our inner existence that we can grow into an adamantine will, and when we use our adamantine will, which we can easily have at our behest, we can conquer the very breath of fear. Here on earth our inner adamantine and indomitable will can and will reign supreme. Only one thing we need: our conscious awareness of the Divine Light which is ours, and it is our birthright to realise and fulfil this inner Light.

There can be no fear, there can be no iota of fear when we

live in the effulgence of our soul. To live constantly in the divine effulgence of our soul only one thing we need, and that is a conscious inner cry. This inner cry is called aspiration, the mounting flame deep within us. When this flame rises up towards the highest, it illumines all around. Darkness is transformed into light, fear into strength, doubt into certainty, ignorance into wisdom, and death into Immortality.

5. Occultism

Occultism is a vast subject. If I am allowed to speak on this subject, I can go on talking for hours and hours. Since time is limited, I wish to give a short talk on occultism.

Occultism is an art. It is an inner art.

Occultism is a science. It is an outer science.

Occultism as an art awakens and inspires our inner life. Occultism as a science energises and stimulates our outer life. A great occultist is a dynamic athlete. He fights against doubt. He fights against impurity. He fights against imperfection.

If you want to be an occultist, a divine athlete, then your life-boat has to ply between the shores of self-observation and self-correction in the river of emotion. That is to say, the human emotion has to be curbed, perfected. But the divine emotion has to be practised, enlarged. This divine emotion makes us feel that we are in God, with God, and for God. Human emotion is otherwise. It binds us, and with the help of this emotion, we try to bind others. Here we play the game of possession — to possess and be possessed. But the divine emotion is something else. Here we enlarge our consciousness. We transform our earth-bound life into the infinite expanse of light.

An occultist has a universal mind. This mind is his watchtower, and he has an eye, which we call the "third eye". Apart from the two eyes, we have a third eye which is in between the eyebrows, a little above. This eye is the eye of vision. This eye an occultist uses as a dynamic, successful and effective weapon.

An occultist has two names, an inner name and an outer name. His inner name is unwavering, unswerving Concentration. His outer name is Dynamic Revelation.

In our spiritual life we notice two brothers: occultism and spirituality. Occultism teaches us how to be brave and quick in the battlefield of life. Spirituality teaches us how to be pure and sure in all spheres and activities of life. Occultism wants to conquer time and space. Spirituality wants to conquer darkness and ignorance. When occultism wants to conquer time and space, it wants to do it in the twinkling of an eye. When spirituality wants to conquer darkness and ignorance, it does it at God's chosen Hour.

Occultism has no time for idle dreams. An occultist has no time for idle daydreams, but he has all the time to see the face of will-power, adamantine will-power within us. He has all the time to see victory's crown here on earth.

Now, there are various types of occultists, but we can put them into three major categories: an ordinary occultist, an occultist who is a little bit higher, and an occultist who is of the highest type. An ordinary occultist will do many things contrary to the divine law, the divine dispensation. For name and fame he will do quite a few things which are damaging and destructive. Here I wish to tell you of an instance.

There were three occultists. One occultist lived near a restaurant and he didn't have enough money to buy anything. Every night he used to threaten the proprietor of the restaurant occultly. He used his occult power, threatened him and commanded him to send him, three times a day, the most delicious meals.

It went on for months and years. The proprietor used to send meals three times a day to this occultist because he was being ruthlessly threatened at night.

Now, the second occultist used to live near a courthouse. Every day he used to see hundreds of people coming out of the court. He used to tell them what was happening in the farthest corners of the globe. They were all wonder-struck to know what was happening in distant countries, and the following morning in the newspaper, everything proved to be true, just as the occultist had said.

Now, the third occultist used to live near a church. Every day when the sincere seekers used to go to the church, he used to pray to the Lord Supreme to increase their aspiration, to expedite their salvation. Then after they had prayed, and as they came out of the church, he used to have the same prayer to the Almighty:

"Oh Father, I pray to You to give them illumination. With my occult power I wish to expedite their spiritual journey. This is my prayer to You. You have given me occult power. I wish to use it for their salvation. I don't want them to wallow in the pleasures of ignorance. These are my brothers and sisters. They are crying for light and illumination and I wish, with Your kind permission, to use my power to expedite their life's inner journey."

Now, when these three occultists passed away, left their bodies, passed behind the curtain of eternity, God said to the first occultist, "I don't need you. I don't want you. The world of greed needs you. You go away. You are meant for the world of greed and temptation."

To the second one God said, "I don't want you. I don't need you. The world of curiosity needs you. You are a miracle-monger. You have to go to the world of miracles. I don't need you."

To the third one who helped the sincere seekers in their spiritual pursuit, God said, "I need you. I need you badly. You have served Me. You have served the divinity in humanity. I need you. You are Mine."

Occultism deals with power. Unfortunately in the West, occultism has been a victim of misunderstanding. Here in the West you have seen that black magic has taken the role of occultism. Proper occultism will never destroy anyone, will not create any calamity for anybody. But black magic, which you see here in the lowest form of occultism, has created millions and millions of problems. I knew personally six or seven persons who were victims of black magic. They came to me for help; I did help them and they are now free. In merciless ways they were attacked by some black magicians. Now, many people will be under the impression that all this was done by real occult power. Real occult power would not create this kind of problem. It is the black magic in the lowest vital plane that creates all these problems.

So, when an occultist lives in the soul and works for the soul, he is a divine occultist. But when an occultist lives in the vital and for the fulfilment of the vital, lower vital, emotional vital, impure vital, then he is not living for the soul. He is living to satisfy his own ego, which is undivine, unrefined, obscure, impure and evil.

A genuine seeker of truth and light will not cry for occult power. Everybody has to realise God, but if one says that occult power is necessary in order to realise God, then I wish to say that one is committing a deplorable mistake. There are many occultists who have not realised God. Yes, in the far distant future, everybody has to realise God. No son of God, no human being will remain unrealised.

What is of paramount importance is God-realisation. When one realises God, if God wants to give him occult power, he will not be able to misuse God's occult power. A sincere seeker will cry only for God's Light, God-realisation and God-fulfilment. He will never cry for occult power.

You all know of the great spiritual Master, Sri Ramakrishna. His dearest disciple was Swami Vivekananda. Once the great Master said to his dearest disciple, "Naren, I have all kinds of occult powers. I want to give you some of my occult powers."

Immediately the disciple said to his Master, "Please tell me, will these occult powers help me in my God-realisation?"

The Master said, "Oh no. Occult power has nothing to do with God-realisation, but if you want to do some work here on earth, at that time occult power can be of some use."

Then Vivekananda said, "No, I want to realise God first — first things first."

So in the spiritual life, a real spiritual seeker will not cry for this kind of occult power. He will only cry for God-realisation, and if God wants that particular person to work for Him, naturally God will give him spiritual power, inner power, to manifest Him on earth.

If one really wants God, if one really wants the transcendental Truth, then one must enter into the realm of Yoga. Yoga means "union with God". Once we become consciously inseparable with our divine consciousness, unlimited consciousness, then we can see, feel and grow into our highest Reality, and the manifestation of this Reality is our birthright.

There are two things we always observe: the power of love and the love of power. When we enter into the lowest form of occultism, we see the love of power; and we do not have to go very far to see the love of power in politics; and in our daily activities also we are exercising our love of power. But the power of love is something different. In the power of love, it is love that exercises power, sweetly, divinely and unconditionally. That is the power of love.

Now a spiritual man, a sincere seeker after the truth, will only care for the power of love and not the love of power. When he is one with God, with the Infinite Consciousness, he will see the power of love; and those who want to show the world their capacity, those who want to exercise their power of ego, will naturally cry for love of power.

We know that when the power of love divinely replaces the love of power, man will have a new name: God.

6. The inner promise

The inner promise is a seeker's inner progress. This progress inspires him, energises him and helps him to please God in God's own Way. The outer promise we make quite often, but the inner promise we make once or twice, not more, during our life's span. The outer promise we make, but the inner promise we keep, we try to live up to it. Finally, we try to manifest this inner promise on earth.

The outer promise we make to ignorance, to teeming ignorance, but the inner promise we make to God. Our outer promise is to torture the world either consciously or unconsciously, or try to destroy the world.

To change the face of the world and to fulfil the world with the divine Will, this is our inner promise that we have made to God.

Now, there are three significant steps to this inner promise.

God is to be seen.

God is to be felt.

God is to be realised.

To see God, we have to be far, far away from the snares of darkness and ignorance.

To feel God, we have to live in the domain and realm of aspiration, the mounting flame within us.

To realise God, we have to grow into divine and constant and supreme surrender.

After we have attained to God-realisation, there are two most significant steps, two more significant promises we have to make. These promises are God-revelation and God-manifestation.

God-revelation is the promise made by the God-realised souls on the strength of their unconditional concern for suffering humanity.

God-manifestation is the unconditional promise of the God-realised souls to love mankind unconditionally and to manifest the reality of Divinity here on earth.

In our day-to-day life, we see a child making promises to his mother: he won't tell a lie, he won't do anything wrong. But unfortunately, he does tell lies, he does make mistakes. But the mother has boundless patience. She feels that sooner or later her child will tell the truth and will do everything right. Then, as a young boy, a teenager, he does quite a few things wrong and he promises to his parents that he will not do them any more. Unfortunately, he fails to keep his promise. But his parents have the capacity to forgive him. They feel that either today or tomorrow he will turn a new leaf. This is the inner confidence that they have in their son.

So in the spiritual life also, many seekers make an inner promise, an inner commitment. They say that they will enter into the spiritual life, they will give real importance to the life of purity, the life of aspiration, the life of realisation; but unfortunately they fail to fulfil their promise. Nevertheless, God's boundless Compassion never leaves them. God, with His adamantine Will and with His Vision of the ever-transcending Beyond, sees that these seekers will sooner or later enter into the right path and they will walk, march, run towards the Destined Goal.

Then there are some advanced seekers who have made considerable progress in their inner life, and who have made a promise to their own inner beings and to God that they will not give up their spiritual quest or journey unless and until they have realised God. God-realisation is their sole aim. As ill-luck would have it, after having some higher experiences, they do not want to march further. They feel that these experiences that they have already acquired are more than enough, at least for this life. So they do not want to go any further. God-realisation at that point they do not need or they do not want. So God-realisation remains a far cry for them.

But God knew that with utmost sincerity these seekers entered into the spiritual life and they have made considerable progress, only now they do not want to run towards their Destined Goal. They do not want to reach the farthest end of the Golden Shore.

God again with His boundless Compassion, observes the situation and tells the seekers, "Look, you will never be fulfilled. You will never see the face of satisfaction until you have seen the Golden Shore. You have not fulfilled your promise. But My Promise to you is unconditional. I shall wait for you. I shall take you, carry you to the destined shore of the Golden All at My choice Hour. If you do not want to run fast, faster, fastest, it is up to you; but you have to know that nobody on earth can remain unrealised, unfulfilled."

God says that this is the supreme decree. Each individual has to realise the highest Truth, but he who aspires will naturally reach the Goal sooner than the others who are still in the world of sleep.

As human beings, most of us are extremely clever. We are clever, but we are not wise. We try to deceive others, human beings. Not only that, we go to the length of deceiving our Inner Pilot, God. In spite of knowing that we can never, never deceive the Inner Pilot, we unconsciously, sometimes consciously, deliberately try to deceive the Inner Pilot, God. We tell God,

"Oh God, if You give us some inner wealth (that is to say, peace, light and bliss), we shall offer half of our peace, light and bliss to mankind. We shall not grab them all. We shall not use them all for ourselves." It is just like saying to God, "If You give me a dollar, I will give half to mankind and only half I shall keep for myself."

Now, God observes our sincerity. He examines the face of sincerity, whether we are really sincere or not. And what happens? God gives us peace, light, bliss and divine qualities to some extent, but we feel that it was not according to our satisfaction. What do we do? Immediately we say, "Oh God, You have not given us the full amount, the full quantity. I wanted to have a dollar, but You have given me half a dollar. You are very clever. You have already kept half a dollar for Yourself, that is to say, for humanity. So I cannot give humanity the peace, light and bliss that I already have, because I feel that You have not given me the full amount."

How we try to deceive the divinity in humanity. Everybody here, here at this place, has something to offer: peace, light or bliss, sincerity, simplicity. There is nobody on earth who is not in a position to help the rest of mankind. This help, this service, if I can use the term service, can be offered by any individual here on earth.

If somebody feels that he is more sincere than somebody else, then let his sincerity be shared with other persons.

If somebody feels that he is pure, purer than somebody else, his neighbours or friends, then let him share his purity.

If somebody feels than he has aspiration, more aspiration than his friends or neighbours, then let him share it.

This is the promise that every moment we can make to God.

Then we come to realise that every time the soul enters into the field of creation and manifestation, the soul makes a most solemn promise to God, the Pilot Supreme, to try its utmost to reveal God here on earth. But unfortunately when the soul enters into the world, ignorance the sea tries to envelop the soul, and then our body, vital, mind and heart consciously or unconsciously get pleasure in identifying themselves with the ignorance-sea. But the soul is all-forgiving. It does not cast aside the body, vital, mind and heart. It has boundless patience.

If this body, vital, mind and heart identify themselves with the soul, and if they want to see the Truth with the soul's eye, if that is their promise, if that is their only promise, inner promise, then the date of God-realisation, God-revelation and God-manifestation on earth is not very far.

Each individual can make a solemn promise to himself, to herself, to humanity at large. This is a promise of dedicated self-service. And when he fulfils his inner promise, God fulfils His highest Promise of absolute Perfection in and through the aspirant.

7. The inner teaching

We get the inner teaching either from a spiritual Master or from our own soul. It is infinitely easier for us to get this inner teaching from a spiritual Master, for we can speak to him and see him daily. He understands our language. He is one with us. Although in the inner world he is infinitely superior to us, he is in us and for us. His inner consciousness is flooded with peace, light and bliss. But we have to know that a day shall dawn when the message of the soul and the spiritual Master's teaching must go together. There can be no difference, no iota of difference between their teachings.

But unless and until one has the capacity to dive deep within, it is always better and safer to listen to one's Master. It is not that one has to have a spiritual Master all his life. No. For some time, especially at the beginning, one must have a spiritual Master. When the seeker himself realises the highest Truth, he does not need any spiritual guidance. He himself grows into effulgent light. The inner soul within him comes to the fore and leads him, guides him and moulds him and perfects his inner and outer nature.

The inner teaching. The inner teaching teaches us how to love mankind and how to serve the divinity in humanity.

Simplicity, sincerity and purity, these are the three things that we need in our inner life: simplicity, sincerity and purity.

Simplicity we need at every moment, for if the mind is not simple, if the mind is complicated, complex, then there can be no peace in our mind. A child is simple. He is all joy. In our day-to-day existence, unfortunately, we do not pay any attention to simplicity. If we go deep within, if we have a simple mind, simple existence, we shall feel how lucky, how happy and how fortunate we are.

Sincerity, it is the life of our heart. If we have sincerity, then we have to know that we are already marching towards our Destined Goal. Sincerity is our safe-guard. Each moment a sincere seeker is running towards his Destined Goal, either consciously or unconsciously. If we want to make constant progress, here on earth, then what we need is sincere heart.

Purity, purity in the body. This purity does not mean that we have to take a bath ten times a day. No. It is the inner purity that we need and not the outer cleanliness. When we are pure, we can receive the divine peace, light, bliss and power in abundant measure. When we can maintain our purity, then peace, joy, light, bliss and power can dawn on earth. Here the whole role of purity is of paramount importance in our spiritual life.

In the inner life we see the roles of fear and doubt, courage and certainty.

Fear, what is it? When we follow the spiritual life, we come to realise sooner than at once that fear is a real enemy. What does it do? It buys our coffin, long before we are destined to die.

Doubt, what does it do? It starts digging our grave while we are still alive, while still we are performing our earthly duties.

Courage. Courage is our inner indomitable will. The outer expression of our inner indomitable will is manifested in the form of outer courage. Each moment we can see the reality, stand in front of the reality, and grow into the reality if our existence is inundated with the inner will and the outer courage.

Certainty. God is ours. God is not the sole monopoly of an individual. It is not that only realised souls can dare to claim that God belongs only to them. No, far from it. Each individual has the right to proclaim that God is his, that he belongs to God. He has to feel that God and he are eternally one and that God-realisation is his birthright.

The inner teaching. What do we learn from the inner teaching? Aspiration. Aspiration is the inner flame, the mounting cry within us. Each individual has this burning flame within. But unfortunately, most of us do not take the trouble to use the flame of aspiration within us. We are fond of using something else in our day-to-day life — desire.

Desire is something that binds us.

Aspiration is something that frees us.

The message of desire is to possess and be possessed.

The message of aspiration is to expand, enlarge and immortalise our earthly existence.

When we desire, we live in the world of anxieties, worries, frustrations, limitations, bondage and death. When we aspire, we live here on earth in our divine consciousness. We feel the message, the life-breath of infinity, eternity, and immortality. These are not vague terms — infinity, eternity and immortality, far from it. He who prays, he who meditates, he who concentrates, he who contemplates daily can easily enter into the domain of infinity, eternity and immortality. His consciousness is bound to be flooded with infinity's peace, eternity's light and immortality's bliss.

The outer knowledge tells us how we can lord it over the world, how we can destroy the world. But the inner knowledge tells us how we can be inseparably one with God's entire creation. Inner teaching means inseparable oneness, not only with the Creator, but also with His creation.

The inner teaching is very simple. As my introducer was kind enough and wise enough to say, that real Indian philosophy is not complicated, but people make it complicated and then they misunderstand it. The inner teaching also similarly at times has become a victim to complicated terms, but it is very, very simple. Anyone, anyone can learn the inner life, can try to live the inner life, can fulfil his inner existence, divine existence here on earth.

Philosophy is not the answer to the inner life. Religion is not the answer. Philosophy helps. Religion too, helps to some extent. But spirituality, let us use the term "Yoga", a Sanskrit word, is by far the best answer to the inner life. Yoga means union, conscious union with God. If we cry for our conscious union with God, then easily, without the least possible hesitation, we can live the inner life.

Now, philosophy. Let us use the Sanskrit word, *darshan*. It means to envision, to see. One of our India's greatest spiritual Masters, Sri Ramakrishna, said, "In days of yore people used to have visions. Now people study darshan!" This is the difference of the Vedic seers who had the highest illumined vision and those who just study philosophy.

Religion. When we go deep inside the religion, without fail we get the message of truth; but we do not go within. I say, "My Hinduism is by far the best." Immediately you tell me, "Stop! Stop! No comparison. Christianity is by far the best." Then a follower of Judaism will not hesitate to contradict both of us. He will say, "No. Judaism is by far the best." So this goes on, no end. This is our outer teaching. Each one is right in his own limited way.

But we have to know the inner oneness, the inseparable oneness with God and His creation. We can consciously achieve this oneness only through proper prayers, concentration, meditation and contemplation. Yoga transcends all religions. Religion is right in its own way. Philosophy is right in its own way. Philosophy can lead us right up to the door. Religion can lead us a few steps inside the room, but real meditation and spirituality, Yoga, not only leads you right up to the throne, but will make you sit on the throne itself.

When you follow the path of Yoga, you will see that there is no quarrel, no conflict. I must add that one has to follow the path meant for him. Otherwise conflicts will arise. Each path claims to be by far the best. No. A sincere seeker, if he is a real sincere seeker, will not find fault with any path.

As you know, there are three principal paths: Karma Yoga, the path of action and dedication; Bhakti Yoga, the path of love and devotion; and Jnana Yoga, the path of knowledge and wisdom. Again, in Jnana Yoga, the path of knowledge and wisdom, there is a special branch. We call it Raja Yoga, which you call in the West "mysticism".

But I wish to say that if one is a true, sincere seeker, a genuine seeker, and if he follows the path of love and devotion, he cannot say a single word against the seeker who is following the path of knowledge, because we know all roads ultimately lead to Rome. I only take one road and you may take some other road, but Rome is there: the Goal. Each road has the right to lead the aspirant to his Destined Goal. So how can I contradict other paths? It is sheer foolishness on our part to discard other's discovery.

Now, our inner teaching tells us that it is true that all paths will lead to Rome, to our Destined Goal, God. But there can be a path that leads us faster than the other paths, and that path is the path of love, devotion and surrender. All roads will lead us to our destination, but one can say that there are short cuts. Here the path of love leads us much faster to our destination.

Now when we follow the path of love, we find our spiritual life, inner life, most satisfactory. Here God is dearest to us, not because He is Omnipotent, Omnipresent or Omniscient, but because He is all Love. A child feels that his father is dearest to him precisely because he feels inside his father all love. He does not care to know how great his father is, whether his father is the magistrate or barrister or president. Just because his father is all love to him, his father is dearest to him.

Similarly, God, our eternal Father, can be approached most successfully and most convincingly with love; and when we approach Him with love, we see that He is all Love; and when we just open our eyes and try to look at Him, we see that He is right in front of us, blessing us, embracing us. He says, "My child, I have been all the time waiting for you." Here, love means one's constant feeling of inseparable oneness with one's Beloved.

The end of all inner teaching is love, the Divine Love, not human love. Human love binds; the result is frustration. And at the end of frustration, destruction looms large. But Divine Love is expansion, enlargement, the feeling of one's true oneness. So if we love a human being, we have to know that we love him precisely because deep inside that particular being is God, not because he is my father, or she is my mother, or he is my brother, or she is my sister. No. I love him just because inside the particular person I feel, I see the living presence of my dearest Beloved.

For those who want to follow the spiritual path, those who want to feel God as their very own, I wish to say, Love Divine is the answer. In Love Divine looms large and important the seeker's real fulfilment and perfect Perfection. This is the easiest path. This love is most convincing, most efficient. We all can practise the inner teaching by offering our true love to God, to the divinity inside humanity. The more we offer this Divine Love, the more we fulfil the Inner Pilot within and without us.

Life Divine is not a far cry here on earth. The fulfilment of divinity here on earth can never remain a far cry, if we know the secret of secrets. And that secret is to grow into the Divine Love, where the lover and the Beloved become one, where the creation and the Creator become one, where the finite and the Infinite become one.

It is here on earth that the message, the soul-stirring flute of Infinity we shall hear. We do not have to go to Heaven, we do not have to go to any realms of consciousness; but right here, here and now, we can hear the message of liberation, enlightenment and divine fulfilment, if we follow the inner teaching, which is Love Divine: love for love's sake, love for God's sake.

8. The universe

>Oxford, to you I bow because you hold
> your tradition.
>Oxford, to you I bow because you own
> English glory.
>Oxford, to you I bow because you are the
> English pride.

Aum. Aum is God. Aum is the Inner Pilot.
Aum is the Universe.

Aum.
Pūrṇam adaḥ, pūrṇam idam, pūrṇāt pūrṇam udacyate.
Pūrṇasya pūrṇam ādāya pūrṇam evāvaśiṣyate.

Infinity is that. Infinity is this.
From Infinity, Infinity has come into existence.
When Infinity is taken away, Infinity remains the same.

Marcus Aurelius said, "The man who does not know what the universe is, does not know where he lives."

The universe.
The universe is God's creation and man's realisation.
The universe is God's Compassion and man's emancipation.
The universe is God's Concentration and man's transformation.
The universe is God's Meditation and man's revelation.
The universe is God's Contemplation and man's manifestation.
The poet in me tells me that the universe is beautiful.
The singer in me tells me that the universe is enchanting.
The philosopher in me tells me that the universe is meaningful.
The Yogi in me tells me that the universe is soulful.
The God-lover in me tells me that the universe is fruitful.

My poet sees the truth.
My singer feels the truth.
My philosopher achieves the truth.
My Yogi realises the truth, and
My God-lover becomes the truth.

Man's dictionary houses millions of words. But God's Dictionary has only two words: aspiration and receptivity. Aspiration and receptivity are the two words we see in God's Dictionary. God out of His boundless Bounty offers these two most significant words, should I say, this significant wealth, to mankind: aspiration and receptivity.

The aspiration of today is tomorrow's salvation.
The receptivity of today is tomorrow's infinity.

In the finite we have to hear the message of the Infinite.
In the fleeting second we have to hear the message of the eternal Beyond.
In the domain of death, we have to hear the message of Immortality.

Here at this point, the immortal poet, Blake, sings through us and for us,

> To see a world in a grain of sand
> And a Heaven in a wild flower,
> Hold infinity in the palm of your hand
> And eternity in an hour.

This is the message a spiritual seeker can cherish. His inner being, inner life can be surcharged with this message, and this message can reverberate in the inmost recesses of his aspiring heart.

The outer universe, the inner universe and the inmost universe. My physics friend, my chemistry friend, my geography friend, my astronomy friend — all of them inform me about the outer universe. I am most grateful to them. My psychology friend and my philosophy friend tell me about the inner universe.

I am most grateful to them. My Yogi friend and my Avatar friend tell me about the inmost universe. I am most grateful to them. I ask them all if they are totally satisfied with their achievements, discoveries and realisations. They flatly say, "No."

My friends in the outer universe tell me that they have much more to discover and unravel. My friends in the inner universe tell me that they have much more to embody and realise. Finally, my friends in the inmost universe tell me that they have much more to reveal and manifest.

The visible universe and the invisible universe. The thinker in us sees the visible universe with the aspiring mind. The knower in us feels the visible universe with the aspiring heart.

Now the invisible universe. In order to enter into the invisible universe, what we need is the soul's illumining light. If we do not see with the soul's illumining light, if we do not listen to the dictates of our soul, it is simply impossible for us to enter into the invisible universe.

The living universe and the evolving universe, the dying universe and the perishing universe. When we aspire, when we try to go beyond the boundaries of the finite consciously, soulfully and spontaneously, we live in the living and the evolving universe. When we consciously or unconsciously cherish doubt, jealousy, fear, imperfections, bondage, limitations and death, we live in the dying and perishing universe.

If we want to live in the universe, the spiritual universe or the real universe, we have to know that we have to abide by the laws of the universe.

What are the laws of the universe? Love and serve.

Love humanity. Serve divinity.

We have to love humanity in divinity. We have to serve the divinity in humanity.

At this point, we can recollect the message of Plato who said,

"Through obedience we learn to command." Now, if we obey the laws of the universe, then we can command ignorance and govern death.

The scientist wants to discover the entire universe. The spiritual person, the seeker of the infinite Truth, wants to discover the universe. Now, the spiritual scientist and the spiritual seeker, will always run together. They have the same message.

The scientist of scientists, Einstein, offers us the most sublime message: "His life is worthwhile who lives for others." This is precisely what a spiritual person, a seeker of boundless light and peace tells us. Only he who lives for others has a meaningful life. Verily this is the message of all secret and hallowed religions: live for others.

Now, science and religion run abreast in this respect, but there is something else. We call it Yoga. It is a Sanskrit word which means union, union with God, union with infinity, eternity and immortality. Now, when we enter into the field of Yoga we feel that our love, our service that we offer to mankind, is not for others, but it is for us, for our enlarged part. There is no such thing as "others". All are members of the same family.

When we remain in the mire of ignorance, we say "I", "you", "him", but when it is a matter of oneness, inseparable oneness, oneness with God, oneness with mankind, oneness with God's creation, then we cannot say that it is for others. It is for our sakes, for the sake of our enlarged and more complete self.

Discovery. Science will discover the truth. Religion, or should I say spirituality, will discover the truth in the universe; and Yoga, oneness with God, will realise the ultimate Truth for the universe.

When the discovery of the scientist is complete, he will see that his universe is manifesting the Truth of the ultimate Beyond.

When religion or spirituality discovers the ultimate Truth, it will see that its universe is realising the Truth of the ever-transcending Beyond.

Finally, when Yoga, or conscious union with God and mankind, completes its journey, it will transform the face of the world. It will illumine the face of the earth.

The discovery of the scientist, the discovery of religion and spirituality, and the discovery of one's highest oneness, inseparable oneness with God, will run together like three brothers, running towards the eternal Father, the Goal.

9. Curiosity or necessity

I am extremely happy, fortunate and proud to be here this evening in your midst. I shall be in the British Isles for about a month. If I go back to New York, where I live, without paying my respectful homage to Wales, it will be the summit of my folly and ignorance.

I understand this is a small university — small in size, but not in height, not in depth. I understand that there are 350 students. I have been to Yale, Princeton, Cornell, Harvard and most of the important universities in the States. There you will find thousands and thousands of students. But what we need is quality and not quantity. What we need is aspiration and nothing else. The search for the Truth, this is the thing that we all need. When we have that inner cry for Truth, we do not need anything else.

Now as you know, yesterday I was at Oxford. Today I am here. On the 23rd I will be in Cambridge. Then I will be visiting Scotland, Ireland, France and Switzerland. What am I doing? I am doing only one thing. Like a bird I fly from one place to another. My wings are love and service. One wing is love, the other wing is service. I try to love mankind. I try to serve mankind. This is what I have been doing so far. So I have come here to love God inside you and to serve the divinity within you.

Curiosity or necessity. Curiosity is not necessity. Necessity is not curiosity. These two are like the North Pole and the South Pole. It is quite simple. A curious man does not want the truth, does not need the truth. He just wants to hear from others what the truth looks like. On very rare occasions, he may want to see the truth from a far distance. He is afraid of personally approaching the truth. He feels that the moment he approaches the truth, the volcanic power of the truth will destroy him, his earthly existence. His earthly existence is nothing other than ignorance.

Curiosity commits two unpardonable sins. It kills our spontaneous love for light, the illumining light that transforms our life and enables us to realise the highest Truth. Curiosity also extinguishes our inner flame, which is a normal and natural fire. This inner flame we call aspiration. The higher this flame of aspiration rises, the sooner we reach the shores of the Golden Beyond.

Curiosity is afraid of two things: the highest reality and divinity. When reality, that is to say, the transcendental Reality, looks at curiosity, curiosity immediately runs and runs, looking for an escape, a hiding place, because curiosity feels that it will be in no time exposed. When divinity looks at curiosity, curiosity, out of tremendous fear, curses divinity. It feels that a perfect stranger is entering into its very breath.

Curiosity has, however, two intimate friends: doubt and jealousy. Doubt feeds curiosity just at the moment when the divine peace, love, bliss and power of the spiritual Master want to help mankind unconditionally. Doubt feeds curiosity at that very moment. Jealousy makes curiosity feel that it is far inferior to the genuine seekers of the infinite Light. So jealousy does not permit curiosity to make friends with the spiritual seekers or to take spiritual help from them. "If the spiritual seeker or Master is so great, then what of it? Let me remain in the meshes of ignorance. No harm." Here jealousy instigates curiosity to remain where it already is.

Now, let us focus our attention on necessity, divine necessity. Necessity is spirituality and spirituality is necessity.

What is spirituality? It is the common language of man and God. Here on earth we have hundreds and thousands of languages to make one understand another, but when it is a matter of God and man, there is only one language, and that is spirituality. If one follows the path of spirituality, one can easily speak to God face to face.

Necessity, divine necessity, is the pressure to see the highest and to feel the deepest. Today we see the highest, tomorrow we feel the deepest, and the day after we grow into the highest and into the deepest.

God is not only *a* necessity, but *the* necessity. How and why is God *the* necessity? We know that everything has failed us or will fail us in one way or another. But God has never failed the sincere seekers of the infinite Truth, and if we really cry for the inner Truth, the infinite Truth, God will not fail us.

We expect from mankind perfection, perfect Perfection. Now, no person on earth is absolutely perfect. Then how can we expect perfect Perfection from anyone? We expect absolute divinity from human beings, but absolute divinity is still a far cry for the individual. But if we want to see perfect Perfection, absolute divinity, then only God can show us perfect Perfection. He can show us His absolute Divinity. What is more, He can offer us His perfect Perfection, His absolute Divinity.

Today's desire compels us to deny and avoid the Truth, God. Tomorrow's aspiration will compel us to see God, the divinity

God, the Inner Pilot. There can be no choice.

Now, God is the only reality, or God is *the* necessity, only necessity. What do we mean by this? When we speak of God, what do we actually mean? We mean God-realisation or self-discovery. Let us use the term God-realisation. God-realisation is not only possible but practicable; and what is more, it is something unavoidable, inevitable.

The outer cry we have. With our outer cry we feel satisfaction is possessing and being possessed.

With our inner cry we enlarge ourselves, we expand ourselves, we fulfil God here on earth.

The immortal poet, Shakespeare, said,

> Teach thy necessity to reason thus;
> There is no virtue like necessity.

Necessity is the greatest blessing. We cannot fathom the depth of necessity.

Man's necessity is God.
God's necessity is man.

Man needs God for his highest transcendental realisation, and he will have it in God. God's necessity is man for His absolute Manifestation here on earth. We need God to realise our highest truth or highest existence. God also needs us to manifest Him here on earth, totally, divinely and supremely.

Without realising God we cannot have abundant peace, light, bliss and power. God-realisation is of absolute necessity here. Without God, we remain unrealised. Similarly, without man, God remains unmanifested.

Philip Sidney said, "Thy need is greater than mine." When

we follow the spiritual life, when we walk along the path of spirituality, one word constantly looms large and important, and that word is "sacrifice". We have to sacrifice our very existence for others — what we have and what we are. What we have is willingness and what we are is cheerfulness. This cheerfulness we can have only when we go deep within. When we are cheerfulness within, we are willingness without. If our inner existence is flooded with joy and delight, then only shall we be eager, more than eager to help the outer world. If there is a barren desert within us, if there is no light within us, how are we going to help or serve mankind? So, if we have joy within, this joy today or tomorrow, sooner or later, we can bring to the fore and offer it to mankind. We have to love mankind soulfully, serve mankind unconditionally.

As I said before, curiosity is not necessity. Curiosity is not spirituality, true. But we all know that we cannot be sincere overnight. If I am not sincere, I cannot become sincere in the twinkling of an eye. If I have not realised the truth, I cannot realise the truth overnight. It is impossible. But if out of curiosity I want to see what is happening in the sincere spiritual seekers who feel that God is the only necessity, then I can try to be sincere, because I see something divine and fulfilling in them.

God-realisation is of the utmost importance. First thing first, and that is God-realisation, self-discovery.

So if out of curiosity one goes to a sincere spiritual seeker or a spiritual Master, then he may see something which he has not seen before in him or around him. So I tell my students or acquaintances who come to me with very limited aspiration (I beg to be excused, I must say that I do have most sincere students, disciples also. But those who are right now unfortunate, and do not have genuine aspiration, I do not throw cold water on them. I tell them,) "Don't worry. If you have come to me just out of curiosity, no harm. Mix with the sincere seekers. See what they are getting from their genuine spiritual life, and then if you feel that their spiritual life has changed their nature or is giving them a new light, new peace, giving a new meaning to their outer life, then try to follow their example. Be one with them."

I have come across quite a few curious, totally and exclusively curious human beings who are now transformed into serious, sincere seekers. Truth, either today or tomorrow, has to be realised, and for that, if we do not have utmost sincerity right now, no harm. Sincerity grows. Everything grows, everything. Like a muscle, everything can be developed. If we do not have implicit aspiration right now, no harm. We can develop aspiration, our inner cry.

So, dear sisters and brothers, here I am seeing many, many sincere seekers. To them I say: run fast, faster, fastest towards your Destined Goal. And I beg to be excused, here I am seeing one or two, very few, curious seekers. To them I say: do not stop with the achievement which is your curiosity. Please try to go one step ahead. Then you will see that today's curiosity is being transformed into tomorrow's sincerity, and in your sincerity you will see the inner cry, the mounting flame which we call aspiration.

Today's aspiration is tomorrow's realisation. This is the only truth. This is the only realisation that I can offer to you, dearest sisters and brothers, seekers of the Infinite Truth. Start here and now.

10. The higher worlds

Cambridge, I bow to your aspiration-height. I bow to your knowledge-light. I bow to your divine pride. True, you are of England, you are in England, but you are of the world at large. The entire world claims you as its very own.

There are seven higher worlds and seven lower worlds. The higher worlds are: *Bhur, Bhuvar, Swar, Jana, Mahar, Tapas* and *Satya*. One of the Upanishads names seven higher regions. These are: *Agniloka, Vāyuloka, Varunaloka, Ādityaloka, Indraloka, Prajāpatiloka* and *Brahmāloka*. Certain spiritual figures are of the opinion that the first-mentioned group of the worlds corresponds to the second. Others, equally qualified, strongly object to this belief. Strangely enough, all, without exception, agree that the world Satya and Brahmāloka are one and the same.

We can enter into these worlds on the strength of our aspiration and receptivity. When we have aspiration, these worlds can never remain a far cry.

Aspiration. What do we mean by this term? The inner cry, the mounting flame within us. Aspiration is reality's constant necessity.

Receptivity. How can we have receptivity? We can have receptivity if we grow into purity and sincerity. When sincerity and purity loom large and important in our earthly existence, then we can easily have receptivity.

A sincere seeker needs aspiration and receptivity. Without aspiration, he is rootless. Without receptivity, he is fruitless.

The higher worlds. Each individual has the divine right to enter into the higher worlds. His aspiration can easily guide him and lead him to God's Throne. To enter into high, higher, highest worlds, what we need is the inner cry. We cry for name and fame. But if we inwardly cry for abundant Peace, Light and

Bliss here on earth, then our entire being can be flooded with Peace, Light and Bliss.

These higher worlds are within us and not without. When we concentrate, when we meditate, when we contemplate, we enter into these higher worlds. When we concentrate dynamically, we near the door of these higher worlds. When we meditate soulfully, we enter into the Room Divine. When we contemplate unreservedly and unconditionally, we reach God's Throne.

Since we aspire to enter into the higher worlds, we pray to the cosmic gods. We feel that the cosmic gods will come to our aid. They will help us enter into the higher worlds.

Here at this point, I would like to invoke the soul of Marcus Aurelius,

> Either the gods have the power to assist us, or they have not. If they have not, what does praying to them signify? If they have, why do you not rather pray that they would remove your desires than satisfy them, and rather set you above fear than keep away the thing you are afraid of?

Now, if we want to enter into the higher worlds with a view to fulfilling our desires, then we can never enter into the higher worlds. We can enter into the higher worlds only because it is the Will of our Inner Pilot, the Lord Supreme. When we go deep within, when we meditate for a couple of hours, if it is most soulful and if the meditation is unconditional at the same time, then we envision the higher worlds. No sincere seeker of the highest Truth, the ultimate Truth, will be denied the higher worlds.

Porphyry throws further light on the matter,

> We must ask of God only such gifts as are worthy
> of God, that is to say, such things as we cannot
> obtain from any except God.

In order to enter into the higher worlds, what we need is sincerity; what we need is purity; what we need is peace; what we need is delight.

Sincerity: Inner beauty's other name is sincerity.

Purity: The name of God's first child is purity.

Peace: Peace is unity's sovereignty and multiplicity's divinity.

Delight: Delight is the name of God's permanent Home.

There are two things we observe in our day-to-day life: human and divine. In everything we do, say or grow into, we see either the divine or the human.

The human world and the divine world. A clever man is he who knows how to deal with his outer world. He does not want to be deceived by the world, by mankind, but unconsciously or consciously he deceives the world, the world of ignorance. A wise man is he who knows all about the inner world, the higher worlds. He does not deceive anybody. He wants to conquer the outer world, the world of ignorance. But his is not the conquest of Caesar, "I came, I saw, I conquered." V*eni, vidi, vici.* Far from it. When a wise man wants to conquer ignorance, he does so only because his inner being compels him to transform the face of the world. He does not take pride in conquering the world. No. He feels the very breath of ignorance, and then he feels that it is his bounden duty to transform ignorance into knowledge, darkness into light, death into Immortality.

There are two ways to enter into the higher worlds. One is the way of knowledge, the other is the way of devotion.

Knowledge. I am the knowledge, I am the known, I am the knower.

Devotion. I am devotion, I am dedication and I am salvation. Knowledge enlarges itself, expands itself into Infinity.

Devotion identifies itself with the absolute Truth. On the strength of its identification, devotion grows into Infinity.

A sincere seeker of the ultimate Truth can either follow the path of knowledge or devotion. But at the end of the journey's close, the seekers who follow the path of knowledge and the seekers who follow the path of devotion will meet together and shake hands, because they have reached the self-same Goal.

We live either in the world of human thought or in the world of divine Will. Human thought slows down and dies out, but the divine Will constantly grows and swiftly flows.

Similarly, human power is born of futility. Divine power is born of reality.

Finally, we observe our love: human love and divine Love. Human love is an express train, destination: frustration. Divine Love is a local train, destination: Illumination. Human physical love is slow poison. Divine Love is the running stream and unceasing source of nectar. Human love can be transcended. Divine Love can be manifested. Human love is fruitless expectation. Divine Love is fulfilled perfection.

Unconditional love God is.
Unreserved devotion man needs.
Mutual surrender God and man offer.

When the power of love replaces the love of power, man will have a new name: God.

The Golden Hour, God's Hour is dawning fast. Let us offer our heart's aspiration to the lofty realisation of the seers of the hoary past,

Ānandādd hy eva khalv imāni bhutāni jāyante,
Ānandena jātāni jīvanti,
Ānandaṁ prayantyabhisaṁ viśanti.

From Delight we came into existence.
In Delight we grow.
At the end of our journey's close, into Delight we retire.

11. How to conquer doubt

A great writer once said, "A philosopher is one who doubts." Now, in my humble opinion, we are all philosophers, for there is nobody on earth who has not doubted at least once. So, in that respect, we are all philosophers.

The Sanskrit word for philosophy is *darshan*. Darshan means vision, to envision the truth. Sri Ramakrishna said, "In days of yore people used to have visions, and now people are studying it." One thing is to have the direct vision of the highest ultimate Truth, another thing is to study it.

Now, here I am in no way throwing cold water on the students of philosophy, far from it. I happen to be also an insignificant philosopher. But what I wish to say is this: philosophy leads us to spirituality, and spirituality offers us God-realisation and self-discovery. So let us start our journey with philosophy. This is the first rung of the spiritual ladder, and then the next rung is spirituality, and then the final is God-realisation.

Doubt. Doubt means absence of real knowledge. Real knowledge is true light, and true light is our inseparable oneness with the world.

Faith and doubt. These are like the North Pole and the South

Pole. Unfortunately, a man of faith is very often misunderstood. We are apt to call a man of faith a fanatic. Here we make a deplorable mistake. A fanatic and a man of faith are two different persons. A fanatic hates reason, ignores the reasoning mind; whereas a man of faith, if he is really a man of faith, will welcome and accept reason and the doubting mind. Then his faith will help the doubting mind to transcend itself into the infinite vast, into something eternal and immortal. This is what faith offers to the doubting mind.

A man of faith is also a man of divine humility. The farther he advances in the realm of spirituality on the strength of his faith, the deeper he grows into the supreme humility.

Here at this point I wish to quote Keats' immortal utterance, "My greatest elevations of soul every time make me humble."

Doubt is our self-imposed ignorance. Faith is our inner vision of the ultimate Truth. Again, faith is our soul's expansion and soul's illumination.

We see darkness all around. We see impurity all around and imperfection all around. Again, it is we who have the inner inspiration, aspiration, capacity and adamantine will to transform the very face of the earth. How? If we conquer doubt, self-doubt, if we conquer our doubt of humanity, of God.

Doubt. Why do we doubt? We doubt because we do not have the conscious oneness with somebody else, with the rest of the world. If somebody doubts me, shall I doubt him in return? If I doubt him, then I sail in the same boat. But if I offer him my faith, my implicit faith, then either today or tomorrow, sooner or later I can transform his nature.

What do we learn from a tree? When we vehemently and ruthlessly shake a tree, what does the tree do? The tree immediately offers us its flowers, its fruits. Now, if others similarly torture us with their teeming doubts, let us offer them our snow-white faith. Then our snow-white faith will transform their life of teeming, darkening and darkened clouds of doubt.

With our eyes wide open we see that the world is ugly. With our ears wide open we hear that the world is impure. Now, we have the mind. Let us use our mind or compel the mind to see only the right thing, the pure thing, unlike the eyes. Let us use our mind or compel the mind to hear only the right thing, the divine thing. It is the mind, the developed mind, the conscious mind, the illumined mind that has the capacity in abundant measure to transport us into the highest regions of consciousness.

We are all under the laws of Mother Earth. Mother Earth is under the laws of Heaven. Heaven is again under the express law of God; and our doubt, cherished doubt, is under its own law. Its law is frustration, and in frustration destruction looms large.

Why do we doubt? Because we are wanting in proper understanding. There was a great spiritual saint named Kavir. He said, "Listen to me, brothers: he understands who loves."

If we love, then we understand; and if we understand the truth, then we have neither the opportunity nor the necessity to cherish even an iota of doubt in our day-to-day existence.

We doubt God at our sweet will. We doubt God precisely because we think He is invisible. We doubt Him because we think He is inaudible. We doubt God because we think He is incomprehensible.

But to see Him, what have we done? To hear Him, what have we done? To understand Him, what have we done?

To see Him, have we prayed soulfully daily? The answer is in the negative, no. To hear Him, have we loved mankind devotedly? No. To understand Him, have we served divinity in humanity? No. We have not prayed to God. We have not loved mankind. We have not served the divinity in humanity. Yet we want to see God face to face. It is impossible.

God can be seen on the strength of our inner cry, which we call aspiration, the mounting flame within us. Every moment this flame is mounting towards the highest. If we know how to cry within, then this flame will mount, will climb up high, higher, highest; and while it is climbing up, it will illumine the world around.

There is an Indian proverb which I am sure most of you have heard, "A strong man fears his enemy when the enemy is far off, but when the enemy is near, he is no longer afraid of the enemy." I wish to add that when doubt attacks a spiritually strong man, he becomes stronger, infinitely stronger. He does this by bringing to the fore his own soul's light which energises him to fight against doubt and conquer it.

There is another way to conquer doubt: if we at this very moment feel that we are children, children of God; and again, if we can feel that God is a Divine Child playing with us. We are human children and He is a Divine Child.

A child does not doubt. He has implicit faith in his parents. He has implicit faith in everyone he comes across. We also can play the same role in our day-to-day life. Let us play with God, the Divine Child. There can be no shadow of doubt in our life when we speak, when we eat, when we move around, if we feel that we have a Divine Child within us, sporting with us. We are not alone. There is someone playing with us at every moment. If we know and feel this, then doubt can never eclipse our mind.

A lover of God, an adorer of God feels that deep within him, in the inmost recesses of his heart, there is an island of ecstasy; and this island can never be submerged by the floods of doubt, for his love has already made him one with this divine certitude.

A seeker of the highest order said, "Some say 'He (God) is too far'. Some say, 'No. He is at home here'. But I have found Him. He is in the cradle of love."

When we love God, our problem is over. True, we all do not see God face to face. But we can imagine for a fleeting second that God with all His Love abides in our dear and near ones. Let us try to see the face of our Beloved in our dear ones. Where there is love, true love, there is all oneness. Where there is oneness, there can be no doubt — no darkening, no threatening, no destructive doubt.

Finally, how to conquer doubt. In order to conquer doubt, we have to be in the process of purification of our nature constantly. This purification has to take place in our physical. The body has to be purified constantly. It is not by washing the body or taking six or seven baths a day that we can purify the body. Our body will be purified only when we feel a living shrine within us. Then we have to install the living deity of light and truth within us. Then the body in no time will be purified. At that time we cannot have any doubt in the body, or in our physical mind.

The vital. The vital has to play the role of dynamism. It is the dynamic energy that we have to offer to the vital, and not the aggressive and destructive power, in order to conquer doubt in the vital.

The mind. Each moment the mind has to be flooded with clarity and right thinking. Each moment the mind has to consciously house divine thoughts, divine ideas and divine ideals. Then doubt will not be able to breathe in the mind.

The heart. Each moment we have to make the heart soulful so that we can easily conquer doubt in the heart. The heart has to offer the message of sacrifice for others, for the rest of the world; and while sacrificing his very life-breath, a sincere seeker feels that he is not sacrificing anything, he is just expanding his own inner consciousness and fulfilling himself here on earth.

Doubt can be conquered. It has to be conquered. How? The only answer is constant and soulful concentration on the mind, meditation on the heart and contemplation on the entire being.

12. Love, devotion and surrender

Love is sweet, devotion is sweeter, surrender is sweetest.

Love is sweet. I have felt this truth in my mother's spontaneous love for me.

Devotion is sweeter. I have discovered this truth in my mother's pure devotion towards the perfection of my life.

Surrender is the sweetest. I have realised this truth in my mother's constant surrender towards the fulfilment of my joy.

Again, love is mighty, devotion is mightier, surrender is the mightiest.

Love is mighty. This truth I feel when I look at my father's face.

Devotion is mightier. This truth I discover when I sit at my father's feet.

Surrender is the mightiest. This truth I realise when I live in the breath of my father's will.

Love, devotion and surrender. St Augustine has blessed us with a profound message, "Love and then do what you like."

Our mind thinks that this is absolutely true. Our heart feels that this is undeniably true. But unfortunately, in our day-to-day life we are not able to practise it. That is to say, we do not know what love is. We do not know why we love something or someone. Finally, we do not know how to love.

What is love? From the spiritual and inner point of view, love is self-expansion. Human love binds and is bound. Divine Love expands, enlarges itself. Here we are dealing with the Divine Love.

Devotion is the intensity in love, and surrender is the fulfilment of love. Why do we love? We love because at every moment we are pinched with hunger to realise the highest, to feel the inmost, to be consciously one with the universe, with the universal truth, universal light, peace and bliss, and to be completely fulfilled.

How to love? If we love with a view of achieving something from others, then that love is no love. Love means constant self-offering on the strength of one's own inner aspiration.

This world of ours needs peace, joy, bliss, harmony, and understanding. We feel that here on earth there is no light, no truth, no divinity, nothing of the sort. All the divine qualities, all aspects of the Lord Supreme are in the skies, in the deep blue skies, not here. This is what we feel. Hence we always look up high for help. We feel that God is in Heaven, not on earth. God will come down into the world to our rescue. He is not to be found here on earth. Here we are wallowing in the pleasures of ignorance. There can be no light, no truth here.

But we must realise that, God being Omnipresent, He is here too. He is within us. He is without us. In the inmost recesses of our heart, we feel His living Presence.

As you all know, George Bernard Shaw has warned us, "Beware of the man whose God is in the skies." But our God is everywhere. He is not only in Heaven, He is here on earth. He is with us, He is within us, and He is for us. We do not have to enter into the highest regions of consciousness to see God. Our inner cry will bring to the fore our inner divinity, which is nothing other than God.

Surrender. Surrender is protection, and surrender is illumination. Surrender is our perfection. We begin our journey at the very commencement of our life. We surrender our existence to our parents and the result is protection. We listen to our parents. We surrender to their will, to their advice and suggestions, and we are protected, well protected. Joy boundless we felt in our day-to-day life when we were children. Why? Because we surrendered our personal will, our own inner thinking to our parents. Here immediately we received joy plus protection. In protection is joy and in joy is protection.

Now in the evening of our life, what happens? If we follow the inner life and the spiritual life, in the evening of our life we surrender. To whom? To the Inner Pilot, the Lord Supreme. At the end of our journey we surrender our very breath to the Supreme. Then we again get joy, perfect joy, unalloyed joy.

To quote Dante, "The happiest man is he who can connect the evening of his life with the beginning."

Now, if we are all sincere seekers of the ultimate Truth, then our journey begins with surrender to our parents, who are our well-wishers, who are our dearest and nearest ones. When we surrender to them our existence, we get joy in abundant measure. Then, when we walk along the path of spirituality, every moment we try to listen to the dictates of our inner being. The more we listen to the inner being, the greater is our joy, the higher is our fulfilment; and then, when our term is over, when we have to enter into another world for a short rest, if we consciously surrender to God's Will, ours will be the supreme joy, ours will be the glory supreme.

It is difficult to love mankind. It is difficult to devote oneself to mankind. It is difficult to surrender oneself to mankind. This is true. In the same way, it is difficult for us to love God, to serve God, to devote ourselves to God, and to surrender our living breath to God.

Now, why? The simple reason is: we want to possess and be possessed. Now, here we are constantly making ourselves victims of ignorance. That is to say, our desire can never be fulfilled. We have countless desires. God will fulfil only those desires that will be of some use, from which we will derive benefit. But if He fulfilled our countless desires, then He would be doing an injustice to our aspiring souls. That He will not do. He knows what is best for us and He has given us beyond our capacity, even beyond our necessity. But unfortunately we are unaware of this fact.

St Francis, from his own experience, has offered a unique truth to the world at large, "He who thinks that God's Love is inadequate is very greedy." Really we are all greedy people. If we go deep within, we see, we feel, we realise that God has given us infinitely more than we need, needless to say, more than we deserve.

Love, devotion and surrender. These are the three rungs in the spiritual ladder, or should we say the ladder of our evolving consciousness. The first rung is love; the second, or you can say the penultimate, is devotion; and the ultimate is surrender.

A tiny drop enters into the ocean and becomes the mighty, the boundless ocean. Unfortunately in the West, surrender is misunderstood. We feel that if we surrender to someone, that means he will lord it over us. We will have no individuality and personality. From the ordinary point of view, the human point of view, this is true. From the spiritual point of view, it is absolutely wrong. When the finite enters into the Infinite, it becomes the Infinite all at once. When a tiny drop enters into the ocean, we cannot trace the drop. It becomes the mighty ocean.

Each moment we are given ample opportunity to love mankind, and if we really love mankind, then we have the feeling of devoted service to mankind. And then when we really want to enlarge our existence, expand our consciousness and be one, inseparably one with the vast, then surrender is the only answer.

Each moment we see right in front of us a barrier between one human being and another human being — an adamantine wall between two human beings. We cannot communicate properly, wholeheartedly and soulfully. Why? Because we are wanting in love. Love is our inseparable oneness with the rest of the world, with God's entire creation. We can break asunder this adamantine wall that we feel between us on the strength of our soulful love.

India's greatest poet, Rabindranath Tagore, said, "He who loves finds the door open." So our heart's door is already open for those who really, truly and soulfully love.

God loves us out of His Infinite Bounty, and His Heart's Door is always wide open. Just because He is all Love, we approach Him. He is our dearest, not because He is Omniscient and Omnipotent, but just because He is all Love.

> Love, devotion and surrender.
> To serve and never be tired is love.
> To learn and never be filled is devotion.
> To offer and never to end is surrender.
> Love is man's reality
> Devotion is man's divinity.
> Surrender is man's immortality.
> Reality is all-pervading.
> Divinity is all-elevating, and
> Immortality is all-fulfilling.

13. The permanent and the impermanent

What is permanent?
What is impermanent?
What is permanent is reality.
What is impermanent is non-reality.

Reality is the existence of light, in light and for light.
Non-reality is the existence of night, in night and for night.
Reality's parents are divinity and immortality.
Non-reality's parents are bondage and ignorance.

When we see the Divine Light we feel happy. When we feel the Divine Light we become strong. And when we grow into the Divine Light our life becomes fruitful.

When we see the undivine night, we become weak, impotent. When we feel the undivine night, we feel sorry, we feel miserable. And when we grow into the undivine night, our life becomes meaningless, fruitless.

Now, illumining light and illumined light; darkening night and darkened night. Illumining light is the light that is within us. Illumined light is the light that is without us. Darkening night is the night that is before us. Darkened night is the night that is around us.

That which is real is permanent, and what is permanent is spiritual. What is spiritual? The life of the ever-transcending Beyond is spiritual. But this life of the ever-transcending Beyond has to be manifested here on earth. This life is real, reality itself.

What is unspiritual? Let us use the term "material". Material is something which is the wealth of the fleeting time.

Divine wealth and material wealth. Divine wealth is our inner aspiration. This aspiration is the song of Infinity, Eternity and

Immortality within us. Material wealth is desire. It is the cry for immediate and constant possession. When we try to possess, unfortunately we feel that we are already possessed. When we try to see someone with our soul's light, we feel that we are already liberated, and he too is already liberated.

A thing permanent is divine. A thing impermanent is undivine. When divine wisdom dawns on earth, we will realise that an impermanent thing is useless.

Divinity and immortality are within us. Immortality tells us what to do and divinity tells us how to do it. Immortality tells us to listen to the dictates of our soul, which is a spark of the Supreme Light. It tells us to be conscious of the Inner Pilot constantly. Divinity tells us how we can do it. We can do it through a self-disciplined life, through dedication to a higher cause, through purification of our outer nature, and through undying and unreserved love for God.

Bondage and ignorance are the parents of night. Ignorance tells us what to do and bondage tells us how to do it. Ignorance tells us to destroy the world and bondage tells us how to do it — through cruelty and brutality, through unfair means.

A spiritual seeker tries to enter into the inmost recesses of his heart, and from there he tries to bring light to the fore. With the help of this light, he wants to grow into the breath of the permanent. Now, to grow into the breath of the permanent, what we need is inner wisdom. What is this inner wisdom?

Lord Krishna, in the Bhagavad-Gita, the Song Celestial, says to Arjuna, his divine instrument, "O Arjuna, a wise man is he who has the mastery over the senses." That is to say, when we conquer the senses, we enter into the realm of wisdom, where reality grows and divinity flows.

Now, to enter into the world of wisdom we need constant love — love for the truth, love for light. But right now we are fond of fleeting truth, fleeting light, fleeting possession. The fleeting wealth that we have or we cherish is terribly afraid of truth. It doubts truth and it fears God. But our divine wealth, aspiration, invokes truth and adores God. Each day we are seeing with our own eyes and feeling with our own heart the impermanence of the man-made world. That is to say, the things that we create with our thoughts and ideas do not last. This moment I have a thought and soon that thought is gone. Perhaps it gives me a result; this result lasts for, again, another fleeting second.

But there is something else we call will-power — soul's will, adamantine will of the soul. If we can exercise an iota of this will-power, then we will see that not only the action but also the result is an everlasting reality. In order to develop the will-power of the soul, we have to enter into the life of the Spirit. We have to have a self-disciplined life. Self-disciplined life does not mean the mortification of life or a conscious torture to the human life. Self-disciplined life means a life that needs the Light and wants to be guided by the Light, moulded and shaped by the Light. And when the life is disciplined, we shall not act like animals. When the life is disciplined enough, the real divinity will grow. At that time we can say that God-realisation or self-discovery is our birthright, and in God-realisation we acquire the wisdom of the everlasting Truth.

It is not that one individual or some individuals are chosen to realise the highest Truth. No, far from it. Each individual is an instrument of God; but he has to be conscious. Right now he is not; he is unconscious. But when he prays, when he meditates, he automatically becomes a constant, conscious instrument of God. And he who becomes a conscious instrument of God hears in the very heart of the finite the message of the Infinite, and feels in the fleeting the Breath of the Eternal.

To think of God, to meditate on God constantly, is to live in

God unreservedly. When we live in God constantly, soulfully, and unreservedly, God unconditionally does everything for us. In infinite measure He offers His Light, Peace and Bliss, and we grow into His very Image.

Here on earth the message of the permanent Truth, the transcendental Truth has to be fulfilled, for God has chosen earth as His field for Manifestation. The eternal Light has to be manifested here on earth, and we, all of us, have to become conscious instruments of God. We can be so if we have the inner cry, and this inner cry has to be the cry of a child. The child cries for his mother. The mother comes running towards the child, no matter where the mother is. The child may be in the living room or he may be in the kitchen, but the mother comes running to feed the child.

Similarly, when we have the inner cry, spontaneous cry for Light and Truth, God out of His Infinite Bounty will show us the Light, and in that Light we will grow.

We shall fulfil God. While fulfilling God, we shall fulfil ourselves, and our only prayer to God is:

Lead us from the unreal to the Real.
Lead us from darkness to Light.
Lead us from death to Immortality,
O Lord Supreme!

14. Attachment and detachment

Attachment and detachment.

Detachment and attachment.

From the body we get the message of attachment.

From the soul we get the message of detachment.

The body is limited, hence the body wants to bind us and limit us. It wants to bind and limit our outer capacity and our inner potentiality.

The soul in its potentiality and capacity, is limitless and endless. Therefore the soul wants to free us from the meshes of ignorance and liberate us from the bondage-night.

What is attachment? Attachment is the dance of our outer pleasure.

What is detachment? Detachment is the song of our inner joy.

Attachment ends in the prison-cell of frustration and destruction.

Detachment fulfils itself in the palace of Divinity and Immortality.

I am a fool if I consciously live in the physical. I am a greater fool if I constantly admire and adore my physical body. I am the greatest fool if I live only to satisfy the needs of my physical existence.

I am a wise person if I know that there is something called the soul. I am a wiser person if I care to see and feel my soul. I will be the wisest person if I live in my soul and for my soul constantly and soulfully, unreservedly and unconditionally.

When we are attached to the body, we become in no time, impulsive. When we are attached to the vital, we become, very soon, explosive. When we are attached to the physical mind, we ultimately become destructive.

But when we are in the body, detached, we consciously feel

our aspiring consciousness. When we are in the vital, detached, we expand and widen our aspiring consciousness. When we are in the mind, detached, we fulfil supremely our unlimited consciousness here on earth.

Many people are unfortunately under the wrong impression that attachment and devotedness are one and the same thing. Attachment is when we are in the finite, when we are attached to the finite. Devotedness is when we devote ourselves to the Infinite and are liberated by the Infinite.

Here in Ireland, nearly a hundred years ago, a young aspirant named Margaret Noble went to India to become the famous disciple of Swami Vivekenanda. This great Yogi had come to the West in 1889 to participate in the Parliament of Religions at the great World's Fair in Chicago. His spiritual stature was immediately recognised, and he became famous overnight.

When he went to England from the United States, Margaret Noble attended his talks and became his dearest disciple. He called her "Nivedita, one who is totally dedicated to the Supreme Cause."

Indian people are all admiration for what Nivedita did for India. She helped Indian women in infinite measure. She helped to awaken their slumbering consciousness so that they could envision themselves as divine instruments and grow into the perfect embodiments of aspiration, dedication and illumination for their Mother India. We Indians are bloated with divine pride when we utter the name of Nivedita.

Her father was a clergyman, a lover of God, a great seeker. Before he breathed his last, on his deathbed, he said to his wife, "Don't stand in Margaret's way. If she wants to go to India, let her go." Margaret's mother had been very upset by her daughter's desire to leave Ireland for distant India, but at her husband's last wish, she did help Margaret and inspired her. Nivedita went to

India and became India's veritable pride. Hers was the heart that knew no despair. Just before she passed behind the curtain of eternity, she uttered under her breath, "The boat is sinking, but I shall see the sunrise."

I wish to offer my humble talk to the hallowed memory of Sister Nivedita, Margaret Noble of Ireland.

Detachment is misunderstood. We feel that if someone is detached, he is indifferent. Spiritual seekers also make the same mistake in thinking that when we want to show detachment to someone, we must show him utter indifference, to the point of total neglect. This is not true. When we are indifferent to someone, we do nothing for him. We have nothing to do with his joy or sorrow, his achievement or failure. But when we are truly detached, we work for him devotedly and selflessly. The results of our actions we offer at the Feet of the Lord Supreme, our Inner Pilot.

It does not matter if the result is success or failure. If we are not at all attached to the results, we get an immediate expansion of consciousness. If we do not care for the fruit of our action, the Supreme rewards us in the Supreme's own Way.

Lord Krishna said, "Thou has the right to act, but not to the fruits of action." The Upanishads declare, "Action cleaves not to a man."

If we work devotedly and selflessly, action does not bind us. There will be no difficulty in working for God's sake if we work without caring about the result. This is true detachment, this is spiritual detachment. When we can renounce the unlit, unaspiring action, we can enter into the divine action which is our real life; and in this real life, there is always perfection and fulfilment.

When we pay all attention to the material world and neglect the inner world, we starve the soul in us. The soul has to be brought to the fore. If we think we can get infinite wealth from the material world, then we are totally mistaken.

Yagnavalka, the great Indian sage, had a wife whose name was Maitreyi. Yagnavalka wanted to spend the evening of his life in meditation and contemplation, so he wanted to give away his earthly possessions. He asked Maitreyi if she wanted his riches. She asked, "Will your riches give me immortal life? Of what use to me are the things that cannot make me immortal?"

We need the material world, undoubtedly, but we cannot give all our energy to it. We feed our body three times a day. Unfortunately we do not have time to feed our soul even once a day. We, the seekers of the infinite Truth, feed the body so that we can become the perfect instrument of the soul.

The soul has divinity, eternity, immortality. The soul wants to offer its world to the body. If the body becomes receptive, it will receive all that the soul wants to offer. The body itself will echo and re-echo in the life of aspiration and dedication. It will march along as the most humble servitor of the soul. Its existence will be the existence of glory and divinity, divine service and supreme fulfilment.

We fulfil the Supreme on earth. He treasures us in His Heart's Heaven.

15. Divine duty and supreme reward

God thinks of His Duty. God meditates on His Duty.
   Man loves his reward. Man cries for his reward.
   Duty performed unconditionally makes God happy, and that is what He at every moment does.
   Reward gained effortlessly and constantly makes man happy, and that is what he always expects and lives for.
   In our human duty, we think of man in man. In our human

duty we see man in man. That is to say, we love bondage in ignorance.

Divine duty is to meditate on God in man. Divine duty is to see God in man. That is to say, to love Divinity in Immortality.

Human duty begins with compulsion and very often ends in frustration and repulsion. Divine duty begins with inner necessity and ends in a flood of ecstasy.

Human reward and Divine reward. Human reward is the fleeting joy from insignificant man. Human reward is the dying love from a weak human being.

Divine reward is the constant Joy that flows from God, the everlasting Joy. Divine reward is the constant Love from God, the all-fulfilling Love.

In our unaspiring life we perform duties, and we feel that duty is another name for labour. We also feel that duty is self-imposed, and reward is a most coveted pleasure. In our aspiring life, duty is voluntary. No, never is it obligatory; and reward is the energising joy of selfless service. In our life of realisation, duty is our divine pride, and reward is our glorious, transcendental height.

In our unaspiring life and even in our aspiring life, we see that duty is first and then reward. Duty comes first, then it is followed by reward. In the life of realisation it is otherwise: reward first, then duty. How? When God offers His transcendental Height, His highest Illumination to someone, it means that God has already granted him full realisation. God has accepted him as His chosen instrument. The very fact that God has accepted him as His chosen instrument indicates that he has already received the highest reward from God. Later God tells him about his duty: to love mankind, to help mankind, to serve divinity in humanity, to reveal God the Eternal Compassion, and to manifest God the Eternal Concern on earth, here and now.

Many years ago, an eminent Indian scientist, PC Ray, was a

student at Edinburgh, here in Scotland. He completed his studies here and went back to Bengal, India and offered his knowledge to his Indian brothers and sisters. Now, it happened that one day somebody asked him how many children he had. He took out from his pocket a list of his children. Can you guess how many children he had? He had only seventy-three children, in spite of the fact that he was a bachelor in the purest sense of the term! Then he said to him, "Look, these are my children: seventy-three brilliant students. They are my true children, and they have given me the opportunity to serve mankind, and this is my duty. I am not married, but I consider them as my own children. I serve them, and by serving these children of mine, I perform my highest duty."

So, here I wish to say that I am also in the same boat, unmarried. I have a few hundred spiritual children. Out of His Infinite Bounty, God has showered His choicest Blessings upon my devoted head, and my spiritual children give me abundant encouragement and opportunities. My spiritual children meet with all my needs when I move around the world. This is my service, dedicated service, and this is my bounden duty.

Today, at this august university, I am offering my selfless service. This is my last talk. My tour has come to an end. I have been away from New York for about a month. I have spoken at Cambridge, Oxford and other universities. I have just come back from Switzerland, Wales, France and Ireland. Yesterday I was in Ireland and today I am here in Scotland. What am I doing? I am trying with utmost sincerity to be of service to the sincere seekers. Each individual has the capacity to be of service to others. Only God can help us, and He always does. What we can do is to serve everybody here on earth. As a servant of God, each individual has the capacity to serve mankind. Service is our matchless duty.

Now, duty and reward from the spiritual point of view, go together. It is like the obverse and reverse of one spiritual coin. Duty is man the aspiration, and reward is God the Realisation and God the Liberation. Again, in reward is man's eternal journey, ever-transcending journey; and in duty is God the ever-transforming, ever-manifesting, ever-fulfilling Reality here on earth, there in Heaven.

Aum.
O Lord Supreme,
Thou art my Mother.
Thou art my Father.
Thou art my Friend.
Thou art my Comrade.
Thou art the Knowledge-Light.
Thou art the Inner Wealth.
Thou art my All.

When we realise this Truth, we fulfil all our duties. There can be no greater duty than to realise the Inner Pilot.

Him to realise, Him to serve, Him to manifest on earth, we saw the light of day.

MY ROSE PETALS

NOTES TO MY ROSE PETALS BOOK 1

1. University of Kent, Canterbury, England,
Monday, 9 November 1970.
2. University of Nottingham, England, Tuesday, 10 November 1970.
3. University of London, England, Wednesday, 11 November 1970.
4. American College, Paris, France, Friday, 13 November 1970.
5. American Centre for Arts, Paris, France, Saturday,
14 November 1970.
6. University of Essex, Colchester, England,
Tuesday, 17 November 1970.
7. University of Leeds, England, Wednesday, 18 November 1970.
8. Keble College, Oxford, England, Thursday, 19 November 1970.
9. St David's College, Lampeter, Wales, Friday, 20 November 1970.
10. King's College, Cambridge, England,
Monday, 23 November 1970.
11. University of Dundee, Dundee, Scotland,
Wednesday, 25 November 1970.
12. American International School, Zurich, Switzerland, Friday, 27 November 1970.
13. University of Bristol, Bristol, England,
Monday, 30 November 1970.
14. Trinity College, Dublin, Ireland, Tuesday, 1 December 1970.
15. University of Glasgow, Glasgow, Scotland,
Wednesday, 2 December 1970.

MY ROSE PETALS

BOOK 2

16. Three lessons in spirituality

Spirituality is our inner growth, inner evolution, inner achievement and inner fulfilment. The day we left the mineral kingdom, we started our spiritual journey. After passing through the plant kingdom, we entered into the animal kingdom and our evolution went faster. Then, from the animal kingdom, we entered into the human kingdom, and our evolution became conscious. Now, from the human kingdom, we are consciously, soulfully, devotedly, divinely and unconditionally trying to enter into the divine kingdom.

All of us here are seekers; we are all spiritual people. On the strength of my own realisation, I wish to say that all of us without exception are studying spirituality. There is no human being on earth who is not studying this subject at least a little. From this subject, everybody learns something according to his capacity or receptivity. There is nobody who has not learned anything. Your learning will not be the same as mine, but that does not mean that you have not studied the subject as well as I have.

What have I learned from spirituality? I have learned only three things. Love of God is the first thing I learned. The second thing is self-discovery. And the third thing is the importance of doing first things first. Love of God. Self-discovery. First things first.

Love of God. Is there anybody who does not love God? No, not even an atheist. The atheist negates God. But to me his very negation is an act of God. And whatever he *does* love is God, because everything comes from God and is of God. Atheists and agnostics are all in the one boat that leads to the destined Goal, though perhaps in spite of themselves. Love of God is oneness with the Universal Consciousness. Conscious oneness with the Universal Consciousness is conscious love of God. God is one;

God is many. He is the tree. He is the branches, the leaves and the flowers. He is unity and multiplicity. When we look within, He is one; when we look without, He is many.

Self-discovery. What do we mean by self-discovery? Self-discovery is our recovery from ignorance-illness. When we are ill, we suffer for a while and then we get better, only to fall sick again. But self-discovery is our permanent recovery from the illness that is called ignorance.

Self-discovery is God-discovery. There is no difference between self-discovery and God-discovery. When you discover yourself, you feel in the inmost recesses of your heart your oneness with God — your inner Divinity, your inner Immortality, your inner Infinity, your inner Eternity, which are nothing other than God Himself. This realisation is not the sole monopoly of a spiritual Master. Everybody without exception can discover it. But when we make a conscious effort, when we pray consciously and devotedly, we come to realise God's Light, Peace and Bliss infinitely faster than those who wallow in the pleasures of ignorance.

First things first. What is the first thing? The first thing in our lives should be God. Our first thought should be: "Let Thy Will be done." When the finite consciously accepts the Infinite as its very own, the finite is blessed with liberation and perfection. When I say, "Let Thy Will be done," it means I am consciously surrendering my lower existence to my higher existence. I can say that my feet are my lower existence and my heart is my higher existence. Both my heart and my feet are mine; they are both part and parcel of my existence. But my feet are in ignorance and my heart is bathing in the Sea of Light and Wisdom. My heart can easily help and guide my feet if my feet are willing to surrender to their higher part, the heart. The feet must feel that now they are in ignorance, but when they enter into the heart, at that time they will be illumined.

I have to know that I embody the lowest and the highest. When I am in the highest, I am consciously one, inseparably one with the Supreme Pilot. In that consciousness I represent Him, and one day I will become what He eternally is. My lowest part is ignorant, imperfect, undivine, hostile, but if I can remember that the highest part also is mine, then I will see nothing wrong in carrying the highest part to the lowest part with the message of Liberation.

So to do the first thing first means to surrender our individual will to the Will of the Supreme, and then to feel that this surrender is the surrender of our lower existence to our higher existence. When we surrender our lower existence to our higher existence, we become the chosen instruments of the Absolute Supreme.

When it comes to studying the spiritual life, we find there are two students in us: the head and the heart. These two students have come to us to learn the higher wisdom, and we have to teach them both. But we have to know which of the two students has more learning capacity and which has less, which is more progressive and which is less progressive, which deserves more attention and which deserves less attention for the time being. Two students, the mind and the heart, have come to learn. The mind is the inferior student and the heart is the superior student. But unfortunately, the inferior one often creates problems for the superior one.

Our inner being is the teacher. It tells the mind-student, "You have learned much. But your knowledge is only information and it is actually standing in your way. We always say that knowledge is our hope, but in your case, knowledge has become a veritable obstruction. You have absorbed too much knowledge. You do not know how to utilise it and you cannot digest it. So please, for God's sake, unlearn. If you can unlearn it, then you will be in a position to learn something really useful from me, your inner being."

Then our inner being tells the heart-student, "You have to learn only one thing: to give. Offer yourself, offer what you have and what you are. Empty yourself." The heart immediately says, "I am ready. What I have right now is insecurity and ignorance. What I am is uncertainty. But I am ready to offer it all immediately. I will offer up all my insecurity, uncertainty and ignorance."

The heart is ready and eager to surrender what it has and what it is, but the mind finds it very difficult to unlearn. What it has learned is how to doubt. This is the most important thing to the mind. If the mind can doubt others, then it really feels that it has some wisdom. The moment I doubt you, I feel I have done something great. Here I have made my doubt a spiritual authority. But this kind of spiritual authority is nothing but slow poison. It kills our spiritual life. The heart, however, is just the opposite. Today it receives, tomorrow it achieves, the day after tomorrow it becomes and finally it realises what it eternally is.

There comes a time when the heart, out of its own inner spontaneous love for its brother, the mind, comes and knocks at the mind's door. With tremendous reluctance, the mind opens its door and, to its wide astonishment, sees that the heart, its own brother, is fully illumined. There is not even an iota of darkness inside the heart. Then the mind asks the heart how it has accomplished this. It says, "You are also a part of the family. How is it that I see in you all illumination, all divinity? What is wrong with me that I am still ignorant and unillumined?"

The heart replies, "I listened to the dictates of the Inner Pilot. I did what the Inner Pilot asked me to do. In your case, the Inner Pilot asked you to unlearn. What you have learned is not illumination. What you have discovered is not realisation. You have learned and discovered information, and on the basis of this information you have built a palace of obscurity and divided consciousness. You have always separated yourself from the rest of the world. You are not accepting my realisation as your very own. You don't claim me as your very own, but I accept you as my very own. I accept each and everyone as my very own. In your case, there is no oneness, but only separation. You do not run to the Light. Your goal is still a far cry. I listened to the Inner Pilot when He asked me to do something, and now I am all illumination."

The mind thinks for some time, and then says, "All right. I will listen to you," and it starts unlearning. First it unlearns doubt, then it unlearns fear, then it unlearns jealousy, then it unlearns the feeling of superiority and inferiority. All the things that divide and separate the mind from the whole, the mind consciously tries to unlearn. The mind chases away doubt; immediately faith grows. It chases away insecurity; immediately confidence dawns. It rejects all feelings of inferiority and embraces the feeling of oneness. Impurity leaves the mind and purity enters. The mind now accepts the Light and thinks of its ultimate goal. The ultimate goal of the mind is Illumination. The ultimate goal of the heart is Liberation. When the two meet together on the way to their destination, they become inseparably one. Then Perfection dawns, and man the seeker becomes the conscious representative of the Absolute Supreme on earth.

17. The seeker's journey

Some of you have come here to see a spiritual teacher. Some of you have come to see a yogi. Some of you have come to see a seeker. I am grateful to those who have come here to see the spiritual teacher in me. I am more grateful to those who have come to see the yogi in me. I am most grateful to those who have come here to see the seeker in me.

As a spiritual teacher, I teach my students or disciples with my heart's love. I have no other way. I have no other knowledge but the knowledge of love. With my heart's love, I try to teach my followers and disciples.

As a yogi who is constantly one with his Inner Pilot, I try to be always at the command of my Inner Pilot. I try to execute His commands and thereby be of service to those who come to me for inner guidance.

As a seeker, I am always at the feet of the Transcendental Supreme. I am a seeker, a seeker of the Infinite Truth. A seeker knows that his journey will never come to an end. He realises the Truth, but he feels that there is no end to his realisation. He discovers the loftiest Truth, the Transcendental Truth, but then he feels there is no end to his Truth-discovery. He comes to realise that because God is infinite, eternal and immortal, there is no end to God's Infinity, Eternity and Immortality. God Himself is constantly transcending His own Infinity, Eternity and Immortality. So we must realise that we are seekers of the ever-transcending Beyond. Each seeker is transcending his own capacity, his own reality, his own dream, his own realisation every day, every hour, every minute and every second.

When one becomes a sincere seeker, he discovers something which a non-seeker has not discovered. A sincere seeker of the highest Truth discovers the fact that he made a solemn promise to the Supreme before he entered into the world arena. This promise was very simple and, at the same time, very soulful. His promise was to be the conscious instrument of the Supreme and to manifest the Supreme here on earth through his dedication, through his aspiration and through his conscious oneness with the world at large. This is the promise each aspiring soul has made, according to the seeker's own vision. All human souls, without exception, make this promise to the Absolute Supreme. Unfortunately, when we enter into the world, we enter into the sea of ignorance. We bathe for thousands of years in this sea of ignorance, but when we become tired of this ignorance-bath, we enter into the Sea of Knowledge and Wisdom. Then we remember our promise, our promise of God-manifestation on earth. Each individual being will one day come to realise that he has made this promise to the Absolute.

Unconsciously everybody is trying to fulfil this promise. But a seeker is trying consciously to fulfil it, and a realised soul has already begun to fulfil it consciously and unconditionally. A seeker of the highest Truth fulfils his promise consciously and soulfully. A spiritual Master fulfils his promise consciously and unconditionally. But the individual who is not aspiring and who does not care for God-realisation or God-manifestation right now, is fulfilling his promise unconsciously.

When one is fulfilling or trying to fulfil God consciously, he is fulfilling God in a perfect manner. When he is fulfilling God unconsciously, he is fulfilling God in an imperfect manner. When one has realised God consciously, one goes a step further and tries to reveal God consciously. Finally, one tries to manifest God consciously. In conscious realisation, conscious revelation and conscious manifestation, we see God the Eternal Perfection. God is for everyone, but one who is conscious of God's Existence-Reality is undoubtedly ahead in the divine race.

Each individual looks for something here on earth and there in Heaven. Here on earth we look for something in God. When we enter into the spiritual life, we pray to God, we meditate on God, we contemplate on God. First we start with our prayers. We learn how to pray from our parents. Then we try to concentrate on something which we want to achieve. We know that when our mind wanders we cannot achieve anything, whereas when we focus our attention and power of concentration on a particular thing we achieve success. We learn the art of concentration, then we go one step ahead to meditation. When we meditate, we try to embody the Vast, the Infinite within us, or we try to dive into the vast, infinite Sea of Light and Delight. The last step is contemplation. When we contemplate, our consciousness becomes one with the thing that we contemplate upon. The lover becomes one with the Beloved. The finite loses its finite existence and becomes one with the Infinite, becoming the Infinite itself. The earth-bound consciousness becomes one with the Heaven-free consciousness.

A seeker wants to see God. When he sees God face to face, he wants to see a certain thing in God, a special thing, and that thing is a sweet smile. Just by seeing God, he will not be satisfied. He wants to see God's exquisite smile. If he sees that God is smiling at him, he will achieve everything. Then the seeker wants to see a certain thing in man and that thing is gratitude. He looks around. He feels that at every moment, consciously or unconsciously, he is offering something to mankind. He feels that if he can observe an iota of gratitude in mankind, then his self-offering will be fulfilled. But mankind is not responding.

Then the seeker looks up to Heaven. He wants to see a certain thing in Heaven, and that thing is Compassion. He feels that if Heaven does not supply him with infinite Compassion, he is helpless. Although he has achieved something in life and the world extols him to the skies, he knows in the inmost recesses of his heart that he is helpless. He feels that if he gets more encouraging and fulfilling Compassion from Heaven, then he will be able to complete his task on earth most convincingly and powerfully.

The seeker expects something from earth. What does he expect? Patience. Earth has given him everything, but when he wants to do something for the earth-consciousness, he feels that the earth-consciousness is restless. It wants everything in the twinkling of an eye. He wants to see patience in the earth-consciousness, and eventually there comes a time when the earth-consciousness does have the necessary patience which permits him to manifest the highest truth on earth.

The seeker expects something from his own life. What does he expect? Unconditional service to mankind. If he can serve mankind unconditionally, then he will be satisfied. If he serves conditionally, then he can never be satisfied or fulfilled. He expects from himself unconditional service to the world at large, and ultimately he grows into that unconditional service-tree.

The seeker expects something when his present earth-pilgrimage comes to an end. What does he expect? He expects the Song of Immortality. He feels that if he can hear the Song of Immortality, then he will someday achieve everything for the earth-consciousness.

Here we are all seekers. Now, there are two categories of seekers: mind seekers and heart seekers, or mental seekers and psychic seekers. The seekers who want to realise the Highest with the help of the mind, through the mind, eventually come to know that they are travelling on a very crowded train. This is the mind-train. While they are travelling on the mind-train, they see that with them are quite a few other passengers, and these passengers are fear, doubt, anxiety, jealousy and other negative and destructive forces. The train is overburdened. It goes slowly, very slowly, creeping sluggishly towards its destination. God alone knows when it will reach its journey's goal. With utmost uncertainty the mind-train crawls towards its destination. But those who want to realise the Highest through the heart and with the help of the heart travel on another train. That is the heart-train. When the seeker travels on the heart-train, there is nobody else with him. He is alone, he and the mounting flame of his aspiration. The train flies towards the destination at top speed because there are very few passengers weighing it down, and it reaches its destination sooner, much sooner than it even expects.

God is an eternal Player. We are His children, who are also playing in the Cosmic Game.

When we live in the physical, we play with sleep, day in and day out. Our consciousness is not awakened.

When we live in the vital, we play with depression and frustration. When we do not achieve our goal in the vital, we are frustrated and depressed; and when we do achieve our goal, we also feel frustrated and depressed, because we feel that it was something else we wanted.

When we live in the mind, we play with doubt. While playing with doubt, at times we feel that doubt is not a good partner, so we suffer a lot.

But there comes a time when faith looms large within us, and then we transfigure our mental doubt. On the strength of our inner faith, we begin to live in our heart and we play with surrender. Sometimes we surrender to the Absolute, sometimes we try to compel the Reality which we are praying for to surrender to us. And Reality, being all one, surrenders, because of our sincere inner cry. But when Reality enters into us in the form of aspiration, it makes us feel that by pleasing us in our own way, it will never be able to satisfy us. Only if we please the ultimate Reality in *its* own way can we be fulfilled. In the spiritual life, many times when we are pleased in our own way, we are not satisfied. Only when we are pleased in the way of the Divine, of the Supreme, can we be inwardly fulfilled.

At the beginning, we start our journey to please ourselves. In order to please ourselves, naturally we have to go through some discipline; for without discipline, we will not have any success. We have to follow mental, vital, psychic and spiritual discipline in order to see the face of inner satisfaction. Even when satisfaction looms large, we are not satisfied unless we please the Inner Pilot in His own Way. Only then does real satisfaction, eternal satisfaction, dawn in our lives. We try to control our lives, we try to perfect our lives and that is good. But when we try to please the Inner Pilot in His own Way on the strength of our unconditional surrender, when we make an unconditional surrender to His Will, when we become His chosen instruments and fulfil Him in His own Way, at that time we become perfect instruments. When today we have the inner dedication to say, "Let Thy Will be done," tomorrow we will have the right to say, "I and my Father are one."

18. Spirituality

Spirituality, according to my knowledge, understanding and realisation, is a house, and God is the resident of this house. Now this is the realisation of the beginning seeker in me. But when the seeker in me is well-advanced, he says that the house and the resident of the house are one and the same.

In the beginning, it is extremely easy for us to think of God as the Creator and not as the creation, because when we look around we see that God's creation is full of imperfection.

At the dawn of his spiritual awakening, a child asks his mother, "Where is God?" The mother immediately answers, "God is in Heaven." Then the child asks, "Where is Heaven?" The mother's immediate answer is, "Heaven is up in the sky." The child is satisfied; he feels that his mother's answer is quite adequate. Then when the child grows older and goes to a church for religious training, the child asks his teacher the same question: "Where is God?" The teacher may say that God is in Heaven or that God is in the child's own heart. Years later, when the child enters into his young adulthood, he may want to go deep within and see for himself where God is. Then eventually he comes to hear about spiritual teachers who have realised God. He goes to a spiritual Master and asks about God's authenticity. When he is convinced that God does exist, his immediate question is, "Where is God?" The spiritual Master will tell him that God is everywhere and in everything. But until the seeker has realised God himself, this will be just mental knowledge. He must go deep within in order to feel these truths.

God is in the "yes" of the heart, and God is in the "no" of the mouth. When the heart says "yes," God exists inside the "yes". God is visible; He is really there. But when we try to speak about God, very often we are subject to doubt and our own inner feelings are confused. The mouth says, "No, no God," but God exists even in the mouth that denies Him. It is only in the heart, however, that we can feel, see and grow into the highest Divinity.

We need God. Why? We need God because we are wanting in satisfaction. We have everything save and except satisfaction. A child is not satisfied with what he has. Today his father can give him ten toys, but tomorrow he will want to have more. An adult may have two cars, but he will feel that he needs three cars or two much more beautiful and expensive cars.

We can easily see that material possession rarely gives a person satisfaction. Only when we aspire and go deep within can we see the face of abiding satisfaction. We try to satisfy ourselves with desire-life, but we fail; we badly fail. Then we try with aspiration-life, and we succeed, we easily succeed. But among those who aspire, there are some who aspire to become great but not necessarily to become good. There are some seekers who enter into the spiritual life because they want to have worldly power, and they hope that God will grant them this boon. These so-called aspirants are not satisfied with the world as it is at present. They want to govern the world in their own way, and show their inner realisation or their spiritual supremacy to the world. Those seekers can never be God's chosen instruments. Only those who aspire for God-realisation, for the sake of fulfilling and manifesting God in His own Way, can offer satisfaction to humanity. The seeker feels that it is his dedicated and unconditional service that can save and transform humanity, and not his wise wisdom.

There is a way to see God face to face. There is a way to grow into our inner Divinity. There is a way to perfect the face of the earth. But who can show the way? The Inner Pilot, the inner Being. But where is that inner Being? Who can tell us about the inner Being? Very often we hear a voice or get a feeling from within, but this is not always the voice of the heart. It may be the voice of our demanding vital, or the voice of our doubting or sceptical mind.

At this point who can help us? Who can take us into the inner realm of our consciousness where we can distinguish the voice of our Inner Pilot? A spiritual Master can do this. A spiritual Master teaches the seeker how to enter into his own heart and how to listen to the dictates of his own inner Being. He can easily lead the seeker to the realm of his inner consciousness and make him feel and hear the voice of the Inner Pilot. The Inner Pilot is the real guide, the only guide. Until one has free access to the Inner Pilot, a spiritual Master is of paramount importance.

How can one know who his spiritual teacher is? One can easily know provided he does just a few things. First he has to silence his mind. There can be no doubt, no thought-waves, no negative or positive forces in the mind — nothing, nothing. When the seeker sees that he has become the possessor of a calm and quiet mind, he asks his dear friend, heart, to choose its proper Master. His heart looks at the spiritual Masters and makes the choice. When the heart sees a spiritual Master, if it is overwhelmed with joy, then there is every probability that that spiritual Master is the right one for the seeker. But when the heart sees a spiritual Master and can make a solemn promise that it will please this Master in his own way, without asking anything in return, then that is most certainly the right Master. When the seeker sees a teacher and finds his entire being inundated with joy, and if he wants to go one step ahead and say, "I will give you my whole existence, my inner and outer existence with no expectation, to serve you, to love you, to fulfil you," then he and his Master will definitely be able to please each other. If the seeker can dare to make that kind of promise to the Master, if this promise comes from the very depth of his heart, then without doubt this particular Master is his.

Otherwise, a seeker may think that because so-and-so has ten thousand disciples, naturally he is a great teacher. Well, he may be a great teacher, but he may not be your teacher. Your spiritual teacher is only he whose very presence will make you swim in the Sea of Light and Delight. Your teacher is the one to whom you will want to surrender your entire existence.

Your Master will make you feel and discover that the inner treasure that you are searching for, and have for millennia been searching for, is within you and at your command. It is not the sole monopoly of the spiritual Master. As he has it, you also have it as your very own; it is your birthright. Inside you is the coffer, inside you is the key. Unfortunately, you do not know where the coffer is hidden or what is inside it. The Master just shows you your key and helps you to open the box. Then, to your wide surprise, you see that the infinite wealth which is inside belongs to you and nobody else.

Right now, realisation is a far cry. It is a distant, unrealised dream. But today's dream is tomorrow's reality. Today we are living in a cottage, let us say the cottage of dreams. Tomorrow we shall be living in the palace of Reality. Today we are crying to see just once the Face of God. If we can see the Face of God only once, we feel that our life will have a purpose. Once we see the face of our Beloved Supreme, our dream will become a reality. And sooner or later, on the strength of our aspiration, we shall definitely see the face of our Beloved Supreme.

But we shall not be satisfied with that joy, with that reality. We will soon have another dream, a higher dream, to be blessed and embraced by our divine Pilot Supreme. This dream, too, will one day be fulfilled. But again, we will not be satisfied with this reality, either, with being blessed and embraced by God. We will have a third and last dream. This is the dream of becoming inseparably one with the Absolute Supreme and of growing into His transcendental Illumination, Perfection and Infinity. This is our last dream, and for that we aspire, aspire for years, for lifetimes, for centuries. But at last all our dreams bear fruit, all our dreams are manifested in the form of reality.

We are now living in the world of dreams, but these dreams are not mental hallucinations. These dreams are not the result of vague ideas. These dreams are the precursors of a new dawn. In the new dawn we will see the God-touch, God-realisation, God-revelation and God-manifestation on earth.

19. Transcendental Height and Aspiration-Light

Dearest brothers and sisters, I have special love and admiration for your country, Ireland. I have been cherishing and treasuring love for this country since I was twelve, when I read a book written about the spiritual Master, Swami Vivekananda. In his biography I read something most striking. A young woman from your country was so deeply inspired by the Swami's spiritual light that she went to India and offered her entire existence to Swami Vivekananda, her spiritual Master. Her name was Miss Margaret Noble, but her Master offered her a new name, a spiritual name, her soul's name: Nivedita. Nivedita means self-offering, total self-offering. She offered her whole existence to India. India's spiritual children will forever remain indebted to her love and sacrifice. India's freedom-boat will forever be indebted to her significant efforts to free Mother India from ignorance. Nivedita embodied dedicated self-offering.

When I was twenty-three years old, for the first time I read her book about her Master, Swami Vivekananda. The great spiritual Master, Sri Aurobindo, once remarked that this book of Nivedita's was written with the breath of her heart. From this book I learned how a disciple can become inseparably one with the Master on the strength of implicit love, devotion and surrender to the Master's will.

There are two types of people on earth: spiritual people and unspiritual people. Spiritual people are often accused by those who are not spiritual of being abnormal. They supposedly want to live in the clouds and eat the moonlight. They have no sense of reality. They are just fooling themselves. This is the accusation that is often thrown at them. Spiritual people, in return, say that they are absolutely normal, whereas the unaspiring people are abnormal.

An unaspiring person accuses a spiritual person of not paying attention to the outer life. But a real spiritual person is bound to pay full attention to the outer life. If he is not sincerely spiritual in the truest sense, then in the name of spirituality he will ignore and revile the outer world. But the outer world is the manifestation of God. If someone wants to realise the highest Truth, how can he ignore God's outer manifestation? A really spiritual person will not ignore the outer world. On the contrary, he will accept the world. He will accept the challenge of the world. Then he will conquer the ignorance of the world and he will offer his Wisdom-Light to the world at large.

Unaspiring people often say that a spiritual person is afraid of the world. He is a coward. He does not brave the world, but runs away and hides like a thief, while the ordinary, unaspiring person shoulders the responsibilities of the entire world. But I wish to say that if a genuine spiritual person does not involve himself in the activities of the world, it is because he is preparing himself to shoulder the responsibilities of the world. He knows very well that it is God alone who can give him infinite Light, infinite Bliss, infinite Peace and infinite Power to change the face of the world. Just by mixing with the multitudes, he will not be able to help the world. But by serving the Inner Pilot, by fulfilling the Inner Pilot, he can one day be of real service to mankind.

Among the spiritual people there are some who are accused of too much spirituality, and there are some who are accused of too little. The latter are like students who go to school for a while, but do not want to complete their studies. They want to stop at grammar school or high school. These seekers are satisfied with an iota of Peace, Light and Bliss. They don't feel that they need infinite Peace, Light and Bliss. But at times frustration looms large in their lives, and they expect infinite Peace, Light and Bliss overnight. God feels that it is absurd on His part to give them infinite Peace, Light and Bliss. They are still children. We do not give a child thousands of dollars. We give him just a penny. That is more than enough for him. Even if this child begs his father to give him a thousand dollars, the father knows that he will not be able to appreciate it or utilise so large a sum properly or wisely.

In the spiritual life, when his aspiration does not immediately satisfy the craving mind of the budding, beginning aspirant, this person very often leaves the spiritual path. He thinks he is wasting his time. He says, "I have tried. I have prayed to God to give me Peace, Light and Bliss, but He has not fulfilled my prayer. I tried so hard, but He has not listened." But his conception of what kind of aspiration he has offered to the Supreme is not the Conception-Light of God. He is a child in the spiritual world. If he meditates fifteen minutes a day, he feels that he has played his role and that it is now God's bounden duty to satisfy him, to fulfil his desires. But when one becomes a sincere seeker, one feels that it is God's duty to bless him with Peace, Light and Bliss only in God's own Time.

At our sweet will, we cannot demand Peace, Light and Bliss from above. Who wins the spiritual race? He who has patience. He who has inner courage. He who has the mounting inner cry, which we call aspiration. Each individual has only two things. When he is not in the inner life or in the life of the spirit, when he is in the body, in the vital and in the mind, at that time he has desire. But when he accepts the inner life, when he lives in the heart and the soul, he has aspiration. Desire has to possess one thing today, two things tomorrow and three things the day after tomorrow. Desire is like that. But aspiration does not go from one to two to three. Aspiration just tries to immerse us in the Sea of Peace, Light and Bliss. It does not try to possess the drops of this sea one by one.

From the ordinary point of view, desire is the most important. From the spiritual point of view, aspiration is the most important. If we desire something strongly, naturally we will get it sooner or later. In the world of desire, if we try very hard to get something or to achieve something, in the course of time we will succeed. And in the world of aspiration, if we desperately cry for Peace, Light and Bliss in infinite measure, we are also destined to achieve our goal in the course of time.

Now what do we need along with our aspiration? We need inner confidence. Right now hesitation looms large in our life. We want to do something, but hesitation does not allow us to do it. Doubt constantly plagues our mind. Hesitation kills our inspiration. It is impossible for us to achieve our purpose. But when we have aspiration, we automatically develop confidence in our life, inner confidence.

Now what is confidence? Confidence is the harbinger of success. With confidence we can accomplish everything sooner or later. Success is a very complicated thing. It is very difficult to achieve. When we think of success, we think of something pleasing and comforting to us. But this is success on the physical plane. On the spiritual plane, success is something that energises us and liberates us from the body-consciousness.

When we achieve success in the ordinary life, we feel that it is not sufficient. Today we achieve success in a particular sphere. Immediately we are subjected to more desires. We achieved success, but success does not satisfy us; success does not please us. We cry for success, but when this success dawns we want to achieve something else.

In the spiritual life, success is a different matter. Success is an inner progress. Progress is success in the process of evolution. We have evolved from the mineral life through the plant life to the animal life, and from the animal life to the human life. Now we are longing for the divine life. We are always in the process of evolution, and success is nothing other than our progress. When we make progress, what do we actually do? We manifest our inner Divinity, our inner Reality, our inner Immortality. When we manifest our Divinity and Reality, we feel that this Divinity and Reality, and God, are one and the same. The manifestation of our inner Divinity is the manifestation of God Himself, and what we call our manifestation is actually God's own manifestation.

When we go deep within, we see that God Himself has chosen us as His instruments in order to manifest Himself in and through us. But when He manifests Himself in and through us we have to play our part, because the Creator and the creation always go together. The player and the instrument always go together. If there is no instrument, the player is useless; and, again, if there is no player, the instrument cannot do anything. Both are equally important in this case. When God manifests Himself in and through us, He gives us equal credit. When manifestation takes place, man and God smile together. The divine man and the Lord Supreme smile together. That is the sign of perfect manifestation.

We talk about aspiration. We talk about concentration, meditation and contemplation. Now why do we need them? We need them because we want to go back to our Eternal Home. Earth is our temporary home. Here we stay for fifty, sixty or seventy years. But we have an Eternal Home where we live forever, and that Eternal Home is deep inside our heart.

Right now we have four homes: Earth, Heaven, Death and God. Earth is our home. But from Earth what do we get? Frustration, only frustration. We work for the world. The world does not care. We work for our near and dear ones. They show no sign of gratitude. They do not fully acknowledge the fact that we are trying to help and serve them. So what happens then is that we look up. The song of aspiration dawns in our life. We want to see our Heavenly home, but we have no idea where Heaven is. We feel that Heaven is in the sky. Spiritual Masters, however, say that Heaven is deep inside our pure heart. We are not in a position to enter into the inmost depths of our heart, so Heaven right now is sheer imagination for us.

Our third home we reach at the end of our earthly journey, and that home is Death. When we enter into this home, we take rest from the battlefield of life. But our vast, eternal Home is God. When we think of God the Home, what happens to us? Consciously or unconsciously, we expect Love, Peace, Bliss, Infinity, Eternity, Immortality. These are the things God the Home is bound to grant us. Whatever we see in God the Home, whatever we expect from God the Home, we will get. If we need Peace, He will flood our being with infinite Peace. If we expect Light, He will surcharge our inner being with divine Light. Anything that we need or expect devotedly, soulfully and unconditionally, God is bound to give us. Why? Because He is all Love.

It is God who has taught us the secret of expectation. It is He who has taken the form of expectation in us, and it is He who meets with our expectation from above. When we expect aspiration from God, He becomes aspiration. It is through aspiration that He enters into His own perfection. Spiritual seekers know that God is the eternal Player. He is playing constantly with His aspiration and His realisation. His highest Transcendental Height and His purest Aspiration-Light go eternally together. His Life-Boat plies between the shores of Aspiration-Light and Transcendental Height.

20. God's School

We here are all seekers, seekers of the Infinite Truth. Although we do not belong to the same class, although our standard may not be the same, we are all studying in the same school. Some are in kindergarten, some are in primary school, some in high school, some in the university. But the name of the school is God's School, and God is our only teacher. He teaches us two important things: how to illumine our inner life and how to sacrifice our outer life on the strength of our feeling of oneness with the world at large.

In this school, as in other schools, there are quite a few steps. We get six degrees or diplomas. The first diploma is the purification of our nature, the purification of our outer being. The second is salvation, salvation from the world of miseries and tribulations. The third is liberation from the snares of ignorance. The fourth is the realisation of our transcendental Self. The fifth is our revelation of the Absolute. The last and highest degree is our manifestation of the Absolute Supreme. These are the degrees we get in God's School.

No seekers who want them will be denied these degrees. In the course of time, in the process of our inner evolution, we are bound to get at least the first three degrees. Each seeker, if he is sincere, has to feel that at every moment his life needs discipline — physical discipline, vital discipline, mental discipline, psychic discipline. If there is no discipline, then the individual will make little or no progress. But if there is discipline or self-control, then he can run very fast towards his goal.

Life has to be taken seriously. But if it is taken too seriously, then we will be pulling the Truth or pushing the Truth. By pulling or pushing we cannot achieve the Truth the way the Supreme within us wants us to achieve it. If we take life too seriously, immediately we expect something grand, great and momentous from life; and if we do not get what we want, immediately we feel frustrated. We feel that we are in a prison of futility. Life is fruitless, work is fruitless, everything is fruitless. We have to take life seriously, but if we take it too seriously, then we demand from life something which it is unable to give us immediately. Slow and steady is the answer here. Slowly, steadily, unerringly, we have to carry life towards its destination. We carry life with our aspiration; life carries us with its patience and perseverance in the journey towards the destined goal.

Some people take life very lightly, however. They think that life has nothing to give, so they wallow in the pleasures of ignorance, either consciously and deliberately or unconsciously. We have to know that these people have made friends with absurdity. Each life has come directly from the Highest Absolute. We cannot squander life. We have to feel that each life has a serious meaning of its own. The individual life will eventually be merged in the Cosmic Life. The finite, the light of the finite, the life of the finite, will be merged in the Infinite. We came from the Infinite. Here on earth we play our roles for fifty, sixty or seventy years, and then we depart. Then after a while with a new message, with a higher light, with a stronger power, we once again enter into the world to fulfil the Universal Life which abides in the individual life on earth. If we take life too lightly, if we do not pay enough attention to life, then we are unconsciously or consciously negating our inner possibilities and destroying our inner potentialities.

There is another way of accepting life, a human way. We can feel that we are, after all, human beings and thus are allowed to do certain things. We can feel that the experiences we get from life will eventually lead us to our destination, but since we are human beings, we may remain in the sea of ignorance for as long as we like. We can constantly err and still expect forgiveness from God. This is the human way of accepting life, or taking part in the human drama. But this attitude is also a deplorable mistake. We should feel that we have to come out of ignorance as soon as possible — not by violence, but on the strength of our aspiration. With our inner strength, inner urge, inner life, we must come out of the sea of ignorance.

There is a fourth way. We can take life divinely. Each moment we can feel that there is something called Divinity that is trying to loom large in our life. Every second Divinity wants to come to the fore. But consciously or unconsciously, we are not allowing it to do so. But if we pray and meditate, Divinity gets ample chance to come forward. That is why a sincere seeker, a seeker of the Absolute Truth, meditates daily. He feels the necessity of bringing his own Divinity forward, for in Divinity he feels a real sense of satisfaction.

Each individual seeker is crying for satisfaction. A child gets satisfaction from a piece of candy. A man of desire becomes satisfied when he gets a million dollars. A seeker who has just launched into the spiritual life is satisfied when he gets an iota of Light and Peace. We are all running after satisfaction. But real satisfaction, complete satisfaction, is still a far cry. Complete satisfaction will dawn only when God-manifestation in its highest aspect has taken place on earth. Right now, God-manifestation is taking place in a veiled and unenlightened way. Many, many people have realised God. Many of them have revealed God. But very few have been able to manifest God because they are surrounded by the unenlightened and unaspiring earth-consciousness. Unless and until the full manifestation of the Supreme takes place on earth, no seeker can be completely satisfied.

Realisation is one thing and manifestation is something else. Until manifestation has taken place, perfect Perfection cannot dawn. To climb up the mango tree is realisation. To climb down again with the mangoes and distribute them to those who do not have is revelation. And after the distribution, to make them feel that this mango is Nectar and Immortality, and that it is from each human being's Immortality that the earth-consciousness will eventually be divinised and fully immortalised — this is manifestation. To climb up the mango tree is great, but it is not enough. We have to climb down again to distribute the mangoes and to make the world aware of their significance. Until we do this, our role is not complete and God will not be satisfied and fulfilled.

Every seeker is playing a significant role. At the very beginning of his journey, he should feel that he is a chosen child of God. If he thinks he is a chosen child of God, then many undivine attributes will automatically drop from his nature. If he can say, "I am a chosen child of God," immediately he will have the inner courage to vehemently fight and chase away doubt, fear and temptation. Doubt will not be able to tell him that God-realisation is something absurd, or that he does not have the capacity to realise the highest Truth. Fear will leave him at once, because he will feel his oneness with God. The Christ used his Realisation-power to say, "I and my Father are one." If an aspirant starts saying, "I and my Father are one," it will be on the strength of his imagination-power. But what today we call imagination will be transformed into reality tomorrow. A scientist imagines the result of an experiment, then he performs it and discovers the reality. Today's dream is tomorrow's reality.

We have to start our spiritual journey with imagination. Inside imagination we have to feel our inner cry, which is aspiration, constantly trying to climb high, higher, highest in a never-ending upward journey. We all have this aspiration, so we are bound to realise the highest Truth.

God-realisation is not the sole monopoly of an individual. Many have realised God and many more will realise God, until a day comes when all will have realised the Highest. But there is something called God's Hour. God's Hour is the hour chosen by God. Today God is pleased with me. Tomorrow God will be pleased with you. The day after tomorrow He will be pleased with somebody else. The moment He is totally pleased with us, He grants us the boon of boons: God-realisation, God-discovery.

There are some seekers who are weak in their aspiration. I wish to tell them that if their aspiration is weak today, they will not always be doomed to disappointment. Carry on slowly, steadily. If you feel that you are weak, then immediately pray to the Lord, to the Inner Pilot, to offer you shelter. He is bound to give it. The cry of the weak seeker is for shelter and protection, and he can expect to get these from his meditation.

There are some seekers here who are strong, who meditate regularly, devotedly and soulfully. To them I wish to say that what they can and should expect from their meditation is joy, inner joy — the joy that conquers limitations, imperfections, bondage and death. Once one has conquered limitations, imperfections and bondage, one's inner being will be flooded with immeasurable joy.

When the seeker is cheerful, when he is flooded with inner joy, inner light and inner delight, he must offer something to the Inner Pilot in order to fulfil and manifest Him. That offering is gratitude. He knows that it is the Inner Pilot who has surcharged his inner being with this Peace, Light and Delight in boundless measure. He now wants to manifest the Inner Pilot, the Supreme, on earth, and he does it through gratitude, soulful gratitude, constant gratitude. When he offers gratitude, the power, the quantity, even the quality of his Joy, Light and Delight automatically increase. How can he offer gratitude?

He can offer gratitude easily and, at the same time, effectively through constant and conscious surrender of his will to the Will of the Supreme. He has to make himself feel that he is nothing other than an unconditional instrument at the Feet of the Lord Supreme. When he becomes an unconditional instrument of the Lord Supreme, the manifestation of Divinity, the manifestation of Reality, the manifestation of Immortality can and will take place here on earth.

Today we are thinking of God, meditating on God, contemplating on God, with the idea that one day we shall see God face to face. When we finally do see God face to face, we will not be satisfied. At that time we will try to have God as our very own. When we get God as our very own, we will then feel the need of consciously and constantly trying to become God. But it is not we who try; it is God within us who aspires. Today's man is God unrealised. Tomorrow's man will be God fully realised.

There is no end to a seeker's journey. Every day we are surpassing our past achievements and transcending our previous goals. If we pray, if we concentrate, if we meditate, we will feel deep within us that we are constantly transcending ourselves. It is not a barrier that we are transcending, but an achievement. Yesterday's goal was to see something. Today's goal is to feel something. Tomorrow's goal will be to become something. We have seen during our meditation that Reality, Divinity and Immortality do exist. We now feel that these are a part of our lives. It is only a matter of time before we grow into these realities and embody them in our lives.

21. Desire and aspiration

Yoga is a Sanskrit word. It means union, conscious union with the Highest, conscious union with the Absolute.

Spirituality is a vast subject. Yoga teaches us how to study this subject. Yoga also teaches us how to have a free access to God, the Absolute.

We are all one, inseparably one with God. But our oneness is an unconscious oneness. But if we follow yoga, if we practise spirituality, then our oneness with God becomes conscious. More than that, it becomes constantly and inseparably conscious.

Two things govern the world, only two things: desire and aspiration. Desire is for those who want to live an ordinary life, practically the life of an animal; and aspiration is for those who would like to live the life of the cosmic gods. The life of desire is immediately followed by destruction. The life of aspiration is followed by revelation, and revelation is followed by manifestation — manifestation of our Divinity, manifestation of the Inner Pilot and manifestation of the Absolute, fully and completely here on earth.

Some people are satisfied with what they have and what they are. What they have is material wealth and what they are is desire. They have desire, but their desires are fulfilled to a great extent and they are satisfied. For these people aspiration is nowhere to be found. They are lifeless, static beings. Those who suffer from frustration and dissatisfaction in the life of desire at least feel that desire is not giving them abiding satisfaction. They want to have something more, to achieve something or grow into something that will give them real satisfaction. In time, these people will feel that the life of desire and material prosperity is not the answer.

There are various reasons why people enter into the spiritual path or want to practise yoga. Some people enter into the spiritual life because the world has disappointed them or deserted them and they are filled with bitter disgust for the world. They feel that spirituality is the only answer.

Some people enter into the spiritual life because they see that suffering is omnipresent. Suffering is within, suffering is without, suffering is in their families, suffering is in themselves, suffering is in the world at large. They know that suffering is not the answer. Something else — Peace, Light and inner Delight — is the answer. And they feel that they can get these only from the spiritual life.

Some people have come to know that the root of suffering is desire. Because people consciously or unconsciously cherish teeming desires, they are compelled to suffer. When their desires are not fulfilled, they suffer from frustration; when their desires are fulfilled still they suffer, for they thought that the fulfilment of their desires would have been infinitely more meaningful and satisfying.

Some people have gone a step further and have come to realise that desire is not the real culprit. It is ignorance that is the real culprit. We wallow in the pleasures of ignorance, and ignorance compels us to desire at every moment. Our inner sky is overcast with clouds, and these clouds are ignorance. We can illumine this inner sky through our constant inner cry, the cry that we hear ceaselessly inside the very depths of our heart, in the inmost recesses of our being. When we cry inwardly, in our inner being we feel that there is a climbing flame. This flame goes high, higher, highest and touches the acme of perfection. This conscious inner cry has a special name, and that name is aspiration.

This inner cry will carry us into the world of infinite Beauty, infinite Delight, infinite Perfection. These worlds are for the people who enter into the spiritual life. They are blessed. They know the Truth. They know that material prosperity cannot give them immortal Life, immortal Light and Delight. It is impossible. Only the inner life, the life of aspiration and dedication, can give them this immortal Peace, Light and Bliss in infinite measure.

Of course, it does not matter why you enter into the spiritual life — whether suffering or frustration or any other factors have compelled you. Once you have accepted the spiritual life soulfully and devotedly, that is enough. Your readiness and eagerness in the spiritual path is the only important thing.

In the spiritual life there should not be any kind of calculation or intellectual approach, but only self-giving to the Inner Pilot. The approach has to stem from the inner being directly, and should not go through the mind or the intellect. This does not mean that you will totally discard and disregard the mind. But the mind that you are using right now is the physical, earthbound mind. Its capacity is very limited; but in spite of that it constantly judges you and others. The mind is always eager to suspect others. It feels that suspicion is the greatest wisdom. It feels that its doubting capacity is the greatest achievement. If the mind suspects or doubts, then it feels that it is doing something very great and significant. Naturally, you very often see that its judgements are totally wrong, because the mind's judgements are based on its preconceived ideas and prejudices. But the heart is all love, all oneness, all spontaneity.

Stand in front of the ocean of spirituality and use the mind. It will say that the ocean is very cold and its waves are dangerous and ferocious. Doubt will tell you that the waves will drown you. But the heart will see the ocean, not as an ocean of destruction, but as an ocean of Illumination, an ocean of Perfection and Fulfilment. It will feel that if you jump into this ocean, you will be jumping into the sea of Reality, and that sooner or later you will become the Reality itself.

Some people are badly frightened by the ocean of spirituality. They feel that there will be no escape for them and that the ocean of spirituality will drown them. Just because they do not care for the ocean of reality, they are now swimming in the ocean of ignorance. We can be in only one place: either in ignorance-night or in Wisdom-Light. Ignorance-night is right in front of us and, at the same time, Wisdom-Light is deep within us. It is we who have to make the choice. If we accept the Wisdom-Light, then our life is bound to be transformed, illumined and perfected. But if we accept ignorance-night, then our life will be devoured and destroyed by ignorance. If we really want to walk along the path of spirituality, then constantly we will be inspired from deep within to follow the path of Light, and to grow into the Light slowly, steadily and unerringly. Then, at the end of our journey's close, we will see the Inner Pilot, the Supreme Beloved, garlanding us with His transcendental Joy and divine Pride.

22. God and love

Dear seekers, dear sisters and brothers, I wish to give a short talk on God and love. God is omniscient. God is omnipotent. God is omnipresent. But knowing this, feeling this, does not satisfy me. Only when I feel that God is all Love, the all-loving Father and Mother, am I most satisfied. His aspect of love pleases me most, enlightens me most and energises me most. Therefore I would like to say a few things on God and love.

We started our journey from Heaven. There we were fond of God's Dream. While we were in the soul's region and not in the gross physical body, we loved God's Dream, or we can say, we loved God the Dream. Now, what was God's Dream? His Dream was to become many. He was one and He wanted to become many so that He could divinely enjoy Himself in infinite forms and shapes. In the realm of the soul, we all loved this Dream of God and wanted to become cosmic players so that we could participate in His Cosmic Drama.

Our soul entered into the world arena to become a conscious player in God's Cosmic Drama. Then, when we entered into the world, we started loving God's Beauty: God's Beauty in nature, God's Beauty in art, God's Beauty in our life. We started loving God the Beauty. His infinite beautiful forms we tried to see with our eyes. We appreciate beauty in various forms in our experiences, in our actions, in our realisations. But there is one thing we want to achieve and grow into, and that is God's Beauty and God the Beauty.

Then we feel the necessity, as we make progress in our spiritual life, of sensing and feeling Infinity. We are finite. We are now in earth-bound time. We are now wallowing in the meshes of ignorance. But we want to free ourselves from the meshes of ignorance. We feel that if we can come out of the finite and enter into the Infinite, then all our problems will be solved, we will have found ourselves. We look for Infinity here, there and everywhere, but we do not even begin to see or feel Infinity. But if we go deep within, if we enter into the inmost recesses of our hearts, we feel Infinity: we feel infinite Peace, Light and Bliss.

In Infinity there is a reality. But what is its source? Its source is Divinity in Immortality and Immortality in Divinity. To see, to feel, to grow into Divinity and Immortality, we enter into God's Heart. How do we enter into God's Heart? How do we have a free access to God's Heart? Only on the strength of our inner cry, which we call aspiration. When our inner aspiration-flame mounts high, we enter into the Supreme, our eternal Pilot.

For an ordinary human being, desire is everything. For a

spiritual seeker, aspiration is everything. In the field of aspiration, there comes a time when a seeker becomes consciously aware of the fact that he has to do the first thing first. Now what is this "first thing"? It is God. "First things first" means that God should come first in his life — not only in his inner life, but also in his daily multifarious activities. It means that God is to be loved first and foremost, both as the Deity and as all human beings. It means that first we have to love God as a personal Being and then as an impersonal Being. It is infinitely easier for us to approach God in His personal aspect than in His impersonal aspect. In His impersonal aspect, God is infinite Peace, infinite Light and infinite Energy, and in His personal aspect He is a most beautiful Being. He is much more beautiful than the most beautiful youth on earth. He has far more beauty than any human being. So first we go through the personal aspect of God and then to the impersonal, but we love both aspects — the personal and the impersonal.

Sometimes it happens that we accept God and enter into the spiritual life, but after a few years we give up the spiritual life. That is to say, we reject consciously and deliberately God's Concern, Compassion, Love and Blessings. What does God do then? When we reject Him deliberately, after having accepted the spiritual path, what does He do? God offers us His compassionate Smile. He tells us, "Children, I am ready to wait for you. I shall wait for you to give Me another chance." He will wait indefinitely. This is how the compassionate Father fulfils Himself in and through us when once we have appreciated God's Love or God the eternal Love.

In our spiritual life, God comes first, then our self-discovery, our unconditional surrender to God and then our God-realisation. If we want to have abiding Peace, Light and Bliss in infinite measure in our inner being, then we have to make an unconditional surrender to the Will of the Lord Supreme.

A difficulty arises at this point in our spiritual life when we start to make progress on the strength of our devoted surrender. Quite often, the mind comes forward. The mind right now is in ignorance. It is unillumined. The mind has acquired much outer knowledge, but the mind is enmeshed in the physical and the vital. So what does this knowledge bring? Doubt and suspicion. The mind is constantly doubting. It doubts others, it doubts God and it even doubts its own existence. Doubt is its own authority. There is a constant battle going on between the doubting mind and the surrendering and surrendered heart. The mind tries to destroy the heart's potentiality. But if we stick to our spiritual life, eventually the heart wins the battle. In the surrendered heart we notice tremendous faith. Faith is our wisdom, our inner wisdom. This inner wisdom tells us that we are of God and we are for God. We came from God and we are going to God, the Light and Delight. Here we are consciously and soulfully trying to manifest God on earth. And at the end of our journey's close, we shall enter into the infinite Peace, Light and Bliss.

Once we have accepted God, it is up to us to continue loving Him and accept Him wholeheartedly, or to reject Him. When we enter into the spiritual life, we feel that we have entered consciously into God's domain. We can make conscious progress, fast progress and fulfilling progress when we accept God wholeheartedly on the strength of our sincerity, purity, humility and love.

Once we have accepted God wholeheartedly, then God becomes our eternal friend and our eternal slave. At that time, when we pray to God, "God, give me this, God, give me that," it becomes His bounden duty to please us. Once we offer our very existence to God, it becomes His responsibility to please us and fulfil us in His divine, supreme Way.

When we pray, when we meditate for a number of years, God,

out of His infinite bounty, offers us a passport. If we have this passport, we can enter into Heaven — the higher worlds. There are seven higher worlds and seven lower worlds. If we do not aspire regularly, devotedly, systematically and soulfully, then this passport is confiscated. We lose our free access to the higher worlds, the inner worlds of Peace, Light and Bliss.

But there comes a time when each individual has to possess Peace, Light and Bliss. God's choice Hour is for everyone. Today God's Hour has struck for you. Tomorrow for him. The day after tomorrow for her. God will not be satisfied unless and until we all have achieved this Peace, Light and Bliss in boundless measure in our inner beings. He will be pleased only when we have discovered our inner existence and only when we consciously, soulfully and unconditionally take part in His Cosmic Game, fulfilling Him in His own Way. This we do only on the strength of our pure love, divine love, devoted and surrendered love to the Will of the Supreme, who is our Inner Pilot.

We are eternal travellers. In Heaven, we were dreamers, and on earth we are travellers along the road of Eternity. We shall reach our Goal of the Golden Beyond. This Golden Beyond is the eternally transcending Beyond. Today's goal will be tomorrow's starting point, just as yesterday's goal is today's starting point. There is no end to our realisation. We are always in the process of cosmic evolution, of our nature's transformation, of our inner illumination and perfection.

23. The spiritual Master

I am extremely happy to be here with you. All of you are aspiring in your own way, so you have given me ample opportunity to be of service to the Supreme in you. There is only one teacher, one Guru, and that is the Supreme. Since we are all seekers, we are all invoking the presence of our eternal Guru, the Supreme.

Most of you are practising spirituality and yoga. It is not a new subject to you. But I wish to say how I approach this particular subject. To me, spirituality is a box and yoga is the key, while God is the wealth or treasure inside the box. Each of you has this box, this key and this wealth. God is not the sole monopoly of spiritual Masters. Never! He is equally yours. Spiritual Masters come into the world to convince you that God-realisation is your birthright. You can claim God as your very own. You can also say the same thing that Christ said two thousand years ago: "I and my Father are one." He said this on the strength of his conscious and constant inseparable oneness with his Father. We do not have that constant, conscious, inseparable oneness. There are days when we feel the Presence of God for a long time. Again, there are days when we feel the Presence of God for only a few minutes. And there are days when we do not feel the Presence of God at all. This being the case, how can we dare to say that God and we are one? We feel that we would be telling a deplorable lie. But like Christ, if we pray, if we meditate, if we discover the highest within ourselves, then the day will come when we will be able to declare the same, when each individual will be able to declare: "I and my Father are one." It is not only possible, not only practicable, but it is inevitable that one day everyone will claim this same realisation.

Yoga is the way to get this realisation. Yoga means union, conscious union with God. Yoga teaches us how we can collect a bumper crop of realisation. This realisation is the realisation of our Divinity, of our Immortality, of the Infinite within us, of the Eternal within us.

According to our traditional Hindu system, there are three major yogas — Karma Yoga, Bhakti Yoga and Jnana Yoga. Karma

Yoga is the yoga of dedicated service. Bhakti Yoga is the yoga of love and devotion. Jnana Yoga is the yoga of knowledge and wisdom. In Jnana Yoga we see an important, most powerful branch called Raja Yoga. In the West, this is what you call mysticism, yoga for the mystics.

There are also other yogas, such as Hatha Yoga and Japa Yoga. Here in the West many people practise Hatha Yoga. This is of great help, supreme help, in keeping the body fit. It relaxes your body and helps you in awakening your consciousness. But you have to know how far Hatha Yoga can take you. In the West, fortunately or unfortunately, many people are under the impression that Hatha Yoga can lead to the destination. But this is not so. Hatha Yoga is the starting point. Practising Hatha Yoga is like studying in kindergarten, whereas concentration, meditation and contemplation are the university courses. Even if you do not study in the kindergarten, you may easily get to the university. There are some good students, brilliant students, who skip some grades. They need not go to kindergarten. They start in primary school and then continue. But if you don't start, then how are you going to reach your destination? Whatever Hatha Yoga can teach us, we should willingly learn, but we must not give undue importance to this small branch of the great tree of yoga.

If our mind is constantly subject to thoughts and ideas, if the thought-monkey is constantly biting us, then we have to take care. We have to fight against the mischievous monkey, thought. Hatha yoga can be of help in this. But there is another type of yoga called Japa Yoga which is a greater help. Japa Yoga is the repetition of a particular word or name of the Lord — Krishna, Rama, Kali, Supreme, Aum, etc. While we practise japa our mind is focused only on our chosen deity, a spiritual quality, a particular aspect of God, or a manifestation of God in a human body. This practice helps considerably in quieting and controlling the mind.

But if we can practise concentration, meditation and contemplation, then it is like taking a modern jet plane to reach our destination. If we want to go to Rome, we can go in various ways. It depends on how fast we want to reach our destination. We can go with the help of an Indian bullock cart, or we can go with the help of a jet plane. Naturally, the plane will take us to our destination much faster.

Now once we reach our destination, the game is not over. We have something else to do. We have to reveal the Truth, the Light that we have achieved and grown into. After revelation, still the game is not over. We have to manifest on earth the Light that we embody. While manifesting the Light of the Supreme, we are fulfilling the Supreme in His own Way. Before we start manifesting the Supreme in His own Way, we are only preparing ourselves to be the divine soldiers, chosen soldiers of the Infinite. But a day comes when we have realised, we are revealing and we have started manifesting. At that time we can claim to be the chosen instruments of the Supreme, the Inner Pilot.

I have been asked many, many times by seekers how yoga fits in with religion. The ultimate aim of each religion is to realise the highest Truth. Therefore, the goal of all religions is one. Yoga expedites one's journey in each religion. That is the role of yoga. Yoga has a big heart. It includes all religions and, at the same time, it tells all religions to go beyond their boundaries. Yoga accepts, embraces all religions as its very own and, at the same time, inspires all religions to go beyond, far beyond their limited domains.

All seekers should follow their own respective paths, and feel that each path is like a boat. You have a boat of your own, I have a boat, she has a boat and he has another boat. If you remain in your boat, sooner or later you will reach your goal. But if you try to keep one foot in one boat and the other foot in another boat, or if you constantly jump from one boat to another, you will soon be drenched in the sea of ignorance, and you will never reach your destination.

But if you have no confidence in your boat, that is a different matter. You have been in school for some time and you feel that you are making no progress. The teacher is not satisfying you. Naturally you have every right to leave the school and find a school that satisfies you. Similarly, if you are not satisfied with your boatman, that is to say, your spiritual leader, you have every right to change the boatman and the boat.

Unfortunately, some seekers are not serious or genuine enough to discover this fact. They start their journey out of curiosity. When they start their spiritual journey out of curiosity, they are misled by outer things. The moment they hear that so-and-so has ten thousand disciples, immediately they want to become disciples of that particular Master. He is very great, they feel, otherwise how can he have ten thousand disciples? These curious seekers tend to accept a Master unwisely, with no proper sense of discrimination.

I wish to say that even though a particular teacher may have ten thousand disciples, he may not be your proper teacher. Your teacher may be somebody who has only two disciples. You may be his third disciple, and then perhaps he will not accept any more. But again, who knows? Your own Master may have thousands of disciples. There is nothing wrong in it. Even though he has thousands of disciples, he can easily have you in his boat, and he can carry you to your destined Goal.

Everything depends on your sincerity. Even after you have accepted a spiritual Master's path, please feel that at every moment you have to play your role, you have to play your part. Some seekers say, "Now that I have a Master, a path, I don't have to do anything. I can sleep day in, day out, in the boat." But it is not like that. Each day you have to offer your own aspiration consciously, devotedly, intensely. Only then is it possible for the Master to give you his Peace, his Light, his Bliss. You have to give to the Master your aspiration, which is your achievement, and the Master has to give to you his achievement, which is his realisation. You have to give what you have, and the Master has to give what he has.

In this way the Master and the seeker, the Master and the disciple, become inseparably one. Your aspiration is of paramount importance and the Master's realisation also is of paramount importance. With your aspiration and his realisation you and the Master are fulfilling the Divine, manifesting the Absolute on earth. You are giving something to the Master which is of infinite value, and on the strength of it he is manifesting the Absolute, the Infinite on earth. The Master and the disciple are of equal importance as players in God's Cosmic Game.

But the seeker needs to have constant faith in his Master, as the Master has faith in him. Once he accepts someone as his disciple, the Master has boundless faith in that particular seeker. But the seeker, the disciple, quite often loses faith in the Master and in himself. Now if he loses faith in his Master, his progress will be delayed but not ended. He can go to some other Master. Perhaps the second one is actually his real Master. So naturally he will make progress. But if the seeker loses faith in himself, then his spiritual life has ended. In the spiritual life, if one loses faith in oneself, then he is lost. He is a babe in the woods. At that time he is not only helpless, but also hopeless.

The Master is your friend, your eternal friend, who helps you to realise the highest in yourself. He helps you to open your inner treasure chest with your key — not his key — and shows you your own treasure. Once he shows you your own treasure, his part of the game is over. In the ordinary life, if you take help from someone to accomplish something, you are under obligation to give that person some fee or compensation. But in the spiritual life, you do not have to give the Master anything but aspiration. When he helps you in your God-realisation, your very aspiration is his fee. You have aspired to find your inner treasure, and he has been of help to you. He feels that if you have accepted him to be of service, that in itself is his fee. The joy of serving God in you is sufficient salary for the Master.

A spiritual Master is he who constantly plays the eternal Game and swims across the sea of ignorance, carrying seekers to the shore of Light and Delight. A spiritual Master is an elder brother, the eldest son. Being the eldest in the family, he knows a little more than his younger brothers and sisters, so he leads or carries the younger ones to the Father. Once he shows his younger brothers and sisters where the Father is, his role is over.

So dear friends, dear seekers, dear sisters and brothers, we are all aiming at the same Goal. We have all started the journey. We have launched into the spiritual path. We are no longer at our starting point. We are on our way to our destination. It is up to us whether to run slowly or to run fast. If we want to run fast, faster, fastest, then we have to simplify our outer life, our life of confusion, our life of desire, our life of anxiety and worry. And at the same time, we have to intensify our inner life, our life of aspiration, our life of dedication and illumination.

24. Yesterday, today and tomorrow

Everybody knows about spirituality according to his own aspiration, according to his capacity and according to his receptivity. Since we are all seekers here, we are supposed to know something about spirituality and we do know a considerable amount. As a seeker of the Absolute, the Transcendental Supreme, I wish to share with you my own knowledge of spirituality.

In my view, spirituality means acceptance of life — acceptance of the inner life first and then acceptance of the outer life, the ordinary life. First we have to accept the inner life. Then, from the inner life, we have to discover and bring to the fore the light, peace and bliss from our soul, to inundate our outer life.

In my view, spirituality can never mean the rejection of life or the total negation of life. To me, spirituality means the true acceptance of life. We have to accept life as it is now. But we must not be satisfied with this life, we cannot be satisfied with this life as such. It is our bounden duty to change the face of the world. But how can we do it? We can do it only when we ourselves are changed within and without. When we are transformed, we are in a position to be of service to mankind. When we can live in the soul and not in the gross physical we are ready to offer our dedicated service to aspiring mankind.

According to my humble philosophy, spirituality should never take shelter in the Himalayan caves. Those days of the hoary past are buried in oblivion. Now we have to face the world. If we enter into the Himalayan caves to look for God, then we are deliberately ignoring the possibility of an integral change, the transformation of our physical, vital, mental and psychic life. Here on earth, amidst multifarious activities, we have to realise the Highest, we have to fulfil the transcendental Supreme.

Our spiritual philosophy tells us that today needs a man of action. Today's man cannot build castles in the air. Today's man cannot remain unillumined. But who are these men of action? If you say that men of action are only those who are practical, it is true to some extent. But really practical men of action are those who have the divine courage to drink of something vast, infinite, eternal and immortal. Men of action are those who challenge ignorance and are ready to fight against ignorance-night, those who want to establish the Kingdom of Heaven here on earth. Yesterday these men of action were all dreamers, but these dreamers were divine dreamers. In their case, dream and reality went together. Dream was the direct vision and reality was the manifestation of this vision. Yesterday's divine dreamers are today's men of action, today's divine warriors. Tomorrow these men have something else to do — tomorrow they have to be the pathfinders and the harbingers of a new dawn, a new light. They have achieved Light; they have grown into Light. Now it is their bounden duty to reveal Light to the world at large. These divine warriors, these men of action, tomorrow have to offer Light to the suffering, bleeding and sinking humanity.

Today we are all seekers. What were we yesterday? Yesterday we were in the world of doubt, teeming doubt. Our mind allowed teeming doubts to enter into us, or our mind cherished teeming doubts and made us feel that doubting others or doubting oneself was the acme of self-discovery. Yesterday we doubted God's existence, we doubted our friends, our relatives, we doubted ourselves, we doubted everyone.

When we doubt others, in the outer world we may not lose anything. When we doubt God, in the outer world we may not lose anything. But when we doubt ourselves, we lose everything. We lose in the outer world and we lose in the inner world as well. We become veritable beggars. The moment we start doubting ourselves we weaken our possibilities and unconsciously destroy our inner potentialities.

Today we are seeking infinite Truth, infinite Light and infinite Peace. Now where can we get infinite Peace, Light and Truth? Here, inside the spiritual heart. We talk about the Universal Consciousness; we talk about the Transcendental Reality. Where is the Universal Consciousness? Where is the Transcendental Reality? Where is the message of the eternal Beyond? They are not in the physical but in the spiritual heart. The spiritual heart houses the Universal Consciousness, the Transcendental Reality, the message of the eternal, ever-transcending Beyond.

Tomorrow, what will we become? Today we are seekers; tomorrow we have to become divine lovers. In human love we are bound to be frustrated sooner or later, but in divine love we establish our oneness with our Beloved consciously, devotedly, soulfully and unconditionally.

We have to offer to the Supreme in humanity everything that we have achieved on the strength of our today's aspiration. Offering is our self-revelation. Self-revelation is our self-offering. When we offer our Peace, Light and Bliss, we have to know that we are offering it to our own ignorant, obscure, impure, unillumined part. We are not offering it to somebody else at all. Let us say that the heart is illumined. But we have to know that the feet are also an integral part of our body. The feet, legs, arms, hands, eyes and every other part complete the whole human body. Similarly, we can take the rest of the world as part and parcel of our being, the part that needs illumination. I do not mean to say that the rest of the world is our feet, far from it. I am only saying that a portion of our entire being is unlit or unillumined.

We have two rooms: the heart and the mind. The heart has achieved or received illumination. It is now obligatory on the part of the heart to enter into the mind to illumine it. We have to feel at every moment that the mind-room — which we can call with utmost simplicity, honesty and humility our unillumined part — is ours. We have to claim the mind-room as our very own, and the mind-room also has every right to claim us. It is we who have to offer Light from the heart-room to the mind-room. And from whom have we already received this Light? From the soul, which is the divine representative of the Supreme.

We who are here on earth have come from somewhere else — far, very far away — into the world arena. What did we do, what did we say to the Lord Supreme when we left our Celestial Abode? We made a solemn promise to the Supreme that here on earth we would realise Him most perfectly, and here on earth we would reveal Him, manifest Him and fulfil Him in His own Way. This was our solemn promise to the Supreme, and He was extremely proud of the soulful promise of His divine children.

But now we do not remember our promise. Now we may consciously and deliberately try to deceive the Supreme and go back on our promise because we want to wallow in the pleasures of ignorance. But He knows that our promise was sincere and genuine, and He knows that we shall fulfil our promise to Him either today or tomorrow, either in the near future or in the distant future. He has that Vision. But we have eclipsed our vision by deliberately making friends with ignorance. We are fond of swimming in the sea of ignorance instead of swimming in the Sea of Knowledge and Light.

Once we actually enter into this world we make an inner promise to our soul and to the world at large that we will help mankind, serve mankind and illumine mankind. In silence we consciously make a solemn promise in the inner world that we will offer constant and conscious service to humanity. Like a beggar, the world looks to us to fulfil our promise. The world looks to each individual to fulfil his promise, but we do not do it. That is why the world is suffering, and still caught in the meshes of ignorance.

Is there anything on earth that can help us fulfil our promise to the Supreme and to the world? Yes. It is called experience, divine experience. Experience carries us into the past. It brings the message of the past and tells us how foolish we were yesterday. Yesterday we did not care for sublime realities, we did not care for God-manifestation. But today we do care for God-realisation, God-revelation and God-manifestation. How foolish we were yesterday! Today we are the same person, but now we earnestly pray and meditate for God-realisation, God-revelation and God-manifestation.

Experience tells us something more. The mistakes that we made in the past can easily be rectified by virtue of our inner awakening and self-discovery. A room can remain unlit for years, for centuries, but the moment we bring light into it, it is lit, it is illumined. We can see that our inner room has been unlit for millennia, but that is no reason why it cannot be illumined as soon as possible. We *can* illumine it and we *have* to illumine it. How do we do it? We do it on the strength of our inner cry, which we call aspiration. In the outer life, when a child cries, the mother runs immediately to the child. Whatever the child wants and needs the mother brings. Likewise, when we cry inwardly for the highest Truth, Light and Bliss which we desperately need, the Transcendental Supreme runs to us and fulfils us in infinite measure.

25. The seeker's four lives

Dear seekers of the infinite Light and Truth, dear sisters and brothers of the Spirit Universal, here in Zurich I see and feel indomitable strength: strength of the body, strength of the vital, strength of the mind and strength of the heart. In the spiritual life nothing is as important as strength and courage. But this strength is not the strength of a hostile force to be utilised for an undivine purpose. Your strength, spiritual strength, is being utilised for a new dawn and a new era. You are inundated with the strength of the spirit, the strength that we call inner strength.

Four thousand years ago the Indian seers of the hoary past, the Vedic seers and sages taught us this sublime truth: *Nayam atma bala-hinena labhyo.* "The soul cannot be won by the weakling." Only the strong can face the teeming ignorance-night and transform it into wisdom-day. He who lacks strength will never dare to enter into the spiritual life.

When we enter into the spiritual life we become fully conscious of our four simultaneous lives. It is only in the spiritual life that we become aware of our animal life, human life, divine life and immortal Life. Before we enter into the spiritual life, these lives are practically unknown to us, simply because we are not conscious of their existence.

What do we mean by the animal life? The animal life is the life of jealousy, doubt and destruction or conscious annihilation. The animal life is like a strong and binding rope. Although the propensity of the animal life is to fight and destroy, there is something in the process of evolution that tries to curb this destructive tendency. That is why from the animal life we enter into a higher form, the human life.

In the human life we still notice a half-animal life. That is to say, we still quarrel, fight, destroy and do many other undivine things. But in the human life we also notice something very meaningful and fruitful, which is called hope. We cherish and treasure an illumining hope. Hope is not something vague and tempting yet millions of miles away from the actual blossoming of reality. No, hope is something that is pushing us forward, pulling us upward to a sublime Reality. Hope is constantly helping us and energising us to run towards the destined Goal.

At times we see that our hopes are smashed into millions of fragments. Why does this happen? It happens precisely because we do not feed our hope with aspiration, with our inner cry. We hope for something, but when difficulties arise we just calmly and peaceably give up our hope. Instead of hope's deserting us, very often we desert hope. We do not give hope a full chance to continue its journey.

In the spiritual life we become aware not only of the animal and the human life, but of the divine life as well. In the divine life we get constant opportunities. We are told that opportunity does not often knock at our door, but when we try to live the divine life, we come to realise that opportunity knocks at our door at every second. We are told that God's choice Hour dawns once in a blue moon, but this is not true. When we enter into the spiritual life we see that God's Hour strikes at every moment. We have only to avail ourselves of each glowing opportunity and of each golden moment.

When we follow the spiritual life we have to make friends with joy. God is constantly offering us this joy, but we are rejecting it ruthlessly at every moment. We prefer to wallow in the pleasures of ignorance. Now, there is an easy and effective way in which we can inundate our being with real joy. It is through our constant inner cry. Outwardly we cry for name and fame, outer achievements and material possessions. But when we cry inwardly, when we cry from deep within, from the inmost recesses of our heart, what we are crying for is Light, Delight, divine Illumination, divine Perfection. The inner life tells us that Delight in infinite measure is at our disposal, that it is our birthright. But because we do not consciously try to claim it as our very own, Delight is still a far cry.

Now what is the difference between pleasure and Joy or Delight? Pleasure is something that is bound to be followed by frustration, and inside frustration what looms large is destruction. We can confidently say that today's pleasure will be tomorrow's frustration and the destruction of the day after tomorrow. But when we follow the spiritual life we see deep within us the fountain of Joy and Delight. This Delight continuously increases in our awakened being. The seeker in us knows perfectly well that our origin was Delight. *Anandadd hy eva khalv imani bhutani jayante...* "From Delight we came into existence. In Delight we grow or expand our consciousness. At the end of our journey's close, into Delight we retire." Delight is our origin, and our goal is to go back consciously to the Source, which is all Delight.

What is Delight or Bliss? It is inner freedom, nothing else. This inner freedom, when properly used, brings to the fore the outer freedom. If the inner freedom does not energise or instruct or illumine the outer freedom, the outer freedom will often act like a mad elephant. In today's world we see how freedom is misused by millions and millions of people. But when the inner freedom comes to the fore and inspires the outer freedom, the outer freedom will reach the destined goal safely and, at the same time, most convincingly and most satisfactorily.

The immortal Life is the life that contains the divine life in its fullest measure. At the same time, it has destroyed the binding rope of the animal life and energised the human life to enter into the divine life. When we enter into the immortal Life, the animal in us is either destroyed or totally transformed, as night is transformed into day. Our human weakness is transformed into strength. Our imperfection is transformed into perfection. All human frailties are illumined and transformed into an ever-growing, ever-fulfilling Light and Delight.

How can we make steady progress, convincing progress, in our spiritual life? We can make satisfactory, conscious and fulfilling progress only by smiling — smiling at the world, smiling at our reality, smiling at Heaven. Each time we smile at any particular reality, if it is a divine reality, our smile immediately increases our capacity, and if it is something undivine, then our smile weakens or destroys its undivine possibilities and potentialities. Now, this smile is not just an ordinary human smile. This smile comes directly from the depths of our heart and from the full awakening of our soul. It immediately makes us feel that we have pleased and fulfilled our Inner Pilot.

We get this inner smile through prayer and meditation. When we pray, we feel that sooner or later God will come to us and fulfil our prayer. Or very often we go to God through our prayer, and then God fulfils us. Either we go to God or God comes to us. Here in the Western world, we give more importance to prayer than to meditation. There is nothing wrong with this. If I like my right eye more than my left eye, and if you like your left eye more than your right eye, there is nothing wrong in it. Prayer and meditation are like two eyes. Both eyes are eager to show us the Light and offer us the Light.

There are many people in the West who go to churches, synagogues and other spiritual places to pray. But their prayers have become mechanical. They are a monotonous routine. You have to eat your breakfast; you eat it, but there is no joy in it. It has become a daily routine. But I wish to say that when we pray, we must pray with a feeling of intensity, with the idea of working for the thing we want to have. If we do this, there is every possibility that our prayers will be sanctioned and granted. We have to envision the result while praying. If we do not envision the reality we are praying for, then immediately there will be a yawning gap between our prayer and the result we are seeking, between the dream and the reality.

But it is only the beginner who will pray in this way, always wanting what he calls satisfactory results from his prayers. When we grow in the spiritual life, in the process of our inner evolution there comes a time when we see that what counts most is not the fulfilment of our prayer at all. We want good results, but if good results come in the form of defeat or failure, so to speak, we accept them with equal joy. In fact we get enormous joy when we can offer our so-called defeat at the Feet of God. In the spiritual life, victory and defeat are like the obverse and the reverse of the same coin. This is the second stage of our development, when we can offer the same joy to God whether our prayer is fulfilled in our own way or not.

The third and last stage is when we pray to God constantly, but do not care for the result whatsoever. We feel that our business is only to pray, and the rest is God's business. We have the inner urge to pray unconditionally, and we feel that it is the divine responsibility of our Inner Pilot to sanction our prayer or not. If He does not sanction it, we do not mind at all. When we can pray unconditionally we make the fastest progress.

There is another way to make the fastest progress, and that is through conscious and constant surrender to the Will of the Supreme. Now, surrender is a very complicated word. An idle human being surrenders to ignorance, to the world. He does not want to make any progress. He has surrendered to his fate, and he will not lift a finger. But that kind of surrender is no surrender. That is only self-deception, and self-deception is nothing other than self-destruction.

Then again, there is the surrender of a slave to his master. A slave surrenders to his master out of fear or outer compulsion. But in the spiritual life there is no outer compulsion, none whatsoever. It is our inner being that compels us from deep within to offer our surrender to the Supreme Pilot. It makes us feel an inner urge to surrender. We feel that we are right now just an iota of the infinite Truth. But when this little iota of truth merges into the Sea of Truth, it loses its individual personality and becomes the Universal Reality, the Universal Individuality, the Universal Immortality.

In the spiritual life, we have to offer our aspiration, our prayer, our concentration, our meditation and our contemplation consciously to God. We have to make a conscious personal effort and, at the same time, we have to offer our inner surrender to God. We must feel that we can sincerely say, "Lord, this much I can do with my hands. This much I can do with my eyes. This much I can do with my physical capacity. The only thing more than that which I have is the capacity to surrender, and this I am giving to You."

In the spiritual life, conscious and divine surrender is the only way to realise the Highest, to grow into the Highest, to reveal the Highest and to manifest the Highest — the Transcendental Reality. When we consciously try to offer all our capacity to God, and to offer Him also our divine unconditional surrender, then in return He will offer us His infinite Joy, Light, Peace and Power. At that time He offers us the message of His divine Victory and gives us the capacity to become His chosen instruments to establish the Kingdom of Heaven here on earth.

26. Spiritual purity

We are all seekers, seekers of Light and seekers of Peace. Each one of us is a seeker in his own way. Each one is spiritual according to his capacity and according to his present necessity. Somebody may be more spiritual than somebody else because he has opened his existence more completely to his inner light. When the sun rises, if we open the doors and windows of our house, naturally we get more sunlight. In the spiritual life also, when we open the door of our heart, then more Light can pass through from our inner being.

In the outer world at every moment we expect something from

others or from ourselves. Very often we do nothing for others, but still we expect quite a few things from them. We may work very hard for others or for ourselves and yet not get anything in return, but we expect. At every moment we expect. But we are making a deplorable mistake here. We should expect only from the right person, and the right person is God. If we knock at the wrong door then we shall never get the result. We have to knock at the right door, which is God's Door: our spiritual heart.

Now we have to know what we can expect from the spiritual life. If we expect from the spiritual life the things that we expect from our material life, our mundane life, then we will be sadly disappointed. If we follow the spiritual life in order to fulfil all our teeming, countless desires, to become the richest or most famous person on earth, or to become the supreme sovereign of this world, then we are not fit for the real spiritual life. But if we follow the spiritual life to get peace of mind, or because we love God, then we can expect results: we can expect Peace, Light and Bliss in abundant measure. Just because God is inside the spiritual life and His constant Blessing is being showered on all seekers, a seeker *can* expect a most comfortable, pleasant life, a life of name and fame. But if he wants to follow the real spiritual life, the life that needs only God, that needs only Peace, Light, Truth and Bliss, then he will not care at all for earthly possessions and earthly achievements.

The world has everything to offer us save and except peace. We can travel the length and breadth of the world and still not find real peace. So where can peace be found? It is deep within us. In the inmost recesses of our heart we all have peace, but unfortunately we have not discovered it. How do we discover it? We discover peace through our constant prayer and meditation. But if this prayer comes only from the physical mind, it will not be very soulful. Only if it comes from the very depths of our heart will this prayer be soulful, and only then will God be bound to answer it.

In the spiritual life, if we can pray well, if we can meditate well, then peace of mind, light and delight are bound to dawn on our devoted heart, searching mind and illumined soul. In order to follow the spiritual life, we must lead a life of purity. Otherwise, like a bad student, we shall always fail our examination and remain in the same class. But if we can establish purity in our physical body, in our vital and in our mind, then we will pass our examination with great honours.

How do we establish purity? We establish purity in the physical through the feeling that we do have inner Light, through our conscious awareness of our inner Light and through the feeling that this Light is eagerly waiting to come to the fore. When we have established purity in the physical, the success we have in any sphere of life becomes permanent. But if we have not established enough purity, then nothing is permanent either in our ordinary life or in our spiritual life. We establish purity in the vital by opening ourselves to the soul's Light. When we have established purity in the vital, the life of aggression leaves us and is replaced by the life of dynamism, vital dynamism. Vital aggression destroys everything but vital dynamism creates. It builds a new world for the seeker within us. When we establish purity in the mind, we consciously and deliberately annihilate doubt, fear and anxiety in ourselves. When we have established purity in our mind, we notice that we do not cherish even an iota of doubt, an iota of suspicion or any wrong, undivine, obscure, unlit or impure thoughts. How do we achieve purity in the mind? We do this by constantly offering our mind to our heart, our spiritual heart, which is in constant touch with the soul. When the mind gets illumination from the heart it has free access to the soul's Light. We can also derive abundant purity from our concentration, meditation and contemplation. But those who do not want to go through this discipline, even those who are not following a strict spiritual life can establish purity in their life, through proper breathing.

The moment we speak of breathing, we find that people become frightened. They feel that if they do not breathe properly, they may get into serious trouble. But I wish to say that even if you do not get a spiritual Master who can teach you how to breathe properly, there is still a way that you can regulate your breathing. It is through constant repetition of the name of your chosen deity or of God. This repetition is called *japa*. If you can repeat the name of God constantly during your prayer and meditation, automatically the sincerity of your japa will regulate your breathing. There are many, many who do not have spiritual Masters to teach them the Indian methods of *pranayama*, or breath control, but they learn to breathe properly on the strength of their most sincere repetition of God's Name.

A child, before his mind is developed, before he knows what thought is, breathes in properly, systematically, in a divine way. But when he grows up, when his mind develops and he enters into the hustle and bustle of life, he loses this capacity. The spiritual life is actually a conscious return to our divine childhood. In the spiritual life we must always feel that we are children of God, chosen children of God. It is a child that makes progress. A child is always open to new feelings, new ideas, new dreams, new ideals. In the spiritual life also, a seeker is always open to higher truths, higher thoughts, sublime ideals and soulful aspiration. It is the bounden duty of the parents to take care of a child. Likewise, in the spiritual life, when we consciously become children of God, it becomes His bounden duty to guide us, mould us and shape us in His very Image.

27. Aspiration and wisdom

Spirituality is a subject to be studied, as we study history, geography, science and other subjects. When we study the subject of spirituality, we discover our inner being, our real being, our true existence. When we become spiritual, that is to say, when we aspire, we see that there are four important things on earth: desire, aspiration, knowledge and wisdom.

Desire is something that binds us constantly. It will not allow us to free ourselves from ignorance. Aspiration is something that tells us about the Infinite and carries us into infinite Peace, Light and Bliss. Knowledge is something mostly of the mental world. Very often what we call knowledge is nothing but mental information. This kind of knowledge is not sufficient; it disappoints us quite often. We soon come to realise that knowledge does not carry us very far. Wisdom is something that comes to the fore from within, from the Light of the soul. When we discover wisdom, we feel that we are in conscious oneness with the Almighty Father.

Since we are all seekers here, let us deal with aspiration and wisdom. When a child cries, his mother runs to him immediately with food. A seeker is a spiritual child. When his aspiration-cry begins, the Almighty Father flies to him with the nectar of Immortality. Wisdom is the Light of the soul. We achieve the Light of the soul, we grow into the Light of the soul, on the strength of our inner cry. The more sincere we are, the sooner our inner wisdom dawns.

How do we get aspiration and wisdom? It is through positive thoughts. There are two types of thoughts, positive and negative. When we follow the spiritual life we always welcome positive thoughts. A positive thought is: "I am of God, I am for God." A negative thought is: "I am nothing, I am useless."

How can we have positive thoughts? We can have positive thoughts, God-thoughts, when we associate with people who pray to God and live a simple, sincere, pure and humble life. But there comes a time when we go beyond even positive thoughts and enter into God's Will. We surrender consciously to the Will of God at every moment. At that time, for us there is no positive thought, no negative thought — only God's Will to regulate and direct our life.

28. The divine host and the divine guest

Dear sisters and brothers, since we are all seekers of the infinite Truth, we are all believers in God and lovers of God. Now, sometimes we believe in something first and then we see that our belief is correct. And sometimes we see something first and then we believe in it. In the spiritual life, when we believe first and then see, we get much more joy than if we see first and then believe. When we see God before we believe in Him, we will only get one per cent joy. But if we first believe in God and then later see Him, at that time we get one hundred per cent joy.

Now, what is belief? It is not only an inner, but also a conscious awareness of truth. After belief, what we feel is faith. Faith is something unshakeable. Faith tells us constantly that our source is God. Once our inner and constant faith dawns, our road to God becomes very clear.

We are all lovers of God, according to our capacity and receptivity. A child is fond of his father, not because his father is a well-educated or a great man, but because his father loves him. There comes a time in the spiritual life when we realise that we love God because He is all love, and not because He is omnipotent, omniscient or omnipresent.

A child cries. The mother feels that it is her duty to come to the child. She offers food, toys or attention. She will give anything to please her child. In the spiritual life, when we become children and cry for Peace, Light and Bliss, God, our Inner Pilot, comes and brings these things to us.

God is our eternal Friend. When there are two friends, today one is the guest and the other is the host, and tomorrow it is reversed. Today I am the guest and God is the host. Tomorrow I am the host and God is the guest.

How can I say this? I can say it on the strength of my aspiration. When I pray, God becomes the host. When I pray, I go to my host, God. When I meditate, I am the host and God is the guest. I invite God in and keep my heart's door fully open. As in the ordinary life two friends visit each other's homes, so in the spiritual life each person can spend time in two homes. One is his heart and the other is God's Heart. There is always a free access between a sincere seeker's heart and God's Heart. Constantly he goes from one to the other. This is how we fulfil God in His Game.

29. Spiritual strength

Dear sisters and brothers, I wish to offer my deepest joy and gratitude to Germany. Here in Germany, mind-power has reached its zenith. Right from my childhood, Germany has always been for me a country of determination and strength. Determination and strength we need in every sphere of life. In the spiritual life, too, at every moment we need abundant strength, for we have to fight bravely against fear, doubt, worry, jealousy and imperfection. Only a brave aspirant can conquer all his inner enemies.

Why do we enter into the spiritual life? Why do we need

God? We need God because God alone can give us abiding and everlasting satisfaction. We cry for material wealth. Eventually, we acquire material wealth, but from material wealth we get practically no satisfaction. Today we have a house, tomorrow we want to have two houses, the next day we want three houses. We may get what we want, but in our acquisition there is no real satisfaction.

When we pray and meditate, we feel that there is something in us, someone in us who is more than eager to satisfy us. That something in us is our inner cry, and that someone in us is our Inner Pilot, God. From the spiritual life, which is the life of pleasing God, we can expect everything. We can and we do get everything if we can truly please God. If we pray to God most soulfully to give us a million dollars, if we can please Him with our sincere aspiration and our soulful prayer, there will come a time when He will make us really rich. Through our prayer, we can fulfil our desires.

But there is another type of prayer which we call aspiration. With aspiration we do not try to get anything. We just try to expand and liberate ourselves and to manifest the Divine on earth.

In the spiritual life, as I said before, will-power and strength are most important. We need strength in the physical, we need strength in the vital, we need strength in the mind, we need strength in the heart. When we have physical strength, when our physical body is full of dynamic energy, we do not fall sick. If we want to meditate early in the morning, the body is ready to help us. If we do not have a healthy, sound body, in spite of our best intention to meditate, the body will revolt and will offer us a stomach upset or a headache or some other ailment that will disturb us.

If we have strength in the vital, then we dare to hope, we dare to accomplish, we dare to conquer all negative forces within us and around us. The strength in the vital we can utilise either to build or to destroy. But we must use this vital strength to build the palace of Light, Peace and Truth, and not to destroy anything.

Two things are constantly trying to destroy our mind: one is fear and the other is doubt. When we have strength in the mind, we do not allow fear or doubt to enter into our mind. Real death comes to us only once in life. But, in a sense, death comes to us almost every day when we allow fear and doubt to enter into our mind. When we welcome or cherish doubt, it is like drinking poison. Doubt negates all our divine possibilities and divine capacities. However, with our prayer and meditation, we strengthen our mind.

If a man does not have strength in the heart, he may have hundreds of friends, but he will feel lonely. He may be very wealthy, but he will feel insecure. But when one prays and meditates, he makes his heart strong and feels there the Presence of the Almighty God. And when one feels the Presence of God in his heart, how can he feel lonely or insecure?

When we have strength in the body, in the vital, in the mind and in the heart, we become fully ready to realise the Highest. God has given the capacity to each and every one of us to discover the real Divinity, the real Reality within us. But we need regular prayer and meditation in order to bring our capacity to the fore and utilise it. If one likes to pray, he can pray. If somebody else likes to meditate, he can meditate. If one wants both to pray and to meditate, he can do so.

It is only through prayer and meditation that we can eventually discover our Dearest, our absolutely Dearest One on earth and in Heaven. And who is this Dearest One? Is He somebody other than ourselves? No! He is our highest and most illumined part. When we pray and meditate, we discover our own highest part.

It is our feet discovering our head. It is a leaf discovering its source, the tree. It is the finite discovering its source, the Infinite.

30. Aspiration and spirituality

To start with, I wish to offer my deepest gratitude to the soul of Sweden. Sweden's soul reminds me of the soul of India. Here I see the simplicity and profundity of heart that I see in India. Also, I see and feel here the eagerness to know something, to do something and to grow into something, which I see and feel in the United States.

Spirituality is a vast subject. If we want to learn this subject in a simple and, at the same time, effective manner, then we must practise yoga. Yoga is a Sanskrit word. It means conscious union with God. We are all seekers here. We are not atheists; for us God exists. But we are not constantly aware of God in our mind or in our day-to-day life. Once a day, perhaps, we become aware of the existence of God, and once a week we may think of God, even though we do believe in His existence. But when we practise yoga, we learn to feel our conscious, constant and inseparable oneness with God, our Inner Pilot.

Spirituality is not something unearthly. It is not something abnormal. It is not something unusual. Spirituality is something normal, natural and most fulfilling. If someone tells you that in order to practise true spirituality and discover the highest Truth, you have to shun society, you have to enter into the Himalayan caves, then I wish to say that this advice is incorrect. Spirituality, real spirituality, tells us to stay here on earth and feel the existence of God in the multifarious activities of our day-to-day life. We have to brave the challenge of the world. We have to fight against the enemies that we have deep within us: fear, doubt, anxiety, jealousy and imperfection. If we retreat to the Himalayan caves or to the farthest reaches of the globe, then our nature will remain imperfect. We have to conquer these undivine, hostile forces right here and now — here on earth, in the midst of society.

We practise spirituality precisely because we need it. We don't do anything on earth if we don't feel the necessity of it. But when we practise spirituality, we should feel that this need is our first and foremost need. Everything else is secondary. If we water the root of a tree, then the leaves, the branches, the flowers and the fruits will all be well nourished. The root, the source of our life, is God. Spirituality brings us this message.

There are two types of love: human love and divine love. Human love wants to possess something or to be possessed by something. Human love is a song of possession. But in possession there is no satisfaction. On the contrary, in possession frustration looms large. We see that the train of destruction immediately follows frustration.

Divine love is the song of expansion. Unlike human love, which binds and is bound, divine love expands and liberates. It liberates our inner being. Our inner being is like a bird, which is in a cage. Divine love allows the bird to come out of the cage and fly into the infinite Vast. We treasure divine Freedom. We can free ourselves, we can free the world at large, on the strength of our divine inner love.

There comes a time when an aspirant feels that only by loving God, seeing God, feeling God and growing into the Light of God can he be totally satisfied. He can be totally satisfied only when he sees God in everything, in every creature, in every human being.

In the spiritual life we start with aspiration, and aspiration soon takes us to realisation. But even realisation feels that it is not sufficient, and it takes us to revelation. Then revelation feels that it is not complete, and it takes us to manifestation. And what is manifestation? Manifestation is the flowering of our inner Divinity. Divinity we always had, but it was implicit; it was dormant. This Divinity has to come to the fore and be manifested here on earth. And this manifestation is called the perfection of nature, the perfection of our earthly existence.

Yoga means conscious and constant oneness with God. Now, how do we establish this conscious and constant oneness with God? It is through self-giving, self-offering. This self-offering is not to somebody outside ourselves. It is to our own highest Reality. The finite is offering its existence to the Infinite, which is our Inner Pilot. And this can be done only through love, devotion and surrender.

The first message of yoga is self-discovery. We have to discover God in ourselves. Then we have to offer our discovery to the world at large. First we shall get the most delicious fruit, and then we shall share it with others. This will give us real joy. Only when we see that we are able to drink the divine nectar together with the world shall we be really satisfied.

There are three principal ways of practising yoga. If we practise the yoga of the heart, then love, devotion and surrender are of paramount importance. If we practise the yoga of the mind, then knowledge and wisdom are of paramount importance. If we practise the yoga of the body, then dedicated, selfless service to mankind is of paramount importance. Yoga unifies our conscious aspiration and God's constant Compassion. What is aspiration? Aspiration is our inner mounting cry. What is Compassion? Compassion is God's all-loving Light and Delight.

We can reach the ultimate Goal no matter which path we follow — the path of the body, the path of the mind or the path of the heart. The Goal is the same. Again, if we sincerely pray and meditate, we will feel that all the three paths go together. When we meditate, we actually offer our purity, our divinity, our reality to the Supreme in mankind; and this is the path of the heart. When we love God and when we devote and surrender ourselves to God in the path of the heart, then we get real inner wisdom, which is the fort of the path of the mind. And when we follow the path of the body, at every moment we feel from deep within an inner urge to love and serve mankind; and in this we find wisdom and a feeling of the heart's inseparable oneness with mankind. So these three paths lead to the same destination.

In the West, unfortunately Hatha Yoga is the most commonly known yoga. But the physical postures and *asanas* of Hatha Yoga are only a small help towards the ultimate goal of union with God. The real yoga is the yoga of concentration, meditation and contemplation. When we concentrate on something, we consciously put an end to all extraneous thought-waves. We throw aside all the thoughts that are in our mind, and we want to walk along the path of reality. Then we go on to meditation. When we meditate, we consciously invoke the Infinite. And the Infinite comes to us with boundless Peace, Bliss and Light. Then, when we contemplate, on the strength of our unconditional surrender, we become one with the Supreme Pilot. Here the divine lover becomes one with the Supreme Beloved. They become inseparable. The creation becomes one with the Source. The finite becomes one with the Infinite. When we practise concentration, meditation and contemplation, slowly, steadily and unerringly we bring to the fore our inner wealth and serve mankind, fulfilling the Inner Pilot, the Supreme, within us.

31. Spirituality: past, present and future

Dear seekers, dear sisters and brothers, today, with greatest joy, I wish to tell you that I am offering you my last talk on spirituality for the summer. I have been away from New York for about a month and have given sixteen or seventeen talks. This will be my last talk on this trip. To each of you I wish to offer my deepest joy, love and blessingful gratitude.

Before we enter into the spiritual life, before we enter into the life of aspiration, there are only three persons in our life: You, He and I. "You" means the world, humanity at large; "He" means God; "I" means myself. We spend all our time thinking about the world or about ourselves or about God. Of course, in the ordinary life we think about ourselves most of the time — how we can become great and famous, how we can do this, how we can get that. Sometimes we also think about the world or about other people. We think that someone else is greater than we, that mankind does not appreciate us, that the world is callous or senseless or useless. We do not think of the world with love; we think of it with jealousy or anger. And very often we think more about the world than we think about ourselves. But in any case, our whole mind is occupied with thoughts, either of ourselves or of others, and poor God comes last. We use up all our time on useless thoughts and think of God once in a blue moon. Ordinary, unaspiring people find their whole life occupied either with their own desires or with feelings of jealousy, insecurity and inferiority. God comes to their minds only on rare occasions.

But once we accept the spiritual life, it is a different story. We actually create a new story. At that time, God comes first and foremost in our thoughts; then comes the world, and last come we, ourselves. First we think of God and pray to God. Then we think of humanity, love humanity and serve humanity. Then, if there is time left, we think of ourselves. First we surrender everything to God's Will. Then we try to offer our lives to humanity. Then, if there is time left, and inclination, we think of ourselves. All the time, God comes first, then man, and last the individual "I".

In the spiritual life, we feel that we can remain in darkness, we can remain unfed, obscure, unrecognised; but let God come to the fore, let humanity be enlightened first, we feel. This is our attitude when we first launch into the spiritual life. But when we make some progress in the spiritual life, we see that we can never separate God, man and ourselves. If I think of God, immediately I am thinking of His creation, His infinite children; and I, myself, am one of His children, because I am also a son of God. So God, humanity and I have to go together.

When we go still higher and deeper, we feel that God is the tree, mankind is the branches, and we, as individuals, are leaves. God is the Eternal Tree, but a tree without branches and leaves looks strange. We do not appreciate it. We appreciate, admire, adore and worship God because He has accepted us as part and parcel of His life, His existence. We are always grateful to God because He has chosen us as His very own.

Spirituality makes us conscious of our past, present and future. There are two types of past. One is our past life of teeming desires, impurity, insecurity, obscurity and imperfection. This past is absolutely useless. We should pay no attention to it. The past that haunts us and reminds us that we were imperfect, we were useless, we were hopeless — this past has to be forgotten completely. Also, the past that has given us limited satisfaction should not be dwelt upon, because it did not inspire us to continue marching towards our goal. Yesterday we had the inner urge to do something. We did it, and we were satisfied. But that satisfaction was not abiding or fulfilling. Yesterday we were satisfied, but today we know that we have to achieve something more, something higher, something deeper and more fulfilling.

But the past that tells us that we tried but have not yet succeeded, that we started running but still have not reached the goal, that we have begun to pray and meditate but have not yet become one with God — this past is the real past. This past is like a train. The past that gives us inspiration and encourages us to go one step forward is the good past. It has left its starting point and is now slowly, steadily travelling towards its destination.

The satisfaction of the past is not enough. We have to go ahead. We have to look forward. We have to run towards our ultimate Goal. This Goal can never be behind us in the past; it is ever before us in the future. Yesterday's achievement was not the final achievement, today's achievement will not be the final achievement, tomorrow's achievement cannot be the final achievement. We are in the process of constant evolution. Today's goal is tomorrow's starting point, tomorrow's goal will be the starting point for the day after tomorrow.

When we follow a spiritual path or make progress in our spiritual life, we feel that satisfaction is something that constantly can be increased, illumined, perfected and fulfilled in boundless measure. It is only in the spiritual life that we get the message of Infinity, Eternity and Immortality. These are vague terms for those who do not want to follow the spiritual life, but for us they are real realities. And where is the reality? The reality is inside our heart, inside the very depths of our heart. There we feel, we see and we grow into infinite Peace, Light and Bliss.

As a spiritual person does not pay any attention to the past, he also does not pay any attention to the future. His future is not like the future of an ordinary person who is hoping to be a king tomorrow although he is a beggar today. A spiritual person does not cherish that kind of hope. A spiritual person feels that here and now he has to realise God. Today he has to become divine, spiritual, pure and illumined. Today he must get his salvation if possible.

This salvation and illumination he will not get by hook or by crook or by exerting himself too much; he will get it by his most intense inner cry. When each morning dawns, he will have an intense cry to see God face to face. Spiritual Masters, before they became realised, were seekers like you. As each day dawned, they felt that this was their last day, their last opportunity to realise God. They felt that they would not be able to survive the day if they did not realise God. But if they did not realise God on that very day, they did not feel sad and miserable or give up the spiritual life. No. The next day they began their journey with the same intense cry from the inmost recesses of their heart. They felt that yesterday they could not fulfil their aspiration, but today, out of His infinite bounty, God had given them another opportunity.

It is by self-giving, unconditional self-offering with the deepest inner cry, that we must try to realise God each day. Only by giving ourselves devotedly and unconditionally to God can we do it. By giving yourself entirely to God, to Light, to Peace, to Delight, you become your highest Reality, which is God, and you grow into the very image of God.

A spiritual person does not want to wait for ten years or twenty years or forty years. If you wait and say that you are trying, you will never succeed. But if you say that you are doing it, you will succeed. So here and now is the answer, not the past or the future. The past has not fulfilled us, and if we depend on the future, we are only building castles in the air. We have to feel that now, today, this moment, is our greatest opportunity.

MY ROSE PETALS

NOTES TO MY ROSE PETALS, PART 2

16. Newman Room, Rose Walk, St Aldates, Oxford, England,
11 June 1973.
17. Keynes Hall, King's College, Cambridge, England, 12 June 1973.
18. Anson Room, University Student Union, Bristol University,
Bristol, England, 13 June 1973.
19. Examination Hall, Trinity College, Dublin, Ireland,
14 June 1973.
20. Catholic Chaplaincy, Glasgow, Scotland, 16 June 1973.
21. The Debater, Marischal College, University of Aberdeen,
Aberdeen, Scotland, 18 June 1973.
22. Debating Chamber, University Student Union,
University of Leeds, Leeds, England, 20 June 1973.
23. Oakland High School, Mansfield, England, 21 June 1973.
24. Botany Lecture Theatre, University College, London, England,
22 June 1973.
25. Hörsaal 120, University of Zurich, Zurich, Switzerland,
25 June 1973.
26. L'Aula, University of Geneva, Geneva, Switzerland,
28 June 1973.
27. Milan, Italy, 30 June 1973.
28. La Grande Salle, Fédération Internationale d'Accueil de Paris,
Paris, France, 2 July 1973.
29. Hörsaal 1, University of Frankfurt, Frankfurt, West Germany,
4 July 1973.
30. Fabiansalen, ABF Huset, Sveavägen, Stockholm, Sweden,
7 July 1973.
31. Sri Chinmoy Centre, Sturegatan 19, Uppsala, Sweden,
8 July 1973.

MY ROSE PETALS

BOOK 3

32. Failure

It is said that the lecturer stands up, speaks up and shuts up. Here the seeker in me is standing up in order to offer his divine love to the audience. The seeker in me is speaking up in order to establish spiritual oneness with the audience. And finally, the seeker in me will shut up when he finds that he has established his inner oneness with the aspiration of the audience.

I wish to speak on failure from the spiritual point of view. There is not a single human being on earth who does not feel that he is a failure. For his failure he blames many others: he blames the world, he blames his friends and acquaintances, he blames his enemies. But he finds it difficult to blame himself. Here we are all seekers, so we are all God-lovers. For true seekers, for God-lovers, for oneness-dreamers, there is no such thing as failure; there *can* be no failure. For earth-transformers, for God-fulfillers on earth there can be no failure.

There are two lives: the human life and the divine life. The human life sings the song of failure. The human life fails, but the divine life succeeds and proceeds. The divine life always succeeds and continuously proceeds. The human life fails precisely because it does not claim God's Eternity, Infinity and Immortality as its very own. The divine life succeeds precisely because it does claim God's Eternity, Infinity and Immortality as its very own. The divine life not only claims them, but also feels that it is always of Immortality and always for Eternity and Infinity.

The human in us binds; the divine in us expands. The human in us wants to wallow in the pleasures of the finite, at times unconsciously and at times consciously and deliberately. The divine in us wants to fly in the firmament of Freedom-Light and Bliss. The human in us and the divine in us both want happiness. Both feel that if they achieve happiness, then there can be no failure.

But the human in us feels that happiness lies in sense-enjoyment or in pleasure-hunting, while the divine in us feels that happiness lies in aspiration, in realisation, in self-transcendence and in God-manifestation.

Aspiration is our inner cry to reach the highest pinnacle of Truth, Light and Bliss. Aspiration is the only key that can unlock God's Door. The very thing that is aspiration today, tomorrow is achievement. Achievement is conquest; self-conquest is self-mastery. Self-mastery and God-discovery are one and the same. In God-discovery, earth-transformation looms large; in earth's transformation, God's Satisfaction-Smile dawns.

Realisation is our conscious, constant and inseparable universal oneness. Self-transcendence is our ever-glowing and ever-expanding receptivity that lets us house God's infinite Truth, eternal Light and immortal Life. God-manifestation is our fulfilled promise. Before we entered into the world arena, we made a solemn promise to the Lord Supreme that we would manifest Him here on earth. When we manifest Him on earth, we fulfil our promise.

I wish to tell you an amusing incident about Oscar Wilde. Oscar Wilde once went to a party after seeing one of his plays. His friends asked him about the play. His reply was that the play was a success but the audience was a failure. In the cosmic game, we are playing with the Supreme. He has allotted a specific role to each of us. If we play our role satisfactorily, then that is our success. World-appreciation and world-admiration cannot elevate our consciousness. It is only in the expansion and heightening of our consciousness that we can see the Face of God and grow into the very image of God.

In the spiritual life first we have to be awakened. Then we have to aspire and then we have to surrender our will to the Will of the Supreme. He who is awakened can never fail. He who aspires can never fail. He who surrenders his earth-bound will to the Heaven-free Will can never fail.

Quite often seekers of the ultimate Truth are misunderstood by unaspiring people. Unaspiring people are very often loud and emphatic in their insistence that God-realisation is of no avail. Without the perfect knowledge of God one can easily exist: this is their discovery. Although they are not atheists, they do not care for the living God. But a seeker cries for the living God. Since we are all seekers, we are crying for a God that is living; at every moment we try to see Him, feel Him and talk to Him face to face. Unaspiring people put forth many tenuous arguments, but we offer them our compassion-smile for we know that they are totally mistaken. When these people become vociferous and supercilious, at that time we have to offer them our forgiveness-weapon. With our forgiveness-weapon we can conquer them in the inmost recesses of our aspiring heart. God is living, and He can also be living for us. What makes Him living for us? It is our inner cry, our aspiration. We can feel Him constantly. When? When the inner flame within us is constantly burning.

We are seekers, but we also work; we do dedicated service. When we work we have to ask ourselves whether or not we work and serve devotedly, cheerfully and unconditionally. If we serve God in man devotedly, soulfully and unconditionally, then success is bound to dawn. Success we attain only through our dedicated service, only by offering our service with joy.

When we offer our success to mankind, we can offer our success as an inspiration, as something to increase the world's aspiration. But very often we offer our success to the world at large only for our own ego-aggrandisement. We want the world to appreciate our success and laud us to the skies. If we offer our success for ego-aggrandisement, we commit a Himalayan blunder. We are all cosmic players in God's divine Game. Let us play the game the way it has been ordained by the Lord Supreme. Let us offer our success to the world in the right way, in the divine way. Otherwise, at the end of our journey we shall miserably fail.

Just because we are seekers, we have to know that success is not our goal. Progress is our goal. Success is earth-bound. It is noticeable mostly in our vital life, the life that struggles and strikes and gets satisfaction when it notices an iota of success. In our life of aspiration, progress is of paramount importance. If we make progress, automatically we are succeeding in our aspiration, in our realisation, in our God-manifestation.

At every moment a seeker should feel that he is a murmuring and flowing river. Eventually he will enter into the vast sea of Knowledge, Light, Peace and Bliss. In this sea of infinite Peace, Light and Bliss, he will feel continuous progress. Today's achievement will be only tomorrow's starting point. A seeker is a divine climber: he climbs up the evolution-tree slowly, steadily and unerringly and reaches the Highest. But when he reaches the Highest, he comes to realise that this height is only the starting point for something still higher. He realises that he is growing into the ever-transcending Beyond.

When a seeker assimilates his realisation, he feels that there can be no failure. In his Heaven-life of aspiration and in his earth-life of self-dedication, his life becomes a life of continuous progress in God's manifestation on earth.

33. Love Divine

I wish to give a short talk on love. As you all know, there is nothing on earth as important as love. In Heaven, too, there is nothing as important as love. My disciples and I are following a path. This path is called "love, devotion and surrender". Love is the root; love is the foundation of our path. We feel that God is dearest to us not because He is omniscient, omnipresent and omnipotent, but just because He is all Love.

To be loved is a good thing. To love others is a better thing. But to love God and man in God's own Way is by far the best thing. When we are loved, our life becomes meaningful. When we love, our life becomes soulful. When we love God and man in God's own Way, our life becomes fruitful.

In ordinary human life we value love and treasure love precisely because we are afraid that the object of our love can be lost at any moment. In the spiritual life we value love because we feel that love is the only thing that can offer us abiding satisfaction. In the spiritual life the love that we experience, the love that we offer, is divine love. Human love is the song of possession. But before we possess others, we see to our utter sorrow that we ourselves are badly possessed. Divine love is the song of emancipation. When we try to emancipate others through divine love, we see that we can emancipate others only after we ourselves have been totally liberated.

Love is courage. Courage is self-giving. Self-giving is God-building, and in God-building God-manifestation takes place. God's total manifestation is today a dream. Tomorrow the dream will be transformed into hope, and the day after tomorrow this hope will be transformed into an inner assurance. When we get the inner assurance, our earth-bound consciousness hears the message of the Heaven-free consciousness. At that time the finite in us consciously, devotedly and soulfully surrenders to the Infinite and becomes inseparably one with the Infinite.

Love is the best form of prayer; love is the best form of worship. There is a striking difference between love and worship. We love because we feel the need of expansion, the need of oneness. When we love God, the lover and the Beloved eventually become one. The lover loses his individuality, his personality, his height, his ego-centred "I" and he and the divine Beloved become one and inseparable. But when we worship we quite often maintain our own individuality and personality. We feel that we are at the foot of the tree while our Saviour is at the top of the tree. Always there is a reverential awe. Because of this reverential awe, we find it difficult to merge totally into the consciousness of our Saviour. But the divine lover, because of his inner oneness, dives deep into the Consciousness-sea of his Beloved and becomes the sea itself. Like a tiny drop, he enters into the mighty ocean and becomes the mighty ocean itself.

In the spiritual life the more we make progress, the more we feel the necessity of love. God has infinite Power, infinite Peace, infinite Light and infinite Bliss. He has everything in infinite measure, but we feel that even an iota of His Love can quench our lifelong thirst. He can and He will give us everything that He has and everything that He is, but we will not be satisfied unless and until He has given us His Love. Needless to say, His Love divine encompasses all His other attributes: Peace, Light, Delight and so on. In this world everything may fail us; we may even fail ourselves. But the divine love within us can never fail us, for this love has a permanent home and Source. That Source is God the infinite Concern, God the infinite Compassion, God the infinite blessingful Pride in mankind. Love ultimately gives us transcendental happiness. This happiness is not a thing that we talk about or see around us, but it is something that we can experience in our day-to-day multifarious activities. We can grow into this inner happiness at God's choice Hour.

As seekers we have to be extremely cautious when we deal with divine love. Very often human love cleverly tries to play the role of divine love. How can we tell whether something is divine love or human love? We can easily know the moment we dare to examine ourselves. Is this love for the truth within us, is it for the light within us? If the answer is in the affirmative, then we can easily know that it is divine love. I wish to tell you an incident that took place in the life of the American President Abraham Lincoln. A certain official said to him that God would be on his side. Lincoln said that he was not concerned about that. His concern was that he would be on God's side. He was concerned only about his acceptance of God's Light. Whether or not God took his side was not the question. He said that God will always be on the right side and it was his bounden duty to be on God's side. Here the real seeker, the real lover in Lincoln spoke.

Through our prayer, meditation and dedication, we can also have God on our side. But this will not satisfy us. If we really love God, we shall offer our love, devotion, surrender, aspiration and dedication to God; at the same time, our fervent prayer and most soulful meditation will be to please God unconditionally in His own Way — to take God's side. If we please God in one way or another, naturally He will please us; but our sincerity will one day loom large and we shall suffer miserably because we have not pleased God in His own Way. We must not expect God to please us in our own way, although He can easily do so. If we want to have something, He can give it to us; but sooner or later that thing will not satisfy us. Our sincere heart will never be satisfied unless and until we have pleased God in His own Way. But if He gives us what He had intended to give us, then the seeker in us is bound to be happy and this happiness will be everlasting.

We can please God in His own Way only when we have discovered and developed within us an unconditional love for our Supreme Beloved. Our love for God is our inmost cry. His Love for us is His life-transforming, life-illumining, life-fulfilling Smile. When we cry for Him, we offer Him our love; when He offers us His Satisfaction-Smile, it is nothing else but His Love that is being expressed.

Love, devotion and surrender. We offer love to God just because we know there is nothing and there can be nothing, there is nobody and there can be nobody other than God who can rightfully claim our love. We offer our devotion to God because He is the only one who can utilise our devotion for a right purpose. We offer our dedicated surrender to Him not because we are His slaves, but because we feel that God and man are one. He is our most illumined part, while the part that we right now represent needs illumination. It is our inner obligation, our bounden duty to be totally illumined from the soles of our feet to the crown of our head. Within and without we must be surcharged with God's infinite Light. When we surrender to the Supreme, we must know that we are surrendering to our own highest part, which is fully illumined. When the lower part enters into the higher part, when the finite in us enters into the Infinite, at that time we become flooded with infinite Light, Peace and Bliss.

34. Confidence

Dear brothers and sisters, dear seekers of the infinite Truth and Light, I wish to speak about confidence from the spiritual point of view. We are now in Oxford University. The seeker in me feels that Oxford first embodies and then represents the art, culture and glory not only of Great Britain, but of the entire European consciousness. Oxford represents world-culture and world-history in the highest form of mental light, knowledge and wisdom in the outer world. Oxford is confidence. It is in the confidence of Oxford that all these supernal qualities are playing their respective roles.

We all know that there are two types of confidence: human and divine. Human confidence is very often founded upon our little "I", our ego. Ego means ignorance-pleasure and sense-enjoyment. This little ego binds us, imprisons us. But divine confidence is founded upon our transcendental Self: the Self that liberates us, the Self that brings us the message of universal Consciousness, the Self that helps us transcend our earth-bound consciousness and enter into the Infinite. I wish to speak about divine confidence.

Confidence is the unification of God the Compassion and man the reliance. Confidence is the expression and revelation of God's Will through the human heart, mind, vital and body. Confidence is the God-Beauty in us. Confidence is truth-unity and truth-multiplicity in us. Confidence is truth-recognition in us, Heaven-vision by us and God-decision for us. Confidence is our life-acceptance and life-transcendence, our earth-transformation and God-manifestation.

Confidence is not pride; it is the conscious awareness of our own height and depth. Confidence is not the aggrandisement of our ego; it is the awareness of our developing strength in the battlefield of life. Confidence is not the precursor of destruction; it is the precursor of achievement, of abundant divine achievement for the Absolute Supreme.

Confidence is our divine contentment which knows what to enjoy, how to enjoy, where to enjoy and why to enjoy. What to enjoy? God's Smile. How to enjoy? Through selfless service, through self-offering. Where to enjoy? In pure consciousness; in the inmost recesses of our aspiring heart, mind, vital and physical. Why to enjoy? Because we need the expression of the inner Self.

In the inner world we feel that divine confidence is housed in our aspiration. Aspiration is the harbinger of Peace, Light and Bliss in infinite measure. He who embodies aspiration in the purest sense of the term can reveal and manifest light, truth and delight. According to the world's receptivity the world receives these qualities from the supreme seeker who embodies confidence in the form of aspiration.

Confidence is like a divine muscle. It can be developed slowly, steadily and unerringly if we know the secret of disciplining our body, vital, mind and heart. In order to discipline ourselves what we need is an inner cry, the cry that carries our entire being into the highest realm of Silence. In this way we develop confidence and with this confidence-muscle we can be strong, stronger, strongest.

Each human being represents the physical world, the vital world, the mental world and the psychic world. In the physical world he is hunting after pleasure. He achieves a little pleasure and feels that his achievement is his confidence. In the vital world he brings the message of Julius Caesar. He declares, *Veni, vidi, vici:* "I came, I saw, I conquered." In the mental world, if his mind is illumined to a certain extent, he feels that through his mind's light earth can be illumined, perfected and liberated. He feels that earth can be a conscious receptacle of divinity, that divinity can be housed in the earth-consciousness. And when he is in the psychic or heart's world he soulfully offers this unique message to the world at large: "I came into the world to love God in mankind and to be of unconditional service to God in mankind."

In our spiritual life belief is of importance, but we have to know whether this belief is mental or psychic. If belief comes to the fore from an inner realm of consciousness, then it is a superior type of belief, psychic belief. This type of belief abides in the silent home of our soul's light, and it is synonymous with divine confidence. It is powerful and unassailable. This type of belief, this divine confidence, inspires and energises us to fight for truth, for light, for world harmony, for world peace and for world salvation. But mental belief can be battered and shattered in a moment by doubt, suspicion and other hostile forces in the world.

In the spiritual life we have two giant friends: faith and confidence. Faith can hear the message of the highest Silence. Faith can guide us and lead us to our soul's Goal of goals. Confidence can hear the message of the cosmic Sound. Confidence can act like a hero-warrior in the battlefield of life. It can change today's world of darkness, imperfection and bondage into a world of light, perfection and freedom.

35. Spirituality as an art

Dear seekers, dear sisters and brothers, I wish to give a talk on spirituality as an art. Spirituality is not only an art, but a divine, illumining and fulfilling art. The work of a human artist very often expresses his individuality, his personality and his earthbound consciousness. The work of a divine artist expresses God the Beauty, God the Divinity and God the Reality. The human artist either surrenders to fate or revolts against fate. The divine artist accepts fate and finally transforms fate.

Art is creation; creation is art. Human art is often a forced creation. In ordinary human art the physical, vital, mind and heart are often forced to try to create something beautiful, lasting and immortal. But in spiritual art nothing is forced. In spiritual art the psychic being comes to the fore and tries to offer the inner art, which is already immortal. The psychic being inspires the body, vital, mind and heart to participate and cooperate in the creation of the work of art.

The great American philosopher Emerson said something most significant with regard to art. He said that in art the hand can never execute anything higher than the heart can inspire. In spiritual art the same rule is applicable. But here we have to say also that the heart can never execute anything higher than the soul can inspire. In ordinary human art we often notice a yawning gulf between the heart's loftiest inspiration and the hand's limited capacity. But in spiritual art there is no yawning gulf between the soul's capacity and the heart's receptivity. The heart becomes a conscious instrument of the soul's capacity and the soul's capacity operates in and through the heart's receptivity. The aspiring receptivity of the heart and the illumining capacity of the soul complement each other.

Each artist has a human artist and a divine artist within himself. The divine artist and the human artist play hide-and-seek within his creativity. When the human artist within him comes to the fore, the person exhibits his art with the hope of receiving appreciation and admiration. He wants the critics and admirers of art to extoll his art to the skies. But when the divine artist comes to the fore, the artist does not need or want appreciation; he wants only to elevate the earth-consciousness through his divine art, to energise and immortalise the earth-consciousness through his divine art.

Both spiritual art and ordinary human art deal with beauty. The human artist has come to feel and realise that the beauty in his art is skin-deep. But the divine artist has discovered something totally different. He has discovered that beauty is soul-deep. When one discovers soul-deep art, one is inspired to dive deeper. When he dives deeper, he discovers God the Art. God the Art is at once the revelation and the manifestation of the ever-transcending consciousness of the Eternal Now. Soul-deep art is constantly leading and guiding the terrestrial consciousness to the ever transcending Reality.

Spiritual art is divine discovery. It realises that the supreme discovery can be made only in and through spirituality. The supreme discovery is God-realisation. The ultimate aim of spiritual art is God-realisation. God-realisation comes only through hard work. Nothing lasting can be achieved overnight. It may take quite a few incarnations, quite a few centuries, before one sees God face to face or merges with the infinite Peace, Light and Bliss. In the ordinary human world we know how hard Hillary and Tenzing worked in order to climb Mount Everest. Spiritual art, the divine discovery, also means climbing up to the highest pinnacle. The motto of this august university is most significant: "Through hard work to the heights." This motto is the universal message, the universal teaching, of all spiritual art.

It is said that one can simplify everything, that everything can be made easy. But if the supreme art, the art of God-realisation, could be made easy through money-power or some other power, then every day thousands or millions of human beings would be able to realise God the supreme Artist. But this is not true. For the art of God-realisation we need aspiration. This aspiration eventually will knock at God's Door, and God will open the Door to the aspiration of each divine artist. If we want to discover the supreme art or the supreme Artist, we have to strengthen our friendship with two divine friends of ours: aspiration and patience. With aspiration and patience eventually we shall reach God's transcendental Height.

Right in front of me is a harmonium. If I tried to draw or paint this harmonium, if I tried to offer all my artistic talent to reveal and manifest the essence of this harmonium, the divinity that I would offer to the world would be very limited and insignificant. But if I placed in front of me a picture of the Saviour Christ and tried to draw him, if with my utmost inner aspiration I used my artistic talents and capacities to try to reveal the quintessence of the Christ Consciousness, then if I succeeded in revealing just an iota of this Consciousness, my achievement would become a unique treasure of Mother Earth. If our painting reveals more of the potentiality of the soul and makes it easier for this potentiality to be assimilated, then we have brought to the fore the essence of all-pervading divinity.

There is a very common maxim that says: "Art for art's sake." But I wish to say that spiritual art cannot be just for art's sake. Spiritual art can be only for God's sake. When God-manifestation can take place in abundant measure, spiritual art is consciously, soulfully and devotedly playing its role. In human art there is a creative motive and a finished product. The cause is followed by the effect. In spiritual art there is no motive or cause; everything is spontaneous. The result, which is already there, is only waiting for God's choice Hour to be manifested. In spiritual art the artist depends entirely on his soul's awakening, his heart's inner mounting cry, his mind's conscious and constant search for the highest Truth, his vital's dynamic approach to the ultimate Reality and his body's unconditional service to divinity's height.

In ordinary art very often the artist and the critic inside him go together. Each must play his respective role; otherwise, the artist will always think that his art is by far the best, and that it transcends all criticism. Each time an artist creates something, if the critic in him also plays a significant role, then the artist may attain a satisfactory standard. But again, if the critic constantly and mercilessly plays his role, then the artist may not survive: he may die through his own self-criticism.

When a spiritual seeker enters into the field of art, he does not criticise his art. He does not play the role of a critic; he plays the role only of a conscious, constant, awakened and unconditional instrument of his Inner Pilot, the supreme Artist. He is not the doer; he is only the conscious instrument of the doer within him. He feels that the supreme Artist within him is the supreme Inspirer, the supreme Revealer, the supreme Liberator and the supreme Fulfiller of the Consciousness divine that is going to be manifested through his art.

Here we are all seekers; we are all spiritual artists. Let us dive deep within and discover the supreme Artist within us, who is constantly supplying us with infinite inspiration and aspiration to reveal the supreme Light, Delight and Perfection through our spiritual art. Our spiritual art is Self-discovery. Self-discovery and God-discovery are one and the same. Today Self-discovery is our Goal. Tomorrow God-manifestation will be our Goal. Today let us dive deep within for God-realisation. Tomorrow we shall dive deeper for God-manifestation, which is the supreme, ever-transcending, eternal Art.

36. Conscience

Dear sisters and brothers, dear members of my spiritual family, here we are all seekers, seekers of the infinite Truth. When I say *my* family, I literally mean it. Because we are all seekers, I claim to be a spiritual brother of yours, an Indian brother of yours. Let us go deep within and try to realise what has prompted us or inspired us to be seekers.

There are millions of people on earth who do not have the inner urge to lead a spiritual life. How is it that we are crying for Light, Delight, Love and Compassion from the Absolute Supreme? How is it that we are trying to lead a better life, a more illumining and fulfilling life, a spiritual life? It is because we have been awakened by the infinite Grace of the Supreme.

The moment we are awakened our conscience plays its most

significant role. The Sanskrit term for conscience is *viveka*. Conscience is the inner voice. It is the voice of inner light. The difference between inner light and outer light I am sure all of us know. Outer light immediately exposes us. If we do something wrong, it will expose us and we will immediately be caught. But inner light acts in a different way. Inner light will never, never expose us. On the contrary, inner light will illumine us. If we make a mistake, if we commit even the worst possible Himalayan blunder, the inner light will come to our rescue. It will illumine us so that we will not do the same thing again.

The inner light tells us what to say, what to do and what to become. What to say? God is for all. God is not only for me, but He is also for you, for everyone. What to do? Love God in every human being. What to become? Conscious, constant and unconditional instruments of God. When we do the right thing, God blesses us. When we say the right thing, God smiles at us. When we become the right thing, God embraces us.

The inner light constantly inspires us and, at the same time, warns us not to go back to our animal life. We all came from the animal kingdom. Even now animal propensities quite often reign supreme in our human consciousness. But the inner light warns us not to go back to the animal life. It tells us to stay at least in the human life proper. There are people on earth who quarrel and fight and lead an animal life. Because we are seekers we have already transcended that life. Now it is our bounden duty to transcend the human life and enter into the divine life. In human life the animal consciousness and the divine consciousness both play their roles. But the animal consciousness plays its role most powerfully and most vehemently, whereas the role of the divine consciousness is very insignificant. Only in an infinitesimal measure do we notice the role of the divine life. But since we are all seekers, we are well determined to do away with our animal life, to transform our human life totally and to enter into the domain of the divine life — the life of light and delight.

It becomes easier for us to illumine the animal life provided we know what the animal life was. The animal life was destruction; the human life that we are now leading is nothing short of frustration; the divine life that we are aiming at is the life of selfless dedication. It is to please our Inner Pilot that we have entered into the world-arena. If we are totally, selflessly and unconditionally dedicated to the Inner Pilot, then we discover the meaning of life. Life is not a chimerical mist, a fantastic dream. Life is a solid reality awaiting transformation; and it is we who can bring down the Kingdom of Heaven into the immediacy of today to transform the earth-consciousness.

The inner light is our creative and conscious evolution. Who is actually evolving in us? God the man is evolving. That is to say, man is ascending towards the topmost height, the pinnacle. And God the Saviour, God the Liberator, is descending into the abyss to transform the darkness-ignorance of millennia with His supernal, infinite Light.

When we are in the process of creative evolution, we notice that God is constantly standing in front of us and pleading with us to enter into His Boat so that He can carry us to the Golden Shore of the Beyond. When we are in the process of conscious evolution, we see God constantly within us and without us, guiding us in our multifarious day-to-day activities.

When the inner light of conscience guides us, we do not care for success; we care only for progress. Success is always limited but progress is unlimited. Success very often plays its role in the vital world, but progress always plays its role in the psychic world, in the inner world. When we make progress we have to know that there is no such thing as failure; success always looms large. If we aim at success, then we shall be bound by our very,

very limited vision. But if we aim at progress, then we are aiming at something that is ever-transcending — an ever-transcending reality of the Beyond.

Conscience is our confidence — inner confidence and outer confidence. Inner confidence tells us that we are *of* God. Outer confidence tells us that we are *for* God. This confidence is not vital aggression. This confidence is the revelation of our soul's light inside the heart. This confidence is perfection in life, and perfection is the transformation of our earth-bound consciousness. When our earth-bound consciousness is transformed into the Heaven-free Consciousness, at that time God-satisfaction dawns both in Heaven and on earth.

Without the evolved, transformed consciousness we cannot realise the Highest. Conscience is just like a tiny drop, whereas consciousness is the mightiest ocean. Consciousness is always present in the spiritual life; consciousness and the spiritual life are synonymous. Consciousness drops and consciousness rises. When the consciousness is low, that means that the inner light is not operating. When consciousness is high, it means that the light of conscience is operating most significantly in that individual.

The desiring man derives satisfaction from his pleasure-life. The aspiring man derives satisfaction from his dedicated and surrendered aspiration-life. For the true seeker there is no such thing as compromise between these two lives. An ordinary human being will always try to make a compromise. Early in the morning he needs God. But when evening sets in, he encounters all the forces of temptation and desire. At that time he hankers after earth-bound limitations. He wants fifty per cent God and fifty per cent ignorance. But a seeker of the highest Truth cannot do that; he has to be totally uncompromising. For him, there is only God and God alone.

There are some human beings who are very clever. They want to remain neutral — neither for God nor for ignorance. But if you enter into the inmost recesses of their hearts, you are bound to notice that they have already taken one side; yet because they fear the consequences of choosing one side, they do not support any path. They do not take God's side; they do not take the side of ignorance. In the ordinary human life, we appreciate the person who is neutral. But in the spiritual life there is no place for a person with a neutral feeling. If you cannot accept God wholeheartedly, you are bound to wallow in the pleasures of ignorance. Millions and millions of people are wallowing in the pleasures of ignorance. You can also add to their ignorance; you can offer your own contribution. But if you are really hungry for Light, for the Truth of the Beyond, then accept God wholeheartedly. You will see how He fulfils your longing — not your temptation, not your desiring life, but your life of aspiration.

When a seeker becomes sincerity itself, God the Infinite plays His role inside the finite consciousness of the seeker. In this case the finite houses the Infinite and the finite becomes the conscious channel, the chosen instrument through which the Infinite operates here in the earth-consciousness. It is the receptivity of the seeker that allows God to manifest in and through him and that enables Mother Earth to be inundated with infinite Peace, Light and Bliss.

I understand there are quite a few teachers here who are teaching Hatha Yoga. That is extremely good. Hatha Yoga is the first step in our spiritual life. In the highest form of spirituality, Hatha Yoga is like kindergarten. We need not start in kindergarten, but we cannot skip all the levels and expect to get our Master's degree. That is impossible. On the other hand, if one thinks that he can complete his kindergarten course and not go any higher, not take any higher courses, then he is making a deplorable mistake. He has to eventually go on to high school and college and take the highest course. In the spiritual life the highest course is God-realisation. Physical discipline is important in the spiritual life. But if we expect God-realisation from Hatha Yoga, then we will be badly disappointed. In any Indian village you will find hundreds of Hatha Yoga experts. But for most of these people, God-realisation is a far cry.

The necessity of physical discipline nobody can deny. But beyond the physical is the spiritual. We have to raise our consciousness to the spiritual. It is inside the spiritual that Divinity, Infinity, Eternity and Immortality are constantly singing and dancing. We have to climb up the mango tree, pluck mangoes and then climb down and eat. If we stay at the foot of the tree and do not climb up, how are we going to get the mangoes?

In no way am I throwing cold water on those who are teaching and practising Hatha Yoga. But please feel the necessity of going on to the highest course. That is to say, you have to go to the inner high school, college and university. The course at the university consists of three subjects: concentration, meditation and contemplation. These three subjects are most important. They are taught through the inner awakened and developed consciousness. First we have to learn how to concentrate. Then we have to learn how to meditate. Finally, we have to learn how to contemplate.

When we concentrate we must not allow even an iota of thought to enter into our mind. We have to focus our concentration on a particular object or subject and nothing else. Then we must enter into it and go beyond it. When we go beyond it, we feel that we have reached the soul. We started from our physical existence. When we reach the soul's plane we see that the soul-consciousness is observing the body-consciousness, and the body-consciousness is entering into the soul-consciousness.

When the body-consciousness is entering into the soul-consciousness, the body is realising the Highest. When the soul is concentrating on the body, the soul is manifesting in the physical consciousness the Light of the Beyond. This is concentration.

The next step is meditation. In meditation the first thing we do is to make the mind absolutely calm and quiet. Then we empty the heart so that God can fill it with His message of Light and Delight. When we meditate, we become the listener and God becomes the talker. God will offer us a message from the Highest and we shall listen to His message. But in order to receive this message we have to make our mind absolutely calm and quiet; we have to make our mind as vast as the sky or the ocean. The aim of meditation is to bring down the Infinite into the finite and carry the finite to the Infinite. The finite enters into Infinity for its highest realisation, and the Infinite enters into the finite for its supreme manifestation.

The third step is called contemplation. This is done only when the seeker is far advanced. We started our studies with concentration. As we became expert in concentration, we began meditation. But contemplation takes years and sometimes incarnations to learn because contemplation can be properly done only when the seeker is on the verge of realisation. Here the seeker totally merges with the Supreme. The divine lover becomes totally one, inseparably one with the Supreme Beloved. The finite totally loses its separativity and becomes one with the infinite Peace, Light and Bliss. At that time infinite Peace, Light and Bliss are housed perfectly in an earthly being.

37. Death

Dear seekers of the transcendental Truth, I wish to give a talk on death. What is death? Death is the immortal pilgrim's short rest along the road of Eternity. Death is a necessary experience for human beings at the present state of their evolving consciousness. Death is a shattering blow for desiring human beings and, at the same time, it is an awakening hand for aspiring human beings.

There are two types of desiring human beings. One type considers death to be an evil force, since death's arrival prevents all his teeming desires from being fulfilled on earth. Therefore, he considers death an enemy, an unwelcome guest. The second type has come to realise that desire itself is painful. When he exercises his capacity and talents in order to fulfil a desire, he sees that this very process is hurtful and painful. When the result comes, it comes either in the form of failure or in the form of success. If it comes in the form of failure, he is doomed to disappointment. And if it comes in the form of success, even then he is not totally happy, for he thought that the success would be something more illumining and more fulfilling than it turns out to be. Alas, he does not get the kind of success that he actually expected from his tireless efforts. So neither desire nor the result of desire is satisfactory; both are extremely discouraging, disappointing and painful. This kind of desiring man welcomes death; he longs for it. Since he cannot stay on earth even for a day without desire and frustration, he wants to leave earth. But again, when death knocks at his door, his whole being is shattered; he cries for life. At that time, he does not want to welcome death. When desire-life proves unsatisfactory he wants death; but when death actually knocks at his door he wants something else; he wants to stay on earth.

As there are two types of desiring persons, even so are there two types of aspiring human beings. One type always longs for the Kingdom of Heaven on earth. For him, the Kingdom of Heaven is not a chimerical mist; it is something within his aspiring heart. He wants to bring it to the fore and manifest it here on earth. But he can do so only by conquering death. He has to conquer death for good; then only will it be possible for him to bring the Kingdom of Heaven to the fore or bring it down from above.

The second type of aspiring person wants to offer another message. He says that no doubt we have to conquer death, but it is not the physical or human body that will conquer death; it is the consciousness within the physical frame that will conquer death. The earth-bound consciousness has to enjoy the Heaven-free Light and Delight. Just by staying on earth for a long span of time — four hundred or five hundred years — we do not accomplish anything significant. If we go to some Indian villages, we see that there are many people who have been on earth for more than one hundred years. But when it is a matter of inner experience, inner growth, spiritual development, divine achievement, they have achieved next to nothing. They are leading an ordinary human life, if not a half-animal life. It is not the mere prolongation of physical life that we need. The consciousness of the reality within us must be expanded, enlarged, energised and immortalised. True, in order to achieve a divine and immortal consciousness, we have to stay on earth for quite a few years. But this is not for the sake of the body's pleasure-life, but for the expansion and enlargement of the consciousness within the body.

The Vedic seers of the hoary past offer a most significant prayer: "Lord Supreme, grant us the eyes to see You for a hundred years. Grant us the ears to hear Your divine Message for a hundred years. Grant us the hearts to serve You for a hundred years." Then they say not just for a hundred years, but far beyond a hundred years. Why? Just to serve God, fulfil God and manifest God here on earth. They want to live on earth for the divine manifestation. They want from God an infinite period of life so that they can realise, reveal and manifest Him. This is their aim. The body will die eventually, but the Immortality of the divinised consciousness must be offered to Mother Earth so that Mother Earth gets something unique, unprecedented, immortal and supreme.

Spiritual people have discovered something else. They are of the opinion that he who does not aspire is a dead soul. One has not to die physically in order to be considered dead. No! He who does not aspire is dead because he is making little or no progress. When we make progress, we are heading towards a new reality. Each time we enter into a new reality, a new life dawns on earth and we are utilised by it. A moment used undivinely increases the reach of the hands of death. A moment used divinely extends and adds to our life.

If we want to live in the eternal Now, we have to feel that the past is dust, that the past is a dead experience. We have to obliterate it from our consciousness. Each second that is disappearing from our life is dead. If we identify ourselves with the passing second and enter into the past with it, then we experience death. But if we utilise each second for a divine purpose, then it has new life. The future we do not know, but we want to grow into the future or we want to bring down the life of the future into the immediacy of today.

The Vedic seers realised that movement is life, that if we do not move in the spiritual life, then death knocks at our door. But again, there is life in deep silence, in the inmost recesses of Silence-Life. In Silence-Life, the sound-body is constantly coming into existence. But this is the deepest and most meaningful discovery: one has to reach the highest realm of Consciousness in order to live in the transcendental Silence-Life. Then one can consciously create at every moment the sound-body that is necessary for God-manifestation on earth.

Death is preparation; death is relaxation. Until it is time to prepare ourselves once more to enter into the battlefield of life, we relax for a short while in death. Life is first of all an experience, the experience that will free us from ignorance-sea and inspire us to swim in the sea of Wisdom-Light. Then life becomes God-satisfaction; in God-satisfaction we experience the height of God's ever-transcending Dream and the depth of God's ever-fulfilling Reality.

The desiring man thinks death is destruction. A beginner-seeker feels death is a supreme mystery. An advanced seeker knows that death is a short rest. A God-realised person has unmistakably discovered that death is an instrument of God. Death is an instrument of God when it frightens the desiring man so that he does not wallow in the pleasures of ignorance, so that he cries for a higher, more illumining and more fulfilling life. Death is also a divine instrument when it plays its role by increasing the aspiration of the seeker. Before death's arrival, a seeker wants to accomplish quite a few things for Mother Earth and Father Heaven, so he invokes Peace, Light and Bliss from above with ever-increasing aspiration, for he wants to inundate his earthly being with these qualities in infinite measure long before death's arrival at his life's door.

Here we are all seekers. Some of us are unconsciously growing into immortal Life or flowing with the river of immortal Life; others are consciously invoking the infinite Light of the ever-transcending Beyond, the Light of immortal Life which we utilise for God's total, complete and perfect manifestation on earth. Each seeker is a creator. Each seeker is a saviour. Each seeker is a liberator. Each seeker is the conscious representative of the Absolute Supreme precisely because in his creation, in his aspiration and in his realisation he discovers a life which is constantly transcending its own height. In this ever-transcending movement, death plays the role of a devoted, surrendered and all-fulfilling instrument of the Absolute Supreme.

When one lived the life of desire, death stood as an obstacle, an ignorance-force. But when one became a seeker, he saw that death is only a loving instrument, that death is nothing but the younger brother of life, As a younger brother, death feels that it is its bounded duty to help its elder brother, life. It does this by offering Immortality's Light, Eternity's Height, Infinity's Smile and Perfection's Satisfaction to earth.

38. Divine hope

Dear seekers, dear brothers and sisters, I wish to speak on hope from the spiritual point of view. Since we are all seekers, it is our soulful aspiration that one day our divine hope will be fulfilled. And what is that hope? That hope is God-realisation.

What is hope? Hope is man's preparation for the unknown. Hope is man's aspiration for the unknowable. The unknown right now is man's ultimate achievement; the unknowable is God's eternal Now.

Hope is man's inner effort. An ordinary man is not aware of this inner effort, but a seeker of the highest Truth is fully aware of it. This inner effort inspires the seeker to see something new, to feel something new, to say something new, to do something new and, finally, to become something new.

When I smile, I see something new around me. When I cry, I feel something new within my heart. When I pray, I say something new to the higher worlds. When I meditate, I do something new for the inner and the outer worlds. When I surrender, I become something new: God's chosen instrument.

In the spiritual life, hope is newness. In this newness is our self-transcendence. Our self-transcendence is God's Pride, His supernal Pride in us. And God's Pride lives in our conscious and constant gratitude.

Hope and faith are two intimate brothers; they always go together. Hope nourishes faith and faith treasures hope. Hope dreams of God-Beauty in God-Reality. Faith dreams of God-Reality in God-Beauty. Hope pulls the heart of tomorrow into the body of today. Faith pushes the body of today into the heart of tomorrow. When tomorrow's heart enters into today's body, man's aspiration is crowned with success. When today's body enters into tomorrow's heart, Heaven's vision is crowned with success. Man's success is the victory of God's Compassion-Light. Heaven's success is the victory of God's Realisation-Height.

To hope is to see with the eye of the heart. To hope is to make the heart captain of the mind, the vital and the body. To hope is to send darkness-night into exile. To hope is to feel the presence of the inner sun. The inner sun is; the outer sun becomes. When we live in the consciousness of the inner sun, we reach the highest Height of God's Silence-Light. When we live in the consciousness of the outer sun, we become one with the sound-life of God's manifestation on earth.

In the spiritual life, hope is humility's light. At the present state of evolution, human humility is a forced humility. But divine humility is soulful, spontaneous humility. Humility is God's Dream-Boat that reaches His Reality-Shore. Humility is God's Beauty in man's reality.

When a spiritual pilgrim starts walking along the road of Eternity, his hope is nothing but humility's light. Eventually it is transformed into divinity's birthright. Then finally divinity's birthright is transformed into Infinity's Smile, Eternity's Light and Immortality's Life.

Divine hope is our soul's promise to the eternal Supreme that here on earth we shall realise Him fully, reveal Him fully and manifest Him completely and perfectly. Again, there are mundane hopes or undivine hopes. We want to become a multi-millionaire overnight. We want to lord it over the world and see the supremacy of our dauntless vital. We want the whole world to be at our feet and accept light from our mind. The world is in darkness; we alone are bathing in the sea of light: this is our firm conviction. Therefore, we feel that we are in a position to offer light to the world at large. We feel that we have everything and we are everything; our only hope is for the world to be at our feet. Mundane hope is not like divine hope. It is an unlit desire that binds us. This desire will eventually bring on frustration, which is immediately followed by utter destruction.

In our spiritual life what we now call hope, hundreds and thousands of years ago we called our soul's promise to the Absolute Supreme: Him to realise, Him to reveal, Him to manifest on earth. At that time our divine hope was our soul's promise that we would enter into the world-scene and participate in God's cosmic Play as conscious players. When we entered into the spiritual life, slowly, steadily and unerringly this promise came to the fore from within. Gradually in our awakened consciousness the power and light of this promise began to loom large. Now we do not see hope as a promise; we feel it as a necessary preparation for our God-manifestation on earth.

In the ordinary, unaspiring world, hope is often no more than building castles in the air. But in the spiritual life, inner hope and the inner cry which we call aspiration always go together. Here our hope is playing the role of a divine harbinger. Hope is like the dream which is always just one step behind the reality. God is using His beckoning Hands to lead and guide the aspiration of the seeker to the destined Goal. God is sailing His Dream-Boat to the Golden Shore of the ever-transcending Beyond.

The hope of a human child is to get the highest degree or diploma. The hope or climbing aspiration of a divine child is to receive and achieve Peace, Light and Bliss in infinite measure. A seeker's hope is his aspiration-light and the Inner Pilot's hope is Perfection-Delight. Each individual seeker represents a conscious and constant promise to his Inner Pilot. Similarly, the Inner Pilot represents a conscious and constant promise to the individual seeker. In his aspiration-light, the seeker enters into the Supreme's cosmic Dream to play his unique role in God's Drama and manifest God in God's own Way. Through His Perfection Delight, God enters into the seeker's aspiration-light to give him what He eternally has and what He eternally is. What He has is the Golden Boat that carries humanity's excruciating pangs; what He is is the Golden Shore of Infinity, Eternity and Immortality. Again, He Himself is the Pilot and He Himself is the Boat that carries humanity's excruciating pangs and teeming ignorance, imperfections, limitations, bondage and death to the Golden Shore of His ever-transcending Beyond.

39. The Way, the Truth, the Life

Dear sisters and brothers, dear seekers of the infinite Truth and Light, I wish to give a short talk on "The Way, the Truth, the Life." This is the motto of your university. It is a lofty motto; therefore, I shall speak on this subject from the spiritual point of view.

Two thousand years ago the Christ proclaimed: "I am the

Way; I am the Goal." His revealed aspiration was the Way; His manifested realisation was the Goal. Humanity's first and foremost achievement is the Way. Humanity's last and most glorious achievement is the Goal. There is a method to shorten the Way. There is a method to bring the Goal closer. How to shorten the Way? Increase our receptivity. How to bring the Goal closer? Surrender our will unconditionally to God's Will. We increase our receptivity through soulful, devoted and ceaseless self-offering. We make our surrender unconditional by realising the fact that our satisfaction lies in God alone and that God alone is our supreme satisfaction. If we have discovered this lofty truth, then only can we make an attempt to grow into unconditional surrender to God's Will.

God has infinite children. In God's family, Truth is the eldest son. Right after Truth is Peace. Truth and Peace are extremely close to each other; they complement each other. They are constantly trying to please each other. Truth offers its transcendental height to its brother Peace, and Peace offers its eternal depth to its brother Truth.

Their Father, the Lord Supreme, observes this act of mutual offering by His two devoted sons. God tells them that they are supremely indispensable in His creation. God says to Truth: "Truth, My son, earth succeeds because of you. If you did not exist, earth could never succeed in anything." God says to Peace: "Peace, My son, just because of you earth is able to receive Me. If you did not remain on earth, earth could never receive or reach Me."

Both Truth and Peace say to their almighty Father: "Father, it is true that we are of some service to You, but we are not indispensable. Never! We are Your creation. You are the Creator and You alone are indispensable. We are extremely grateful to You for granting us the opportunity to be of service to You.

We wish to become; we wish to be. We wish to become Your messengers. We wish to be the carriers of earth's sufferings to Heaven-Delight. We wish to bring down Heaven's Delight into earth's excruciating pangs. Please allow us to perform this task so that through us You may fulfil Yourself, Father."

This is their hope and desire. They want to be constantly at the Feet of their Lord Supreme. They feel that if they stay at the Feet of their Supreme Beloved, then only will earth know how to value the supreme Height and the eternal Depth of the Absolute Supreme. Truth and Peace feel that they can act as intermediaries or representatives to show earth who the Supreme is and how He can be approached. How can He be approached? He can be approached only through the aspirant's devoted surrender to the transcending height of Truth and the illumining depth of Peace.

Truth is the connecting link between the Way and the Life. Truth energises and illumines the Way that the seekers of the Infinite travel: Eternity's road. It is Truth that feeds the life divine. It is Truth that helps the life divine in its total manifestation on earth. Truth is the connecting link between the path to the Goal and the Goal itself, which is the divinely perfect life on earth.

Human life and divine life. Human life is the life of earth. What we need on earth is the transformation of our nature, the transformation of our limited consciousness, the transformation of our earthbound necessity and reality. The divine life is the life in which we manifest the highest Reality. The Reality-Song we have already learned, but we have not yet started singing it here on earth.

The realisation of the human life is this:

> A sea of Peace and Joy and Light
> Beyond my reach, I know.
> In me the storm-tossed weeping night

Finds room to rage and flow.
A raft am I on the sea of Time,
My oars are washed away.
How can I hope to reach the clime
Of God's eternal Day?

But the realisation of the divine life is this:

But hark, I hear Thy golden Flute.
Its notes bring the Summit down.
Now safe am I, O Absolute!
Gone death! Gone night's stark frown!

Human life and responsibility need not go together; human life and duty do not *want* to go together. Most human beings find it very distasteful to accept responsibility and duty. They do not want to be responsible even for their own actions, let alone for others' actions. Human life is afraid of responsibility. Human life is afraid of duty. But the divine life takes responsibility as a golden opportunity. The divine life takes duty as a golden opportunity. The divine life realises that we can expedite our Heavenward journey by fulfilling our God-ordained responsibilities, for this is what satisfies God. And the divine life knows that satisfaction can dawn in our life only when God is satisfied. If we do not satisfy God, no matter what we say, what we do or what we achieve, our true satisfaction will always remain a far cry.

The seekers who are walking along Eternity's road always feel it is their bounden duty to do the first thing first. The first thing is God-realisation. God-satisfaction blossoms into reality only when God-realisation has taken place. If we can satisfy God even in an infinitesimal measure through our divine love, divine devotion and divine surrender, then our life of insufficiency, desire and frustration will be transformed into a life of considerable satisfaction. But if God is missing inside our achievement, there will not be an iota of satisfaction there. So seekers of the infinite Truth have come to realise that it is in God and God alone that supreme satisfaction resides.

The human truth tells us that God is in Heaven or somewhere else, but not inside us. He is a foreigner or a stranger to us. He is in the highest Heaven and we are wallowing in the pleasures of ignorance on earth. How can God's Existence loom large in our life of impurity, in our life of inconscience, in our life of death? This is what the human truth says. But the divine truth tells us in soulful and unmistakable terms that God is bound to be within us. It tells us that the Heaven we are talking about is not somewhere else, not in the highest plane of imaginary consciousness. Heaven is not a location; Heaven is a plane of consciousness inside our illumined heart. This plane of consciousness which is fully illumined lives for the illumination of earth, the illumination of human consciousness. If we know what Heaven is and where Heaven is, then it is extremely easy for us to lead a divine life, for we see that Heaven is part and parcel of ourselves.

God is nearer to us than our eyes and nose, only we do not have the vision to see Him. When we keep our human eyes closed, we cannot see anything; we cannot see even the things that are near us. Similarly, if we keep the inner eye shut, then we cannot see God. When we open this inner eye, this third eye, we can see the past, we can see the future, we can see God's Height, we can see God's Depth.

Unfortunately, our third eye is fast asleep precisely because we do not feel the need of that eye. Most human beings are afraid of seeing their past and their future because they know what they were in the past. They know what kind of animal life they led and they don't want to see it again. Also, if they see the enormity of the future, the vastness of Infinity, Eternity and Immortality, they will be frightened to death. Again, some people are eager to open their third eye, but God's Hour has not struck for them. They meditate for a few years to open up the third eye, yet it does not open. But if the third eye does not open in the span of five years, they should feel either that they are not praying and meditating well or that this boon is not meant for them.

In the spiritual life aspiration is of paramount importance, but patience is also of paramount importance. We have to wait for God's Hour. Aspiration is like the runner's starting point. Then, when the starter fires the gun, he runs at his top speed. This is his aspiration. The goal is God's Hour. He has to run fast, very fast to reach the goal. The distance he has to run to reach the goal is fixed by God. If God wants the seeker to run one hundred metres, and if the seeker runs only seventy metres and then feels that he should have reached the goal by then, whose fault is it? The seeker has to cover the whole distance; he must run the full one hundred metres. Then only will he see God's Hour waiting for him. In the spiritual life aspiration is the starting point and patience is God's Hour. If the seeker starts his journey with aspiration and continues with aspiration plus patience, then he is destined to reach his Goal.

The unlit, obscure, ignorant and earth-bound human life can get its realisation, liberation and salvation only when it enters into Heaven's conscious and constant Blessings, Love, Compassion and Concern. How do we discover Heaven? In self-offering — self-offering according to God's Will and not our will. In the human way of life, the offering of reciprocal understanding or misunderstanding is the order of the day. I give to you and you give back to me. I strike you; you strike me. I speak well of you; you speak well of me. This is the human way. But the divine way is totally different. If it is God's Will, without the least possible hesitation I give to you what I have and what I am. What I have is the inner cry to climb up high, higher, highest. What I am is constant dedication to you and to the world at large, without expecting anything in return. Our life of aspiration is the life of constant awareness, constant self-giving, constant feeling of inseparable oneness with God and humanity. This is the divine way.

Sometimes we give of ourselves and feel that we are most generous. But it may happen that our offering is going to the wrong person, to one who does not need it or want it right now, to one who is fast asleep. The hour has struck for us to get up and to go to the inner school to learn, but our friends may still be fast asleep. We feel that we are doing them a favour by waking them, but they may not like the idea of getting up at this early hour. They may be irritated and angry. Our self-offering should be to the Divinity in humanity, but not to each individual as such. We will make a Himalayan blunder if we offer our dedication to someone who is still fast asleep in the inner world. He does not want our help right now. If we obey God's Will, we will help the right person, the person who is ready to come out of his ignorance-sleep and run with us to the Golden Shore. When we follow the divine life, when we lead a divine life, we always place God first in all our activities. His Will we execute. It is He who chooses the person or persons in whom we shall serve Him.

40. The inner hunger

Dear sisters and brothers, dear seekers of the infinite Truth, here we are all seated in a boat. The name of this boat is God's Dream-Boat. This Dream-Boat is sailed by our Inner Pilot. In it we are safe and it shall take us to the Golden Shore of the Beyond.

Is there anybody on earth who has never been hungry? No! Is there any soul in Heaven who has never been hungry? No! Each human being on earth is suffering from inner hunger. Each soul in Heaven also is suffering from inner hunger. Here we are all seekers. A seeker is hungry for God-realisation. A soul in Heaven is hungry for God-manifestation.

As an ordinary human being, an unaspiring being, we have already known what earthly hunger is. To fulfil earthly hunger we need material food and material possessions; we need a distinct individuality and personality and we need the pride of supremacy. This is what we notice in our unaspiring earthly hunger, our ordinary human hunger. But when we become spiritual seekers, we have a different hunger. At that time we hunger for God's Light, Truth, divine Beauty, Peace and Bliss. We hunger for Infinity, Eternity and Immortality.

When we have earthly hunger, very often we adopt foul means to satisfy our hunger. We try to feed ourselves in our own human way without knowing, without feeling and without becoming the inner light. But when we try to satisfy our divine hunger, we try to satisfy it by pleasing God in His own Way. We are able to satisfy it only by pleasing the Supreme in His own Way. We become the song of unconditional surrender, divine surrender to God's adamantine Will. This Will is also His all-loving Will.

A human child has hunger. He is hungry for affection and love from his parents, but his hunger is not illumined. His hunger is unlit. Within each human seeker there is a divine child. Call it a soul or anything else you want to. This divine child also needs Affection, Love, Concern and Compassion from God the Father and from God the Mother. But there is a striking difference between these two children. When the human child sees that his parents show affection and love to others, he immediately falls victim to jealousy. He feels sad and miserable. The divine child is pleased only when his divine, transcendental Parents offer equal Love, Affection, Concern and Compassion to all his friends, relatives and acquaintances. This child will never be pleased in a selfish way. He will be pleased only if everybody gets the same things that he gets. This child is pleased only when it sees satisfaction within and satisfaction without.

Each individual soul is hungry for God's Smile. It knows that there is nothing as important as God's Light in the life of aspiration and dedication. God too is hungry, hungry for the seeker's smile. That is the only thing He wants from us. He waits for millennia in order to get a smiling face from His earth-children.

We pray to God for millions of things; we pray to God to fulfil our countless desires. But when we become seekers we feel that there is only one thing that will satisfy us and that is God's Smile. If a seeker is not advanced, if he is not on the verge of Self-realisation, he finds it difficult to feel that God is constantly smiling at him from His transcendental Height of divine Concern and Compassion. Because this seeker does not dive deep within, he finds it difficult to believe that God is smiling at him while transforming his agelong ignorance into eternal Wisdom-Light.

It has been said that no clock is more regular than the sun. This truth is undeniable. But in the spiritual world we can say that no clock is more regular than our Heart's inner mounting cry. This inner cry wants to climb high, higher, highest and reach the acme of perfection. This cry is constant inside each fleeting second, and its climbing flame is birthless and deathless.

When we become soulful seekers, we become consciously aware of the inner cry of aspiration. Before that, this inner cry remained hidden inside; we did not feel it. But once we begin to consciously aspire, we feel the need of something eternal and perpetual; once we feel that terrestrial things do not please us, at that time we get the inner cry for something that can satisfy us permanently.

Right now we are beginners in the spiritual life, but we are not going to remain beginners forever. One does not remain in the kindergarten all his life. One hungers for ever-increasing wisdom until there comes a time when he gets his Master's degree and Ph.D. Similarly, the beginner-seekers will not be doomed to disappointment. Everyone plays the role of a beginner at some time. But ultimately the beginner becomes advanced and reaches the highest Height.

The body has a hunger of its own. The vital has a hunger of its own. The mind has a hunger of its own. The heart has a hunger of its own. The body's hunger can be satisfied by material food or by wallowing in the pleasures of ignorance. But the same body-consciousness eventually comes to realise that in pleasure-life there is not and cannot be any abiding satisfaction. Pleasure-life is eventually followed by a sense of tremendous frustration, and inside frustration what looms large is a sense of utter destruction.

The vital's hunger can be satisfied by domination. To lord it over the world like Napoleon or Julius Caesar is its desire. But the vital, too, eventually comes to realise that in domination there is no abiding satisfaction. There is only an ever-increasing craving and an ever-mounting frustration which houses destruction within its breast.

The hunger of the mind can be satisfied by doubting the world. If it can doubt the entire creation and nullify or annihilate the whole world, the physical mind gets tremendous satisfaction. The mind feels it is the highest member of the human family and that it alone can illumine the whole being. At times the mind goes so far as to feel that it is in a position to add to the light of the soul, although this idea is most ridiculous. The soul is the guide and representative of the Lord Supreme. The soul has infinitely more light than the mind even at its highest. Nevertheless, the mind cherishes this kind of absurdity. Frustration and destruction loom large in the hunger of the mind.

The hunger of the human heart is to love and to be loved. When the heart is hungry for love, the heart does not see in itself the light of the soul. This is because it consciously or unconsciously mixes with the vital, or we can say that the vital enters into the heart. Rather than inspire, the vital instructs or instigates the human heart to claim love from others, and the heart tries to force its way into others. This is absolutely wrong! When the human heart plays the game of possession, which is not a positive or divine quality, it finds no satisfaction because the person it possesses is a bundle of ignorance. Once again frustration and destruction play their roles. When the heart itself becomes a flood of sincerity, it sees its mistakes and feels miserable that realisation is still a far cry.

When we are insincere, we feel not only that we have reached the goal but also that we are ready to offer the goal to the world at large. When we are sincere, all our imperfections come to the fore and we realise how far we are from our goal. When we pray and meditate, our heart does become sincere. When this sincerity speaks, our heart feels miserable and immediately runs to the soul, to its elder divine brother, for guidance and illumination. Then the soul guides the heart. When the heart establishes a free access to the soul, the heart is safe. The human heart at that time becomes the perfect instrument for God-manifestation on earth.

Earth has a hunger, a special hunger. Earth hungers to see the face of Heaven. Earth has had the vision of Heaven's face only in silence during its highest plane of wakeful consciousness. But earth wants to see the face of Heaven inside its multifarious activities twenty-four hours a day. Earth wants to see the reality of Heaven not in a dream but in its waking hours. Earth feels that Heaven embraces all the Glory, Divinity, Infinity, Eternity and Immortality of the Absolute Supreme. Earth feels that by establishing a deep friendship with Heaven it will be able to get God's Grace, Compassion, Love and Blessing in the twinkling of an eye.

Heaven too has a special hunger. Heaven hungers to feed the heart of earth. It feels that earth's heart is simple, sincere, genuine, pure and all-loving. Heaven feels that its dream can be manifested only through the aspiring heart of Mother Earth. Heaven tries to make friends with the heart of earth because it feels that this is the only way it can manifest and transform its dream into reality.

Earth feels that by pleasing and becoming one with Heaven's consciousness it will be able to bring down God's Light sooner than at once. Heaven feels that by establishing a deep friendship with the heart of earth it will be able to fulfil its dream as soon as possible. This dream was Heaven's promise to the Absolute Supreme that, with the cooperation of earth, it would manifest God's Light, God's Beauty, God's Truth, God's Peace and all His divine qualities here on earth.

Human hunger starts with "I", but when it turns spiritual it becomes "we". When it turns absolutely divine, this hunger becomes nothing short of "God-existence". When we are hungry to achieve and fulfil God the Root, then only can we begin to fulfil the God-Tree's branches. If we do not have a hunger for the Source, our hunger will not be perpetual, everlasting and immortal. A seeker of the highest Truth comes to realise that with human hunger there will be no satisfaction. Only if we are hungry for the infinite Light will real satisfaction dawn in our lives. The human satisfaction of claiming others we shall deny for the divine satisfaction of self-giving. Not by claiming others as our very own, but only by constant self-offering to the world at large do we attain lasting satisfaction. When we offer ourselves totally and unconditionally to our Inner Pilot, our life-long hunger for oneness with our Source is satisfied for Eternity.

41. Fear in the spiritual life

Dear sisters and brothers, here we are all seekers, seekers of the infinite Truth and Light. We are all seated in God's Dream-Boat. At God's choice Hour, we shall reach the Golden Shore of the Beyond. I wish to give a short talk on fear, fear of the inner life and fear of the outer life.

What is fear? Fear is an experience of the finite life. Fear is an experience of the earth-bound consciousness. Where is fear? Fear is inside the heart of the life that does not proceed. Man is afraid of the animal life because he feels that the animal life will destroy him. Man is afraid of the human life because he feels that the human life will fail him in the long run. Man is afraid of the divine life because he feels that the divine life will expose his teeming weaknesses.

Man is right when he feels that the animal life will destroy him. He is perfectly right when he feels that the human life will eventually fail him. But he is totally wrong when he feels that the divine life will expose him.

The divine life is the life of God the Divine Mother. Let us think of a human mother and a human child. When a human mother notices the shortcomings, imperfections and weaknesses of her son, what does she do? She hides them carefully and secretly. She will never even think of exposing her own child to the world. So the Divine Mother, who is infinitely more loving and compassionate than the human mother, can never expose Her son. Like the human mother, She hides the teeming imperfections of Her son from others; then She makes Her son aware of his shortcomings because She does not want Her son to repeat the same mistake. If he repeats the same mistake again and again, God-realisation will always remain a far cry for him. When She makes him aware of his mistakes, of his ignorance, She does it with the best intentions in order that he may know the difference between an ignorant life and a life of wisdom. The Mother Divine does not delay. She carries the child one step forward. She transforms the child's ignorance into wisdom-light. She transforms his weakness into strength. She transforms his life of night into a life of light.

There can be no fear when we are aware of our universal oneness. We know a human child is very small, limited, weak and ignorant. But the human father is tall, strong and full of knowledge. The father may be commander-in-chief of a vast army: thousands of soldiers are afraid of him and even the nation is afraid of him. But look at his child! The child runs to his father and does anything he wants to. He does it precisely because he has established an inner oneness with his father. Where there is inner oneness, there can be no fear. A tiny drop is afraid of the mighty ocean as long as it retains its individuality and personality. But when the same drop feels its oneness with the vast ocean, it just enters into the mighty ocean and feels not only that the entire ocean belongs to it, but also that it has actually become the entire ocean. When we have a sense of separativity, we are bound to suffer from fear. But when we establish unity or oneness, there can be no fear.

Thousands of years ago the Vedic seers of the hoary past offered us a significant message: "The soul cannot be won by the weakling." A weak person is he who is always afraid of something.

He is even afraid of his own life. Yesterday he was afraid of today. He thought that today would try to fool him or deceive him. He had a dream yesterday and thought that today would not allow him to fulfil his dream. Today he is afraid of tomorrow. He is afraid of tomorrow because he feels that tomorrow is a stranger. He cannot have faith in a stranger; he cannot trust a stranger, for a stranger may cause tremendous trouble for him.

Now we are seekers; but there was a time when we were not seekers. Once we lived a desiring life, but now we are living the life of aspiration. When we led a desiring life we were afraid of the aspiring life. We thought that the aspiring life, which is God-life, would not make us happy. We thought it would inspire us to enter into the Himalayan caves to spend the rest of our lives in seclusion. Unfortunately, we cherished a wrong belief. Now we can easily see that although we have accepted the spiritual life we don't have to go into the Himalayan caves. We can practise the life of aspiration here in the everyday world.

We are afraid that God-realisation is not meant for us; we feel that it is only for the selected few, so at times we are afraid of what we are doing. But if we are sincere, then we know that there *have* been people on earth who have realised God. And if we have the same inner cry, then we shall also realise God one day.

In the Western world, unfortunately, there is a peculiar kind of seeker who feels that if he accepts the spiritual life which is advocated by Indian Masters, he will have to give up his Christian religion. That is a deplorable mistake. One does not have to give up his religion in order to practise the spirituality that is taught by Indian Masters. The heart of spirituality is Yoga. Yoga means conscious oneness with God. Yoga is the path that leads to God. Religion is a house. You have to live in your house as a Christian, I have to live in my house as a Hindu, and somebody else has to live in his house as a Buddhist. Each one has to live in his own house, but everyone has the right to walk along the same road, which leads to his school where he gets his knowledge. The road belongs to everyone. But the houses do not belong to everyone. If it is your house, it belongs to you. If it is my house, it belongs to me. But the road belongs to all. In the inner life we can walk along the same road, no matter in which house we live; for the ultimate destination is always the same.

Again, we do not *have* to walk along the same road. There can be many roads which will lead us to the same destination. But we have to be wise. One road may be short and sunlit, another road may be very long and a little bit obscure. If we follow the road of the heart, then we are walking along the short and sunlit road. But if we walk along the path of the mind, then we are walking along the long, dark road.

We have to give due value and importance to time. If we can arrive sooner at our destination, then we can continue on to our next destination. When we reach our destination, we realise God; but this is not the end of our achievement. Once we realise God, we have to reveal God. After we have revealed God, we have to manifest God here on earth. God-realisation is our first goal, God-revelation is our second goal and God-manifestation is our third goal. The sooner we can reach our first destination, the better for us. I have come from New York to Europe. I came by plane, but I could have come by boat. Just because I came by plane, it took me only a few hours to make the journey. This is the short cut. If I had come by boat, it would have taken me a few days or a week to arrive. My first goal was to come to Europe and I came the fastest, shortest way. Because I took the fastest route, I am now in a position to reach my second goal. My second goal is to give talks and to offer my dedicated service to the aspiring people here. My third goal will be to go back to New York, my source, where I have to do a great many things.

Fear causes worry. We always worry about our physical body. We worry because our physical is sleeping or because it suffers from ailments. We worry about our vital. We feel that our vital will destroy us or others. We are afraid of our mind and we worry about our mind. We feel that our mind may become full of doubt; then we shall not be able to believe anybody. Or we feel that our mind may not have enough doubt, and people will call us a fool. We are afraid of our own heart and we worry about our heart. We feel that if our heart does not feel its oneness with everyone, then we shall suffer much. We are worried that if our heart does not accept the light of the soul, then we will remain always in darkness.

Finally, we are afraid of death and we worry about death. We are afraid of death because death is unknown to us. Anything that is unknown to us creates terrible fear in us. But we do not know that death is also afraid of us. Death is afraid of us when we become seekers of the transcendental Truth. Death is afraid of us when we become one with the Love of God. When we become one with God's transcendental and universal Love, at that time we grow into an eternal Life. This eternal Life is always unknowable to death. Before we grow into eternal Life, we are afraid of death. After we have become eternal Life, death is afraid of us.

SRI CHINMOY

NOTES TO MY ROSE PETALS, PART 3

32. Riverside Lounge, Cambridge University Centre, Cambridge University, Cambridge, England, 12:30 pm, 24 June 1974.
33. Conference Room, University College, London University Union, 15 Gordon Street, London WC 2, England, 8 pm, 24 June 1974.
33. Paragraph 6. In the original, this part of the sentence was published as "His outer attributes".
34. Oxford University, Oxford, England, 12:30 pm, 25 June 1974.
35. University of Birmingham, Birmingham, England, 7:30 pm, 25 June 1974.
36. Sherwood Hall Boys' School, Stuart Avenue, Forest Town, Nottinghamshire, Mansfield, England, 26 June 1974.
37. Curtis Auditorium, Physics Building, University Precinct, University of Newcastle, Newcastle-upon-Tyne, England, 27 June 1974.
38. Faculty Room South, David Hume Tower, University of Edinburgh, George Square, Edinburgh, Scotland, 28 June 1974.
39. Queen Margaret Union, University Gardens, Glasgow University, Glasgow, Scotland, 29 June 1974.
39. Paragraph 12. From *My Flute*, 1972.
40. Graduates' Memorial Building, Trinity College, Dublin, Ireland, 1 July 1974.
41. Biblioteca Comunale, Piazzale Accursio, Milan, Italy, 3 July 1974.

MY ROSE PETALS

BOOK 4

42. Miracles

Dear seekers, dear sisters and brothers, today I shall give a short talk on miracles. A miracle is something unusual, something unimaginable. If a man walks on water, then he performs a great miracle. If a man flies in the sky, then he performs a great miracle. If a man can destroy a whole country, then he performs a miracle.

A boat sails on water, an aeroplane flies in the sky and a hydrogen bomb can destroy a country. Who has built the boat, who has built the plane and who has made the bomb? Man! Without a man's consent, the boat cannot sail; without a man's will, a plane cannot fly; without a man's conscious approval, the bomb cannot drop. A human being is necessary to sail the boat, to fly the plane and to destroy the country. Poor man! Unfortunately, he has totally forgotten that he is the creator of these things.

Who is superior, the creator or the creation? Undoubtedly, the creator! If the creator does not want the boat to sail, the boat cannot sail on its own. If the creator does not want the plane to fly, the plane cannot fly on its own. If the creator does not want the bomb to drop, the bomb cannot drop on its own. We are compelled to run after miracles just because we forget the undeniable fact that we are the miracle-creators.

Here we are all seekers, seekers of the infinite Truth and Light. What can be a greater miracle than when a finite human being cries to the Infinite for Peace, Light and Bliss? The finite wants to house the Infinite. The earth-bound consciousness wants to be transformed into the Heaven-free consciousness. The infinite Spirit wants to reveal itself in and through the finite body. Are these not miracles of the highest order? Can there be any greater miracle achieved by a human being than God-realisation? God-realisation means one's conscious awareness of a living God.

God-realisation means one's embodiment of infinite Peace, Light and Bliss here in an earthly body. A beginning seeker feels that the greatest miracle on earth is God-realisation. But when he becomes advanced or when he realises God, he comes to know that God-realisation is something absolutely normal — more normal than our day-to-day habits of working, eating, sleeping and playing.

God is the cosmic Tree. A tree has branches, leaves, flowers and fruits. A tree without branches, leaves, flowers and fruits is no tree at all. By the example of the tree we can learn that God needs us and we need God. The tree needs leaves, flowers and fruits; and the leaves, flowers and fruits need the source, which is the tree. The vast sea cannot become a sea without countless drops of water. The sea needs the existence of countless drops of water, and the drops need the existence of the sea. We need God as tiny drops need the ocean, and God needs us as the ocean needs the drops. We need God for our highest realisation and God needs us for His supreme manifestation here on earth. When we are aware of the Supreme's need, God-realisation is no miracle. But when we are not aware of it, for weaklings like us to think of God-realisation, and for God the Infinite to manifest Himself in and through a tiny, finite body, seems like the Supreme Miracle. On the physical plane, indeed, it is a miracle. But on the inner plane it is not a miracle because God and man are interdependent.

If we want to acquire miraculous power, we can concentrate on certain spiritual centres in the body. We first start concentrating on the base of the spine. Then we move two inches higher for the second centre. The navel is the level for the third centre; then the heart, the throat, the forehead and finally, the crown of the head. These centres are not in the gross physical body; they are located inside our subtle body. If they were in the physical body, by this time the doctors would have discovered them. Unfortunately, they are not for medical science to discover, but only for the seeker to discover through his inner cry.

The question at this point is whether or not these miraculous powers can be of any help to our God-realisation. The answer is definitely not. The great spiritual Master Sri Ramakrishna one day said to his dearest disciple, Vivekananda, "My son, I have practised so much meditation. I have achieved many miraculous powers, and I want to give them all to you. You know that I do not care for these things. I want to lead a most simple life; I want to wear the most simple clothes and eat the most simple food. Since you are my dearest disciple, let me give these powers to you."

Vivekananda said, "Please tell me one thing first. Will these occult powers help me in any way to realise God?"

"Oh, no! Occult powers can never help you in God-realisation."

Vivekananda said, "Then I do not want them. I want only God."

Here we see the aspiration of a really sincere seeker. Because of his sincere aspiration, Vivekananda did realise God. If a less sincere seeker had been offered this gift by his Master, he would have immediately tried to grab the occult powers from his Master. But a sincere seeker knows that God must come first. Another spiritual Master of the highest order, Sri Krishna, told his dearest disciple, Arjuna, that if one cares for occult power, then he is millions of miles away from his inner existence, the divine existence.

The creator is superior to his creation. These occult powers, miraculous powers, come from God; they cannot come from anywhere else. If there is a mango tree in front of me, if I want to eat a mango, I can. But if I eat a mango without permission from the owner of the tree, then I take a risk. I may be scolded and insulted. But if I take permission from the owner first, then I may eat as much as I want.

The goal is very far. If we do not start walking along the way, then how are we going to reach it? There are many roads that lead to our goal. On one road we find occult powers or miraculous powers. They are like beautiful trees and flowers in a garden alongside the road that is leading to our destination. If we walk along this particular road, we may be tempted to enter into the garden. We may eat some fruits and enjoy ourselves there for a long time; we may forget that we even have a goal to reach. We enjoy the garden to such an extent that we just stay there, or we may go back home with the idea that we shall return to enjoy the garden every day. Then we totally forget about our destination. So this garden of occult powers is a garden of temptation.

There is another road we can also follow. If we walk along this road we find that there is no garden, no park, no trees, nothing to distract us. There is only the road with the golden goal at the end. If we walk along this road steadily, then we will unmistakably reach our destination. This is the advantage of the plain road. When we walk along the road that does not offer us the temptation of occult power, there is every possibility that we will reach our goal much sooner.

What is miracle-power, after all? Miracle-power is something I can do that you cannot do. If something can be done by both of us, then it is no longer a miracle. Here on earth when a thing is extremely difficult to do, when it is next to impossible, it is like a miracle. I will tell you an incident. A little boy of five came to my house with his elder brother. I told him I could spell his name properly. I spelled his name properly and he was wonder-struck. How was it possible for me to correctly spell his name? It was beyond his imagination! He himself did not know how to spell his name, but I knew how. To him it was a miracle because he could not do it. But to his elder brother and to me, it was no miracle at all. It was a most ordinary, everyday matter.

A child studies in the kindergarten and his elder brother studies at the university. When the child sees his elder brother studying big, big books on so many different subjects, when he sees him reading, writing and committing things to memory, to the child this is nothing but a miracle. But in fifteen years or so this very child will easily be able to do the same. He will study big books and go to the university and read and write like his elder brother. Right now he does not know that he himself will soon have the same capacity, and just because he does not know, he thinks his elder brother is performing a miracle.

Here we are all seekers. Some of us are half-sincere; some of us are fully sincere. Others are only curious to know what is going on. In the spiritual life we tell people that curiosity is not spirituality; but it can become half-sincerity and half-sincerity can become spirituality. It is better to start with a little than not to start at all. Today you are nothing but a curious seeker. But if you continue, tomorrow you can become a half-sincere seeker and the following day you can become a fully sincere seeker.

Even as we need a teacher to help us in our studies at school, so also do we need a spiritual teacher to help us in our inner studies. I happen to be the spiritual teacher of a small group of disciples. I wish to say that I am also a performer of miracles. Not what I do, not what I say, but what I am inwardly is the most important thing. The real miracle is my meditation. This is the miracle that you people cannot yet perform, but which you will definitely be able to perform one day if you aspire sincerely and devotedly.

The great spiritual Masters like the Christ, Sri Krishna and the Buddha performed a great many miracles in the outer world.

But a far greater miracle was their very presence on earth. Outwardly, the Christ performed about forty-five supreme miracles, but in his inner life he performed millions and millions of miracles which were not recorded and which can never be recorded, except in the Heart of the Supreme. A far greater miracle than any of his outer miracles was his physical presence on earth, and the greatest miracle of all was his immortal Consciousness that guided and uplifted the earth-consciousness. The same thing is true of all real spiritual Masters from all countries.

We are all seekers. Just because we all have some inner cry for God, for Truth, for Light, for Bliss, we are here. If we did not have this inner cry, we would have gone out to a movie or to a party or somewhere else. But to those who have not come, to those who know that we are here listening to a spiritual talk or inwardly praying to God and meditating on God, it is nothing short of a miracle, because they do not dare to do what we are doing here. Not only do they not dare, but they cannot dare; so undoubtedly it is a miracle for them.

We do not need miracles. We do not need occult powers. What we need is God's Compassion. In God's Compassion alone abides our God-realisation. God-realisation is our birthright. If we want to acquire occult or miraculous powers, we easily can. If we feel that we don't need them or don't care for them, then we don't have to take them ever. We have to know that God-realisation is something that everybody has to have. No one can escape it. If we don't want God-realisation now, it is only a matter of time until we do. If we do not want God right now, God will not allow us to remain unrealised forever. Someday we will want Him; nay, we will need Him badly. At that time God-realisation, the supreme miracle, will be ours.

43. The aspiring life

Dear seekers, dear sisters and brothers, I wish to give a short talk on life. Needless to say, I shall speak on life from the spiritual point of view.

> Life is a lost opportunity if I do not aspire.
> Life is a gained prosperity if I aspire.
> Life is a lost soul if I do not aspire.
> Life is a gained goal if I aspire.
> Life is an animal-destruction if I do not aspire.
> Life is God-Perfection if I aspire.

When I do not aspire, earth does not need me and Heaven does not need me. When I aspire, earth needs me and Heaven needs me; also, God needs me. There was a time when I lived the desiring life. At that time, I wanted to capture the world; I wanted to own the world. Now I aspire. I wish to become a perfect instrument of God. I wish to serve humanity and be constantly dedicated to humanity.

> For me, life is a forward march.
> For me, life is an upward climb.
> For me, life is an inward dive.
> When I march forward, I see God's Sound-Power.
> When I climb upward, I see God's Silence-Power.
> When I dive deep within, I feel God's Love-Power.
> God's Sound-Power has awakened my life.
> God's Silence-Power has liberated my life.
> God's Love-Power has immortalised my life.

My life needs inner guidance. When I am guided by my Inner

Pilot, my life is safe amid earth's storms. When I am guided by my Inner Pilot, I am certain amid the world's insecurity. Life does not mean only to know the truths about God. Life means an intimate connection, an inseparable union, with my Inner Pilot. In order to be guided by my Inner Pilot, in order to know Him intimately, I have to pray and meditate. I have to know that each thought that I think is a prayer. I have to know that each action that I take is a meditation. In order to pray well and have a good meditation I have to offer my gratitude to my Pilot-Supreme. It is His Compassion that has given me the capacity to pray and meditate.

When I pray, I climb up God the Tree. When I meditate, I bring down the mangoes from above and distribute them to aspiring souls. Both my prayer and my meditation are of paramount importance. If I do not climb up God the Tree, then I remain unrealised. If I do not climb down with the fruits, then God remains unmanifested. Perfection dawns only when I am realised and God is manifested.

Countless human beings are afraid of the spiritual life because they feel that it will take them away from the life they are now living. They feel that their present life is a life of satisfaction. At times, when they are mercilessly frustrated by the life that they are now living, they feel the necessity of God and the divine life. But to them, God is a stranger and the divine life is something unknown. They feel that a stranger and an unknown life cannot be trusted. But here they are totally mistaken. God is not and cannot be a stranger. And the divine life is the real life. The real life is something that inspires us and makes us feel that Infinity, Eternity and Immortality are our birthright.

Nothing can be more normal and natural than a divine life. The life that we are leading now is abnormal and unnatural. Why? Because it has made friends with darkness, ignorance and bondage. How can ignorance offer us God-Beauty, God-Light and absolute Truth?

When we make progress in our spiritual life we feel that our life is of God and our life is for God. What we want from life is satisfaction and nothing else. When we live the desiring life, no matter what we gain, there can be no satisfaction. We have an unceasing hunger that constantly wants to devour others and the entire world. By devouring others and devouring the world we cannot have satisfaction. We can have satisfaction only by establishing our inner oneness with the rest of the world. In order to achieve satisfaction we must walk along the road of aspiration and not along the road of desire.

We have seen that the world's richest man wants to become still richer. No matter how much money he gets, his needs increase more, and the more his needs increase, the more he becomes a beggar. The seeker wants to decrease his desires. The more he decreases his desires, the sooner he sees the Face of God. When he decreases his desiring life, only one desire remains; that desire is the aspiration which comes from the very depth of his heart. This aspiration wants only one thing: God. Aspiration feels that just realising God is not enough; it also wants to manifest God here on earth in His own Way. When our aspiration has realised God and manifested God in His own Way, then supreme Satisfaction dawns both in Heaven and on earth.

44. Spirituality

Dear sisters and brothers, dear seekers of the transcendental Truth, I wish to give a short talk on spirituality. When we use the term "spirituality", we mean God. We are with God, we are in God, we are of God and we are for God. This is an experience that can be living and spontaneous in our day-to-day life. To be with God we have to withdraw from our little "I", our ego, which binds us, limits us and finally leads us to death. To be in God we have to purify our body, vital and mind. To be of God we have to please God in His own Way. To be for God we have to offer God on earth the promise that we made to Him in Heaven: Him to realise, Him to reveal and Him to manifest — for this we came onto the earth-scene.

Self-reliance is good. Dependence on God is far better. But when we offer our surrender to God's Will, and when God's Compassion accepts our surrender, this is by far the best. We say that we love God. If we really love God, then we have to serve God in humanity. In order to serve humanity, we must liberate ourselves from vital depression, mental suspicion and psychic disintegration. We have to be fully ready to love humanity even though humanity misunderstands us. A divinely crucified earthly life glorifies the Heavenly promise.

Earlier I mentioned the little "I", the ego. Now I wish to speak about the big "I", the universal "I", which we can call the universal Consciousness. When we live in this Consciousness, we feel that we are the chosen children of God. If we are the chosen children of God, how can we mix with falsehood, darkness and ignorance? It is impossible. If we are God's chosen children, then our friends are Peace, Light and Bliss.

Here we are all seekers of the highest Truth. At every moment our thoughts are judged, our prayer is judged, our meditation is judged, our surrender is judged by our Inner Pilot. If we have a pure thought, we then acquire solid strength. If we have a soulful prayer, then we gain divine confidence. If we have a sublime meditation, then we come closer to God. If we make an unconditional surrender to God's Will, then we can claim God as our very own.

Among the seekers there are some who are afraid of light. There was a time when we were all afraid of light. We thought that our evil thoughts and evil deeds would be exposed by light. But now that we have become seekers we clearly see that light has not exposed us; on the contrary, light has illumined us. The outer light exposes us; the inner light only illumines us. This is the difference between inner light and outer light.

In the spiritual life we cannot and must not make earthly plans. Very often when we make plans, five-year plans or ten-year plans, we wait and wait until the last moment before acting on our plans. Then at the last moment it is too late and we achieve nothing. A spiritual seeker does not need any plan. He depends entirely on his inner guidance, which is spontaneous and constant. When we listen to the guidance of the Inner Pilot, we achieve everything immediately.

Life means action. Action is based upon meditation. Meditation eventually reveals God and manifests Him on earth. We pray to God and meditate on God — not because we have done many things wrong in this life, not because we want to compensate for our ego-directed actions, not because we have to offer Him a petition so that He can forgive us, but because we feel that our life is a constant preparation for God. This preparation is the indication of God's revelation in and through us. This preparation makes us feel that God needs us for His manifestation. We need God to reach the highest Truth, highest Light and highest Bliss. God needs us to reveal His Dream and manifest His Divinity. What is His Dream? His Dream is earth-transformation. His Dream is nature's perfection. Our real reality lies in our conscious embodiment of God, our conscious revelation of God's Light and our conscious manifestation of God's Perfection.

Here we are all seekers; some are beginners, some are a little advanced. The beginners may have some curiosity about God's existence. But those who are a little advanced know that God does exist. They feel that it is God who is guiding them in a divine way. But when? Only when they inwardly cry. To love God and God alone, we have to cry inwardly at every moment and become a helpless inner cry. I always tell people in the spiritual life to start no matter where they are, no matter how developed or undeveloped they are. Unless we start, we can never reach our destination. Even if we start with curiosity, we will see that our curiosity will eventually lead us to faith. Faith is something divine within us. When we have faith in God, God gives us faith in ourselves. When our faith in God and our faith in ourselves work together, we become a perfect instrument of God. At that time, we gain inner experiences and these experiences carry us along the road of Immortality.

For those who follow the spiritual life there comes a time when we distinctly hear God's Voice. God offers us His highest message: today's imperfect man is tomorrow's perfect God. Today's unfulfilled man becomes tomorrow's fulfilled God. But how? Through divine love, divine devotion and divine surrender. Human love binds us. Human devotion is nothing but attachment. Human surrender is nothing but compulsion. Divine love is the heart's expansion. Divine devotion is the sweetest intimacy with God. Divine surrender is the complete satisfaction of our life. This surrender is the surrender of our unlit life to our own fully illumined soul. In the real spiritual life if we have divine love, divine devotion and divine surrender, then we accomplish everything. The Kingdom of Heaven we bring down into the world, and earth's cry we carry up to Heaven's Smile.

45. The secret of joy

Dear seekers, dear sisters and brothers, today I shall talk on the secret of joy. There is nobody on earth who does not want joy. There is nobody on earth who does not need joy. But there are only very, very few people who know the secret of joy.

The secret of joy is not to be found in the life of desires; the secret of joy is in the life of aspiration. The life of desire blinds us and binds us. The life of aspiration illumines us and liberates us. The life of desire makes us feel that we are all beggars. The life of aspiration makes us feel that we are all God's divine children. The life of desire is the life of pleasure. A life of pleasure can never be a life of joy, because pleasure is followed by frustration and frustration is followed by destruction. But joy is followed by deeper joy, deeper joy is followed by deepest joy and deepest joy is followed by infinite Joy.

In the spiritual life, we can have joy only when we surrender ourselves to God's Will. Two thousand years ago the Saviour Christ taught us the supreme message: "Let Thy Will be done." There can be no higher message, no deeper secret, than this. If we want to have infinite Joy, then here is the secret. As long as I am in the finite my joy is bound to be finite. I can have unlimited joy only when I enter into the Infinite. How much joy can a drop of water contain? But when this drop enters into the mighty ocean and becomes inseparably one with the mighty ocean, the joy it can contain becomes infinite.

We get joy from self-conquest. To conquer ourselves we have to discipline our life. From a disciplined life we get self-mastery. From self-mastery we get the message of self-discovery. Self-discovery and God-realisation are one and the same. When we realise God, our inner consciousness is flooded with Light and Delight. At that time we have infinite Joy, infinite Peace and infinite Light.

There are various ways to get joy, but the easiest and most effective way is through love. When the mother loves her child, how happy the child is! But the mother remains on earth for seventy or eighty years and then she dies. Her son, who has now become a grown-up man, does not get any more joy from his mother because she is no longer on earth. He has received love, which is joy, from his mother for thirty or forty years. This joy we call the joy of the finite. But when we love God, the Inner Pilot, who is eternal, then our joy will be permanent and eternal. I am not saying here that we should not give importance to a mother's love. We can enter into infinite Joy without throwing aside finite joy.

In our life of joy service is as important as love. If we serve God in mankind, we can become happy. If we serve those who need our help, then we can become happy. Each time we serve, we expand our consciousness, and real joy grows in the expansion of our consciousness. Service means going from one to many, from many to the Infinite. First I eat and serve myself. Then I feed my near and dear ones. And then I try to feed the whole of humanity. As I serve more and more seekers, as I increase my service, I also increase my joy.

Something which is quite important in our spiritual life is freedom. Freedom from what? Freedom from falsehood, darkness and ignorance. Every day God gives us freedom. It is we who have to use this freedom. With our freedom we need not pray to human beings to give us things. We can easily pray only to our Lord Supreme, who is our Liberator. We can love only God, who is our Beloved Supreme. But in order to pray to God, meditate on God and love God, we need inspiration. This inspiration we may get from a flower, from a flame, from the sky, from the mountains, from the sea, from the moon, from the stars, from the sun. Or we can get this inspiration from a God-realised man. We may look at a flower for inspiration or we may look at the flame of a candle, but we have to know that the flower has not realised God, the flame has not realised God. If we meditate on the picture of a Master, we get a kind of inspiration which is much more powerful than the inspiration that we get from a flower or a candle flame. If we meditate on a picture of the Christ, Sri Krishna, the Buddha or other spiritual Masters in whom we have faith, then naturally we shall get infinitely more inspiration than if we meditate on a flower or a candle flame.

Here on earth we are caught by the animal in us, by the human in us and by the Divine in us. When we are caught by the animal in us, we fight vehemently to free ourselves. What are the animals inside us? Doubt, jealousy and aggression. When we are caught by the human in us, it compels us to be satisfied only with a small, insignificant thing. It forces us to remain inside a tiny cave. It tells us that we cannot realise the Infinite. The Divine in us catches us most lovingly. The Supreme holds His divine child most lovingly and tells him that He is dreaming in and through him. He wants His child to grow up and one day become as great as He is.

In our daily practical life there is a way for us to get joy. If we lead a simple life and go to our goal on a direct path, if we walk along a sunlit path, then we can have joy. A simple life is the life of happiness. A direct path is the path of joy. A sunlit path is the path of constant joy.

We do not get joy because the world is full of chaos. Who has created this chaos? You and I. It is we who have to be blamed. When our body only sleeps and snores, we create chaos. When our vital strikes others, we create chaos. When our mind doubts others, we create chaos. But if we use our body to serve God in man, if we use our vital to inspire others, if we use our mind to illumine others, then we are bound to get joy.

We have made many, many promises to God. Every day we promise God that we shall do this for Him, we shall do that for Him, but we never, never do what we promise. God has made only one promise to us and that promise is that He will give us His Joy. His Joy He wants to give us in infinite measure, but when He wants to give it to us, we do not receive it. God is like the sun, an inner sun; He is all Light. If we keep our windows and doors shut, then the sunlight cannot come in. Similarly, if we keep our heart's door shut, then God's Joy cannot come in. But if we keep our heart's door open, then we get light and illumination from God the inner Sun.

We have three special rooms: the room of the soul, the room of the heart and the room of the mind. There are two more rooms: the room of the vital and the room of the body, but most of the time we keep the doors to these two rooms closed. When we live in the soul's room, we see that there is nowhere for death to stay. When there is nowhere for death, naturally we will be extremely happy. When we live in the heart-room, we see that at times there is a seat for death. Naturally, we cannot be as happy as when we are in the soul's room. This moment, when our heart identifies with Light divine, naturally there can be no death; but the next moment, when our heart identifies with the ignorance of the world, at that time all is depression, frustration, destruction and death. In the room of the mind, not only is there a seat for death, but death is welcome to sit on any seat he wants to. Death comes in and sits either on its own seat or on any other seat it wants to occupy. So there can be no joy at all in the room of the mind. If we are in the mind-room, we have to pray to enter into the heart-room. If we are in the heart-room, let us pray and meditate to enter into the soul's room. It is only in the soul's room that we will find infinite Joy, infinite

Satisfaction and infinite Perfection.

46. Capacity

Dear sisters and brothers, dear seekers of the highest Truth, I wish to give a short talk on capacity. Capacity is something that everybody is familiar with; it is not something new to any human being. God grants us capacity the moment we take human birth. In fact, the soul is inundated with capacity in the soul's world before we ever take human birth. The soul then assumes a physical body and uses this capacity to reveal and manifest God here on earth.

A child that is one day old knows how to move his hands and legs and how to cry. These are some of his capacities. As the child grows up, his capacities increase. When he becomes a fully-fledged man, either he misuses his capacities or he uses them properly. If he properly uses his capacities, he eventually realises the highest Truth on earth. If he misuses his capacities, then here on earth he lives in the world of ignorance and death.

Since we are all seekers, we all have some capacity to love God, to serve God and to surrender ourselves to God's Will. If we love God, then we are doing the first thing first; we are watering the roots of the tree. If we serve God, we come closer to God and God comes closer to us. If we surrender ourselves to God's Will, then we feel that we are complete.

Yesterday we cried and cried for God's Love. Today we are smiling and smiling with God's Love. Tomorrow with our smile we shall bring down the Kingdom of Heaven to earth. When we bring down the Kingdom of Heaven to earth, our Beloved Supreme will enjoy His rest on earth and all human beings will at last find their all-nourishing, all-protecting nest.

We must try to serve God in every human being. This service of ours has to be unconditional. If it is conditional service we will never be happy. Whenever we serve God or love mankind we have to do it unconditionally. Then only can we be continuously happy.

Two thousand years ago the Saviour Christ taught us the supreme lesson: "Let Thy Will be done." Millions, billions and trillions of prayers have been offered to God, but there can be no better, no greater, no more fulfilling prayer than this. If we love God we become happy. If we serve God we become happier. If we surrender our individual will to God's Will we become happiest.

There is a special way to become happy. If we know how to follow the inner guidance, then we can really be happy. This guidance comes directly from the soul. Unfortunately, quite often our vital being cleverly deceives us. It makes us feel that its own message is actually coming from the soul. How are we going to know whether a message is coming from the vital or from the soul? There is an easy, most effective way to know this. If it is the voice of the vital, then we will know immediately from the way we feel after we complete the action. After we act, the result of our action will come in the form of either success or failure. If we fail in something and then feel miserable, we can know that it was not the voice of the soul that told us to do that thing; it was the voice of the vital being. If we are successful and then become extremely happy and proud and try to dominate the world with our happiness and pride, again we can know that it was not the soul's voice. The moment we get a message from the soul or hear its voice, we get an inner thrill. Whether we succeed or fail, we have an inner joy. This joy does not make us want to dominate the world; rather, it makes us feel our oneness with the world. With this joy we can enter into others' hearts and help them to lead a better and higher life.

A life of peace is a life of tremendous capacity. How do we get peace? There are many ways to achieve peace but I wish to tell you of two main ways. One way is to minimise our desires. Since we are seekers, a day will come when we shall have no desires at all. But before that day dawns, our peace of mind will increase if we try to minimise our desires every day. The second way to get peace is to feel that we are not indispensable here on earth for anything or for anyone. Long before we came into the world, the world existed; long after we leave this world, the world will still exist. So how can we be indispensable? We stay here on earth for sixty, seventy or eighty years. Then we see our children, grandchildren and great grandchildren carry on where we left off in the supreme process of evolution.

In our daily life, sometimes we see good in others and sometimes we see bad. This is a form of capacity that we exercise every day. But we have to know that when we see bad in others we multiply our own bad qualities. When we see good in others we find that we can bring forward our own good qualities and see our own Source. This Source is the Unity which is trying to manifest itself through multiplicity.

Life is a constant battle between good forces and bad forces, between divine forces and undivine forces. When we lose in the battlefield of life we feel that we are doomed to disappointment. This disappointment is itself a negative force. During the fight we have already spent a considerable amount of energy. But if we pay attention to our disappointment and despair, we lose even more of our precious energy. To pay attention to anyone or anything is to expend energy. If we pay attention to the right people or the right things, then we get energy back from them in abundant measure. We offer our capacity to the human in them; then the soul or the divine in them gives us back even more capacity, out of gratitude. In the outer life, the more we offer knowledge to others, the more there comes to us a higher and deeper knowledge to illumine our mind and heart. In the spiritual life also, the more we serve others, the more capacity God grants us for service.

When we have earthly power, physical power, we feel that we shall be able to dominate the earth. When we have spiritual power, we feel that we can be of service to mankind. Spiritual power is the power of our inner cry. Spiritual power climbs high, higher, highest and brings down from above God's Light, Peace and Delight. Then it distributes these qualities in the physical world. Spiritual power is the power of inseparable oneness. Physical, earthly power is the power of division and destruction. But when physical power is illumined and guided by spiritual power, then the physical power adds to the spiritual power in the tug-of-war against ignorance. Physical power, the younger brother, takes the side of spiritual power, the older brother, and together they battle against ignorance. When two strong persons are on one side and only one is on the other side, naturally the side that has two persons will win.

In the spiritual life there is a special way to increase our capacity every day, every hour, every minute. It can be done through gratitude. When we offer our soulful gratitude to God, our capacity for receptivity immediately increases. Our receptivity is like a vessel; this vessel can be enlarged. Naturally, the larger the vessel the more it will be able to hold of God's Light and Delight.

The life of a seeker is the life of inner faith. Faith is something that constantly brings us the message of the Beyond. Faith is the foundation of our real life. We must have faith in God; we must have faith in ourselves. If we have faith only in God and not in ourselves, or if we have faith only in ourselves and not in God, then we cannot go very far. What is our faith? Our faith is our inner cry for God's Light and Bliss in infinite measure. Our faith is God's transcendental Smile, which transforms our life and carries us from the sea of ignorance to the sea of Wisdom. Our inner faith in God constantly helps us to run the fastest and constantly makes God run towards us in the fastest possible way. Because God's speed is far greater than our speed, when we take one step towards God we see that God has taken ninety-nine steps towards us. Then we meet together.

Capacity means to give and to receive. What can we give God? We can give Him only what we have. What we have is a sea of ignorance. What He has is a sea of infinite Light and Delight. God is anxious and more than eager to give us what He has and what He is. It is we who do not want to give our ignorance to God. We feel that if we give our ignorance away to God, then there will be nothing that we will have or be able to claim as our own. But when we pray and meditate, we realise that we can claim God's treasures as our own.

An unaspiring person feels that he can create a better universe. God not only feels that He can create a better universe but He actually has the capacity to do so. Seekers can help God in creating a better universe through selfless, dedicated service and through constant aspiration. If God wants me to be perfect, if I cry most sincerely and most devotedly, one day God will make me perfect. Then there will be one less imperfect person in this world. Tomorrow, if you also try most sincerely the way I have tried, then there will be two persons on the side of perfection. If every day one person takes the side of perfection, then this world of ours will eventually become perfect. The process goes from the one to the many, from the individual to the universal, from the earth-bound consciousness to the Heaven-free consciousness, from the finite reality to the infinite Reality which is God's Song of the ever-transcending Beyond.

We can do something for everyone: for earth, for God and for Heaven. We can bring down Heaven's Smile for earth. We can offer our earth-cry to Heaven. We can offer our surrendered life to God. Finally, if we really want to love earth in a divine and supreme way, then we must remind ourselves of the long-forgotten promise that we are here on earth to embody God consciously, to reveal God devotedly, to manifest God unmistakably. Our embodiment of God, our revelation of God and our manifestation of God must be unconditional. If we do this, God's infinite capacities will shower on us. At that time we become God's ambassadors, His most perfect instruments on earth. And it is in and through us that He will then sail His Dream-Boat to the Golden Shore of the ever-transcending Beyond.

47. Satisfaction

Dear seekers, dear brothers and sisters, I wish to give a short talk on satisfaction. Earth needs satisfaction, Heaven needs satisfaction, man needs satisfaction; even God needs satisfaction. Where is satisfaction found? Satisfaction is found in being, in achieving and in becoming. What are we? We are God veiled and unmanifested. What do we achieve? We achieve God-realisation. What do we become? We become God revealed and manifested.

What is satisfaction? Satisfaction is perfection. Yesterday our perfection was God-realisation. Today our perfection is God-revelation. Tomorrow our perfection shall be God-manifestation.

Who is satisfied? Not he who has material wealth in boundless measure. Who is satisfied? Not he who rules a country. Who is satisfied? Not he who performs constant miracles. He alone is satisfied who is in constant communion with his Inner Pilot. He alone is satisfied who loves God unconditionally. He alone is satisfied who serves God in God's own Way. In order to commune with God inwardly, love God unconditionally and serve God in His own Way, we need aspiration. Aspiration is the inner cry that rises from the very depths of our heart. It climbs high, higher, highest and touches the pinnacle of Light and Truth. Aspiration is the creation of God's Compassion. Compassion is God's highest and best divine quality. God has infinite divine qualities, but His Compassion far surpasses all His other divine qualities. God's Compassion and man's salvation are inseparable.

Satisfaction lies in our self-giving. Through self-giving we enter into the universal Consciousness and the limited human consciousness grows into the boundless divine Consciousness. Self-giving precedes God-becoming. God-becoming experiences the universal Consciousness in both its static and its dynamic forms. In His static form God enjoys His supreme Silence. In His dynamic form God enjoys His all-manifesting Sound.

On the physical plane we try to get satisfaction at every moment, but we try to get satisfaction by fulfilling our desires. We feel that each time we fulfil a desire we shall see the face of satisfaction. But unfortunately, each time a desire is fulfilled we feel tremendous dissatisfaction. We feel that something higher, something more powerful, exists; yet that very thing we have not yet achieved. We blame our circumstances. We blame others. We blame the world. We blame God. We blame circumstances because we feel that circumstances could have been on our side, but were not. We blame others because we feel that they could have been of considerable help to us, but were not. We blame the world because we feel that the world did not encourage us enough to win the victory. We blame God because we feel that God was indifferent to us and did not play His part. We feel that God did not give us the tremendous will-power we needed to achieve victory in life. We feel that He did not show us the

Compassion we needed. But if we are sincere, we will see that it is we ourselves who have to be blamed; for no matter what we do or achieve, we will always have a sense of dissatisfaction unless and until we have realised the highest Truth, the Lord Supreme.

There are a few enemies we have within us that do not allow us to be satisfied. They are doubt, jealousy and despair. Doubt-power is contagious. It starts in the mind and then spreads to the vital and the physical. Gradually it poisons the whole of our physical existence. Jealousy acts like a ferocious animal. If it gets the opportunity it will not hesitate to devour the whole world. Despair is a destructive power, a negative power that feels that everything is lost and there is only darkness. Despair invokes frustration and frustration invokes destruction. In a negative way despair obtains satisfaction, but this satisfaction is nothing but self-destruction.

Divine satisfaction lies in renunciation. What do we renounce? We do not renounce the body. We renounce the things in us that are not aspiring — qualities like fear, doubt, anxiety and worry. After we have renounced these, we bring faith, joy, love, devotion and confidence into our life. These divine qualities give us real satisfaction. If we want to be satisfied in our spiritual life we have to cultivate devotion. Devotion can give us considerable joy and satisfaction. If we kneel down before our Lord Supreme, He blesses us and gives us joy. If we cry like a child, He embraces us, and in His embrace we get satisfaction. If we pray soulfully to Him, He employs us to serve Him in aspiring humanity, and through our soulful service we get satisfaction.

As ordinary human beings want satisfaction, spiritual Masters also want satisfaction. While they are here on earth they serve God. This is their satisfaction. They also make a solemn promise to the world at large that they will come back again and again to serve God in mankind and to fight the evil forces and help the divine forces.

"Whenever the undivine qualities prevail and the divine qualities decline, I embody myself for the protection of the good and for the destruction of the wicked." This is the message that Lord Krishna offered to mankind. He also taught us that if we really want satisfaction, we have to live in the consciousness of the soul and not in the physical consciousness. The soul is the divine representative of God on earth. This is Lord Krishna's description of the soul: "Weapons cannot cleave it; fire cannot burn it; water cannot drench it; wind cannot dry it. Eternal and immutable is the soul." If we can remain inside the soul, we cannot be affected by the buffets of life, for we become immortal. It is in Immortality that we will find eternal satisfaction. In the finite there can be no satisfaction because the finite always wants to possess. In possession there can be no satisfaction. But in the Infinite there is all satisfaction.

The modern world is getting satisfaction from new scientific discoveries. What is God's latest discovery? If we say that God's latest discovery is man, then we are mistaken. If we say that God's latest discovery is human aspiration, we are mistaken. If we say that God's latest discovery is man's dedication, we are mistaken. If we say that God's latest discovery is man's surrender to God's Will, we are also mistaken. What, then, is God's latest discovery? It is man's gratitude, which is absolutely the rarest thing on earth. Each time God discovers it, He feels that it is really His latest discovery. When man offers gratitude to the Supreme, his power of receptivity increases in infinite measure. As his receptivity increases, his satisfaction-power also increases. The supreme Satisfaction lies in man's constant offering of gratitude to God.

48. Inner experiences

Dear sisters and brothers, here we are all seekers of the highest transcendental Truth and Light. Just because you have been kind enough to come here today to see the seeker in me, I wish to share with you a few inner experiences of mine.

My first and foremost experience is the discovery of the importance of the spiritual heart. This heart constantly aspires to climb high, higher, highest in order to reach the highest pinnacle of Truth and Light. This heart is the heart of inseparable oneness — oneness with you, with God, with the world at large. Inside this heart, the seeker in me has discovered three most intimate friends and eternal friends: love, devotion and surrender. This love is divine love. This devotion is divine devotion. This surrender is divine surrender.

Human love we all know. It is a song of temptation, a song of frustration, a song of destruction. But divine love is the song of aspiration, the song of realisation, the song of perfection and, finally, the song of Satisfaction supreme here on earth and there in Heaven.

Human devotion is the song of attachment, conscious or unconscious. There is practically no light in the song of attachment. But when we have divine devotion, which is the devotion we offer to the Highest in order to become one with its Light and Delight, the seeker in us becomes the Lover divine. At that time, the seeker in us devotes his entire life and his entire being to a higher, more fulfilling reality, to the Supreme Beloved and the supreme Cause. He is devoted only to the Truth, Light, Beauty and Delight which abound in infinite measure in the heart of the universal Consciousness. His song offers him deepest joy, which he feels in the inmost recesses of his heart. The song of devotion leads him to the sea of Nectar-Bliss.

The third eternal friend that I have discovered inside the heart is divine surrender. This surrender is not imposed; this is not the surrender of a slave to his master, which is founded upon fear. The divine surrender that I am speaking of is the feeling of oneness with the Highest. This surrender is founded upon oneness, inseparable oneness. The unillumined in us is crying to enter into the illumined in us and become totally illumined itself. The finite has become conscious of its own infinite existence on the highest plane of consciousness; therefore, the finite aspires to become consciously one, inseparably one, with its own highest reality: Infinity. This surrender is not being compelled; it is spontaneous, willing and cheerful. Divine surrender has discovered that self-giving to the Divine is nothing other than God-becoming.

The seeker in me has discovered a cosmic tree. This cosmic tree has many, many branches, but the three most significant branches are love, devotion and surrender. When we climb up the tree and try to sit on the love-branch, we see God's Door, His Heart's Door, which is immediately opened for us. When we climb up a little higher and sit on the devotion-branch, we see someone inside God's Room beckoning us to enter. And finally, when we climb up still higher and sit on the surrender-branch, we again see someone beckoning to us. But this time it is not a representative of God; it is God Himself. God Himself comes out and signals us to enter into His Room. He says to us, "My children, now you have seen in Me the perennial Truth, Light and Bliss. Here is My Crown. Here is My Throne. These are all for you. You have been wallowing in the pleasures of ignorance from time immemorial. There was a time when you claimed ignorance as your very own. Now is the time to claim Me, My infinite Light, Peace and Bliss, as your very own. It is time to claim Me as your birthright."

A life of love divine tells us who God is.

A life of devotion divine tells us where God is.

A life of surrender divine makes us sit on the Throne of God and wear the Crown of God.

The seeker in me has discovered the path of the heart. There is another path — the path of the mind. There are people who want to follow that path, but there one encounters many risks. When one walks along that path, a few so-called friends make his acquaintance: fear, doubt, anxiety and worry. These so-called friends eventually prove to be veritable enemies. In the beginning, doubt makes the seeker feel that if he can doubt everything and everyone in the world, then he can play the role of a supreme judge. The seeker soon comes to realise, however, that his doubting faculty has not made him a chief justice; it has only created a malignant cancer in him.

Fear, in a tricky way, wants to make the seeker feel that it is warning him and cautioning him. But the seeker eventually comes to realise that fear is only blocking his mind and tormenting his entire being. He has not done anything wrong, so why should he be afraid of anything or anyone? Only a criminal, only someone who has done something wrong, need be afraid. So the seeker comes to know that the message of fear has no validity; then fear becomes forceless.

Worries and anxieties make the seeker feel that he needs them in order to keep alert. They make him feel that the reason he is so stricken by worries and anxieties is because he has concern for his outer and inner wants. But alas, there comes a time when the seeker who is following the mental path realises that it is not anxiety or worry that show real concern for his outer and inner wants or for mankind. When we are in the physical, we may say that worries and anxieties show our concern for others. But when we are in the soul, we discover that real concern is the feeling of oneness, the oneness of our expanded, unlimited self with the various parts of our own being and with the rest of the world.

Real concern for ourselves lies in our conscious awareness of our integral oneness with the body, vital, mind, heart and soul. Right now, we have established a physical unity from the soles of our feet to the crown of our head. In all our limbs we feel unity. When our feet and hands hurt, we feel pain all over our body. Similarly, if our brain-power has achieved something, if we have stood first in a university examination, then immediately our entire body-consciousness becomes full of joy, delight and pride. Why? Precisely because our whole body has established inseparable oneness with the mind. This same kind of oneness that exists in the physical we have to establish with all the parts of our being — physical, vital, mind, heart and soul. If we can do this, we will have real concern for our own existence. But if we want to have concern for the world, we have to know that genuine concern has to come from our feeling of inseparable and indispensable oneness with our infinite existence, with our countless brothers and sisters.

When we live in the heart, our road is short. When we live in the mind, the road is long; also there are quite a few hooligans that come to rob us. If we are very brave and powerful and have indomitable will, then we can walk along the path of the mind successfully. But if we walk along the path of the heart, we find that it is at once the safest and the most effective way, for it is the path of divine children. When we follow the path of the heart, we automatically become divine children. When we become divine children, we spontaneously follow the path of the heart. If we follow the path of the mind, we feel that we can accomplish everything all by ourselves; we need very little help or practically no help from above. We feel that we are the doers, that we can do everything. But a child never feels that he is the doer. He always feels that his mother and father will do everything for him. He has the feeling because he has established his oneness with his parents. One smile from the child is enough to give the parents infinite pleasure. In the child's smile, the Kingdom of Heaven is immediately brought down to earth. One cry from the child is enough to make the parents muster all their love-power, compassion-power and concern-power. It immediately builds a bridge between Heaven and earth. The child cries in the living room and the mother comes running from the kitchen, for she feels that it is her bounden duty to come and please the child. The divine child's cry has the power of uniting earth and Heaven.

It is children who make constant progress. They live in the world of dreams, and dreams are nothing other than realities in the making. Today's dreams are tomorrow's realities. Today's imperfect human being will be tomorrow's perfect human being. Today's weakness is tomorrow's strength. A child is God's Dream-Boat today. Tomorrow he will not only reach the Golden Shore, but he will also become the Shore itself. This is the path of the heart which the seeker in me has discovered.

Dear sisters and brothers, I wanted to share with you the experiences that I have had. Now I have offered them to the seeker in each of you with my heart's deepest love, my soul's deepest gratitude and with my feeling of inseparable oneness with each of you.

49. Inner obedience

Dear spiritual sisters and brothers, dear seekers of the supreme Truth, I wish to give a short talk on obedience from the spiritual point of view.

Obedience is a forced life; obedience is the surrender of an inferior man to a superior man. These are the realisations of an ordinary, unaspiring human being. But the obedience that I am going to talk about is the inner obedience. This obedience is our conscious recognition of our higher life, higher reality and higher height. This obedience represents the achievement of true knowledge. When we obey the higher principles, the higher law, we come to realise that we are living eternally in the eternal Now.

A child obeys his parents. While obeying he walks along the path of truth, light and beauty. Although his outer life may be full of fear, his inner life is approaching the destination of perfection. In the spiritual life we are all eternal children. As sincere seekers we become devoted children and surrendered instruments of God; we listen to the Voice of the Inner Pilot who is guiding our destiny and moulding and shaping us in His own Way. When we go deep within we feel that we are an exact prototype of His Being. We obey our Inner Pilot, not because He is all-powerful or because we fear He may punish us if we do not obey Him. No, this is not our realisation. Our illumined love-power wants to be one with His infinite Love and Light. We obey Him because He is all Love.

From the spiritual point of view, obedience is our self-giving to the illumined consciousness. The individual consciousness, the personal consciousness that we embody, is very limited. But we can offer our individual and personal life to something that is universal. Then the limited becomes universal and unlimited. A spark of divine light we are. When we enter into the vast Sun, we offer our individuality and personality to our highest source and then we become part and parcel of this vast Sun of Universality. From the finite we go to the Infinite; from the Infinite we go to the transcendental Absolute where all is universal oneness.

Our feet take us to school where we get mental knowledge and wisdom. This is because the feet and the mind have established their inseparable oneness. It is not obedience but inner necessity that makes them help one another. My legs will serve my mind when it is a matter of learning, and when it is a matter of running, my mind and heart come to the aid of my legs with their conscious concern and will-power. Obedience is our conscious acceptance of our entire existence. When one part of our being needs special attention, another part comes to its rescue. "United we stand; divided we fall." This is the motto of our inner obedience.

In the spiritual life inner obedience and self-discipline go together; they are inseparable. When we discipline our life, we feel that we are no longer in the animal kingdom but in the human kingdom and, at the same time, we are aspiring for the divine kingdom. This divine kingdom is bound to dawn. In fact, on the strength of our aspiration, it is we who will give birth to the divine kingdom here on earth. Self-discipline leads us to self-discovery, which is God-discovery. God-discovery is followed by God-revelation and God-revelation is followed by God-manifestation. Finally, God-manifestation is followed by God-perfection and God-satisfaction.

Hesitation comes into our life when we do not obey the Inner Guide. Hesitation comes into our life when we do not nourish our inner existence with prayer and meditation. When do we hesitate? We hesitate when we live in the mind-room instead of the heart-room. When we are in the mind-room, we see a tiger in front of us, a lion behind us and other destructive animals all around us. We also hesitate when we shake hands with gloom, either consciously or unconsciously. When we open our inner door to the Prince of Gloom, we constantly hesitate. But if we obey the Inner Pilot, we are always cheerful. At that time the Prince of Gloom has no access to us. We also hesitate when we do not claim God as our very own. Our highest and only real

Reality is God's Dream-Boat. But if we do not realise that in us and for us is God's Reality-Shore, then we are bound to hesitate.

If we follow the Will of our Inner Pilot, there is never any hesitation in our life. We must know that the moment an individual seeker obeys the Inner Pilot, a most beautiful rose comes into existence in the garden of God's Heart. This heart-rose emanates a celestial fragrance that elevates the whole earth-consciousness.

How can the seeker know what the Will of the Inner Pilot is? How can he differentiate between the voice of the soul and the voice of the mind or the vital, which can create unimaginable problems for him? How will he separate the real from the unreal, the wrong from the right? The sincere seeker will be able to detect easily the wrong, the unreal voice. If the voice wants him to get satisfaction from the results of his efforts, then it is the unreal voice. After obeying the voice, if he will be satisfied only if victory dawns, and disappointed if failure comes, then he knows it is the wrong voice. The right voice, the divine voice, the voice of his soul will only inspire him to do selfless action and right action. This is not always the same as successful action in the outer world.

In India's Bible, the Bhagavad-Gita, Lord Krishna says to his dearest disciple: "Thou hast the right to action, but claim not the fruits thereof." Action divinely performed is the supreme Victory. The result can come in the form of either success or failure. When a child learns how to crawl, he feels that he has achieved a tremendous success. But when he knows how to walk properly, he feels that yesterday's accomplishment was very insignificant. Today's success is never enough. Tomorrow we will try to get another, more gratifying kind of success. What we feel we want is something to satisfy our immediate need. But when it is a question of continual progress, our immediate need is also the eternal need. Our eternal need is progress. Progress is the continuous fruitful, ever-transcending fulfilment of our eternal need. Success is pleasing to the human in us, but when we take the side of progress, we get tremendous divine satisfaction. We see progress in the growth of a tree. A seed germinates and grows into a tiny plant. Gradually it becomes a huge Banyan Tree with hundreds of branches and thousands of leaves which can offer shelter to countless human beings. If we take life as a song of gradual progress, then life is constant satisfaction.

Inner obedience is responsibility and duty. When we look at responsibility with our unaspiring human consciousness, it seems like an unbearably heavy burden that we have to shoulder. But when we follow the spiritual life, we look upon responsibility as a divine opportunity. The more responsibility we have, the more we are able to fulfil both Heaven-consciousness and earth-consciousness. Responsibility is our immediate necessity. It is the necessity of our soul, the necessity of the real in us, the necessity of the ideal in us and the necessity of the ever-transcending in us.

A sincere seeker feels that it is his inner and outer necessity that has compelled him to cry for God and become inseparably one with God's infinite Light, Truth, Peace and Bliss. He also feels that God's Necessity and God's Divinity are constantly in need of his existence. God's Divinity needs him for God-realisation, and God's Necessity needs him for God-manifestation. Necessity is founded upon mutual responsibility. The son has made a solemn promise to the Father that to realise and manifest Him he will go into the world-arena again and again. The Father has made a solemn promise to the son that in him and through him He will manifest His infinite Peace, Light and Bliss.

A sincere seeker, an obedient seeker, feels that the desire-life is a dangerous thing. It is constantly destroying his inner power and inner realisation. When he becomes really sincere, really devoted, really obedient, he feels that his aspiration-life is constantly taking him away from the desire-life and animal-life. Each human being first lives the desire-life, then the aspiration-life and finally the realisation-life. When he lives the realisation-life, he finally comes to see that his animal-life and desire-life served a purpose, but were only stages in the soul's slow and steady evolution.

Aspiration-life is the life of inner obedience. When we obey someone outwardly, even out of fear, we gain something. But when we obey someone inwardly because he is divine, then we grow into his very image, into his own divinity. When we inwardly and outwardly offer our obedience to the Inner Pilot, our first experience tells us that we are on earth and our Father is in Heaven. Our second experience tells us that we are where our Father is, or our Father is where we are. Our third and ultimate experience is that no matter where He is or where we are, our only wish is that His Will be done. Let Him be in Heaven, let us be in hell. Our only prayer to the ever-compassionate Father is this: "Let Thy Will be done." This is the highest perfection founded upon the beauty of inner obedience.

50. Force

Dear sisters and brothers, dear seekers of the supreme Truth and Light, I wish to give a short talk on force, human force and force divine.

Forgiveness is a powerful divine force. To forgive others in the physical plane is a difficult task. To forget others' imperfections is more difficult. Not to notice anything wrong in others is most difficult. But when we think of God it becomes easy for us to forgive others; when we pray to God it becomes easy to forget others' shortcomings, limitations and imperfections. When we meditate on God, it becomes easy for us not to notice anything wrong in others.

Self-discipline is a force that every aspirant needs. In the total perfection of our self-discipline we discover our true self. In order to discipline our physical we have to cry for light. In order to discipline our vital life, the life of pleasure, we need light from above and from within in abundant measure. In order to discipline our mind we need peace, boundless peace.

To conquer the heart, we need love-light. To conquer the soul, we need oneness-light. When physical force conquers something, it tries to destroy it. When spiritual force conquers something, it tries to illumine and perfect it. Human force often conquers and quite often destroys. Divine force ultimately conquers and always illumines darkness and ignorance with its light.

Unconditional surrender to the Will of the Supreme is the most significant force in our human life. This force must inevitably precede God-realisation. When we surrender to the Will of God, when our earthly existence becomes a song of surrender, a flower of surrender, we can place it devotedly at the Feet of the Lord Supreme.

Undivine human forces rule most of the outer world. Divine forces guide the inner world. God's Compassion for humanity does not allow the undivine human forces to destroy the world. God's Love for divinity encourages the divine forces to try to liberate the world of ignorance, imperfection, limitation and bondage.

When our consciousness is in the animal world, the force that enters us is destructive. When our consciousness is in the human world, the force that enters cries for domination. When our consciousness is in the divine world, the force that enters expands our consciousness and perfects our nature. If we are good, if we are divine, if we are perfect, we will not have to use human force, for our very presence will be a divine force that will inspire others to become good, divine and perfect.

When we live in the body, vital and mind we do not and cannot see the ideal of life and the ideal in life. Life has no ideal at that time; life is only a pleasure-hunt. When we live in the heart and the soul we see and feel an ideal. At each second a divine ideal looms large in our life. Inside each ideal there is something called reality. This reality is the message of divinity; it is Immortality's life in us. The seeker wants to see this inner reality.

Our ideal is the highest Truth, Light and Bliss. We shall not cease crying unless and until we have achieved these qualities in boundless measure as our own inner reality. This is the goal that a seeker aims at.

The force of the body, vital and mind is very limited. The force of the heart and soul is boundless. The vital force will sing with Caesar and Napoleon: "I came, I saw, I conquered." The spiritual force will say, "I came, I loved the world, I became one with humanity. Why did I come? I came because I was commissioned by the Lord Supreme to serve Him and to manifest Him here on earth." In order to serve and manifest the Supreme, we need to love the world. If we do not love the world and become one with humanity's excruciating pangs, then we cannot serve and manifest God on earth.

Physical force does not and cannot equal the force of the heart's oneness. Thousands of years ago Lord Krishna, the Buddha and the Christ lived on earth, yet even now their consciousness is guiding and illumining the length and breadth of the world. This is because the force which they used was not the force of the body, vital or mind. When we use the force of the physical plane, we feel that it is the ultimate force, that there cannot be any superior force. If someone drops a bomb, he feels that since he is destroying everything, his is the greatest force. He does not realise that the force that is used in the physical can easily be conquered by a stronger force, and that force is his mental force. If his mind does not allow him or instigate him, he will not drop the bomb.

Even the force of the limited human mind is stronger than that of the destructive body. But spiritual force is infinitely stronger than mental force. The highest spiritual force is love. There can be no force as effective as love. Love on the physical plane binds and limits us. It is a song of possession and attachment. But spiritual love expands and liberates us. It is a song of illumination and liberation for ourselves and for others.

The force that is used by spiritual Masters is not physical force; it is not vital force or mental force. It is the divine love-force. Love-force is also perfection-force. If the Master loves someone, then it is his bounden duty to perfect that person. If the sweetest love-force does not bring about the necessary response in the seeker's outer being, then the Master uses whatever other form of love-force is applicable at that time. Once we have an iota of peace, light and bliss, what will happen if we lose it? It will be an incalculable loss. A spiritual Master knows this far better than we do. That is why he uses his love-force, his perfection-force in us, for us.

51. Yesterday, today, tomorrow

Desire was death. I discovered this supreme truth.

Aspiration is life. I discover this sublime truth.

Realisation is satisfaction. I will discover this unparalleled truth.

Yesterday I wrote good things; therefore, my Lord Supreme was pleased with me. He shook hands with me.

Today I have good thoughts; therefore, my Lord Supreme

is more pleased with me. He is blessing my devoted head and surrendered heart.

Tomorrow I shall do good things; therefore, my Lord Supreme shall be most pleased with me. He shall bless me unreservedly.

Yesterday I was a power-hungry animal.

Today I am a peace-hungry man.

Tomorrow I shall try to become a love-hungry God.

Yesterday I was God-preparation.

Today I am God-dedication.

Tomorrow I shall be God-perfection.

I knock at God's Heart-Door because my sweet Lord has once shown me His Heart's Door.

I pray to God because my sweet Lord has once taken me into His Soul-Room.

I cry and cry for my Lord Supreme because my sweet Lord has once made me sit on His Silence-Throne.

I have seen God once; therefore, I wish to see Him again.

I have loved God once; therefore, I wish to love Him again.

I have surrendered to God's Will once; therefore, I wish to surrender my existence to God's Will again.

I know it will not be difficult for me to see God once again. I know it will not be difficult for me to love Him again. I know it will not be difficult for me to surrender my earthly existence to His Heavenly Will again. But there is something that will be extremely difficult for me, for I have not yet done it before. I have not claimed God as my own, very own, for it is difficult, extremely difficult, for me to claim Him as my very own. The day I claim God as my very own, He will proclaim me as His chosen instrument, His Dream-fulfilled Boat.

52. Aspiration and dedication

In our spiritual life two things are of paramount importance: aspiration and dedication. They are like complementary souls; each adds to the other. Aspiration is our heart's ascent; dedication is our heart's descent. Aspiration is our life's beauty; dedication is our life's plenitude. When we aspire, we try to see man in God; when we dedicate ourselves, we try to see God in man. Aspiration tells us where God is; dedication tells us who God is. Where is God? God is inside the heartbeat of our acceptance-light. Who is God? God is none other than ourselves in our transcendental Height.

There was a time when we walked along the desire-road. At the end of our journey's close we discovered that our destination was nothing but frustration. Frustration then persuaded us to meet with its most intimate friend, destruction. Together we sang with frustration; together we danced with destruction.

But now we are walking along the road of aspiration. This road is endless and the seeker's journey is eternal. On this road life is progress, life is God-preparation, life is God-manifestation, life is God-satisfaction. On this road we sing with Eternity's Silence and we dance with Infinity's Sound.

There was a time when we dedicated ourselves to someone or to something with the hope of world-appreciation, world-admiration and world-adoration. But when we discovered that world-appreciation, world-admiration and world-adoration fell short of our expectation, we tried to console ourselves with a new hope. This hope was world-recognition. We thought that if the world recognised us, this was enough. But world-recognition was also not to our satisfaction. At this point, our self-styled knowledge-light revolted against God's lack of Compassion. We despised the height of the world's ingratitude.

But now we are sincere, dedicated seekers. We feel that world-recognition is absolutely unnecessary, not to speak of world-appreciation, world-admiration and world-adoration. At this point, we have discovered something most significant: world-appreciation, world-admiration and world-adoration are like devouring animals. They can devour us at any moment on our way to God-realisation unless we are well protected by God's adamantine Will and unconditional Compassion.

In the spiritual life quite often we are disappointed. Why? Because every day our aspiration is not intense, because every day our dedication is not genuine. How can we have intense aspiration and genuine dedication in our daily multifarious activities? We can have these unparalleled divine qualities if every day we offer our soulful gratitude to the Inner Pilot. Gratitude is the only prayer that is immediately answered by our Inner Pilot.

We are seekers, but there are millions and millions of unaspiring people on earth. They may ask us what they consider a difficult question. They may ask us how we live on earth amidst countless sufferings, excruciating pangs and world-ignorance. We immediately tell them that our aspiration has the answer. We tell them that aspiration not only *has* the answer but also *is* the answer. They ask us how we can love people who are full of ignorance, full of imperfections and full of animal propensities. We immediately tell them that our dedication has the answer. We tell them that dedication not only *has* the answer but also *is* the answer. We employ our aspiration, our heart's cry, to help us propel the Dream-Boat of God. We employ our dedication to be of service to God with the hope that the Reality-Shore will come closer to us.

Our life of aspiration and dedication is the payment of our personal debt to our Mother Earth. Our life of vision and satisfaction is the payment of our personal debt to our Father

Heaven. Our life of perfection and ever-transcendence is the payment of our personal debt to our Supreme Lord.

When we do not aspire we notice that human life is full of rules and regulations. When we do aspire we feel that there are no rules and regulations; we are flowing with the river of freedom and entering into the Perfection-Sea. When we realise the highest Truth we come to realise that there is only one rule and that rule is: God comes first. Then we go one step further and see that the sole rule is: God for God's sake, and not for our personal satisfaction. It is our unconditional surrender to God's Will that can make us really happy and fulfilled.

Aspiration and dedication have three most intimate friends to help them reach their destined goal. These friends are concentration, meditation and contemplation. Time will not permit me to speak on them at length, but I wish to demonstrate for a few seconds what concentration meditation and contemplation are.

First let us try to concentrate. When we concentrate we focus all our attention on a particular subject or object. Our concentration is like a divine arrow entering into the object. It pierces the veil of ignorance. I shall be concentrating on my heart. You can also concentrate on your heart or on anything or anyone you want to. [Sri Chinmoy demonstrates concentration for a few moments, in silence.]

Now I shall meditate. When we meditate we do not focus on a particular thing; we merge into something vast, endless, infinite. I shall meditate on the sky. You can also meditate on the sky or on something else if you like. [Sri Chinmoy demonstrates meditation.]

Now I shall contemplate. When we contemplate the seeker in us becomes the divine Lover, inseparably one with the Supreme Beloved. [Sri Chinmoy demonstrates contemplation.]

Dear seekers, exactly a month ago I left New York for Europe.

I have visited quite a few European countries and I have given talks at several well-known universities. Today marks the end of my lecture tour, or rather, the end of my dedicated service here.

I am a spiritual farmer. God, out of His infinite Bounty, has entrusted me with the task of plowing the spiritual land. This is my first visit to your beautiful island. I have been here for about four hours. During these four hours, I have felt the Indian consciousness here in Iceland. India's natural beauty I have observed here; India's inner peace I have felt here. My presence here makes me feel that my life of aspiration and your life of aspiration in the inner world have built a bridge between spiritual India and spiritual Iceland. My Indian heart offers its soulful gratitude to your hearts of aspiration, for it is you who have given me the opportunity to be of dedicated service to you today. Nothing gives me greater joy than to be of dedicated service to the Supreme inside aspiring human beings.

Usually at the end of my talks, I answer questions from the seekers. With your kind permission, I wish to tell you that I have answered thousands and thousands of questions. But during this visit to Europe, I have not invited any questions from the audience. Now I do not know why, but I am inspired at the end of this journey to welcome a few spiritual questions from you. Your genuine enthusiasm and cry for God have impressed my heart deeply.

[Sri Chinmoy answers a few spiritual questions.]

SRI CHINMOY

NOTES TO MY ROSE PETALS PART 4

42. Hörsaal 101, University of Zurich, Rämistrasse 71, Zurich, Switzerland, 5 July 1974.
43. L'Aula, University of Geneva, Geneva, Switzerland, 7 July 1974.
44. ABF Huset, Sveavagen 41, Stockholm, Sweden, 9 July 1974.
45. Room 10, University of Uppsala, Uppsala, Sweden, 10 July 1974.
46. St Thomas' Church Hall, Vasteras, Sweden, 11 July 1974.
47. La Grande Salle, Fédération Internationale d'Acceuil de Paris, 30 rue Cabanis, Paris, France, 12 July 1974.
48. Friends' House, Ship Street, Brighton, England, 15 July 1974.
49. University of Bristol, Bristol, England, 16 July 1974.
50. University of Swansea, Swansea, Wales, 17 July 1974.
51. Grand Hall, Caxton Hall, Caxton Street, London SW 1, England, 19 July 1974.
52. University of Reykjavik, Reykjavik, Iceland, 21 July 1974.

MY ROSE PETALS

BOOK 5

53. Two instruments: mind and heart

Two instruments: mind and heart. The mind is division: world-division and self-division. World-division is nothing short of world-poverty. Self-division is the beginning of self-destruction. The heart is acceptance: acceptance of the inner life and acceptance of the outer life. The inner life is aspiration. The outer life is dedication.

Again, aspiration is a kind of dedication and dedication is a kind of aspiration. When we aspire we climb up high, higher, highest. While we are climbing up, like a bird we are spreading our wings. And while we are dedicating ourselves to the cause of humanity, while we are spreading our wings, at that time we also climb up.

Aspiration and dedication form a life-tree within us. The branches of this tree symbolise dedication, while the trunk of the tree looks up in order to reach the skies of aspiration. So our life-tree at once embodies aspiration to reach God's transcendental Heights and dedication to reach God's universal Reality.

Usually we have two types of mind, the human mind and the divine mind. The human mind is apt to choose; while choosing it loses. What does it choose? It chooses doubt, it chooses to be with countless doubts. What does it lose? It loses its innate, illumining Light. The divine mind unfolds itself at every moment; while unfolding it becomes. What does it unfold? It unfolds its illumining beauty. What does it become? It becomes, on earth and in Heaven, an ever-increasing, ever-fulfilling Reality.

As a human being, very often we use the human mind, the earth-bound mind. On rare occasions we use the divine mind, the Heaven-free mind. The earth-bound mind embodies doubt, suspicion, fear, jealousy, insecurity and many other unaspiring qualities. The earth-bound mind tells us to be always cautious because the world around us is treacherous.

The Heaven-free mind, which we feel deep within us on very rare occasions, tells us to be sincere, dedicated, devoted and loving. It asks us not to be suspicious. It tells us to love the world, because to love mankind means to serve our absolute, eternal Father. The Heaven-free mind brings to us the message of peace in self-giving, the message of light in self-giving, the message of perfection in self-giving.

As we have the human mind and the divine mind, even so we have the human heart and the divine heart. The human heart has a fearful beginning. The divine heart has a birthless song. The human heart has a tearful end. The divine heart has a deathless dance. The human heart has a fearful beginning and a tearful end. The divine heart has a birthless song and a deathless dance.

The human heart quite often mixes with the vital, the vital that is always hungry like a wolf. Just because it mixes with the vital, it takes upon itself quite a few of the problems and imperfections of the vital. At that time, the human heart teaches us to possess the world.

Alas, when we listen to the human heart, we only discover that possession is not satisfaction. There is not an iota of satisfaction in world-possession. Therefore, we change teachers and go to the divine heart. The divine heart always teaches us the message of give, give and give; and while we are giving, we see that we have also become. What do we give and what do we become? We give a soulful cry and we become a fruitful smile. Our soulful cry is blessed by God's transcendental Vision. Our fruitful smile is blessed by God's universal Reality.

The earth-binding heart and the Heaven-liberating heart. When we wallow in the pleasures of ignorance, when we lead the life of desire, the earth-binding heart cannot enjoy a free access to the Real in us. But when we walk along the road of aspiration, the Heaven-liberating, Heaven-enjoying heart enters into us and offers us its divinity, its supreme satisfaction, its supreme perfection.

Desire gives us the earth-binding heart; the earth-binding heart gives us desire. The Heaven-enjoying heart gives us aspiration; aspiration gives us the Heaven-enjoying heart.

Here we are all seekers. There was a time when we felt the fulfilment of desires was necessary in order to become happy. So we have fulfilled quite a few desires of ours. And what have we realised in the fulfilment of our desires? We have realised that we have acted like beggars. A beggar can never claim the plenitude, the infinitude of God's entire creation, for he knows that there is a yawning gulf between his reality and the vast reality which is owned by somebody else.

Now we are aspiring and, in our aspiration, we have come to realise that we do not want to possess. We want only to give what we have and what we are. What we have and what we are is an inner cry to become perfect instruments of the Absolute Supreme; and what we shall establish is our conscious, constant, inseparable, unconditional oneness with the Absolute Supreme.

54. Two instruments: doubt and faith

Two instruments: doubt and faith, a destructive force and a constructive force, a negative force and a positive force. Doubt bewilders us; doubt baffles us. Doubt is nothing short of physical poverty, vital insecurity and mental impurity. Faith loves us; faith teaches us. Faith loves us because we are of God and God is for us. Faith teaches us precisely because God wants us to be His chosen instruments, His perfect instruments, so that we can distribute His Light in the world and manifest His Love on earth.

Self-doubt and doubt of God. He who doubts himself discovers that self-doubt is the precursor of self-destruction. He who doubts God discovers birthless and deathless futility. He who has faith in himself becomes a hero-warrior in the inner world and achieves immediate success. He who has faith in God becomes a supreme God-lover and a reality which continuously proceeds. A continuous progress becomes his name.

Doubt itself is a treacherous theory and a destructive practice, whereas faith is precious and prosperous. This is what we hear from God in our heart. This is what we hear from God in our entire being. Whenever we doubt, we not only weaken ourselves but also separate ourselves from the whole, from the Universal Reality. Each time we doubt, we lose an opportunity. Each time we show faith in others, we fulfil that opportunity and grow into a larger reality. And at that time, the fulfilling reality becomes ours. What is opportunity? Opportunity is an unconditional boon which descends from above to illumine the consciousness of humanity.

Doubt is always over-active. It wants to destroy the world in a shockingly horrid manner. Faith is active, selflessly active, continuously active. Faith begins the Cosmic Game at God's choice Hour and ends the Cosmic Game at God's choice Hour. But when we follow the road of faith, we come to see that there is no real end. We are all walking along Eternity's Road. Each time we reach a particular destination, that destination becomes the starting point for a higher, more fulfilling and more illumining goal. Today's goal is tomorrow's starting point. So when we live in faith, glowing faith, we grow into this ever-transcending Reality, into this ever-transcending Reality's Goal.

Doubt is capacity. This capacity can take us back to our animal life, the life of destruction. Even now, when we cherish anger, jealousy and other destructive forces, we feel that we are roaming in the animal kingdom. Unless and until each human being is totally transformed and illumined, there will always remain in him an amount of animal qualities and propensities. But if the same human being invokes Light from above, then there comes a time when his life is inundated with Light and Delight. At that time, he not only gives up totally the animal in himself, but he also grows into the divine in himself. The divine in him is his transcendental Vision and universal Reality.

Each human being starts his journey with faith. A child has implicit faith in his parents. The mother tells the child, "This is the letter 'A', this is 'B'." The child listens to the mother and learns the alphabet. The child goes to school and listens to what the teacher teaches. He learns. But when his mind develops, it unconsciously, if not consciously, wants to establish a free access to the doubt-world. Anything that is new to the mind offers temptation, fascination. So the mind tends to enter into the world of doubt. The journey was started with faith, with the heart's implicit faith. But while the seeker is walking along the road, the mind takes over. The mind finds it easier to divide and destroy than to unify and build. But when we start aspiring and try to compel the mind to swim in the sea of the soul's light, the mind eventually surrenders to the soul's light.

There are two minds. One is the doubtful mind, the suspicious mind, the mind that does not care for light, for the inner wealth. There comes a time when this mind sees that there is no satisfaction, not to speak of abiding satisfaction, in the domain that it inhabits. So it surrenders to the heart. The heart always tries to play the role of identification. The heart of a child maintains its oneness-feeling with his parents, his brothers and sisters and the members of his world-family. A seeker is he who is in the aspiring heart, of the illumining soul and for the fulfilling God.

Here we are all seekers. Our heart tells us that oneness is satisfaction and satisfaction is perfection. Again, when we descend for world-illumination, we go from the rung of perfection to the rung of satisfaction, and from satisfaction we come down to oneness. Satisfaction is founded on oneness and perfection is founded on satisfaction. If we walk along the road of the heart, we discover the supremely divine Reality, which we eternally are. And this Reality is nothing but oneness — our oneness with the Supreme, the Inner Pilot.

Questions and answers

55. Question: How can we overcome fear in the spiritual life?

Sri Chinmoy: In the spiritual life there should be no fear. Why should you be afraid of anything or anyone? Since you are praying to God the Almighty, meditating on God the Almighty, why should you be afraid of anything or anyone? A child feels his mother has all the power of the world. So when he is afraid of anything, he runs to his mother because the mother has all affection for him. Here also, you are a spiritual child of God, so when you are attacked by any kind of fear — either in the physical, the mental or the vital — immediately try to run towards the sweet Supreme, who is all Compassion, all Love, all Blessings.

When ordinary human beings pray to God, their prayer is full of desire. We pray to God to grant us Peace, Light and Bliss in infinite measure, but unaspiring people pray to God to give them material wealth, worldly prosperity. When one prays to God with desire, it is all through fear, because one has no idea whether God is going to fulfil one's desires. But if the prayer is soulful, there will be no fear. Say you are praying to God for Peace, but you are not getting it. But just because you are praying for something good and divine, God will come to you and give you the necessary patience to wait for God's Hour. In one hour you cannot get a Master's degree. You study in school from kindergarten to university in order to get your Master's degree. In the spiritual life also, when you ask for something very high, very deep, very profound, it takes a long time. So if you pray for divine things, for Peace, Light and Bliss, you are bound to feel that there is something called God's Hour. If you live in His Hour, there can be no fear. But in the ordinary life, if you crave earthly or mundane things, naturally fear will always assail you. In your case, since you are a seeker, there should be no fear, for you are taking shelter inside the infinite Affection of the Absolute Supreme.

56. Question: How can we be conscious of God all the time in our mental work, such as when we are studying?

Sri Chinmoy: When you are driving a car, your hands are on the wheel, your feet are on the gas and your eyes are looking forward and sideways. Look how many things you are doing. It is the same thing when you are studying. Easily you can keep God in mind. Before you begin to study, before you open up your book, pray to God most soulfully that your study will be no different from your prayerful thought. Then, while you are studying, you have to feel the prayerful consciousness which you had just before you started studying. It is like a flow. Once you start running properly on the right track, automatically you continue along that same track. But if you go the wrong way or take a wrong turn, then you follow in that direction.

An ordinary person will study so that he will get a diploma

and become extremely great or prosperous in life. In your case, you are not studying for name and fame. No, you are studying to please the Inner Pilot. You are studying in order to become a good, divine instrument of God. And there shall come a time when the Inner Pilot will utilise you in His own Way to serve others. You will acquire knowledge and this knowledge you will distribute to aspiring mankind. So your studying will be totally different from the studying of others.

If you have that kind of attitude towards your studies, then there will be no problem. When you are studying, you have to try to feel the purpose behind it: you are studying to please the Supreme in His own Way. Then, when the time comes for you to teach, you will not teach like other teachers. You will try to bring to the fore the divinity inside each of your students so that they also can become chosen instruments of God. If you can have this idea when you study, you will see that your mental life will not be an obstruction to your spiritual life. But if you separate the outer study from the inner study, which is your prayer and meditation, then there will always be problems. At that time, you will see a yawning gulf between your mental study and your psychic or spiritual studies. They have to be blended. The capacity of the mind has to be illumined by your psychic capacity, spiritual capacity. Then there can be no problem.

57. Question: If we are in a place or circumstance where we feel our consciousness falling, is there a way we can immediately raise it again?

Sri Chinmoy: You have to become more alert, more soulful. You have to feel that once upon a time you had the capacity to climb up the consciousness-tree, but now you are climbing down. The capacity you had to climb to the highest, topmost branch you still have. And this same capacity you can apply today. Only you have to feel that your goal is to remain as high as possible. Always try to keep the goal right in front of you. You always have to be conscious of your purpose, the reason you are following the spiritual life, the reason you must remain in your highest consciousness.

This is the time for you to go up high, higher, highest and discover yourself. Then you have to come down to distribute the Peace, Light and Delight that you have achieved. Right now your brothers and sisters are hungry and you don't have the means to feed them. If you stay with them, you will be one other hungry person, and there will be no one to feed you. So you have to climb up the tree and pluck the mangoes. If you just climb up and come down without plucking any fruit, then what will you have to distribute to mankind? You won't be able to give anything to mankind. You go up and collect the fruits and then you come down to distribute the fruits to your brothers and sisters. Then again you have to go up.

But before you are well established in your inner life, spiritual life, it is always advisable to be alert. If you see that by mixing with someone your consciousness is brought down, then don't mix with that person. That person is not bad. No, in everybody there is God, so you can't say that person is bad. Only you have to know that right now you do not have enough inner strength and capacity to mix with that person. Right now God is giving you the opportunity to mix with those who have already established some Peace, Light and Bliss. Birds of a feather flock together; you are a spiritual person, so you should mix only with spiritual people. But once you become strong, there shall come a time when you can mix with unaspiring people — not out of self-indulgence, but out of love, out of compassion, so that they shall also be lifted. Their consciousness also has to be elevated, but for that you need aspiration and determination. First you have to ascend the consciousness-tree yourself; only then can you help others ascend.

So right now, if your consciousness is descending when you are mixing with unaspiring people, do not mix with them. Mix only with those who will help you increase your aspiration. But it is not forever. There shall definitely come a time when you will be sufficiently strong that you will be able to go out and help them.

58. Question: When a child asks you, "Who is God?" what is the best answer to give him?

Sri Chinmoy: When a child asks you, "Who is God?" just ask the child to look into a mirror and to smile as soulfully as possible. The word "soulfully" the child may not understand, but the child can easily see how beautiful he looks. Tell the child to try to give the most beautiful, absolutely the most beautiful smile, and to look at himself. The child will know whether it is a beautiful smile or just an ordinary smile. So, the more beautiful the smile the child gives, the more divinity comes forward. When the child looks at his own face, at his most beautiful, glowing consciousness, you tell him that that is God and nobody else.

Who is God? God is our own highest reality. If you can give a most soulful smile that will immediately illumine you and the whole world, that smile is nothing other than God. Let the child remain in the consciousness of his most beautiful smile, a smile that pervades the length and breadth of the world. The child's most beautiful smile is the most convincing answer. In the case of adults, they have to pray and meditate and develop a divine consciousness. But for a child, this is the easiest and most effective answer. And at the same time, it is absolutely true. You are in no way fooling the child.

59. Question: *Is the feeling that the outside world is futile really a form of aspiration?*

Sri Chinmoy: If you feel this, it means that you are approaching the truth in a complicated manner, a perverse manner. You should not think that the outside world is futile. You have to feel that the outside world is yours. You have to accept it, but not the way the world wants you to accept it. You will accept the world with the idea that a day will come when with your own light, with your own delight, with your own divine capacity, you will transform and illumine it. Right now, if you accept the world the way it wants you to accept it, you shall only wallow in the pleasures and meshes of ignorance, for the outer world is much stronger than your own capacity. But one day you will be strong, you will be stronger, you will be strongest. While you are developing your courage and strength, you can't say that the outside world is hopeless, useless. Only you have to feel that you don't have enough capacity to illumine it. If you criticise the outside world, if you feel that it is futile and useless, then you will cherish a kind of superior feeling. That superior feeling will bloat your ego and you will feel that it is beneath your dignity to mix with the world even after you get Power, Light and Bliss.

The outside world is like a child, the youngest member in the family. You know your little brother or sister is not doing the right thing. At the same time, you do not have the capacity to correct and perfect the child. But a day will come when you will have enough strength. At that time when you request the child to do something good and divine, the child will do it because he will see something in *you* that is divine, luminous, supreme.

But if you look down upon the child, thinking that the child is doing everything wrong and leading an undivine life, then you will automatically cherish a kind of superior feeling. This superior feeling will separate your reality and existence from that of a child. Today you are aspiring only to strengthen yourself; tomorrow you will aspire to strengthen the ones that are around you. But if you think that everything in the outer life is futile and meaningless, if you do not feel your oneness with the world, then how are you going to illumine it?

Right now the capacity that you have is very limited. But one day you will have boundless capacity and then, at God's choice Hour, you shall be a perfect instrument to serve the weak ones. But if you think that others are useless, you shall never do any service for the outside world. There will always be a big gap between you and others: "I am all good and they are all bad people. So let good people remain together and forget about the bad." No. Good people will stay together in the beginning only to gain strength. But once they have gained strength, good people will go and mix with others. The rest of the world is not bad; only you have to say that it is less good. But if you say you represent day and they represent night, then that will be a serious mistake. You have to feel that you have an iota of light more than the world has, and with that iota you are trying to be of help.

60. Question: If somebody is angry with you, what should your reaction to the person be?

Sri Chinmoy: There are a few ways to solve this problem. Anger is undoubtedly a negative power, a destructive power. When that negative power attacks you, you can resort to an infinitely superior power. That power is the Supreme's Compassion. When anger has come and attacked you, at that time if you invoke the Compassion of the Supreme, which is infinitely more powerful than human anger, then you will be able to inundate the other person with the Supreme's Compassion. Even if he hurls all his anger-arrows at you, if you can invoke the Supreme's Compassion, then these arrows will not be able to hurt you. On the contrary, these arrows will eventually illumine you. This is the best approach, the divine approach, for only this approach will bring abiding satisfaction. But if you cannot go to the Highest and get the highest power, then you have to take the second-best course, the human approach.

Just remain indifferent. Your power of indifference is extremely powerful. You have no idea to what extent indifference-power can solve your problems. With your indifference-power you can create a solid, adamantine wall that nothing can approach. If you remain indifferent, then between you and the other person there will be a wall, a solid wall, which his anger will not be able to pass through. If somebody is angry with you and wants to destroy you, just feel that you don't belong to him and he does not belong to you. Feel that there are two worlds and your world is totally different from his. When you are indifferent, automatically you create another world inside you. So you remain in your indifference-world and let him remain in his anger-world.

But if you take this approach, the human approach, and use your indifference-power, you have to know that you won't be able to remain indifferent for a long time. Your own aggressive power will come forward: "If he can strike me, then I can also strike him: tit for tat." But in the spiritual life it is not like that. If somebody attacks you, your attitude will be different. He will attack you to destroy you, but you will only touch him in order to transform him. So your view is totally different from his. He is trying to devour you; but you will only touch him, for if you don't touch him, how are you going to transform him? If the potter does not touch the clay, then he cannot give shape to any pots. If someone is angry, he will catch hold of all the pots and smash them, break them to pieces. But the potter will only touch them and give them shape. When you have superior power, you will touch the earth-consciousness in order to change it, transform it, illumine it.

We are all seekers of the infinite Truth and Light. If unaspiring persons attack us, they will attack us according to their capacity, according to their understanding, according to their realisation. But our understanding is far superior to theirs, so we have to illumine them. If we do that, then their vital will feel that it is the worst possible punishment that we have given. Their soul will immediately be grateful, but their vital, their unaspiring or aggressive vital, will feel that it has received a most powerful punishment.

61. Sorrow and joy

I wish to give a short talk on sorrow and joy. Sorrow is an inner experience. From this experience we come to feel that life has no meaning and no purpose, that we are travelling along a road that has no goal.

Joy is also an inner experience. From this experience we come to feel that life at every moment has some special meaning, that life has joy as its goal right from the beginning. Early in the morning the sun dawns. As soon as we look at the sun, we get joy. Then we pray and meditate. From our prayer and meditation we also get joy. Then the members of the family meet together and sit to eat. Here they get joy from the union of the family. Then each human being enters into his respective work. Work is nothing but self-giving, and self-giving is the best kind of joy.

What does sorrow do? In the beginning sorrow breaks our heart; then it strengthens our heart. In the beginning sorrow darkens our mind; then it illumines our mind. In the beginning sorrow takes away all the life-energy from our vital; then it gives our vital a new hope, a new promise and a new light. It strengthens and inspires our vital with a new determination. Sorrow throws our body into a sea of helplessness; then it lifts our body up and teaches our body how to swim in the infinite sea of Light and Delight.

Joy, in the beginning, gives our heart infinite peace. Then it gives our heart continual confidence to do something higher, better and more divine. Joy, in the beginning, expands our mind, expands the vision of our mind. Then joy gives our mind the capacity to hold the whole world inside it. Joy, in the beginning, gives our vital the strength of a roaring lion. Then it looks around and inspires everyone who wants to lead a better life. Joy, in the beginning, gives our body the capacity to grow into something beautiful, luminous and fruitful. Then it gives our body the capacity to see, feel and talk to God inside itself.

We are living on this earth planet. The earth planet is full of sorrow. There are many reasons why our earth planet is full of sorrow. But the main reason is this: earth wants to realise the highest, the absolute highest, but it feels that it is simply impossible because there are millions and millions of people who do not want to lead a spiritual life.

Like the earth-consciousness, Heaven is also unhappy. Heaven wants to manifest itself on earth. It wants to manifest God's Peace, God's Light, God's Beauty on earth. But earth is not receptive at all. Therefore, Heaven is also unhappy.

On very rare occasions, when earth sees even one person who wants to lead a pure life, a life of aspiration and dedication, at that time earth is happy. When one person wants to go up, when one of her children is going up, earth feels extremely happy. Similarly, on very rare occasions, when one person is receptive, Heaven becomes very happy, because that person makes a pathway for Heaven to descend and manifest something of God's Light.

God has two aspects. One aspect is His human aspect, the other aspect is His divine aspect. God is inside each of us. When He uses His human aspect He feels sad, because He feels it will take man such a long time to reach his goal. When He uses His divine aspect, He does not feel sad. At that time He is dealing with eternal time.

Man also has two aspects. One aspect is his desiring self, the other aspect is his aspiring self. When man lives the life of desire, he finds only frustration; and frustration is the harbinger of destruction. When man lives the life of aspiration, he eventually gets everything that God has and is: infinite Light and infinite Delight.

62. Success and failure

Dear seekers, dear friends, dear brothers and sisters, I wish to give a short talk on failure and success from the spiritual point of view.

Failure is a discouraging force. Success is an encouraging force. Failure makes us feel that we have been forced to climb down the life-tree. Success makes us feel that we have climbed up the life-tree and enjoyed the most delicious fruit.

What is failure? It is a tearful cry. What is success? It is a fruitful smile. When we fail, whose failure is it? It is the failure of our unlit vital. When we succeed, whose success is it? It is the success of our satisfied vital.

Why do we fail? Is it because we are unlucky? Is it because we have not worked very hard? Is it because we have not invoked God's Compassion and Blessings? Is it because God has accepted this failure as an experience He wanted to have in our life? Is it because God has granted this failure to us? Is it because God has willed that we should lose? No! No! It is for a different reason that we experience failure. It is for the strengthening of our consciousness that, at times, God grants us defeat.

Why do we succeed? Is it because we are lucky? Is it because we have worked very hard? Is it because God's Compassion and Blessings we have invoked? No, it is not because of these things that we achieve success. We succeed because God, out of His infinite Kindness, wants us to win in the battlefield of life. God grants us defeat in order to strengthen us: He grants us success in order to encourage us.

The body of the man of failure says to God, "Father, You do not love me. Therefore, I have failed." The vital of the man of failure says to God, "Father, You do not care for me. Therefore, I have failed." The mind of the man of failure says to God, "Father You are indifferent to me. Therefore, I have failed."

But the Father says to His children, "No, My children, you are wrong."

The body of the man of success says to the Father, "Father, You love me only. Therefore, I have succeeded." The vital of the man of success says to the Father, "Father, You care for me only. Therefore, I have succeeded." The mind of the man of success says to God, "Father, You have most special Compassion for me. You show Your Compassion to me only. Therefore, I have succeeded."

But the Father says to these children of His, "No, My children, you are wrong. It is not because I love you more than others that you get success and they do not. In the inner life there is no such thing as failure and success. There is only an ever-transcending progress. Through repeated defeats, I want you to become a spiritual giant so you can defeat the ignorance-giant that wants to devour the world. Through success, I want you to run faster than the fastest. I want you to defeat the ignorance-animal, the ignorance-donkey. If you reach the goal sooner than ignorance, then you will be able to realise Me, reveal Me and manifest Me. And once I am manifested through you, there will be no suffering, no bondage, no limitation, no death, no darkness."

The Father says to failure, "I want you to be stronger than the strongest. It is you who have to be responsible for My full Manifestation on earth. I want to entrust you with the supreme Duty. Therefore, I am making you strong, divinely and supremely strong.

"Failure and success, I have equal love for both of you. Do not judge Me; only love Me. If you love Me, then you will feel that I am fulfilling Myself in and through you, through both of you in a unique way."

Failure says to the Father, "Father, is there any way I can succeed?"

"Yes, My son, there is a way. If you are more careful, more alert, more conscious at every moment, then success will be yours."

Success says to the Father, "Father, is there any way I can have success all the time?"

"Yes, there is a way. You have to be cheerful and self-giving. If you give yourself cheerfully, then you are bound to achieve success all the time."

Progress says to the Father, "Father, is there any way I can always make progress?"

"Yes, there is a way, My child. You should always aim at ever-transcending Perfection. If your goal is to reach perfection, then at every moment you will always make progress. Perfection is not a stagnant pool but a running river; it is always moving towards the infinite Sea, its Source. Therefore, you should always try to make your goal the ever-transcending Reality. If you do this, you will always be able to make progress and satisfy Me."

When we love God, when we serve God, when we surrender ourselves totally to God, at that time failure cannot make us sad. We do not care for success, we do not even care for progress. Our love, devotion and surrender lifts our consciousness far above the heights of failure and success and progress, and we become surrendered to God's Omnipotent Will. When we become inseparably one with God's Will, we enjoy divine satisfaction in our inner life and in our outer life. This divine satisfaction is what God wants from all of us. He created us so that we could be divinely satisfied; this was the only purpose He had in His Vision. His Vision was transcendental, but He wanted to manifest His transcendental Vision here in the universal Reality. The Real in us wants from us not failure, not success, not even progress, but only God-satisfaction and God-fulfilment in and through us, through our surrender to God's Will.

Questions and answers

63. Question: What is the spiritual significance of the seven notes in the scale: "do", "re", "mi", etc.?

Sri Chinmoy: The seven notes that we have in the scale correspond to the seven higher worlds. Each note comes down from a specific inner world.

64. Question: What should one eat in the spiritual life?

Sri Chinmoy: The kind of food that keeps the body and mind calm and quiet is the best food for those following the spiritual life. Naturally, vegetables are far better than meat. Meat comes from the animals, which are always fighting and destroying one another. If we eat meat, then the animal consciousness enters into us. And it is this animal consciousness that we want to transcend. But the consciousness of vegetables and fruits is very mild. They are not destructive like animals.

65. Question: What is spirituality and meditation? Is spirituality peace?

Sri Chinmoy: Spirituality is peace, peace within and peace without. In the spiritual life, we should do everything that will help us to acquire peace.

Meditation is our conscious attempt to become consciously aware of God. When we say God is everywhere, God is only a vague idea for us. If we don't feel God, see God or talk to God consciously, then what is the use of having a God? Unconsciously if we do something, we do not get the real result. Consciously we have to do things. So many times a day we move our hands, legs and everything without being conscious of it. If we just do it unconsciously, we do not develop our strength. But if we do the same things consciously, it is called exercise; we develop our strength. Then, when we have strength, we try to conquer lethargy, disease and other wrong forces. Similarly, if we consciously meditate, then we feel God, see God and talk to God. Otherwise, God will be right in front of us and we won't be able to see Him.

66. Question: What is the Indian view of suicide?

Sri Chinmoy: If one commits suicide, then one is doing something extremely wrong. One commits suicide because of some emotional problems or some weakness in his life. But we are God's children and we have to fight against weakness and ignorance. God has given us this body, vital, mind, heart and soul in order to realise Him and manifest Him on earth. But if we destroy the body, then how can the vital, mind, heart and soul act for God? The body is a house. Without a house, how can we live? If we destroy the body, then we cannot live on earth. So God does not want us to destroy the body. He wants us to face the world. If we fight against temptation, ignorance, weakness, emotional problems, then only we can realise God and please God.

According to strict Indian philosophy, the act of suicide is the worst possible inner crime. Once the body is consciously destroyed, it takes hundreds and hundreds of years for the soul to reincarnate. If it is a natural death, then the soul gets the opportunity to come down again and reveal God's Light in the normal way. But if it is an abnormal death, it becomes extremely difficult for the soul to come back on schedule. It is not only difficult, but almost impossible, unless God out of His infinite Compassion or some very great spiritual Master helps the particular soul.

67. Question: Is the capacity of the thinking mind a power?

Sri Chinmoy: The capacity of the thinking mind is always a power, but it is very limited. It is very limited because often it contradicts itself. The thinking mind will say that so and so is good. It is positive thought that the thinking mind has applied. But after five minutes the same mind will say, "So and so is a very bad person." Now it is a negative thought. The negative force and the positive force will fight and then both sides will become weak. Again, sometimes it is even worse than that. The thinking mind will say, "Who am I to judge whether you are a good man or bad man?" Then the mind starts doubting itself. When the thinking mind starts doubting itself, it becomes an extremely weak force instead of becoming a strong force.

68. Question: Is perfection perfect?

Sri Chinmoy: Perfection is always perfect. But again, perfection is always transcending itself. Perfection is not a stagnant pool. As I said in my talk, it is a river that is flowing, flowing.

69. Question: What do you think about outer progress?

Sri Chinmoy: When we increase our faith in God, that is our inner progress. But when it is a matter of outer progress, we are always looking for the results. If the result is success, then we are happy; if the result is failure or defeat, then we are unhappy. And when in our outer life we can offer both success and defeat with a cheerful heart to God, that is our true outer progress.

70. Unreality and reality

Dear seekers, dear friends, dear sisters and brothers, I wish to give a short talk on unreality and reality.

Unreality is a discouraging reality and nothing short of a negative reality. Reality is a positive and encouraging divinity. Unreality is the conscious fear of reality. Unreality is the continuous non-acceptance of reality. Unreality is the constant rejection of reality. Even from the dawn of creation, seekers of the Absolute Truth wanted to discover reality in unreality. But the Vedic seers came to realise that it is from the unreal that we come to the real. They said, *Asato ma sad gamaya* ... Lead me from the unreal to the real." They also thought that anything that is dark within us is less than reality. Again, inside the night they felt and saw an abundance of light. Inside human imperfection they found an iota of perfection. And inside that iota of perfection, they found that life was immortal.

Then there came a time when the Vedic seers of the hoary past wanted to discover reality in unreality in a different manner. They saw how much suffering there was in the world, and they felt that the only way to have satisfaction or joy was to renounce the world. They said that suffering is unreal and joy is real. They also felt that anything that exists creates problems for human life. Therefore, they sang, *Rupena* ... "Enjoy through renunciation. Do not try to possess the world, for possession is nothing short of frustration."

But in the course of inner evolution, the seekers discovered something else. They discovered that renunciation is not the way; acceptance is the only way. They felt that if they claimed to be children of God, it was their bounden duty to please God in His own Way. They felt that if God was real, then His creation must also be real. God the Creator is reality; therefore, God the creation is also reality. It is the seeker within us that consciously tries to unify both God the Creator and God the creation.

The seeker tries to elevate his consciousness through prayer and meditation and reach the highest state of consciousness. This state of consciousness is God's Transcendental Consciousness. The Transcendental Consciousness houses at once the reality of the Infinite and the reality of the finite. The real reality of the finite and the real reality of the Infinite is to grow into everlasting love. The unreal reality of the finite is to live with limitation, ignorance, bondage and death.

Reality has a consciousness in the inner world and also a consciousness in the outer world. In the outer world, reality deals with the body, vital, mind and heart. In the inner world, reality deals exclusively with the soul. The consciousness of the body-reality is to give and take. The consciousness of the vital-reality is to take and take only. The consciousness of the mind-reality is to take and give. The consciousness of the heart-reality is to give, only to give. The consciousness of the soul-reality is to fulfil God in God's own Way. The soul does not maintain any role of its own. It always soulfully and cheerfully abides by the Supreme's adamantine Will.

Each individual offers to the world at large unreality and reality in a unique manner. In the outer world, when an individual says that he knows everything in God's creation, he is offering unreality to the world. In the outer world, consciously or unconsciously, he is forced to be in the realm of division and partition. Therefore, he cannot know the Absolute Truth in its infinite reality. Again, if the same individual says that in the inner world he knows everything, then he is not exaggerating. What he says is true, absolutely true, for in the inner world, his oneness with deep, abiding wisdom is complete. On the strength of his inner oneness with the Absolute Lord, he is knowledge itself.

In the outer world, on the physical plane, each thought unfulfilled is a symbol of unreality; each thought fulfilled is a symbol of reality. But in the inner plane, the spiritual plane, each thought is real in itself, each thought is a world itself. Whether it is manifested or not manifested on the earth-scene is of no consequence. As long as it represents a world, it is undoubtedly a reality.

In the outer world, if an individual says that he loves God, then he is not telling the absolute truth, he is not offering the absolute reality. The outer world is the world of countless desires. In the outer world, God does not get the love, the loving life-breath of the individual. Unless and until God gets the life-breath of love, which gives Him total satisfaction, God does not call it real love.

In the inner world, the same individual offers love to God on the strength of his aspiration. And what is his aspiration? His aspiration is nothing short of God's illumining Compassion. This illumining Compassion has the capacity to please God in God's own Way. When a seeker acquires God's illumining Compassion, he becomes not only the divine love, but also God the Love Himself.

Questions and answers

71. Question: What is the meaning of our life?

Sri Chinmoy: The meaning of our life is to become one with the absolute Truth, the absolute Reality. This absolute Truth is God the infinite Compassion and God the infinite Satisfaction.

72. Question: How can we achieve that?

Sri Chinmoy: It is through inner meditation that we can achieve it. When we pray for ordinary things, mundane things, our prayers are quite often fulfilled. But we have to pray for something divine; we have to pray for Peace, Light and Bliss. Quite often we meditate on the things that give us satisfaction. But from now on, we have to meditate only on the things that give God satisfaction. One of the things that give God satisfaction is our conscious self-surrender and conscious self-giving, not to the human in us, but to the divine in us. Through our conscious self-giving and constant self-surrender, we can realise the Highest.

73. Question: What does one do during meditation?

Sri Chinmoy: Meditation has quite a few stages. In the beginning, the seeker's meditation has to be of one type. Then, when the seeker becomes mature, his meditation becomes of a totally different type. If the seeker is a beginner, then he has to try to control his thoughts and ideas. He has to make his mind absolutely vacant, calm and quiet. If any thought comes, he has to watch and see whether it is a good thought or a bad thought, whether it is a divine thought or an undivine thought. If it is an undivine thought, then immediately he will try to destroy it; and if it is a divine thought, he will allow it to enter and grow inside him. Then, when he is advanced, there should be no thought at all. There comes a time when the seeker makes continuous progress and goes far beyond those good thoughts and bad thoughts, divine thoughts and undivine thoughts. He goes far beyond the duality-life, far beyond the thought-world, to where there is he and God and nobody else: God the Creator and God the creation. At that time, he is God the creation and God the Creator unified in the Transcendental Consciousness.

74. Question: Why do desires exist?

Sri Chinmoy: Desires exist because we want to do something, we want to become something, we want to grow into something. But when we want to do something, we have to know whether we are doing the right thing. When we want to become something, we have to know whether we are becoming the right thing.

75. Question: Why should the past be forgotten?

Sri Chinmoy: If he drags out his past, his painful past, then he is not moving forward. One has to look forward; one has to proceed. Suppose yesterday an individual committed a Himalayan blunder. If he drags yesterday's Himalayan blunder into today's reality, he will only curse himself. But if he can totally obliterate it from his mind, if he can feel that yesterday didn't exist, then he will only look forward towards the light.

The past drags us to the death-consciousness. It makes us feel that life has no value. If we do not forget the past, we are only carrying a heavy load on our shoulders and we won't be able to move forward. Suppose in a past incarnation someone was a low type, a thief, and in this incarnation he comes to know that he was a thief. Then, in this incarnation, if he wants to grow out of his previous incarnation, he is not going to budge an inch. He will feel, "Oh, I was such a bad fellow; it is impossible for me to become a saint." So he has to consciously obliterate the past from his mind; he has to go forward, and not stay with the achievements or the sorrowful experiences that the past has given. Then, when he becomes a saint, he can easily deal with the past, if such is God's Will.

76. Question: Would you call what unites us a religion?

Sri Chinmoy: It is the life-principle that unites us. If an individual wants to call the life-principle a religion, then he is perfectly right to do so. If he wishes to call it a philosophy, again he is perfectly right. But whatever we call it, we have to know that it is the code of life, the life-principle, that unites us with the rest of the world. If we call it the universal religion, then we feel it is all one. If we call it the universal God, then it is all one. But if we say that ours is the only religion and that all the other religions are useless, then our religion cannot unite the universe. Whatever claims to be the best cannot unite. Only the universal feeling which grows within us and around us can unite us.

77. Question: Is the self-consciousness that we discover the same as God-realisation?

Sri Chinmoy: If we discover the self-consciousness that we keep only to ourselves, this self-consciousness is only the discovery of the ego. But if we discover the consciousness which is universal and transcendental, then naturally we have realised God.

78. Question: How can we come up from thought?

Sri Chinmoy: It is quite possible. It is a kind of exercise that we have to practise. We have taken one kind of exercise for centuries; therefore, we are now getting the result of that exercise. But if we want to take another kind of exercise, we can do that too. When we take exercise to develop our arm muscles, we do develop them. Then, if we take exercise to develop our leg muscles, we will do that too. With our will-power, our human will-power, we can create millions and millions of illumining and fulfilling thoughts. Again, with the same will-power we can stop thoughts. It is like a knife. With a knife we can stab someone or we can cut a fruit and distribute it to our friends.

79. Tree of meditation

Sri Chinmoy: I wish to thank you deeply for having given us the opportunity to have this tree planted here. I am offering you my soulful gratitude, and I also wish to offer a blessingful message to my students, my spiritual children.

This tree is a Himalayan Pine. The Himalayas are not only the tallest mountains, but also the most inspiring, the most generously blessed with divine grandeur. The Himalayas are not only the tallest in terms of earthly reality, but also the highest in terms of spiritual reality. Many, many, many seekers have prayed at the foot of the Himalayas or inside the Himalayan caves and have realised the highest absolute Truth. So the Himalayas embody the inner height of the highest magnitude and also the outer height of the highest magnitude.

In the Himalayas we see the outer achievement and the inner achievement together, serving one cause: realisation. As soon as one sees the Himalayas, one is reminded of his own inner divine qualities: peace, light and bliss in boundless measure, as well as his outer qualities: concern, patience, compassion and dedication.

Here in Zurich we have created our own Himalayas. Our Himalayas are our inner aspiration and our outer dedication. Today we have here about twenty-five seekers. Our aspiration and dedication we are offering to this Himalayan Pine. This tree is not only for the very few who are here today, or for those who belong or will belong to our Zurich Centre. It is for all who are aspiring in all our Centres, and for all the seekers who are aspiring all over the world, for this tree symbolises aspiration and dedication.

We have come here to be blessed by the aspiration of this tree and, at the same time, we are blessing the tree with our souls' delight. It is a mutual blessing. Also, we have come here to spread the inner fragrance of this tree. Our aspiration will carry the inner fragrance, which is peace and light, from this tree, and wherever we go, we shall consciously or unconsciously spread this inner fragrance.

I wish to make a soulful request: that at least once a month my students from the Zurich Centre come here to pray and meditate most soulfully, as our San Francisco disciples do around their tree. Every month you will remind yourself on the physical plane of the aspiration and dedication that you are now offering to the tree and at the same time receiving from the tree.

This tree is at once our child and our parent. When we sit at the foot of the tree and look at its height, we feel that we are the children and the tree is our parent. But when our inner aspiration merges consciously into the transcendental Heights of the Absolute, at that time this earthly reality — this tree that is in front of us — is our child. So this moment our parent feeds us and nourishes us with its beauty, fragrance and protection, and the next moment we bless the child with our aspiration-might and realisation-height.

A tree is sacrifice, right from its root to its topmost branch. Let our lives also be a true sacrifice in the physical world, in the vital world, in the mental world and in the spiritual world. As a tree is constant sacrifice from the top to the bottom — from the root to the highest part of its existence — even so, what we have inside us, outside us and around us we must sacrifice to bring forward our inner divinity. This tree has only one message: sacrifice. By virtue of sacrifice we reach the Highest. Constantly this tree is aspiring to reach the Highest, and this highest Reality the tree achieves or receives on the strength of its constant sacrifice.

Mr Schmid: I would like to express a few words of appreciation. Honourable Sri Chinmoy, dear pupils of his, seemingly for two reasons we have come together here. One is the tree, the other is the presence of Sri Chinmoy. But, as you are fully aware, we are here this morning because of the significance of what the tree stands for.

A year ago, when we expected your visit, the selection was made, and the tree was planted then. So please don't feel disappointed that the tree has actually been here for a full year. It is still with the original purpose in mind that you have dedicated this tree today.

A year ago, the City Fathers considered what kind of tree they would like to have in honour of meditation. And as you see, it is a somewhat exotic species. There are only very few of its kind in Switzerland. The other ones are all in Geneva, which happens to be the European centre of the United Nations. So we got a tree that had been in Geneva before, and it was planted here.

It took a full year for you to come and, of course, we are extremely happy that you are here. The City Council and the Mayor were extremely grateful for your thoughts. The city is also happy, indeed, that it was in a position to offer what we believe is an extremely beautiful spot for this "Tree of Meditation", as we have started to call it ourselves. And in the name of the City Council I would like to present you with a book on the City of Zurich, which says in the introductory caption that a tree of meditation has been planted in this Rieterberg Park, out of respect for the goals you pursue, and it is overlooking the heart of the City.

I think it is not by coincidence that the City also has a heart. And when you look through the gap over there, that is the heart of the city of Zurich.

Thank you again very much for the idea. We hope that the tree will prosper.

Sri Chinmoy: I am extremely grateful to you for your soulful and encouraging words. I wish to offer you, on behalf of all my students, on behalf of myself and in the name of my Inner Pilot Supreme, our most soulful gratitude. You have not only given us this opportunity, but also you have given us your heart's assurance that our prayer, meditation and dedication will bear fruit. And for that, my soul, my heart and my life of aspiration are all gratitude to you.

Mr Schmid: Thank you.

[After the tree dedication, Sri Chinmoy visited a museum in the park. Afterwards, he wrote this in the guest book:]

I happen to be an Indian. Therefore, I wish to say a few words about the Indian sculpture divinely displayed here. To me, this is not only an art-feat, but a feast of the inner spirit. The spiritual India's, nay, spiritual Asia's pristine beauty, soulful fragrance and fruitful vision are distinctly visible in this sweet, pure, elevating and illumining museum. The divine seeker-lover of art in me finds his true satisfaction here. Therefore, I leave here a soulful gratitude-heart.

NOTES TO MY ROSE PETALS PART 5

53. Friends' House, York, England, 4 June 1976.
54. Friends' House, Canterbury, England, 5 June 1976.
55-60. Ealing, London, England, 6 June 1976.
61. YMCA, Rome, Italy, 9 June 1976.
62. Milan, Italy, 10 June 1976.
63-69. Milan, Italy, 10 June 1976.
70. University of Zurich, Zurich, Switzerland, 11 June 1976.
71-78. University of Zurich, Zurich, Switzerland, 11 June 1976.
79. On 12 June 1976 a ceremony was held in Rieterberg Park in Zurich, dedicating a tree of meditation which had been planted there some months earlier in Sri Chinmoy's honour. Officiating at the dedication was Mr Schmid, First Adjunct of City Planning. Both Sri Chinmoy and Mr Schmid spoke briefly about the meaning of the tree. These were their words.

MY ROSE PETALS

BOOK 6

80. Fear and courage

We are afraid of God. God's infinite Vastness frightens us. God's transcendental Height frightens us. God's immeasurable Depth frightens us.

God is both Truth and Light. God the Truth tries to lead us to the perfect Truth. But we unfortunately feel that God the Truth is always examining us. We feel that since we are a mountain of falsehood, since we are making mistakes at every moment, God the Truth will punish us. But God is all Compassion. He does not punish us. On the contrary, He tries to illumine our mistakes and make us perfect. In the process of evolution, He tells us that falsehood is nothing but lesser Truth. We have to transcend falsehood and then enter into Truth. And for that, we need a constant inner cry, which we call aspiration.

Just as we are afraid of God the Truth, so also are we afraid of God the Light. We feel that God the Light will expose us, since we have done many undivine things. If someone commits a theft, he wants to hide. He is afraid of light. He feels that if he is in light, he will be exposed. But God the Light is totally different. Here the Light does not expose us; it illumines us. The Light tells us that darkness also has a little light, that night too has a little bit of light. God, being all Light, is all-pervading. Therefore, He is bound to be in darkness as well as in Light. Of course, when He is in darkness, He will have only a very small amount of Light, whereas in an aspiring human being He will manifest boundless Light. Again, even if there is just a little light, this light will grow into boundless Light. It is like the seed that grows into a Banyan Tree.

Fear and courage. Fear has capacity in a negative way. It rejects oneness. It wants to remain always individual and separate. Fear is like the tiny drop that does not want to merge into the vast ocean. It wants to maintain its individuality and personality. The finite is afraid of the Infinite and, at the same time, it does not want to confess its fear. But the vast ocean knows that its individuality and personality are composed of countless drops of water. The infinite knows that it has become infinite precisely because it houses the finite in infinite measure.

On the physical plane, there are two types of fear: fear of the imaginary and fear of the real. Imaginary fear is far worse than real fear because we are afraid of something that we can only imagine. We are afraid of death because we feel that death will take away all our earth's wants, all our earth's love, all our earth's oneness. Here we achieve, here we accomplish; but we have no idea what is going to happen to us in the other world. We have no idea if we shall go to Heaven or to hell. Here on earth at least we know that we have our dear ones and relatives to look after us. But we do not know whether we shall meet with our dear ones in the other world or whether there will be anyone to look after us. In fact, we do not even know if there is another world. Therefore, the very thought, the very idea, the very conception of death frightens us.

Like imaginary fear, we can have imaginary courage. The worst possible imaginary courage is the courage of an atheist. He is infinitely more insignificant than an atom in that he challenges and denies God's existence. God is infinite. God is eternal. God is immortal. Yet the atheist challenges God's existence; he denies God's existence or speaks ill of God.

There are some human beings who do not pray and do not meditate, yet they feel that they have boundless peace to offer to the world at large. This is their imaginary courage. Or there are some human beings who feel that they can have the world drop down at their feet at the twinkling of an eye. Like Julius Caesar, they feel that they will be able to say, "I came, I saw, I conquered." This is all imaginary courage, for they are afraid of something or other. They are afraid of a tiny, imaginary thought. A tiny thought will enter into them, say, that their parents or dear ones are being attacked and are in very serious condition. Then for quite a few years this wicked thought can command them most mercilessly. Yet these human beings say that the whole world can be placed at their feet if they want it.

Fear of the known, fear of the unknown and fear of the unknowable. We have done many things undivine; therefore, we are afraid of the consequences. We know that as we sow, so we shall reap. The law of karma nobody can deny. If we have done something wrong, then we have to pay the penalty. Here what we fear is quite known. But there is also the unknown fear. If we do something wrong today, then we feel that in the near future we are going to suffer for it. We have no idea if the punishment will be severe or not. But we do know that we will be punished. The very thought of the punishment tortures us. Although the real punishment we shall get later on, right now the unknown fear, the fear of the unknown, tortures us.

Fear of the unknowable is fear of what is going to happen in our life or after our death — fear, for example, that there may be a catastrophe and this world of ours will not last. This unknowable can be positive or negative. Infinite Light is an unknowable Reality and it can frighten us. Infinite night, darkness, is also an unknowable reality that can frighten us. The infinite Light is a positive force; the infinite night is a negative force.

We speak of the Universal Consciousness; we speak of the Transcendental Consciousness. We achieve both the Universal Consciousness and the Transcendental Consciousness on the strength of our inner courage. Inner courage is nothing but constant self-giving. Here we are all seekers. Before we became seekers we stayed with our desire-friends, but now our friend is aspiration. God granted courage to our body before we were spiritual, before we aspired. He thought that with this courage we would be fully alert. He gave courage to our vital. He thought that with this courage our vital would be dynamic. He gave courage to our mind. He felt that with this courage our mind would be completely clear. He gave courage to our heart. He thought that with this courage our heart would be totally pure. Then we became seekers. Now God has given our heart the power of oneness. He has given our mind the power of wideness. He has given our vital the power of compassion. He has given our body the power of sacrifice.

Then He tells us, "Children, don't be afraid of the known, don't be afraid of the unknown, don't be afraid of the unknowable. Have courage in the known. And then, after a while, you will have courage in the unknown. And have courage that even the unknowable will one day become not only knowable but completely known.

"Your parents, your grandparents, your ancestors prayed to Me. Therefore they received Light from Me. Their light has entered into you and you have become spiritual. And now, if you pray and you meditate, you will also get Light from Me. Your light far surpasses that of your parents, grandparents and ancestors. There is no competition, but in the process of evolution I am manifesting Myself in and through human beings more and more. There shall come a time when I, the Unknowable, will appear before you with My infinite Peace, Light and Bliss, and these will all become known to you. At that time, you shall have courage within, courage without. When you dive deep within, with your inner courage, you play with God the Creator. And when you bring your outer courage to the fore, you play with God the Creation. This is how you participate in My cosmic Game."

81. The cry and the smile

I wish to give a short talk on the cry and the smile: the outer cry and the inner cry, the outer smile and the inner smile.

The outer cry is for name and fame. The inner cry is for Truth and Light.

When we walk along the road of name and fame, there comes a time when frustration makes friends with us. This frustration-friend takes us to destruction and there our journey ends.

When we walk along the road of Truth and Light, perfection becomes our friend and perfection leads us to satisfaction. But there our journey does not end; on the contrary, there a new and unprecedented journey starts. For this satisfaction is nothing but the ever-transcending Reality. Each time we are satisfied, a new reality inspires us to transcend ourselves.

The outer cry lives in the outer world. The outer cry is to possess the world, to bring it under our dominion, under our jurisdiction for us to use in our own way. We want to possess the world precisely because the outer world is not within us. Anything that is not within us, we feel is not ours.

The inner cry lives in the world of aspiration. Aspiration ultimately grants us realisation. Realisation means oneness with the Infinite. As individual seekers, we become inseparably one with the Infinite when we realise our transcendental Self. Inside our transcendental Reality we see the entire world with its cries and smiles.

The outer smile is the smile of the face. Quite often the outer smile consoles us, although it is not always encouraging and illumining. We notice at times that there is a motive behind the outer smile. The outer smile at times wants to be reciprocated; we smile and we want the world to smile back at us.

The inner smile is the smile of the heart. This smile inspires the seeker and elevates his consciousness. When the inner smile manifests itself through the outer smile, it reminds the seeker of his promise to the Absolute Supreme. His promise is to realise God, reveal God and manifest God here on earth. When the outer smile manifests itself through the inner smile, it is assurance that the outer life offers to the inner life. The outer life says to the inner life, "I am sorry I have stayed away from you for so long. But from now on, I shall become inseparably one with you. I shall help you in every possible way. Not only that, I shall please you and fulfil you in your own way. I shall fulfil you in your own way because I know that your way and God's Way are absolutely one."

Human life itself is a cry right from dawn to sunset. The moment a child is born, he offers a cry to Mother Earth. Again, when he is about to pass behind the curtain of Eternity, he offers a cry to Mother Earth. From the outer point of view, the child cries because the world is a stranger. The world is a stranger to the new-born babe; therefore he cries. And the same person, when he is ready to die, is afraid of the other world. Therefore, he offers a cry. This is a human, outer explanation of the reality that we see.

But there is also an inner explanation, an esoteric explanation of the cry. When the soul enters into the world of manifestation with a human body, it offers its gratitude to Mother Earth through its cry. The soul enters into the world-arena and it offers gratitude to Mother Earth for accepting it. And the same soul, at the end of its journey, again offers gratitude to Mother Earth through the physical cry, for the physical body was granted the opportunity by Mother Earth to realise, reveal and manifest Truth and Light on earth.

The human child cries for the mother's milk. But this human child, on the strength of his aspiration, becomes a divine child.

When he becomes a divine child, he prays to the Universal Mother, to the Absolute Supreme, to grant him Nectar, Delight, Immortality. In his human existence, he cries for the milk which nourishes the human existence. In his divine existence, he cries for something divine and immortal.

The human cry and the divine smile at times go together. The human cry in the physical world and the divine smile in the vital world at times go together. When a dear one dies, we cry. When we cry, the soul that is close to us smiles in the vital world. In the vital world, the souls that are attached to us, that still have kept a close connection with the world, get tremendous joy when we cry for them, and their joy they express with a smile. But if these souls are in the inner worlds that are far beyond the vital world, in the intuitive world or in the soul's world, they only watch the progress of the individuals on earth. If they see that their dear ones who are on earth have manifested everything that they were supposed to manifest before leaving the body, then they are happy. If not, then they feel sad and miserable for their dear ones.

The souls that remain in the soul's world always abide by the Will of the Supreme. Sometimes the Will of the Supreme tolerates certain things, sometimes it approves and sometimes it is totally committed to certain things taking place on earth. When the soul mixes with the vital, especially the lower vital, it loses its pristine divinity for the time being and it does not always abide by the Will of the Supreme. But it never loses its inmost divinity, which is eternally immortal. The souls that lose a bit of their universal Reality, a bit of their divinity, become one with ignorance and become a miserable cry. Again, the souls that do not mix with the lower vital and remain always above the vital world, here and elsewhere, remain always in perfect peace and bliss. These souls constantly offer smiles both to Heaven and to earth. Again, it is not only ordinary human beings who cry and smile, but also the spiritual Masters of the highest magnitude who offer their cries and smiles to mankind.

Here in the West, the Saviour is Christ. The Christ cried for humanity's salvation from sin. And sin is nothing but limited consciousness, which unfortunately we claim to be ours. Again, out of his infinite Bounty, the Christ gave us the most luminous Smile when He said, "Let Thy Will be done." When the human in the Christ became one with our cry, he said, "Father, what have I done? Why hast Thou forsaken me?" Again, when the Christ became one with his own divinity, his own transcendental Reality, he offered to the world at large his highest wisdom, his smile: "I and my Father are one."

In the East, we recall the Buddha's human cry for a little bird before he got his enlightenment. To save the life of a bird his heart literally bled; and he did save the bird. Again, in his later years, the Lord Buddha cried for the enlightenment of humanity. He got his illumination and his heart cried to offer it to the world at large. He told humanity two most sublime things. First he said, "This world is transitory. Here, if you expect abiding satisfaction, then you are bound to be disappointed." The second message he offered to the world at large was this: "Discover the Light within. Be the Light unto yourself."

The Christ taught us to free ourselves from sin-consciousness. The Buddha taught us to free ourselves from ignorance and bondage-consciousness. The Christ, out of his infinite Compassion, taught us the message of salvation; and the Buddha, out of his infinite Compassion, taught us the message of liberation. When we achieve salvation, anything within us that is inferior to the highest Reality becomes one with the highest Reality. When we achieve liberation, anything within us that is limited, anything within us that limits or binds us, becomes totally liberated, illumined, perfected and fulfilled.

Aspiration is an inner cry; again, aspiration is an inner smile. When we aspire to reach the highest Height, it is an inner cry that we embody. When we climb down to serve God in each human being, we are embodying an inner smile. Each human life is composed of a cry and a smile. The cry strengthens, the smile expedites. Therefore both the cry and the smile are of paramount importance.

God's Vision is the inner Cry to manifest His infinite Divinity. God's Reality is the inner Smile that grows and glows in humanity's aspiring consciousness. As long as man and God exist, man will cry to God for fulfilment in his own human way and God will cry for fulfilment in and through man in His divine Way. Man will cry to God to give him the capacity to bind the world; God will cry for man to liberate himself and to liberate others. If someone is a desiring person, there will come a time when he becomes an aspiring person. At that time he says to God, "O Lord Supreme, I shall be pleased only when I please You in Your own Way." God and the seeker smile simultaneously. The earth consciousness accepts the divine Consciousness and the divine Consciousness accepts the earth consciousness for Reality's transcendental Satisfaction.

Questions and answers

82. Question: How can a sincere seeker distinguish a true teacher from an untrue teacher?

Sri Chinmoy: A sincere Master will always say that he and the seeker have to work together. The Master says he will not be able to grant the seeker realisation overnight. If the Master says he will grant the seeker realisation if the seeker gives him millions of dollars, then that Master is false. The true teacher says to the seeker, "You show me your aspiration and I shall show you God's Compassion. I shall unite both God's Compassion and your aspiration. When they come together, then you become perfect." The real Master will always tell the seeker that there is something called God's Hour. It is then that God grants the seeker realisation. There is an hour for preparation and an hour for realisation. When we sow a seed, it takes time to germinate; then gradually it becomes a sapling and finally a tree. Until it becomes a tree, until it offers fruit, it is in the process of preparation. But when the tree bears fruit, it completes its journey. It is no longer preparation; it is realisation.

83. Question: I feel that there is a reality which is expressed through different religions, but I have read in the Upanishads that one must be able to transcend this reality. However, I find it very difficult.

Sri Chinmoy: You have to pray and meditate. Each religion has a way of expressing the Truth. Reality is One. But it expresses itself through each religion according to the receptivity of that particular religion. When you realise the Highest, then naturally you go through all the religions at once and, at the same time, you reach the Highest.

84. Question: There are many different spiritual paths to reach the one Reality. What is the difference between these paths and do they all go to the same point?

Sri Chinmoy: If the paths are real, then they lead to the same destination. It is like a school. A school has hundreds of students. Suppose ten or twenty students walk along one road to come to the school. Again, there are a few students who will walk along another road to come to the same school. So there are many roads, but the school remains the same.

But you have to know that some students are more advanced than others. Some will go to kindergarten and some will go to college or university. Again, the kindergarten student will one day graduate and go to elementary school, high school and college and eventually he will get his Master's degree or Ph.D. So today's goal may not be tomorrow's goal. In the beginning, the seeker aims at a particular goal. Then he wants to achieve a higher goal, grow into a higher goal. So collectively, all individuals are coming to the same goal according to their receptivity and capacity. If one's capacity right now is the high school capacity, then he is coming to the high school. If his capacity is for college, then he is going to college. And no matter what level he goes to, there are many of his standard who will come to the same school. Many will come to the high school; many will come to the college. But the goal for the seekers of one height will be one particular thing, and for the seekers of another standard there will be another goal.

85. Question: Who determines the capacities and standards?

Sri Chinmoy: The capacity is aspiration; the capacity comes from the inner cry. If you really do need God, if you desperately need God, then your standard is very high. If God comes first, Truth comes first, Light comes first in your life, then automatically the inner cry increases.

86. Question: Is there a way to increase the inner cry?

Sri Chinmoy: Certainly. Suppose there are four or five good swimmers. If you want to become a good swimmer, then you will mix with the swimmers. If somebody knows how to swim better than you do, then you will mix with that particular swimmer in order to learn how to swim better. Similarly, if you want to accelerate your spiritual progress, you have to mix with those in whom you have some confidence, some trust that they will be able to guide you and accelerate your progress.

87. Question: How does one come to know which is one's dharma?

Sri Chinmoy: If one really wants to know, one can. If one wants to learn, one goes to school. If one wants to sing, one goes to a musician, a singer. If one wants to know anything, then one goes to someone who already knows. If someone wants to know what his *dharma* is, then he has to go to someone who knows everybody's dharma.

88. Question: What exactly is realisation?

Sri Chinmoy: Realisation is self-discovery and God-discovery. When one realises God, or the highest Truth, one becomes inseparably one with humanity's cry and Divinity's Smile. When he identifies himself with humanity, he cries for humanity because humanity is hungry; and when he identifies himself with Divinity, then he becomes happy because he has got the opportunity to feed humanity. Oneness with Heaven, oneness with earth — conscious, complete, inseparable and eternal oneness — is called realisation.

89. Question: What role does conscious will play in the spiritual life?

Sri Chinmoy: Conscious will is of paramount importance in the spiritual life. Unconsciously we do many things, good and bad. But when we do them consciously, with conscious will, then we get the effect immediately.

If we use our conscious will, then we shall get up early in the morning, take a shower and pray to God. But if it is unconscious will, we shall keep in the back of our mind the thought that we have to pray, and that is all. Meanwhile, we shall remain lying down. While sleeping, we may repeat God's Name once or twice, and then we shall feel that we have prayed or meditated. But we are lethargic, idle; we will not leave the bed. For one second we shall meditate and for ten minutes we shall sleep. This is called unconscious will.

Conscious will is like an express train. It just starts and then it goes to the destination as fast as possible. Unconscious will stops at many stations before it reaches the destination. Each time it reaches a station, it takes a rest there and relaxes its capacity. Then it has to regain its capacity to go to the next station. This way it takes a very, very long time. People who pray and meditate unconsciously will take thousands and millions of years to realise God.

Conscious will values time. It knows the necessity of time. Conscious will teaches us that time is very precious. If we do not realise God today, then how are we going to reveal and manifest God tomorrow? Therefore we have to realise Him as soon as possible. Again, realisation has no end, revelation has no end, manifestation has no end. So we feel that it is the supreme necessity to realise at least some height and then reveal and manifest that height.

90. The third eye

Dear seekers, I am extremely happy to be here with you. This art gallery is called the Third Eye Centre; therefore, I shall give a short talk on the third eye. I wish to invoke the third eye of all the seekers here, and if you want to, you can be of help to me. There is a special way to invoke the third eye, and that is to chant AUM. We have six major psychic centres. Each centre has a sacred seed sound. The seed sound of the third eye is AUM. Before I begin my talk, I wish the seekers to join me in chanting AUM three times.

AUM... AUM... AUM.

AUM is a Sanskrit syllable. It is the combination of three letters: A, U and M. A represents God the Creator. U represents God the Preserver. M represents God the Transformer. There was a time when seekers felt that God the Creator needed God the Preserver, and that God the Preserver, as necessity demanded, would need God the Destroyer. But in the spiritual process of evolution, seekers of the highest magnitude have discovered that God does not destroy. He only transforms. Anything that is unlit, obscure or impure in us, He transforms into purity, beauty and divinity. So when we chant AUM, at one time we invoke God the Creator, God the Preserver and God the Transformer.

The third eye is located between the eyebrows, a little above. This eye is also called "the commanding eye". What does it command? It commands our past, our present, our immediate future and our distant future. That is to say, past, present and future are at its command. The third eye, when it envisions the past, feels and sees the beginning of humanity's evolution. When it enters into the present, into the immediacy of today, it sees the capacity and receptivity of humanity. And when it enters into the near or distant future, it sees not only the possibility and practicality, but also the inevitability of humanity's progress, perfection and satisfaction.

There are quite a few ways one can open the third eye, but the two most significant ways are through prayer and through concentration. If one soulfully prays to the Absolute Supreme to open one's third eye, the Lord Supreme may open it. And if one concentrates on the third eye soulfully, devotedly and consciously, then one can open the third eye oneself. But even in this case, the seeker owes his success ninety-nine per cent to the divine Grace, for without it he cannot even make the sincere effort. Although he may want to become sincere, sincerity does not come to the fore all at once. It takes a very, very long time. Therefore, the seeker has to know that God's Grace has given him the necessary sincerity to open his third eye.

Some of you may be curious to know what actually happens before the third eye opens. Before the third eye opens, the seeker feels a kind of sensation in that spot. In the beginning, it may feel as though a tiny ant were moving around there. A few days or a few months later, the seeker will inwardly see a disc. At first it rotates from left to right. Then, when it starts rotating very fast, it changes its direction and rotates from right to left.

After a few months or a few years, the seeker will see a fully illumined sun in his forehead, like a bright midday sun. This sun indicates the complete opening of the third eye. When the third eye is completely opened, the infinite Vast, the eternal Height and the immeasurable Depth can be seen inside the third eye.

At that time, the seeker sees himself as the seed of the entire creation, as the tree of the entire creation and as the fruit of the entire creation. The seed is the past, the tree is the present and the fruit is the future.

For absolutely sincere seekers, highly advanced seekers and seekers who have totally surrendered to God's Will, to have the third eye opened is a veritable blessing, a great boon. But if the seeker still has many earthly desires to be fulfilled, then it is nothing but a curse. There have been many seekers who made considerable progress before their third eye was opened. But when their third eye was opened on the strength of their eagerness or on the strength of their dynamic will, and not on the strength of their surrender to God's Will, their progress stopped almost immediately. When the third eye is opened while the vital is still impure, the power of the third eye creates problems for the seeker. The impurity of the vital enters into his divine vision and blinds it. Then the human being, at times, acts like a mad elephant.

If the seeker wants to open his third eye in order to know his past, and if he sees that in his past life he was an atheist, then despondency assails him. He feels that if he did not even believe in God in his previous incarnation, how can he realise God in this incarnation? If the past was not satisfactory, being able to see it with the third eye can create problems for the seeker. And if the distant future is not promising, the seeker will feel doomed to disappointment if he can see the future. If the future is threatening and frightening, then the third eye may create tremendous fear. But when the third eye is opened in accordance with God's Will, no matter what the seeker did in the past, no matter what is going to happen today or tomorrow, no matter what will take place in the distant future, the seeker will not be affected, for God's Will will liberate him, illumine him, perfect him and immortalise him.

There are some spiritual Masters who tell their students that it is not advisable for them to try to open the third eye. What is of paramount importance right from the beginning is to surrender to God's Will. The easiest and safest way to become aware of God's Will and to surrender to God's Will is to open the heart centre. If the seeker opens the heart centre first, then he becomes inseparably one with God's Will. After that, if God wants to grant the seeker that Vision which He Himself is, if God wants to open the seeker's third eye, then it will not cause any problem. At that time the happenings of the hoary past, the immediate present or the ultimate future are no longer matters of concern to the seeker, for the seeker has become inseparably one with God's universal Vision and transcendental Reality. Inside God's universal Vision and God's transcendental Reality, all the things that he sees, feels and grows into can be perfectly housed without any problem whatsoever. So if God wants to give Vision to a certain seeker, He will give it. Why? Just because the hour has struck for Him to make a perfect instrument of that person. But if a seeker untimely pulls the Vision-Reality of the third eye, it will be a disaster for him. The third eye is the eye of illumination for sincere seekers. But for curiosity-mongers the third eye is nothing but temptation.

The third eye is like a toy that a child plays with. After a few years he does not want to play with toys any more and he gives it up. At that time he studies for knowledge; he prays and meditates for inner wisdom. After the seeker has played for a few years with the third eye toy, he wants to acquire infinite wisdom-light. This wisdom-light he gets on the strength of his constant surrender to God's Will and by virtue of his inmost cry.

The opening of the third eye does not determine God-realisation at all. Some people think that if the third eye is opened, that means they have realised God. No, the third eye can see the Face of God, but this does not indicate that conscious oneness with God has been established.

The third eye can see the past, the present and the future, but it cannot change humanity's cry into divinity's Smile. With it we can see something, but we don't have the capacity to change it. If we can't change it, then it remains imperfect. But if we see something and have the capacity to perfect it, then it is worth seeing. If one has discovered oneself and has realised the highest Truth, then if one sees something that needs perfection, at that time he can perfect it. It is the seeker's self-discovery that can make the third eye an effective divine instrument. When the third eye observes something that needs perfection, the third eye can get the necessary help from the inner light of the seeker's self-discovery.

The earthly eyes, the two human eyes, are side by side, but they cannot see each other. Why? Because of the human limitations, because of the earthly bondage that each eye embodies. But if we stand in front of a mirror, then we see both the eyes at once. Similarly, when we stand in front of our highest Reality, God, and see God with our third eye, then only can we see human life in its acme of perfection. Otherwise, the third eye will see, but what it sees will not offer any abiding satisfaction to the seekers of the ultimate Truth. Only if it sees God, only if it sees infinite Truth and Light, only if it can embody God's divine Presence at all times and feel God's universal Reality inside its Vision, only then can the opening of the third eye be a perfect spiritual experience.

91. Ignorance and knowledge

Dear seekers, dear brothers and sisters, I wish to give a short talk on ignorance and knowledge. This subject is familiar to each and every human being. Again, each human being deals with ignorance and with knowledge according to his inner receptivity and his outer capacity.

Ignorance wants to conquer; knowledge wants to illumine. Ignorance wants to conquer the world by fighting, strangling and killing. Knowledge wants to illumine the world by loving and by becoming one with the world. Ignorance is hunger for constant separativity. Knowledge is hunger for constant unity. Ignorance teaches us how to consciously or unconsciously bring to the fore the destructive, animal qualities of the world. Knowledge teaches us how to dive deep within and bring to the fore the illumining, divine qualities of the world.

I come, I see, I conquer: this is the message of ignorance. *I love, I serve, I become:* this is the message of knowledge. I come into the world, I see and feel God's creation around me and I want to conquer it, dominate it, lord over it. This is the message of the ignorance-teacher within me. The knowledge-teacher within me teaches me to love and serve the world and to become God's instrument in the world. By listening to the knowledge-teacher within me, I love and serve God and I grow into my inner Being, the Highest Reality that is at one with God Himself.

When we pray to God to fulfil our desires — our teeming, countless desires — at that time it is ignorance that is playing its role in and through us. When we request God to take our side, to be on our side, then again it is ignorance that is playing its role in and through us. But when we pray to God to fulfil our aspiration and grant us the capacity to be on His side, at that time it is knowledge that is playing its role in and through us.

Aspiration is our inner cry, the cry that climbs up high, higher, highest. While climbing, it illumines the unlit human in us, purifies the impure animal in us and serves the divine in us for God's manifestation on earth. When we are on God's side, the finite in us consciously merges into the Infinite and the individual "I" becomes one with the Universal Reality.

In the world envisioned by God, there are two divine members of God's family that have been playing the eternal game of Light and Delight on earth: faith and purity. Each human being is constantly attacked by ignorance-forces. These ignorance-forces are doubt and impurity. Faith is the Supreme within us, the divine representative within us, the divine child within us that is growing and glowing, illumining and fulfilling. Doubt tries to conquer the faith within us and poison it. Faith also wants to conquer doubt. But when faith conquers doubt, it does not poison doubt, it does not destroy doubt. Only it illumines doubt, for faith regards doubt as the younger member of its family. Therefore, faith feels that it is its bounden duty to illumine doubt, which is a younger, destructive member of the family.

Just as doubt tries to destroy our faith, so does impurity try to destroy the purity that is within us and around us. It tries to destroy not only our purity, but also our divinity. If impurity is successful, then it does destroy our purity, but it can never destroy our divinity. Purity is of the heart and for the heart, so it can be destroyed. But divinity is of the soul and for the soul; therefore, it can never be destroyed. In the course of time, slowly, steadily and unerringly purity and divinity conquer impurity. They do not destroy impurity, but they purify its very existence. They show impurity a part of the divine reality that is within.

Doubt is a destructive force that will destroy not only faith but also itself. Impurity also is a destructive force. When faith, purity and divinity conquer these ignorance-forces, these forces are illumined, perfected and fulfilled. Let us say ignorance is a thorn that has entered into our foot. It takes another thorn to rid ourselves of this ignorance-thorn. This second thorn is temporarily our saving-power. Then what do we do? We throw away both the thorns because we fear that the thorn that has become our saviour will eventually create problems for us.

At this point, wisdom has to enter into the picture. Wisdom is not the information that we get from the world around us. Wisdom is what we get from our soul.

Wisdom at every moment energises the physical in us, the vital in us, the mind in us and the heart in us. When the physical is energised, it opens its door to the supreme Reality. When the vital is energised, it opens its door to the supreme Power. When the mind is energised, it opens its door to the universal Peace. When the heart is energised, it reaches the height of transcendental Oneness.

The finite in us is not aware of the Infinite, but when it is made aware of the Infinite, it has an inferiority complex, and it does not want to be consciously one with the Infinite. The finite is an ignorance-force. But the Infinite feels its oneness with the finite. It feels that there was a time when it was not the entire ocean. It was just a tiny drop, like the finite. And then, from that tiny drop, it widened its consciousness and expanded into the ocean itself. This occurred through the process of evolution. Again, the Highest, the absolute Truth, was originally One. God was One, and then He decided to become many. The Infinite consciously decided to become the finite. Knowledge tells us that within the Infinite, there we can find the finite; and within the finite, there we can find the Infinite. Just because God is infinite, He can enjoy Himself in the tiniest atom as well as in the infinite Vast.

Knowledge tells us something more. Divine knowledge tells us that the many and the One were, from the very beginning, identical; they were made together. The One is the Vision; the many is the Reality. God the Vision and God the Reality are all the time together. From God's Vision-power, immediately Reality came into existence. Again, with Reality-power, Vision came into existence. God wanted to enjoy Himself. He wanted to offer Nectar, Immortality, to His whole creation. With the creation He felt the expansion of His Self-Form, His manifested Form. When He first created the world, with His inner Vision He saw the ultimate future. Now, slowly, steadily and unerringly, He is unfolding His Vision.

92. Ingratitude and gratitude

Dear seekers, dear brothers and sisters, I wish to give a short talk on ingratitude and gratitude. These are two forces. Ingratitude is a destructive force, whereas gratitude is a constructive force. Every day in our multifarious activities, either we express ingratitude or we express gratitude to our fellow beings.

Ingratitude is not our inability to acknowledge the gifts we receive from others. Ingratitude is our deliberate unwillingness to acknowledge the gifts we receive from others. Gratitude is receptivity, the receptivity that acknowledges others' gifts, others' love and concern. Each time we express gratitude, we expand our hearts.

Receptivity can be increased. How can we increase our receptivity? We can increase it by cultivating it. The farmer cultivates the ground and then he sows the seed. He waters it and eventually the seed germinates and grows into a sapling and a tree. Here also, when we cultivate our gratitude-heart, we get the opportunity to sow our pure love there. This pure love grows into true concern, and true concern eventually becomes inseparable oneness.

When we want to pick a beautiful flower from a tree, we look around to see if anybody is observing us. We feel that nobody should know that we had to take the flower from some other place. We want to show the world at large that this flower was ours right from the beginning. In order to do that, we try to destroy the branches of the tree.

We receive gifts from our friends in the inner worlds but we don't want others to know about it. So we speak ill of our inner friends, consciously or unconsciously. We want to make the world believe that we are self-sufficient, but the rest of the world knows that we are receiving something from others. Ingratitude is nothing but a sense of inferiority, an inferiority complex. The gifts we get from others we do not want to acknowledge. We are afraid to expose ourselves to others.

Ingratitude, impurity and the doubting mind go together. It is impurity that divides and separates us and does not allow us to have the feeling of oneness or gratitude. And this impurity unconsciously or consciously is treasured by the doubtful mind. Gratitude, purity and the loving heart always go together. The gratitude-flower grows in our purity-heart. Purity expands our heart. Purity awakens our entire being within to the highest level of consciousness. The heart is self-giving. And what is self-giving today becomes tomorrow God-Delight and God-Perfection.

Here we are all seekers. Some of us are extremely sincere, while others are to some extent sincere. Those who are sincere seekers of the highest magnitude are all gratitude to the Supreme. When they observe their relationship with the Beloved Supreme, they see that He showers upon them Peace, Light and Bliss in abundant measure from above. If they forget to offer their gratitude to their Inner Pilot, the Inner Pilot does not mind. He immediately forgives them. The Beloved Supreme is bound to forgive even insincere seekers if they forget to offer their loving gratitude while on the way to the Ultimate Goal. God is infinitely above our ingratitude-heart. But although God may forgive the seeker, the sincere seeker may find it impossible to forgive himself. When his sincerity-flower petal by petal fully blossoms, he gets tremendous pangs in the inmost recesses of his heart if he has not offered gratitude to the Supreme.

God does everything unconditionally. We try to become His perfect instruments and we try our utmost to become worthy of His infinite Compassion, infinite Love and infinite Light, Peace and Bliss. Our ideal is to be like Him. Our inner cry is to become exactly the same as our transcendental, universal Pilot Supreme.

Within us is the animal kingdom, the human kingdom and the divine kingdom. The animal in us does not allow us to become fully human. The human in us does not allow us to be fully divine. The animal in us is anger, jealousy, impure thoughts; these are the animal forces within us. They don't want us to become properly human. The animal in us is a hungry tiger. The human in us often feeds the tiger. But instead of being grateful, sometimes the tiger devours us. The human in us is our sense of division. The human in us wants to control itself without being part and parcel of any collective group. Always it wants to remain off by itself. It does not want to go to the divine, to the all-pervading, the all-loving, all-illumining and all-fulfilling divine. The divine in us brings us joy, love and satisfaction. But the human in us devours this joy and then does not care for the divine. It speaks ill of the divine. It falls short of the divine and then it becomes totally indifferent to the divine. It remains aloof and makes us feel that the divine does not exist. So the animal in us does not want the gift that it gets from the human in us, and the human in us does not want the gift from above.

But again, we are all evolving. The animal in us is evolving into the human and the human in us is evolving into the divine. The divine in us wants to go to its Source, the Supreme. The human in us tries to become divine by mixing with someone who consciously embodies divinity and spirituality. When we see a spiritual Master, when we see a saint or a sage, someone who is embodying Peace, Light and Bliss, we try to serve him, please him, become a member of his inner family, spiritual family. Then when we become spiritual, we try to please our Eternity's Beloved Supreme. We try to become the exact prototype of His universal and transcendental Existence.

The animal grows into the human by serving, the human grows into the divine by serving, the divine grows into the Absolute by serving. While serving, we offer our gratitude, for it is the higher force that has granted us the opportunity to develop through our service. There are millions and millions on earth who are still fast asleep. But we have been awakened. By whom? By a higher force. So each time we get the opportunity to serve, we feel that it is because a higher force has kindled the flame of aspiration and dedication inside us. Therefore we are grateful. Gratitude looms large when we are given the opportunity to be of service to the Supreme in mankind. This gratitude-power is our expansion-power, our self-expansion-power. Each time we offer our gratitude to the Supreme, we expand our hearts and grow into the universal Heart and transcendental Reality.

93. Satisfaction

Dear seekers, dear spiritual brothers and sisters, I wish to give a talk on satisfaction from the spiritual point of view. It is only human beings that need satisfaction from God. God Himself is all Satisfaction. At the same time, He wants to see and achieve satisfaction inside each and every individual. Here we are all seekers. Inside us is the animal existence to some extent, the human life as such, and the divine life that we are longing for. Finally, Light Supreme abides within us, in the inmost recesses of our hearts.

The animal in us wants satisfaction through destruction. The animal in us is jealousy, doubt and anger.

The human in us wants to aspire, but then it drowns in the pleasures of ignorance. At times it does want to aspire, and when it aspires it feels the supreme necessity of realisation: realisation of its inseparable oneness with the world of Love, God's Love.

The divine in us consciously and constantly longs for satisfaction, satisfaction within and satisfaction without.

The Supreme within us wants the supreme Satisfaction. God is granting us His unconditional Satisfaction. He is showering His infinite Compassion on us. And we receive according to our inner receptivity and capacity. Our capacity is our devoted head and our receptivity is our surrendered heart.

We want satisfaction; therefore, we make a personal effort. From our personal effort we gain satisfaction. Again, from our inner surrender to God's Will we gain higher satisfaction. When we combine soulful personal effort with surrender, at that time we get supreme satisfaction.

Being a seeker myself, I wish to say that there are three principal ways to achieve satisfaction in life. First is the way of concentration, second is the way of meditation and third is the way of contemplation. Through concentration, meditation and contemplation we achieve satisfaction. Dear, dearer, dearest satisfaction; sweet, sweeter, sweetest satisfaction. Satisfaction that is dearer than the dearest, sweeter than the sweetest.

Concentration is speed; it wants to grant us satisfaction sooner than at once. When we concentrate, we can achieve and receive considerable satisfaction on earth. It is like a man reaching his goal; deep in our destination is satisfaction.

Meditation is slightly different. Meditation will give us peace, which is another kind of satisfaction.

Contemplation gives us satisfaction through delight. It helps us to discover the delight within us. Contemplation tells us that delight is our Source, that in delight we actually grow and that at the end of our earthly journey, into delight we shall retire.

Concentration is speed-satisfaction, meditation is peace-satisfaction and contemplation is delight-satisfaction. Concentration, meditation and contemplation are the three members of the divine self. Each member plays a distinctive role in bringing satisfaction. Concentration plays the role of the hero-warrior. Meditation plays the role of the wisest instrument of the Supreme. Contemplation plays the role of the divine Lover and the Beloved Supreme.

Concentration joyously declares, "God is for me." Meditation soulfully declares, "I am for God." Contemplation unconditionally declares, "God and I are eternal. I am for God and God is for me. I am unconditionally for God and God is unconditionally for me." This is the blessing and wisdom-light that contemplation offers to us.

Concentration has the capacity to discover the tiniest drop inside the vast ocean and to concentrate on it. It can separate the tiniest drop from the infinite Vast and then it can do anything it wants to do with the tiniest drop.

Meditation has the power, on the strength of its inner spiritual capacity, to transform the tiny drop into the vast ocean. The power of meditation has the capacity to transform the finite into the infinite Vast.

Contemplation has the capacity to see unification between the tiny drop and the vast ocean. In contemplation, they combine their capacity in order to achieve satisfaction.

Creation is satisfaction and the Creator is satisfaction. If we see creation with the eye of our Inner Pilot, it is nothing short of satisfaction, supreme satisfaction. But if we see creation with our own human eyes, with our limited vision, then we see and feel nothing like satisfaction. If we use our limited vision, we see all around us confusion and frustration. But if we invoke God-Vision, we see God's creation in us, through us and around us. Then, we notice continuous preparation and ever-transcending perfection in His creation. Confusion and frustration offer dissatisfaction: continuous preparation and ever-transcending perfection grant us divine satisfaction.

Expectation is satisfaction when we want something from others. We expect something from others; others expect something from us. Each of us gives and we both derive satisfaction. Then we go one step ahead and feel that there is no satisfaction in expectation. If we expect, we act like a beggar. A beggar is one who does not have the things that he wants. If we have expectation, I tell you that we act like beggars; but we are like an emperor if we don't expect. Instead of expectation, we have to have surrender, constant surrender to God's Will. We shall evoke God's Presence and then it is up to Him if He will grant us satisfaction. If we seek only to be His perfect instruments, and if He allows us to be His perfect instruments, at that time we shall derive true satisfaction.

Each individual seeker can pray and meditate and in this way grow into satisfaction supreme. When he wants his satisfaction to be high beyond the skies, he climbs up high, higher, highest in order to see His Heavenly Father and thus grow into divine, supreme satisfaction. And the same seeker, when he meditates, realises that God's Heavenly satisfaction is not only in Heaven but also on earth. Therefore, when he wants to feel his Father's

Heaven in the highest realm of consciousness, he climbs up on the strength of his prayer; and when he wants to see His Father's Universal Form as well as His Transcendental Form, at that time he prays.

We pray, meditate, concentrate and contemplate only for one thing: the satisfaction of our Lord Supreme. If we fulfil ourselves in our own way, out of His boundless Compassion, God without fail will grant us satisfaction in our own way. But just because we are spiritual seekers, our sincerity will not allow us to derive supreme satisfaction unless and until we can please God in His own Way.

How will we please God in His own Way? There is only one way and that is through self-giving. Self-giving is founded upon our constant inner cry. This inner cry we see, we feel and we grow into only when we put God first in our life.

94. Greatness and goodness

I wish to give a very short talk on greatness and goodness. Here we are in Oxford. Oxford is a place of greatness and goodness. Oxford, I bow to your greatness and I bow to your goodness. Your greatness is divinely meaningful and your goodness is supremely soulful. Anything that is great in England is to be found here in microcosm. Greatness and goodness combined are what Oxford is.

Students who want to cultivate mental knowledge of the highest degree come here from all over the world to achieve greatness. Then they go back to their respective countries to offer the knowledge-light that they have achieved from here. This knowledge-light that they spread is goodness.

To have greatness is to have faith in oneself: in one's physical, in one's vital, in one's mind and in one's heart. If one has a strong body, he has faith in his physical strength. If one has a dynamic vital, then he has implicit faith in his vital. If one is blessed with a brilliant mind, then he has faith in his mind. And if one is blessed with a pure heart, a pure and unalloyed heart, then he has tremendous faith in his heart.

Goodness is faith only in God, in Truth, in Light. When one becomes part and parcel of Truth, then one takes the side of Truth and Light. And when one is always for God, this is nothing but goodness. Goodness always has faith in God, Truth and Light.

Greatness is a universally acknowledged fact. Goodness is also a universally acknowledged fact. But it is something more. It is universally loved reality. Greatness we observe in our outer life. Goodness we observe in our inner life. With our human eyes, we observe greatness around us, all over the world. With our divine heart, we feel goodness within us and within others.

God is great because He has created this world. This is a fact that we have been taught by our parents, by our friends, by the world body. God is also good, kind, compassionate. He is our Source within us; He is for us, eternally for us. He wants to liberate us, He wants to illumine us, He wants to grant us realisation, satisfaction and fulfilment. He is the Author of all good. This is God the Goodness. God the Creator is Greatness and God the Lover of His creation is Goodness. We love God not because He is supremely great, but because He is universally, transcendentally good. Greatness astonishes us. Goodness illumines us, liberates us from the shackles of bondage.

Greatness we can express in an animal way when we quarrel, fight and try to destroy one another. When we stay together in a family and love one another, then greatness is expressed in a human way. When we try to elevate one another and help one another reach the highest heights, at that time greatness is expressed in a divine way. Finally, greatness is expressed in the supreme way when we tell the world that God the Eternal Reality is also eternally good; He is the Source. He is waiting for us, Him to please in His own Way. Here we reach greatness, supreme greatness, on the strength of our conscious and constant surrender to God's Will.

Usually our human mind craves greatness, whereas our divine heart longs for goodness. Sometimes we notice a yawning gulf between the mind and the heart, between the goal that the mind wants to reach and the goal that the heart wants to reach. The mind tries to see its goal by separating one reality from another. Everything it wants to see in an infinitesimal measure, whereas the heart wants to see the goal, the reality, as a unit, one and inseparable. The mind and the heart approach reality in different ways, but they cannot always remain separated. They have to be unified in order to achieve the highest truth. There are two kinds of mind: the physical mind and the illumined mind. The physical mind is bound by the physical world. It wants to lord it over the world. It wants to stay at least an inch above others so that it can dominate others. Consciously or unconsciously, willingly or unwillingly, it gets tremendous joy from its sense of separativity. The illumined mind is totally different. It longs for vastness within and without. It wants nothing but vastness; and inside vastness, it wants to grow and glow.

The human heart, which is very near the vital centre, is quite often insecure. It does not want to house others inside it. It feels that when others want to take shelter in it, they may break the vessel. It feels it is too small. Therefore, the human heart is quite often insecure, timid. And just because it is quite near the vital, unconsciously or consciously, like a magnet it pulls impurity from the undisciplined vital. But there is also the spiritual heart.

This heart is always united with the soul; it has established its oneness with the soul. The soul, which is the direct representative of the Lord Supreme, has Light in boundless measure. And the spiritual heart has a free access to the soul. Therefore, it can easily bring down the soul's light into its system.

The oneness of the spiritual heart and the vastness of the illumined mind must be brought together. Oneness we can establish with another individual or with some tiny object. But if we have vastness along with the oneness, if we can establish our oneness with God's vast creation, then we become perfect. Likewise, vastness without oneness is of no avail. God's creation is very vast, but if we fail to establish our oneness with this vastness, then vastness remains a barren desert. In order to become perfect, we have to create within us vastness and oneness, and we have to grow into both vastness and oneness.

There are two worlds. One is the world of desire; the other is the world of aspiration. When we remain in the desire-world, greatness looms large. But when we remain in the aspiration-world, goodness looms large. Just because we are seekers, we are consciously trying to come out of the domain of the desire-world and establish our abode in the aspiration-world.

The desire to know the world and the desire to know oneself are totally different things. When we want to know the world around us, without caring for our oneness with the world, unconsciously we are aiming at greatness. And this greatness, without fail, separates us from the world. But when we want to know ourselves implicitly, what we realise is that we are part and parcel of the whole, of the integral reality. Even if we start with the desire-world and try to become great, no harm. It is far better than remaining in the world of lethargy and somnolence. But there shall come a time when we see that our greatness has not given us an iota of satisfaction; for inside greatness what we see is frustration. There comes a time when our greatness is challenged. An individual feels that he is a great singer. But sooner or later his pride is smashed when he sees that another singer is far better than he. Then what does he do? He resorts to goodness.

Goodness is not in competing with the world around; only it offers the message of self-transcendence. If we at all have to compare, then the comparison is with ourselves. If we at all have to compete, then we will compete with our own previous capacities. Here there is no other world. There is only our own world of constant and continuous progress. We try only to transcend ourselves. In the desire-world there is comparison and competition. But in the aspiration-world, we do not want to make others feel that we are superior. No. When we feel that we have an iota of light, we aspire to have abundant light, infinite Light. Only by virtue of our constant aspiration do we transcend our own capacities. We feel that the more we increase our capacity and the more we utilise our capacity to please the Inner Pilot in His own Way, the sooner we become His perfect instruments.

SRI CHINMOY

NOTES TO MY ROSE PETALS PART 6

80. Université de Genève, Geneva, Switzerland, 14 June 1976.
81-89. American Church, Paris, France, 15 June 1976.
90. The Third Eye Centre, Glasgow, Scotland, 16 June 1976.
91. Glasgow University, Glasgow, Scotland, 16 June 1976.
92. University of Edinburgh, Edinburgh, Scotland, 17 June 1976.
93. Friends' Meeting House, London, England, 18 June 1976.
94. Oxford University, Oxford, England, 19 June 1976.

MY ROSE PETALS

BOOK 7

MY ROSE PETALS

I — "Reflections": a radio broadcast

95. Interviewer: This morning we have a different "Reflections", and I think this music really sets the scene. There you had Yehudi Menuhin playing violin with the Eastern musician Ravi Shankar playing sitar: the meeting of the East and the West.

And this is what we're going to be talking about this morning — a meeting of the spiritual life of the East with the spiritual life of the West — because we are very lucky here at Medway to have a Guru, a Master from India, who has Centres of spirituality all over the world. And we've also got some of his students here. The Master, or Guru, is Sri Chinmoy.

You were born in India?
Sri Chinmoy: Yes, I was born in India.
Interviewer: Where?
Sri Chinmoy: In Bengal, in 1931.

96. Interviewer: And what happened to you in those early years to make you a spiritual Master today?

Sri Chinmoy: As a young boy I was brought to a spiritual community in South India. I stayed there for twenty years and practised spirituality. I prayed and meditated every day for a considerable amount of time until I realised deep within me something very high, powerful and supreme. Then, in 1964, I was commanded by my Inner Pilot to come to the West to be of service to the Supreme inside aspiring seekers in the Western world.

97. Interviewer: You are a teacher. You are bringing to us the spirituality which you have discovered, and teaching it to us in the West. Does it matter that I'm not a Hindu, but a Christian?

Sri Chinmoy: In our path there is no problem whatsoever with regard to religion. One may practise Christianity, one may practise Judaism and one may practise Buddhism. I tell my students that religion is nothing but a house. You as an individual live in one house, and I as an individual live in another house. But although we live in different houses, if we both want to learn a certain subject, which is God-realisation, we will both go to the same school. This school is our inner school. When we pray to God and meditate on God, we go to our inner school, and in order to go there we may or may not walk along the same road. But both of us leave aside the limitations of our respective houses when we go to study in our inner school. Irrespective of religion, one can practise spirituality.

98. *Interviewer: I accept the fact that you are a Master, a Guru, a teacher. As a Christian, what am I expected to do, or what, in fact, would you teach me that would deepen my inner silence, my spiritual life?*

Sri Chinmoy: Thank you. I deeply appreciate your sincerity and humility. Your soul is full of aspiration and dedication. When somebody comes to me as a seeker, I tell that person that each individual teacher has a way of teaching. Each teacher is right in his own way, and each student is right in his own way. On the basis of my own inner realisation, I advise each seeker to be as simple as possible, as sincere as possible, as humble as possible. Each teacher has a special path, and ours is the path of love, devotion and surrender: divine love for God, divine devotion to God and divine surrender to God.

Human love ultimately fails. It ends in frustration and destruction. But divine love constantly expands. From the limited individual it grows into the Unlimited, the Infinite, the Vast, and there we feel our inseparable oneness with the entire universe.

Human devotion is nothing but unrecognised attachment. We say that we are devoted to someone or to something, but if we go deep within, we discover that this feeling is nothing short of our attachment to that individual or to that cause. But divine devotion is totally different. Divine devotion is to something high, deep, sublime. It helps us to grow into the infinite Consciousness. We know that there is a goal, and that we have to reach this destination; therefore, we devote ourselves wholeheartedly to the supreme Cause.

Human surrender is the surrender of a slave to his master. He is under compulsion to please the master; otherwise the master will punish him. But divine surrender is totally different. Here the finite in us tries to recognise the Infinite in us and become one with it; but there is no compulsion. Cheerfully, devotedly and unconditionally our lower part surrenders to our own highest part.

We have within us both the highest and the lowest. Right now, unfortunately, we are wallowing in the pleasures of ignorance. We have totally forgotten our own divinity, our own highest Reality. But on the strength of our prayer and meditation, there comes a time when we realise the highest part that is within us, and we surrender to our own highest part. We do not surrender to somebody else or to something else. This is what I try to share with my students.

99. Interviewer: You have written a number of books, and after reading what you have written, it seems to me that peace, the inner peace, is the thing that is the result of all this. I am very interested to see that you emphasise that to get this peace is not a matter of departing from the life of work and retreating into the Himalayan caves or sitting on snow-capped mountains, but that it can be achieved here on earth in the hustle and bustle of life. Can I move from you, Master, for just a moment, to one of your disciples?

What has this really meant to you as a human being? Has it obviously enriched your life very much over the past years?

Ms Siegerman: Sri Chinmoy has given me my source. In him I have seen a being who embodies the divine Consciousness, and this has inspired my whole life. It tells me to follow his teachings and to make within myself some reflection of what I see in him. I see a great soul full of majesty and inner divinity.

He has touched my soul, has given me my own inner existence, so that the outer world which I had been involved in before is now flowering with a new significance because it is impelled and activated by my inner life. That is to say, my whole existence has a purpose and a meaning because in touching my own soul I have seen a link between my own soul and the Supreme.

So my outer life has meaning and purpose now. And the activities of the Sri Chinmoy Centres are all done with the purpose of putting us into a higher consciousness so that everything we do, everything we involve ourselves in, is something good, something progressive and something of a higher consciousness. In Sri Chinmoy I see the most perfect spiritual Master, because in him I found a perfect balance of acceptance of the world and God-realisation.

Interviewer: You are not retreating from the world? This isn't sort of a retreat; this isn't sort of getting away from it all?

Ms Siegerman: It's not an isolated community at all. We are involved completely in the outside world. Sri Chinmoy's disciples are in every kind of occupation. There are students, nurses, secretaries, businessmen, teachers, musicians, artists. Our lives in the Centres are full of very normal activities. We have dramas, choirs, sports, music, jokes. We are like a community that wants to operate in every field from a yogic consciousness, from the Consciousness of the Supreme.

Interviewer: I know that there is a Centre in London. And Mary Plumbly here, comes from London. You run the London Centre?

Mrs Plumbly: Yes, I do.

Interviewer: How long have you been with Sri Chinmoy?

Mrs Plumbly: It will be five years in October, on 14 October.

Interviewer: What did meeting Sri Chinmoy mean to you?

Mrs Plumbly: Longing to meet Sri Chinmoy and being able to become his student have given purpose to my life, given it some real meaning and depth which it didn't have before. I was looking for something which I didn't have, and now I have got it.

Interviewer: If I had known you ten years ago, and then I hadn't met you for ten years and I met you now, do you think that I would have seen a great difference?

Mrs Plumbly: Oh yes, I think so.

Interviewer: Peter Orsell also belongs to the London Centre. Peter, what has this meant to you in your life?

Mr Orsell: When I first saw Sri Chinmoy, I was feeling at that time a sense of frustration with the world around me. But now I feel a sense of expansion and progression towards the higher life which is deep inside myself. I feel a true sense of progression in my inner life, and I feel different in the outer life also. Before I met Sri Chinmoy, I felt very inadequate to deal with the world. Now I am starting to feel a sense of oneness in my own way. I feel more peace; I can accept peace much more now. I can accept the world more.

Interviewer: Were you a Christian?

Mr Orsell: I never had any religious faith.

Interviewer: What about you?

Ms Siegerman: I was from a Jewish background, a Russian Jewish family. But when I graduated from college, I went to India because I had become very interested in Oriental philosophy and I was searching for the source of that philosophy in India. I wanted to transcend the background I had been brought up in, because I had a great leaning towards the Orient.

Mrs Plumbly: I was brought up in a Christian background and I had a complete education. I found it very helpful to have a Christian background.

Interviewer: But you're not a Christian now?

Mrs Plumbly: Oh, yes. Although I don't attend any church, I couldn't say I'm not a Christian now. I haven't accepted any other religion and Sri Chinmoy's teachings easily embrace Christianity. Spirituality doesn't really reject anything one truly believes in. I've learned to understand Christianity more than I ever did before.

Interviewer: Maybe the spiritual life is missing in Christianity today?

Mrs Plumbly: Unfortunately, I think a lot of it has become just paying lip service to something people don't really understand. In the spiritual life, we are trying to live what we believe. That is something, I think, that the majority of Christians do not sincerely try to do.

100. Interviewer: Master, I'll come back to you now. I think we know a little more about it all now. You mentioned Yoga. One of your books is called *Yoga and the spiritual life*. For many people, Yoga is nothing more nor less than a set of physical exercises where you stand on your head, or fold your legs into impossible positions. But that's not what you mean by the word "Yoga", is it? Are there exercises? Are there physical postures that you try to teach your students?

Sri Chinmoy: No, not at all. "Yoga" means conscious union with

God. The fastest way to achieve this is to concentrate, meditate and contemplate. This is the most effective way to realise God, to discover one's own Reality. If one practises hatha yoga, which is the physical exercises, it may help to some extent. But there are thousands of people, especially in India, who can do all the physical exercises most correctly. But God-realisation is still a far cry for them. If it were only by practising physical exercises that one could realise God, then everybody would have done it by now. These are like kindergarten courses. If one wants to study in kindergarten, one can. But if one wants to skip that course, one can easily do so.

Spirituality, which is true Yoga, demands concentration, meditation and contemplation. These three steps only are of paramount importance. As far as we all know, the Christ did not practise physical postures. Lord Krishna did not do it. Lord Buddha did not do it. But all of them did realise God and become one with God on the strength of their prayer, meditation and contemplation. They did not practise hatha yoga, but they did pray, they did meditate, and on the strength of their prayer and meditation they became one with the transcendental Consciousness and the universal Reality of the Supreme.

Interviewer: So Yoga really means union with God?
Sri Chinmoy: Conscious union with God.
Interviewer: God is within each one of us?
Sri Chinmoy: God has always been within each one of us. Each individual has to realise God according to his inner capacity. And each individual can choose to accept the aspect of God that pleases him most. Somebody may like God's personal aspect, as a most luminous Being, while another person may like the impersonal aspect: God as infinite Energy. Again, somebody else will be pleased only if the God he realises is a God beyond his imagination.

God is both personal and impersonal. God will come to each individual according to that individual's choice, to please him in his own way. If you care for the impersonal aspect, God will come to you as the impersonal Existence. If I care for God in His personal aspect, then He will come to me as a personal Being.

101. Interviewer: Now, for the many listeners who are living in this county of Kent in England, how can your spirituality, your teachings, help them?

Sri Chinmoy: As you know, there are two lives: the inner life and the outer life. The inner life is the seed, and the outer life is the plant. If we sow the seed, then only will it germinate and grow into a plant. So before we go to work, before we enter into the hustle and bustle of the world, we should pray and meditate for a few minutes in order to inundate our inner life with peace, light and bliss. Then we can enter into the battlefield of outer life with inner strength, inner courage and inner light. When we do this, we see that there is no difficulty, no insurmountable problem, in the outer world. First we must have inner courage, inner strength, inner peace, light and bliss. Then we can regulate our lives most satisfactorily.

Interviewer: Mrs Plumbly, what can interested people from here do who are listening to us now? Can they write to you at the London Centre?

Mrs Plumbly: Yes, they can write to me at the London Centre for literature or come talk to us in London. The address of the Sri Chinmoy London Centre is 31 Niagara Avenue, Ealing, London W5, England.

102. Interviewer: Thank you. Master, in addition you seem to have done many things. You paint, you write, you compose and play music.

Sri Chinmoy: Yes, right from my childhood I have been composing songs and poems, and I have written considerably. Over two hundred and fifty books I have completed. I have also done thousands of paintings. All this I do with one view, one purpose: to share with aspirants all over the world my aspiration and my realisation. One individual may be inspired by a particular painting or a particular song or a particular poem. Another individual may like another painting, another song, another poem. At the same time, I wish to say that I will remain an eternal seeker. While seeking ever higher Truth and Light, by the Grace of the Supreme, I am able to express my aspiration in various ways. I am trying to share with other seekers my own aspiration in various forms.

103. Interviewer: I notice, too, that you were a decathlon champion in your youth, that you were a fine athlete.

Sri Chinmoy: I was a very good sprinter. Now I am trying to run in the inner world as I once did in the outer world. So I am encouraging my students to run both in the inner world and the outer world. When we run in the inner world, we realise our divinity, and when we run in the outer world, we manifest our divinity. First we realise, then we manifest. These two worlds, the inner and the outer, must go side by side. This is our acceptance of life. When we pray and meditate, we go up high, higher, highest. Then, when we serve humanity, we come down and share with humanity whatever we got at the top of the tree.

104. Interviewer: Now we are going to end this morning's "Reflections". I want to read out one poem you have written, called "The

Absolute". And while I read it we will hear the music of Yehudi Menuhin and Ravi Shankar again. But before we end, I would like to go around the table and ask each of you for one very short sentence about what life really means to you now.

Ms Siegerman: For me, the meaning of life is to know what one really is, to discover one's inner life, which is the soul, the representative of God in the human body. And when we find the soul, then our lives find purpose, meaning, joy and fulfilment.

Mrs Plumbly: It means development and progress, spiritual progress.

Interviewer: Something which is so lacking in many people's lives.

Mr Orsell: For me it has taken me from sadness and frustration to joy. I think joy, divine joy, is what life really means to me.

Interviewer: Master, for once you are not going to have the final word. But, in a way, you *will* have the final word, because I am going to read your poem. This is a poem by Sri Chinmoy, called "The Absolute".

105. The Absolute

> No mind, no form, I only exist:
> Now ceased all will and thought.
> The final end of Nature's dance,
> I am It whom I have sought.
> A realm of Bliss bare, ultimate;
> Beyond both knower and known:
> A rest immense I enjoy at last;
> I face the One alone.

I have crossed the secret ways of life,
I have become the Goal.
The Truth immutable is revealed:
I am the way, the God-Soul.
My spirit aware of all the heights,
I am mute in the core of the Sun.
I barter nothing with time and deeds;
My cosmic play is done.

II — Talks

106. Confidence

Dear friends, dear brothers and sisters, dear seekers, I wish to give a short talk on confidence. Here we are in Cambridge. Cambridge immediately awakens confidence in us. What we call confidence in the outer world is nothing short of assurance in the inner world. Therefore, I bow to the confidence and the assurance in Cambridge.

Confidence awakens our physical. Confidence energises our vital. Confidence illumines our mind. Confidence purifies our heart. A pure heart, an illumined mind, an energetic and dynamic vital and a wakeful body can and will manifest the divine realities here on earth.

Confidence is a divine revelation of our inner assurance. There is an unseen reality within us, a divine Pilot, an Inner Pilot who moulds and shapes our lives. When we hear the message of the Inner Pilot, in our outer life we feel confidence. Confidence is an outer gift from above, whereas assurance is an inner gift from above. Confidence is self-awareness. We want to be aware of ourselves. We want to know what our source is, where we came from, what we are doing here on earth. We want to know our respective roles in this cosmic Game, this *Lila*. Our confidence brings to the fore the inner vision, the reality that we are aiming at, that we want to grow into.

Confidence is not a display of our egocentric life. Confidence is a divine force. Ego binds us, blinds us. Ego offers us the message of separativity and self-enjoyment. Confidence, on the other hand, wants to express its universal oneness. It is for all; it is for the Infinite, the Vast. Confidence cannot be satisfied all by itself. It wants to grow into the Universal Light and Transcendental Height.

When we have confidence in ourselves, we realise the ultimate Truth and Light, the Absolute Supreme. When God has confidence in us, He makes us not only His perfect instruments, but conscious representatives of His Divinity, His Reality, His Infinity, His Eternity and His Immortality on earth. With our confidence in God, we go up and reach His Transcendental Height. With God's Confidence in us, God comes down and makes us His Infinity, His Eternity, His Immortality. And this is not the end of His Game. Then He wants us to manifest what we have become.

Confidence is introduction. Confidence introduces our earthly reality to the divine Reality. And the divine Reality introduces its wealth — infinite Peace, Light and Bliss — to us when we are confident.

Life is either meaningful or meaningless. For those who do not seek, life is meaningless, a barren desert. For seekers, at every moment life is meaningful and fruitful; life has a purpose, a meaning, a reality and an ultimate Goal. What brings us the message of the ultimate Goal, what brings us the reality of the inner world, the more illumining, more fulfilling higher world?

It is our confidence. With our confidence-light, we dig deep within; and while digging within we cultivate the bumper-crop of realisation, liberation and perfection.

An unaspiring person talks to himself and talks to the world. But he cannot talk to the Ultimate Reality. It is only a man of confidence, inner confidence, divine confidence, supreme confidence who can talk to the Highest Reality: the Transcendental Vision and the Universal Reality.

One portion of divinity comes down into the world and another remains above. The one that remains above is known as the Father-Reality and the one that comes down is known as the Son-Reality. Again, there comes a time when the two realities become inseparably one and tell the world of their oneness. Jesus Christ, the Saviour, announced, "I and my Father are one." His confidence-light he brought down into the world; and it was his confidence-light that uttered, "I and my Father are one." When divinity enters into humanity and illumines humanity, at that time humanity claims divinity as its very own.

Confidence is oneness with the Beyond, the oneness of earth-life with Heaven-life. Where God is, confidence is bound to be. God has given us the secret key to open up His Heart's Door and that secret key is confidence. We pray, we meditate, only to cultivate one divine quality and that one divine quality is confidence. Confidence shows us the way to go ahead, the way to dive deep within, the way to fly above. Confidence is the pioneer that constantly leads us, guides us, beckons us to the ultimate Source.

Each individual has teeming questions: "Who am I? Where do I come from? What is my ultimate goal?" All the questions of our inner and outer life can be answered by one solitary thing: confidence. If we have confidence, then we can explore the inner world. If we have confidence, then we can explore the outer world.

Here we are all seekers. We want to know the reality that we eternally are and that we are going to offer to the world at large. And for that what we need is perfection, self-perfection. It is only in self-perfection that we can please the Inner Pilot, the Supreme Pilot, the world around us, the world within us. This perfection is our constant confidence in ourselves and in our Inner Pilot.

Again, this confidence has a Source. Its Source is God's Compassion-Light and Compassion-Delight. God grants us Light in boundless measure at our journey's start. And it is He, the Supreme, the Eternal Pilot, who grants us eternal, boundless Delight. Light energises us. Light leads us, guides us to our ultimate destination, where we see the transformation of Light into Delight. Delight fulfils us. Delight immortalises us.

We aspire to become good, to become loving, to become devoted, to become useful to the world at large. But this aspiration also needs something from us. It is confidence that aspiration expects from each seeker. If the seeker is wanting in confidence, then his aspiration can never be regular, it can never be spontaneous, it can never be continuous. But if inside his aspiration confidence looms large, then he walks along a sunlit road to his destined goal.

A child has confidence in his parents. He feels that his parents know everything, have everything and are everything for him. Similarly, a seeker has all confidence in his Inner Pilot, the Supreme, who is guiding his destiny, his life, his aspiration, his realisation, his reality to the ultimate Goal.

Each day we are granted by the Author of all good, out of His infinite Bounty, confidence both in our inner life and in our outer life. But if we use our physical mind — our earth-bound, sophisticated, obscure, unlit, unaspiring, intellectual mind — to search, we may not feel God's Confidence-Light. For the earth-bound mind feels that it is complete in itself; it does not need any reality other than its own existence.

But the heart constantly feels that it can house something more, that it can see something more, that it can grow into something more, that it has something more to offer to the world at large. The heart has the eagerness to receive and to achieve from the world within and from the world without. The heart has a constant inner thirst to be universal, to be transcendental. Therefore, the heart always looks within and around to grasp and invoke the infinite Realities that abide in God's entire Creation. The heart comes to realise that there is only one way to achieve and grow into these infinite Realities and that is the way of self-giving. And what is self-giving today, tomorrow that very thing is God-becoming. So, on the strength of self-giving, our aspiring heart becomes both universal and transcendental. And this self-giving heart has a source of its own and that source is confidence. Confidence also has its source. Its source is God's Compassion, God's infinite, unconditional, immortal Compassion in man, for man.

107. Human teachers and divine teachers

Man has many teachers. A child comes into existence. His first and foremost teacher is his mother. The mother teaches the child everything with her boundless affection, boundless love and boundless concern. The child responds with a smile. A child learns everything from his mother with a soulful smile. Then the mother teaches the child to recognise the father. The father becomes the child's second teacher. He also offers the child affection, love and concern in boundless measure. The mother offers everything to the child with a tremendous feeling of oneness, whereas the father does everything for the child with a feeling of vastness. Oneness is there, no doubt, but vastness is the lesson that the child learns from the father.

God has granted each individual being a small house and a big house. Both houses are of equal importance. The mother teaches the child everything that the small house has to offer: affection, love, concern, sweetness and oneness. The mother offers the message of the happy family. The father teaches something more. He offers the message of a larger family: a few friends and the outside world.

Two teachers are teaching us two things which are of equal value and equal importance. Just because the child is the student, he has to learn. In later years he will learn many subjects from many teachers. When the child goes to school, he will have a teacher for history, geography, science, mathematics; for everything he will have a teacher. Each teacher teaches the student a different thing. Since the student is young, he may not know what his future career will be. So, the best thing is for him to know everything to some extent. Then later on, he can make a choice. It is not that the teacher wishes the student to be a jack of all trades and master of none. No! The teacher wants the student to know a little bit about everything, so that in the future he can easily decide what career he wants. A student spends a few years in high school and then he goes to college. There the professors offer him a higher type of knowledge. Then, when he goes on to the university, he takes one or two subjects in order to get his Master's degree or Ph.D. At that time his future career begins to blossom. The student eventually gets his diploma and becomes a man of knowledge. All these years may bring what he has worked for: satisfaction, a higher satisfaction, a deeper, more illumining and more fulfilling satisfaction.

As a child he learned the alphabet and studied a few books. When he went to college he studied a higher and more illumining knowledge. Then he came to the university to get the vast ocean of knowledge. But in spite of that, he does not have satisfaction. He feels that there are still many things he does not know. At one time he thought that if he had the highest degree, he would be by far the best, and everybody would be under him. But now he sees that there are others who are as good as he is, or even better than he. So his pride is smashed and he feels that in this world of competition there can be no joy. He has got earth-knowledge, he has become an authority on a particular subject, but he feels that there are others who know more than he. He realises that as long as he remains in the world of desires, trying to compete with others and defeat others, as long as he feels the necessity in his heart to outdo others or lord it over others, then there will be no happiness. Happiness does not lie in mental achievements, in his outer achievements. Happiness lies only in inner achievements. The human teachers who have taught him his earthly lessons have played their role. Now he wants to go to a spiritual Master who has studied inner subjects and has a free access to inner life, inner wisdom. He feels that if he studies inner subjects, then he will have peace of mind, abiding joy and a sense of satisfaction.

On the mental plane he has achieved something, but on the spiritual plane, the inner plane, the plane that has abiding joy and satisfaction, he is a veritable beggar. So he comes to a spiritual Master to have inner lessons and study inner subjects. The spiritual Master tells him that there are quite a few inner subjects, but there are two main subjects he has to learn if he really wants to achieve satisfaction from life, if he really wants to be successful in a divine sense. These two subjects are prayer and meditation. If he studies prayer and meditation and learns them well, then he will definitely have joy and satisfaction in his life.

The spiritual Master says to the student, "If you want to learn how to pray, then you have to become simple, you have to become sincere, you have to become humble. Your prayers will be answered only when you have become totally simple, utterly sincere and unmistakably humble." So the student brings to the fore simplicity, sincerity and humility from within, and he prays. When he prays, he feels that his whole inner being, his whole life, is being elevated to a higher plane of consciousness. He is praying for peace, light and bliss, for illumination and perfection. His prayer itself is giving him joy. Even if he does not receive from above an iota of peace, light or bliss, he does not mind; for he gets tremendous satisfaction from prayer itself. Of course, if he is going to be a true seeker of the highest order, then only is it possible for him to pray unconditionally. If not, he will pray for peace, light and bliss conditionally. That is to say, he will be simple, he will be sincere, he will be humble and on the strength of his simplicity, sincerity and humility, he will expect to be rewarded.

But if he prays unconditionally, at that time he prays only for the fulfilment of God's Will.

The other subject the student has to learn is meditation. Here the teacher tells the student that he has to make his heart as pure as possible; he has to become purity itself. The teacher says, "Simplicity, sincerity and humility are needed, but if you want to be successful in meditation, you also need something else, and that is purity. A pure heart is of paramount importance. If there is impurity either in your physical consciousness, your vital consciousness or your mind, then you will not be able to study this subject well. If you lack purity, your mind will never be able to achieve the divine vastness and enter into Delight, Ecstasy and Light. So purity is of paramount importance: purity in thought, purity in deed, purity in the result of each action, purity at the journey's start and purity at the journey's close."

What is purity? Purity is our constant love of oneness, within and without. To love the entire world as one's own, to feel inseparable oneness with the rest of the world: this is purity. Each time the seeker breathes in, he must feel that his entire being is purified, that he has drawn cosmic energy to purify his whole body, vital, mind and heart. And when he breathes out, he has to feel that all the impurity from his body, vital, mind and heart he has thrown into the Universal Consciousness. He purifies and empties his system, and then brings down Peace, Light and Bliss in infinite measure so that he can become a true instrument of God.

The teacher tells the student, "If you want to become extremely successful, if you want to become an expert in the subject of meditation, then you should learn something else, and that is concentration. You have to concentrate on only one thing: the positive side of life, not the negative side of life. Concentrate on the reality that creates, not the reality that destroys. You have to feel the necessity of running towards your goal as swiftly as possible. You can reach the goal by walking and again by flying. It is you who have to make the decision. If your aim is to run the fastest towards your goal, then you have to concentrate. While concentrating, you are unburdening your many thoughts, your many ideas, your worldly activities; the incidents that are inside your mind you have to cast aside. In this way you have to unburden yourself. Concentration has to be like an arrow aimed at the target. At every moment you have to run the fastest, like a deer. You must not carry any burden: no thoughts, no worldly ideas. Only then can you run the fastest."

So the student devotedly listens to the spiritual Master, and anything that has to be cast aside, he casts aside. He only concentrates on the positive side of life, and he does make considerable progress. Simplicity is the first step to the goal. When the student becomes sincere, he comes to the second step; and when he becomes humble, he is at the third step. Then, if he can cultivate purity, that is the fourth step. At that time, inside his purity, simplicity, sincerity and humility, he will see something else: love. He has love for simplicity and his love for simplicity is giving him joy. He has love for sincerity and his love for sincerity is giving him joy. He has love for humility and his love for humility is giving him joy. He has love for purity and his love for purity is giving him joy. Everything that he has and is embodies love. This love he offers to the subject that he is studying: meditation.

When he meditates soulfully, on the strength of his simplicity, sincerity, humility and purity, the student feels that this world belongs not only to God, but to him as well. He feels that this world, God's creation, is not only *for* him but also *of* him. His sublime meditation makes him feel that God the Creator and he the creation are inseparable. They complete God's cosmic Vision, cosmic Game. The Creator without the creation remains unfulfilled; the creation without the Creator remains unrealised. So the Creator needs the creation for His manifestation, for His fulfilment, and the creation needs the Creator for its ultimate, transcendental, absolute realisation.

The student has learned how to pray, how to concentrate and how to meditate. Then the teacher says, "Are you getting joy in what you are doing?"

The student says, "Definitely I am getting joy. From my prayer I am getting joy, from my meditation I am getting joy, from my concentration I am getting joy."

Then the teacher says, "Now I wish to teach you another subject. It is the most important subject. From this subject you will get utmost joy, ever-transcending joy. Here the joy is limitless and, at the same time, it is transcending its own Infinity. This subject is called contemplation."

Here the student becomes the divine lover and God is the supreme Beloved. In each second of his earthly life, the seeker feels he is inundated with his Beloved's Presence. He sees a continuous growth of his receptivity. In each act, in each thought of his, in everything that he has, in everything that he does and everything that he has become, he feels the glowing Presence of his Beloved in the inmost recesses of his heart.

When one runs the fastest with concentration, one gets joy. When one goes up high, higher, highest with prayer, one gets joy. When one enjoys vastness from his meditation, one gets joy, but this joy may not be and cannot be constant. But when the student becomes the divine lover and at every moment sees and feels the Presence of his supreme Beloved, his Beloved Supreme, then his joy is constant and, at the same time, infinite and ever-transcending.

Now the teacher says to the student, "My child, I have taught you everything that I have learned from my teacher."

The student asks, "Do you have a teacher?"

The Master replies, "Yes, my teacher is God Himself. You may call me a teacher, but to be absolutely honest with you, I am not a teacher; I am only a messenger. I carried God's messages to you. The lessons that you have learned from me are nothing but messages that I received from God. And the inner cry that you have shown me, the hunger, the thirst, the eagerness that you have shown me, are nothing but your messages. These messages I have taken to my Teacher, who is the only Teacher. I am the messenger, common messenger. I have taken your hunger to Him and from Him I have brought His feast for you. You gave me what you had, your hunger; and He gave me what He had, His Food, Nectar, for you. Now I want you to go to my teacher who is also your Teacher, everybody's Teacher, and in silence give Him your infinite love and concern."

Then the spiritual Master takes the student to God. At that time God says to the student, "What do you want from Me? Do you want to serve Me?"

The student says, "I want to serve You."

Then God says, "Do I have to give you something in return?"

At that time the student may say, "In return I expect a smile from You, which is my salary. I will do everything that You want me to do, but I shall be grateful if You give me a smile, which will be my fee." If this is what the student says, then the Teacher, the Supreme Teacher, will grant it. But the student may say something else to God. He may say, "I will do everything that You want me to do, and I don't expect anything from You, no smile, no love, no concern, nothing. Only I want to please You in Your own Way, unconditionally and cheerfully. That is my goal."

If this is the promise that the student can make to the real Teacher, the only Teacher, God, then God says to him, "My child, you are My most perfect instrument. I shall be able to manifest in and through you on earth, for it is you who will carry me into the world and manifest Me fully on earth."

One seeker wanted to serve God conditionally. God said to him, "You have abundant Peace, Light and Bliss. You have also made tremendous progress. Therefore, undoubtedly, you are a very great seeker, and you will be My instrument." But the unconditional seeker is something more. This seeker God makes His Representative. To the one seeker God says, "You are My instrument and you will fulfil Me according to the capacity that you have." But to the other seeker God says, "You are a Representative of Mine, who will manifest Me according to My Will, according to My own Capacity, which is unlimited."

So the student either becomes a Representative of the Absolute Supreme, absolutely one with His Will, on the strength of his unconditional love, unconditional devotion and unconditional surrender; or the seeker expects a smile, recognition, as a salary for his work. So it is up to the student to make the choice. Here we are all seekers, all sincere seekers. We have started our journey right from our childhood. Our mother was our teacher, our father was our teacher, our kindergarten teacher and our college professors were our teachers. These were all our human teachers. Now we are knocking at God's Door and asking Him to accept us as His students. This is how we end our journey. But this end is not the real end, for God is endless in every way. When we reach our first goal, then He places before us a second goal, a higher goal. Each moment today's goal becomes the starting point for tomorrow's higher goal. At every moment God is taking us, carrying us with Him, to His own ever-transcending Vision and ever-transcending Reality.

III — Ipswich television interview

108. Interviewer: Yoga is becoming highly respectable. One Guru at least has been welcomed in the corridors of power. He's Guru Sri Chinmoy, who's Guru to the United Nations Meditation Group in New York. Sri Chinmoy was taking a break from his UN work today and enjoying a visit to Ipswich. For six years now, Sri Chinmoy has been Guru at the United Nations in New York, ministering to the spiritual needs of a growing number of the UN's official staff. The Indian-born teacher and philosopher sees meditation as essential to world unity and peace, a view shared by his UN disciples, who see meditation as "Our Hope for Mankind".

Today his English disciples meditated with their Master in a room that was heavy with the scent of flowers and incense.

Afterwards, I talked with Sri Chinmoy about his role at the UN.

Sri Chinmoy: At the United Nations they are giving me the opportunity to be of service to them. I am not a teacher; I am a server. There is a great difference between a teacher and a server. I serve the United Nations according to the capacity that the Supreme has granted me, and there are people who are kind enough to accept my service.

109. Interviewer: Why does there seem to be an increase in interest in what meditation can do for mankind? I notice that on the UN Meditation Group book here, they call meditation "Our Hope for Mankind".

Sri Chinmoy: United Nations members have already tried other ways and have not been successful. So now some of them are trying this way, the inner way. The outer way they have tried; through politics and various outer means they have tried to bring about peace. But, unfortunately, they have not succeeded. So now they are trying to cultivate the inner way.

110. Interviewer: When you talk about peace are you talking about individual peace of mind or world peace?

Sri Chinmoy: I am talking about both: individual peace of mind and also world peace. The world is composed of you and I, he and she. So if you have peace of mind, I have peace of mind and he has peace of mind, then automatically it becomes universal peace.

111. Interviewer: So you think that an increased awareness of meditation and interest in meditation in lots of nations throughout the world brings hope for world peace and unity?

Sri Chinmoy: That is the only way, I feel. When a nation cares for peace, then another nation joins it and also cares for peace. In this way all the nations eventually will care for peace. At that time there cannot be any war or any ill feeling among nations.

Interviewer: Thank you, Sri Chinmoy.

IV — Talks

112. Life

Dear seekers, dear friends, dear brothers and sisters, I wish to give a short talk on the subject of life. This subject is at once most familiar to us and most significant to us. Each individual can claim to be an authority on this subject. So I am grateful to you for having given me the opportunity to speak on this subject and be of service to you this evening.

There can be a philosophical approach to life, there can be a religious approach to life, there can be a spiritual approach to life and finally there can be God's approach to life. I wish to discuss each of these approaches from the spiritual point of view.

Philosophy is of two types. One is the outer philosophy; the other is the inner philosophy. The outer philosophy deals with some philosophical books and remains exclusively in the mental world. The inner philosophy deals with light and divinity, and with Heaven and earth. According to Indian tradition, philosophy itself is vision, for the Sanskrit word for philosophy is *darshan*, which means vision. We envision the inner world that is trying to come forward and manifest itself in our outer life. This inner world is the world of Peace, Light and Bliss. The outer world that we live in is full of conflicts and negativity and destructive forces. So we pray and meditate to bring to the fore the inner world and replace the outer world with it. But from the strict spiritual point of view, it is not a replacement but a transformation. The outer world is not replaced. It is transformed and illumined by the light of the inner world.

Now, let us deal with the religious approach to life. Usually there are two main religious approaches to life. One is the occidental approach; the other is the oriental approach. Eastern religion, especially the religion of the hoary past, tells us that we need only one thing: liberation. Western religion, mainly the Christian religion, teaches us the message of salvation: salvation from sin. In the East, we learn how to liberate ourselves from the finite consciousness and enter into the infinite Consciousness. In the West, we learn how to raise ourselves from the sin-reality and enter into Heaven to enjoy our salvation-light. Western religion tells us that our body, vital, mind and everything that we have is impure. In order to purify the body, vital and mind, what we need is constant prayer. When we sincerely and soulfully pray, our Heavenly Father listens to our prayer and grants us salvation. In the East, since our goal is to achieve liberation from the limited body, limited vital, limited mind, we have to practise meditation, for liberation we can achieve only through proper meditation.

What is meditation? Meditation is our conscious awareness of something vast and infinite within us. Meditation grants us Peace, Light and Bliss. With this Peace, Light and Bliss, we enter into our body, vital and mind and expand and transform them into vastness. Prayer and meditation are two approaches that lead to the same goal. This goal is called perfection.

In the spiritual approach to life, we have to know that there is a true approach and a false approach. If it is a false approach, then we want to give up life. If it is a real approach, a divine approach, then our spirituality teaches how to accept life and be fulfilled in life. If the approach is not real, we want to leave aside the members of our family, we want to discard society and the world itself. We say that the world is full of suffering, that it is all illusion; therefore, we want to leave the world. But the real approach is totally different. In this approach we accept life as such and we love life. We know that the world we live in is far from perfection, but if we give up life, if we shun life, we know that the world will always remain imperfect. Therefore, we feel it is our duty to accept life, love life and transform life.

How do we transform life? We transform life with our inner cry. There is an outer cry and also there is an inner cry. When we cry outwardly, we cry for name and fame and material prosperity. When we cry inwardly, we cry for divine Love, divine Peace and divine Light. When we get Peace, Love and Light from above, we start transforming the world around us.

Finally, I wish to deal with God's Vision-approach to our life. There is no difference between God's Vision-approach and God's Reality-approach to life. We feel that vision is one thing and reality is something else, that vision is at one place and reality is at another place. I am sitting here and you are facing me. You are the reality and I am the vision. We are not sitting together and we are not inside one another; therefore, you as reality and I as vision are two totally different things.

But this experience is only on the physical plane. On the inner plane, we get a totally different experience. There we see God's Vision and God's Reality together; there we see God's Silence and God's Sound together. For us, God the Creator and God the creation are two different things. But when we pray and meditate, we see that there is no difference between the two; both are part and parcel of God the Infinite, God the Eternal and God the Immortal.

Our physical mind tries to understand what God is on earth and what God is in Heaven. For this reason, we have created two separate existences for the reality and the vision. The mind cannot truly understand or even conceive of two things at the same time. One thought must follow another. We cannot at the same time observe two things with the same kind of concentration; one is bound to get more attention than the other. But when we pray and meditate, not only two things, but countless things we see simultaneously. Also, our focus of concentration will be equally distributed. And what are these countless things we see? They are nothing but God the creation. It is through our prayer and meditation that God the Creator makes us feel that His creation and He Himself are absolutely one. We cry inwardly to go up and be with our Heavenly Father and then He gives us a smile and sends us back to do His work here on earth in His Way.

113. Two instruments: impurity and purity

Two instruments: impurity and purity. Here we are all seekers, seekers of the highest Transcendental Truth. In our life of aspiration and dedication, purity and impurity play two significant roles: purity in a positive way and impurity in a negative way.

Impurity tells us, "I am of myself and I am for myself. Although I am limited, I want to expand myself, I want to cover the length and breadth of the world." This is what impurity tells us.

Purity tells us, "I am of God's infinite Beauty and I am for God's constant Satisfaction." This is what we learn from purity. Its source is God and at every moment it wants to please God in God's own Way.

Impurity is nothing short of division, world-division and

self-division. But purity is all the time playing the role of creation, new creativity; and this new creativity is founded upon conscious oneness with the world at large.

Impurity is an inner disease and a contagious disease. Consciously and unconsciously the seeker is attacked by this disease. If a seeker even unconsciously mixes with impure human beings, then his consciousness is lowered considerably. If a seeker unconsciously walks along a road that an impure person has just travelled, then he is affected. If he sits at the foot of a tree where an impure person has previously sat, then he becomes a victim to impure thoughts, although he cannot account for them.

Similarly, if a seeker walks along a road that a spiritual person has just travelled, if a seeker sits at the foot of a tree where a spiritual person has sat a few minutes earlier, then he gets good thoughts, divine thoughts, illumining thoughts and fulfilling thoughts.

Impurity plays the role of a thief. It enters into the physical proper and from there it tries to steal a few divine things that the physical embodies. Then it enters into the vital proper and steals away a few divine things from the vital. Then it enters into the mind proper and steals a few significant things, precious things from the mind.

The soul, which is the eldest and wisest member of the family, looks at the body, the physical, and feels sad over the deplorable condition of the body. This body does not know what has actually happened; the body does not know that a part of its reality has been stolen, but the soul knows. Then the soul looks at the vital and feels miserable over the deplorable condition of the vital. Then the soul looks at the mind and again feels very sad. The soul looks at all the younger members of its family and feels sorry that impurity, the thief, has stolen so many of their divine qualities. The soul searches for the thief and at long last it discovers the thief in the tiny cave of the mind. In spite of having divine power, the soul pleads with the impurity-thief to change its ways. It tells impurity that only if it changes its life and grows into purity will it have satisfaction. The thief has robbed the physical, vital and mind of quite a few spiritual qualities, but still it is not satisfied: whereas if the thief is illumined and transformed into purity, then it will have abiding satisfaction. The soul convinces impurity and impurity gives way to purity slowly, steadily and unerringly. Yesterday's impurity grows into purity through the illumining light of the soul.

The seeker continues to walk along the road of Eternity with patience, perseverance and devoted service. But after a few years it may happen that another attack of impurity will assail the human mind. Impurity offers the message that temptation is everything; there is nothing save and except temptation. "Live in the world of temptation and then you will have satisfaction." If the seeker enters into the world of temptation, he discovers frustration; and inside frustration what looms large is destruction. Yesterday impurity was astounding temptation. Today it is frustrating frustration. Tomorrow it becomes petrified destruction. This is what impurity teaches us.

Purity teaches us something else. Yesterday purity taught us how to pray soulfully. Today purity teaches us how to meditate with a calm, quiet, vacant and tranquil mind. Tomorrow purity will teach us how to contemplate soulfully and unconditionally. What is prayer? Prayer is something that lifts us high, higher, highest, to where we can see face to face our highest Reality, God. With prayer we reach the Highest and there we see our Beloved Supreme. When we meditate, our Beloved Supreme descends and stands right in front of us. When we pray, God plays the role of a magnet; He pulls us up to His Height. And when we meditate, we play the role of a magnet; we pull God down to our height, to our consciousness. Then, when we contemplate, we see that wherever God is, we are there also. We see that we are in the same play; we are playing the cosmic game of oneness. In this game, this moment God is playing the role of the Beloved Supreme and we are playing the role of the divine lover, the supreme lover; the next moment God changes roles and makes us, out of His infinite Bounty, the Supreme Beloved while He plays the role of the Supreme Lover. This is what contemplation is: oneness inseparable, oneness at the same height, which God grants us out of His infinite Compassion.

The Scriptures teach us the value of purity; the spiritual Masters teach us the value of purity. Now, what is purity, after all? Purity is our sincerity and our willingness. A sincere heart embodies purity to a great extent. If the sincere heart goes one step ahead with willingness, then it becomes all purity. A man may commit Himalayan blunders; therefore he falls down and begins crawling. Then he confesses that he has made a mistake. But just by confessing his mistake, he cannot rectify it. Just because he has confessed, he is infinitely better than one who has made countless mistakes, serious mistakes, but who is unwilling to confess. Sincerity is something most valuable; it gives him the added divine energy to enable him to stand up. Then comes the willingness to walk ahead, to walk forward. He may be frightened to death. He may think that if he walks forward he will again fall down; he will again be tempted and suffer defeat, so the best thing is not to stand up at all. At this point, he is making a serious blunder. He has to know that, in spite of making repeated mistakes, there is a way to reach his destination. And, for that, he has to grow inside him the willingness, the divine willingness to move forward constantly, consciously, devotedly and unconditionally, so that at God's choice Hour he can reach the Golden Shore of the Beyond.

When sincerity and willingness go together, the aspiring heart automatically becomes pure. Our heart that wants to aspire, that wants to dedicate itself to a supreme cause, is bound to be inundated with purity when there is conscious and constant sincerity and spontaneous, conscious and constant willingness to grow into the absolute Reality. This absolute Reality we eternally are, but unfortunately we are oblivious of the Reality. Through constant practice, constant awareness and constant self-giving, we can become fully aware of the Highest Reality which we inwardly, eternally are. But if we remain in the mind — the doubting mind, the suspicious mind, the mind that belittles others — then God-discovery will always remain a far cry.

Purity's role is unique: no purity, no God-discovery. If the heart and the entire existence become purity's flood, then God-realisation can never remain a far cry. A pure heart can and does claim God as its very own. Within easy reach of the purity-heart is God with His infinite Compassion, with His infinite Love, with His infinite Reality.

V — Questions and answers

114. Question: Can you explain what is the meaning of the word AUM?

Sri Chinmoy: AUM is a Sanskrit word. It is the combination of three letters: A, U and M. A stands for God the Creator, U stands for God the Preserver and M stands for God the Transformer. God creates us, then He preserves us and then, if something goes wrong, He transforms it in order to keep it perfect. AUM is the mother of all Indian mantras. All the mantras have a source and AUM is the source of all the mantras.

115. Question: I am a Christian, and although I pray, I never get any higher than I am now. How can I start to do the things that you are talking about? What is the first step to take in order to learn how to meditate?

Sri Chinmoy: If you could learn how to concentrate on only one thing, that would be very good. When you are concentrating, if many thoughts come to your mind, you will discard them. When you concentrate, there should not be anything inside your mind. When it is possible for you to concentrate only on the thing that you want to, then you are ready for real meditation. As I said before, if you can lead a simple life, a sincere life, a humble life and a pure life, then it will help you considerably in your meditation. And if you read spiritual books, that will also help you. If you listen to the talks of spiritual Masters, if you mix with spiritual people, if you listen to spiritual music, all this will help. There are so many ways that you can get benefit.

116. Question: Thank you very much for your message. Would you be so kind as to give us further explanation about concentration and meditation?

Sri Chinmoy: When we concentrate, we focus all our attention on a particular object or subject. Concentration is one-pointed attention, focusing on the tiniest particle. When we concentrate, we do not have the need to have any thought inside the mind. We want to run the fastest, like a deer; we want only to reach our goal. When we meditate, we want to see the vastness, not only inside our mind but also inside our entire being. We meditate in order to feel within ourselves the vastness of the sky, the ocean.

So, we can say that concentration deals with the smallest reality and meditation deals with the largest reality. But both realities are equally important at a particular stage of our evolution. Concentration paves the way for proper meditation. Suppose right now I want to meditate but there are thousands of ideas entering into my mind. How am I going to meditate? If I want to meditate with these thoughts, then I will never get any peace of mind or vastness inside of me. In the spiritual life there are three stages. Concentration is the first stage, then comes meditation and finally, contemplation.

117. Question: Is the spiritual reality involved in other activities? Is it bound to other realities?

Sri Chinmoy: Spiritual reality is not bound by any reality. It is inside all the realities that we see, but it is not bound by any of them. It is like God. God is not bound by anything, but out of His infinite Compassion He is within you, within me, within her, within everybody. God is omnipotent, omnipresent, omniscient; He is under no obligation to do anything for us. But, out of His infinite Bounty, at every moment He is working in and through us on our behalf. Spirituality is God's language; it is an inner language that we learn. Therefore, it is also unlimited, but it works in and through us for our joy and perfection.

118. Question: What is the real meaning of love between man and woman? What is the spiritual significance of marriage?

Sri Chinmoy: There is human love and there is divine love. The human love that exists between a man and a woman is a dance of possession. Each wants to possess the other, but to their astonishment, they see that they are already possessed before they possess each other. If one is possessed by someone, he is at the mercy of that person. When he is possessed, when he is caught, he is terribly frustrated. Today's possession becomes tomorrow's frustration. And, the day after tomorrow, frustration becomes total destruction. This is what we see and know as human marriage.

But there is also something known as divine marriage. Here it is not possession, but oneness. On the strength of our oneness we try to illumine and liberate others. Lo and behold, before we illumine and liberate others, we find that others have illumined and liberated us. Divine love is all-giving; here there is no demand. In divine love, we make constant sacrifice and we see that our heart and our whole vision is enlarged.

God Himself was one in the beginning. Then He became many in order to divinely and supremely enjoy Himself. When an ordinary human being enjoys, he enjoys the pleasure-life, lower vital life, emotional life. But when a God-lover enjoys, he enjoys God's Love, God's Light, God's Bliss; and this Joy, Love, Peace and Bliss he sees inside others.

When it is a divine marriage, one head becomes two heads, two hands become four hands. Everything is doubled; our capacity automatically increases. If one has increased everything and walks positively towards the goal, naturally he will run the fastest. But if there is a constant battle going on between husband and wife, if one wants to run the fastest and the other does not, then one will be a heavy burden on the other's shoulders.

How can one run the fastest when one is carrying something very heavy that is unwilling to reach the destination?

So, it is the individual who has to make the decision whether he is going to marry and whether it is to be a divine marriage. If it is a human marriage, then it will be all frustration. If it is a divine marriage, it will be all illumination. Divine marriage is oneness. Oneness is perfection and perfection is complete satisfaction. It is satisfaction that both man and God need. God gets satisfaction by manifesting Himself through His creation, through us. We get satisfaction by climbing up high, higher, highest, to the highest plane of consciousness. We climb up for our satisfaction in and through God, and God climbs down in and through us for His Manifestation, His own Satisfaction, which is in and through us. The act of climbing up and the act of climbing down are one, inseparably one.

MY ROSE PETALS

NOTES TO MY ROSE PETALS PART 7

95-105. Medway Radio, Chatham, Kent, England, 20 June 1976.
99. Paragraph 8. Mrs Mary Plumbly's spiritual name is Sushumna. Her daughter, Swarnodaya, was one of the first British disciples of Sri Chinmoy, having joined the Sri Chinmoy Centre in New York. Her mother Sushumna joined shortly after, and later became the first London Centre leader.
105. From *My Flute*.
106. Cambridge University, Cambridge, England, 21 June 1976.
107. Ipswich, England, 21 June 1976.
107-111. ITV, Ipswich, England, 21 June 1976.
112. ABF Huset, Stockholm, Sweden, 22 June 1976.
113. Indian Cultural Society, London, England, 6 July 1976.

PART 2

FIFTY FREEDOM-BOATS TO
ONE GOLDEN SHORE

FIFTY FREEDOM-BOATS TO
ONE GOLDEN SHORE

BOOK 1

Part I — Lectures

1. Thought-waves

From the spiritual point of view, each thought carries a special weight in our mind. Each thought has a special signification. In our ordinary life, we all know what a thought is. We create thought. We cherish thought. There is nobody who does not know how to think — do ordinary thinking, that is. If someone does not know how to think, we call him a fool. But if one who has a developed mind chooses to stop thinking, if he has learnt the art of stopping the mind, he makes tremendous progress in the spiritual life. When a thought enters into a seeker's aspiring mind, he has to feel that it is like meeting an enemy on the battlefield. The more one can silence the mind, the sooner one realises the Goal.

The human mind feels that thought is the ultimate power and light. Unfortunately, this is a deplorable mistake. The aspiring heart constantly receives the supreme message from the soul. Only by silencing the mind can one receive this message and reach the highest absolute Supreme.

The Lord Buddha silenced his mind and entered into *Nirvana*, the bliss unfathomable of the Transcendental Height. The Christ opened his heart and embraced all humanity on the strength of his universal oneness with his Father, the ultimate Goal. Either by silencing the mind or by opening the heart, today's man can become tomorrow's God, tomorrow's Divinity. And embodied Divinity soon becomes revealed Immortality.

Desire and aspiration are two simple words, but they embody tremendous power. Aspiration consciously follows the road of light, whereas desire consciously or unconsciously follows the path of darkness. Darkness means satisfaction in limitation. Our desire wants to grab and possess, but before it possesses, it is possessed. While being possessed, while enjoying consciously or unconsciously the role of subjugation and imperfection, desire is to some extent satisfied. At the same time, desire embodies power which very often ends in frustration. And this frustration gives birth to destruction and annihilation.

Each human being has aspiration; each human being embodies aspiration. This aspiration in him builds up the tower of Truth, Light and Bliss. Aspiration is never satisfied with imperfection. It climbs up high, higher, highest. At each moment the mounting flame in us, while climbing towards the highest, illumines the obscure, impure, unaspiring elements of our gross physical. Then finally, he not only realises but also manifests the Kingdom of Heaven in his inner being.

Desire is the product of our thought-waves. Aspiration is the product of our soul's will. The soul's will we can possess and claim as our very own only when we consciously surrender what we have and what we are to the Supreme. What we have is an inner longing for Truth, Light and Bliss. We have to offer this longing unconditionally to the Supreme, our Inner Pilot. What we are is ignorance, unfathomable ignorance. This ignorance, too, we can and must offer to the Supreme consciously, devotedly and unconditionally. But instead of doing this, we wallow in the pleasures of ignorance and, what is worse, we often do it consciously and deliberately.

The desire in us demands that the physical in us rest eternally in the sea of ignorance. The aspiration within us warns us that once we go to sleep we will find it extremely difficult to awaken our consciousness and get up. The realisation in us, our soul's realisation, tells us that we are already fast asleep in the domain of ignorance, and that we have been sleeping there for millennia.

A sincere seeker of the highest transcendental Truth can transform and purify the desire-life with the life of aspiration. In order to do this, he must know what desire has done for him. Desire has offered him a sense of dissatisfaction. Even after his desires are fulfilled, still he is dissatisfied. The seeker sees that in the depth of his desire and in the very fulfilment of his desire there looms a sense of complete dissatisfaction. Why is this so? It is because desire is not the ultimate Truth. Desire cannot offer us the ultimate Truth, which is all-satisfying. But when we follow the path of aspiration, even an iota of Light satisfies us. Although we know perfectly well that an iota of Peace, Light and Bliss cannot quench our eternal inner thirst, each iota of divine Truth, Peace, Light and Bliss carries tremendous satisfaction for us. And gradually, on the strength of our aspiration, each tiny drop of Divinity grows into a vast ocean of Fulfilment.

Aspiration embodies satisfaction. Desire embodies dissatisfaction. Each human being has the right to stay either in the desire-world or in the aspiration-world. Here we are all seekers of the Truth. For us, aspiration is the road. We shall walk joyfully along the road of aspiration. Today the very thing that we call aspiration, tomorrow we shall call realisation. The day after, we shall call the same thing revelation, and the following day we shall call it manifestation, our manifestation of Divinity.

A sincere seeker is blessed with inner vision when he has free access to the Source. He continually and constantly depends on his inner vision. Once he has established his connection with the Source, his life becomes the realisation-message of God, the illumination-message of God, the perfection-message of God. And in the course of time, in either the near or the distant future, in the process of evolution humanity is bound to accept these messages. What is the essence of these messages? Love, love divine, which is the song of universal oneness. If we silence our thought-waves and listen to our heart-waves, we can spread the love-message of the Supreme. We can offer this love-message to the world at large, and we can sing the song universal to kindle the flame of aspiration in all individuals.

We are now conscious of the supreme Tree. We are climbing up the Tree. Eventually we can grow into the cosmic Tree and then we can watch the multifarious leaves, which are our brothers and sisters, grow and unfold. It is we, the seekers of the ultimate Truth, who can feed the inner hunger of these leaves of the supreme Tree.

2. Realisation, revelation and perfection

With your kind permission, I wish to say that this is my fourth visit to Harvard University. In 1969 I spoke on *The Vedanta philosophy*; in 1971, on *The Upanishads: the crown of India's Soul;* last year, on *The glowing consciousness of Vedic Truth;* and now, my fourth talk will be on *Realisation, revelation and perfection.* Since I am a spiritual seeker, a seeker of the highest transcendental Truth, the subject of today's talk is one with which my heart and soul are intimately familiar.

Realisation, revelation and perfection. The animal in us has realised that destruction is perfection. The human in us has realised that separation or partition is perfection. The divine in us has realised that the transformation of our human nature is perfection. The Supreme in us has realised that the manifestation of our inner divinity and reality is perfection.

Destruction is power. Separation or partition is power. Transformation is power. Manifestation is power. Destruction-power is the animal revelation. Separation-power is the human revelation. Transformation-power is the divine revelation. And manifestation-power is the supreme revelation.

As we advance in our spiritual life, we come to realise that destruction-power is abominable and separation-power is deplorable, but that transformation-power is admirable and manifestation-power, the divine manifestation-power, is most adorable.

A sincere and genuine seeker goes deep within and discovers the truth that animal life is sheer futility; that human life, if it does not aspire, is stark stupidity; that divine life is immediate necessity; and that spiritual life is deathless and birthless immortality.

> For God-realisation, we need aspiration-cry.
> For God-revelation, we need dedication-smile.
> For God-manifestation, we need patience-wisdom.

Aspiration is a perfect stranger to rejection. It accepts everything within and without. Then, the things that have to be transformed, it transforms on the strength of its climbing cry.

Dedication is a perfect stranger to calculation. When a sincere seeker dedicates himself to the right cause, to the inner goal, he forgets how to calculate. He goes far beyond the domain of calculation. His dedication is soulful giving, unconditional giving, self-giving, of what he has and what he is.

Patience is a perfect stranger to imperfection. When aspiration and dedication loom large in our spiritual life, patience, our third friend, plays its role most satisfactorily. Patience and God's infinite Compassion play together and dance together. At that time, we see that our teeming imperfections are ready to be transformed into perfect Perfection.

Realising God is like climbing up a tree. Revealing God is like climbing up and down the tree time and again at God's choice Hour. Manifesting God is offering the fruits of the tree to the world at large.

Love, always love. When we love soulfully, realisation does not and cannot remain a far cry. Serve, always serve. When we serve and serve devotedly, revelation cannot remain a far cry. And when we unconditionally become the transcendental Truth and Reality, God-manifestation does not and cannot remain a far cry.

Sri Krishna realised God, the absolute Supreme. After he had realised the Lord Supreme, he became God the eternal Lover and God the eternal Beloved. The Christ realised God, the transcendental Father. On the strength of his supreme realisation he declared, "I and my Father are one." The Christ became the universal brother. We too, if we are humble and sincere seekers, can realise God the Supreme Pilot. After realising God the Supreme Pilot, we can become universal servers of Truth and Light.

Realisation tells us who God is. Revelation tells us what we can do for God. Manifestation and perfection tell us what God does for us and what we do for God.

Who is God? God is our inner cry and our outer smile. He cries with us and for us on earth. He smiles with us and at us in Heaven. God is at once our heart's eternal Lover and our soul's supreme Beloved.

What can we do for God? We can do one thing, and that is to establish the Kingdom of Heaven on earth. The Kingdom of Heaven is not a chimerical mist. It is a reality within us trying to come to the fore and reveal and manifest itself on earth.

What does God do for us? What God does for us is simple, spontaneous, illumining and fulfilling. He liberates us from our teeming imperfections with His unconditional and transcendental Compassion. And what do we do for God? What we do for God is equally simple, spontaneous, illumining and fulfilling. On the strength of our heart's constant, inner mounting cry, we try to make Him smile, smile with joy at His creation vast.

3. The world within and the world without

Dear seekers of the infinite Truth and Light, I wish to give a short talk on the two worlds: the world within and the world without, the inner world and the outer world.

The citizens of the outer world are brooding doubt, teeming fear and strangling jealousy.

The citizens of the inner world are blossoming faith, soaring courage and glowing love.

> Doubt destroys the universal Brother in us.
> Fear destroys the supernal Dreamer in us.
> Jealousy destroys the transcendental Lover in us.
>
> Without the Brother, our body is helpless.
> Without the Dreamer, our mind is hopeless.
> Without the Lover, our heart is fruitless.
>
> Faith inspires the divine seeker in us.
> Courage feeds the eternal server in us.
> Love fulfils the immortal runner in us.

With our soulful faith, we knock at God's Heart-door.
With our adamantine courage, we confidently walk to God's

Heart-room.

With our serene and pure love, we run to God's Heart-room and occupy the special seat right beside God's Throne.

Two worlds: the outer world and the inner world. The outer world constantly demands. There is no end to its demand. When its demands are not fulfilled, the outer world begins to expect. When its expectations are not fulfilled, the outer world becomes frustrated and wants to destroy everything around it.

The inner world does not demand, does not expect. The inner world only accepts. It accepts human beings as they are. Once it accepts them, it tries either to transform or to fulfil them. Each human being has imperfections and limitations. The inner world tries to transform our limitations into plenitude, our imperfections into perfections. And again, within each individual there are divine qualities like hope, dream and promise. The inner world fulfils our hope, fulfils our dream and fulfils our promise. What is our hope? Our hope is to become good and divine. What is our dream? Our dream is to enter into the vastness of the Infinite and become the Infinite itself. And what is our promise? Our promise is to create here on earth the Kingdom of Heaven. The inner world helps us, inspires us, energises us and finally fulfils our promise at God's choice Hour.

In the outer world, the highest achievement is the mind. There are three types of mind: the physical mind, the intellectual mind and the intuitive mind. The physical mind is the mind that is involved in and controlled by the gross physical consciousness, the mind that operates in and through the physical only. The intellectual mind is the mind that dissects and examines everything and everyone from a distance without becoming inseparably one with the object of its scrutiny. The intuitive mind is the mind that runs like the fastest deer. It enters instantly into something and becomes the very essence of that thing on the strength of its God-given capacity to feel its oneness with everything around it.

Most of us do not have this intuitive mind, but we try to cultivate it. When we pray and meditate we gradually cultivate the intuitive mind. Once we have developed the intuitive mind we have free access to our inner realms where the bumper crop of realisation grows. Realisation is the song of plenitude, fulfilment and God-victory in our still obscure, impure, unaspiring and unfulfilled life.

In the inner world the highest achievement is the heart — the aspiring heart, the surrendering heart, the ever-transcending heart. The aspiring heart wants to climb up high, higher, highest, and while climbing it illumines the world around it. The surrendering heart offers its very existence to the Will of the omniscient, omnipotent and omnipresent God, the Inner Pilot. The surrendering heart knows that it is a tiny drop that has to merge into the mighty Ocean, God. By surrendering to this Ocean it does not lose its individuality and personality. On the contrary, it gains the individuality and personality of the Ocean, itself. When it merges into the Ocean, the tiniest drop becomes the mighty Ocean. The ever-transcending heart knows that there is no end to our progress and achievement. Today's goal is tomorrow's starting point. Again, tomorrow's goal will be the starting point for the day after tomorrow, since God Himself is endlessly progressing and eternally transcending His own infinite Heights.

The inner world and the outer world can and will eventually go together. But we have to know that, at the outset of our spiritual journey, we have to change our priorities. That is to say, we have now to pay utmost attention to the inner world, instead of to the outer world. We have to go without from within, not the other way around. Once we are well established in the inner world, we can again turn our attention to the outer world. First we shall give utmost importance to the inner world, then gradually to the outer world, until finally we love and serve both worlds equally and simultaneously. When we are fully established in the outer world on the strength of the divinity we have acquired in the inner world, at that time we shall successfully unite both the outer and the inner worlds.

The inner world is the seed. The outer world is the banyan tree. We have to pay attention to the seed first. When the seed germinates, it grows eventually into a banyan tree. Without the seed the tree cannot come into existence, and without the tree our expectations from the seed can never be fulfilled. So in the beginning the seed is important. In the end the tree is important, because it has grown from divine origins.

The inner world is the soul and the outer world is the body. Without the body the soul cannot manifest. But without the soul the body cannot realise. If we pay attention to the soul and allow our inner being to be surcharged with the soul's light, then we can successfully enter into and illumine the obscurity, impurity and darkness of the outer world. Once the outer world is illumined, it can live harmoniously hand in glove with the inner world.

The outer world is the horse. The inner world is the rider. The horse has to carry the rider or master to the destined goal. If there is no rider to inspire and energise the horse and direct it to the destined goal, the horse will reach the goal very slowly, if at all. So the rider needs the help of the horse, which is the body; and the horse needs the guidance of the rider, which is the soul.

In our ordinary life, no matter how much material wealth we have, no matter how much outer authority we can exercise, we shall not be satisfied. Satisfaction is not to be found in the present-day outer world, no matter what we do, what we say or what we achieve. But today's insufficiency is not and cannot be a permanent reality in our lives. When the light of the inner world looms large and comes to the fore, satisfaction automatically dawns in our devoted mind and surrendered heart. What we want from our lives is satisfaction — nothing more, nothing less. This satisfaction we are bound to achieve, provided we dive deep within and approach the outer world from the inner world.

Let us enter into the inner world and bring forward the plenitude, the Eldorado, of the inner world, and share it with the outer world. Today we are having a kind of experience, an unfulfilling or unfulfilled experience. But tomorrow we can, without fail, have fulfilling and fulfilled experiences of Divinity and Immortality, provided we aspire. What do we aspire for? We aspire only for the Highest, for the Ultimate, for the absolute Supreme. How do we aspire? We aspire through constant self-giving. And today's self-giving is tomorrow's God-becoming.

4. You

You want God. You need God. You have God. You are God.
   You want God and you need God.
   When you are in your vital, you want God.
   When you are in your heart, you need God.
   Your vital demands God's choice Hour.
   Your heart devotedly waits for God's choice Hour.
   When your vital knocks at God's door, no answer.
   Frustrated, you break open God's door.

Alas, alas, God is not to be found in His room. He is elsewhere.

God knocks at your heart's door.
You immediately answer.
God blesses your devoted head.
God embraces your surrendered heart.
You want God in order to dominate His vast creation.
You need God in order to emancipate your little world.
You have God and you are God.
You have God; therefore you can look up.
You are God; therefore you can dive within.
You have God; therefore the world loves you.
You are God; therefore it is you alone who can expand your universal consciousness, it is you alone who can always transcend your ever-transcending height.
You have God. Your sea-deep eyes can prove it.
You are God. Your sun-vast heart is the proof.
You have God. Your body of sound can prove it.
You are God. Your soul of silence is the proof.
You have God; therefore death bows to you.
You are God; therefore Immortality claims you.
You have God; therefore you are unmistakably great.
You are God; therefore you are ceaselessly good.
God you want?
Then your first friend is temptation,
Your second friend is frustration,
Your third friend is destruction.
God you need?
Then your first friend is love,
Your second friend is devotion,
Your third friend is surrender.
God you have.

FIFTY FREEDOM-BOATS TO ONE GOLDEN SHORE

Your first friend is aspiration,
Your second friend is liberation,
Your third friend is realisation.
God you are.
Your first friend is revelation,
Your second friend is manifestation,
Your third friend is perfection.

God you want? Be careful.
God you need? Be hopeful.
God you have. Whom else do you need? No one!
God you are. Who does not need you? No one!

Everybody needs you, for you have God and you are God.
You are the body,
You are the vital,
You are the mind,
You are the heart,
You are the soul,
Of what you have and what you are.
What you have is a vast heart.
What you are is a glowing soul.
God you want.
God you need.
God you have.
God you are.

5. Self-examination

Dear seekers of the infinite Truth, just because we are all seekers we are all in God's Boat. God's Boat will carry us to our destined Goal. Today I wish to give a short talk on self-examination. Most of us here are students. To be precise, all of us are students. Some of us are studying at the university, while others are studying in the outer world or in the inner world. We work very hard to pass our examinations. Our teachers and professors work very hard to be impartial.

When the human teacher wants to examine us, very often his pride pleads with him. It wants to examine us on the teacher's behalf. When God, the divine Teacher, wants to examine us, His Compassion pleads with Him. It wants to examine us on God's behalf. The human teacher gladly agrees to the proposal made by his pride. The divine Teacher immediately agrees to the proposal offered by His Compassion.

When the human teacher examines us, we either pass or fail the examination. But when the divine Teacher examines us, we never fail. Why? We never fail because the divine Teacher is at once our examiner and our private tutor. He privately teaches us what He is going to ask us on His examination. Naturally we never fail. First He teaches us devotedly, constantly and unconditionally. Then He openly examines us, and we all pass His examination without any difficulty.

Self-examination and deception are total strangers. They are constantly at daggers drawn. Deception hates self-examination. Self-examination is fond of perfection, and perfection is proud of self-examination. Deception runs backward. Self-examination runs forward to its goal of perfection. At the end of the backward journey, Satan, the evil force, shakes hands with deception. And at the end of the forward journey, God, the

Supreme Pilot, garlands self-examination.

Self-examination is our aspiration for the higher world and the inner world. The higher world is immortal Light. The inner world is infinite Peace. Light shows us the face of Truth and then makes us the body of Truth. Peace makes us the body of Truth and then shows us the face of Truth. Light says to Peace, "Sister, I need your Length. What you have and what you are is Infinity's Length." Peace immediately tells Light, "Brother, my Length is equally yours. What you have and what you are is Transcendental Height. I need your Light and your Height." The immortal Light says, "My sister, take it. My Light and my Height are equally yours."

Unlike us, God examines Himself constantly. We are reluctant to examine ourselves, but God is fond of examining Himself at every moment. He examines Himself in order to see whether His infinite Compassion is operating most effectively in the heart of mankind. And unlike us, God is fond of perfecting Himself at every moment. He feels that He is perfect only when we can offer Him a soulful smile. We pray to God for countless things, but He inwardly prays to us for only one thing: a smile, a soulful smile.

Self-discovery and God-discovery are one and the same thing, but they usually work in two specific ways. In God-discovery, we see the infinite Infinity crying in the heart of the finite. In self-discovery, we see the finite smiling through the soul of the Infinite.

Self-examination leads us to self-control. Self-control leads us to self-mastery. Self-mastery is the denial of ignorance-sea and the affirmation of Illumination-sky. Self-examination is our journey's start. Our first Goal is self-discovery. Our second goal is God-revelation. Our third and last goal is God-manifestation.

God-discovery or God-realisation, God-revelation and God-manifestation: these are the three rungs in the ladder of our spiritual evolution. Early in the morning, Mother Earth offers God-realisation to Father Heaven as her first gift. At noon, Mother Earth offers God-revelation to Father Heaven as her second gift. And in the evening, Mother Earth offers God-manifestation to Father Heaven as her third and ultimate gift.

All seekers of the Transcendental are receiving Truth, Peace, Light and Bliss according to their capacity and receptivity. Everyone starts his spiritual journey as a beginner-seeker. When a beginner-seeker examines his body, he discovers a stupid donkey. When he examines his vital, he discovers a mad elephant. When he examines his mind, he discovers a restless and mischievous monkey. And when he examines his heart, he discovers a feeble ant. His sincerity sees and feels it. But at the end of his journey's close, his sincerity makes him see and feel something else. He examines his body and discovers a sea of Purity. He examines his vital and discovers a sea of divine Power. He examines his mind and discovers a sea of infinite Peace. He examines his heart and discovers an infinite expanse of Light and Delight.

[The University of Connecticut in 1973 became the first academic institution to offer a credit course on Sri Chinmoy's philosophy. The course was developed and taught by Professor Peter Pitzele (Brihaspati). These remarks were addressed by Sri Chinmoy to Brihaspati's wife, Indira, and to Brihaspati's students, who attended the talk.]

[To Indira]: You are Brihaspati's inspiration. You inspire him outwardly and I inspire him inwardly. He needs inspiration both from the outer world and from the inner world. Our deep inspiration and his lofty aspiration have made him what he is — a professor who is loved and admired by all his students. In the name of the Supreme, I offer my loving gratitude to you and to Brihaspati.

[To Brihaspati's students]: I am most grateful to you. You have studied our philosophy. I pray to the Supreme to shower His choicest, highest blessings upon your devoted heads and your aspiring hearts. By studying our philosophy, you have given us the opportunity to serve the Supreme in your aspiring hearts. Brihaspati will offer our light to the Supreme in you. For that I am offering you my soul's deepest love and my heart's blessingful gratitude.

6. Choice

Dear seekers, dear sisters and brothers, dear aspirants for the highest ultimate Goal, I wish to give a talk on the subject of choice. Who has made the first choice: God or I? My mind thinks that it is I who have chosen God. My heart feels God and I have chosen each other simultaneously. My soul knows that it was God who chose me first, long before I even dreamt of choosing Him.

Each human being is a chooser. He chooses mankind to obey his express orders. He chooses God to listen to his soulful prayers. The animal in man chooses life-destruction. The human in man chooses world-admiration. The divine in man chooses God-realisation. The Supreme in man chooses perfect Perfection.

We choose God when we come to realise that the world does not need us, that the world does not care for our wisdom-light.

Only when the outer world has disappointed us and our immediate world has deserted us do we think of choosing God. God chooses us because He does not want to drink the nectar of Immortality alone. God chooses us because He does not want to reveal His transcendental Reality alone. God chooses us because He does not want to manifest His universal Oneness alone.

Our body chooses rest, pleasure-loving rest. Our vital chooses aggression, titanic aggression. Our mind chooses information, encyclopaedic information. Our heart chooses love, all-fulfilling love. And God chooses perfection within and perfection without — perfection in our inner life of realisation and perfection in our outer life of manifestation.

Before we enter into the spiritual life we choose the might of the outer world. But once we enter into the spiritual life we choose only the Light of the inner world. Before we enter into the spiritual life we choose the name and fame of the outer world. But once we enter into the spiritual life we choose to participate most soulfully and devotedly in God's cosmic Game in order to please Him and fulfil Him in His own Way.

Now what is the spiritual life? The spiritual life is the life of our conscious God-awareness. What else is the spiritual life? The spiritual life is the life of our constant God-loving and our ultimate God-becoming. I choose God, not because He is all-Power, not because He is all-Wisdom, not because He is all-Light and all-Peace, not even because He is all-Love, but because He and I are one, eternally one. God and I are eternally one. You and God are eternally one. We are all eternally and inseparably one with God.

I am the Dream-Boat of God's Heart and God is the Reality-Shore of my life. This is the realisation each individual seeker here and everywhere is bound to achieve sooner or later. We are all inseparably one with God. It is for this reason and no other reason that we choose God. As long as we are unconscious of the fact that we are one with God, we wallow contentedly in the pleasures of ignorance. But once our inner being is awakened, our soul comes to the fore and convinces our outer physical mind of the fact that we are not only God's chosen instruments but also God's eternal comrades. He needs us, as we need Him. He is the Tree and we are the branches and leaves. The Tree trunk and the branches and leaves need each other. We choose Him for our realisation, as He chooses us for His manifestation. Without Him we cannot realise our highest absolute Height. Again, without us He cannot manifest His Vision-in-Reality, His Reality-in-Vision.

Each human being on earth represents God according to his own capacity and receptivity. In and through each human being God manifests Himself in a specific way. Each individual is of paramount importance to Him, for He Himself has chosen each individual to play a significant role in His cosmic Drama. But we have to know that it is God who chooses us first, and not we who choose God. The Creator creates the creation, and then the creation admires the Creator. The creation is the choice of the Creator and admiration is the choice of the creation. It is through our heart's admiration and adoration that we become consciously one with the Supreme Pilot, and it is through His conscious, compassionate choice that He has established His inseparable oneness with each human being, each child of His on earth.

Duty is the supreme choice of God. He feels there can be nothing more important than duty. He discharges His Duty at every moment, for He feels that in performing His Duty He is not only awakening the earth-consciousness but also bringing down the Heaven-Delight into the very heart of earth.

We are at once the representatives of both Mother Earth and Father Heaven. As the representatives of Father Heaven, our first and foremost choice should be self-giving to the Supreme Beloved. It is in our self-giving that we can manifest the transcendental Reality on earth. As the representatives of Mother Earth, we feel that it is our bounden duty to spread our wings like a bird — not to cover the length and breadth of the world, but to expand our earthbound consciousness, to transcend the limits of our earthly existence. Here on earth we have to go deep within and try to spread our wings of Light and Delight so that we can consciously grow into the ever-transcending and ever-widening Universal Consciousness.

God made His choice in choosing us; now let us make our choice in choosing Him. His choice is the song of manifestation. Our choice is the song of realisation. And today's realisation is tomorrow's manifestation. Again, tomorrow's manifestation is only the beginning of a forward and upward and inward journey. Today, on the strength of our inner choice, we move forward, upward and inward and reach our chosen destination. But today's destination will only be the starting point for our farther, higher and more fulfilling goal of tomorrow. There is no fixed Goal, for we are all evolving. In the process of evolution we are running, flying and diving towards an ever-transcending, deepening and widening Goal. To run farther, fly higher and dive deeper is the only choice that each individual seeker on earth should consciously, devotedly, unmistakably and unconditionally make.

7. Meditation and the inner education

Dear seekers, dear sisters and brothers, this evening I shall give a short talk on meditation and education. Since my subject will be meditation and education, with your kind permission I wish to meditate for a while. I shall be extremely grateful to each of you if you would join me in my meditation...

Meditation and the inner education. Meditation is a vast subject. Being a spiritual man, I know a little bit about meditation, and I can speak on this subject for hours. But I wish to tell you, with all the sincerity at my command, that if we can meditate soulfully even for a fleeting minute, the result of our meditation will far surpass the effect of any talk given by anybody on earth on this subject.

But since we have to convince our physical mind, we talk and we listen. We are in the mind, and we feel that we are of the mind and for the mind. Such being the case, at times it is of paramount importance to give talks on meditation; but meditation is best done in utmost silence, in pin-drop silence.

Since we want to convince our physical mind, let us try to know what meditation actually means. Unfortunately, in the West, many people have misconceptions about meditation. They think meditation means living a life of self-abnegation, and that meditation cannot be applied to our daily needs. They think meditation is for those who want to live in the Himalayan caves, for those who want to shun society. But I wish to say that these notions are all ill-founded. A seeker who knows how to meditate properly, effectively and soulfully is a practical man. Meditation is not theoretical, but practical. Since God is Himself practical, a seeker of the highest Truth cannot be otherwise.

In this world either we desire or we aspire. At each moment we are given ample opportunity to possess and grab the world or to become inseparably one with the world. Meditation teaches us how to become inseparably one with the world at large. When we cry for the Vast, for the ultimate Truth, meditation is the immediate answer. When we want to achieve boundless Peace, boundless Light, boundless Bliss, meditation is the only answer. The world needs one thing, and that is peace, and meditation is the only answer.

Everybody meditates. If you tell me, "No, I do not know how to meditate," unfortunately I cannot see eye to eye with you. Everybody meditates, but there is a difference between my way of meditation and your way and his or her way of meditation. Since the dawn of Heaven, and the creation, everybody has been meditating, but we all meditate according to our capacity and receptivity. When we think of God and meditate on God, this is one form of meditation. When we cherish or treasure a good thought, even for a fleeting second, this is another kind of meditation. Anything that helps us in our self-expansion is meditation.

In the West, we most often speak of prayer, while in the East, especially in India, we speak of meditation. The Western belief is that prayer can and will do everything. In the East, we feel that meditation can give us everything, that meditation will help us to grow into the ever-transcending Beyond. Prayer and meditation are bosom friends. When we pray, our entire being climbs up high, higher, highest and reaches the ultimate Truth. At that time we offer ourselves to the Supreme, the ultimate Source. With our prayer we commune with God, we establish a free access to the highest Absolute Father. When we meditate, we make our mind calm, quiet, vacant and tranquil, and we receive Light from above in infinite measure.

Meditation and prayer are two different types of conversation, but they serve the same purpose. When we pray, we talk to God; we tell Him all about our needs and all our soulful expectations. Through our prayer we ask God for anything that we want; and anything that we would like to offer God from our very existence we offer through our prayer. But when we meditate we remain silent, absolutely silent, and we beg of God to work in and through us. He dictates and we try to execute His express Will.

In the beginning, we see and feel on the strength of our meditation that God alone is doing everything, and that we are mere instruments. But, in time, when we go deep within, we come to realise that He is not only the doer but also the action itself, and He is not only the action, but also the result thereof. To simplify the matter, we can say that meditation means God's conscious and compassionate dictates to us and prayer means our soulful conversation with God. When we meditate, God talks to us and we most devotedly listen. When we pray, we talk to God and He most compassionately listens.

Meditation and the inner education are one an the same thing; meditation *is* the inner education. To be a proper human being we have to be integrally educated. To be a proper divine being we have to be supremely liberated in our inner life and in our outer life. The outer education tells us what the world is doing. The inner education tells us what we can do. The outer education helps us make a decent living. The inner education helps us live for God in the heart of man. The outer education is an observation, an observed fact. The inner education is an experience, an experienced reality. With our outer education we can at best knock at God's Door. With our inner education we can not only enter into God's Room, but actually sit on God's transcendental Throne. The outer education is the fulfilment of the physical mind, the vital and the earthbound consciousness. The inner education is the song of liberation, salvation and divine freedom.

Each human being has two teachers. As there is outer education and inner education, even so is there a teacher for us in the outer world and a teacher for us in the inner world. The teacher in the outer world tells us, "Accept me. If you don't accept me, you are bound to remain always a most deplorable fool. So the sooner you accept me, the better for you." The teacher in the inner life tells us, "Accept me, please, for if you do not accept me I shall always remain incomplete. You and I are one. If one part of my existence remains unlit, obscure and unaspiring, then I myself remain imperfect. Therefore, I beg of you, O seeker, accept me, for I wish to become complete and perfect with your kind acceptance of my reality's Light." The outer teacher tells me, "Follow me. I can show you the goal. If you don't follow me, there is no goal for you. It is I alone who can show you the goal, so follow me." But the inner teacher tells us, "Believe me, once and for all, the supernal Light is in you. The transcendental Light is of you. The eternal Father is for you. Finally, O seeker, I wish to offer you this message: you are the way and you are also the Goal. Believe me, once and for all."

8. Experience

Dear seekers, dear spiritual brothers and sisters, I wish to give a short talk on inner experience. In the spiritual life there are few things as important and significant as inner experience. To have an inner experience is to have many millions of spiritual dollars. Inner experience is a seeker's most precious wealth. Since we are all seekers here, what is of paramount importance in our lives is inner experience.

An inner experience is the seeker's conscious awareness of his Immortality.

An inner experience is the seeker's conscious expansion of his Infinity.

An inner experience is the seeker's conscious fulfilment of his Eternity.

There are three things that we have to experience in our inner life, our life of aspiration and dedication. These things are: Light, divine Light; Power, divine Power; and Peace, divine Peace.

Ordinary light will expose us if we do something wrong, but divine Light never exposes us. On the contrary, it illumines us and tries to perfect us.

Human power is the power that urges us to break and destroy, to dominate and crush others. Human power is the power of separativity. But divine Power inspires us to create and build. It is the power of oneness.

Human peace is usually a forced compromise. But divine Peace is our fulfilment in the perfection-song of the Universal Consciousness, the all-pervading Consciousness that abides deep within us.

When we experience the divine Light, we feel that the soul-seed within us begins to germinate.

When we experience the divine Power, we see our life-plant growing slowly, steadily, unerringly, convincingly and fruitfully.

When we experience the divine Peace, we see the blossoming of the perfection-flower of our life-plant.

When we have the soul's need for inner experience, we grow into true seekers. But before we feel the necessity for inner experience, we are all ordinary human beings. For an ordinary human being, what is necessary is progress. And this comes through outer experience.

An outer experience is the insecurity of our human heart.

An outer experience is the obscurity of our human mind.

An outer experience is the immaturity of our human vital.

An outer experience is the impurity of our human body.

A human being at times represents his own divine qualities and at times represents his human qualities. At times, unfortunately, he even represents the animal qualities that still remain within him.

Destruction-night is the animal experience.

Aspiration-height is the human experience.

Perfection-light is the divine experience.

In our spiritual life, there is something infinitely more important than experience, and that is called realisation. When we have an experience of the highest magnitude, we feel that we are touching or are about to touch God the Tree. But when we have the highest realisation, we feel that we are not only touching the God-Tree but also climbing up the Tree and reaching the highest bough, where we then enjoy the nectar-fruits.

An experience of God can be denied and rejected by the doubting mind, but the realisation of God far transcends the domain of doubt and the judgement of the mind. It goes far beyond the jurisdiction of the human mind. Realisation has the power to remain constantly in tune with the highest Source, so the human mind cannot disturb its poise, confidence and certainty.

Man's inner experience of God makes man aware of the possibility of God-becoming. That is to say, when man has an iota of God-experience, he begins to feel that sooner or later he will be able to grow into the very image of God. God's experience in man makes God feel that the perfection of His Manifestation-Light on earth is not only possible and practicable, but also inevitable.

In man, God is a dream. This experience both man and God achieve. In God, man is a reality. This experience man and God simultaneously receive. In man, God is a dream. In God, man is a reality.

With God, man smiles. He smiles the smile of Perfection, transcendental Perfection. With man, God cries. He cries the cry that has been inside the human heart from time immemorial.

God's Compassion-experience and man's Liberation-experience are inseparable. When God's Compassion descends, the meshes of ignorance dissolve and man's Liberation dawns.

When we have an inner experience, we spontaneously learn something higher, something deeper, something more soulful and more fruitful than any ordinary human learning. One inner experience will teach us how to run towards the Goal, how to discover our higher and deeper reality. Another inner experience will teach us how to unlearn everything that has caught our mind in the outer world — everything undivine, unillumined, unaspiring, unfulfilled. The things that are fulfilling, we shall learn from our ever-evolving experience. And the things that are discouraging and destructive, these we shall unlearn. Every day, on the strength of our inner experience, we have the opportunity to learn the higher Truth and unlearn the many hostile and undivine things that our mind has mistaken for Truth.

When we are in the process of learning and unlearning, there comes a time when we achieve perfection both in our inner life and in our outer life. Today's experience grows into tomorrow's realisation. For a seeker, inner experience is the precursor of God-realisation, which is the most important, most significant experience. Then tomorrow's realisation grows into the perfection of the following day. Experience is the first rung, realisation is the second rung and perfection is the third rung of the Cosmic Ladder.

Outer experiences we can share with others when we are suffering and also when we are in a cheerful frame of mind. Whether we have something to be proud of or whether we have inner pangs, we can easily share these experiences. But if we share our inner experiences with others, we are just inviting doubt to snatch them away. And once we allow others to inject doubt into our mind and heart, our progress stops. No seeker will be able to go further if he prematurely shares his inner experiences with others. But once a seeker has reached the highest Height or has at least achieved something solid and concrete in his spiritual life, then he can share his experiences with others without the risk of losing the inspiration and illumination of those experiences. Indeed, at that time, his inner experiences will inspire and illumine his friends.

One may have hundreds and thousands of experiences during his life of aspiration. But two or three major experiences are more than enough for a seeker to realise the Highest, the Absolute. Now, we have to be careful about our inner experiences; we have to know whether these deeper experiences are real or not. When a seeker gets an experience, he has to go deep within in order to get a still higher and deeper experience so that he can know the true meaning of his previous experience. Or, if he has a spiritual Master, the Master can tell him the true meaning of his experience.

Let us start our journey with aspiration. If we have sincere aspiration, we are bound to have inner experiences, and then our realisation cannot remain a far cry. And once realisation dawns, perfect Perfection is bound to blossom in our life of aspiration on earth. We have to aspire to bring down the Kingdom of Heaven to earth. The Kingdom of Heaven automatically descends to earth when we grow into Perfection, when we dive into the Heart of the highest Absolute Supreme.

9. The heart

Dear seekers of the transcendental Truth, dear sisters and brothers of the one transcendental Spirit, this evening I wish to give a talk on the heart.

I wish to tell all my friends and my spiritual brothers and sisters here in Philadelphia that inside the heart of each individual seeker rings the Liberty Bell. The Liberty Bell that we see here in Philadelphia has a large crack, and therefore it does not ring properly. But in the inner life, our Liberty Bell rings perfectly. It is up to each individual to listen to his inner bell every day. This bell has been ringing from time immemorial in each individual soul, inspiring the soul to take part in God's cosmic Drama and to run fast, faster, fastest towards the destined Goal.

We have a loving heart, an aspiring heart, an inspiring heart, an illumining heart and a fulfilling heart. With our loving heart we welcome the world at large. With our aspiring heart we climb up to the highest pinnacle of divinity. With our inspiring heart we inspire not only the world within us, but also the world without — the world of God's entire creation. With our illumining heart we illumine our ignorance, darkness, imperfection and bondage. With our fulfilling heart we fulfil God the Dreamer in us, God the Player in us, God the Lover in us and God the Beloved Supreme in us.

Also, with our loving heart we can unconditionally surrender ourselves to the Will of God. With our aspiring heart we can grow into the very image of God. With our inspiring heart we can spread the message of God throughout the length and breadth of the world. With our illumining heart we can manifest our inner divinity on the outer plane. And with our fulfilling heart we can fulfil both God the Creator and God the creation at once. Our fulfilling heart is nothing other than our unconditionally surrendered heart flying with the wings of the Supreme.

When we enter into the spiritual life, we come to realise that we also have a soulful heart, a heart of peace and a heart of delight. The soulful heart we need at every moment in our life of aspiration. Without it we cannot make an iota of inner progress. The peaceful heart we need because when peace is wanting in our life, this life has no abiding satisfaction. The heart of delight we need because it is the very source of our divine plenitude and infinitude. We came from delight, we live in delight and, at the end of our journey's close, into delight we retire.

Ānandādd hy eva khalv imāni bhutāni jāyante...

How can a beginner in the spiritual life have a soulful heart? Let him look into the sky in the evening when the sun starts to set. When the beginner-seeker looks at the sky and becomes deeply absorbed in the setting sun, his soulful heart comes to the fore. If the beginner needs a peaceful heart, let him concentrate, meditate and contemplate on the very depths of the ocean, the ocean of life. And if he needs a heart of delight, let him look at the ocean surface and allow his inner being to get in tune with the waves of the ocean.

The heart is most intimate to us and most significant in our life. When our physical heart fails, we pass behind the curtain of Eternity and die. Similarly, in the spiritual life, when our heart of aspiration fails even while we are living here on earth, we will be living in the world of death. Medical science will tell us that the physical heart is located within the chest on the left side. Some spiritual Masters are of the opinion that the spiritual heart is on the right side, and others are of the opinion that it is in the middle. Then again, there are still others who are of the opinion that it is inside the forehead, a little above the eyebrows. Naturally these spiritual Masters are dealing with the spiritual heart, and each is right in his own way. Each has discovered the heart according to his own inner light and inner wisdom.

When we are told that the heart is between and a little above the eyebrows, at the outset we are bound to be puzzled and somewhat disturbed. Whether it is on the left side or the right side of the chest may be immaterial to us. But when we are told that the heart is located between the eyebrows, naturally we are thrown into a sea of confusion. But I wish to say that those who are of the opinion that the heart is located there are perfectly right in their way, for that place is the source of our intuition, of our intuitive light. Heart means light. Wherever we feel the presence of light, without the least possible hesitation we can say that that very place is the heart, heart and light are one and the same thing.

Now we have to know that the heart is not the highest or the most perfect member of our inner family. It is the soul that is the highest, because the soul is all light. In the soul there is no darkness at all. The human heart receives light from the soul, and that is why the soul is superior. It is the source of the heart's light. The human heart identifies with the soul's light, whereas the mind finds it extremely difficult to do this. That is why the heart is superior to the mind. Again, the mind is superior to the vital because the mind searches for the truth, for light — at times consciously, at times unconsciously. But the vital does not care for the highest truth. The vital cares for the truth only when the truth offers satisfaction in the vital's own undivine way. But the vital does at least care for light, whereas the gross physical does not want light at all. It is ready to remain imperfect and incomplete for millennia.

When we enter into the spiritual life, we discover that there are two significant roads that can lead us towards our destined Goal. One road is the mental road, the road of the mind; the other is the psychic road, the road of the heart. Now both of these roads will take us to our destined Goal. But one road is shorter and safer, and that is the road of the heart. When we follow the road of the mind, at any moment doubt can snatch us away. The world's information can pull down human aspiration. But the road of the heart is sunlit. When he follows this road, a seeker always feels deep within himself a deer running towards the destined Goal. Each individual has to know whether he listens more to his mind or more to his heart. The message of the heart is altogether different from the message of the mind. Since we want to reach our Goal as soon as possible, we feel the supreme necessity of the heart.

There are two ways of approaching the ultimate Reality: one is the way of knowledge and the other is the way of love. Those who follow the path of the heart become convinced, on their way to self-discovery, that love itself is the supreme Knowledge. Right now, knowledge and love seem like two different things. The mind supplies us with knowledge and the heart supplies us with love. But the deeper we go, the clearer it becomes to us that love and knowledge are one and the same. God is omniscient, God is omnipotent, God is omnipresent. He is everything. He embodies Infinity, Eternity and Immortality. But when we go deep within, we find that these qualities do not satisfy us. There is only one aspect of God that satisfies us totally and most convincingly, and that aspect is God's Love. When on the strength of our own love we approach God's infinite Love, we are totally satisfied. We will not be satisfied when we see or feel God the all-awesome. Only the Love aspect of God quenches our eternal thirst.

In the spiritual life we see that two hearts can and often do become inseparably one with each other. One is the heart of the seeker or disciple, and the other is the heart of the teacher, the spiritual Master. These two hearts are constantly singing one song, the song of self-giving. When a true disciple meets his Master for the first time, his inner and outer promise to the Master is this: "I want nothing from you. Although I have come to you so that you can help me in my God-realisation, even if you never grant me God-realisation, my love for you, my devotion to you and my oneness with you will always remain total and unconditional." So a real seeker uses his heart of oneness, his heart of self-giving, when he accepts his Master. And he will grow into spiritual perfection through his love and devotion for the Highest in his Master, the Inner Pilot, God the Supreme. The spiritual Master also uses his heart when he accepts a disciple who comes to him for inner guidance. On the strength of his own self-giving heart, the Master tells his disciple, "I have already accepted you, no matter what you do for God. Even if you do not do anything for God, for God's manifestation, still I shall go on loving you."

So the disciple's heart becomes one with the Master's heart and makes the solemn promise: "Whether or not you help me in my God-realisation is up to you, but I shall go on loving the Supreme in you forever." And the Master also makes a solemn, soulful promise to the disciple: "Whether you care for God-manifestation or not is up to you, but my love for you and my self-offering to you shall remain unconditional forever."

It is said that a pure heart is everything. Now what does it mean to have a pure heart? First of all, there must be sanctity and serenity in the heart. But I wish to say that that is not actually enough. A pure heart means a heart that embodies the constantly climbing flame of aspiration. If within the heart there is an ever-mounting flame that wants to reach the Highest, then that is the heart of purity. All of us here have a pure heart to some degree. Since we are all seekers here, we are bound to have the inner flame of aspiration in our heart. Let us try to feed this inner flame through our constant spiritual practice, through our daily prayer, meditation and contemplation. The highest transcendental Goal resides deep within each of us. Our Goal can never be a far cry; it is within our reach, provided we constantly look ahead, look deep within and look upward to the highest Height.

We leave the starting point the moment we feel in the inmost recesses of our heart the flame of aspiration. Once we have left the starting point, it is only a matter of time before we reach the Goal. Those who are awakened can run the fastest towards the destined Goal. Those who are in the process of awakening may rest assured that the Goal is awaiting them. And those who still cannot get up will not be belittled by those who are in the process of awakening or by those who are already awakened. The spiritual life is not a life of competition. If competition is at all necessary, then each should compete with his own weaknesses, imperfections and limitations, with his own bondage and death.

If we practise meditation regularly, faithfully and devotedly, not only do we come closer to our Goal, but the Goal itself comes running towards us. Halfway along the path, the Goal and the runner meet to fulfil each other's needs. By reaching the Goal, the runner fulfils his task, the task of realising the highest possible Truth. And by reaching the runner, the Goal makes the manifestation of the highest Truth not only possible and practicable but also inevitable. The Goal and the runner fulfil themselves as they fulfil their respective roles in the life of aspiration and in the life of manifestation.

10. Time

Dear brothers and sisters, dear spiritual seekers, this morning I wish to give a talk on time.

> Time is love.
> If we love time,
> Then time gives us what we want: pleasure.
> Time is love.
> If we love time,
> Then time gives us what we need: joy.
> Time is love.
> If we love time,
> Then God accepts from us what we have: ignorance.
> Time is love.
> If we love time,
> Then God gives us what He has: Light.

Pleasure. Pleasure on the physical plane, the vital plane and the mental plane is very short-lived, but during its brief span pleasure injures the real in us. The real in us is our cry for God, for Truth, for Light — our cry for Infinity's heart, Eternity's body and Immortality's soul. Today's pleasure ends in tomorrow's frustration and destruction. Tomorrow's frustration and destruction end in the total eclipse of our inner divinity. Therefore, a sincere seeker of the transcendental Truth tries to avoid pleasure.

Joy. In the spiritual life, joy is of paramount importance.

Joy grows, joy flows and joy soars.
God the climbing Tree grows with our joy, our inner joy.
God the dancing River flows with our joy, our fulfilling joy.
God the flying Bird soars with our joy, our illumining joy.

If a spiritual seeker remains in a cheerful frame of mind he makes very fast progress. Joy means confidence in his life of aspiration. Joy is self-discovery and self-fulfilment.

Ignorance. When we go deep within, we see that we have nothing to give to God but ignorance. This ignorance God accepts from us most gladly, most devotedly and most unconditionally. Our life of ignorance we offer to God, and in return God offers to us a life of beauty, a life of plenitude, a life of infinitude.

Light. Light is self-revelation. Self-revelation grows into self-manifestation, and self-manifestation grows into self-perfection. Self-perfection and God-perfection are one and the same thing, operating on two different levels. We notice self-perfection in the heart of the finite. We notice God-perfection in the body of the Infinite.

Time is our oneness with God, our conscious oneness with God. We establish our conscious oneness with God on the strength of our inner cry. Mother Earth offers us her wealth: patience, sacrifice and compassion. Father Heaven offers us His wealth: love, wisdom and illumination. With the help we get from Mother Earth, we prepare ourselves for salvation. With the help we get from Father Heaven, we prepare ourselves for divine glorification. Salvation we get from earth, and divine glorification we get from Heaven. When we receive salvation, we feel that we are growing into the very image of our Beloved Supreme. When we are offered glorification, we feel that our

Beloved Supreme is playing in and through us. In the finite He is singing His Song Celestial, His song of infinite Beauty, Light, Melody and Harmony.

The animal in us does not care to know about time. The human in us knows that there exists something called time, but it does not value time. The divine in us utilises time most effectively and divinely. The Supreme in us, the Inner Pilot, fulfils His dream and His reality here on earth through time.

Here on earth a child has no time even to eat his candy. A young boy has no time to study. A young man has no time to think. An old man has no time to rest. But a seeker knows that his God has the time to eat candy, to study, to think, to rest. His God has time for everything. The seeker also knows that God has the time to do everything because He takes the help of time. Only with the co-operation of time can He achieve everything in and through His aspiring, devoted and surrendered children.

Unaspiring human beings do not enlist the help of time. They do not know the value of time. They think that achievement is of paramount importance, and not the time required for the achievement. So they do not care for time; they neglect time. They do not realise that time is the bridge that will carry them to the other shore. If they do not use the bridge, they cannot go on to the other shore where there is Light, Peace and Bliss in boundless measure.

But the aspiring person, the seeker, appreciates time and utilises it. When it is time to eat, he will eat; when it is time to think, he will think; when it is time to study spiritual books, he will study; and when it is time to rest, he will rest. For him, each day is a new challenge, a new opportunity. He enters into the battlefield of life to conquer darkness, limitation, bondage and death. He has to fight and rest at the appropriate times. He has to do all the things that are necessary to invoke Peace, Light and Bliss from Above in infinite measure so that he can bring to the fore his inner divinity and offer it to the world at large.

There are two types of time in the spiritual life: earth-time and Heaven-time. Earth-time is necessity, and Heaven-time is reality, while necessity's reality is God-intoxication. The seeker in us feels that it is of supreme necessity for him to see the face of reality. And when he sees the face of reality he becomes a God-intoxicated soul. Reality on its part enters into our necessity and fulfils our necessity by illumining us within and without.

A God-intoxicated soul comes to realise that he has to achieve the eternal Truth first and then serve the divinity in humanity. First he has to achieve the Highest, the Absolute, and only then can he serve the Absolute in mankind. In this way he will be able to grow into the transcendental reality. God's Reality, on the other hand, feels that since it already is eternal, it must always serve its own all-pervading consciousness. The tree feels that it is its bounden duty to fulfil the needs of the branches, leaves, flowers and fruits. It also knows that it has the capacity to do this. So Reality starts serving its infinite manifestations immediately, for it knows that it has what it requires: consciousness in infinite measure. So the one climbs up the tree and then brings down the fruit to share it with humanity, while the other, who is already seated on the top of the tree, comes down immediately and shares the fruit with the aspiring humanity.

In the spiritual life, a sincere seeker knows that there is a God-appointed hour, a God-ordained hour. We call it God's Hour. This hour we can neither pull towards us nor push aside, but we can expedite it. We can shorten our road to God-realisation provided we are ready to sacrifice ourselves, to offer to the Divine at every moment all that we have within us — our ignorant, undivine and unaspiring qualities, as well as our aspiring qualities.

There is one thing in our physical that is unwanted now and forever, and that is lethargy.

In the vital there is something that we have to get rid of, and that is aggression, or the feeling of superiority and supremacy.

In the mind there is something that we must get rid of, and that is doubt. We doubt others and we doubt ourselves. When we doubt others, nothing happens to them. They go on perfecting themselves through their daily experiences. It is we who suffer each time we doubt, for we eclipse our inner sun. This is the sun that is ready to offer us its light in abundant measure; it is ready to kindle the flame of aspiration within us so that we can climb up high, higher, highest into our transcendental Divinity.

In the heart we also have something to get rid of, and that is insecurity. Very often we feel that we are helpless, we are hopeless, we are useless. But this wrong notion we must not cherish. Once we become sincere seekers on the path of Truth and Light, we know that deep within us is the Inner Pilot. It was He who inspired us to walk along the road of Infinity, Eternity and Immortality. If He Himself had not inspired us, we could not have launched into the sea of spirituality. But He did inspire us, and He continues to inspire us every day. So we can never be helpless, we can never be insecure. We know there is Light within us. Just because we do not now have the Light at our disposal, we cannot say that this Light will remain always a far cry. On the contrary, today's impossibility is tomorrow's destined achievement. There is simply no such thing as impossibility in our spiritual life.

We know that we are aiming at a Goal, the Goal that has everything divine for us in infinite measure. We are trying to establish our conscious oneness with Someone who is infinite, eternal and immortal — our God. Since He is our Source, since He is our Goal, how can our ultimate achievement be limited? Everything that we want to achieve, everything that we want to grow into, needs time; and our time is determined by God. We shall not pull God's Hour. We shall not push God's Hour. We shall simply play our role. We shall pray, we shall meditate the way we feel best from deep within. And God will select His Hour to illumine us so that He can fulfil Himself in and through us. In His fulfilment is our real achievement and real perfection.

Part II — Questions and answers — New York University

11. Question: Is the potential that anybody has for spiritual growth limited by astrological possibilities or some other possibilities which are available to them, or can everything be overcome with a great enough effort?

Sri Chinmoy: It depends on the eagerness of the aspirant and the intensity of his aspiration. There is no such thing as impossibility, but we have to know how much opposition we have to face. If we constantly pray and most soulfully meditate, then there is no difficulty that cannot be surmounted.

It often happens that when we cannot conquer some undivine forces during this lifetime, we feel that we will never be able to conquer these imperfections. But if we are real followers of Truth, eternal Truth, then we know this is not our first or last incarnation. At the age of four, let us say, we had a desire, and at the age of forty we fulfilled that desire. At the age of four we wanted something; at the age of forty we got it. But if we had died at the age of thirty-eight or thirty-nine, then we would not have fulfilled that desire. We would still have felt that it was impossible at the time of our death.

Now, at the age of forty, we have sincere aspiration to realise God. It may be that with this aspiration we will be able to realise God in two hundred years. But when we reach eighty we are totally tired, exhausted in the battlefield of life, so we go to the other world for rest. This does not mean that our opportunity to realise God is ended. Again we will come back and fight against ignorance like real soldiers in the battlefield of life. Then, after two hundred years of aspiration, we will realise God.

There is no such thing as impossibility. It is only a matter of time. But if we are really sincere and earnest, we can greatly expedite our spiritual journey. If something would take two years in the natural and normal course, we can achieve that very thing in three months or two months, or even a month if we are very devoted and sincere. Our achievements entirely depend on our sincerity, earnestness and the strength of our inner cry for the ultimate Truth.

12. Question: Why is there creation?

Sri Chinmoy: Creation is for satisfaction. When we create we get joy. When we compose a song we get joy; when we write a poem we get joy. God felt the necessity of satisfaction for Himself and for all of us. Without satisfaction we cannot last even for a second.

God was quite perfect when He was the silent Brahman, when He was in the trance-bound state. But He felt the necessity for creation because He felt that remaining alone could not satisfy Him. He was a tree without a branch. Then He said, "No, I want to have quite a few branches." Then He said, "No, branches are not enough. I want to have leaves." Then He created millions of leaves. So we are all His creation.

13. Question: If I am God and I have God, then why do I need God and want God?

Sri Chinmoy: Intrinsically, and by the very fact of your created existence, you are God and you have God. But since you are not consciously aware of it, at the same time you want God and you need God. What you really want and need is not God Himself, but conscious and constant knowledge of God and union with God.

14. Question: Does the divine Will predetermine what will happen in our life?

Sri Chinmoy: To some extent it is predetermined. Again we have God's Compassion, God's Love, to change our fate. As you sow, so you reap: this is one theory. Two young boys are playing. One has struck the other, so naturally he will be beaten by the one he has hurt. But if the first boy goes running to his father for protection, then the fellow he has hurt cannot strike him back. He is under the protection of somebody who has much more strength than the ordinary retributive justice. If you have made some mistake or done something wrong in your previous incarnation, the time will come for you to receive punishment. But before that, if you consciously feel that you have done something wrong, you can invoke the protection of the Supreme, the Almighty Father.

15. Question: What does God have to do with suffering, pain and sickness?

Sri Chinmoy: If you go deep within, then you will see that it is God who is suffering, that it is God who is going through each experience. Now you feel separated from God. That is why you say, "I am suffering, my friends are suffering, my relatives are suffering." But when you have the capacity for universal oneness, you will feel that it is only God who is having this experience in and through you and everybody else. He Himself is the disease, He Himself is the remedy. You call it suffering, but in God's Eye it is an experience that He Himself is going through in the process of His own evolution.

Part III — Questions and answers — University of Connecticut

16. Question: How can a person be sure that he really has aspiration?

Sri Chinmoy: A person can be sure that he has aspiration by the mere fact that the question has entered into his life. You have aspiration. Otherwise you would not have come here. You would have become a perfect friend to desire. Whoever comes to a spiritual place or wants to see a spiritual Master most certainly has aspiration. Now you may say that some people have come here out of curiosity. But even in curiosity there is aspiration. Otherwise the person would say, "Who cares for spiritual life? It is all useless." But if a person has some curiosity, he will say, "Let me see what a spiritual man looks like and what others are doing." Curiosity is a kind of subtle eagerness, an unconscious eagerness to learn something, to do something, to grow into something. Curiosity is the precursor of aspiration. Here there are many, many people who are sincere, and one or two who are just curious. Now the many who are sincere will be able to inspire the curious people easily.

To come back to your question, you do have aspiration. But if you are conscious of your aspiration, if you are confident about it, then you will make better progress. If you are doubtful of its existence in your life, you will not be able to march like a hero. You *do* have aspiration, so you should try to run as fast as possible, like a deer. If you do not try, you will just plod along like an Indian bullock cart. We are all given the opportunity to walk slowly or to run the fastest. Please try to run.

17. Question: When we find ourselves encountering difficulties in the spiritual life, is the best thing just to surrender to God's Will and leave it all up to Him?

Sri Chinmoy: It entirely depends on your own spiritual height, your own achievement. There are two types of seekers. One seeker is very idle, extremely idle. He has heard the idea of surrender to God's Will, so he will not lift a finger. "Let me surrender everything to God's Will and not do anything," he says. The other seeker will pray, meditate and devote his life dynamically to God. "I am offering the result of my aspiration to God," he says.

If one is sincere and really aspiring, he prays and meditates in a divine way, according to his capacity. He does what he can, and at the same time he watches all the situations, calamities and forces around him. He says, "I have done my part. Now it is up to God to free me from these undivine forces or unpleasant experiences." This is the best attitude. If we can go deep within every day during our meditation, we will become the observer, the witness, *Purusha*. But if we cannot go deep within every day in our meditation, the next best thing is to act like a hero. It is a kind of heroism when we offer the results of our actions to God. The result may take the form of defeat. But if we can gladly offer the result to God, we are a divine hero.

Unfortunately, most of us do not do that. We try a little, but when we see an enormous elephant in front of us, we give up. "It is simply useless," we say. And sometimes we blame God. Since we are encountering so many difficulties now that we have entered into the spiritual life, we think it would be better to return to the ordinary life. But at this point we are making a serious mistake. When we go deep within, we will realise that the difficulties we now are encountering did exist before. But at that time ignorance knew that we were absolutely at its mercy. Ignorance was our lord. We were fast asleep in the ignorance-room, so ignorance did not take the trouble to bother us much. Now that we are trying to come out of the sea of ignorance, ignorance is trying to pull us back. "Where are you going?" it demands. "You have to stay with me!" When we are conscious of the struggle, we are on our way out of the ignorance-room. The difficulties were there inside, but at that time we were totally unconscious of them. Now we are aware of them.

So if you can go deep within, please ask God to take care of you. Let your aspiration go high, higher, highest. But if you don't feel that you have very free access to God's Will, the best thing is to fight ignorance on the physical plane with your own eagerness and capacity. When wrong forces disturb you, you have to fight. If you surrender, many more wrong forces will attack you.

18. Question: What is the cause of ignorance?

Sri Chinmoy: The cause of ignorance is our fondness for limitations. Although we say we want to be vast, we get real pleasure in separating ourselves from others. We always have a sense of demarcation, partition. We speak about peace, universal peace, but every day it is "I" and "Mine". "I am for myself and I do not need anybody. I want to stay with myself. I will have nothing to do with you. Don't bother me." Ignorance comes when we bind ourselves consciously. But when we expand ourselves and feel the universe itself as our home, when we feel that we are for all and of all, then there is no ignorance. Ignorance comes into the picture only when we limit and bind ourselves and feel that this limitation is our real satisfaction. If we can feel real satisfaction lies only in our self-expansion, then there is no ignorance.

Part IV — Questions and answers — University of Maryland

19. Question: Is there any reason for doubt?

Sri Chinmoy: There is no reason for doubt. The only thing is that we cherish doubt because we are in ignorance. A child eats mud and dirt. What is the reason? He gets pleasure; he feels it is nourishing food. But when he grows up he will never touch it. He knows that he has to eat proper food. Like the child, we doubt because we have not seen the face of Reality. Once we have seen the face of Reality, how can we doubt? When I look at my hand, how can I doubt my hand? I may doubt a thought, a judgement, a feeling inside me, but my hand, which I see and feel, how can I doubt? But unless and until we have the vision of Reality, we will be subject to doubt.

Again, there are some people who believe in others. They may not have seen the face of Reality, but they believe because they know someone else has seen it. If a child has faith in his elder brother, he will immediately believe what his elder brother tells him. And then, when he grows up, he will see for himself that it was true.

In the spiritual life, you have to know that the act of doubting is useless. If you doubt yourself, you are consciously weakening your own possibilities and delaying your own progress. If you say, "I have done so many things wrong, I am not meant for the spiritual life. God does not care for me," then you are making a serious mistake. If you see that somebody is superior to you in the spiritual life, you should not become discouraged. Do not think that he was always superior to you. No! Once upon a time he was also a beginner like yourself. Everybody was a beginner. You do not get your Master's degree all at once. So the best thing is to allow yourself to grow inwardly, silently, with cheerfulness and patience.

When we doubt others, consciously or unconsciously we betray our own ignorance. When we see an elephant, if we doubt the elephant and say, "This is just a dog or a cat," the elephant is not going to lose anything. But we will be simply indulging in stupidity. Similarly, if we doubt God, then God will not lose even an iota of His Divinity. God will simply say that we are walking along the long road. There is a very short road and a very long road. If we walk along the path of doubt, the road is very long, arduous and, what is worse, it is constantly lengthening. There is no end to it. But when we follow the path of faith, not only do we run along an easy road, but every day the road shortens itself.

Inside us there is a white tablet of inner purity. The moment we doubt, we create a dark spot on it. If we persist, there comes a time when the whole tablet is covered with dark spots. But the moment we have faith, that tablet becomes clear and pure again, and we can write on it according to our soul's dictates. After we have written, then we can try to manifest the reality that we have seen, felt and realised in our inner life.

Part V — Questions and answers — University of Delaware

20. Question: What is the difference between the inner teacher and the outer teacher?

Sri Chinmoy: The ordinary teacher, the outer teacher, very often imposes certain ideas on the students. Although this is the land of freedom, there are some preconceived ideas which teachers unfortunately thrust upon the minds of students. But the inner teacher will not impose anything; he will not thrust any ideas on his disciples. On the contrary, he will consciously and devotedly try to bring forward the seeker's own inner wisdom. The spiritual Master knows perfectly well that he is not the ultimate Truth. He is not the Guru. The only real Guru is the Supreme. The Master will tell the disciple that the disciple has everything. "You have the treasure, you have the box and you have the key. But unfortunately you have not used the key for a long time and you have misplaced it. You cannot get to your inner wealth. I have come here to show you where you have put the key and I will help you open the box. Then, once you get the treasure, it all belongs to you. Then my role is over."

21. Question: Why is it that so many Indian spiritual Masters come to America instead of trying to help the people in their own country, where there is so much poverty and hunger?

Sri Chinmoy: Now, dear seeker, you have to know that a real spiritual man is not bound by any geographical or religious boundaries. Once you belong to God, you become universal. If you are a true seeker, you will feel that you are not an American or a Canadian or an Indian, but a citizen of the world. I am a spiritual man, and on the strength of my prayer and meditation I dare to say that I am a cosmopolitan. A spiritual Master is not bound by east or west or north or south; he will go wherever his Inner Pilot commands him. We are all spiritual brothers and sisters, and God is our common Father. If He wants a particular child of His to help His other children, then He will send the child to them.

If there is poverty and hunger in India, then certainly it is God's concern. And it is also God's concern if many people in the West are not living a spiritual life. Since it is God's concern, it is He who asks the spiritual Masters to come to the West. The same God sends Westerners who have scientific and material knowledge to the East.

To confine any human being to his native land is foolishness. It is the mind that creates this problem. The mind gets satisfaction only in separation, whereas the heart gets satisfaction in identification and oneness. If you can remain in the heart, then you will feel the joy of identification with the vast reality. At that time there is no "I" or "you", but all "we".

Part VI — Questions and answers — Princeton University

22. Question: How can we have more joy and less tension in our daily life?

Sri Chinmoy: We can have more joy only in self-giving, not in demanding. When there is tension, it is because we want something to be done in our own way while others want it done in their way. Tension starts in the mind because we see light in one way and others see light in some other way. So there is no peace, no poise, only tension.

Tension also comes when we want to do something in the twinkling of an eye that takes two hours or two days to do. We have to know that God has not thought of it in that way. God wants us to take two hours or two days to achieve it. If we can keep God's Hour in our minds and not our own hour, we will get joy. Tension goes away from the seeker's mind when he knows the art of surrendering to God's Will.

We must see that God operates not only in us but in others as well. God also operates in our so-called enemies. But these are not our real enemies. Our real enemies are our doubt, fear, anxiety and worry. When we do not cry to perfect others, but only try to perfect our own lives then we will have joy. Also, if we do not expect anything from anybody else but expect everything only from God, then we will get joy. If we can feel that we are not indispensable, that without us the world can go on perfectly well, then we will have joy. This is the way we can all get abundant joy in our spiritual life.

23. Question: *If we have a job that involves a lot of thinking and activity, how can we maintain any sense of spirituality or light?*

Sri Chinmoy: Undoubtedly, it is a difficult task. But early in the morning, before you enter into the hustle and bustle of life, before you go to your office, you are given ample opportunity by God to meditate on your heart. When you meditate early in the morning, you gain something from God: Peace, Light and Bliss. Then, when you go to your office after you have meditated early in the morning, inside your heart you have to feel that you are carrying some spiritual dollars. There you keep your spiritual wealth safe and protected. Then, while you are in the office, and are involved in your multifarious daily activities, you are carrying this inner wealth with you. When you need peace of mind or poise, immediately try to think of the wealth that you have inside you. It is as if you have kept a candle burning inside your heart. The moment you bring the candle out, the darkness of the outer world around you is illumined.

You always have the capacity to bring something forward which you have earned from your morning meditation. When you work you get a salary. In the inner life your work is your meditation. When you pray and meditate you get your salary, which is light. You put it inside your heart and then, when you need some peace or light or joy in your outer life, you can bring it out from deep within you to illumine you and save you in moments of crisis.

Part VII — Questions and answers — University of Pennsylvania

24. Question: What dies?

Sri Chinmoy: Ignorance in us dies. But if we see ignorance with our inner eye, inner vision, we see that ignorance does not actually die but becomes transformed into light. When we use our earthly knowledge, we see that something lives for a long time and then it dies. But when we use our intuition we see that everything is in the process of transformation, illumination and perfection.

In India we have the trinity of God in three aspects. They are Brahma, Vishnu and Shiva; the Creator, the Preserver and the Destroyer or Transformer. Some people use the term "Destroyer", but inner philosophy uses the term "Transformer". God has created the world and He wants to preserve it. Who wants to destroy his own children? The mother will not destroy her children. The mother will only try to transform them. If the children are naughty and mischievous, the mother will not throw them out of the house. The mother will say, "My child only needs illumination and perfection." There is a feeling of oneness that the mother has with her children.

Creator and creation are one. When someone creates something, immediately he identifies himself with the creation. God has created us. So He is not going to destroy us. He is only going to transform us. But when we feel separated from God, the Source, when we feel that He is the Creator and we are the creation, then the problem arises. But if we go deep within, we see that there is nothing to be killed. That which needs transformation will naturally undergo transformation, that which needs illumination will undergo illumination and that which needs perfection will undergo perfection.

25. Question: Can we make as much spiritual progress living in the world and leading the life of a householder as we would living an ashram life?

Sri Chinmoy: Unfortunately, it is not possible. Again, we have to know what kind of ashram life we are speaking of. One may live in an ashram, but at the same time think constantly of ordinary life — "That person has become a success and the world is appreciating him. This person everybody is extolling to the skies. But I am doing nothing but living in an ashram." This kind of thing is not real ashram life at all. If you live a proper ashram life, if you are constantly aspiring and have no outer bondage, then there is no one to come between you and God. If your whole life is given totally and unconditionally to God-realisation, if you are running towards the Goal all alone with only God in mind, naturally you will make the fastest progress, while someone who has family problems and has to deal all the time with the unaspiring world will naturally make slower progress.

But there is a way that the householder can make very fast progress. If the householder feels that he is looking after his near and dear ones, not because they are near and dear to him, but because the Living Presence of God is inside them, this is very good. If God comes into the picture all the time, then there will always be a soulful feeling towards the near and dear ones. It is the same thing with a student. If someone is studying to get world information or world knowledge which he feels is necessary, or if he is studying so he can get a good job, then that person will make no progress. But if the person studying feels that he has the capacity to receive and reveal God's Light only in a small quantity right now, but that the knowledge he is getting from books and the outer world is only a preparation for the inner knowledge, then this is the right attitude. Right now he is reading books written by others. But a day will come when he will be in a position to read his own book, which is already written inside his soul. Right now he does not have the capacity to read his inner book, but he feels that the inner life is leading him and guiding him in and through the outer knowledge. Today you have the capacity only to receive just a little of God's Light, through books. But tomorrow you will have a larger vessel and enter into the Ocean of God's Light.

If you have this divine attitude towards studies or towards your family, then you will make very fast progress. Then, if you are sincere and surrendered to God's Will, when the Hour strikes and God feels the necessity of your entering into ashram life, you will do so. If, in the beginning, you are not given the opportunity, do not feel that you are not meant for the spiritual life. Far from it! God knows His Will far better than you do. There are certain reasons why He wants you to go through the householder life or the student life — the life of outer responsibilities.

Part VIII — Questions and answers — Marlboro College

26. Question: *When you speak of someone seeking enlightenment, doesn't that imply that the person does not have it inside him? And how can one ever attain it by seeking it?*

Sri Chinmoy: It is like this: I had something, but I have misplaced it. Suppose I had something precious in my room. It was I who had it and I who misplaced it, and now it is I who am searching for it. It has always been mine, but I do not know where it is. But when I begin searching for it, I know that after some time I will find it. Through constant seeking I will get back my inner wealth, which is illumination.

27. Question: *Do you have any idea of why it was lost?*

Sri Chinmoy: When we came into the world we felt that temptation was more important than actual realisation. It is as though two coins were put in front of us. One was a counterfeit or false coin; the other was authentic. But the counterfeit coin was more charming on the outer plane than the real one. So we were attracted by the one that was outwardly charming, while we ignored the genuine one.

28. Question: *Why are we more attracted to temptation, or the unreal coin?*

Sri Chinmoy: In the ordinary life, on the superficial plane, we always feel that the unreal is more charming. Here on earth, if we can get something by hook or by crook, if we can achieve something in the twinkling of an eye, we are pleased. To discipline our lives for five minutes seems most difficult. Anything that is difficult for us we immediately shun; while that which is within our immediate reach we try to grasp. That is why we do not get the real. The real is always there, but to achieve it we have to work very hard. Nevertheless, we have to know that true satisfaction, abiding satisfaction, can come only from the attainment of the real.

29. Question: Is meditation the only way to achieve enlightenment?

Sri Chinmoy: No. Prayer is another way. In the Western world you pray, and in the Eastern world we prefer to meditate. These are two roads which eventually converge and lead to the same destination. If you pray most soulfully, you will definitely get illumination. Again, if you meditate soulfully, you are sure to get illumination.

Some people like to pray while others like to meditate. If you feel that prayer is most effective in your life, then naturally you will pray most soulfully. And if you feel that meditation helps you most convincingly in your life of aspiration, then you try to meditate. It is the individual who has to make the choice.

FIFTY FREEDOM-BOATS TO ONE GOLDEN SHORE

NOTES TO FIFTY FREEDOM-BOATS TO ONE GOLDEN SHORE,
BOOK 1

1. Manning Hall, Brown University, Providence, Rhode Island,
9 January 1974 — 2:00 pm.
2. Paine Hall, Harvard University, Cambridge, Massachusetts,
9 January 1974 — 8:00 pm.
3. College Hall, Dartmouth College, Hanover, New Hampshire,
11 January 1974.
4. Meyer Hall, New York University, New York, New York,
12 January 1974.
5. St Thomas Aquinas Chapel, University of Connecticut, Storrs,
Connecticut, 14 January 1974.
6. West Chapel, University of Maryland, College Park,
Maryland, 16 January 1974 — 2:00 pm.
7. Smith Hall, University of Delaware, Newark, Delaware,
16 January 1974 — 8:00 pm.
8. Commons Room, Graduate School, Princeton University,
Princeton, New Jersey, 22 January 1974.
9. David Rittenhouse Auditorium, University of Pennsylvania,
Philadelphia, Pennsylvania, 22 January 1974 — 8:00 pm.
10. Happy Valley Common Room, Marlboro College, Marlboro,
Vermont, 25 January 1974.
11-15. Meyer Hall, New York University, New
York, New York, 12 January 1974.
16-18. St Thomas Aquinas Chapel, University of Connecticut,
Storrs, Connecticut, 14 January 1974.
19. West Chapel, University of Maryland, College Park, Maryland,
16 January 1974 — 2:00 pm.
20-21. Smith Hall, University of Delaware, Newark, Delaware,
16 January 1974 — 8:00 pm.
22-23. Commons Room, Graduate School, Princeton University, Princeton, New Jersey, 22 January 1974.
24-25. David Rittenhouse Auditorium, University of Pennsylvania,
Philadelphia, Pennsylvania, 22 January 1974 — 8:00 pm

26-29. Happy Valley Common Room, Marlboro College, Marlboro, Vermont, 25 January 1974.

FIFTY FREEDOM-BOATS
TO ONE GOLDEN SHORE

BOOK 2

Part IX — Lectures

30. Power

Dear sisters and brothers, dear seekers of the ultimate Truth, I wish to give a talk on power. We all know what power is. Everyone from a child to an octogenarian can tell us what power is. But I wish to say a few words on power from the spiritual point of view, based on my own inner experiences.

Life is action and action is power. Now, whom does this power belong to? Is it mine? No, never! Were it my power, I could use it at any time. But there have been many times when I wanted to use power and could not, precisely because this power does not belong to me. This power does not belong to any individual. It belongs to some higher realm.

Why do we want power? We want power because we feel that it will satisfy us in various ways. Within us we have the animal, the human and the divine. Although we have come out of the animal kingdom, we still have a good many animal propensities in our life. Although we are aspiring for a divine and higher life, the unlit, the obscure, the undivine animal and human in us are still predominant. To satisfy the animal in us, we want power to destroy the world. To satisfy the human in us, we want power to gain supremacy over others and lord it over them; we want power so that we can bring others under our control and make them extol us to the skies. To satisfy the divine in us, we want power so we can identify ourselves with all and sundry. The divine in us wants to become inseparably one with all human beings on earth. With the divine, there is no question of destruction, no question of supremacy; there is only the universal song of oneness.

Here we all are seekers. Before we entered into the inner life, the life of self-discipline, we noticed quite a few things about the members of our family: body, vital, mind and heart. We discovered that our body was exceedingly weak, impotent; our vital was extremely aggressive, dangerous; our mind was constantly confused, obscure, doubtful; and our heart was continually insecure. We stayed with our weak body, aggressive vital, unlit mind and insecure heart for a good many years.

Then something deep within prompted us to enter into the spiritual life, the life that could give us the message of the Infinite, the Eternal and the Immortal. Now that we have started making progress in the spiritual life, we have come to realise that this very body of ours can become most powerful. Our vital, our mind and our heart can also become most powerful. But we must know that the power of the body is not the power that we outwardly see, the power that takes the form of destruction. The infinite Power that we now see in the body is expressed in the body's self-dedication to the Supreme Lord. The boundless Power that we now see in the vital is expressed in the vital's dynamic, enthusiastic urge to welcome the vast world as its very own. The infinite Power that we now notice in the mind is expressed in the mind's clear, perfect vision of the ever-transcending Beyond. Finally, the infinite Power that we now notice in the sun-vast heart reveals that there, in the heart, our divinity grows and our reality constantly fulfils its own immortality.

There are three types of power usually seen in the present-day world: machine-power, man-power and soul-power. Machine-power is to some extent blind. It takes tremendous joy in destroying the world. Although machine-power is unconscious, even in its unconsciousness we notice that, in a subtle way, it enjoys destruction. But we must remember that this machine-power is utilised by man-power, by the power of man's fertile brain. So machine-power can easily be brought under our control if we use our human brain-power or, preferably, our heart-power. Heart-power is the power of love, the power of oneness. If we use the power of our love and the power of our oneness, then the power of destruction can easily be nullified.

Our soul-power is constantly, incessantly trying to come to the fore and guide our outer consciousness, our outer life. Unfortunately, right now we do not pay any attention to the soul-power; but once we go deep within and become familiar with it, we shall be able to use it most effectively. The soul-power is the power of universal oneness. The soul-power is the power of real fulfilment and complete perfection in our aspiring lives.

There is a negative power and there is a positive power. Negative power we see in our idleness. When we live a lethargic, *tamasic* life, we tell God that we are tired and exhausted, that we do not want to budge an inch. We say, "If it is true that You are all Compassion, then please offer us what You have: Peace, Light and Bliss." But if an idle person invokes God in this way, God is not going to listen to his prayer. Never! Again, a *rajasic* person, a man of unpolished, undisciplined dynamism — or, rather, aggression — wants to pull down Peace, Light and Bliss from Above by dint of his unillumined will for power. If he succeeds, it will be a disaster; for when something is achieved untimely, it is never given due value or utilised for a divine purpose. If we utilise power for an undivine purpose, we invite destruction into our life of aspiration. If we utilise power for a divine purpose, we shall be fulfilled in a spiritual, divine and immortal way.

Positive power can be all-fulfilling. The Upanishads, the sacred Vedic lore of India, tell us that a weakling can never realise the highest Absolute.

Nāyam ātmā bala hīnena labhy

The soul cannot be won by the weakling…

If we at all want to dive into the inner life, if we want to be guided and moulded by the soul, then we have to be extremely strong. The strength we need is not so much physical strength, but the strength of self-discipline, the strength of self-enquiry, the strength of self-withdrawal from the life of the senses, the strength of self-effacement in the world of offering and self-fulfilment in the world of aspiration and meditation. The Upanishads again inspire us most profoundly:

uttiṣṭhata jāgrata prāpya varān nibodhata…

Arise, awake, realise and achieve the Highest with the help of the illumining, guiding and fulfilling Masters.

The path is as sharp as the edge of a razor, difficult to cross, hard to tread — so declare the wise sages.

But the Upanishads in no way want to discourage us. On the contrary, this sacred message will always inspire us to run towards the Goal. But we have to know that only he who is awakened can run towards the ultimate Goal. The Goal, God-realisation, cannot forever remain unattained or unattainable. Today's impossibility will not always remain an impossibility. No! If the seeker's cry is strong and powerful, the Smile from Above is bound to dawn.

In our day-to-day life we constantly exercise power, either in accepting or in rejecting reality. When we use power to accept reality with a view to transforming it, if necessity demands, then this power is called the soul's power, the power of the Source. But if we exercise power to reject the world-situation, to reject the possibilities of the world, to reject this world because we feel that its sufferings and turmoil are past correction, then our own transformation and illumination will always remain for us a far cry.

Each human being gets the opportunity to invoke power in various ways. Every day he gets the golden opportunity to invoke power with his hope. Hope is nothing but concealed power. When we cherish hope, we must know that we are consciously or unconsciously invoking an inner or higher power. Today's hope turns into tomorrow's actuality. Today's dream is bound to be fulfilled in tomorrow's reality.

As hope is a power, so also is expectation a power. We expect many things from ourselves and from the world. We feel that today's expectation is going to bring down tomorrow's realisation. But in the spiritual life, we play the role without any expectation whatsoever. We feel that our role is to perform divine service, but not to expect the fruits thereof. If we can love, serve, pray and meditate with utmost sincerity, purity and self-offering, then our God-appointed realisation is bound to dawn. It will far transcend our highest expectation and far surpass the flights of our loftiest imagination.

In the spiritual life we deal with silence and we deal with sound and finally, we deal with a Consciousness which is beyond both silence and sound. Silence is power. This silence creates the world within us and without. Sound, the cosmic sound, is also power. As the transcendental Silence creates the world, so does the cosmic Sound sustain and maintain the world. Finally, the Consciousness which transcends both sound and silence immortalises the seeker's aspiring being.

We cannot separate the Power of God from His other divine aspects. Power is one aspect of God; Love is another. In the ordinary life, power is power and love is love. But in the spiritual life, in God's Life, Power and Love are inseparable; they are like the obverse and reverse of the same coin. Now, if we do not properly understand the power of love and the love of power, we run into the most deplorable difficulties. Before we realise the highest transcendental Truth, what we have is the love of power. But after we realise the Truth, we come to feel that there is only one thing in our life, and that is the power of love. As long as we remain in the world of desire, we cherish the love of power. But the moment we enter into the world of aspiration, dedication and illumination, we come to realise the power of love. The love of power destroys the Palace of Truth within us. The power of love builds the Palace of Truth within us and creates the Kingdom of Heaven within and without us, bringing down Infinity to play in the heart of the finite. When the power of love replaces the love of power, man will have a new name: God.

31. Spirituality

Dear sisters and brothers, dear seekers of the ultimate Truth, I wish to give a talk on spirituality. As we all know, spirituality is a vast subject, and here, in an hour, I can never do justice to it. But let me at least make a beginning.

In spirituality we come to learn of two significant terms: "meditation" and "dedicated service". All of us here are fully aware of these two terms. Some of you may use the terms "knowledge" and "work". Knowledge is the result of meditation.

When we dive deep within, we see, we feel and we grow into the highest Knowledge. Work, when it is done in a divine spirit and for a divine purpose, is dedicated service. The combination of meditation and dedicated service makes a man perfect.

In this world, many are of the opinion that spirituality cannot offer a balanced life, but I wish to say that they are badly mistaken. It is spirituality alone that can offer us a real life, a balanced life, a practical life. Who is practical? He who knows the truth and who knows how to apply the truth in his daily life. A spiritual person is he who tries to know the truth today, to discover the truth tomorrow and to apply the truth the following day in all his multifarious activities. A spiritual person is someone who goes to the very root of the Truth, for he knows that if there is no root there cannot be any tree. And the root of the Truth is love. A spiritual person meditates not for his own sake alone; he meditates for all and sundry. He meditates for his dear ones, and he meditates for every human being on earth. His is a life of love and dedication.

Each individual has his own way of reaching the ultimate Truth. One may find it easier to reach the Truth through dedicated service, by loving God in each human being, by seeing and feeling the divinity in humanity. Another may want to dive deep within and first reach the Source, and then work on the earth-plane. Both are doing the right thing. But the person who does not aspire and does not want to aspire in any way — who is useless in society — is either a fool or a dead soul.

Each seeker should feel that it is his bounden duty to realise the Highest. But each seeker must know that God-realisation, the realisation of the ultimate Truth, need not and cannot be the sole monopoly of any one individual. Everyone is destined to reach the Highest. But there is a way that leads a seeker to his destination quite fast, and that is the way of the heart. If we empty the heart and welcome the eternal Guest, our eternal Beloved, He comes in and fulfils His own transcendental Reality in our day-to-day existence. The other way, the way of the mind, is lengthier and more difficult. But if we can silence the mind, then Peace, Light, Bliss and Power in infinite measure can enter into us also.

We are all seekers. In our inner life, our spiritual life, we have already travelled millions of miles. Although we may at times fall victims to our animal qualities and indulge in quarrelling, fighting and other negative and destructive actions, still we no longer cherish or appreciate the animal in us. We know that what we actually want from our lives is Peace, Light and Bliss. The animal in us has played its role, and now the human in us is playing its role. We are cherishing the hope that today's human qualities will be transcended and transformed into divine Reality. When we meditate, we feel that this is no longer a hope, but a certainty. When we meditate deeply, profoundly, in the very depths of our heart, we feel that there is no such thing as impossibility. As we have transcended the animal kingdom, so also must we transcend our human weaknesses, imperfections, limitations and bondage.

In the Western world, meditation is not as common as prayer, but I wish to say that prayer and meditation are like two most intimate brothers. If we pray soulfully, we can get what meditation offers us. When we pray, we feel that something from within, from our very depths, from the inmost recesses of our heart, is climbing high, higher, highest. And we feel that somebody is there to listen to our prayer, or somebody is there to receive us at the pinnacle of our aspiration's height. When we meditate soulfully, devotedly, in pin-drop silence, we feel that a divine Guest is descending into our heart to guide us, to illumine us, to perfect us and to fulfil His own transcendental

Reality within us. We feel that the Infinite is entering into the finite for their mutual fulfilment.

In this world there is a need for peace. This peace comes only from within, and we can bring it to the fore only through meditation. If we can meditate soulfully for ten minutes every day, we will energise our entire being with Peace. Peace houses Light, Bliss, Fulfilment and Satisfaction. We can have Peace not by possessing the world or leading the world, but by becoming a lover of the world.

Now when we become a lover of the world, we may commit a most deplorable mistake: we may expect something from the world in return for our love. We are ready to accept the limitations and imperfections of the world as our very own. But if in spite of our best efforts, our best intentions, our deepest love and compassion for the world, the world does not listen to us or does not offer us enough gratitude, at that time we make an inner demand on the world. At the beginning of our service, we demand everything from the world in return for our offering, our life of sacrifice. If we give something, we expect the same amount in return, if not more. Then there comes a time when we give as much as we have, we give to the utmost of our capacity, and we expect in return only an infinitesimal measure of what we have given. But even if we expect just an infinitesimal quantity of appreciation from the world, I wish to say that we are bound to be unhappy; we are bound to be wanting in peace. Let us give to the world unconditionally what we have and what we are: Love. The message of love we get only from our daily prayer and meditation. We know that love means oneness, inseparable oneness. And in oneness there is no expectation, no demand.

There are two ways to love. One way is to go first to the human love and then reach upward to the ultimate Love, the divine Love. The other way is to reach the divine Love first and then enter into and transform the human love. The divine Love always inspires us, guides us and moulds us into something immortal, which we can offer to humanity. The human love frustrates us, disappoints us, and finally constrains us to try to enter into the kingdom of divine Love.

We have to love life and also love truth. Truth and life can never be separated. When we try to separate truth and life we cannot make any progress. In our human love, frustration may loom large. But in the divine life, love is constantly building us and shaping us into the very image of God.

We have spoken about peace and love. If someone asks us to speak about peace, we will be able to speak most eloquently. But speech does not help us to establish the kingdom of peace on earth. It is our silent prayer and soulful meditation that can give us the peace of mind which our little world, our own personal world, badly needs, just as the entire outer world needs it. To begin at the beginning with ourselves is the only way we can eventually bring peace to the world. If I do not have peace myself, how can I offer peace to others? Impossible!

We have a body, which we regard as the only reality. When we satisfy the need of the body for earthly food, for nourishment, we feel that we have fulfilled our task. But in our inner life also we have someone to feed every day, and that is our soul, the divine being within us, the conscious representative of God on earth. Although we feed our body every day, somehow we fail to feed this divine child within us. Since we never do the first thing first, we remain unsatisfied here on earth. First we must go deep within, and then — from within — we must go without. The inner life must constantly embrace, guide and inspire the outer life. The outer life is eventually liberated by the inner life, which already has liberation in fullest measure.

The inner life and the outer life can and must run abreast. The inner life will constantly receive messages from Above, messages of Infinity, Eternity and Immortality. Infinity, Eternity and Immortality are not vague terms. When one becomes an advanced seeker, he sees and feels infinite Peace, Light and Bliss within himself. One need not be a God-realised soul to have this experience. All of us have Peace, Light and Bliss in infinite measure in the very depths of our aspiring spiritual heart.

But right now the door of our heart is locked by ignorance. We have to open the door and dive deep within to go beyond ignorance to where our own Peace, Light and Truth reside.

We are God's children, His chosen instruments. God abides within us as a constant Dream, and we live in God as His only reality. He lives in us as a Dream that will ultimately be transformed into reality; and we live in Him as a reality that will grow into His ever-ascending, ever-blossoming Dream. We are all seekers, and we are all in a boat. Our journey can never come to an end, for God, the eternal Pilot, is our Pilot, and we are in His Boat. He is the Boatman, He Himself is the Boat and He is the Golden Shore of the Beyond.

32. Freedom

Dear seekers of Truth, Light and Bliss, I am extremely glad to be at this august university today. This university loves progress more than anything. In our spiritual life also, we care for only one thing — progress. We do not care for success; we care only for progress, and in our progress looms large our success. Today's success is the starting point for tomorrow's achievement. Success never gives satisfaction, but when we make progress we do get satisfaction. Progress is the Will of God working in and through us, carrying us safely to our ultimate Goal.

Today I wish to give a short talk on Freedom. We all know something about what freedom is, for freedom is very familiar to each individual soul. As a freedom-loving country, America stands in the vanguard of the freedom-loving countries. So, dear sisters and brothers, perhaps you know more about freedom than I do. But from the spiritual point of view, for the seeker of the Infinite Truth, I would like to say a few words on spiritual freedom, inner freedom.

What is freedom? Freedom is our conscious, spontaneous and selfless search for Light, abundant Light, infinite Light.

There are two kinds of Light: the outer light and the inner light. The outer light exposes us, examines us and judges us. The inner light awakens us, illumines us and fulfils us.

Once we enter into the world of aspiration, we come to realise that there are three types of freedom: animal freedom, human freedom and divine freedom. Animal freedom enjoys total destruction. Human freedom enjoys fleeting or deluding pleasure. Divine freedom enjoys illumining and fulfilling oneness. Animal freedom and human freedom are earth-bound freedom. Divine freedom is Heaven-free freedom. Earth-bound freedom is the song of our unlit ego's supremacy. Heaven-free freedom is the song of our reality's perfection and divinity's manifestation.

In today's world, man and perfection are perfect strangers. In tomorrow's world, man and perfection will be bosom friends, illumining friends and fulfilling brothers. In the mind of today's world, divine manifestation is sheer impossibility; but in the heart of tomorrow's world, the divine manifestation is an unmistakable inevitability.

Spiritual freedom is our liberation from the mire of self-created bondage. When the body is liberated from the mire of ignorance, the body divinely serves God in man. When the vital is liberated from the aggression of ignorance-dream, the vital divinely loves God in man. When the mind is liberated from its tiny, limited ignorance-cave, the mind divinely manifests God in man. When the heart is liberated from its insecurity-prison cell, the heart constantly feels the Supreme Pilot here on earth, there in Heaven.

In the spiritual life, we need speed. To my great joy, we are very close to Detroit, the capital of the automobile world, the city of speed. In the inner life, speed is aspiration. If there is no aspiration, then there is no speed, and God-realisation remains a far cry. We know the speed of an Indian bullock cart and the speed of a modern jet plane. Aspiration has the speed of a modern jet plane. Aspiration is the heart's mounting cry that finds its satisfaction only when it reaches the goal of the ever-transcending Beyond. Once it reaches the Goal, the inner being is inundated with freedom, the freedom that feeds us, energises us and fulfils the hunger of humanity.

Right now, if you ask, "Who needs freedom?" our answer is that everyone needs freedom. If you ask, "Who has freedom?" the answer is that nobody has it. But if we launch into the spiritual life, if we follow the path devotedly, soulfully and unconditionally, then today's bondage can be transformed into tomorrow's freedom. Outer freedom is fleeting and badly lacking in satisfaction. Inner freedom gives us real and abiding satisfaction. Unless and until we have attained satisfaction, we shall always remain unfulfilled and empty.

In order to bring satisfaction into our life, we cry deep within. When God's Hour strikes in our life of aspiration, we become not only men of freedom but also lovers of freedom. At that time we transform mankind with our embodied, revealed and manifested Freedom Divine.

Now we are in the state of Michigan. The state motto is extremely significant from the spiritual point of view: "If you seek a pleasant peninsula, look about you." In the spiritual life, we are looking for a spiritual peninsula. The peninsula is Love, Devotion and Surrender — Divine Love, Divine Devotion and Divine Surrender. Human love binds; Divine Love expands. Human devotion is our unconscious attachment; Divine Devotion is our conscious awareness of our ultimate reality. Human surrender is the surrender of a slave to his master; Divine Surrender is the surrender of the finite to the Infinite. This surrender is conscious, wholehearted and unconditional, and it allows the human being to realise his Source, God.

After God-realisation, the finite human life becomes inseparably one with the Infinite. At that time, the Infinite sings its most soulful song, the song of God-Reality, and the finite sings its eternal song, the cry of millennia.

The moment we enter the spiritual life, one sublime thought, word and idea becomes paramount to us, and that is "consciousness". Strangely enough, this state of being abounds in lakes. Lakes consist of water, which signifies consciousness. Consciousness and spirituality are inseparable.

When we elevate our consciousness to the highest level of awareness, illumination dawns. When we spread the wings of our consciousness, we fly into the sky of Immortality. Each seeker consciously tries to expand his consciousness, illumine his consciousness and fulfil his consciousness; for in the expansion, illumination and fulfilment of his consciousness, he becomes one with the real, divine Supreme, his Source and his Goal.

33. Peace

Dear sisters and brothers, dear seekers of the ultimate Truth, I wish to give a talk on peace.

Peace is a most familiar word. Each seeker knows what peace is according to his receptivity's capacity. I am a seeker. I wish to share with you the peace that I have experienced. By offering my experience, I wish to become totally one, inseparably one, with your life of aspiration and dedication.

What is peace? Peace is our liberation from bondage. What is liberation? Liberation is our universal oneness with God the Unity and God the Multiplicity. What is bondage? Bondage is the dance of our unlit ego. What is ego? Ego is the unreal in us. And what is the real in us? The real in us is Truth; the real in us is God. God and Truth are inseparable, the obverse and reverse of the same coin.

What is peace? Peace is our satisfaction. What is satisfaction? Satisfaction is our conscious and constant oneness with the Will of the Supreme Pilot. Where does this satisfaction lie? It lies in our self-giving and in our God-becoming.

Peace, the world needs. We all need peace. But when we think of peace we try to discover it in our mind. We use the term "peace of mind". We feel that peace can be found only in the mind, and if once we can discover peace in the mind, then our problems will be solved for good. But at this point I wish to say that the mind we are referring to is the physical mind. This mind is the doubting mind, and in the doubting mind we can never feel the presence of peace. We can feel the presence of peace only in the loving heart. The doubting mind leads us to total frustration. The loving heart leads us to complete satisfaction. We doubt, and then we feel a barren desert within us. We love, and then we feel a sea of Reality and Divinity within us.

Peace is not to be found in external knowledge. Most of our external knowledge is founded on information, and information cannot give us any abiding satisfaction. Peace is not to be found in outer efficiency. Peace is found in self-mastery.

If we want to achieve peace in our inner and outer life, then we must know the necessity of reciprocal inclusiveness and not mutual exclusiveness. Earth and Heaven must be united. Heaven has the silence of the soul. Earth has the sound of life. The silence of the soul leads us to our Source, the highest Reality; and the sound of life allows us to manifest what is within that highest Reality. In the inclusiveness of earth and Heaven we can achieve peace.

Peace is the only authority in our life of ascent and descent. When we ascend, we learn the song of unity in multiplicity. When we descend, we learn the song of multiplicity in unity.

All of us here are seekers. We are all children of God. We are progressing according to our inner intensity and our soul's necessity. Each individual member of the world family has a special way of achieving peace. A child feels that he can achieve peace only by making noise. Inside noise, what looms large for him is peace. An adolescent finds peace only in constant activity. A youth finds peace only by creating a new world or by destroying the old world. An old man finds peace in unlearning most of the things he has learnt from the ignorant world. When he unlearns, he feels considerable peace. He also achieves peace by placing himself at the Feet of the Supreme Pilot.

Peace is our inner wealth. This inner wealth we can bring to the fore only when we expect nothing from the outer world and everything from the Supreme Pilot within us, at God's Choice Hour. Often, when we work for the world and serve the world we feel that it is the world's bounden duty to offer us gratitude or to acknowledge our service. When we expect something from the world, we are bound to meet with frustration. But when we expect from the Inner Pilot, He fulfils us beyond the flight of our imagination. But one thing we must know, and that is that God has an Hour of His own.

Our duty is to pray for peace, meditate on peace, concentrate on peace and contemplate on peace. God's duty is to inundate us with His Peace. When we know the art of surrender, the kingdom of peace within us cannot separate itself from our living reality. It is our conscious inner surrender, our unconditional surrender to the Inner Pilot that expedites our journey towards the discovery of the all-illumining and all-fulfilling Peace.

Now we are in the state of Ohio. The state motto is most significant for all seekers: "With God, all things are possible." The moment we enter into the spiritual life, we feel there can be no better, more encouraging and more illumining message than this. A beginner-seeker believes in it. An advanced seeker goes one step further and feels that God is the Doer, God is the Action and God is the Fruit thereof. So, our first lesson in the spiritual life is that everything is possible with God. Then later we come to feel that we do nothing, that it is God who does everything in and through us. This is the great lesson, the ultimate lesson, that we learn from our inner school.

The capital of the state of Ohio is Columbus. In the state of spirituality, there is only one capital, and that is aspiration. On the strength of aspiration we can achieve our Goal. On the strength of aspiration we transcend constantly our earthly reality and existence. No matter in which field we apply aspiration, the mounting flame within us, we are bound to achieve success. The state of Ohio offers us a shining example. From Ohio, seven American Presidents came, and offered their loftiest height and light to the whole country. Not only in the field of politics, but in every walk of life, when we aspire, our aspiration leads us to the destined goal.

Every day the Almighty Father, the ever-Compassionate Father, gives us ample opportunity to discover something new. The thing that we are discovering is love, love divine. Love divine is at once eternally ancient and eternally new. When we discover love divine within us, we grow into the very image of God the eternal Lover and God the eternal Beloved, who ever abides within us.

34. Success and progress

[Excerpt from the introduction by Dr John Philip Posey, Associate Professor of History and Director of Non-Western Core Programme: "I was delighted that a rather eminent religious leader was going to be in the Midwest giving a series of lectures here. He seemed to be interested in coming down to Indiana, so I jumped at the opportunity. I was a little bit concerned that this Wednesday morning would not be a time to get too many people to a lecture, but somehow my illusions have been smashed..."]

Dr Posey, I am most grateful to you for your kind words. Since last evening, your heart of magnanimity has touched my heart most deeply. In silence I pray to the Almighty Father to grant you His choicest Love and Blessings. Human life is a series of experiences. Six years ago, while I was in Puerto Rico, I went to a chapel and was insulted and scolded vehemently by the Mother Superior. What was my crime? That I was an Indian, a Hindu, and I entered a Christian chapel. But today at St Joseph's College I am basking in the kindness of everyone here. Both experiences I offer at the Feet of the Almighty Father.

I am a seeker. I am a devoted brother of mankind. I try to

serve the Almighty Father in each of my brothers and sisters. And if anybody asks, my foremost qualification is that I am a humble lover of humanity. Dear sisters and brothers, dear seekers of the Infinite Truth, we are all seated in a boat. The name of this boat is God's Dream-Boat, and our Pilot is the Lord Supreme. He is carrying us to the shores of the Golden Beyond. I wish to give a short talk on success in the life of desire and progress in the life of aspiration.

Success we want; progress we need. When we live in the word of desire, teeming desire, we want success. We feel that it is everything. But when we live in the world of aspiration, we come to realise that what we actually need is progress, continual and constant progress.

Success gives us name and fame. Progress gives us a higher inspiration, a deeper faith and a stronger assurance.

Our success is immediately claimed by many. It is claimed even by those who had nothing to do with its advent. But our progress is treasured by only one Person, our eternally beloved Father Supreme.

Success is the song of possession. We want to possess the world, but to our wide surprise we see that before we can possess even one person on earth, we have been mercilessly possessed and bound by the world at large.

Possession, ambition and outer success go together. The strength of ambition finally offers us success. But the strength of surrender to the Almighty Father grants us progress, which is what the Supreme wants from our lives.

When ambition becomes our bosom friend, when our inner being is surcharged with determination, we achieve success. But we have to realise that in the spiritual life when we offer and surrender our ambition to the Source, we make true progress. And in this progress we find real fulfilment. When we succeed in something in the outer world, we feel that we have done it in spite of opposition from the entire world. We feel that it is by virtue of our own capacities that we have achieved our desired success. But when we make progress — no matter in which field — within the inmost recesses of our heart we come to feel that the entire world helped us, that each individual on earth has helped us in some way or other according to his capacity.

A man of success, the moment he achieves success, starts adding up all the difficulties and dangers he encountered before success dawned in his life. A man of progress, the moment he makes progress in his life of experience or in his life of realisation, starts counting all the blessings he received from Above. Finally, he realises that the door of opportunity is marked by both "push" and "pull". He pushes aside his life of bondage, his life of ignorance, his life of countless imperfections. He pulls down from Above Peace, Light and Bliss in boundless measure — slowly, steadily, devotedly and unerringly.

Renunciation is progress. We renounce our life of ignorance, our life of teeming doubts. Here I wish to recall the message of the Upanishadic lore:

Īśāvāsyam idaṁ sarvam...

> The whole world is owned by the Lord Supreme. Let us not hunger after others' possessions. In renunciation is the satisfaction everlasting: in renunciation we drink the Nectar-Delight of the Absolute.

Progress is like a lotus that blossoms petal by petal. Each time a petal comes into existence we feel that a new dedication, a new hope, a new self-mastery dawns in our life of service to aspiring mankind.

Success and progress on the human level are two so-called rivals. Success wants to please itself according to its own receptivity's capacity. Progress wants to please God unconditionally in His own Way. My experience tells me that success has a short life which, at the same time, is dubious and precarious. My realisation tells me that progress has an everlasting and ever-transcending life. We achieve today's goal on the strength of our progress, which is founded on aspiration — our mounting inner cry. But then, today's goal becomes tomorrow's starting point. Tomorrow we have to start for a higher goal. Each time we reach a goal, our aspiration tells us that it is only the starting point for a higher, more meaningful and more fruitful goal. We are in the process of constantly transcending our reality. And the ever-transcending Reality is the Golden Shore of the ever-transcending Beyond.

Today's imperfect man, today's unlit man, grows into tomorrow's perfect and fully illumined man only when he feels that progress is the only thing that he needs. Each time we climb to a higher rung of the ladder of progress, we automatically achieve success — inner success. But if we run after success, there is every possibility that we may adopt foul means and do undivine things, because we are competing with others with whom we have not yet established a sense of inseparable oneness. When we want progress, we feel that if we have to compete with anyone or anything at all, our enemies are within us: fear, doubt, anxiety, worries, insecurity.

In order to reach the highest Goal, we must have faith in abundant measure, both in ourselves and in the Almighty Father. If we do not have faith in the Almighty Father all at once, no harm. Out of His infinite Bounty, He will illumine us, guide us, perfect us and fulfil us at His choice Hour. But if we lose faith in ourselves or if we are wanting in faith in our life of aspiration and dedication, then we shall be devoured by the ignorance-tiger. At that time nobody will come to our rescue.

We and God must have reciprocal faith. Our faith in God will make us His chosen instruments. His faith in us will inspire us to manifest Him totally, unreservedly and perfectly here on earth. Our faith in Him will give us what we desperately need — realisation. His faith in us will give Him the opportunity to manifest Himself in and through us. We need Him for our highest realisation; He, out of His infinite Kindness, needs us for His divine Manifestation.

Faith is the only thing that makes us feel that we are part and parcel of Eternity, Infinity and Immortality. Eternity, Infinity and Immortality are not vague terms. They are realities growing and glowing in the heart of the genuine seeker. When we have faith in abundant measure, the Lord Supreme assures us that in and through us He will manifest His perfect Perfection.

35. Wisdom-Light

Dear sisters and brothers, dear seekers of the infinite and eternal Truth, I wish to give a talk on Wisdom-Light. Each individual present here has Wisdom-Light. Today I will share with you my Wisdom-Light; tomorrow, easily and effectively you can share with many your Wisdom-Light.

What is Wisdom-Light? Wisdom-Light is something that eternally glows inside our heart and around our life eternal. Wisdom-Light tells us that there are only two mighty powers on earth. These powers are temptation-power and liberation-power. When we surrender to temptation-power, we come to realise that our body is unawakened, our vital is undisciplined, our mind is unillumined and our heart is unfulfilled.

When we aspire for liberation-power, we come to realise that our soul is a fulfilled and, at the same time, a constantly fulfilling reality; that our soul is an illumined and, at the same time, an ever-illumining reality.

When we enter into the spiritual life, we come to realise that we have three teachers: ignorance-teacher, knowledge-teacher and wisdom-teacher. Ignorance-teacher teaches us how to talk. Knowledge-teacher teaches us how to talk and act. But wisdom-teacher teaches us only how to act spontaneously and unconditionally.

When we talk and talk, we enter consciously and deliberately into the domain of ignorance. When we talk and act, at times we see a yawning gulf between our speech and our action. We say something and we do something totally different. We make a solemn promise to do something, but when reality dawns we see a vast gulf between our promise and its fulfilment. But when we act spontaneously, soulfully and unconditionally — when we offer our dedicated service — an unseen Hand guides us, shapes us and moulds us into the very image of our Inner Pilot. It is only by devotedly serving the Inner Pilot in each individual that we can make our life meaningful and fruitful.

The brotherhood of man can never be achieved by talking, but only by becoming something, by achieving conscious oneness with the Tree which is God. Unless we establish our conscious, inseparable oneness with the Almighty Father, the Absolute Supreme, we can never establish in our inner life or outer life the full brotherhood of man. We have to touch the tree and climb up the tree. Only then can we approach the branches and enter into the millions and billions of leaves, which are our brothers and sisters. If we do not go to the tree and climb up the tree, how can we enter into the consciousness of the leaves, which are our brothers and sisters?

Ignorance is self-enjoyment, knowledge is self-examination and wisdom is self-perfection. When we swim in the sea of ignorance, we enjoy. This enjoyment is followed by frustration, and frustration is followed by destruction. When we try to examine ourselves, we see imperfection looming large. But, at the same time, perfection is within our easy reach. Self-perfection is wisdom. When we pray and meditate, we enter into the reality of silence, and this gives us the opportunity to perfect our life within and without. Silence embodies perfection. Silence is ready to reveal its perfection in and through us on the physical plane, which is now inundated with ignorance, darkness, bondage and imperfection.

How do we discriminate Light from night, Truth from falsehood, Immortality from death? We discriminate the one from the other by praying and meditating, by trying and crying. When a child cries, his mother comes to the rescue and offers him toys or food or anything else that he wants. Similarly, when we cry in the inmost recesses of our heart, the Mother Divine, the Mother Supreme, comes to our rescue and inundates our inner and outer being with infinite Light. This Light is our real Divinity, Immortality and perfect Perfection.

Very often we feel that knowledge and wisdom are one and the same thing. But when we enter into the spiritual life and get inner experiences, we come to realise that knowledge and wisdom are two totally different things. Knowledge is like the younger brother in the family, and wisdom is the older brother. Naturally, the older brother will be infinitely wiser than the younger one. Knowledge sees something and then wants to utilise that thing. Wisdom feels the Truth, wants to grow into the Truth and finally becomes the Truth. Knowledge and wisdom are two brothers at the foot of the Realisation-tree. Let us call it a mango tree. Knowledge starts counting the leaves, the branches and fruit, but wisdom climbs up the tree, plucks a mango and eats to its heart's content.

Now, where can wisdom exist? It can exist everywhere. It can exist in knowledge, in intelligence, in the intellect, in intuition. But the wisdom that abides in the soul is the wisdom that leads us and guides us fastest towards our destination. When we pray and meditate we go deep within and hear the dictates of our soul. Once we hear the dictates of our soul, we establish a free access to the world of divine Reality, Infinity, Eternity and Immortality.

Here I wish to quote the words of Benjamin Franklin: "Work as if you were to live a hundred years. Pray as if you were to die tomorrow." Work I take as dedicated service in the spiritual life. Every day it is our bounden duty to offer our dedicated service to the Supreme in all human beings. Dedicated service greatly helps us to reach our destined goal. Now, we have to know that today's goal is not and cannot be the goal forever. Today our goal is realisation of the highest Truth and the highest Light. Tomorrow our goal will be the revelation of the highest Truth and Light. And the day after tomorrow our goal will be the perfect manifestation of the highest Truth and Light, which we will then embody.

"Pray as if you were to die tomorrow." A seeker of infinite Truth must feel that each moment is a most sacred opportunity for him. Tomorrow death may snatch us away from the world arena. So we have to feel that this is the last time, the last opportunity, the last moment we have to realise the ultimate Truth. On the one hand, we know that death is nothing but a short rest in the flow of Eternal Time. On the other hand, we know that here on earth we have to accomplish quite a few things for God's fulfilment and for our fulfilment. Right now, our fulfilment and God's fulfilment are diametrically opposed.

But when we pray and meditate, we come to feel that God's fulfilment is our fulfilment, that God's fulfilment is the only fulfilment. If we pay considerable attention to the value of time, we do not wallow consciously in the pleasures of lethargy and ignorance. We can utilise each moment for our ever-increasing fulfilment and ever-fulfilling illumination on the strength of our inner cry to see something, to grow into something and to become something.

About an hour ago when I arrived here, I was deeply moved to see the motto of this august college: "Equal opportunity for all, freedom to see and discriminate the truth and the brotherhood of man."

Equal opportunity for all. Now who can give us equal opportunity? Only the Inner Pilot can give and does give equal opportunity to all. Every day, early in the morning, He knocks at our heart's door. When He knocks at our door, some of us wake up and answer the door while others remain in the world of sleep, inconscience and ignorance. In our outer life, once we lose an opportunity we seldom get it back. But in the inner life we get a new opportunity every day, every hour, every minute. He who responds to the inner opportunity immediately runs fast, faster, fastest towards the ultimate Goal.

Each individual has to be given freedom to seek the Truth in his own way. We cannot thrust our truth on others. Each has to go deep within to the Truth. Truth is the Goal, but in order to reach the Goal, we can and do adopt different paths, different roads. Different roads allow different individuals to run the fastest. If others force their freedom upon us, it will be totally valueless for us. But if we search deep within, our freedom is our revelation, our illumination, our perfection. The Vedic lore offers us a momentous message:

FIFTY FREEDOM-BOATS TO ONE GOLDEN SHORE

Asato mā sad gamaya,
Tamaso mā jyotir gamaya
Mrityor ma amritaṃ gamaya.

Lead me from the unreal to the Real.
Lead me from darkness to Light.
Lead me from death to Immortality.

I am extremely happy that the state of Illinois is proud of calling itself "Land of Lincoln". Lincoln was a seeker in the pure sense of the term. God gave him a magnanimous heart. Emerson said of him, "His heart was as great as the world, but there was no room in it to hold a wrong." I wish to elaborate on this most significant utterance.

When we become a seeker, we try to have a heart as vast as the world itself, or try to have a heart even vaster than the world. In this vast heart, a real seeker does not see the ignorance of the world as belonging to others. The heart of a true seeker sees the imperfections, limitations and bondage of others as its very own. Emerson says Lincoln's heart did not hold a wrong, but I wish to say that his heart did not hold a wrong *of his own*. His heart did hold the wrongs of millions and billions of human beings, and he accepted these wrongs of others as his very own — not with a sense of pride, but with a sense of oneness.

Since we are all seekers, the world is within us, not outside us. Each individual that we see around us is within us as well. Also, when we go deep within we see that we have a large family, a very large inner family of doubts, fears, anxieties, worries, imperfections and limitations. When we transform them on the strength of our conscious concentration, meditation and contemplation, we see that our outer world is also totally transformed.

I am here in Chicago. The very name of this city gives me enormous joy and delight. When I was eleven years old, I read a biography of the great spiritual figure, Swami Vivekananda. In 1893, when they held the Parliament of Religions here, Swami Vivekananda came and offered the eternal wisdom of the soul's light. My young heart was so delighted and moved, for he came from the same place where I was born, Bengal. So the younger brother feels a oneness with his elder brother. Vivekananda was divinely and supremely blessed to be able to offer the wisdom-light of India here at the Parliament of Religions.

To me, each religion is a soulful, powerful, meaningful and fruitful house. Each individual should live in a house; he cannot live in the street. But a man need not stay all the time in his house. He comes out to study. Here our inner school and our inner subject is Yoga. Yoga is conscious oneness with God. We are all seekers, sincere seekers. For us God does exist. And it is only a matter of time before we will be able to see Him, feel Him, fulfil Him and grow into His Image.

36. Forward!

Dear seekers of the highest Truth, dear sisters and brothers of the spiritual family, as we all know, each state has a motto of its own. To my deepest joy the motto of your state, Wisconsin, is very significant in the spiritual life. *Forward*. To me, "forward" is not a mere word or an idea, but a secret and sacred key to open God's Door.

Forward. There can be nothing as significant as moving forward in our life of aspiration. The Vedic seers of the hoary past uttered a significant mantra: *Charai veti*, "Move on, forward!" We shall move forward towards the farthest Beyond. Today we are in the Dream-Boat; tomorrow we shall touch the Reality-Shore. Forward, ever forward.

We are all seekers; we are all in the world of spirituality. To me spirituality is a one-way road that leads us to our destination. Once we start our journey, we may stumble, we may walk slowly, we may march or we may run fast, faster, fastest towards our Goal. There may come a time when we proceed backwards on our way towards the Goal, but this is only a temporary experience. After a while we go forward again.

We do not belong to the past; we belong to the future, the future that grows and glows in the immediacy of today. I tell my students that the past is dust no matter how much we have achieved in the past or what we were in the past. The past has not given us Truth, Light and Bliss in infinite measure. Therefore, we can and must expect these things only from today, or from the future that is looming large in the heart of today.

In the spiritual life we come to realise that we have four good friends: simplicity, sincerity, humility and purity. With the help of these friends, we move forward.

Simplicity-friend wants us to be as simple as possible. It tells us that our mind makes us feel that God is very complex, but actually He is very simple, simplicity itself. Therefore we, too, have to be simple in order to receive and achieve Him.

Sincerity-friend tells us that God is all sincerity. Although we do not know or understand His operation, His way of working in and through us, still God is very sincere. Therefore we, too, must be sincere in order to be God-like.

Humility-friend tells us that God is very humble. Although He is the Highest, the Lord Supreme, His Humility-power and Oneness-power make us feel that if we, too, are humble, one day we will be able to reach the Highest. God is like a tree. When the tree has no fruit, it stands erect and may look proud and haughty. But when the tree is laden with fruit, it bows down. So God, who is always full of inner fruits, bends and bows so that His children can climb up the tree and eat to their heart's content.

Purity-friend tells us that God is all purity. It tells us that our living breath must be purity's flood if we want to hold, cherish and treasure the Presence of God within us.

When we are sincere in our forward journey, we see that our road is very straight. When we are simple, we feel and we see with our inner vision that the road is sunlit. When we are humble, we feel that the road is short and, at the same time, shortened still further by the Grace of God. When we are pure, we see clearly with our inner vision that the ultimate Goal itself is running towards us as we are running towards the Goal. And our meeting place is where the finite unites with the Infinite.

Charai veti! "Move on, forward!" There was a time when we were in the mineral world, but when the necessity came from within, we moved on and entered into the plant world. From the plant world, we moved on into the animal world. From the animal kingdom we entered into the human kingdom. Now it is our inner urge that will lead us to the Divine Kingdom.

In the mineral world, the ruler is Ignorance-Emperor. In the plant world, the ruler is Ignorance-King. In the animal world, the ruler is Ignorance-Commander. In the human world, the ruler is Ignorance-Captain. In the Divine World, the ruler is the Light Supreme of the ever-transcending and ever-fulfilling Beyond.

We move forward on the strength of our outer and inner education. Outer education at times fails to tell us that there is something called inner education. Or it happens that outer education discourages us from entering into inner education. Now, outer education has to offer what it has and inner education has to offer what *it* has. But it sometimes happens that when we have too much outer education we accumulate too much world-information and not so much knowledge, not to speak of wisdom. At this time we find it difficult to enter into the world of inner education. Again, too much of the intellect, too much of the physical mind surcharged with doubt, fear, anxieties, worries and other discouraging elements, makes it difficult for us to enter into the inner education and make progress.

We need the mind, but only the mind that listens to the heart, for the heart listens to the soul. Otherwise the mind, the vital and the body become unruly members in our spiritual family. So we have to try very hard to stay in the heart, since this heart has to listen to the eldest member of its family, the soul. Similarly, the mind must listen to the heart, the vital must listen to the mind, and the body must listen to the vital. In this way, the spiritual family can grow together and fulfil the message of the Absolute Supreme.

From the inner education we come to realise that Truth and Wisdom-Light are already within us. But sometimes we need help convincing our outer being that we do have within us what we actually seek. In outer education, we feel that the knowledge is somewhere else and we have to search for it and get it. In the inner education the ultimate Knowledge, the Wisdom-Light, is all within us, but somebody has to convince us of this. The inner teacher tells us, "Inside you is the treasure, inside you is the box, but unfortunately you have misplaced the key. It is your treasure and not mine. It is your box and not mine. But I will show you where the treasure is and, if you want me to, I will also help you open the box. Once you open the box, all the treasure will be yours." The inner teacher is like a river. Just follow the river and it will take you to the sea, which is your own Reality, your own Divinity, your own Immortality.

Before we enter into the spiritual life, we are small people. Once we enter into the spiritual life, we are great people. But after we start making real progress in the spiritual life, we become good people. A small man never thinks that he is small. A great man thinks that he is great. A good man thinks that he is neither good nor bad. He sees that he is just an iota of Light, just an iota of Truth, while God is the infinite sea of Light and Truth. When we make real progress, we come to know how small, how insignificant we really are. But again, there comes a time when the finite, the infinitesimal drop, merges into the ocean of Truth, Light and Bliss and becomes the vast ocean itself.

The small man is afraid of moving forward because he feels that the unknowable may destroy him altogether. For him, to step forward is to enter into the unknowable. A great man is reluctant to step forward because he feels that this forward step may take him into something unknown, which may be unfriendly. A good man feels that the unknowable or the unknown is nothing but God veiled. Once we enter the unknowable and the unknown, God becomes unveiled — unveiled Reality, unveiled Divinity. So a good man is never afraid of progress. He knows that right ahead of him is the veiled Reality and, if he approaches this veiled Reality, it will become the unveiled Reality.

We can move forward only when we have confidence. Before we enter into the spiritual life, we have very little confidence, even in ourselves. We do not know or do not care to know that there is someone called God who can inundate us with confidence. But once we enter into the spiritual life, we see that it is God who offers us confidence. That is why we make progress and walk, march, run towards our destined Goal. At every moment God tells us that unless and until we also have divine confidence, we will not be able to make the fastest progress.

Only when we have divine confidence can God's Confidence operate most successfully and gloriously in us. And what is our divine confidence? It is the confidence that tells us we came from God, and so cannot mix with ignorance. We cannot swim in the sea of ignorance. No! We have to swim in the sea of Light and Delight.

The forward march, the inward march and the upward march are the same. If we take one step forward, we have to feel that simultaneously we have taken a step inward and a step upward. In our forward step, we see the Body of God. In our inward step, we see the Heart of God. In our upward step, we see the Soul of God. When we have the Body of God, the Heart of God and the Soul of God, at that time we do not need anything else.

We have to move on, move on far, farther, farthest; deep, deeper, deepest; high, higher, highest. Since we are seekers, there is no end to our achievement. We achieve on the strength of inner assurance — our assurance to God and God's assurance to us. God's constant assurance to us is this: "Children, you are all of Me, of My Infinity, Eternity and Immortality." Our assurance to God is this: "Father, we are for You. We are for Your manifestation, Your complete manifestation, Your perfect manifestation here on earth." In this way, when God assures us and we assure God, then our journey towards the highest Height, the deepest Depth and the farthest Beyond reaches its destined Goal; the Dream-Boat touches the Reality-Shore.

37. Wisdom, justice and moderation

Dear seekers, dear friends, I wish to give a talk on "Wisdom, justice and moderation", which is the motto of Georgia. "Wisdom, justice and moderation" is a most significant motto. If we can apply these ideals in our daily life, then we can derive much Peace, Light and Joy from our earthly existence.

Wisdom. Wisdom is our liberal self-giving and not our selfish self-seeking. Wisdom is the beauty of our inner flame. Our inner flame is our upward aspiration-flight. Our aspiration-flight is our immortal Reality's height. The man of wisdom serves God in man. The man of wisdom loves man in God. By serving God in man, the man of wisdom gets boundless Peace, Light and Bliss. By loving man in God, the man of wisdom expands his vision. He feels himself an extension of the ever-increasing vision, inner and outer. Wisdom is at once experience and realisation. Experience tells the seeker what he can eventually become: a perfect instrument of God. Realisation tells the seeker what he eternally is: an eternal player, divine and supreme.

Justice. Justice human and justice divine. "As you sow, so you reap" — this is human justice. "Tit for tat." "An eye for an eye and a tooth for a tooth." But Divine Justice is this: give what you have. You have to become what God is. Give your treasured possession, ignorance, to God. God will give you, in return, His very existence, which is Light flooded with Delight. In our human world, justice is more painful than heartful. In the divine world, justice is meaningful and fruitful. In the vital of night, justice threatens and frightens us. In the heart of Light, justice inspires and perfects us. In the human world, justice forces and punishes us. In the divine world, justice awakens us, illumines us and liberates us from the meshes of ignorance.

The great philosopher, Aristotle, once remarked, "Justice is what every man considers his very own." Now, in the spiritual life, only God is our very own. But this God of ours also belongs to every other soul as well. This God can be claimed by each and every soul as its very own. In order to make others feel that God is equally theirs, we have to become one, inseparably one, with them. And in order to become inseparably one with them, we have to become a Concern-sky and a Love-sea. It is our Concern-sky and Love-sea that can make others feel that they belong to us and we belong to them.

On the strength of our oneness, we can make others see what they want and what they really need. What they want is desire; what they really need is aspiration. We have to tell them that if we give them what they want — the fulfilment of desire — then this is bound to be followed by frustration; whereas if we offer them what they need — aspiration — then this aspiration will be the harbinger of realisation. And realisation is an ever-lasting, ever-growing, ever-fulfilling achievement in man's aspiring consciousness.

Moderation. Moderation means balance. A moderate life is a balanced life. The Buddha taught the path of moderation, the middle path. He warned us not to go to extremes, for he himself had gone to the extremes and found that that was not the answer. A real seeker shuns all extremes. An austere, severe life is not meant for him; nor is a life of constant enjoyment and pleasure meant for him. We have to adopt the middle path. We have to be normal and natural. And in our normal and natural life, we have to invoke the supernatural life, the life of Divinity, Infinity and Immortality.

A real seeker accepts the outer world. In his acceptance he pays considerable attention to the outer world. He accepts the inner world. There, too, he pays considerable attention. In his life of acceptance, he accepts the reality as such and wants to transform it with his inner cry, with his love of God, Light, Truth. In his rejection of darkness, he rejects the things that are unhealthy, the things that destroy his inner potentiality. But again, there are many undivine things in a person that can be transformed into divine realities. So he accepts these things and tries to transform them.

Life is a challenge for us. From a human point of view our earthly experience is like being in a battlefield. But if we go deep within, we come to realise that every day is an opportunity, every hour is an opportunity, every moment is an opportunity. If we can utilise these golden opportunities, then the imperfection that looms large in our life of today can easily be transformed into perfection in our life of tomorrow.

In our spiritual life there is a divine ladder that reaches to the highest pinnacle of Truth, Light and Bliss. This ladder has three rungs. The first rung is moderation, the second rung is justice and the third is wisdom. When we step on the first rung, we read the message: "Know Good." When we step on the second rung we read the message: "Do Good." And when we step on the third, we read the message: "Be Good." The moderation-rung teaches us how to know good in everything in God's entire creation. The justice-rung teaches us how to do good in all our multifarious activities. The wisdom-rung teaches us how to become good and how to grow into the very image of God.

When we are wanting in wisdom, it is a loss. When we are wanting in justice, it is a double loss. And finally, when we are wanting in moderation, it is a triple loss. But if we discover faith, inner faith, then it is a veritable gain. And along with it, if we can discover our aspiration, then it is a double gain. Finally if we can discover our divine surrender, our constant and unconditional surrender to the Light to the inner Source, to the real Source, then it is a triple gain. So, if we can have faith, aspiration and surrender, then the destined Goal can never remain a far cry.

A seeker is a man of wisdom. He wants to see the root of the Reality-tree. Then he wants to feel the necessity of becoming the seed of the Reality-tree. Finally, he wants to actually become the seed of the Reality-tree. When he becomes the seed of the Reality-tree, he sees that there is only one thing that was, is and forever shall be, and that is Love: the Love that created, the Love that nourishes, the Love that sustains God's universe.

If we practise what we preach, then wisdom becomes our profession. What we practise and what we preach should be the same: love. We tell the world to love, but we may not actually offer love to the world. But if we offer love and become love, then we can most assuredly expect to see love in the world at large. It is God's Love-Power that compels us to think of Him, to pray to Him, to meditate on Him and to claim Him as our very own. As God claims us as His very own on the strength of His own Love-Power, so also He tells us and inspires us and begs us to claim Him as our very own on the strength of our love for Him.

When we come face to face with God, He asks us to offer Him what we have. If we can offer Him our real treasure, a heart of love, He immediately accepts it and says, "You have passed your examination." But if we offer God all our world-possessions — physical, vital, mental possessions — but do not bring Him love, then He will not be satisfied. God will say, "No, bring Me your heart of love; that is your true treasure. And once I have your true treasure, then I will give you My Treasure, which is Light and Delight in infinite measure."

38. Hope and Life

I wish to give a short talk on one of the mottos of South Carolina. As you all know, South Carolina has two mottos. "Prepared in mind and resources", is one motto; the other motto is, "While I breathe, I hope." I wish to say a few words on the second motto, from a spiritual point of view.

Hope is Life. Hope is progress. Each individual life is an Idea of God's, a Plan of God's and a dream-fulfilling Reality of God's. Hope likes the God-idea; Hope loves the God-plan; Hope serves the dream-fulfilling Reality of God.

There are two lives: desire-life and aspiration-life. Desire-life starts with self-enjoyment and ends in self-destruction. Aspiration-life starts with self-enquiry and ends in God-discovery. Today's life for us is God in preparation, and tomorrow's life for us will be God in perfect Perfection, God in His Manifestation on earth.

Two lives: human life and divine life. Human life cries to live; divine Life lives to offer. Human life is counted in years; divine Life is measured by progress — illumining and fulfilling progress. Human life always wants to enjoy without learning; Divine Life wants to learn first and then enjoy. Human life does not want to learn and does not learn anything. It is satisfied with what it gets, which is ignorance. It enjoys ignorance to its heart's content. Divine Life wants to learn, it wants to learn the lessons of Eternity. While learning the lessons of Eternity, divine Life is enjoying the Bliss of Immortality.

Life and hope are inseparable. Life is the body, and hope is the intuitive divinity in us, the divinity that wants to transcend the reality which we presently are. Hope is man's seeking, hope is man's inner urge, hope is man's upward flight into the Beyond.

We are all walking along the road of Eternity. When an unaspiring, ordinary human being walks along this road, he is followed by some of his so-called friends: fear, doubt and anxiety. When these friends reach him they make of him what they themselves are: fearful, doubtful and anxiety-stricken. God is the Goal; He is the Way; He is the eternal Traveller. When God walks along His eternal road towards the ever-transcending Beyond, all the world can follow Him, led by hope. When hope reaches Him, God makes hope His dearest friend, eternal partner and eternal fulfiller of His Dream.

Life and hope entirely depend on inner wisdom. Here on earth we have two types of wisdom: earthly wisdom or earthly knowledge and heavenly wisdom or heavenly knowledge. Here on earth *vidya* and *avidya*, knowledge and ignorance, together move, together dance. Thousands of years ago, the Vedic seers offered this message:

> *Vidyam cavidyam ca yas tad vedobhyam saha*
> *Avidyaya mrtyum tirtva vidyayamrtam asnute*

> He who knows and understands knowledge and ignorance as one, through ignorance passes beyond the domain of death, through knowledge attains to an eternal Life and drinks deep the Light of Immortality.

What they call "ignorance" is earthly knowledge, and what they call "knowledge" is heavenly wisdom. With earthly knowledge we try to go beyond the domain of death, and with heavenly wisdom we try to enjoy the Bliss of Immortality.

When we enter into the spiritual life we see and feel at every moment that God is the Doer, God is the Action and God is the

Fruit. On the strength of this realisation, we feel we have ample opportunity to reveal our inner divinity. A life on earth is not meant for pleasure; a life on earth is meant for self-offering. Self-offering eventually makes us what God is.

Each day is a golden opportunity for us to bring to the fore a new life, a new dawn. With each day we expedite our earthly progress. We enter into God's Domain, which is within us, in the inmost recesses of our heart. When we pray and meditate regularly, devotedly and soulfully, we come to realise that life is not only meaningful and fruitful, but is actually God's manifesting Reality on earth. And we come to understand that hope is the precursor of tomorrow's all-revealing and all-fulfilling Reality.

Life is the car. Hope is the engine. Aspiration is the fuel. God is the Destination.

39. Success, failure and progress

> We shall not fail; we are bound to succeed, for God Himself is our Boat, God Himself is our Boatman and God Himself is our journey's Goal.

Fear and doubt are two self-styled friends of ours who want to accompany us to God's Palace of infinite Light and Delight. They tell us what we should do. Our fear tells us that we shall blame God. Our doubt tells us that we shall fail God. But this journey of ours is a long one. At a certain point along the way, our teeming fear and brooding doubt become tired and remain behind.

We also have two real friends: courage and faith. We have invited these two friends to accompany us on our Godward journey, and they have accepted our invitation. They tell us that they will give us what they have. Courage will give us inspiration; faith will give us aspiration. Courage will inundate our being with inspiration so that we can envision the highest Goal. Faith will inundate our being with aspiration so that we can reach our destined Goal.

From the spiritual point of view, what is failure? Failure is an experience which awakens us. What is success? Success is an experience which energises us to strive for a higher and greater success. And what is progress? Progress is an experience which illumines us and fulfils us.

Failure indicates our lack of adamantine determination. Success indicates our tremendous power of concentration. Progress indicates that the crown of God's Will is in us and for us.

In our day-to-day life, when we fail in something we feel that the whole world is lost. We find it extremely hard to bury our sad experience in oblivion. When we succeed, at times we are bloated with pride. We cherish this pride because of our ego. At times we exaggerate our achievement beyond imagination. At times we want to prove to the world that we have or we are something when, in the purest sense of the term, it is not true. We try to make others feel we are exceptional, but in the inner recesses of our heart we know that this is false. When we care for progress, we want to be only what God wants us to be. We do not want any appreciation whatsoever from the world. We do not want the world to overestimate or underestimate us; we want the world just to accept us.

In our outer life, we fail because we do not give proper value to our goal, to our achievement. We have to appreciate and admire the Goal. If we give it proper value, we are bound to succeed. After darkness, dawn appears. Now, while we are living in inner darkness, if wisdom brings inner dawn into our consciousness and we do not appreciate or accept the dawn, then the dawn is not going to remain in us. When we become sincerely spiritual, we give the utmost value to Light, to the effulgence of Light. Now we live in darkness, but we will not be always in darkness. We are now fast asleep, but we need not sleep forever. Provided we have an intense inner cry, provided we give value to our Goal, we shall most assuredly reach our Goal.

A sincere seeker has a peculiar way of spelling the word "sincere". The inner philosopher spells the word "sin-seer". Now, in our philosophy there is no such thing as sin. What Westerners call sin is actually imperfection, limitation and bondage. A sincere seeker is a seer, for he sees his imperfections, limitations and bondage. Once he is fully aware of his limitations and weaknesses, he has already taken one step forward towards his liberation from bondage. At that time his goal is no longer a far cry.

We shall not fail. On the strength of our inner cry, on the strength of our inner mounting flame, we shall succeed. What we have is our inner cry. What God has is His transcending, revealing, fulfilling Smile. When our ascending cry and God's descending Smile meet together, we reach the supreme Goal.

We shall not fail, we cannot fail. We shall succeed on the strength of our one-pointed devotion to our Inner Pilot. How do we acquire this one-pointed devotion? We can acquire one-pointed devotion only when we have peace of mind. How can we have peace of mind? We can have peace of mind only when we detach ourselves from the tempting world about us and dive deep within to see the root of the Reality-tree.

We shall not fail God because we know what we have and we know what God has for us. There is a saying that "God helps those who help themselves." Now, some people may ask, "If we know how to help ourselves, why do we need God's Help? Or, if God is kind enough to help us, then why does He want us to use our puny personal effort?" Here we have to know that God's task is to fill us with Light only when we have emptied ourselves of darkness. We have to empty our vessel, and then God will fill the vessel. We empty ourselves of the ignorance of millennia, and God enters into us and fills us with Light and Delight. If we do not play our role, how shall we satisfy God? God is playing His Cosmic Game and we are consciously following the spiritual life, consciously accepting His Cosmic Game and playing with Him. While consciously and devotedly playing the Cosmic Game, we offer what we have. God accepts our capacities, our achievements, our possessions, and He gives us His capacities, His achievements, His possessions. He gives us perfectly, eternally and unconditionally.

We shall not fail God because we love God and because God loves us. Love is oneness, inseparable oneness. When we sing the song of inseparable oneness, we cannot fail.

Part X — Questions and answers — University of Maine

40. Question: Is there a possibility of complete fulfilment in this world?

Sri Chinmoy: It depends on what kind of fulfilment you are referring to. If it is fulfilment of our teeming desires, then we shall never be fulfilled. Today if one desire is fulfilled, tomorrow we will have another desire, and the moment that desire is fulfilled, we will have yet another desire. If we expect fulfilment in life through desire, then we shall never be fulfilled.

But if we follow the other road — the road of aspiration —

even if we get just an iota of Peace, Light and Bliss, we shall feel a real sense of fulfilment. And as we grow inwardly, our Peace, Light and Bliss increase. When we take exercise daily, we gradually develop our muscles and become strong, stronger, strongest. So also in the spiritual life, when our aspiration — our inner strength — is built up, there comes a time when we get Light, Peace and Bliss in infinite measure and feel total satisfaction and fulfilment in our life.

If we accept the life of aspiration, sooner or later fulfilment is bound to come. But as long as we wallow in the pleasures of ordinary life and feel that desire will be able to satisfy us, then we cannot know fulfilment. Our human desires will never be totally fulfilled. They must be transcended. Desire does not have the capacity to free us. On the contrary, the very nature of desire is to bind us, for desire itself is bound; whereas the very nature of aspiration is to free us, for aspiration is always free. That which has freedom can eventually free us, but that which has no freedom but is only a slave cannot offer us anything.

41. Question: Sometimes I feel that I am competing with others and trying to realise God ahead of them. Could you say something about this?

Sri Chinmoy: In the spiritual life, there is no such thing as competition. We do not compete with others because we know they are our brothers and sisters. If we feel that everyone is a brother or sister, we begin to get a feeling of oneness with them. If you *have* to enter into the field of competition, then I tell my students to compete with themselves. Right inside us there are so many competitors — fear, doubt, jealousy, insecurity — which are always ready to compete with our aspiration. When we want to go one step ahead towards our goal, immediately fear enters into our mind, doubt darkens our mind and other undivine forces immediately try to stop our onward journey.

So if you must enter into the field of competition, then compete with yourself, your inner undivine, unruly members. Since we have all entered sincerely into the spiritual life, we should not compete with others. We only look forward. We feel that when our time comes we will reach our destination: when our hour strikes we shall reach our goal. The destination is there for everybody, but the hour has to strike. If the hour strikes for you then you will reach your goal. If it strikes for me, then I will reach my goal. If it strikes for somebody else, then that person will reach his goal.

42. Question: How can we stop thoughts from bothering us during meditation?

Sri Chinmoy: We have to make an effort to calm and quiet our mind. We can call this a kind of inner exercise. If we do it every day, sooner or later we are bound to succeed. Let the fly bother me as many times as it wants to, but each time it comes I will try to chase it away. Each time an undivine thought enters into my mind, I will throw it out of my mind. It is like a foreign element, a thief, that has entered into my room. Why should I consciously allow a thief to remain in my room when I have the capacity to throw him out? Here also, when an undivine thought enters into my mind, I will just capture the thought and throw it into the blazing fire of inner aspiration.

43. Question: If we killed off all our desires and lived all the time in the inner world, it seems to me there would be no progress in the world and everything would stagnate.

Sri Chinmoy: If you feel that we cannot live all the time in light, that we have to live in darkness for twelve hours and in light for twelve hours, that philosophy is perfectly all right according to the standard of certain individuals. Someone meditates for one or two hours, and then goes out and enters into ordinary life. Someone else can meditate for several hours and there are some people who can meditate all day and night. It is all a matter of necessity. Inner necessity compels one person to meditate for one hour and someone else to meditate for twelve hours or twenty-four hours.

Now, when somebody meditates for an hour, he gets a kind of satisfaction. During that hour, he could have done something totally different, but he did not care for it. He preferred to meditate. He felt that the satisfaction he would get from meditation was more worthwhile than the satisfaction he would get from working or gossiping or whatever else he would have done during that hour. But after that hour, he wants to go back to the worldly life and its kind of satisfaction. But someone else may be able to meditate for twelve or twenty-four hours. Again, it is a matter of inner necessity, of what kind of satisfaction the person wants and needs.

There are two rooms. One room is unlit and obscure right now; the other room is fully illumined. One person may say that he wants both rooms equally: "I want to remain in the unlit room for twelve hours and in the well-illumined room for twelve hours." So he is most welcome to do that. But somebody else may not feel the necessity of staying in the unlit room at all. He says, "I want to remain only in the room which is illumined."

Then there is another person who says, "I have remained in this illumined room for twenty-four hours and now I have gotten illumination. Now let me go into the other room which is still dark and illumine it with my light." This person has a big heart, so he enters into the dark room to illumine his brothers who are still in darkness. He was getting satisfaction, abiding satisfaction, in the illumined room, but this was not enough. He will be fully satisfied only when he goes into the dark room and transforms it with his light. So there are some people on earth who have come back into the world of suffering even though they have the perfect capacity to remain eternally in the world of light and delight.

If we can bring the wealth of the inner world into the outer world, which is now obscure, then easily we can illumine this world. But first we must enter the inner world — the world of light — and receive something ourselves before we can offer it to the outer world. When we can do this, the inner and outer worlds will become united, and the outer world will become fully ready for the inner message. Right now the outer world is not ready, but a day will come when the outer world and the inner world will go perfectly together.

Part XI — Questions and answers —
Virginia Commonwealth University

44. Question: Which sound or chakra would be best for me to meditate upon?

Sri Chinmoy: For you, and all of us here, the best chakra to meditate upon is the heart. The heart chakra is called *Anahata*, which means "the soundless sound". Here on earth we need some physical action to produce a sound. But in the spiritual heart nothing is required, yet we continually hear a sound. And inside that sound a new creation is constantly being born.

If you meditate on the heart chakra, gradually you will come to feel that your own spiritual heart is larger than the largest. At that time you will see that the universal consciousness is inside your heart, and not outside. If you want to grow into something infinite, divine, eternal and immortal, then the heart chakra is by far the best. There you are always safe. The other chakras have boundless capacities, but if you are not totally pure then many, many problems may arise from meditating on them. But the heart chakra itself embodies purity. When you meditate on the heart, your entire being is flooded with purity. And only in purity can divinity abide permanently.

45. Question: I'm not sure I understand what you mean when you say the inner life is like a journey, which eventually takes you to the ever-transcending shore.

Sri Chinmoy: On the one hand I say "the boat", "the journey" and "the shore". On the other hand I use the term "ever-transcending". When I say you reach the shore, I mean that today's goal can be achieved. But today's goal is just tomorrow's starting point. A child's goal is to have a dollar. When he gets a dollar he has reached his goal, but he is not satisfied. He wants to get two dollars or ten dollars. So that one dollar which was his original goal becomes the starting point for an ever-growing and expanding goal.

When we start practising spirituality, we feel that if we get an iota of Peace, Light and Bliss, that is enough. But in a few years, we cry for abundant Peace, Light and Bliss in our life. We have reached our goal, but that is only the starting point for a vaster goal because our inner hunger is not satisfied. Eventually we will care for infinite Peace, Light and Bliss, and when it is a matter of infinity, there is no end.

46. Question: According to reincarnation, our next life is supposed to be a reflection and extension of this life. Could you please elaborate on this?

Sri Chinmoy: Our next life need not be a reflection of the previous life. Suppose somebody has played his role most satisfactorily. Suppose you were a great artist in your previous incarnation and your soul does not want to have that experience again. If your soul wants you to have the experience of being a politician, then your previous experience as an artist may not come to the fore at all. If the soul has not completed its role in a specific field and wants to continue the same process, only then will one life be a reflection of the previous life. Otherwise, the soul may change the characteristics, nature and propensities of the human being totally.

47. Question: You say that one should have a love for life. Does this encompass all living things, all forms of life?

Sri Chinmoy: We shall love all life, but we have to use our wisdom. When I say we should love all life, I mean that inside each life form we should try to see and feel the presence of God. God is playing His Cosmic Game in many different roles. But we have to know that in the field of manifestation, life embodies different levels of divinity. We shall love all life, but we cannot be foolishly undiscriminating. Some forms of life are the embodiment of destruction. With these forms, we have to be careful. I will not go and stand in front of a tiger just because I know that God is inside the tiger. The tiger will kill me. I will not love a snake in a very personal way, or I will soon be transported to the other world. If there is a mad elephant right in front of me, I will not go and touch its feet. When I want to express my devotion, I will go to a spiritual Master or to someone in whom I see the conscious presence of divinity. God is in a tiger, God is in a chair and God is also in a holy man. If we are wise, we will know which one to expect inner enlightenment from.

48. Question: You spoke about the mind during your talk. How does one go about transforming the mind?

Sri Chinmoy: Let us take the mind as a room and let us take the heart as another room. You have two rooms. Right now you are living in the mind room, which is unlit and obscure. The other room, your heart, is fully illumined, because it has free access to the soul, which is all illumination. The heart room, too, you can claim as your very own, only you do not stay there. But if you can live for a few weeks or a few months or a few years in the illumined room, then easily you will be able to transform the unillumined room when you return there. Stay in the heart room for however long it takes you to get abundant light. The other room will not go away; the other room will wait for you to give it illumination. When you feel that you have attained illumination in your heart room, then come to your mind room and flood it with your heart's light. But if you stay with the mind room all the time with the hope of illumining it from within, you will waste your time. If I want to light a candle, I must use a flame that is already burning, already illumined. The heart room, fortunately, is already illumined. So if you go there, you can become fully inundated with light, and with that light you can illumine your mind.

49. Question: How can a human being function on earth without using the mind?

Sri Chinmoy: We must not think that when there is nothing in our mind, we have become a fool or will act like an idiot. This is not true. If you can keep your mind calm and quiet for ten or fifteen minutes, I tell you a new world will dawn within you. This is the root of all spiritual progress. Right now you can make your mind calm and quiet for only a few seconds, or for a minute. But if you can maintain your calmness, poise and tranquillity for half an hour or even for fifteen minutes, I assure you that inside your tranquillity a new world with tremendous divine light and power will grow.

When you do not have any thought in your mind, please do not feel that you are totally lost. On the contrary, feel that something divine is being prepared in your pure and aspiring nature. You cannot expect immediate results. The farmer sows the seed and then he waits; he never expects the crop to spring forth all at once. It takes a few weeks or a few months to germinate. Your mind can be like a fertile field. If you plant the seed of silence and poise and cultivate it patiently, sooner or later you are bound to reap the bumper crop of illumination.

50. Question: How often should we fast in order to help our spiritual life?

Sri Chinmoy: Fasting does not necessarily help us to make spiritual progress. A snake eats only twice a year or so, but the consciousness of a snake is not better than my consciousness or your consciousness, even though we eat every day. But if you want to fast once a month for a full day, or if you want to eat only breakfast and no lunch or dinner on a particular day, it helps in purification. Fasting does help to purify our nature, without doubt. It brings to the fore the subtle purity inside our nature. But everything has a limit. If you go to extremes it will tell upon your health. Once a month is fine. Once a week is all right if you are strong and healthy, and if you feel that it helps you. But if you want to fast every other day, that will absolutely ruin your subtle nerves. Once a week strong people can try, but once a month is enough.

Part XII — Questions and answers — University of Michigan

51. Question: Do you feel that mankind is making spiritual progress?

Sri Chinmoy: Humanity is progressing towards its destined goal. Sometimes we notice clouds of doubt and teeming imperfections, but these things will always be around until we have achieved perfect Perfection. Each individual has left the starting point. Now, one individual may be behind another in the Godward race, but we all are running towards the same goal. Each individual is progressing. This progress may not be noticeable in our outer life. It will become noticeable only when a tremendous amount of light has dawned in our devoted life, our life of surrender to the Will of the Almighty Father. Even though there are calamities, crises, wars and so forth on the outer plane as well as on the inner plane, still we are definitely progressing.

Part XIII — Questions and answers — University of Toledo

52. Question: Is it easy to realise God while living in the world, instead of renouncing the world?

Sri Chinmoy: Some spiritual Masters, including myself, are of the opinion that it is not necessary to renounce the world and enter into a life of solitude. We have to face the world and we have to realise the Highest in the world. We do not want to lead the life of an escapist. Who escapes? He who feels that he has done something seriously wrong or he who is afraid. We have not done anything wrong and we have not to be afraid of the world around us. If we are afraid of the world, then we shall be afraid of everything.

Now we see a giant world of imperfection around us. We try to escape it in order to protect ourselves. But I wish to say that a far more formidable enemy than the present-day world is nothing other than our own mind. When we enter into the caves, we cannot escape our mind. We carry that mind with us — a mind which is full of anxiety, jealousy, confusion, doubt, fear and other undivine qualities. This mind of ours forces us to remain in the battlefield of life. If we do not conquer our mind while living in the world, what good will it do us to remove merely our body from this everyday world?

Here in the ordinary world we have to live amongst our

friends. But we can easily choose our friends, and we must do so carefully. If we want to be spiritual, then we have to spend most of our time with spiritual people. If we spend most of our time with unaspiring people, then their consciousness will enter into us, and then our God-realisation and inner illumination will remain a far cry. But if we have proper guidance from within, if we know that we are walking along the right path, and if we mix with aspiring people, a day will come when we will be inundated with divinity. Then we will be in a position to reveal our inner wealth, and at that time we will be able to associate with all and sundry, to offer and share our experiences with them without endangering our own spiritual consciousness.

53. Question: What is the art of surrender?

Sri Chinmoy: There are two types of surrender. One type of surrender comes under compulsion. This is the surrender of a slave to his master. He knows that if he does not serve his master, if he is not constantly at his master's beck and call, he will be punished. This surrender is based on fear. But the divine surrender is otherwise. Here we surrender our ignorance, incapacity and imperfection to the Inner Pilot, who is all-Light, all-Illumination, all-Perfection. When we enter into the spiritual life, we come to realise that when we surrender our ignorance, we are just surrendering our lowest reality to our own highest Reality. This surrender is based on love and oneness.

In the ordinary world, the servant is one individual and the master is another. There is a constant sense of separativity. But when we pray and meditate, we discover a kind of divine surrender within us which makes us feel that God and we are essentially one. He is our Eternal Father; He is our most illumined part, our Source, which we are now climbing up to and entering into. So, by surrendering, we do not lose anything; on the contrary, we return to our Source and become what we originally were. The finite consciously and cheerfully enters into the Infinite. Each one of us is now like a tiny drop. When it enters into the ocean, a tiny drop loses its individuality and becomes one with the infinite expanse of the ocean.

54. Question: In other words, to become one with God is to surrender one's identity?

Sri Chinmoy: We don't surrender our identity; we only surrender our limited, earth-bound individuality, the individuality that binds us, that says "I and mine", instead of "we". What we do is develop our conscious identity with God and God's Will, in order to achieve an inseparable oneness with Him. At that time we do not worry about losing our puny human individuality, for we gain God's infinite Vastness in its place.

55. Question: Is it necessary to meditate in the lotus position?

Sri Chinmoy: It depends on the individual. If an individual is a beginner, it is advisable for him to sit in the lotus position or in a similar upright position. I tell my students to try and sit in a comfortable position but to keep their backs straight. When the spinal column is straight, one can breathe properly. So long as we keep our back erect and feel that we can breathe properly, we do not have to go through any austere postures. Certainly, if the lotus position is painful or uncomfortable, you should not use it.

Now, it is not only the physical posture that counts, but how pure we are in our thoughts. No matter how well we do our lotus position, we cannot make any progress in our meditation if our minds roam uncontrollably and we become victims to unpleasant and undivine thoughts. Certainly it does help to some extent if we can sit in the lotus position, but real meditation comes only when we know how to silence the mind and open the heart. When we silence the mind and open the heart, God can enter into us with His Peace, Light and Truth.

56. Question: How can we use meditation to get rid of pain?

Sri Chinmoy: You should try to invoke Light in order to cure pain. Pain is, after all, a kind of darkness within us. When the inner Light or the Light from above starts functioning in the pain itself, then the pain is removed or transformed into joy. Really advanced seekers can actually feel joy in the pain itself. But for that, one has to be very highly advanced. In your case, during your prayer or meditation you should try to bring down Light from Above and feel that the pain is a darkness within you. If you bring down Light, then the pain will either be illumined and transformed or removed from your system.

57. Question: When we silence the mind, do we get any kind of messages?

Sri Chinmoy: When we silence the mind, we come to hear a message both from within and from Above — from our soul and from God. We hear the dictates of the soul when we silence the mind. And again, we feel the constant flow of God's Love when we silence the mind. When we silence the mind, God talks to us and we listen. When we do not silence the mind, we go on talking and talking and talking endlessly, and usually we waste others' precious time as well as our own time. But when God talks, we feel at every moment that He is illumining our entire being.

58. Question: How do we go about silencing the mind?

Sri Chinmoy: There are two ways. One way is to fight it out. The mind is like a monkey. If you are attacked by a monkey, which constantly bites and pinches you, you have to threaten the monkey. Then, each time it comes, if you strike it vehemently, eventually the monkey will feel that it is hopeless to try to bother you. You must always remain as vigilant as possible. When an undivine thought enters into your mind, immediately you will chase it away. If you are constantly vigilant, eventually these thoughts will give up and no longer come to disturb you.

Try to feel that you are standing at your heart's door, and it is up to you to allow anybody in. If you bolt the door from the inside and don't allow anybody in, then how can thoughts come? But what actually happens is that we sometimes cherish our thoughts, not consciously but unconsciously. Then it becomes very difficult for us to terminate the thoughts when we wish to.

The other way to silence the mind is to invoke Peace from Above. No matter how many thoughts enter into your mind, pay no attention to them. Let them come and attack you, for when you invoke Peace from Above, you are like a solid wall that they cannot penetrate. At that time, no thought will dare to strike you.

Part XIV — Questions and answers — St Joseph's College

59. Question: In one of your poems you wrote, "Above the toil of life, my soul is a bird of fire winging the Infinite." I wish you would explain that to me.

Sri Chinmoy: I am very happy that you have read my poem. This poem describes an experience I had when I was fourteen years old. My soul was flying in the sky of Infinity, Eternity and Immortality.

There comes a time in the life of each seeker when he has a new awakening, a higher awakening. At that time, he sees and feels higher Truth in a different way. When our consciousness is awakened to a higher realm of reality, we sense that the things that once seemed impossible or out of reach are not only possible and practicable, but also inevitable.

Right now we are all encaged. Right now, when we think of ourselves, we think of the body. Inside the body are the vital, the mind, the heart and so forth. But the body-consciousness generally dominates us, whereas the soul-reality seems like something foreign and strange. But when we regularly pray and meditate, we feed the aspiring soul. Then one day we smash asunder the tiny cage where we have been trapped for millennia, and once we come out, our body-consciousness disappears. At that time we grow into and become the soul-reality. And the soul-reality is the song of Infinity, Eternity and Immortality. At that time, we become the soul itself. Inside our aspiring heart we see a universal consciousness, and inside that universal consciousness we see our own soul, which is our eternal Reality. It is flying, offering its hidden treasure to those who need it, who want it and who claim it as their very own.

60. Question: To what extent does your emphasis on the soul flying "above the toil of life" lead to our ignoring the needs of our fellow man?

Sri Chinmoy: We have to know that a blind man cannot lead another blind man. One of the two has to be endowed with vision. Now, I am hungry and you are hungry. Suppose I know that there is a tree which has many fruits. If I have the capacity to climb up but, unfortunately, for the time being you do not have the capacity, what shall I do? Both of us are hungry. Just because one of us does not know how to climb, will the other person stop climbing? No! My bounden duty at that time is to climb up, pick a few fruits and then come down and share them with the one who does not know how to climb.

God has granted me this capacity, and it is my duty to utilise it. The world is in suffering and in darkness. True! But if I remain always in the world's darkness, then what do I add? I add only my own ignorance and my own darkness to the world. But if, on the strength of my aspiration, I can enter into the world of light, that does not mean I am not going to help the world. I will come back into the world where my brothers and sisters are still in darkness, and bring them light from the other world.

61. Question: What is your path?

Sri Chinmoy: I walk along the road of love, devotion and surrender. First, I offer my love to God, then I offer my devotion to God and finally I offer my surrender to God. When I offer my love to God I feel that He is the only one whose love I need in order to make progress. When I love Him, I discover that He is none other than my own self, my higher existence, my most illumined existence. Normally, when we love someone, it is a different individuality and personality that we love. But when we love God, we feel that He is our own highest, most illumined Reality.

Since God is our highest and most illumined Reality, it is easy to devote our existence to Him. When we offer our devotion to Him, we feel that He is the only person who can take us to our highest Height.

As an individual, I know how weak, how ignorant, how imperfect I am. I am like a tiny drop. But my aspiration is to become vast, infinite, eternal and immortal. So when I — the tiny drop — enter consciously into the ocean of consciousness, I do not lose my individuality or personality. On the contrary, I claim the infinite expanse as my very own and I grow into that infinite expanse of Peace, Light and Bliss. Here my surrender does not take away anything of my existence or reality. On the contrary, when I surrender my limited consciousness, my finite consciousness, to the Highest, I feel that I enter into my real Reality, which is your Reality and everybody's Reality as well.

Part XV — Questions and answers — Roosevelt University

62. Question: You said it is good to serve God. But is the only way to serve God to serve the God in other people?

Sri Chinmoy: Yes. But only if you pray and meditate will you feel that God is inside everybody, that He is a living Reality. You know that God is everywhere and in everything, true. But if you pray and meditate, then this mental belief becomes a real, living truth to you. At that time you consciously serve each person precisely because you know and feel that God is inside him.

If you do not see the Face of God, of Truth, of Light, then your physical mind will not be convinced of the value of the things that you are doing. Today you will serve someone and tomorrow you will say, "Oh, he is such a fool. He has no aspiration, nothing! Why should I serve him?" If you look at an individual without prayer and meditation, you will separate the man from the soul. But if you pray and meditate, then you will see the soul, the divinity inside that man, and you will try to bring to the fore that person's divinity. Otherwise, it will be impossible to bring to the fore the inner divinity of someone you are serving.

If you don't pray, if you don't meditate, then your work may not be dedicated service. And if it is not dedicated service, then it will not help you to make any spiritual progress. There are many people who work fifteen, sixteen hours a day. But their action is not dedicated service. They are only working mechanically to make money and take care of their outer responsibilities and so forth. But if you wish to really dedicate your life to God and mankind, then prayer and meditation must come first.

63. Question: You said that time is short. Were you referring to the spiritual life or to the life on earth?

Sri Chinmoy: In the spiritual life we are living in eternal Time. But here on earth we stay for only fifty, sixty or seventy years. Some people do not enter into the spiritual life until the age of thirty or forty or even sixty, and some do not enter at all in a given lifetime. So what are they going to accomplish during all those years? The sooner we enter into the spiritual life, the inner life, the better.

Today's goal cannot be tomorrow's goal. Tomorrow we have to have a higher goal. Because we are restless and lack peace of mind or any joy or sense of illumination, today our goal is to have an iota of Peace, Light and Bliss. But when we get that iota we feel that it is not enough for us. We are not acting greedy. It is just that we realise that the promise we have made to God that we shall please Him, that we shall realise Him, that we shall reveal and manifest Him, is not yet fulfilled.

If we are alert, we can avail ourselves of each moment as an opportunity. Otherwise, as time passes, either our ignorance increases or we do not allow the Light to enter into us. On the one hand, we have to know that we cannot bring God's living Presence into our lives by hook or by crook. But at the same time, we should feel an inner urge and intensity to see His Face immediately. Again, if we do not see Him and feel His Presence, we must not be doomed to disappointment. At that time, we shall have to use another type of wisdom, which is called patience. We want to see God because we feel that we need Him badly. But if He does not want to come to us at that particular moment, it is up to Him. Our business is to pray and meditate, and we have to leave the results at His Feet.

64. Question: How can we eliminate fear?

Sri Chinmoy: We can eliminate fear by increasing or expanding our consciousness. Fear comes into existence because we constantly or deliberately isolate ourselves. You are afraid of someone because you have a sense of separateness. You and I are separate individuals. But if you expand your consciousness, you will feel that my nose, my ears, my eyes all belong to you — they are part and parcel of your existence. I know the strength of my fist. If I strike myself with it I will definitely be hurt. But I know that my arm and my hand belong to me. My hand is not going to hurt me. My nose is not going to be attacked by my fist. Why? Because my entire body is one existence, and all its parts know and feel this. So when we expand our consciousness we can feel this same identity, this same oneness with someone whom we now call a stranger. In this way we can easily eliminate fear.

65. Question: I'd like to know if there is any way that we can still meditate and practise yoga without giving up our own religion?

Sri Chinmoy: It is very easy. Yoga is not a religion, and at the same time, it is not at all against religion. Religion is a house. I have to stay in my house; you have to stay in your house. We will not be able to stay in the street. But we have to know that there are quite a few things that we do not get in the house. Yoga we may get somewhere else, but we can easily bring it into our house. Aspiration, prayer, meditation will not conflict with any religion. Yoga is just like a course in school. It is a path that we can all walk along together, regardless of our religion.

66. Question: What is the experience of God like?

Sri Chinmoy: God can be seen, felt and realised as a personal being, most luminous, infinitely more beautiful than a human being. And again, we can experience God as an infinite expanse of Light, Bliss, Power, or any divine quality. Each individual will realise God in both the personal and the impersonal aspect. But if we think of God in His personal aspect first it is easier, because right now we are in the finite. If we can imagine God as a person, then from the form we can go to the formless aspect. But for us to think of something formless, of God as an infinite expanse, would be sheer exercise in mental gymnastics at this point. Reality grows in us most effectively when we go the proper way, from the personal God to the impersonal God.

God has everything. But when you touch the God-tree, you may get the experience of Peace, while somebody else will get the experience of Bliss. So you will say that God is all Peace and he will say that God is all Bliss. But it is the same God, the same Goal. In the process of reaching the Goal we may see it in different ways, but once we really reach it, we can see that it is everything. Then, if we have to describe it, give a definition, we will describe the God-tree in whichever aspect we like best. We can experience everything, but in our expression, our revelation, we will reveal the aspect we like best.

In my conception, God is not somebody other than ourselves, not a separate person. The God that we are referring to is our highest and most illumined part. Right now when we think of ourselves, we think of our body and not of our soul. We identify ourselves all the time with our lowest part. Our being is like a house that belongs to us. We do not use the third floor at all, but spend most of our time in the basement or on the first floor. Since we spend most of our time there, we feel the basement is our real reality. But the third floor is also ours, if we can only find our way there.

67. Question: How can I improve my morning meditation?

Sri Chinmoy: Every morning you have to offer your gratitude to God for having awakened your consciousness while others are still sleeping, and for all His infinite Blessings to you. If you offer just a fragment of your gratitude, you will feel God's Compassion. Then, when you feel God's Compassion, try to offer yourself. Say, "I will try to please You only in Your own Way. So far, I have asked You to please me in my own way, to give me this and that so that I can be happy. But today I am asking for the capacity to please You in Your own Way." If you can say this sincerely, automatically your morning meditation will be strengthened.

68. *Question: Can you suggest a method of meditation?*

Sri Chinmoy: Everybody has a soul. Your soul may try to express its divinity through Light; somebody else's will express itself through Power. Although each soul has infinite Peace, Light and Bliss, in each incarnation it will express itself in different ways. So each individual has to pray and meditate in his own way. To discover the best way of meditation, go deep within; or, if you have a Master, he will teach you inwardly or outwardly.

There is no common rule that everybody will meditate in a certain way. There are certain things that everybody can benefit by doing, but everybody has his own way of discovering and experiencing the Truth. The Goal is the same, but there are different roads. So everybody cannot do the same type of meditation. There is one type of meditation which will not interfere with anybody's inner path, and that is to silence the mind and open the heart. But again, everybody will have his own way of doing this. If you can silence the mind and open the heart, then you will feel the presence of your heart's eternal Guest, the Supreme.

Part XVI — Questions and answers — University of Wisconsin

69. Question: My aspiration seems very feeble, and I'm worried it won't get any stronger in the future.

Sri Chinmoy: Let us not worry over the future. Let us think of the present. As you sow, so you reap. In the past perhaps you have not sown the proper seed. Let us say your inner cry was not intense in the past and that is why your aspiration is not strong right now. You are not crying for God all the time; you do not have the feeling that without God you cannot exist. You feel that as long as there is the world, as long as you have friends, as long as there is food, you can go on. But when you feel that you can exist without water, without air, without everything, but not without God, at that time you can be certain that you will find fulfilment in the near future or in the future that is growing within you. If you sow a seed now, it will germinate and become a plant and eventually grow into a giant banyan tree. So if we sow the proper seed — that is to say, aspiration — then the aspiration-tree will bear fruit, which we call realisation. But if we do not sow the proper seed inside ourselves, then how can we get the proper fruit? So let us not worry about the future. Let us only do the right thing today, at this moment, here and now. Try to aspire now, today, and let the future take care of itself.

70. Question: I have a Master in India who told me to meditate on my navel chakra. But I'm not exactly sure how to do this. Could you comment on his advice?

Sri Chinmoy: You are in a boat that belongs to somebody. So your Master would be the right person to help you and guide you. If you are following a path, I feel I should not interfere. Your own Master knows infinitely better than I do what is right for you. I can only advise my own students and those who are not following any specific path. When the students of others come to me, I try to encourage them and inspire them to be absolutely faithful to their own Masters. You are asking about your Master's instructions. He who has given you the instructions should also be able to give you the capacity to understand his message. I am the wrong person to advise you in this matter. I know what is in my room and if somebody asks me, I can tell him. But if somebody asks me about somebody else's room, I will be totally ignorant. So I am very glad that you have a Master, and I wish to say that he is absolutely the only person to tell you how to follow his instructions.

71. Question: How can a seeker come to terms with the consequences of his past mistakes?

Sri Chinmoy: The seeker can only try to do the right thing, try to realise God. He himself is imperfect, but he knows there is Somebody who is perfect, and that is God. A real seeker feels that if he goes to God and gets Light, and if he is able to transform his own life, then he will be able to help others whom he has caused to suffer. Just because he was ignorant, he did something wrong. If he wants to make up for his past bad actions, first he must get something higher than or superior to what he had, and that something he can get only from God. So when he gets Peace, Love and Light from God, he can offer it to those whom he has caused to suffer. This is the best thing he can do for them.

Part XVII — Questions and answers — Georgia Institute of Technology

72. Question: What is the difference between the transcendental Self and the ordinary self?

Sri Chinmoy: Considerable. There is a Self that is the transcendental Self — the silent Self. When we go deep within, in our highest, most sublime meditation, we discover this Self. This is the transcendental Self. The self that we use in our day-to-day life, in our earthly reality, is the self of the physical world, of the mental and of the vital world. Each world has a kind of self.

When we speak of the higher Self, the transcendental Self, we are referring to something that deals with Silence — eternal Silence, infinite Silence, immortal Silence. When we live in the world of Silence, we come to know what the transcendental Self is. We come to know that the entire creation came into existence from it. Now we are living in the world of sound. Here we do not see or feel the transcendental Self. It is a stranger to us. But when we realise our highest divinity, the transcendental Self becomes our real friend here on earth in all our multifarious activities. In the life of sound, in the hustle and bustle of our daily activities, that Self will keep Peace for us and offer it to us. We are in motion, in constant movement, but there is Peace inside us, like the peace and tranquillity at the bottom of a rough sea. This Self we gain when we attain constant oneness with Infinity, Eternity and Immortality.

73. Question: It seems like it will take such a long time to realise this transcendental Self.

Sri Chinmoy: The task we have set before us takes a great amount of time. Our goal is to bring down into the earth atmosphere Peace, Light and Bliss in infinite measure, although now we do not have perhaps even an iota of Peace. But we have to know that when God's Hour dawns, everything will come. For a child to become a multi-millionaire is just a dream; now he does not have a penny. But this dream can become a reality when he grows up if he has tremendous determination.

We are all God's children. We are trying to get Peace, Light and Bliss in infinite measure. When we deal with Infinity, naturally we have to pay attention to Eternity also, because Infinity and Eternity go together. We have to be in the presence of Eternal Light. The man may get his million dollars, but when he dies he offers it back to Mother Earth. And when a spiritual child, when a seeker achieves and grows into Peace, Light and Bliss, he also leaves it here for Mother Earth to use when he leaves the body. As a human being leaves his material wealth on earth, so also does a spiritual person leave his spiritual wealth on earth when he departs. But in his case, in addition to leaving his spiritual wealth on earth for the benefit of his spiritual descendants, he also is fully able to enjoy this wealth during his rest in Heaven.

Part XVIII — Questions and answers — Clemson University

74. Question: *You seem to feel that the mind is not that important. What about students, who go to school?*

Sri Chinmoy: As a student, you certainly have to develop your mind. But we have to know that there are two types of mind. One is the physical mind, which is constantly doubting and subject to undivine thoughts. The physical mind is constantly judging everything and then examining itself to see whether its judgement is true. The physical mind is fond of accumulating information, but information is not going to give us an iota of inner wisdom. This mind does not help us at all in our inner development. But there is also the pure mind, the higher mind, the mind that is far beyond the domain of doubt. That mind is clear; that mind sees the Reality as such and wants to grow into the Reality. The higher mind and the loving heart go together.

The physical mind will bring us information or world-knowledge. Inside this world-knowledge there is not true wisdom, but still we cannot look down upon this knowledge. Only we have to feel that this knowledge must be transcended so we may enter into the higher mind. Right now we do not really know Infinity, Eternity and Immortality. These are vague terms that the physical mind cannot grasp. But if we enter into the higher mind, then we see these things as the real Reality.

Part XIX — Questions and answers — University of North Carolina

75. Question: You talk about God, but we do not have any concept at all of who God is. Who is God?

Sri Chinmoy: God is all Love. God is all Light. God is all Beauty. God is everything: Truth, Peace, Light, Bliss in infinite measure. He is with form; He is without form. If you experience God as Peace, then you will say God is Peace. If you experience God as Light, then you will say God is Light. If you experience God as Love, then you will say God is Love.

Since we are human beings, according to our limited understanding we say God is this or God is that. But God is really everything. If we want to experience Him as an infinite expanse without any form, we can do so. But again, if we want to experience Him intimately as a most illumined being right in front of us, then He becomes that. So He is this, He is that. Again, He transcends everything. To our human mind, he can be either this or that. But when we have our Highest Realisation, we see that God is constantly transcending all our inner and outer conceptions.

SRI CHINMOY

NOTES TO FIFTY FREEDOM-BOATS TO ONE GOLDEN
SHORE, PART 2

30. Luther I Bonney Hall, University of Maine, Portland, Maine, 2
5 January 1974.
31. Pace Memorial United Methodist Church, Virginia
Commonwealth University, Richmond, Virginia, 6 February 1974.
32. Rackham Hall, University of Michigan, Ann Arbor, Michigan,
12 February 1974 — morning.
33. Ingman Room, New Student Union, University of Toledo,
Toledo, Ohio, 12 February 1974 — afternoon.
34. Conference Room 1, Halleck Building, St Joseph's College,
Rensselaer, Indiana, 13 February 1974 — morning.
35. Congress Room, Roosevelt University, Chicago,
Illinois, 13 February 1974 — afternoon.
36. Union Cinema, University of Wisconsin, Milwaukee, Wisconsin,
14 February 1974.
37. Student Center Chapel, Georgia Institute of Technology, Atlanta,
Georgia, 20 February 1974 — morning.
38. Foreign Student Lounge, Clemson University, Clemson,
South Carolina, 20 February 1974 — afternoon.
39. Humanities Lecture Hall, University of North Carolina,
Asheville, North Carolina, 20 February 1974 — evening.
40-43. Luther I Bonney Hall, University of Maine, Portland, Maine,
25 January 1974.
44-50. Pace Memorial United Methodist Church, Virginia
Commonwealth University, Richmond, Virginia, 6 February 1974.
51. Rackham Hall, University of Michigan, Ann Arbor, Michigan,
12 February 1974 — morning.
52-58. Ingman Room, New Student Union, University of Toledo,
Toledo, Ohio, 12 February 1974 — afternoon.
59-61. Conference Room 1, Halleck Building, St Joseph's College,
Rensselaer, Indiana, 13 February 1974 — morning.
62-68. Congress Room, Roosevelt University, Chicago,
Illinois, 13 February 1974 — afternoon.

69-71. Union Cinema, University of Wisconsin, Milwaukee, Wisconsin, 14 February 1974.
72-73. Student Center Chapel, Georgia Institute of Technology, Atlanta, Georgia, 20 February 1974 — morning.
74. Foreign Student Lounge, Clemson University, Clemson, South Carolina, 20 February 1974 — afternoon.
75. Humanities Lecture Hall, University of North Carolina, Asheville, North Carolina, 20 February 1974 — evening.

FIFTY FREEDOM-BOATS TO ONE
GOLDEN SHORE

BOOK 3

Part XX — Lectures

76. God's Love

God loves us. He loves us constantly and unconditionally. No matter what we have done, what we are doing or what we shall do, He will always love us. God loves us much more than He loves Himself. If we use our thinking and doubting minds, this may seem hard to believe. But if we use our loving and surrendering hearts, then we are bound to feel that God loves us infinitely more than He loves Himself. Why does He love us so much? He loves us because He feels that His Dream remains unfulfilled without us, His Reality remains unmanifested without us; without us, he is incomplete. Right now we feel that it is only we who really love ourselves. Then there may come a time when we think that God, too, loves us. But for us to believe that God loves us infinitely more than we love ourselves seems sheer impossibility.

There have been many, many times in our lives when we have felt miserable because we told a lie or deceived someone or became jealous of others. After we do something wrong or undivine, our inner consciousness comes to the fore and we feel miserable. We curse ourselves and try to punish ourselves. But God's Love for us remains exactly the same. We hate ourselves for our mistakes, but God still loves us and will always continue to love us. Our justice-power condemns us, but God's Compassion-power forgives us, illumines us and transforms our weakness into strength with its adamantine will-power. God gets satisfaction when, with His blessingful Smile, He gives us His Compassion-flood, His Concern-sky and His Love-sea so that we can grow into His very Image.

God loves us, and in return He wants us to smile, to love and to transcend. The moment we offer Him a soulful smile, God is pleased with us. The moment we offer Him an iota of our love, God is pleased with us. The moment we want to transcend our earthbound consciousness, God is pleased with us.

Our human love constantly tries to separate and divide, but the divine Love we get from God always adds and multiplies. God used His Delight-power when He created the world, and now He uses His Love-power to protect the world and bring perfection to earth, His creation.

Here on earth we have everything save and except one thing: satisfaction. It is only by loving God that we will get true satisfaction. God is our own highest, most illumined Reality. "United we stand, divided we fall": this is the motto of the State of Kentucky. In the inner life also, when we become consciously one with God, we feel a real sense of satisfaction. But when we are separated from God, when we are divided into two, we feel incomplete, unfulfilled and dissatisfied.

If we are not seekers, we love God once in a blue moon; but if we are seekers of the highest Truth, then we try to love God soulfully and constantly. There is an easy way to love God soulfully and constantly. When we separate darkness from light, the transient from the eternal, and outer knowledge from inner wisdom, then it becomes extremely easy for us to love God soulfully and constantly. After we love God soulfully and constantly, we can go one step ahead and love God unconditionally by giving Him what we have and what we are. What we have within is inner aspiration to grow into the vast Beyond. What we are without is a sea of ignorance.

God also gives us what He has and what He is. What He has is infinite Peace, Light and Bliss, and what He is is constant Concern, Concern for our liberation from the meshes of ignorance and Concern for our perfection. God loves us. We love God. By loving God, we gain victory over our age-old ignorance. By loving us, God makes us consciously feel that we are eternal players, divine players in His cosmic Game.

The great pioneer, Daniel Boone, called Kentucky a second paradise. In the spiritual life, every day we can have a sense of paradise. Paradise means infinite Peace, Light and Bliss. When the seeker prays and meditates, he enters into paradise. When his mind is calm and quiet, when his mind is tranquillity's flood, his heart becomes all-giving and his life becomes Divinity's Reality. Paradise is not a place; it is a state of consciousness. When we free our mind from the meshes of ignorance, when we liberate our existence from the mire of earth, we see, feel and grow into paradise.

77. Self-Transcendence

Dear sisters and brothers, dear seekers of the highest Transcendental Truth, I wish to give a short talk on self-transcendence.

We are all seekers who wish to transcend our present realities. Why do we want to transcend? We want to transcend because the life of ignorance, bondage, imperfection and death cannot satisfy us. We want to achieve something. We want to grow into something which is eternal; we want to grow into the very image of Immortality.

Right in front of us there are two worlds: the world of desire and the world of aspiration. When our life belongs to the desire-world, we feel that satisfaction is always a far cry. When our life belongs to the aspiration-world, we feel that satisfaction is our birthright. The life of desire is a life of self-chosen bondage. The life of aspiration is a life of God-chosen transcendence.

In our life of self-transcendence, from the lower we grow into the higher. The lower is transformed into the higher, the less perfect is transformed into the more perfect. Things that have to be rejected, we reject; things that have to be transformed, we transform; things that have to be transcended, we transcend. This process of transcendence is beyond the thinking of the mental man. It finds its existence in the self-giving of the psychic man. The psychic man becomes part and parcel of reality by identifying with reality itself. The thinking man, the doubting man, finds it extremely difficult or impossible to identify himself with that reality.

In our ordinary life we deal with constant possibility, and at the end of our efforts we meet with either success or failure. But in the spiritual life, we do not care for failure or success; we care only for progress. In this way, possibility is transformed into inevitability.

A seeker of the Highest Truth, the moment he enters into the spiritual life, feels that he has transcended his life of conscious impurity and obscurity. The life of desire he has transcended; now he is living the life of aspiration. At every moment he has the golden opportunity to go high, higher, highest on the strength of his inner mounting cry.

Each time our aspiration, our mounting cry, touches the highest pinnacle, it is fired again. The goal that it touches need not and cannot be the ultimate Goal, for today's goal is tomorrow's starting point. Again, tomorrow's goal will be the starting point for the day after tomorrow. There is no end to our realisation. There is no end to our self-transcendence. Our aspiration ascends, our realisation transcends, our satisfaction dawns, finally our God smiles. With our inner cry we ascend to God's descending Smile. When we feed our inner cry, and when we become our inner cry, at that time our song of realisation and transcendence begins.

In order to transcend, two things are of paramount importance: our personal effort and God's Grace. By personal effort alone, we cannot transcend ourselves. Again, God's Grace will not do anything unless and until we are receptive. If we can receive God's Grace and properly use it, then only can we reach the Highest. A sincere seeker is transcending his previous reality at every moment. When he transcends, he does not reject anything. The sincere seeker accepts the world as his very own. Like a potter who accepts clay and moulds it into something beautiful, a spiritual seeker accepts the life of ignorance and tries to transform it with his inner wisdom-light.

In our deepest philosophy, we consider past achievements of no value. We say the past is dust. The past has given us what it has to offer, but it has not given us what we need: liberation, realisation, salvation and perfection. So it is today, it is in the immediacy of the present, that we have to grow into the spiritual life. Since most of us are beginners in the spiritual life we try to meditate for five minutes, ten minutes, half an hour, or an hour a day, and to keep our best consciousness always to the fore. If we can meditate an hour a day, we try to extend the effects of this meditation throughout the whole day. As soon as a child throws a ball, its momentum keeps it going, and it covers a considerable distance. So also our soulful prayer and meditation, even if it only lasts half an hour, projects our aspiring consciousness into the heart of each day and enters into all our multifarious activities as they unfold hour by hour.

As in the world of desire we want to grow and expand, so also do we want to grow and expand in the spiritual life. In the beginning we want an iota of Light, then we wish to have abundant Light, and then infinite Light. But there is a great difference between the expansion of our earthly desires and the expansion of our divine aspiration. When we possess mortal life, the desire-life, we are not actually satisfied. Even when our desires are fulfilled, we discover that we have new desires, and there is no abiding satisfaction. We have always the same hunger, the same unsaturated, unfulfilled hunger. But in the spiritual life, when we get an iota of Peace, Light and Bliss — although our ultimate aim is to have these in infinite measure — even an iota gives us a sense of satisfaction. And, in the long run, at God's choice Hour, we do get Peace, Light and Bliss in infinite measure. Each time we are divinely satisfied and fulfilled, we transcend our earthbound reality and enter into the Heaven-free Reality.

The motto of this state is "Agriculture and commerce". The spiritual seeker is a farmer. He cultivates his heart here in this world and receives from Above, like falling rain, the divine Grace. At the time when the seeker develops one-pointed devotion to the Inner Pilot, he collects the bumper crop of realisation. It is like an exchange of natural capacities. The seeker identifies himself with the consciousness of earth, increasing his receptivity through surrender. And at the same time he invokes the transcendental consciousness from Above. When the earth consciousness and the Transcendental Consciousness meet, when earth's surrender and Heaven's Grace join together, at that time realisation dawns in the seeker's aspiring life. There is a royal road that leads to self-transcendence. That road is our surrender, our conscious, unconditional surrender to the Will of the Absolute Supreme.

78. Compassion

Dear seekers, I wish to give a talk on compassion. When we use our mind to understand the meaning of compassion, very often we are misled and we mislead others. But when we use our heart, we understand the meaning immediately, and we make others understand as well.

Compassion is God's immense and intense Concern for mankind. When we show compassion to others at the time of their need, compassion is sweet. When we receive compassion from others while we are in dire need, compassion is sweeter. And when we come to realise that it is God's Compassion that is enabling us to fulfil our promise both to Heaven and to earth, Compassion is sweetest. Our promise to Heaven is to reveal our divine qualities here on earth. Our promise to earth is to manifest all our divine capacities so that Mother Earth can utilise them for her own purposes.

We are all seekers here, and we feel that if we can receive God's most illumining Compassion, then our spiritual journey will be expedited. But how are we going to receive this Compassion from Above? We can easily do it if we can feel that we are like a child, a little divine child. When a human child cries, no matter where the mother is, she comes to comfort him, for by pleasing the child she gets satisfaction. Similarly, when we soulfully cry for God's Compassion, God immediately descends with His Compassion-power.

A child cries helplessly because he feels that without his mother's help and guidance he cannot do anything. But the spiritual child does not cry with a sense of helplessness. He feels that there is a Source, and that Source is omniscient, omnipotent and omnipresent. When we become soulful in our cry, we establish a free access to the Source. So the seeker in us, the divine child in us, cries soulfully and not helplessly.

In our ordinary day-to-day life, in our multifarious activities, we speak of Grace, divine Grace. From the spiritual point of view, there is a subtle difference between Grace and Compassion. Let us imagine a vast expanse of water all around — this is Grace. But when there is a heavy downpour, a shower, this is called Compassion. Compassion is Grace, but in a very intensified, one-pointed form. Grace is something general, which is for everyone whether he aspires or does not aspire. But divine Compassion, real Compassion, enters into our aspiring consciousness, our aspiring life, only when we feel the inner urge to fly into the Beyond.

Compassion wants to operate in us at every moment, but quite often, because of our ignorance, we resist Compassion consciously or unconsciously, even after we have begun to cry for it. In the ordinary life, if somebody wants to give us something out of his infinite kindness, and we don't take it, then the person immediately withdraws his gift, as if to say that we do not deserve it. But in the case of God, it is not like that. God never withdraws His Compassion from us. On the contrary, He tries to offer more of His divine, unconditional Compassion.

Compassion is a power, an illumining power. But when we are extremely stubborn and reject Compassion totally and mercilessly, God at times relies on His Patience-power. He knows that Eternity is at His disposal and that one day in the process of evolution we shall be able to receive His Compassion. Today if we do not achieve and receive His Compassion devotedly or gratefully, He does not mind. Tomorrow He will give us another opportunity, and in either the near or the distant future, we are bound to accept His Compassion-power, for this alone can transform our nature. So God does not withdraw; He only uses another type of Power, which we call patience.

Before we enter into the spiritual life, Compassion is something abstract. But when we enter into the spiritual life, and live a divine life, Compassion becomes concrete. At every moment we feel God's Compassion in us in either a subtle or a solid, palpable form. At every moment we can see it, feel it and grow into it.

Aum.

The state motto of Louisiana is "Union, justice, confidence". These terms are extremely spiritual. *Union*. Union occurs between the finite and the Infinite. Right now we are in the physical, so we are all living finite, individual, separate existences. But when the finite enters into the Infinite in order to realise the highest Absolute, or when the Infinite enters into the finite to manifest its own Divinity, then this union immediately establishes one reality, one fulfilling reality. In the union of the finite and the Infinite we realise the highest plane of consciousness and, at the same time, we manifest Divinity on earth.

Now, what actually is being united when the Infinite and the finite join? It is God's Compassion and man's surrender. God's greatest gift to mankind is His Compassion-power, and man's greatest gift to God is his surrender-power. When man surrenders to God soulfully and unconditionally, when he surrenders to God's Will cheerfully, at that time God's Capacity, God's Reality, God's Infinitude become his. Compassion is the magnet in God, and surrender is the magnet in the seeker. When God uses His Compassion, it is like a magnet from above pulling us up to the Highest. And when we use our surrender, this magnet immediately pulls God down into our living breath. So when our magnet and God's magnet come together, the Hour of

God dawns for us in our life of aspiration and self-dedication.

Justice. In the ordinary human life, justice says, "As you sow, so you reap." This is justice: tit for tat. If somebody has done something wrong, we feel we have every right to threaten him, frighten him, warn him, punish him. But this kind of justice is on the lowest rung of the human ladder. When we step up to a higher rung, justice becomes a kind of forgiveness. If we can forgive someone who has done something wrong, if we have the capacity, then we feel that forgiveness itself is justice. When we enter into the highest level of consciousness, at that time there is no question of either punishment or forgiveness. It is only a matter of illumination. The highest Self encompasses and embodies all of Reality. So if one part of its existence is unillumined, it does not punish or forgive. It tries to illumine that part of its own existence. When we watch the world from the highest plane of consciousness, we feel that the ignorant, obscure, impure, imperfect world needs illumination. Here justice is the feeling of oneness. Divine Justice is the transformation of our own unlit existence. Divine Justice is self-illumination.

In the ordinary life, we feel that equality is justice. But in the divine world, if somebody has the capacity to receive more Peace, more Light, more Bliss from Above, then he should be given more. Equal opportunity should be given, but if you have more capacity or receptivity than I have, then you should progress according to your own speed and not slow down to my speed. If you wait for me, then God's Hour will have to wait for you, and you will not reach the Goal at God's choice Hour. This kind of equality is not an act of illumination. If your time has come, you go. God has given me the same opportunity, but you have developed more capacity. That is why you have received more light and you can run faster towards your Goal. When

God gives me the capacity at His choice Hour, at that time I also will reach the Goal. This is called divine Justice. God is constantly giving us all the same opportunity, but our individual capacity is not the same.

Confidence. Confidence is a most important quality in both our human life and our divine life. In the human life, usually our confidence is based on our ego, our unruly vital. The unruly vital makes us feel that we can do everything, that there is nothing on earth we cannot do. Nevertheless, it is true that in our human life, if we do not have confidence, we cannot do anything. But in the divine life when we have confidence, it is a different matter. This confidence comes from an inner awareness of our Source. We feel, "I am God's son, I am part and parcel of God. Since He has infinite Peace, Light and Bliss, since He has infinite capacity, I also have the same within me. Right now I am not aware of it, but a day will come when I will not only be aware of it but will actually be able to manifest it." This is called divine confidence.

Now, some people have confidence only in God and not in themselves. This is a deplorable mistake. They should have confidence in themselves, but they should feel that this confidence is coming directly from God. They have to feel that their faith in their own personal effort is their confidence in a capacity which has come directly from God. God has given us this confidence and God is the one who is experiencing this confidence in and through us. This confidence is nothing other than the confidence God has in Himself.

God always has confidence in us, but very often we lose confidence in ourselves. When we have been defeated once or twice in the battlefield of life, we lose all our confidence. But God never loses His confidence in us because He knows that He is the Root and we are the branches. Since the root is firm and solid, how can the branches fail? God knows His capacity, His potentiality, His Plenitude and Infinitude; therefore He has all confidence, not only in Himself but also in us, for He feels that we are His direct manifestation. Without us He cannot manifest what He has and what He is; and without Him we cannot realise what we have and what we are. We are part and parcel of God's Divinity, His integral Reality; therefore He always has boundless confidence in our capacity.

79. Love human and Love Divine

Dear sisters and brothers, I wish to share with you my humble philosophy, which is based on love. We know that there are two types of love: human love and Love Divine. In human love, what we actually try to do is to possess the many without caring for the One, the Source. But if we do not possess the Source, then the many cannot be of any help to us. If there is no root, then how will the tree grow? How will we be able to claim the branches or the flowers and leaves as our very own? With the divine Love, we go first to the One, the Source, and from there we go to the many. We become one with the root, and then we grow into the tree, which will manifest itself through the branches and leaves, the flowers and fruits. Divine Love is the song of multiplicity in unity.

In human love there is demand or, at least, expectation. Very often we start with demand, and when a higher wisdom dawns we no longer demand, but still we expect something from others. We convince ourselves that this expectation is justified. Since we have done something for others — offered our love — we feel it is quite legitimate to expect something in return.

But in divine Love there is no such thing as demand or

expectation. In divine Love we just give what we have and what we are. What we have and what we are is dedicated service. In the human life, before we give our love, we try to discover love in others — that is, their love for us. In the divine Life, before we give our love to others, we try to discover Love in its reality and integrality within ourselves. Only then are we in a position to offer love to others. At first our satisfaction dawns when we feel that those to whom we offer our love accept it wholeheartedly. But there is an even higher form of divine Love when we go beyond this feeling, and give love just for the sake of self-giving. We give, and even if our love is not accepted, we do not mind. We shall go on giving, for we are all love, our Source is all Love.

In human love there is not only demand and expectation, but there is something even worse: withdrawal. First we demand, then we expect. When our expectation is not fulfilled, we sometimes try to withdraw from the person to whom we have offered our love. In divine Love, it is never like that. With divine Love we try to become one with the weakness, imperfection and bondage of others. Although we have inner freedom, we use this inner freedom not to lord it over others, but to become one, consciously one with their imperfections. In this way we can understand them and serve them at their own level, with a view to transforming their imperfections.

The capacity of human love is so limited that we cannot expand ourselves and totally embrace one another. There is bound to be a feeling of supremacy. I shall love you, no doubt, but I wish to remain an inch higher than you. On that condition I shall love you. The superior loves the inferior because he is satisfied to some extent with his position in this relationship. The inferior very often loves the superior because of his insecurity. So love binds them and gives them both some sense of satisfaction. But in divine Love there is no such thing as superiority and inferiority. Divine Love always gives itself freely and wholeheartedly. Divine Love gets satisfaction only by offering itself totally and unconditionally.

In divine Love, we come to notice that the personal and the impersonal perfectly go together. There is a balance between the two. The personal in us enters into the vast, which is impersonal; and the impersonal in us enters into the personal to manifest its unmanifested Reality, Divinity and Immortality. In human love, the personal and the impersonal are two strangers; worse, they are at daggers drawn. The personal and the impersonal at best try to reach a compromise, but this compromise brings no satisfaction at all; in the very depth of human love, there is always a rivalry and competition between the two. On rare occasions, the personal says to the impersonal, which is inside the human being, "Let us alternate our reality, our height, our wisdom, our capacity. This moment you stand up and I shall remain seated; the next moment I shall stand up and you will sit."

In human love, very often the physical mind, the doubting mind, the suspecting mind, comes to the fore. But in divine Love, we see only the loving heart, the surrendering heart, the all-beckoning heart. The mind loves a reality because it sees the reality according to its own understanding and vision. But the heart loves a reality because it sees the reality in the reality's own form. The heart becomes inseparably one with the reality, with the very existence of that reality, both inner and outer. It sees the living breath of the reality in its own form and shape; it sees the body and soul of the reality all together.

In human love, the lover and the beloved are two separate persons. The lover is running towards the beloved, and when he reaches the beloved he finds his satisfaction. In divine Love, the lover and the beloved are one and inseparable. In divine Love, the Lover is the Supreme and the Beloved is the Supreme. In human love, we feel that satisfaction lies somewhere else — not within us, but in somebody else. But in divine Love, satisfaction is found nowhere else but in ourselves. The Lover and the Beloved are one and the same — the Supreme dwelling within and the Supreme outside us. When we speak of our "self" as the divine Lover or Beloved, we have to know that this is the "Self" which is both the One and the many. This Self, the Supreme, finds its satisfaction only when It gets a glimpse of God's Reality, Infinity, Eternity and Immortality in the many. This "Self" is the One, and It wants to see and feel its Reality in the many.

Love is duty. In our human life we see duty as something mechanical, lifeless, forced — something thrust upon us. But in the divine Life, duty is something full of opportunity. At every second an opportunity is dawning for us to expand our life's consciousness, our life's reality, our life's delight. So in the divine Life we welcome duty, for it increases our capacity and potentiality and expands the dream of our divine, unhorizoned Reality.

Life is the lesson of Love. Love is the lesson of Life. When we study Life's lesson in our human life, the lesson is composed of fear, doubt, anxiety, worry and frustration. But in the divine Life, we see that Love is the lesson not only *of* Life, but also *for* Life — for the Life that is everlasting, ever-illumining and ever-fulfilling.

A divine Lover is he who believes in the divine miracle. A human miracle is something that feeds our curiosity, something that lasts for a fleeting second. But the divine miracle is the elevation of consciousness. To raise somebody else's consciousness, to raise humanity's consciousness even an iota is the true divine miracle. The conscious help the divine Lover gives to the seeker performs this divine miracle.

We are of God the eternal Love and we are for God the eternal Love. We are of God the Infinite Love and we are for God the Infinite Love. Eternity is the Source of the Silence-life; and Infinity is the message of the sound-life. From the One we came and for the many we exist. This is the real message of divine Love. We are of the One and we are for the many — the many in the One. This is the quintessence of Love Divine.

80. The human and the divine

Dear seekers of the highest Truth, I wish to give a short talk on the human and the divine.

Our outer essence is human; our inner essence is divine. The human world is the desire-world. The divine world is the aspiration-world. In the desire-world, when we get something we immediately cry out, "Eureka, I have found it! This is it." But in the divine world, when we get something we say to ourselves, "There is something else I need, something higher, deeper, more illumining and more fulfilling." This sense of dissatisfaction is not bad or undivine. This kind of dissatisfaction makes us feel that we are destined to grow into something infinitely higher than what we are now.

Human right and divine right. Human right tells us that we dare to defend our rights. This is the motto of the State of Alabama: "We dare defend our rights." Now why do we want to defend our rights? Because we feel that our skills and capacities are not properly appreciated and admired, that we are to some extent exploited. Therefore we feel that it is our bounden duty to defend our rights. The divine in us also tells us that we must dare to defend our rights. But in this case, it is our divine right to offer our inner message to the world at large, our divine right to tell ignorance that we belong to the Supreme alone. We are of the divine and we are for the divine. We cannot mix with ignorance and we must not allow ourselves to be devoured by ignorance. True, we have wallowed in the pleasures of ignorance for millennia. But that does not mean that we shall not exercise our divine right to go deep within and bring to the fore the Light infinite to inundate the world of suffering and darkness.

The human in us wants to discover if there is any Truth, Light and Divinity in others. It is in doubt whether others have these qualities. But the divine in us knows that Truth, Light and Divinity are everywhere. They are not the monopoly of any individual; everybody has deep within him Peace, Light and Bliss in infinite measure.

The human in us wants to see the face of reality, so that it can change the reality to suit its own desires. The divine in us wants to see the face of reality so it can grow into the very image of the transcendental Reality.

The human in us constantly cries for success, more success, abundant success. But the divine in us wants progress, constant progress, inner and outer. This progress is founded entirely upon self-giving, and self-giving is the precursor of God-becoming.

The human in us wants to possess the world so it can utilise the world in its own way. Alas, to its extreme sorrow it sees that before it possesses the world, the world has already possessed it mercilessly. The divine in us wants to offer its very existence to the world; it wants to illumine the world with its love and selfless dedication. Lo and behold, it sees that before it has illumined the world, the world has illumined it totally.

The human in us wants to realise God the Power so that

it can lord it over the world. The divine in us needs the God who is all Good. The human in us prays to God and meditates on God and hopes to bring God down to satisfy its teeming desires. The human in us prays to God for its own satisfaction. But the divine in us prays and meditates so that God can utilise us in His own Way, in a divine Way, in a supreme Way.

The human in us wants to move from the door of the body to the room of the soul. It wants to go from the body to the soul through the vital, the mind and the heart. The divine in us wants to do the same thing, but the other way around. It wants to go from the soul to the heart, from the heart to the mind, from the mind to the vital, from the vital to the body. The divine in us feels that since the soul has Light, we have to enter into the soul's room first and from there enter into the other rooms, which are obscure, unlit and undivine.

When the human in us becomes sincere, we realise the undeniable fact that we need transformation: the transformation of the body, the transformation of the vital, the transformation of the mind and the transformation of the heart.

Right now, the body is constantly wallowing in the pleasures of ignorance, consciously and deliberately. But there shall come a time when this very body will try to aspire and try to serve the divine, here on earth and there in Heaven.

Right now, the vital in us is aggressive and destructive, but this very vital will one day aspire to become dynamic and progressive. Right now the vital in us will say, like Julius Caesar, *Veni, vidi, vici:* "I came, I saw, I conquered." But this same vital, when it gets illumination, will say, "I came into the world to love the world, to embrace the world, to become one with the world."

Right now, the mind in us suspects the world, judges the world, doubts the world. But the same mind, when it cries for illumination in the near or distant future, will realise that it has come into the world to perfect the world's ignorance and illumine others. But before it illumines others, it will feel the necessity of self-illumination; it will realise that its ability to perfect others entirely depends on its own perfection. So the mind will perfect itself first and then offer its perfection to the aspiring world.

Right now, the heart in us is insecure, weak and impotent. It sees the Vast, but it does not want to establish its inseparable oneness with the Vast, precisely because it is badly frightened. But when the human heart is transformed into the divine heart, it will throw open its door to the world at large and there all humanity will find a haven. The heart will become inseparably one with God's creation. By becoming one with God's entire creation, it will feel that it has fulfilled its promise to the soul and its mission on earth. Its promise was that it would receive the soul's light in boundless measure, and its mission was consciously to serve humanity with this light.

The soul, too, has made a promise, a promise to God and to man. To God, the soul has made the solemn promise that it will manifest divinity on earth; and to mankind, the soul has promised that it will liberate the body from the meshes of ignorance. Here "body" means the body-consciousness, which includes the physical, the vital, the mental and the psychic. The soul is bound to fulfil its promises to God and man.

Each human being becomes a conscious instrument of God when he enters sincerely into the spiritual life, the life of aspiration and dedication. Before that, he is in the world of ignorance, the world of sleep. But the impossibility which looms large in this human life need not and cannot forever remain with us. Our life of ignorance will eventually be transcended. Our essence, deep within us, is divine, and what we have within is bound to come to the fore at God's choice Hour.

The human in us wants to discover the Light; the divine in us wants to reveal the Light, which it feels it has always had. When the human in us aspires, it wants to grow and become. But the divine in us constantly knows that it eternally is.

The human in us will be fulfilled only when it consciously accepts the dictates of our inner divinity. The divine in us will fulfil itself only when it transforms, illumines and perfects the human in us. By the transformation of the human in us and the manifestation of the divine in us, we grow into perfect Perfection.

The human in us prays:

> *Hiraṇmayena pātreṇa satyasyāpihitaṁ mukham*
> *Tat tvaṁ pūṣan apāvṛiṇu satyadharmāya dṛiṣṭaye*

> The Face of Truth is covered with a brilliant golden orb.
> Remove it, O Sun, so that I who am devoted to the Truth may behold the Truth.

The progressive divine in us says:

> *Vedāham etaṃ puruṣaṃ mahāntam*
> *Aditya varṇaṃ tamasaḥ parastāt*

> I have known this Great Being, effulgent as the sun beyond the boundaries of tenebrous gloom.

And the Transcendental, the all-pervading Divine in us, says:

> He the Absolute and we the aspiring consciousness
> are inseparably one.

81. Problems

Dear seekers of the Transcendental Truth, I wish to give a talk on the subject of problems.

Problems within, problems without, problems everywhere. True, we do have some problems; but unfortunately we multiply them into countless problems. How do we multiply our problems? There are two ways. First, we invite the past and the future to come and stay with us in the heart of today. And second, we try to solve all our problems in the twinkling of an eye.

Let us consider the past — the unfulfilled past, the sad past, the past that has not given us what we actually wanted — an enemy or a useless friend. And let us take the unmanifested future as a perfect stranger. If we know that somebody is useless, that he has not encouraged, inspired or liberated us, then let us not invite that particular friend to stay with us. Again, let us not invite a stranger, either. A stranger may not please us. He may do something harmful and hurtful. Let us not have faith in a stranger; let us have all faith only in today. Today is our friend, our only friend. Let us take morning as a dream-boat and evening as the reality-shore. Right now we are all in the sea of aspiration. Once we cross the sea, we will reach our destined Goal.

Each human being, from a child to an octogenarian, has problems. A child has a problem when he wants to learn the alphabet. But he studies, and there comes a time when he not only learns the alphabet, but can easily read any book he wants. Similarly, a beginner in the spiritual life finds it extremely difficult to get even an iota of Peace, Light and Bliss no matter how bitterly he cries for it. But this beginner does not remain always a beginner. After a while he becomes an advanced seeker and finally, at God's choice Hour, he realises the ultimate Truth.

At that time, his inner being becomes flooded with Light and Delight. But this cannot take place overnight. If we try to pull down God's Hour prematurely, we will only be frustrated.

We have the body, the vital, the mind, the heart and the soul. The problem of the body is impurity. The problem of the vital is aggression. The problem of the mind is doubt. The problem of the heart is insecurity. And the problem of the soul is that it has not yet manifested its inner divinity here on earth.

The body's problem can be solved only when purity dawns. The vital's problem can be solved only when dynamism enters into the vital and energises it. The mind's problem is solved when the mind is illumined by divine faith. The heart's problem is solved when the heart becomes flooded with the light of love. And the soul's problem is solved when the soul becomes the breath of supreme confidence.

In order to achieve purity, dynamism, faith, security and confidence, we must listen constantly to the dictates of the Inner Pilot, and consciously surrender to the Will of the Supreme. Now what is the Will of the Supreme? The Will of the Supreme is our conscious acceptance of the divine Light within us and our acceptance of earth as the field for the divine manifestation. We have to bring to the fore our inner Light in order to offer it to the world at large for its salvation and illumination. And we have to accept earth for the manifestation of God's Divinity.

In each individual there are two beings. One being wants material success; the other wants the life of inner solitude. Now, when the individual achieves material success, he feels that something is lacking, something is missing. His life is still filled with problems. What is he missing? He is missing peace and tranquillity. The material life has not given him Peace, Light and Bliss. He feels that if he can achieve Peace, Light and Bliss, then all his problems will be over, and he will be able to rest for good. The other being within him wants only the life of inner peace. Only the inner life is real for that being. The outer life it discards or negates; it feels the outer life is of no use. Then the individual goes deep within and realises Peace, Light and Bliss. But when this Peace, Light and Bliss remain unmanifested, the individual again feels miserable. He feels that the things that he has or has grown into must be manifested in the outer life, the outer world.

The first being cried for material wealth, but material wealth did not satisfy it because inner realisation was lacking. And the second being had inner realisation, but the outer manifestation was missing. So the second also had a problem.

Before we realise God, our problem is ignorance; we ourselves are the problem. After we realise God, our problem is manifestation. It is like earth's problem and Heaven's problem. Earth's problem is realisation; Heaven's problem is manifestation. Even God has problems. God's problem is to make us feel that we are His children, His chosen children, that we are of Him and for Him. His problem is to make us feel that He is the root and we are the branches of the self-same tree.

How do we solve our problems? We solve our problems by going deep within. The Christ said, "The Kingdom of Heaven is within you." The Kingdom of Heaven means the Kingdom of Light and Bliss. Only if we go deep within, will we see the face of the Kingdom of Heaven. And once we have free access to the Kingdom of Heaven, all our problems are solved once and for all.

There are two types of people: desiring people and aspiring people. A desiring man takes a problem as a shattering experience, but an aspiring man considers a problem a strengthening experience. Whenever a problem arises, a desiring man feels that this problem is going to shatter his hopes. Then he is doomed to disappointment. This disappointment gives birth to frustration, and in frustration looms large his destruction. But an aspiring man sees a problem as a foundation stone. He accepts the problem as a challenge. He seeks to get a firm footing on the problem and use it as an opportunity to progress. In each experience, the Compassion of the Highest, the Beyond, is there to guide us and help us first to surmount the problem and then to transform it into a radiant opportunity to grow into the very image of our Lord Supreme.

There is a Zen saying that before one studies Zen, mountains are mountains. But after one enters into Zen practice, mountains no longer remain mountains. And finally, when one gets illumination, mountains become mountains again. We can say that mountains are the difficulties that we encounter when we enter into the spiritual life. After a while, we see that these mountains of difficulties can easily be surmounted. They are like passing clouds, and the inner sun is bound to reappear. Finally, when we realise the Highest, we see that the mountains of difficulties that we previously encountered have been transformed into mountains of opportunities — opportunities for progress, achievement and greater awakening in the ever-transcending experience of the highest Reality. The difficulties have become opportunities carrying us to the ever-transcending Beyond.

The motto of the State of West Virginia is "Mountaineers are always free." This is a significant motto from the inner point of view, because mountaineers are climbers. We aspirants, too, are all climbers, trying to climb up to the highest Height, the Pinnacle, on the strength of our inner cry. The higher we go, the more freedom we enjoy. The higher we go, the more the freedom of the Absolute is bound to inundate our existence, inner and outer. This freedom is the freedom of the Divinity within us, the freedom of the Infinity that belongs to us, the freedom of the Immortality of which we are made.

82. Do we love God?

Dear friends, dear sisters and brothers, I wish to pose a question. Do we love God? Do we really love God? The immediate answer is, "We do, we do love God."

We love God. Therefore we do not want to live a semi-animal life; we do not want to live a life of temptation; we do not want to live in the world of falsehood, darkness, limitation, bondage and death. We love God. Therefore we wish to feel and grow into His Presence in all that we do and say. When we do not aspire, we love God only to fulfil our desires. But when we aspire, we love God for His own sake. We want to be freed from the snares of desire, from the teeming clouds of desire, so that we can claim our birthright in God and for God.

We love God. Therefore we try to live within. To live within is to divinely glow at every moment. We love God. Therefore we try to reveal without. What do we reveal? We reveal our inner divinity, our conscious, inseparable oneness with our Inner Pilot, the Absolute Supreme.

We love God. Therefore, if we see defects in others, we feel that it is our bounden duty to perfect these defects, for our sweet Lord can never be pleased with us when we consciously or deliberately fail to perfect the imperfections that we notice in others. But when we perfect others, we come to realise that our task is just an expansion of our own self-awakening. We are all members of the same family. The root and the trunk is God, and we are the branches and leaves and fruits and flowers of God, the Tree.

We love God. Therefore we live on earth and try to manifest

Him and fulfil Him in His own Way. We play our roles like divine warriors. Every day we enter the battlefield of life to fight against fear, doubt, ignorance and bondage. And at the end of our journey on the physical plane, we leave the body behind and our soul-bird flies to the highest region of Light and Delight. There we take rest for some time before coming back once more to this earth. We come to earth in order to manifest our inner divinity and to fulfil the promise that our souls have made to the Absolute Supreme, our promise to manifest and fulfil Him here on earth as well as there in Heaven.

We love God. Therefore we want to live not in the unreal, but in the real. The unreal in us is the egocentric "I", the "I" that binds us and sings the song of separation. This is the personal "I", which tells us that we are of the finite and cannot come out of the finite. But the real in us is the universal "I". This "I" tells us that we are of the Infinite and we are for the Infinite. With this "I" we come into the world to sing the song of perfection, and when we retire from the earth-scene, with this same "I" we sing the song of realisation which we learnt here.

We love God. Divine Love is the first and foremost among our friends, here on earth, there in Heaven. Inside the heart of Love, we find two other friends: faith and devotion. Without faith we feel that our journey is insecure and that there is constant danger looming in our path. But when we see the face of our faith-friend, feel faith within us and grow into faith, we feel that our journey is quite safe. And when we see the face of our devotion-friend we know that we have found a short-cut, a sunlit road, to our destined Goal.

What makes us love God? It is God's boundless Compassion, His unconditional Compassion, that makes us love Him. God's divine Pride in us also makes us love Him. In addition, our inner cry, the climbing flame within us, makes us love God, for this flame knows that, unless and until it reaches the Highest, we can never see the face of abiding satisfaction. The world can offer us many things, but it cannot offer abiding satisfaction. This we must get from our inner life, our inner world. On the strength of our inner cry we have to reach the highest Pinnacle; and then we have to come down and distribute to the world at large what we have received and achieved in the highest plane of our consciousness.

We are all seekers. A seeker is one whose inner being is inundated with opportunity. There are three hundred and sixty-five days in a year. For a genuine sincere seeker, each day offers a new opportunity, and each opportunity is one rung in the ladder leading to our destined Goal. The seeker knows that if he cries soulfully from the inmost recesses of his heart, then each day he will climb up to a new and higher rung. Once we climb up the ladder of inner evolution and reach the Highest, we will see that the Highest is not something new; it was always within us, only we had not yet discovered it as our very own. Once we feel that the Highest is our very own, we have to reveal and manifest it. This is the cosmic Game that we play and that we have been playing from time immemorial.

The deeper we go, the sooner we discover that not only do we love God, but also God loves us. But God loves us in His own Way, not in our way. Right now we feel that God loves us if He fulfils our desires or aspirations. But when we go deep within and experience real Love, the divine Love, we will feel at every moment that we are God's chosen children. And whether He fulfils our immediate wishes or not, we know that whatever He does He is doing for our own good. Furthermore, we come to realise that He is constantly fulfilling Himself in and through us.

God is within each individual. He is found in unity and He

is found in multiplicity. This moment God is unity and the next moment God is multiplicity. Again, He is unity in multiplicity and multiplicity in unity. When we love God unconditionally, we feel that at every moment we are facing Reality and growing into Reality, and finally we realise that we are also transcending Reality, that we are flowing in the stream of the ever-transcending Reality, which is our perfect Immortality. Only when we are aware of our divine, transcendental Reality can we establish our perfect Immortality here on earth and there in Heaven.

Aum.

83. The spiritual life

Dear brothers and sisters, we are all students, students of the higher knowledge of the eternal Truth. A student learns and unlearns. A student learns the things that are inspiring, illumining and fulfilling; and he unlearns the things that are useless, the things that make him feel at every moment that his life is doomed. He learns the message of Light, inner Light; and he unlearns the message of ignorance and darkness.

How do we become spiritual? We become spiritual by emptying the mind, the mind that unconsciously cherishes fear and doubt. We try to empty fear, doubt and other undivine thoughts or foreign elements from the mind. We can also become spiritual by silencing the mind. When we can silence the mind, our life becomes a fertile field where a bumper crop can grow. There is still another way to become spiritual: by purifying the heart. In a pure heart, God can manifest Himself with all His Radiance. A heart of purity can easily become one, inseparably one, with God's eternal Reality, Divinity and

Omnipresence. When we empty the mind, we welcome God; but when we purify the heart, we actually place a throne for God inside our heart, which is His Home.

To become spiritual is to represent the ideal within us. What is this ideal? Our ideal is God the infinite Light and eternal Truth. On the strength of our aspiration, our inner cry, we grow into our ideal, then we reveal the ideal and finally we manifest the ideal.

Before we become spiritual, life is meaningless, life is a most deplorable burden. But after we become spiritual, we do not feel the heavy weight of life. On the contrary, we feel that we have become like birds flying in the welkin of Infinity and Immortality. Our life offers us real meaning, for it is a life of love and divinity.

Before we become spiritual, we do not see or feel God's loving Hand and ever-compassionate Heart. But after we become spiritual we feel God's guidance consciously and constantly in all our multifarious activities. When we become spiritual, God unites our heart with His own Heart of eternal Truth and infinite Light, Peace and Bliss.

An ordinary person wants to possess God; a spiritual person wants God to possess him. The ordinary person feels that if he gets God, then he will be able to lord it over the world; the entire world will be at his feet. But a spiritual person wants to be possessed by God. He feels that if he possesses God, at any moment the world of temptation may lure him and he may fall. But if God the Almighty possesses him, he will never be able to fall. The seeker always wants God to look after him and guide him. He feels that if he is possessed by God, then at every moment he can be of dedicated service to mankind. And only by serving God in mankind will he have abiding satisfaction.

Not by establishing an empire can man achieve abiding satisfaction, but only by self-awakening and self-giving. The seeker knows this truth; therefore he wants to renounce the undivine in himself and embrace the divine. The undivine in him is fear, doubt, anxiety and worry; the divine in him is strength, courage, faith, the feeling of oneness and the sense of perfection. An unspiritual person wants to discover peace in the world. But a spiritual person knows that he can discover peace only in the inmost recesses of his own heart. An unaspiring person will not find satisfaction or peace of mind, no matter how favourable the outer conditions are, because he does not know where to look or how to look for it. But a spiritual person, whatever opposition or unpropitious circumstances he has to face, will always have abundant peace and satisfaction, for they will flow from within him in an unquenchable flood. For the sincere seeker, peace reigns supreme because of his life of aspiration.

For an ordinary person, the aggressive vital is normal and necessary. But for a spiritual person, the vital does not always have to be aggressive. It can become pure and dynamic. When we have a pure, dynamic vital, we feel that we can really establish the kingdom of Truth on earth. When our vital is dynamic, we expand our consciousness. But when our vital is aggressive, we just destroy others; and while destroying others, we diminish our own reality, which is the universal reality.

There is also a divine vital within us. This vital operates only in our sincerity, humility, clarity and self-giving. The aggressive vital or the dynamic vital can say, in the words of Julius Caesar, *Veni, vidi, vici*. "I came, I saw, I conquered." But the divine vital says, "I came, I surrendered, I became. I came to God; I surrendered my existence to God; I became God the infinite Compassion, God the infinite Love, God the infinite Concern."

In our day-to-day existence, we discover that life is nothing but duty. This duty is a constant source of discouragement and frustration, as though somebody has placed a heavy load on our shoulders. But in the spiritual life, duty is taken in a different way. Duty means opportunity. Each time we fulfil our duty, we feel that we have gone one step further towards the Ultimate Goal. And each time we fulfil our divine duty, God entrusts us with more Peace, Light and Bliss.

A sincere spiritual seeker feels that human life is a constant blessing. Life is not bondage or frustration; life is opportunity. Here on earth is where we have to see the face of Truth and grow into the very image of the transcendental Reality. Life has to be utilised for a high purpose, for a divine purpose, for a fulfilling purpose. As an ordinary person cries for name and fame, for worldly satisfaction, a sincere seeker also cries; but he cries for Truth, for Light, for Bliss. He cries for God. He wants God to make him His perfect instrument. He does not want to be the doer, he does not want to be the action, he does not want to be the observer. He wants God to be the doer, he wants God to be the deed, he wants God to be the witness and he wants God to fulfil Himself in every way in and through him.

An ordinary, unaspiring person may see the Reality-tree from a distance, but he is afraid of it. He feels that the Reality-tree is all Light, and he is afraid that this Light will expose his ignorance. But a sincere seeker just runs towards the Reality-tree, touches the root, sits at the foot of the tree for a few seconds, and then tries to climb up the tree. He feels that the Light of the Reality-tree does not expose; on the contrary, he feels that it illumines, and illumination is perfect fulfilment. There are people who do not launch into the spiritual life because they are afraid that their weaknesses will be exposed, or they feel that there is nothing worth having in the spiritual life. But a sincere seeker knows that life has true meaning only when we enter into the spiritual life, for the spiritual life is the root of the tree of eternal life. If there is no root, then the tree cannot grow, and he can never climb up to the highest branch.

A spiritual seeker wants to achieve Truth, Light, Peace and Bliss on the strength of his self-giving, for his self-giving is his God-becoming. When he consciously becomes what he eternally has been, he knows that life is not a dream but a reality; that life is not only the messenger or harbinger of satisfaction, but also the real satisfaction itself. God is experiencing Himself in and through life, which is a manifestation of His Light and Delight. The seeker knows that today he is of God and tomorrow he will be for God. He is of God: that is his realisation; he is for God: that is his revelation and manifestation.

84. Silence

Dear seekers, dear sisters and brothers, I wish to give a very short talk on silence. Therefore, with your kind permission, I wish to maintain silence for a few minutes...

[Sri Chinmoy meditates with the audience briefly.]

Life needs and wants victory, but the victory that we achieve in the world of sound does not last for long. This victory is very fleeting. The victory that we achieve in the world of silence is everlasting, and each time a victory dawns in this inner world we feel that we are being prepared for a higher and more fulfilling victory in tomorrow's Dawn.

An ordinary man thinks either that silence cannot be achieved or that it is of no avail. But a seeker knows that silence can be achieved on the strength of his inner cry. He also knows that silence is of tremendous importance, for without silence we cannot see the face of Truth or grow into the very image of Truth and Light. Silence is within, but we have to discover it. Unless and until we discover our inner silence, we cannot feel that we are of God and for God. Inner silence is not just the absence of thoughts. No! Silence is the blossoming of our indomitable inner will. Silence is our inner wisdom-light. This wisdom-light is our conscious and constant surrender to the Will of our Inner Pilot, who inspires us, encourages us and guides us to the Shores of the Golden Beyond.

Silence is preparation, our preparation for God's examination. We come to know God's Hour only when we observe silence, only when we dive deep within. An unaspiring person does not and cannot know God's Hour. If God's Hour dawns in his life he fails to notice it. But a seeker who practises silence every day for half an hour or an hour knows when God's Hour is going to strike. And God not only tells him when the Hour will strike but also, like a private tutor, helps the seeker to pass his inner examination.

Silence is our protection. When we live in silence, we are protected by God's mightiest Power, His all-illumining Light. At that time the negative forces of fear, doubt, anxiety, worry, insecurity and selfishness can have no access to our inner being. We are protected by God within and without at every moment.

Silence is our transformation. When we observe silence consciously, our outer being is transformed. This transformation is a great achievement for Mother Earth. When a human being is transformed, Mother Earth feels that she has achieved something momentous, something that can be kept for eternity for the rest of humanity to treasure. And this transformation becomes a foundation for a higher and mightier achievement in the ever-continuing process of evolution.

Silence is our will-power. This will-power conquers the very pride of ignorance-night and manifests the Light of Divinity's Delight in aspiring souls who want to climb up to the highest Pinnacle and bring down the message of Immortality to earth. Our human mind says, "Silence is emptiness; it is sheer emptiness and nothingness." But our aspiring heart knows that silence is the fulness and plenitude of our Eternity's Height and Infinity's Light.

Aum

Pūrṇam adaḥ, pūrṇam idam, pūrṇāt pūrṇam udacyate.
Pūrṇasya pūrṇam ādāya pūrṇam evāvaśiṣyate

Infinity is that.
Infinity is this.
From Infinity, Infinity has come into existence.
From Infinity, when Infinity is taken away,
Infinity remains.

This is the message that we get from silence. Again, the soul tells us that silence is oneness, our inseparable oneness, our universal oneness with the Pilot Supreme.

Silence is our Truth-consciousness, our highest Reality. This Reality in the inner world is our divine Love, our supreme Love for the world at large. And this Reality in the outer world is the supreme Glory of the Supreme for aspiring humanity.

Here we are all seekers. At times we are prone to watch our weaknesses, incapacities, limitations and imperfections. When we do this we are bound to be disappointed with ourselves. But our inner silence illumines us. It says, "Don't be disappointed. It is God within you who is going through a series of experiences in and through your imperfections." When we realise God, we see that these imperfections were necessary at the time for our evolution. And then, when they were no longer necessary, these imperfections were turned into perfections. From darkness we enter into Light. From the unreal we enter into Reality. From death we enter into Immortality.

Asato mā sadgamaya,
Tamaso mā jyotirgamaya,
Mrityor mā amritaṃ gamaya.

Lead me from the unreal to the Real.
Lead me from darkness to Light.
Lead me from death to Immortality.

Silence tells the seeker in us to love, to love himself. It tells us it is wrong to hate ourselves because of our imperfections. When the seeker loves himself, loves the Divine within himself, he eventually realises the Ultimate Truth. Then he comes to realise that it was not he who loved the Divine in himself, but it was God the Lover who loved God the eternal Beloved Supreme within him.

In Heaven God is Silence-dream. On earth God is Reality-sound. In His Silence, God prepares Himself. Through His cosmic Sound, God manifests Himself. The transcendental Silence is our Source, and the emanating sound is our manifestation. The higher we go, the deeper the silence we enjoy. And the deeper the silence we enjoy, the more fulfilling the manifestation of our divinity.

85. Prayer

I pray. I pray to become God's perfect instrument. I pray to God to free me from the little "I" and to make me the big "I", the universal "I". The little "I" tells me what it can do for me. It tells me that it can destroy the world or bring the whole world to my feet. The universal "I" tells me that I am of God and for God. It tells me that I am all love for God the Creator and for God the Creation.

I pray. I pray to God to act through me and for me. When I act for myself, I create constant problems, untold problems. But when God acts in and through me, it is all divine achievement, fulfilling achievement.

I pray to God to choose for me. When I choose, I choose desire unconsciously or consciously. Then there comes a time when I consciously treasure desire, imperfection, limitation and bondage. I consciously want to remain in the finite and wallow in the pleasures of ignorance. But when God chooses for me, He chooses aspiration, the inner cry. This inner mounting flame takes me high, higher, highest and then brings me down to offer my realisation-fruit to aspiring humanity. When God chooses for me, He chooses Infinity, Eternity and Immortality. Infinity, Eternity and Immortality — these are only vague terms for those who do not aspire. But for those who aspire, these are living realities in the very heart of the seeker's aspiration.

I pray to God to make me one with suffering humanity. I pray to God to make me one with aspiring humanity. I pray to God to make me one with illumined humanity.

When I pray to God to make me one with suffering humanity, it is because the physical in me is at last seeing the truth that there is no end to suffering in the unenlightened physical consciousness. When I expand my physical consciousness, I share and thus lighten the burden of the suffering earth.

But now suffering humanity does not want to remain forever in its deplorable condition, so it begins to aspire. When it aspires, I have a free access to its aspiration, for when I expand my psychic consciousness, I become one with aspiring humanity. Then, when suffering has been ended by aspiration, when humanity is flying with the wings of aspiration, it enters into the world of illumined humanity. It is here, when we become part and parcel of illumined humanity, that we discover the meaning of life.

When I pray, I converse with God. I tell God that I need Him. God tells me, "My son, you need Me now. But I always needed you, I need you now, and I shall always need you." Then God asks, "Son, why do you need Me?" I reply, "Father, I need You because with You I am safe, with You I am happy; without You I am unsafe, without You I am unhappy." God says, "Son, I needed you to become My Dream-Boat. I need you to become My ever-flowing Life-River. I shall need you to become the Golden Shore of My ever-transcending Beyond."

When I pray loudly, my prayer is not soulful, and I cannot hear the faint Voice of God. But when I pray in silence, when I pray soulfully, I hear God's powerful Voice clearly and most significantly. When I pray to God out of fear, my fearful prayer does not reach God's door. But when I pray to God with love, my prayer reaches God's very Heart. And my loving prayer places me at the very Feet of God, my eternal Haven.

My prayer is a magnet and God's Concern is another magnet. When I pray, my magnet-prayer reaches the Highest and pulls God down into the very breath of my earthly consciousness. At that time, God offers me what He eternally is: Immortality's Smile. And when God's Concern-magnet pulls me up, I give Him what I have always been: inner cry, the inner cry of millennia.

When I reach the Highest on the strength of my prayer, God makes me His Dream-fulfilling Reality. When God comes down and feeds my heart on the strength of His unconditional Compassion, He makes me His Dream-fulfilled Reality.

It is our reciprocal self-giving that makes us inseparably one. Through my prayer, I offer to God all that I have and all that I am: ignorance. And through His Compassion, God offers to me what He has and what He is: Peace, Light and Divinity's ever-flowing Bliss.

In the Western world, we use the vehicle of prayer to reach the Highest. In the Eastern world, especially in India, we use the vehicle of meditation. Both are of paramount importance; both are of equal value. Prayer and meditation will give us the same result provided they are both soulful. But we have to know what actually happens when we pray, and what actually happens when we meditate, even though the result is the same. When we pray, we feel that God is the listener, and we are the talker. We cry from within, and God listens to our cry and consoles us. Our prayer is our conversation with God. But when we meditate, we empty our minds and purify our hearts and become receptivity itself. At that time, God the Guest, the eternal Guest, enters into us and sits on the throne of our hearts. When this happens, God talks and we listen. In this way the conversation is always perfect. In prayer, we talk and God listens; and in meditation, God talks and we listen. Let us pray; God is bound to listen to our prayers, our inner cry. Let us meditate; we are bound to listen to God's Voice, His inner Voice.

Prayer tells us that we are for God, for Him alone. Meditation tells us that we are of God, of Him alone. It was through the power of meditation, the soul's meditation, that the soul came down into the physical world. And now the soul will go back to its own transcendental Height by offering its prayer. The soul becomes one with earth-bound prayer, and this earth-bound prayer eventually grows into Heaven-free realisation.

Let us pray; God is listening to us. Let us meditate; we shall hear God's Voice. When we pray, God becomes our Beloved

Supreme and we His eternal Lover. When we meditate, we become God's Beloved and He our Divine Lover Supreme.

Part XXI — Questions and answers — Berea College

86. Question: What is the purpose of reincarnation?

Sri Chinmoy: Let us take a new incarnation as tomorrow's reality. Today we exist; we know today is a reality to us. But when tomorrow dawns we see that there is a new life. Reincarnation means new life. Life for me is today, but when tomorrow dawns the consciousness that I enter into tomorrow will be a new life. Now, why do we need tomorrow? We need tomorrow because we have not accomplished everything that we wanted to accomplish today. Let us take each incarnation as another today. We come into the world for satisfaction. While we follow the path of desire we find that we are never satisfied. Each time we fulfil one desire, more desires take its place. There is no end to our desires. So we come back to earth again and again to fulfil our endless desires. But when we enter into the path of aspiration we do get satisfaction. If we get an iota of Peace, Light and Bliss we are satisfied to some extent. But still we feel the need, the inner urge, for more Light, infinite Light, so we come back until we realise the Highest. Then, after realisation, God wants us to reveal and manifest the Highest. In this way we fulfil God and God fulfils Himself in and through us.

87. Question: What kind of powers do we get from meditation?

Sri Chinmoy: When we have human power, earthly power, we try to lord it over others; we want to show our supremacy. But when we acquire power from our meditation we try to offer it to the world at large; we use it to fight the world's ignorance. And if we still have ignorance in ourselves, we use the power that we get from meditation to illumine our own imperfections and to perfect our own individual consciousness.

88. Question: If we meditate, will this in any way help our friends and neighbours?

Sri Chinmoy: It is through constant prayer and meditation that the inner world will come to the outer world. If you pray and meditate early in the morning, if you treasure divine thoughts, they will immediately enter into your friends and dear ones. But if you cherish undivine thoughts, destructive thoughts, these also will affect the world around you. We can feel that our soul wants to be friendly, wants to illumine the world around us. First we have to know that the entire world has a common source, the Supreme. If we water the root, then only will the branches and the leaves be able to drink. If we don't feed the root, then the branches and leaves will all die. So the first thing we do in the morning is go to the root, the source: the Almighty Father, the Supreme. And from the Source we move out to the rest of the world.

Part XXII — Questions and answers — University of Tennessee

89. Question: What has been your experience of God?

Sri Chinmoy: I have experienced God in the personal as well as the impersonal form. At this moment, I see Him as an expanse of Light and Delight. The next moment He may take the form of a most luminous being. When we realise the Highest, we see that He is at once personal and impersonal. Like water and ice, He can be with form or without. Sometimes water is liquid, and we can swim in it. Other times it is solid, and we can walk on it. In the spiritual life also, sometimes we are fond of the impersonal aspect of the Highest Absolute, sometimes we are fond of the personal aspect. The Highest is beyond personal and impersonal but, at the same time, He embodies both. The Highest is formless, and at the same time He is with form. If we have to state in a word what He is, we have to say that He is both, and again, that He is beyond both. We cannot grasp God with the human mind. In the beginning He is this; then He is that. Then there comes a time when He is beyond both. The Highest is the ever-transcending Reality. Today's Beyond is tomorrow's starting point.

90. Question: What is the relation between aspiration and prayer and meditation?

Sri Chinmoy: When we aspire, we find that we have the capacity to pray and the capacity to meditate. Prayer takes us up into the highest Beyond and shows us the face of the Ultimate Truth.

Meditation brings down the reality of the Beyond into the vastness of our own inner silence and enables us to offer this reality to the world at large.

91. Question: Are you right now in your highest plane of consciousness?

Sri Chinmoy: I am now in a high plane of consciousness, but not in my highest plane of consciousness. I am in a calm plane of consciousness, where I can observe what is taking place in both the inner world and the outer world. I am right now in the psychic world, the world of the heart, where there is all love, all oneness. Here my heart is wide open. I have come here to be of service to the seeker in each of you, so my consciousness is the consciousness of inner dedication. We are sharing here. You are sharing your aspiration with me and I am sharing my realisation with you.

Part XXIII — Questions and answers — Tulane University

92. Question: Why are some people receptive to God's Light and others not?

Sri Chinmoy: A farmer sows thousands of seeds, but perhaps only a few hundred of the seeds ever germinate. He offers equal concern while he is throwing the seeds, but the seed itself must have some power of receptivity. God is giving what He has: His Light. But each individual has to feel the necessity of receiving it. One person is hungry and somebody else is not hungry. One person is fast asleep when God's Hour dawns; somebody else jumps up and runs. It is the same Hour, the same opportunity. But when the Hour strikes, if somebody is still fast asleep, what can he accomplish? Because he is not receptive, he does not get up; but the other one immediately gets up and runs towards the goal.

Opportunity comes for everyone. The hour strikes at the same time, and all have been given limited freedom. But one wants to utilise freedom by accepting the Light, the other wants to utilise freedom by not accepting Light at all. With my freedom of choice, my free will, I can accept the Light. But if I choose to remain in the vital, then I can show my individuality and not accept the Light. Showing one's individuality expresses one kind of freedom. That is one kind of capacity. But showing one's universality, becoming one with God's Will, is also a capacity, and a much greater capacity. If someone wants to utilise his freedom in that way, naturally he will receive God's infinite Light.

93. Question: If two persons choose to accept God's Light, will they both absorb an equal amount?

Sri Chinmoy: We both accept God's Light, but if your inner hunger is not as intense as mine, naturally you will not be able to eat the same quantity. If one person has an insatiable hunger and someone else is satisfied with only a little, naturally the former will accept more.

94. Question: And if we are both equally hungry?

Sri Chinmoy: Then we shall run together. But I wish to tell you that very few people are equally hungry. For me, perhaps just a drop of nectar is enough. For someone else it will be ten drops. And a third person will say, "I need the infinite ocean." If two persons are of the same type, or the same capacity, naturally they will run together. But the inner hunger is rarely the same.

Part XIV — Questions and answers — Mississippi Gulf Coast Junior College

95. Question: What do you feel about astrology?

Sri Chinmoy: I feel it has helped and will continue to help mankind greatly. But astrology is not the highest Truth. Astrology is not the Highest; God is the Highest. If a seeker reaches the Highest and prays to God to change his fate, God can easily do it. So astrology is not the Absolute Truth; the Absolute Truth is God.

But astrology does have some truth. So it is up to the individual whether to be satisfied with astrology or with God. If the seeker finds it difficult to go to the Absolute all at once, naturally he can go step by step. If he has faith, tremendous faith, in astrology, then naturally he will benefit from greater understanding of it. But one's fate can be changed by an unchanging Will, by the Divine Will, by the Omnipotent Will. And that Will is within us. If we can have a free access to that Will, then we can go far beyond the domain of astrology.

96. Question: Can you say something about the other worlds or other planes of consciousness?

Sri Chinmoy: This is not the only world; there are other worlds and other planes of consciousness. As we know, there are seven higher worlds and seven lower worlds. Each world has its own kind of love. The higher we go, the more we feel love as an expansion of consciousness — constant expansion, constant freedom. And the lower we go, the more we see love as something that is binding us, the more we find ourselves at the mercy of love.

When we pray and meditate, when we go deep within, we become aware of a ladder of consciousness leading to the higher worlds. Consciousness itself is a ladder which has seven rungs. So each time we step on a rung we know that we are in a different world.

Part XV — Questions and answers — University of South Alabama

97. Question: Do you teach any mantra or any meditation techniques to your disciples?

Sri Chinmoy: We have a path of our own, but we do not teach any outer technique as such. Our path is the path of love, devotion and surrender. We feel that this approach can lead us to our destined Goal. Outwardly, I do not give any specific mantra to my disciples. But inwardly I do help them when they meditate. When my disciples meditate with me, or when they invoke me in their meditation, I bring down Peace, Light and Bliss from

Above, and in silence they learn how to meditate properly from within. This technique cannot be demonstrated outwardly or taught by means of words. Our technique is the practice of conscious surrender to God's Will, divine love for God, and constant self-dedication to the Supreme within us. This is the technique which my disciples follow.

98. Question: You said that the human in us is scared to death when it sees vastness. Could you explain this a little more?

Sri Chinmoy: When the human in us does not have any illumination, when we see vastness we are immediately frightened by it because it is something totally alien to us. It is completely outside the bounds of our experience. But when we aspire and the divine in us begins to come to the fore, we see some Light, at least a tiny ray of Light, within us. And because we have an iota of Light within us, then we see that the infinite Light of the vastness in front of us is like a friend or a relative. Now we are in darkness, and we do not dare to claim Light as our own. But if we have a little Light, then we feel that eventually we can grow into the infinite Light. If I have one dollar, I feel that if I try then I can get much more. But if I don't have even a dollar, then I feel that money is simply beyond my capacity to attain.

A child has very limited strength, limited knowledge, limited power. But he feels his identity, his oneness, with his father and knows that his father's capacity will eventually grow into him. If his father has material wealth, then he will also have material wealth in the course of time. Because of his oneness with his father, the child knows his wealth and claims it as his birthright. So when we establish some sense of oneness with the Vast, with the Light which is our Source, we feel that the boundless Reality of Peace, Light and Bliss is going to be ours.

Our heart of insecurity will not remain always a heart of insecurity. If every day we pray and meditate, then Light will descend into our heart. First a little Light descends, then more Light, then vast, boundless Light. With our inner Light we can approach the Light that is around us with no fear at all. For what we see around us is a manifestation, a projection, of what we have within. There is nothing which we cannot claim as ours, for our root is God. If our root is God, the omnipresent Reality, then we shall not be afraid of anything.

Right now we identify with ignorance, and feel that God is somebody or something separate from us. We feel a yawning gulf between our existence and God's. Because we have not tried to go deep within, our own reality is a stranger to us. Naturally we are afraid of this reality since it is a stranger. But once we go deep within we see that our reality is not a stranger. It is only a manifestation of the one Reality, and that Reality is the Supreme, the Source within us.

99. Question: Is it possible to have peace but not happiness?

Sri Chinmoy: No! Real peace and happiness are inseparable. But we have to know that peace must be established on all the levels of our being. Perhaps we have established peace inside our heart, but not inside our mind. If we do not have peace of mind, then how will we have happiness? If one part of the being remains without peace — either the heart, the mind, the vital or the physical — then happiness will remain a far cry. Real peace — divine peace, illumining peace, fulfilling peace — is bound to give us happiness when the entire being is inundated with it. We are bound to be happy if the entire being is peaceful.

100. Question: Do you believe that Jesus was the son of God? Do you believe that Jesus was a transcendental Being?

Sri Chinmoy: I consider Jesus the son of God and also a transcendental Being. Jesus is called the son of man, but he brought down to earth with him the divine Consciousness. The son of God means the conscious possessor of the infinite divine Consciousness. Jesus consciously embodied the Almighty Father, the Supreme, the Absolute. At times in his life he called himself the son of God. "Our Father who is in Heaven," he used to say. But also, there came a time when he said, "I and my Father are one."

Jesus had to present himself to the world at large as the son of man so that people would have faith in their own possibility. Otherwise people would have thought, "Oh, he is divine; that is why he can do everything." But when they could say, "If he can reach the Highest, we also can," they were encouraged and inspired to go deep within and aspire. Again, Jesus had to show that Heaven and earth are not at two different places. He showed that Heaven is inside our hearts, inside our consciousness, and that we can all be conscious children of God. And at times he had to offer his divine authority to the world, for only in this way could he establish his consciousness on earth. At these times it was necessary for him to reveal himself to the world as a transcendental Being, and he did so.

At one moment Jesus was the son of man, bound by the limitations of the physical nature. At other moments he was the conscious son of God leading the world to its destined Goal. And at still other moments he said, "Where is the Goal if not within me?" When Jesus said, "I am the Way, the Truth and the Light," he meant that within him, within his divine consciousness, was the Goal itself. So he had to play three roles simultaneously during his stay on earth.

101. Question: If truth is in us and boundless consciousness is in us, then why do we always look for them outside ourselves?

Sri Chinmoy: Our heart, our spiritual heart, is as large as the Universal Consciousness Itself. Truth is always inside our heart; it is not something outside of us. But when we think of ourselves, we think of the body with height and weight and certain features; we do not think of ourselves as something vast or infinite. But when we begin our spiritual search for truth and boundless consciousness, it is always an inner search. We do not look outside of ourselves for these things. When we realise the Highest, when we are in the inner world, in the world of divine Reality, at that time this physical body is not our only reality. Our true Reality we see as something vast and infinite. Right now we do not identify ourselves with that inner Reality, so we often feel that truth and boundless consciousness are something outside us. Once we begin to think of ourselves as infinite, eternal and immortal, then we will know where to look for these and all other divine qualities.

Part XXVI — Questions and answers — Wheeling College

102. Question: I understand that you are speaking in fifty states. What is the purpose of this tour?

Sri Chinmoy: I have come here to serve. I feel that my service is like sowing a seed, a spiritual seed. If I see that somebody is aspiring, I know that God has given me the capacity to increase the flame of aspiration within him. My service is for those who are ready to accept, not necessarily my path, but some kind of inner life. I try to bring to the fore their own inner life. I try to encourage and inspire those who are a little bit awakened so that, instead of walking, they will march or run towards their Goal. It is to offer further inspiration to sincere seekers that I go from one place to another.

Being a lover of God, I see each state as a different home. All houses belong to God, and I am a son of God. So I go from one home to another to visit all my brothers and sisters. I feel it is my bounden duty to be of service to my brothers and sisters according to my capacity, the capacity that the Supreme has given me.

103. Question: You talk about first getting truth from within and then bringing it out to the world. I am wondering how much of an involvement you would allow for things like politics, marriage and other secular activities while one is engaged in the inner search.

Sri Chinmoy: We must try to live a balanced life. The outer life and the inner life must go together. We must not exclude the world, but we must also use our wisdom. We have to know our own inner strength and how much we can be involved in ordinary earthly activities without being distracted or pulled down from our inner life. If we receive enough strength from within, we can easily handle the outer life. But if we are inwardly weak, the outer life can be like a mad elephant, which we are unable to control.

If we do not go deep within, if we give all our attention to the material aspect of life, then we find that even the achievement of material success does not satisfy us. Again, if we withdraw totally from the outer life and live a sheltered and withdrawn life, manifestation of our inner progress will be lacking. So we have to know that a true divine life is a life of realisation and manifestation. If there is only manifestation and realisation is lacking, then there can be no perfection. On the other hand, if we care only for realisation and not for manifestation, there will be no perfection there either.

Perfection means the oneness or the flowering of realisation and manifestation together. But light must come from the inner life to illumine the outer life, for in this way everything which the outer life offers to the world will be divine. The inner life will give what the inner life has to offer, and the outer life will give what the divinised outer life has to offer. The inner life will offer Peace, Light and Bliss to the outer life, and the outer life will gladly accept it. When the outer life is ready to serve, when the outer life is purified and illumined to some extent, then it will work in the world and offer its achievements and capacities to the world at large as a dedicated service. It is mutual acceptance that will offer us perfection in our lives. Those involved in the inner life will accept the outer life as well, and those in the outer world will accept the inner life as another necessity. In this way the Kingdom of Heaven will be born on earth.

104. Question: Could you tell us a bit more about what being a disciple involves?

Sri Chinmoy: Whoever becomes my disciple naturally feels something in me, and if I accept him as a disciple, naturally I see something in him. A disciple and a Master make individual promises to each other. The disciple promises that he will follow the Master's path devotedly and soulfully. And the Master makes a solemn promise that he shall lead and guide the disciple to the destined Goal. The disciple makes his promise only to the Master, because for him right now the goal is the Master. He cannot conceive of the ultimate Goal, so he goes to an individual who has some Peace, Light and Bliss. Gradually, as he approaches his Master's consciousness, his only Goal becomes the Supreme. But the Master, right from the beginning, makes his promise to the soul of the disciple and also to the Supreme. He promises that he will take this seeker to God. The acceptance of a disciple and the acceptance of a Master are like mutual offerings. The disciple has tremendous aspiration; that is why he has come to the Master. So he gives what he has, his aspiration, to the Master. And the Master, just because he is a Master, has inner illumination. The Master selflessly offers his illumination to the disciple.

105. Question: Does the Master remain in contact with the disciple through prayer and meditation?

Sri Chinmoy: Yes. Prayer and meditation are the real communication. The disciple prays, not to the Master, but to the Supreme, the Highest, the Absolute within the Master; and he also meditates in this way. But the Master observes the disciple and sees whether his prayer is sincere and his meditation is soulful. If it is, then the Master carries the disciple's prayer or meditation directly to the Supreme, and brings back Peace, Light and Bliss from the Supreme to the disciple.

The Master is like a beggar. He comes to the disciple with folded hands and says, "Pray sincerely, meditate soulfully." Then he goes to the Supreme and says, "Please grant me Your Peace, Light and Bliss so that I can offer it to my spiritual children, who are praying and meditating so soulfully." The Master cries to the disciples to pray and meditate soulfully, and he cries to the Supreme to grant them Peace, Light and Bliss.

106. Question: Is it necessary for the Master and disciple to come together on occasion?

Sri Chinmoy: Yes, it is absolutely necessary. It is always advisable to visit the Master occasionally if you are not in the same city or same state. We have a physical mind, and the physical mind is satisfied only when it receives a very solid, positive experience. If we do not see the Master, then the world may tell us that our Master is like this or that, and our physical minds may start doubting our inner experiences. But if we see our Master personally, then our physical minds will have a better conception of him. This does not mean that the disciple will have more faith in his Master or make more progress if he stays with the Master twenty-four hours a day. Far from it! The disciple has to pay attention to developing an inner connection as well as an outer connection with his Master. But as long as the Master is on earth, it is good to remain in contact with him outwardly through seeing him, by telephone or by letter, so that on the physical plane the Master knows what is happening in the disciple's life, and the disciple knows that his Master knows. When the Master is no longer on the physical plane, then the disciple has to remain in contact with the Master through his most sincere and intense meditation.

107. Question: How do the Master and the disciple deal with a problem that seems to separate them rather than bring them together?

Sri Chinmoy: When a problem arises in a disciple, the disciple should immediately offer that problem to the Master. The Master will gratefully accept the problem as his very own. The relationship is like that of a child and his parents. If the child has some difficulty, he immediately tells his parents, who then take full responsibility. If the child has a headache or a sore throat, he tells his parents. They call the doctor, who gives him medicine. Similarly, when one of my disciples has a problem, he tells me inwardly or outwardly. Then I go to the doctor, the Supreme Doctor, to whom I have free access. From Him I bring down Peace, Light and Bliss and offer it to the disciple. Then the problem is illumined and solved. As an ordinary father is responsible for his child when the child is suffering, so also the spiritual father takes responsibility for the problems of his disciples when the disciples freely and sincerely offer them to him.

NOTES TO FIFTY FREEDOM-BOATS TO
ONE GOLDEN SHORE, BOOK 3

76. Baird Lounge, Berea College, Berea, Kentucky, 21 February 1974 — 9:00 am.
77. Student Center, University of Tennessee, Knoxville, Tennessee, 21 February 1974 — 1:30 pm.
78. Kendall Cram Room, Tulane University, New Orleans, Louisiana, 27 February 1974 — 9:00 am.
79. Room 132, Jefferson Davis Campus, Mississippi Gulf Coast Junior College, Gulfport, Mississippi, 27 February 1974 — 2:00 pm.
80. Student Center Ballroom, University of South Alabama, Mobile, Alabama, 27 February 1974 — 8:00 pm.
81. The Chapel, Wheeling College, Wheeling, West Virginia, 28 February 1974 — 1:30 pm.
82. Omaha Milo Bail Student Center, University of Nebraska, Omaha, Nebraska, 5 March 1974 — 12:30 pm.
83. Room 103, Iowa Western Community College, Council Bluffs, Iowa, 5 March 1974 — 2:00 pm.
84. Battenfield Auditorium, Student Center, Kansas City College of Osteopathic Medicine, Kansas City, Kansas, 5 March 1974 - 7.00p
85. Room 217, Haag Hall, University of Missouri, Kansas City, Missouri, 5 March 1974 — 9:00 pm.
86-88. Baird Lounge, Berea College, Berea, Kentucky, 21 February 1974 — 9:00 am.
89-91. Student Center, University of Tennessee, Knoxville, Tennessee, 21 February 1974 — 1:30 pm.
92-94. Kendall Cram Room, Tulane University, New Orleans, Louisiana, 27 February 1974 — 9:00 am.
95-96. Room 132, Jefferson Davis Campus, Mississippi Gulf Coast Junior College, Gulfport, Mississippi, 27 February 1974 — 2:00 pm.
97-101. Student Center Ballroom, University of South Alabama, Mobile, Alabama, 27 February 1974 — 8:00 pm.
102-107. The Chapel, Wheeling College, Wheeling, West Virginia, 28 February 1974 — 1:30 pm.

FIFTY FREEDOM-BOATS TO ONE
GOLDEN SHORE

BOOK 4

Part XXVII — Lectures

108. Service

Dear seekers, dear sisters and brothers, I wish to give a short talk from the spiritual point of view on service. I am a seeker, and I feel that a seeker is under a divine obligation to be of constant, dedicated service to mankind. I serve humanity, not because I am helpless, but because I long to be deathless. When I become deathless, I serve both man and God. I serve man, the unrealised God; I serve God, the unmanifested man.

My service has to be unconditional. My unconditional service is my transcendental Freedom. My transcendental Freedom is my eternal satisfaction. And my eternal satisfaction is God's universal manifestation, the manifestation of Divinity's Perfection and Reality's Immortality.

Service is love and love is service. When I love God, humanity cheerfully loves me and God blessingfully serves me. When God serves me, He serves me with His boundless Concern, and when humanity loves me, it loves me with its dedicated, immortalised oneness.

As a seeker, I serve both earth and Heaven. I serve earth with my inspiration-race. I serve Heaven with my aspiration-face. My inspiration-race and my aspiration-face have a common source: God's Grace, His infinite and unconditional Grace. God's Grace enables me to have a free access to my soul.

I frequently go to my soul's realm, for my soul has given me permission to take anything that I want from there. Such being the case, I take my soul's purity and offer it to my body. In this way I serve my body. I take my soul's dynamism and offer it to my vital. In this way I serve my vital. I take my soul's light and offer it to my mind. In this way I serve my mind. And then I take my soul's delight and offer it to my heart. In this way I serve my heart.

I serve my inner existence with faith, love, devotion and surrender. Faith is my reality. Love brings me the message of universal Oneness. Devotion makes my existence on earth sweet. Surrender to God's Will makes my life constantly meaningful and fruitful. I serve my outer existence with concentration, meditation and contemplation. Concentration means the one-pointed focus of attention on an object. First we concentrate on an object, and then we grow into it. Meditation means the invocation of vastness within our hearts. Contemplation means the absolute, inseparable union of the seeker and the Sought, the lover and the Beloved.

I serve the desiring man with my renunciation-light. This renunciation-light I get from my prayer, my meditation and my love of Light and Truth. I serve the aspiring man with my Realisation-height. This Realisation-height is my oneness with the Source, which is all Light and Delight. This oneness I discover only in and through my self-giving. I serve the liberated man, the man who is freed from the meshes of ignorance, with my earth-bound cry and my Heaven-free smile.

I serve the unknown with my imagination. Today my capacity is imagination; tomorrow my capacity will be aspiration. Aspiration is the inner flame within us that climbs up to the Highest and then comes down to offer its divine wealth to the world at large. Today imagination is my capacity; tomorrow aspiration will be my capacity; the day after tomorrow realisation will be my capacity. And in realisation, God-revelation and God-manifestation can take place.

The state motto of Arkansas is "The people rule." Here we see the importance of collectivity. In the spiritual life, we have to go together in a collective, unified way. Individual assertiveness has to be totally negated; collectivity has to be constantly embraced. And what is collectivity, but the song of oneness. It is our oneness, our inseparable oneness with the vast, that rules. If we are seekers, then we will feel in our inner life a connection with the entire universe. We will feel that we exist not for ourselves alone, but for all. I give to you what I have; you give to me what you have. It is through reciprocal self-giving that we exist. Oneness is the flowering of our reciprocal self-giving. What we call self-giving today, tomorrow that same thing we call God-becoming. God is the root of the tree and He is also the branches, leaves, flowers and fruits. By collectivity we mean the leaves, flowers, fruits, branches, trunk, root, everything. Inside this collectivity is the divine Harmony, the all-loving, all-illumining, all-fulfilling Harmony of the Supreme.

109. Renunciation

Dear seekers, dear brothers and sisters, I wish to give a talk on renunciation. We are all seekers here, so we are not afraid of the word "renunciation". An ordinary, unaspiring person is usually alarmed the moment he hears the word "renunciation". For him, renunciation means giving up everything he loves and cherishes, whatever he claims to be his own. But as spiritual people, we know that renunciation means something else. It means giving up the things that are undivine, unreal, imperfect — things that are compelling us constantly to lag behind in our Godward march. Anything that is real in us, anything that is divine in us, anything that is perfect in us we will never renounce. As seekers of the transcendental Truth, we are not afraid of renunciation precisely because we know what we are going to renounce, and what we are going to achieve by renunciation. We are going to renounce the finite in order to achieve the Infinite, Eternal and Immortal that abides within us.

What do we renounce? We renounce our ego. We renounce ego precisely because our ego is limited and blind. What else do we renounce? We renounce our doubt. We renounce doubt because doubt is slow poison which will eventually kill us. We renounce our ignorance. We renounce ignorance because ignorance binds us and makes us feel that we are forever doomed to the earth-bound consciousness. Ignorance makes us feel that we are weak and impotent, and that a life of Infinity, Eternity and Immortality is a far cry.

Renunciation cannot be achieved overnight. Nor can we get it by accident. For renunciation, we have to go deep within and pray and meditate. Also, we have to know the necessity of self-conquest. This self-conquest is nothing but our self-discovery, nothing short of God-realisation. Self-discovery and God-realisation are one and the same, the obverse and the reverse of the same divine, spiritual, immortal coin.

India's greatest poet, Tagore, once remarked that he would renounce, but not in an austere manner. There are people who want to renounce everything and embrace the life of austerity, but austerity is not real renunciation. Real renunciation says we must enjoy the freedom of liberation here amidst our multifarious activities; we must achieve liberation through the purification, illumination and transformation of our limitations, imperfections and bondage. We must lead a normal, natural life but be constantly aware of the things that must be inwardly renounced for a higher, better, more fulfilling life.

The motto of the state of Oklahoma is most significant: "Labour conquers all things." Renunciation is dedicated labour, dedicated service. When we soulfully offer our dedicated service, we conquer everything and achieve everything. What is the thing that houses everything? God's Smile. When we offer our dedicated labour to God, God's Smile dawns in our life of dedication. A sincere, dedicated worker knows that his life is like a tree. A tree works very hard to offer us flowers and fruits, to offer us shade and shelter. From its root to its topmost bough, everything a tree has is a selfless offering. From the beginning to the end, the life of a tree is sacrifice. Even when we cut off a branch of the tree, the tree continues to offer us shelter and protection with its remaining branches. Similarly, when our dedicated service is misunderstood, we shall not stop serving or offering our Light. We shall go on with our dedicated service, for we know we came into the world for self-giving. A man of dedicated service gets constant and abiding satisfaction from his labour regardless of whether or not the world accepts it.

This is the prayer of a sincere, genuine server of mankind, a divine labourer:

> O ignorance, I wish to be a tree of compassion.
> O man, I wish to be a tree of dedicated service.
> O earth, I wish to be a tree of patience.
> O Heaven, I wish to be a tree of constant aspiration, climbing up high, higher, highest.

Conscious renunciation is the manifestation of peace. An ordinary person is satisfied with the kind of peace which spiritual seekers see as mere compromise. It is a compromise between husband and wife, between nation and nation, between one adversary and another. This world needs real peace, but the moment some temporary agreement, some compromise, is reached, the world thinks it has achieved peace. But real peace is something infinitely more meaningful and fruitful than this.

Real peace is our heart's infinite ecstasy and our soul's eternal satisfaction.

Renunciation is the manifestation of our awakened consciousness. An awakened consciousness is the bridge between Heaven and earth. In consciousness, man becomes; in consciousness, God is. Man becomes his highest Reality, which he once upon a time was. God is His all-pervading, transcendental and universal Consciousness, which He eternally has been.

A man of renunciation raises the consciousness of others who are aspiring or who are about to aspire. This selfless act of his is the greatest gift that he can offer to humanity. The world is fascinated by miracles, but the greatest, the most fulfilling of all, is to raise the consciousness of others. An ordinary miracle lasts for a fleeting second, and when it ends we find ourselves in the same consciousness that we were in before. But when the true miracle takes place, our consciousness is elevated and illumined. As the man of renunciation marches forward towards the farthest Beyond, he climbs up an evolving ladder of transforming, divinised consciousness. By his very act of self-transcendence, the man of renunciation inspires and elevates the consciousness of his brothers and sisters who want to climb up the same ladder.

An ordinary person is afraid of transcendence. He feels that transcendence is something unknown, and perhaps unknowable. He feels that the moment he enters into the unknown, he will be thrown into the very jaws of a devouring tiger. But for true seekers, the unknown is not a ferocious animal. The unknown is something or someone whom we have not yet seen, but whose friendship we shall one day cherish and treasure. We are not afraid of the unknown because we pray and meditate. Our prayer and meditation is like a searchlight that lets us see far ahead. If we do not use this searchlight of prayer and meditation, we will not be able to see anything ahead of us. The unaspiring person feels that the only light is where he now stands, and that one step ahead of him is all unknown darkness. But in us, as seekers, there is a constantly burning lamp which illumines our path until we see that it has become sunlit and quite safe. And what is this lamp? It is our faith — our faith in God and our faith in ourselves.

For the beginner, for one who has just started walking along the path, renunciation is necessary and obligatory. But for an advanced seeker, renunciation is not necessary. If someone is on the verge of realisation or has made tremendous progress in the inner life, renunciation takes a different form for him. He does not actually renounce any more, but he tries to transform. If he feels fear in the world or in himself, he does not renounce fear, but with his inner light and wisdom he transforms it into courage. If he sees the world's doubt or his own doubt, with his inner light he transforms it into faith. When he transforms fear into courage, this courage is nothing short of divine manifestation. And when he transforms doubt into faith, this faith is the eternally sunlit path towards the ultimate Beyond. At this point, renunciation is the transformation of our earth-bound consciousness into the Heaven-free consciousness. Earth's pangs and privations are transformed into Heaven's boundless yet ever-increasing Delight. Ignorance is transformed into divine Wisdom, darkness into Light, imperfection into Perfection, and human bondage into transcendental Liberation.

110. Love

Divine Love is a flowering of delight and self-giving.
Human love is the gambol of sufferings and limitations.

111. Friendship

Dear sisters and brothers, dear seekers of the transcendental Truth, I wish to give a talk on friendship, which is the motto of Texas. Friendship is extremely significant in all phases of our life. Friendship is the bridge between two human beings. Friendship is the bridge between earth and Heaven. Friendship is the bridge between the known and the unknown.

Here on earth we try to establish friendship with our fellow human beings. Sometimes we are successful, sometimes we are not. But even when we are successful, this friendship does not satisfy us completely. Then we go deep within and discover our Eternal Friend, God, the Inner Pilot. God and each individual on earth are eternal friends. But only when we begin to aspire do we come to realise this truth.

There are three types of friendship: animal friendship, human friendship and divine friendship. The friendship that exploits us is animal friendship. The friendship that mutually helps two persons is human friendship. The friendship that unconditionally gives, that gives with no expectation whatsoever, is divine friendship.

Friendship can arise out of necessity and also out of generosity. If two human beings are in the desiring world, their friendship is founded upon necessity. But if one is in the desiring world and the other is in the aspiring world, then we have to know that the friendship of the aspirant is founded upon generosity, while the friendship of the desiring person is based upon necessity.

Desire makes unending demands; its hunger can never be appeased. No matter how much experience or possession is accumulated, still satisfaction does not dawn in the heart of a desiring individual. Aspiration also has an eternal hunger, but when aspiration achieves an iota of Peace, Light and Bliss, it feels a kind of satisfaction. Although an aspirant aims to reach the Highest, the Absolute Pinnacle, although he longs for infinite Peace, Light and Bliss, an iota of Peace, Light and Bliss satisfies his grateful heart. But he knows that today's achievement is not complete. If he looks forward, or dives deep within, or climbs high, higher, highest, he knows he is bound to be inundated with Peace, Light and Bliss in boundless measure. At God's choice Hour, God will give the aspirant infinite Peace, Light and Bliss.

In our ordinary human life we have two friends: fear and doubt. Fear tells us, "Stay inside your body-cage, where you are safe. If you come out, the ferocious world-tiger will devour you, so don't come out of the cage of your body." Doubt tells us that our real friend is our physical mind, the mind that cautions us, that warns us, that tells us that the outer world is a real stranger. Doubt says, "If you allow the outer world to enter into you, it is like dealing with a stranger. At any moment you may be exploited, deserted and destroyed for good. Have no faith in anybody on earth. Expect nothing good from anyone on earth. You are your own saviour, you are your own salvation — you and nobody else. Exist for yourself."

Here we are all seekers, so we shall have faith in God. If it is impossible for us to establish divine faith today, we can start with faith in ourselves. In spite of knowing that we are limited and bound, let us have faith in ourselves. Then this limitation and bondage of ours can be transcended on the strength of our inner cry. But if we have faith in an undivine force, a force that destroys, then in addition to destroying others, we will ourselves be destroyed. A similar thing happens when we have faith only in ourselves. We try to possess others, but before we can actually possess them, we are ourselves possessed. It is only in divine faith that we do not possess. There we just expand — expand our consciousness, expand our reality, expand what we have and what we are. But let us start, if necessary, with faith in ourselves, and then go beyond and attain divine faith. In divine faith we see that there is no end to our journey and achievement. We are in the flow of an ever-transcending, ever-illumining Reality, which is perfection.

Friendship is harmony, friendship is peace, friendship is bliss. Friendship is harmony. Mutual harmony removes all dark conflicts. Each individual has opinions of his own, but when friendship becomes the connecting link between two persons, all conflicts are removed and they become one.

Friendship is peace. Here, peace means confidence. I have confidence in you and you have confidence in me; our mutual confidence is peace. I shall not speak ill of you or try to ruin you; you will not speak ill of me or try to ruin me. On the contrary, I shall give you what I have: my love, my sympathy, my concern, my compassion, my total support of your cause, and you will do the same for me.

Friendship is bliss. When friendship lasts, it offers bliss. The Kingdom of Heaven is established when love inundates our beings, when the feeling of oneness reigns supreme and there is no sense of separativity. At that time illumining, fulfilling and perfect Perfection dawns in our life of aspiration. Thousands of years ago the Vedic seers offered us the message of bliss.

Ānandādd hy eva khalv imāni bhutāni jāyante,..

From Delight we came into existence.
In Delight we grow.
At the end of our journey's close, into Delight we retire.

Friendship is sweet when it is all harmony.
Friendship is sweeter when it is all peace.
Friendship is sweetest when it is all bliss.

Now, the moment we are awakened, the moment our inner light comes to the fore and awakens us from our ignorance-sleep of millennia, we discover that fear and doubt are not our friends at all. Our true friends are courage, indomitable courage, and faith, boundless faith. Our inner courage tells us, "Go out, look around the rest of the world; all of earth's inhabitants are your friends, your brothers and sisters. If you stay in your physical consciousness, you are binding yourself, you are limiting your possibilities and potentialities. Go out. The world is eagerly awaiting your arrival." Our dear friend, faith, tells us, "We are all of the same Source and for the same Source, so how can we be afraid of others? The Source is one, but the One wanted to play the game of many. The tree is the Source, and the branches, flowers, leaves and fruits are the many. From the same root we all came into existence, so let us consciously establish our inseparable oneness with all human beings. Let us sing together, dance together and play together. In this way we will please and fulfil the Absolute Supreme with our universal oneness."

Each individual has faith in something or in someone. We cannot say that someone has no faith at all. This moment he has faith in God, another moment he may have faith in himself and a third moment he may have faith in somebody or in something else. Now, when an individual has faith in God, he is in the world of aspiration and vastness, in the world of Infinity, Eternity and Immortality. When he has faith in himself, he is in the world of desire, in the world of possession, limitation, bondage and death. When he has faith in neither God nor himself, then he has faith in destruction — in world-destruction or in self-destruction. But he always has faith either in God or in himself or in some undivine force.

Friendship is service, the dedicated service we offer to Mother Earth and Father Heaven. When we want to offer our dedicated service to Mother Earth, we pray to the Lord Supreme to grant us a life of ceaseless duration. When we want to offer our dedicated service to Father Heaven, we pray to the Lord Supreme to grant us a life of selfless contribution. With our service, Heaven gets the opportunity to manifest itself here on earth, and earth gets the opportunity to realise the Highest, the Absolute.

In the spiritual life friendship is founded on inner acceptance. A spiritual teacher and a seeker become one on the strength of their inner friendship. The seeker goes to a Master and says, "Master, I love you, I trust you, I give you my life." The Master immediately says, "My son, I love you, I trust you and I give you my life and also God's Life." The disciple says, "Master, I offer you my solemn promise that I shall serve the Supreme in you." The Master says, "Son, I offer you *my* solemn promise that unless and until I have taken you to our Father, the Absolute Supreme, I shall not rest. Your promise is just to me, but my promise is to two persons. Here on earth I am promising you that I shall carry you and guide you to the Golden Shores of the Beyond, and the same promise I am making to the Inner Pilot, who is your Master, my Master, the Eternal Master; to Him I am giving the same promise. With your friendship you will give me what you have: ignorance. With my friendship I will give you what I have and what I am: Wisdom-Light. This Wisdom-Light the Supreme has granted me out of His infinite Bounty, and this I offer to you. If you think that you are a beggar, then you must know that I am more of a beggar than you.

You have to go begging only to one place, but my condition is more deplorable; I have to go to two places. I go to you with folded hands and beg you to give me your ignorance. Then I go to God with folded hands and beg Him to give me His Compassion-Light for you. I am the messenger between you and God. This is the friendship that I have established with earth and Heaven. Earth's pangs and penuries I take to Heaven, to the Eternal Father in Heaven, and from Heaven I bring down Peace, Light and Bliss in abundant measure for sincere seekers." This is the eternal friendship between the Master and the disciple.

The Master also says something else to his disciples. He says, "Your Master is not and can never be myself. The real Master is somebody else — the Supreme, the Absolute Supreme." A spiritual teacher is only an elder brother to humanity. When seekers are aspiring for the Highest, the teacher shows them where the Father is. Once he leads them to the Father, his role is over. And the seeker of today becomes the leader, the teacher of mankind tomorrow. When his time comes, he shows aspiring humanity, his younger brothers and sisters, the same God, the same eternal Friend, the same transcendental Supreme, that his own teacher once showed him.

112. Intuition

Intuition selflessly feeds the inner life and recognises, inspires and fulfils the outer life.

113. The practical reality

Dear seekers, dear friends, dear brothers and sisters, I wish to give a short talk on the practical reality. Reality is at once a simple and a complicated word. For an ordinary, unaspiring human being, reality is a far cry. At every moment life offers him frustration. His life is the life of desire. When his desires are not fulfilled, he is frustrated, and when his desires *are* fulfilled, still he feels no abiding satisfaction; therefore, according to him everything is unreal. This is his realisation. But we here are all seekers. We feel that everything is real, for we see the soul in everything and the soul of everything, while an unaspiring person sees the body in everything and the body of everything. But the body is ephemeral, whereas the soul is eternal, and reality abides only in the heart of Eternity.

Practical reality is the conquest of our teeming earth-bound desires. This conquest has another name: Freedom-light. Freedom-light liberates the seeker from the hunger of the finite. Freedom-light liberates the seeker from the darkness of bondage-night. Freedom-light does not permit ignorance to lord it over the heart of the sincere, loving, devoted and surrendered seeker. Freedom-light is the inner necessity of one who seeks the highest transcendental Truth, which is the perennial Source. Freedom-light is the outer necessity of one who seeks the Ultimate Truth, which is the transcendental Goal.

When we approach reality with our earth-bound consciousness, we feel that reality is not at all practical. But when we approach reality with our Heaven-free consciousness, we realise that reality is always practical. Reality is the ideal in human life. Reality is the natural beauty of the life divine. The animal in us does not know or feel the existence of reality. The human in us at times knows and feels the value of reality, but it does not strive for reality's breath. The divine in us always wants to grow in the heart of reality. The Supreme in us is all-Reality in us, with us and for us.

What is practical reality? Practical reality is silence. Silence does not date from any particular point in time. Silence owes its origin to no particular being. Silence is eternal. Silence is universal. For its validity, silence does not depend on our worldwide proclamation or on our genuine and implicit acceptance. Silence transcendental has God; Silence transcendental is God. God's transcendental Silence wants total and perfect manifestation here on earth. Why do we need silence? We need silence precisely because we need abiding satisfaction. Why do we need satisfaction? We need satisfaction because of our inner divinity's Immortality. How do we achieve satisfaction? We achieve satisfaction by purifying our mind, illumining our heart and liberating our life.

Practical reality is also sound. Silence prepares the life of aspiration. Sound reveals the life of aspiration. Love fulfils the life of aspiration. Silence immortalises the life of aspiration. A life without silence is a goalless life. A life without sound is a meaningless life. A life without love is a helpless life.

The man who knows that God is within him feels his goal within and without. The man who knows that he is for God is bound to feel that his life is meaningful. He who has discovered the truth that he is of God is bound to feel that his life can never be hopeless. On the contrary, his is the life of adamantine will; his is the life of all-energising, all-fulfilling, all-pervading reality. When a seeker feels God's Presence within him, he smiles the smile of God-transcendence. When he feels that he is for God, he sings the song of God-compassion. When he feels that he is eternally of God, he dances the dance of God-perfection.

Practical reality is Delight. Delight is God's Eye of Compassion and Liberation. When God's flood of Delight enters the very breath of the seeker's aspiring life, God's Reality-dream looms large and God's inner Promise comes to the fore. The seeker feels that his life of imperfection will be transformed before long into a life of perfect Perfection. When the seeker's heart is liberated from the meshes of ignorance, God's unfulfilled Dream gets the opportunity to expedite its earthbound journey and ultimately to fulfil its Dream-Reality in and through the loving and unconditionally surrendered divine warrior-seeker.

Practical reality is the seeker's attainment of perfection — perfection within, perfection without. The seeker achieves perfection in the outer life by disciplining his life, by acquiring mastery over his outgoing energy. The seeker achieves perfection in the inner life through constant and unconditional surrender to the Will of his Inner Pilot.

Practical reality is the attainment of supernal peace. The state motto of Nevada is "All for our country." The undivine critic may find this lofty message sentimental or emotional. But the sincere seeker of the Highest Truth, from the spiritual point of view, will observe this message in a divine way. From the spiritual point of view, "country" signifies the "abode of peace". In the motto, "All for our country", "all" signifies simplicity, sincerity, purity and humility. These qualities are to be found in the abode of peace. When we live in the abode of peace, impossibility cannot knock at our heart's door. Nothing is impossible. Everything is not only possible, practical and practicable, but also inevitable.

Earth has glowing aspiration. Heaven has descending illumination. When earth's aspiration and Heaven's illumination meet together, the dream-boat of the seeker reaches the Reality-Shore of the Beyond. Earth aspires; Heaven inspires. Earth aspires for the Heaven-soul; Heaven inspires the heart, the reality of earth. Because earth aspires, earth is supremely great; because Heaven inspires, Heaven is divinely good. Each individual seeker has the golden opportunity to knock at his own heart's door at God's choice Hour, not only to see the face of Reality, but also to grow into the Reality itself, provided his life is a life of constant dedication to the Inner Pilot.

114. What has life taught me?

What has life taught me? Life has taught me how to exclude and include — how to exclude unreality and how to include reality. When I feel that I am of God and for God, I become the fulfilling reality. When I feel that I am of myself and for myself, I become the self-deceiving unreality.

> Reality unveils, reveals and fulfils.
> Unreality veils, conceals and kills.
> Reality expands and transcends.
> Unreality cries and dies.

What has life taught me? Life has taught me conscience, common sense and God-sense. My heart utilises conscience; therefore, my heart is pure and brave. My mind utilises common sense; therefore, my mind is clear and direct. My soul utilises God-sense; therefore, my soul is divine and perfect.

Life has taught me how to live and learn, how to learn and live, how to live and live, how to learn and learn. When I live and learn, I try to jump up onto the topmost bough of the tree instead of climbing up right from the foot. When I learn and live, I do the first thing first — I walk and then I run. When

I live and live without first learning the inner lesson and discovering the real essence of my life, I deliberately deceive the divine within me and the divine in others. When I learn and learn, I constantly expand my earth-bound consciousness and transcend my earth-bound reality.

Life has taught me how to learn, unlearn and relearn. I learn. I learn the song of divine duty. By performing the duty divine, I know that I fulfil the divine within me, the Supreme within me. I learn the song of the childlike heart, for I know that if I have a childlike heart, I will always have the eagerness and inner urge to fulfil the divine by learning and discovering the Reality itself.

Each time I learn something, I march forward towards my destined Goal, my transcendental Goal. When I learn that my life is God-Light, then during my soulful prayer and meditation I feel God the Infinite Peace, God the Eternal Light, God the Immortal Life claim me in the inmost recesses of my heart as His very own. At that time, I claim God's Infinity as my length, God's Eternity as my height and God's Immortality as my depth — the depth of my silent being. At that time I consciously become one, inseparably, eternally one, with the Inner Pilot, the Absolute Supreme.

I unlearn. I unlearn the song of self-importance and self-aggrandisement. As a seeker, I have to unlearn many other things, as well. My mind is full of information and empty of illumination. If my mind is filled with information, then I feel that I am a donkey carrying a heavy load on my back. What I need is not world-information, but world-illumination. So first I have to unlearn this world-information, for in order to get world-illumination I need a mind of clarity, a mind of luminosity. Also, I have to unlearn the capacity of the physical mind. The physical mind teaches me how to doubt, how to suspect, how to belittle and how to bind myself and others. When I doubt others with my physical mind, I do not gain anything; at the same time, they do not lose anything. And when I doubt myself, I immediately dig my own grave.

I relearn. I relearn the song of God-union, of conscious God-union. When I am in Heaven, I am the soul. There God and I are one, inseparably one. But when I, as a soul, enter into the world arena and take on a physical frame, then I enter into the world of bondage, limitation, darkness and ignorance. There I become the body-consciousness. If I take the body-consciousness as my reality, then I cannot learn anything from life, for the body-consciousness is limited, unlit, obscure, impure, undivine. But when I think of myself as the Soul-Reality, I get the opportunity to relearn the truth that God and I are eternally one.

Life has taught me how to examine the essence of God's Silence and God's Sound. When I use my human eyes to examine God's Reality, I am totally lost. But when I use my heart to examine God's Reality, my heart immediately sees the true Reality, on the strength of its total identification with Reality. The physical eyes are very often misled, but the inner heart cannot be misled. The inner heart is the direct representative of the illumining soul, which is one with the Source. As long as I use the physical mind, I see others as others; but when I use the aspiring heart there is no *you*, no *he*, no *she*, only *I* — the Universal *I*, and not the limited ego. So when I use my heart, I become the Reality. But when I use my mind or my physical eyes, I am quite often deceived, and I remain unfulfilled.

When I do not aspire, my life teaches me frustration, and I push and pull. I push my life towards something, but eventually I come to realise that this something is a goalless nothing. I pull myself towards the little, puny ego-consciousness, and

I see that I have pulled myself towards an empty reality. But when I neither push nor pull, just offer my existence in its totality to the Inner Pilot, I consciously become what I eternally am: God-consciousness.

As a seeker, I know that my life has taught me how to love and whom to love. How to love? Devotedly, soulfully and unconditionally. Whom to love? God in man and man in God. When I love God in man devotedly, soulfully and unconditionally, I become one with God the Unity. When I love man in God, I become one with God the Multiplicity. One is the Source; many are the manifestations of the One. The tree needs branches; the branches need the tree. By loving God, the seeker in me becomes the tree itself, and by loving man, he becomes the branches.

Life has taught the seeker in me how to devote myself to my higher part and to my lower part. When the lower part in me devotes itself to the higher part, the higher part gets additional strength for its manifestation. When the higher part devotes itself to the lower part of my being, the lower part gets the opportunity for transformation.

Life has taught the seeker in me how to surrender. I surrender soulfully, devotedly and unconditionally to my own higher reality. This higher reality encompasses and embodies everything as its very own, so when I divinely surrender, I feel that the unillumined part of me is surrendering to the fully illumined part of me. When God's Hour strikes and the unillumined becomes fully illumined, and the illumined becomes fully manifested, then my entire being becomes totally divine and perfect.

When I live the animal life, I see darkness all around and feel that this darkness is my only reality. When I live the human life, I see an iota of light and feel that one day I will be able to bathe in an infinite sea of Light. When I try to lead the divine life,

I feel that my Inner Pilot has already paved the way for me to walk along the path to His ultimate Reality. At that time, I feel that God's Dream-Boat is carrying me to His Reality-Shore — the Golden Shore of the ever-transcending Beyond.

The soul tells me that life is perfection. We are not travelling from imperfection towards perfection, but from less perfection to greater perfection, to the greatest perfection. In the process of evolution, life is continuous progress. This progress is perfection aiming at the highest Absolute Perfection. When life began from the mineral world, it was the beginning of life's perfection. But there is no end to our progress. Today's perfection is the starting point for tomorrow's higher, deeper, more illumining and more fulfilling perfection.

Life has taught me something sublime: that I am not indispensable; only the Supreme in me is indispensable. Life wants to offer me happiness, and real happiness lies only in this discovery. When someone feels that only the Supreme in him is indispensable, then his life is all happiness.

Finally, life has taught me the most important thing: that God and I need each other. I need God for my perfect perfection, and God needs me for His total Manifestation on earth. This is the supreme lesson that life has to teach, and I am offering it to each seeker present here.

115. Kindness

Yesterday I discovered kindness in myself.
Today I see how beautiful and soulful I am.
Yesterday I discovered kindness in humanity.
Today I see how meaningful and fruitful humanity is.

116. Transformation, liberation, revelation, manifestation

Dear seekers, dear brothers and sisters, I wish to give a short talk on transformation, liberation, revelation and manifestation — four sublime realities in our life of aspiration.

The animal in us needs immediate transformation. The human in us needs conscious liberation. The divine in us needs perfect revelation. The Supreme in us needs complete manifestation. To see God we need transformation. To be invited by God we need liberation. To be loved by God we need revelation. To be immortalised by God we need manifestation.

Transformation of the body shows us how pure we can be. Liberation of the vital shows us how dynamic we can be. Revelation of the mind shows us how vast we can be. Manifestation of the heart shows us how divine we can be. We can be as pure as the dawn. We can be as dynamic as a divine warrior. We can be as vast as the sky. We can be as divine as the soul. Transformation is walking along the road of Infinity. Liberation is marching along the road of Immortality. Revelation is running along the road of Eternity. Manifestation is flying the fastest towards the ever-transcending Reality.

When we are freed from the binding past and transformed, we do not remain in the body-cage; we start living in the soul-palace. When we are transformed we change our friendships. Ignorance-night no longer remains our friend. Instead, knowledge-light becomes our true and dear friend. When we are transformed we sing a different song. We cease to sing the song of the finite. We sing the song of the Eternal in order to become the Infinite.

When we are liberated from the meshes of ignorance, we come to realise what we eternally are: God the dreamer, God the lover and God the fulfiller. At that time, we want to reveal ourselves. Unless and until we have revealed our divinity, we cannot prove God's existence on earth. The world may think that all our sublime experiences are mental hallucinations, chimerical mists and acts of self-deception unless we can reveal God's Divinity within ourselves. But when we can reveal our inner divinity to others, they will see that our dream-boat has touched the Reality-Shore. And when we manifest our inner divinity, at that time the Golden Shore of the Beyond becomes firmly established in the here-and-now.

Transformation. In the hoary past, the seekers of the Highest did not care so much for nature's transformation, for physical, vital, emotional transformation. They cared only for their own realisation. They realised the Highest, but in spite of that, their physical nature remained unlit, obscure, imperfect.

Liberation. In the hoary past, many liberated souls cared only for their own liberation. They did not care for the liberation of the world at large. They felt that because it was so hard for them to get liberation, everybody else should also have to work hard. Also, they felt that everybody would realise God, everybody would be liberated at God's choice Hour, and that it was not their business to expedite this Hour.

Revelation. In the hoary past, the seekers of the highest magnitude did not care for revelation. They thought that if they revealed what they had realised, then there was every possibility that the world's ignorance would capture their knowledge-light and wisdom-height. They were afraid of revealing their inner divinity. They realised the highest Truth, but they did not want to share it with the rest of the world because fear, fear of the unknown, tortured their inner existence.

Manifestation. In the hoary past, seekers of the highest magnitude, liberated souls, great Yogis, did not care for manifestation. They felt that here on earth nothing is worth manifesting, because nothing can last for good. They felt that this planet is the abode of sorrow, of suffering, so why try to establish something divine here permanently? They felt that there was no assurance, no guarantee that this world would be transformed into divinity's flood; therefore, they did not care for manifestation.

But the present-day seeker wants perfection within, perfection without. Unless and until the body is perfect, the vital is perfect, the mind is perfect and the heart is perfect, we feel that perfect Perfection is a far cry. The process is long and arduous, but once we succeed in this sublimely significant task, we reach the Golden Shore of the Beyond.

The motto of the state of Oregon is "The Union". Here we are all seekers. A seeker is he who practices spirituality. Now, spirituality has a secret and sacred word to offer: the word is *Yoga*. Yoga means conscious union with God. I am truly happy that the motto of this state encompasses the same ideal as the breath of spirituality, which is Yoga. Union has to be established between the finite and the Infinite, between today's imperfect man and tomorrow's perfect God.

How do we establish our conscious union with God? There are various ways to do this. First, we can minimise our earthly needs and thus establish ourselves to increase our Heavenly needs. Then, we have to cry for God inwardly, as a child cries for his mother. The Lord Supreme will fulfil our inner cry of aspiration. Two concepts govern the length and breadth of the world: desire and aspiration. Desire binds us; aspiration liberates us. Desire makes us feel that we are of the finite and we are compelled to be for the finite. Aspiration tells us that we are of the Eternal and for the Infinite. Infinity, Eternity and Immortality are not vague terms, but divine realities that are trying to come to the fore so that we can become tomorrow's God.

Besides crying inwardly, we also have to feel consciously that God needs us as much as we need God. As ordinary human beings we need God to fulfil our teeming desires. When we become spiritual seekers we need God for only one thing: to discover our highest transcendental Height, our deepest transcendental Depth. And we do discover these when we realise God. Now, just as we need God for our realisation, so God needs us for His own Manifestation. He has to manifest Himself in and through us. He was one; that was His Silence-realisation. He wanted to become many; that was His Sound-manifestation. When we achieve His Realisation and He achieves in and through us His Manifestation, perfect Perfection dawns. When we feel that we are of God and for God, we see that we are of the all-pervading Silence and for the all-fulfilling cosmic Sound. At that time we are totally liberated, revealed and transformed.

Each seeker represents a promise to God. The promise is his own physical transformation. He wants to free his earth-bound life and he does free his earthbound life on the strength of the boundless Compassion of the highest Absolute Supreme. Each seeker's promise to God is to manifest God on earth in God's own Way. The seeker fulfils his promise only when he gladly, cheerfully and unconditionally gives to God what he has and what he is. What he has is inner cry, and what he is is ignorance. When he gives to God devotedly, soulfully and unconditionally his achievement: inner cry, and his present reality: ignorance, then the seeker is transformed, liberated, revealed and manifested in God's own Way.

117. Just for today

Just for today, I shall pray to God. My prayer is my inner, climbing cry. I know this cry will reach God's Palace. My snow-white prayer will knock at God's Door. God will open His Door and ask me what I need. I shall tell God that I need His infinite Compassion to awaken me from my slumbering life. God will grant my prayer.

Just for today, I shall meditate on God. I know that when I meditate on God, I empty my heart. When my heart is empty, my Eternal Friend, my Eternal Divine Guest comes in and sits on His Throne inside the very depths of my heart. In the inmost recesses of my heart His Life of infinite Concern, Compassion, Love and Blessings abides.

When I pray, my Eternal Friend listens to my prayer and fulfils my prayer. When I meditate, my Eternal Friend comes in and fulfils my inner need. When I pray, I talk and He listens to me. When I meditate, He talks and I listen to Him. This is how we converse. My prayer and my meditation are of paramount importance in my life of aspiration, dedication and surrender to the Will of my Inner Pilot.

Just for today, I shall love my God, my Supreme. I shall not love anybody else, not even my own existence. I shall love only God, God alone. Has He not loved me from time immemorial? Will He not love me throughout Eternity? Since He is all love for me, it is my bounden duty to love Him, at least for this day. I shall love Him, and my love for Him will immortalise my earthly reality and my heavenly dream.

Just for today, I shall become the divine lover and call my Lord the Supreme Beloved. In human love there is constant demand, constant expectation and constant disappointment. In love divine there is no demand, no expectation and no frustration; there is only self-giving. This self-giving is eventually transformed into God-becoming.

Just for today, I shall love God unconditionally. I shall feel His infinite Compassion, His blessingful Love in and through my life of aspiration. I shall feel that God loves me infinitely more than I love myself. When fear, doubt, anxiety and jealousy assail my life of aspiration, when I cherish and treasure limitation, bondage, ignorance and death, at that time, I hate my life. But my Eternal Friend, my Pilot Supreme, loves me still.

Just for today, I shall serve God. I have come to realise that there is nothing and there can be nothing as sweet and as fulfilling as service. When I serve God, I feel that my life of frustration is transformed into a life of illumination. My service to God makes me feel that my existence on earth is meaningful and fruitful. When I serve God I feel that I have expanded my earth-bound consciousness into the Heaven-free consciousness.

Just for today, I shall surrender my will to God's Will, His all-loving, all-pervading, universal Will. Yesterday God surrendered compassionately and unconditionally to my animal greed. Today God surrenders lovingly and compassionately to my human wants. Tomorrow God shall surrender joyfully and proudly to my divine needs. Just because He has surrendered to my animal greed, just because He surrenders to my human wants, just because He will surrender to my divine needs, I feel it is obligatory on my part to surrender my earthly life just for a day to His Will, so that His Will can be done on earth in and through my life of aspiration and dedication.

Just for today, I wish to share my supreme secret with my Supreme Pilot. My secret is this: that I shall no longer call ignorance my friend. My friendship with ignorance terminates today. From today on I shall have God as my only friend, my sempiternal Friend. I shall have Him not only as my Friend, but also as my All.

Just for today, I wish to have peace of mind. In order to have peace of mind I must feel that I am not indispensable at all. I must end my song of self-importance and realise that the world does not need me. The world existed before I was born; the world shall exist long after I pass behind the curtain of Eternity. Who is needed? Only the Supreme Pilot in me is needed. When I feel that I am not indispensable I receive an iota of light and achieve peace of mind.

Just for today, I shall be the all-loving child to the Supreme Pilot. Just for today, I shall be the hero-warrior walking along the path of Eternity. Just for today, I shall feel that I need God and God needs me, and ultimately I have to feel that God needs me more than I need Him. At times, because of my ignorance, I feel that I do not need Him. But God, being perfect, sees me always with His all-illumining Light. He knows that I am destined to be His seeker, His lover, His instrument for manifestation. He knows my potentiality and my capacity. He knows that I am an exact prototype of His ultimate transcendental Reality; therefore, He needs me more than I need Him.

I need myself this moment to fulfil my countless, teeming desires. But when my desires are not fulfilled and when I realise that I do not have the capacity to fulfil them, I feel that I do not need this earthly existence. I want to discard this body-consciousness, for this body-consciousness does not give me an iota of satisfaction. Since I am a failure, I feel that this life is of no avail. But God knows that there is no such thing as failure. There is only experience. We work, we serve, we pray, we meditate each moment in conscious dedication, and the result of this dedication takes the outer form of either success or failure. But when we go deep within, we feel that there is no such thing as success or failure. We see everything as an experience that has come to us in the march of evolution. Finally, we realise that even this experience is not our possession. It is actually God's experience, for He is the doer, He is the action and He is the fruit thereof.

Just for today, I wish to be a conscious garland of gratitude to be placed at the Feet of my Inner Pilot.

Just for today...

118. The existence of God

Here we are all seekers. Some of us may not be as sincere as others. Some of us may be curiosity-seekers. Some of us, at times, may be doubters. Some, at times, may be atheists. Yet we are all seekers. Just because we are seekers, one day — at God's choice Hour — we shall realise God.

The motto of the state of Idaho is "Let It Live Forever." We know that the human body does not live forever. It exists only for sixty, seventy, or eighty years, and then its role is over. But there is something within us that does exist forever, and that is the soul. Just because we are seekers, we do believe in the soul.

How is it that the soul exists forever and not the body? The soul exists forever precisely because the soul is the direct representative of God on earth. The soul, from its very beginning, has embodied the message of Divinity, Eternity, Infinity and Immortality, whereas the body has not. The soul exists forever because the soul is an immortal part of its ultimate Source: God, the Eternal Pilot.

Our next question is: does God exist? The atheist in us says, "No, God does not exist. God does not and cannot exist; therefore, I don't need Him." The agnostic in us says, "I doubt it, I doubt it. And since I am not even sure of God's existence, why should I pay attention to God?" The desiring man in us immediately says, "Yes, God exists. I can see Him; I can feel Him. When? When my desires are fulfilled! At that time, I imagine God according to my sweet fancy. But when my desires are not fulfilled, then God does not exist for me. And if I see that others' desires are being fulfilled and not mine, then I may say that God exists for them but not for me."

Now, the aspiring man in us also has something to say with regard to God's existence. The aspiring man in us says, "God exists even though I cannot prove it to the world at large. I see and feel His Presence, and I know a day will come when I will be able to bring Him to the fore and show Him to the world at large." When we become one with the aspiring man, something within us tells us that God exists, and this something is our inner urge, our inner cry.

As a human being, one moment I can be an atheist, the next moment an agnostic, the next a desiring man or an aspiring man. I can also be a dreamer and can dream all the time. Now, when I dream of God, I feel that although God exists, He is far away — very, very far. I see a yawning gulf between my dream-boat and my reality-shore. I can also be a lover. When I become a lover of God, I see God as nearer than my eyes and dearer than my heart. Or I can become a server. When I serve God, it is because I get the utmost joy in serving God. There are many things I have done, many things I have said, many things I have offered in my life, but nothing has given me real and lasting joy. Only my service to God has given me everlasting joy; therefore, the server in me feels that God's existence is for my own happiness.

As a seeker, I have three friends: concentration, meditation and contemplation. I ask them, "Friends, have you seen God?" They immediately say, "Yes, we have seen God. Not only have we seen God, but also we can make you see God." When I ask them how, my friends tell me that they work together, one after the other, in a successive manner. They say that they are like three rungs of a ladder. My concentration friend tells me, "Just take any object and concentrate on it. Don't allow any wave of thought to enter into your mind, whether good or bad, divine or undivine. Make your mind absolutely thoughtless." I listen to my concentration friend and abide by his dictates. Then my meditation friend offers me his advice. He says, "Your heart is full of fear, impurity, insecurity and ignorance. Just empty it, empty it." I empty my heart, and immediately I feel tremendous joy, for then the Eternal Guest, God, comes in and sits on His Throne inside the inmost recesses of my heart. Finally, my contemplation friend tells me, "When you contemplate, try to feel in the beginning that you are playing a game of hide-and-seek with an intimate friend. This moment you hide and *he* seeks; the next moment he hides and *you* seek. Now, how long can you play hide-and-seek? For fifteen minutes, half an hour, an hour. Then it is all over and you come together as real friends, intimate friends, freely and totally revealed to each other. This is what happens between you and God when you contemplate."

I ask my three friends who has taught them all about God. They tell me that it was their parents who showed them the Face of God and taught them all about God. I ask them who their parents are. They say that their parents are aspiration and will-power. Aspiration is their mother; will-power is their father. When we become one with our aspiration, with our aspiring heart, we acquire knowledge from our conscious identification and oneness with the ultimate Reality. And just as our heart's identification with the supreme Reality can show us God's existence in Heaven, so, too, can our soul's light show us

God's existence on earth. And what is our soul's light? It is our will-power. In the spiritual life, aspiration and will-power go together. We need both mother and father.

What is aspiration? Aspiration is our inner cry for the Highest. And what does aspiration do? Aspiration helps us to minimise our desires. Once our desires are diminished, we feel peace within and joy without.

Ānandādd hy eva khalv imāni bhutāni jāyante,
Ānandena jātāni jīvanti,
Ānandaṁ prayantyabhisaṁ viśanti

Thousands of years ago the Vedic seers of ancient India sang this message. "From Delight we came into existence. In Delight we grow. At the end of our journey's close, into Delight we retire."

What is will-power? Will-power is something that expedites our journey. We know that we have a starting point and a destination. If we take the help of an Indian bullock cart to reach our destination, it will take us years and years. But if we make use of a modern jet plane, it will be only a matter of a few hours. Similarly, with our adamantine will-power we accelerate our progress. While we are proceeding along the path, concentration enters into us like a divine bullet, energises us and makes us feel that we can run the fastest to our goal. Meditation tells us that we have to dive the deepest to find our goal. Finally, contemplation tells us that we do not have to go anywhere. We do not have to run; we do not have to go deep within. We can stay where we are. Only we must give to God what we have. What we have is soulful gratitude to the Inner Pilot. We have gratitude because we feel that our aspiration and our power of receptivity have come directly from God.

Receptivity grows only when gratitude flows. God's existence can be proved only when our receptivity is complete, for if we cannot receive Him, no matter how many times He appears before us we will not be able to claim Him as our very own. And unless and until we can claim God as our very own, we will not be able to prove His existence.

Right now we are in the finite and we are for the finite. We find it very difficult to imagine the Infinite as our very own. But this is the limitation of the physical mind. There is also an intuitive mind, an illumined mind, but right now we do not have this mind. The physical mind always wants to experience the truth by cutting it into little pieces. For the mind to accept God or any reality as a whole is impossible. The mind limits; the mind binds. But the heart does not do that. The heart expands; the heart liberates. The heart wants to see the truth in its entirety; it wants to feel, possess and claim the truth as its very own. How does the heart do this? The heart is very wise. It secretly enters into the room of its elder brother, its most illumined brother, the soul, and brings back to its own abode boundless light. When the aspiring heart is inundated with light, whatever it sees it accepts in its entirety. Eventually there comes a time when the physical mind enters into the heart, which takes it into the soul. At that time the mind becomes liberated, just as the heart has been liberated by the light of the soul, and the soul has been liberated by the Consciousness-light of the Supreme.

We are all seekers. For us God does exist. It is only a matter of time before we become consciously one with Him. He who has already left the starting point will naturally reach the goal sooner than those who are still lingering behind. But spirituality is not a matter of competition. If we have to compete at all, then let us compete with the fear, doubt, anxiety, jealousy and other negative forces within ourselves. Let us defeat them, which means transform them. If we can transform our fear into courage, our doubt into faith, our insecurity into security, our impurity into purity and our imperfection into perfection, that is a worthwhile success and a significant progress. In the spiritual life we give all importance to progress, because progress is our soul's constant necessity. We are part of an eternal progress. From the unmanifest we entered into the mineral kingdom, then into the plant kingdom, then from the plant to the animal and from the animal to the human. Now we are trying to enter into the divine kingdom. When we think of ourselves as a song of progress and not as a song of success, then God-realisation is within our sure reach.

119. Beauty

Beauty is my body's purity. Beauty is my vital's humility. Beauty is my mind's serenity. Beauty is my heart's magnanimity. Beauty is my life's sincerity.

As a seeker, when I develop these divine qualities, I become all beauty. A child is beautiful, a flower is beautiful, a flame is beautiful. When I have a childlike heart, God talks to me. When my life becomes a flower of gratitude, I get the opportunity to sing with God His universal Song. When my life grows into a climbing flame, I play with God and take conscious part in His cosmic Game.

Beauty is in giving. Beauty is in receiving. Beauty is in giving and giving alone. Beauty is in receiving and receiving alone. When I give, I see that before I have given anything, Heaven is already smiling through my offering, my self-giving. When I receive, I see that earth is smiling in and through me. When I give and give, I see that God the divine Pilot is offering Himself to aspiring humanity in and through me. When I receive and receive, I see that God the infinite Compassion is entering into me and expanding my earthbound consciousness, finally transforming it into the Heaven-free Reality.

When I invoke the soul and become one with the soul, I have the capacity to reveal the Source at God's choice Hour. At that time, I have a most significant message to offer to my brothers and sisters of the world:

Vedāham etaṃ puruṣaṃ mahāntam...

I have known this Great Being, effulgent as the sun
beyond the boundaries of tenebrous gloom.

When I have attained this capacity, my own soul shines with the effulgent beauty of that one great Being.

When I invoke the heart, become one with the heart and try to offer the wealth of the heart to the world at large, I see a new beauty growing within me and flowing around me. At that time my message is:

Twameva mata pita twameva...

Thou art the Mother.
Thou art the Father.
Thou art the Friend.
Thou art the Comrade.
Thou art Knowledge.
Thou art Wealth.
Thou art my All.
Thou art my Lord Supreme.

This message that I offer to the world is founded upon my heart's oneness with my Inner Pilot. This is the sweetest and, at the same time, the most convincing feeling of inseparable oneness with the Inner Pilot. When I establish my inseparable oneness with my Inner Pilot, I feel Him as my Mother and Father of Eternity; as my Friend and Comrade from time immemorial; and as my Lord Supreme, my All. This is the beauty of the heart that a seeker embodies, reveals and manifests here on earth.

When I invoke the mind and become one with the mind, I offer the wealth of the mind on the strength of my soulful prayer.

Aum bhūr bhuvaḥ svaḥ...

This is the *Gayatri Mantra,* the prayer for the mind, for the illumination of the mind. This is India's peerless mantra or incantation. All the other mantras of India are derived from this one. This is the loftiest prayer that the Indian seers of the hoary past realised and offered to aspiring humanity.

We have already discovered beauty in the soul, beauty in the heart and beauty in the mind. Now we have to discover beauty in the vital. When beauty in the vital dawns, we become energetic, dynamic, progressive and fulfilling. At that time we pray to the Supreme to inundate our vital with power infinite, power divine, the power that builds, not the power that breaks; the power that energises us, the power the vital needs for the full manifestation of divinity on earth. The message of divine power which I offer to the world is:

Tejo asi tejo mayi dhehi...

Thy fiery spirit I invoke.
Thy manly vigour I invoke.
Thy power and energy I invoke.
Thy battle fury I invoke.
Thy conquering mind I invoke.

This power in the vital is the beauty of the vital for the manifestation of God here on earth.

I also try to invoke the body-consciousness and become one with the aspiring body in order to discover beauty in the body. For this, I pray to the Supreme to grant me sound health and an aspiring body. This is the prayer of my body:

Tach chaks ur debahitam...

May we, for a hundred autumns, see that lustrous
Eye, God-ordained, arise before us...

In this case a hundred years means an infinite or indefinite expanse of time. If we have a long life of aspiration on earth, then we can realise God, reveal God and manifest God. We need a long life of aspiration, dedication, devotion and surrender. This is the beauty in the body and of the body, for the soul and for God, the Supreme.

If we want to discover more beauty here in the earth-consciousness, we have to realise what is essential and what is not essential. Another most significant message of the Upanishadic seers is:

Neti, neti

Not this, not that.

Ignorance, no! Darkness, no! Bondage, no! Limitation, imperfection, no! We do not need them. We need faith, courage, humility, purity, sincerity and all the divine qualities. We renounce the unillumined parts in us and invoke the parts that are illumined, the consciousness that is illumined. Not this; not the ignorance which we now claim as our very own and which claims us as its very own, but light, the light that claims us as its very own and the light that we are going to claim as our very own.

There is also a supreme Beauty. The supreme Beauty is in our conscious, inseparable oneness with the Supreme. This supreme Beauty we discover on the strength of our conscious, constant and unconditional self-giving. When we dare to say, "Not my will, but Thy Will be done," then we can also say, "I and my Father are one." When we sincerely say, "Let Thy Will be done," at that time the supreme Beauty reveals itself in and through us. And when we say, "I and my Father are one," at that time the supreme Beauty finds its complete manifestation on earth here and now.

I have given a short talk on beauty. Now my students and I will sing a Bengali song on beauty.

[This is a translation of the song which Sri Chinmoy and his disciples sang. The words and music were written by Sri Chinmoy.]

Sundara hate sundara tumi
Nandana bana majhe...

You are beautiful, more beautiful, most beautiful,
Beauty unparalleled in the garden of Paradise.
Day and night may Thy Image abide in the very depth of my heart.

Without You my eyes have no vision;
Everything is an illusion, everything is barren.
All around me, within and without,
The melody of tenebrous pangs I hear.
My world is filled with excruciating pangs.
O Lord, O my beautiful Lord,
O my Lord of Beauty, in this lifetime, even for a fleeting second,
May I be blessed with the boon to see Thy Face.

120

Stop pushing! Your ignorance-night is too heavy.
Stop pulling! God's knowledge-Light is too vast.
Pushing is frustration.
Pulling is temptation.
Prepare yourself slowly, steadily and unerringly.
Yours will be the Goal of goals.

121. Philosophy, religion and spirituality

Dear seekers of the highest Truth, dear brothers and sisters, I wish to give a short talk on philosophy, religion and spirituality. As you all know, philosophy is a vast subject. Religion is a vast subject. Spirituality is a vast subject. Time will not permit me to do justice to these lofty subjects. Yet, with your kind permission, with your loving goodwill, I shall say a few words from the spiritual point of view on each one.

Philosophy is in the thinking mind. Philosophy is of the searching mind. Philosophy is for the illumining mind.

Religion is our conscious or unconscious response to the beckoning Light. Religion is our firm belief in the lofty experiences of our predecessors. Religion is our great satisfaction in our glorious past.

Spirituality is in the aspiring heart. Spirituality is of the liberating soul. Spirituality is for the fulfilling and immortalising God.

A lover of philosophy talks about God's Vision. A lover of religion talks about God's Power. A lover of spirituality talks about God's Compassion. A lover of philosophy wants to see God's Face. A lover of religion wants to see God's Eye. A lover of spirituality wishes to grow into God's all compassionate Heart.

A man of philosophy is a dreamer. A man of religion is an observer. A man of spirituality is a divine lover. A divine dreamer, a divine observer and a divine lover are good friends.

A man of philosophy wants to see the height of life. A man of religion wants to see the depth of life. A man of spirituality wants to see the reality of life and the reality in life.

There is a human philosophy and there is a divine philosophy. The human philosophy is a dry piece of wood. The human philosophy is a soulless goal. The divine philosophy is a fruitful tree. The divine philosophy is an all-illumining life and an all-fulfilling goal. The divine philosophy knows that its Source is transcendental Silence. The divine philosophy knows that its Source is transcendental Delight.

There is a human religion and a divine religion. The human religion is a baseless self-aggrandisement. The human religion is a lifeless confidence. The divine religion is a constant God-proclamation from the very depth of the seeker's heart. It is in the inmost recesses of his heart that a seeker proclaims God's Reality, God's Divinity, God's Immortality.

There is a human spirituality and a divine spirituality. The human spirituality, in the name of God, deceives mankind. The human spirituality, in the name of God, deceives its own true being by offering a false God-realisation to aspiring humanity. The divine spirituality knows that at God's choice Hour each follower of religion will be inundated with infinite Light, Peace and Bliss. The divine spirituality is fully aware of the fact that each practitioner of spirituality is a conscious, chosen instrument of God, crying for the dawn of Life immortal here on earth.

A man of true philosophy, a man of true religion and a man of true spirituality need God. For them there is no other choice.

I am extremely happy to learn that the motto of the state of Colorado is "Nothing without Deity". Without God, without the Inner Pilot, we are nothing. With the Inner Pilot, we are everything. God is the Realisation-tree, and this Realisation-tree has many branches. Philosophy, religion and spirituality are three branches of God the Realisation-tree. The man of philosophy can sit under the philosophy branch, the man of religion can sit under the religion branch, and the man of spirituality can sit under the spirituality branch. It is in the protection and shelter of the Divinity that we can grow into Immortality.

The man of philosophy, the man of religion and the man of spirituality are three brothers walking along three different roads. But they have started their journey, and they are destined to reach their goal at God's choice Hour. Each human being has philosophy to some extent, religion to some extent and spirituality to some extent. But if a seeker enters into the life of aspiration, and if his inner being compels him to love God for God's sake, then automatically the wealth of philosophy, the wealth of religion and the wealth of spirituality will all loom large in his life of aspiration. Philosophy will tell him who God is. Religion will tell him where God is. Spirituality will tell him why God is.

Part XXVIII — Questions and answers — University of Arkansas

122. Love

The heart's love claims God but does not blame God.

The mind's love doubts God in the morning, fears God in the afternoon, hates God in the evening and cries for God's Love at midnight.

123. *Question: What do you concentrate on?*

Sri Chinmoy: You can concentrate on anything, but if you are a spiritual seeker you will choose something that has some spiritual significance. Suppose you have a flower in front of you. A flower signifies purity. First you focus all your concentration on the flower, and then try to feel that you have become the flower itself, that is to say, purity. First you concentrate, and then you try to become part and parcel of the object you are concentrating on. The flame of a candle signifies aspiration, so you can concentrate on the flame of a candle, also. If you wish, you can concentrate on a divine quality, such as love or peace. Each person can make his own choice.

124. Question: Do you respect other religions?

Sri Chinmoy: I do respect other religions with utmost joy and utmost reverence. Just because I am a spiritual man, I feel I can treasure all religions and claim them as my very own. If one is not spiritual, then one is bound by a particular religion. But because I have become a spiritual seeker, I feel that all religions are like branches of a tree, and the tree is God. How can I deny the existence of the branches when I accept the tree as my very own? If I accept the tree as my very own, then whatever is part of the tree I also claim as an undeniable reality.

125. Question: How can one work for God?

Sri Chinmoy: Whenever we work, we can and should feel that we are working for God. Right now when you are working, you may not think of God, or you may not feel the reality of God. You see physical work as just work. But if you can see work as an opportunity to express your capacity, or to reveal your goodness, your divinity, then most certainly you are working for God at that time. By working, or serving, you have to feel that you are moving towards your goal.

If you are a labourer and are working with your hands, your mind can be inside God, your heart can be inside God, and you can consciously place your very action inside God. Otherwise, your action will be in somebody else — in somebody's appreciation or admiration or judgement — and you will be concerned with what he thinks about your work. But if you are working to please one person, the Inner Pilot within you, the Inner Pilot will naturally expect you to work perfectly. He will not tell you to cheat or deceive the person who has asked you to work, for the real employer of everybody is the Supreme.

Right now when we finish a difficult job, we are very pleased with ourselves. We say, "Ah, I've done it. It was such a hard job, but I did it." But there comes a time in the spiritual life when we feel that all the work we accomplish is actually being done through us by the Inner Pilot. We realise that we can do nothing by ourselves; we are mere instruments. It is God who does everything in and through us.

Until we have that kind of feeling, let us try to offer the fruits, the results of our actions to God. If success comes from our work, let us offer it at the Feet of God. And if failure comes, let us offer this also at the Feet of God. Both success and failure are experiences that God is having in and through us. If we do not have this attitude, then we shall only try for success by hook or by crook. And this success may lead us to a kind of confusion. Today's success may be transformed into tomorrow's frustration. But if we offer the results of each action of ours at the Feet of God instead of trying to claim them as our own, then we are free.

126. Question: I am a vegetarian but I work as a meat handler. Is this increasing my karma?

Sri Chinmoy: If you are a vegetarian, and if your earthly duty demands that you work at a place where you have to handle meat, do not feel that you are increasing your karma or doing something wrong. As long as you do not feel the necessity of eating meat, and your consciousness is not in the aggressive animal consciousness, then there is no harm.

Sometimes, I know, there is something called compulsion. If this is the only place that you can get a job, then you should do it. But your consciousness must not be in the meat; your consciousness must be in something pure and divine. You have to know where your consciousness remains while you work. There are some people in the spiritual life who do not eat meat, but when they see meat and fish immediately their greed and desire comes to the fore. This kind of vegetarianism is only self-deception. But if you do not want to eat meat and do not feel the need of it, then even if you touch meat there will be no problem.

If you are extremely sincere, and if you feel that touching meat lowers your consciousness, then your sincere aspiration will knock at God's Door and God will provide you with some other job. If He feels that your consciousness is being lowered by touching meat and if you are sincerely crying and searching for another job, then He will not allow you to remain with this one. But if your consciousness is not lowered, then God will say, "There is no harm in it."

127. Question: How do you see the physical body as entering into the scheme of things?

Sri Chinmoy: The physical body is a temple. We have to keep the physical clean and purified and in good repair. Otherwise, even if we achieve something high we will not be able to keep it permanently. We must not discard the physical, but we must try to keep it pure and divine for the soul to work through. And when the soul comes to the fore, the physical has to invite and accept the Light, and become part and parcel of the soul's consciousness. Only then can the physical be properly used for the divine manifestation.

Part XXIX — Questions and answers — University of Tulsa

128. Question: Is it necessary to transcend all emotions for the spiritual life?

Sri Chinmoy: There are two types of emotion. One is vital emotion, which wants to possess. Unfortunately, before we possess, we are possessed. The other type of emotion is divine emotion. This emotion is not bad. It says, "Since I am God's chosen child, how can I do this? How can I wallow in the pleasures of ignorance? I have to work for God, I have to realise God, I have to serve God in aspiring mankind." This is an emotional approach. But this is a purified emotion. This kind of emotion will illumine and liberate us. If we can transcend the vital, earth-bound emotion, then we can feel freedom, real freedom, infinite freedom.

129. Question: Is it important for spiritual seekers to spend time with one another?

Sri Chinmoy: It is always advisable for seekers to mix with other seekers, for then they will be inspired. If you stay with somebody who is not aspiring at all, that means you are constantly struggling. It is very difficult for a seeker — especially in the beginning — to maintain his highest consciousness. As soon as he goes someplace immediately he sees unaspiring people. Even if he does not talk to them, still they are spreading their vibration. If a saint comes here, immediately you will feel his vibration. And if a thief comes, immediately you will feel that vibration. But if you are a seeker and another seeker is with you, then immediately your strength increases tremendously. So it is always advisable for seekers to be in a community together or to meet together often.

130. Question: How many levels of initiation are there, and how many times will a Master initiate a disciple?

Sri Chinmoy: No matter on what plane the Master initiates you here on earth, that is more than enough. Initiation means that the Master teaches you how to swim. Once he teaches you how to swim, he will constantly inspire you to swim across the sea of ignorance. He will not have to teach you again and again how to swim. Once he teaches you, that is enough. He will constantly inspire you, guide you, shape you and mould you until you reach your Goal, your transcendental Self, your highest Reality.

Part XXX — Questions and answers — Southern Methodist University

131. Question: How important do you think it is to have a spiritual teacher if one is very eager to make fast progress? And also, how long does one have to stay with the teacher?

Sri Chinmoy: It entirely depends on how sincerely the seeker wants to go to the highest plane of consciousness, how deeply he needs Peace, Light and Bliss. If his need is great, he will immediately try to get someone who can be of help to him. If he feels the necessity of making the fastest progress, then a teacher is of paramount importance, for even if he is able to make some inner progress alone, he may be doubtful of his achievement.

If he has an experience, he may doubt the experience or not know its actual significance. A teacher is bound to clarify his experiences and expedite his inner progress. In the ordinary life, a teacher examines you and either passes or fails you. But a spiritual teacher is more like a private tutor. He does not examine. He just teaches his students how to pass God's examination.

A teacher is necessary unless and until we have reached our own highest goal. In the ordinary life, we start our schooling with kindergarten, and progress to the university. Once we complete our course in the university, we do not go to school any more. In fact, we may become teachers ourselves. Similarly, once we have reached the highest Absolute, we no longer need a teacher.

132. Question: How is it best to cope with the occasional fears and doubts that plague us?

Sri Chinmoy: Why are we afraid of something or someone? Because we have not established our oneness with that person or thing. When a child stands in front of his father, his father seems as tall and strong as a giant to this little child. If he had not established his oneness with his father, he would be scared to death. But he is not afraid of his father, for he knows that his father loves him and that his father's strength is all for his use and his protection. In the spiritual life also, we are only afraid of something or someone because we have not spread our wings of consciousness. If we spread our wings, then the whole world becomes ours.

To cope with doubt we should ask ourselves whether we accomplish anything by doubting others. If we doubt somebody's achievement to the very end of our days, our doubt will not take away from his achievement. If he has achieved something, it is done and our doubt cannot diminish it. But if we start doubting ourselves, that is our real destruction. The moment we start doubting our own possibilities, potentialities and capacities, we can no longer progress. If you now doubt me and feel that I am not a sincere seeker, a few moments later you will feel that I am a sincere seeker, and a few moments later you will doubt your own capacity and authority to judge. Now, when you doubted me, I did not lose anything, and when you had faith in me, you did not lose anything. But when you started doubting your own judgement, then you reached a stalemate. If you cannot now accept a Master wholeheartedly, it is best to try to create aspiration within yourself, so that you can conquer doubt.

Let us take fear, doubt, courage and faith as four persons knocking at your door: two friends and two enemies. Since it is your door, you can allow your friends to come in, but not your enemies. Allow courage and faith to enter, then bolt the door to keep out fear and doubt, for once you allow your enemies in, they will exploit you. They will try to take every advantage of your weakness. It is you who can accept or reject fear and doubt, faith and courage. At every moment a seeker must be conscious and cautious about when he should open his heart's door and his mind's door.

When the seeker has become very advanced and has travelled far, very far, towards his goal, at that time he does not reject fear, he does not reject doubt. With his inner wisdom, he transforms fear into courage and doubt into faith. When a seeker is on the verge of realisation, when he has the inner will-power, he does not want to leave any imperfection on earth untransformed. He feels, "If I do not conquer this fear, then it will go and torture my younger brothers and sisters, who are my very near and dear ones. Let me conquer it and transform it once and for all."

133. Question: For spiritual beginners, it seems that it is necessary to make some compromise between their family life and their spiritual life. Do you think that this compromise will always have to exist, or can it be transcended by some other kind of relationship?

Sri Chinmoy: In the beginning, if your eagerness and love for God are not intense, if you feel that you can live with God, but not with God alone; if you feel that other human beings are also necessary for your happiness, then you have to make a compromise. Otherwise, you will not be able to remain in the spiritual life. But if you feel that you can live only in God's Luminosity, if you feel that you cannot live even for a second without Him, then go to Him and do not think of compromise. He will take care of you and He will also take care of the members of your family.

If God wants you to run the fastest, at that time you have to know who is dearest to you — God or the members of your family. Right now you are making a compromise so that your near and dear ones can be happy. But you know that your capacity is very limited, whereas the One you are approaching has unlimited capacity. You do not want to neglect your family, but you have to know that you do not have infinite capacity to make your mother or father or brother or sister happy. In trying to please them, you reach a kind of compromise. But if you reach the Source with your intense inner urge, then you can ask the Supreme, your Inner Pilot, to take full responsibility for your near and dear ones. And He has infinite capacity to make them happy.

Who looked after your near and dear ones twenty or thirty

years ago, before you came into this life? And in fifty or sixty years, when you go away from this earthly scene, who will take care of them? Right now, we feel that we are indispensable. But when we enter deeply into the spiritual life, we feel that only one person is indispensable, and that is God. If you need God badly, He will allow you to go to Him directly. He will give you the capacity to deal with the members of your family without having to compromise your spiritual life, and He will give your near and dear ones the strength to lead their own lives without hampering your spiritual progress.

Part XXXI — Questions and answers — University of Nevada

134. Question: How can one know the God inside himself without becoming confused by the mind?

Sri Chinmoy: I am glad you have come to realise the limitations of the mind and the confusion it creates. Our philosophy is the philosophy of the heart, for the heart accepts and becomes one with reality in its pristine form. If you live in the mind, you will always be confused. This moment the mind accepts reality, and the next moment it rejects reality as something unreal. The mind that I am speaking of is the physical mind, the mind which is in the physical body and which is constantly seeking satisfaction in and through the physical. But there is also a higher mind, which we call the illumined mind. This illumined mind is ours when the heart offers light from the soul to the mind, and the mind accepts the light devotedly and soulfully. But until the mind becomes illumined, nothing will be lost or destroyed if the seeker tries to separate his mind from the aspiring consciousness of the heart.

For the time being the seeker knows that he has two rooms — one is the mind room, the other is the heart room. Unfortunately, in the mind room there is no light. If the seeker remains there all the time, there is no guarantee that one day he will be illumined. But if the seeker enters into the heart room and stays there for a few months or a few years, then his entire being will be surcharged with light. Then, when he is convinced that his inner being is surcharged with light, he can enter into the mind room with his inner light and illumine the darkness there. The mind also has to be illumined at the proper hour, but right now we have to pay all attention to the aspiring heart. And because God does not want a seeker to remain imperfect in any part of his being, from the aspiring heart, the illumining heart, we have to bring light slowly, steadily and unerringly into the limited, doubting, suspicious earth-bound mind. Then all confusion there disappears and the earth-bound mind becomes the Heaven-free mind, the illumined mind.

135. Question: Is there but one Satguru *in any one age or are there many Satgurus at one time?*

Sri Chinmoy: There can be more than one *Satguru* at one time. As on the human level there are many teachers, so also there can be many spiritual Masters on earth. But the only real Satguru is God; not any human being. I always tell my disciples that I am not the Guru. The real Guru is the Supreme. Spiritual Masters are His representatives; they represent God for their own spiritual children.

136. Question: If we fall asleep during meditation, does that mean we should sleep more at night so we can stay awake?

Sri Chinmoy: Some people may sleep twelve hours a night, but when the time comes to meditate, they will still fall asleep. So you have to know whether you fall asleep during meditation because you did not have enough sleep or because you are lethargy-prone. If you sleep for only three or four hours, then probably your body needs more sleep. But if you sleep for seven or eight hours at night and still fall asleep during your meditation, then I wish to say that it is not because of lack of sleep. It is because of lack of aspiration, lack of determination.

137. Question: How can we see the divine in another human being when each human being has so many faults?

Sri Chinmoy: Since you would like to see the divine in others, you have already covered half the distance. Some people do not want to see the divine in others. On the contrary, they want to see only the undivine in others so that they can criticise and ridicule. But when you become a sincere seeker, at that time you try to see the divine in others in spite of their limitations. By seeing someone's limitations, we only delay our own progress. And, at the same time, we do not help the other person in any way. If we find fault with somebody, his undivine qualities are not going to disappear, nor are ours going to decrease. On the contrary, his undivine qualities will come to the fore in his defence, and our pride, arrogance and feeling of superiority will also come to the fore. But by seeing the divine in someone we expedite our progress and help the other person to establish his own life of reality on something divine.

In the spiritual life, we have to see others with the heart of a lover and not with the eye of a critic. Each individual knows his own limitations, but still he should think primarily of his divine possibilities and divine potentialities. By constantly thinking of his divine potentialities, by focusing his attention on his divine possibilities, he is able to enter into the realm of fulfilling reality.

To see the divine in others, we have to love. Where love is thick, faults are thin. If you really love someone, then it is difficult to find fault with him. His faults seem negligible, for love means oneness. This oneness comes from our conscious acceptance of his reality as it is. A mother, in spite of knowing her child's countless limitations, does not stop loving him, because she has established her oneness with him. If there is imperfection in the child, the mother claims this imperfection as her very own. And when the child grows up, he feels that his mother's weaknesses are his own.

If you find it difficult to love the human in someone, then love the divine in him. The divine in him is God. Just because you are a seeker, you know that God exists in that person just as God exists in your own life. Even if it is difficult to love the human as such, for you to love God is extremely easy because you know that God is divine and perfect. So each time you look at an individual, if you can become consciously aware of God's existence in him, then you cannot consciously be disturbed by his imperfections or limitations.

Part XXXII — Questions and answers — Stanford University

138. Question: I've heard that when one accepts a spiritual path, there is a point at which one must surrender oneself to a Guru who is higher than himself. But I've also heard that one must constantly question his teachings and listen to his own inner voice. These two injunctions seem to conflict.

Sri Chinmoy: First of all, you have to know that if one goes to the trouble of getting a Guru, then he has to listen to his Guru all the time. It is better for one not to accept a Guru if he cannot accept his teachings, for the words of a real spiritual Master are directly inspired by the Supreme. A human being may be the leader of a few hundred or a few thousand, or a few million people. But the real Guru, the Guru within him, is God.

When you accept a spiritual Master as your teacher, it is because he is more illumined than you. As I said during my talk, you have to listen to your higher part. Right now your mind is superior to your physical or vital. When the mind asks you to do something, the physical and the vital in you obey. But again, the heart is superior to the mind, for the mind doubts and suspects, whereas the heart gets illumination from the soul. Similarly, the spiritual teacher, if he is really illumined, is the seeker's own highest part. He is not a different person. So just as the mind must listen to the heart, which is its more illumined part, in order for the seeker to make spiritual progress, so too the seeker must listen to his Guru, whose illumination is that of total oneness with the Supreme. There should be no sense of separativity when the disciple listens to his Guru, for the unillumined part of him is listening to the illumined part.

In the matter of surrender, we do not surrender to somebody

else. We are only abiding by the soulful dictates of some part of us which is already illumined. It is not somebody else we are listening to; it is our own highest part. As beginners, we cannot remain constantly in contact with our higher part. But if we know that there is someone who represents and embodies the Highest, we can try to listen to him. When my legs listen to my mind, I do not feel that it is beneath the dignity of my legs to do so. I know that my head and my legs are part of the same body. The spiritual Master and his disciples are in that sense inseparably one.

The questioning mind can never realise the Highest; only the aspiring heart can realise the Truth. If you want Light, then you have to have implicit faith. Faith in whom? Faith in yourself, faith in God and faith in the one whom you choose as your guide or leader. Once you reach the highest Goal, you do not need a guide. At that time, you and the Goal are together. But if you start questioning your own sincerity, or the sincerity and the capacity of your Guru, or the existence of the Goal itself, then you will never arrive there. If you really want to follow the spiritual life, you must have implicit faith in yourself, in your teacher and in God. Only then can you make the fastest progress.

139. Question: How does one begin on the spiritual path?

Sri Chinmoy: If you want to follow a specific spiritual path, then you need inspiration to start with. This inspiration you can get from spiritual books, preferably those written by the real spiritual Masters. If you do not get adequate inspiration from books, or if books do not satisfy you, you should mix with the disciples of spiritual Masters. If you associate with seekers who have already found a path, you will get inspiration, encouragement and assurance. Then you have to go to a teacher.

The Master and the path are one. If you follow a specific path, naturally there will be a Master for that path. There are quite a few teachers and paths, but you have to make a choice. The teacher who gives you the greatest joy is meant for you.

140. Question: Why is it that you always speak of God in masculine terms?

Sri Chinmoy: God is both masculine and feminine. The Christ always called God the Father, so the term "Father" is more commonly used in the Western world. In the East, we quite often speak of the Supreme Goddess. But when I am with Westerners, I use the term which is more familiar to you, because I feel that it will be easier for me to share my experiences with you in that way. Nevertheless, God is both masculine and feminine. Again, God is neither masculine nor feminine, but transcendental. He is what He eternally is: He is His Vision and He is His Reality. This Reality embodies both masculine and feminine and also transcends both.

141. Question: What is the nature and purpose of the soul?

Sri Chinmoy: Each soul is a direct representative of God. God is one, yet He wants to experience Himself or enjoy Himself divinely and supremely in infinite forms. When we enter into the world, we aspire in order to realise the Highest. There are many worlds, but God-discovery or Self-discovery can take place only here on earth. In order to reach the Highest, the Absolute, we have to come here, to Mother Earth. The soul, the inner bird, comes here in order to fulfil the promise that it has made to the Absolute in the highest plane of consciousness — let us say, in Heaven. Each soul has to manifest the Light here on earth in a specific way. Nature is the field. A farmer needs a field in order to cultivate. So the soul comes to Mother Earth and cultivates Light, Peace, Bliss and Delight in the physical manifestation. The soul is like a divine farmer. The body is a field, the vital is a field, the mind is a field and the heart is a field. In each field the divine farmer cultivates, and from each field he expects a bumper crop of realisation. When the body-consciousness or the body as a field becomes fertile, and when the vital, the mind and the heart become fertile, the soul fulfils its promise to God and manifests divinity on earth. It is through the revelation of the soul's Light that the Transcendental Supreme becomes manifested. So the soul and nature go together. One is the divine farmer, and the other is the ground for cultivation.

142. *Question: Was the Christ an avatar?*

Sri Chinmoy: On the strength of my own highest realisation I wish to say that the Christ was, is and shall always be an avatar. Avatar means the direct representative of God — God in human form. An avatar embodies God's Vision and Reality all at once. With him, Vision and Reality go together. The Christ, Sri Krishna, the Buddha, Sri Ramakrishna, all came from the same Source, but had different names. This moment I call Him Krishna because I like the Krishna form; the next moment I like the Buddha form and I call Him the Buddha; and then I may call Him Ramakrishna or Christ. But they are all eternally one.

Part XXXIII — Questions and answers — Portland State University

143. Question: Is there a difference between sleep and meditation?

Sri Chinmoy: Yes, there is the greatest possible difference between sleep and meditation. In a sense ordinary people are always sleeping as long as they are in ignorance. Even when they are physically working or running, unless and until they are spiritually awakened, they are fast asleep. From the spiritual point of view, he who is not aspiring is fast asleep.

Physical sleep is necessary, for the body needs rest. Every day the seeker goes out into the battlefield of life and fights against fear, doubt, anxiety, jealousy and other undivine forces, so he does need rest. When the body is tired and exhausted, it needs sleep. But we have to know whether our desire for sleep is the body's necessity or the necessity of pleasure-life, whether it is the body's need or merely its demand. If the body has worked very hard, then certainly the body deserves rest. But if the body demands ten hours or twelve hours of sleep, unless we are sick we are only making friends with inertia, lethargy, ignorance and death.

When we indulge in excessive amounts of sleep, we do not create anything; we just add our own contribution to ignorance, to death's capacity-might. Because of lethargy and our love for idleness, if we wallow in the pleasures of ignorance, then the time that we are offering to sleep, we are unable to offer to God. Time does not wait for us. Time comes to us, and we can use it either to pray or meditate or to take rest. But when we have established inner peace, we diminish our need for sleep, because peace itself is rest. We can sleep for only two hours or we may not sleep at all for days and nights. For the beginner it is advisable to sleep for seven hours; but eight, nine or ten hours is too much.

The great spiritual Masters have a different kind of sleep. It is called *Yoga-nidra*. Because of their realisation, they are constantly one with the soul. When they sleep, others may see and feel that they are fast asleep, but their souls are all vigilance. These Masters may snore, and their bodies may be totally inert, but at that time they have separated the body from the soul and have become inseparably one with the soul. They are allowing the body to take rest because it has worked hard and it needs and deserves rest, but they know that they are not asleep, their consciousness is not asleep. Their real reality, which is the soul's reality, is absolutely alert. The soul is meditating most powerfully. For ordinary seekers this is not possible. This dreamless sleep, which is at a very high state of consciousness, is experienced only by seekers on the verge of realisation or actually realised. This kind of sleep is inseparable from meditation. But normally, sleep is sleep and meditation is meditation. If it is beyond what is necessary, sleep is friendship with ignorance. Meditation is always friendship with illumination.

144. Question: Could you tell us what Christ is?

Sri Chinmoy: Christ is the Infinite Consciousness, the Eternal Reality. Christ as the physical man, the son of a carpenter, stayed on earth for thirty-three years. But if we care for the spiritual, for the divine, for the immortal, then we will say that Christ is infinite, eternal, immortal. Two thousand years ago Christ came in the physical form, but even now He is with us in spiritual form, and He shall eternally remain with us. For spiritual seekers He is always inside their hearts. For ordinary people, even if He comes and stands in front of them, still they will doubt Him and suspect Him.

145. Question: Why is it so difficult to unite one's worldly work with the spiritual life?

Sri Chinmoy: The difficulty is that we do not really try to follow the spiritual life. The moment we get up in the morning, we think of our school, our office, our family problems and our earthly duties. We do not do the first thing first. We do not think of God. Consciously or unconsciously we forget the existence of God, but we never forget the existence of mankind. God does not exist in our mind; what exists in our mind is man alone. Naturally we cannot combine the two. If God took precedence in our mind early in the morning, before humanity came into the picture, then we could combine them. But we have not invited our Eternal Friend to enter our room and stay with us; we have invited only man. When we do not invite our first and foremost Friend, naturally we cannot introduce our other friend to Him. We want to tell God, "This is my friend man," and we want to tell man, "This is my Friend God." But one of the friends is missing. So we have to make sure to invite both friends. But again, we shall be wise if we know which of the two friends has more capacity to please us and should come first. Before we invite the world at large, before we invite mankind into our mind and heart, let us invite God, our Eternal Friend. If He comes and we feel His presence in our heart, then easily we can combine both the outer world and the inner world.

146. Question: How should one meditate?

Sri Chinmoy: It entirely depends on the individual. Somebody may find it easier to meditate inside the mind; somebody else finds it very easy to meditate inside the heart, or to meditate on a flower or a candle, or to meditate while looking at the vast sky or at the blue ocean. If you have a Master, you can meditate on your Master's picture. Whichever form of meditation gives you utmost joy or the utmost sense of satisfaction is the best form of meditation for you.

Part XXXIV — Questions and answers — North Idaho Junior College

147. Question: When a disciple meditates on you or on your photograph, how much does he actually feel your presence?

Sri Chinmoy: It depends on the disciple's aspiration. If the disciple is meditating most devotedly, most soulfully, then he is bound to feel my inner presence strongly. Either he will feel me inside his heart, or he will feel his own existence inside my heart, or both. But in order to be able to meditate soulfully, the seeker has to meditate daily, with love, joy and concern for his own progress and for his Master's divine manifestation.

Every day we do not eat most delicious food. One day we eat delicious food and then, for a week, the food we eat may be quite ordinary. Similarly, one day a disciple may feel his Master's presence strongly, and then for a few days he may not. No one can become an expert all at once. Everyone needs practice. In the beginning, it may not be possible for a seeker to feel the

Master's presence every day, but there comes a time when he is bound to feel the Master's presence within him, not only during the time of his meditation, but also during his multifarious activities.

How does one become a sincere, devoted, genuine seeker? He does so by feeling in each thought, in each action, that his Master is within him and for him. Naturally, when the disciple constantly feels his Master's presence, the Master will feel the disciple's conscious, constant inner cry, which is called aspiration.

148. Question: What is the Will of the Supreme?

Sri Chinmoy: The Will of the Supreme is to make each of us His perfect instrument. Right now we are all imperfect instruments, but His Will is to make us perfect so that he can manifest Himself in and through us most perfectly. Perfect Perfection has not yet dawned on earth, but His Will is to make everybody in His creation perfect. In His Vision He saw perfection, but in His manifestation, perfection is still a far cry. So, His Will is to manifest perfection in the earth-consciousness.

149. Question: How can we achieve peace in our outer life?

Sri Chinmoy: We can achieve peace in our outer life provided we do the first thing first. Early in the morning, before we enter into the hustle and bustle of life, if we meditate for ten or fifteen minutes, then peace will enter into us. If we bring forward our divine qualities of aspiration, dedication, love, devotion and surrender to the Will of God, they are bound to bring down peace from Above. These qualities are like divine friends, eternal friends within us; they are more than eager to be of service. If we invoke them early in the morning before we leave our house, then we will go outside with peace. But if we do not feel the conscious need for peace and do not invoke it, why should peace come to us? Unless and until we invoke it, peace will remain in its own world.

The power of peace is similar to the power of money. If we put money in our pocket early in the morning, we can buy things all day. Similarly, if we meditate early in the morning for peace, and peace descends, then when we enter into the mad, insane world, we are surcharged, inundated with peace which we can utilise all day. Peace itself is adamantine power. If we are powerful and strong, then the restlessness of the world cannot torture us. But if we are weak and lack inner peace, naturally we will be overwhelmed by the restlessness and undivine qualities of the world.

Part XXXV — Questions and answers — University of Montana

150. Question: What is the difference between seeing God and realising God?

Sri Chinmoy: There is a great difference between seeing God and realising God. When we see God, we can see Him as an individual or as an object or as something else. But we do not consciously and continuously embody Him and feel that He is our very own. When we see God, it is like seeing a tree. We do not at that time consciously embody the tree-consciousness.

And since we do not embody it, we cannot reveal or manifest it. But when we realise something, at that time it becomes part and parcel of our life. We may see a flower, but when we realise the flower we actually become one with the consciousness of the flower.

When we merely see something, we cannot claim it as our very own, and that particular thing also will not claim us. Seeing is on the physical plane, while realising is on the inner plane. Seeing does not last, whereas realising does remain with us. If we see something, the vision may last for a short while; but when we realise something, this knowledge lasts forever. In the spiritual life we always say that there is a great difference between experience and realisation. Experience is something that lasts for a few hours or a few days or months or years; but it does not last forever. Experience enters into our life but does not and cannot make its permanent abode within us. But once we have realisation it becomes part and parcel of our life and lasts for eternity.

151. Question: Could you please talk about attachment and detachment in love?

Sri Chinmoy: Human love is attachment; divine love is detachment. Why is human love attachment? Because human love constantly demands. Human love wants to possess and be possessed; otherwise it is not satisfied. But even when we are possessed or when we possess, there is no satisfaction, because we see the limitations inside the other person and the limitations in our own being. When we see limitations in ourselves or in others we are not satisfied, for the soul in us can never be satisfied with imperfection. It wants constant illumination and perfection.

When we love divinely, we are not attached to anybody. We care only for the expansion of our own consciousness and of the consciousness of others. We feel that it is not right to bind them. By binding an individual we do not accomplish anything. When we really love we feel that we should expand our consciousness into Infinity and should allow and help those with whom we are closely connected to expand their consciousness as well. Divine love is the song of expansion. Constantly we try to expand our reality and help others to expand their reality. And while we are expanding, one day, at God's choice Hour, we will become one with His universal Consciousness, His transcendental Consciousness.

Attachment is in the body; detachment is in the soul. If we live in the body-consciousness, we will always be attached to people and objects around us. But if we live in the soul-consciousness, we will try to illumine the things in us that have to be illumined, we will try to perfect the things in us that have to be perfected and to manifest the things that have to be manifested fully here on earth for God's purpose.

152. Question: How may one realise God?

Sri Chinmoy: If one wants to learn history or geography, one studies these subjects. In the same way, to realise God inner study is necessary. This inner study we call aspiration. In the field of aspiration there are three significant friends or guides: concentration, meditation and contemplation. When we practice these disciplines sincerely and devotedly, they lead us inevitably to God-realisation.

153. Question: How do we deal with negative emotions like anger, jealousy and fear?

Sri Chinmoy: Sometimes people feel that the more they think of their negative qualities, the more they are conscious of them, the sooner they will be able to get rid of them. Unfortunately, this is not true. In the spiritual life, the more we think of our negative qualities, the more they lord it over us and the more we are caught by them. What we have to do is to see if there is anything in us that we can invoke to solve our problems.

Suppose we are constantly at the mercy of anger. Now, if we can establish peace in our being, we will not have anger. How do we do this? We do not think of anger at all; we pray and meditate only for peace. The very nature of peace is to spread. When peace spreads its wings inside our being, our anger is bound to be transformed because it comes under the influence of peace.

Suppose we are assailed by jealousy. We are jealous of others because we have not established our oneness with them. But if I put the shot with my right hand, my left hand will not be jealous even though it will not be able to throw as far. My left hand and right hand have established their oneness. When one part of my body does something, the other part does not feel miserable, because each knows that it belongs to the same body, and that the entire body is its reality. When I work with my mind, my feet do not feel miserable, because they have established their oneness with my mind. In the spiritual life also, when we establish oneness with the Source, which is God, then we are not jealous of anybody. If we feel that our reality is God, then each individual is like a limb of our conscious, dedicated, devoted spiritual body. If they are all limbs of my body, then they are part and parcel of my existence. So how can I be jealous of them? So if we pray for inseparable oneness with the Source, the problem of jealousy will easily be solved, because God is the root and the tree and the branches. Jealousy can be overcome only by our constant feeling of oneness with others. Unless and until we have realised others as our very own, we call them different personalities, different individualities. But if we can see and feel them inside ourselves as members of our own larger family, jealousy will disappear from our life of aspiration.

Similarly, with all other undivine qualities, the best way to deal with them is to invoke the divine qualities which will illumine and transform them.

Part XXXVI — Questions and answers — University of Colorado

154. Question: Could you please tell us about your path to God-realisation?

Sri Chinmoy: Our path is the path of love, devotion and surrender. We feel that if we can love God truly and soulfully, we will be able to run to God faster. We feel that if we love God truly and soulfully, we will want to devote our lives to Him, to please Him and fulfil Him. Finally, we feel that we must surrender our human will to the Will of God consciously and unconditionally. We feel that if we surrender our will to God, then we will be able to realise Him in His own Way. If we want to realise God in our own way, we shall have to be satisfied with only an iota of divine Reality. But if we want to realise God in God's Way and at His choice Hour, then He will inundate us with His Infinity,

Eternity and Immortality.

Love, devotion, surrender — this is our path. Divine love, divine devotion and divine surrender. Human love, we know, ends in frustration, and inside frustration what looms large is destruction. Human devotion is attachment. As with human love, with human devotion we try to possess and we are possessed. In this song of possession, we do not get any sense of satisfaction. But when we devote ourselves to the Supreme, to the Inner Pilot, we feel boundless satisfaction. When someone devotes his life to an ordinary human being, one imperfect being is devoting himself to another imperfect being. And two imperfect beings, when they come together, cannot make one perfect being. So we try instead to offer our devotion to the Perfect One, who is God, and from Him we expect perfection through our dedicated, devoted service.

Divine surrender, too, is totally different from human surrender. A slave surrenders to his master under compulsion, because he is at the mercy of his master. But in the spiritual life, when we make divine surrender to God, it is not the same kind of surrender. We feel that we are a tiny drop entering into the vast ocean. When the tiny drop, the individual consciousness, enters into the vast ocean of infinite Consciousness, it does not lose its individuality or personality. Rather, it grows into the infinite Individuality and Personality.

Who is God, after all? God is not a third person. God is our own highest and most illumined part. A real seeker can feel that there is no difference between his existence and God's existence. It is only that God's existence is his most illumined existence, while his personal existence is right now still wallowing in the pleasures of ignorance. When he surrenders, he is surrendering his lowest self consciously, soulfully and unconditionally to his highest and most illumined Self, so that his highest Self can mould him, shape him and guide him according to its own transcendental Vision.

155. Question: How does a person surrender? What does a person do to achieve divine surrender?

Sri Chinmoy: We all know that a human being is expected to work on the physical plane. This kind of work is noticeable. On the mental plane and the psychic plane we also work, but this work is not so noticeable. Now, when we work on the physical plane, immediately we expect some result. This result takes the form of either success or failure. If we can offer the result of our work at the Feet of the Supreme, this is divine surrender. When we dive deep within, we see that we are not the doer. God Himself is the doer, as well as the action and the fruit thereof. When success comes, if we take it as an experience, and when failure comes, if we take it as another experience, then we will not be disturbed by failure and not allow pride to enter into our heart because of success. It is in our dedicated action and the surrender of our achievements to God's omniscient, omnipresent and all-loving Will that divine surrender lies.

156. Question: In the highest state of samadhi, when you look at other human beings, what kind of consciousness do you feel in them?

Sri Chinmoy: When one is in the highest transcendental samadhi, the physical personality of others disappears. We do not see others as human beings. We see only a flow of consciousness, like a river that is entering into the ocean. He who is in the highest trance becomes the ocean. And he who is in a lower state of consciousness is the river. The river flows into the sea and becomes one with the sea. But there is no individuality, no personality that the one who is enjoying the highest samadhi notices in the other. A human being who is not in this state of samadhi is a flowing river of consciousness, while the one who is in samadhi has become the sea itself, the sea of Peace and Light.

157. Question: If God is the only doer, what is the role of man's free will?

Sri Chinmoy: God is the doer, but our free will has to be united with God's Will. Free will is our soul's consciousness-light. We can use the light of the soul for God-manifestation, or we may not use it at all. If we do not use it, then the aggressive part of the vital or the lethargy of the physical or the doubt of the mind comes into the picture and captures us. God does everything through the soul, which is His direct representative. God is the sun and the soul is like a lamp. This lamp embodies and represents the sun here on earth. But we usually do not remain in the soul's light and take full advantage of it, so our free will takes the form of lower vital movements, our free will becomes our friendship with lethargy, our friendship with the doubting mind, our oneness with the heart's insecurity. Our free will decides that the body, the vital and the mind have enough light to guide us, or it tells us that we are helpless without the guidance of our Lord Supreme.

158. Question: Why must a seeker love God?

Sri Chinmoy: A seeker is not forced to love anybody, not even

God. A seeker's love is always spontaneous; it comes from the inmost recesses of his heart. In the heart, everything is spontaneous. In the mind, love is something we force, and in the vital, also, sometimes we force it. But in the aspiring heart, the love that we see and feel for God and for aspiring humanity is spontaneous. We cannot separate the heart's consciousness or the psychic consciousness from spontaneity. We cannot say that a seeker *must* love God, but we can easily say that a sincere, genuine seeker *will* love God, for God Himself is all Love.

159. Forgiveness

Forgiveness means the freedom of the mind, the bliss of the heart, the oneness of the soul.

FIFTY FREEDOM-BOATS TO ONE GOLDEN SHORE

NOTES TO FIFTY FREEDOM-BOATS TO ONE GOLDEN SHORE, BOOK 4

108. Student Union Theatre, University of Arkansas, Fayetteville, Arkansas, 6 March 1974 — 12:00 noon.
109. Great Hall, Westby Student Center, University of Tulsa, Tulsa, Oklahoma, 6 March 1974 — 4:00 pm.
111. Room 104, Student Center, Southern Methodist University, Dallas, Texas, 7 March 1974 — 9:00 am.
113. The Center for Religion and Life, University of Nevada, Reno, Nevada, 17 April 1974 — 2:00 pm.
114. Memorial Chapel, Stanford University, Stanford, California, 19 April 1974 — 8:00 pm.
116. Portland State University, Portland, Oregon, 22 April 1974 — 10:00 am.
117. Hughes Auditorium, Gonzaga University, Spokane, Washington, 22 April 1974 — 4:00 pm.
118. Administration Building, North Idaho Junior College, Coeur d'Alene, Idaho, 22 April 1974 — 7:30 pm.
119. Montana Rooms, The Student Center, University of Montana, Missoula, Montana, 23 April 1974 — 9:30 am.
121. The Physics Building, University of Colorado, Boulder, Colorado, 23 April 1974 — 9:00 pm.
123-127. Student Union Theatre, University of Arkansas, Fayetteville, Arkansas, 6 March 1974 — 12:00 noon.
128-130. Great Hall, Westby Student Center, University of Tulsa, Tulsa, Oklahoma, 6 March 1974 — 4:00 pm.
131-133. Room 104, Student Center, Southern Methodist University, Dallas, Texas, 7 March 1974 — 9:00 am.
134-137. The Center for Religion and Life, University of Nevada, Reno, Nevada, 17 April 1974 — 2:00 pm.
138-142. Memorial Chapel, Stanford University, Stanford, California, 19 April 1974 — 8:00 pm.
143-146. Portland State University, Portland, Oregon, 22 April 1974 — 10:00 am.

147-149. Administration Building, North Idaho Junior College, Coeur d'Alene, Idaho, 22 April 1974 — 7:30 pm.
150-153. Montana Rooms, The Student Center, University of Montana, Missoula, Montana, 23 April 1974 — 9:30 am.
154-158. The Physics Building, University of Colorado, Boulder, Colorado, 23 April 1974 — 9:00 pm.

FIFTY FREEDOM-BOATS TO
ONE GOLDEN SHORE

BOOK 5

Part XXXVII — Lectures

160. Concentration

Dear seekers, I wish to give a short talk on concentration. In the spiritual life concentration is of paramount importance. Without concentration we cannot make any satisfactory progress. With concentration we can run like a deer. Concentration accelerates our progress towards the Golden Beyond.

> Concentration in the physical is attention.
> Concentration in the vital is penetration.
> Concentration in the mind is observation.
> Concentration in the heart is assimilation.
> Concentration in the soul is illumination.
> Concentration in God is perfection.

Concentration is a seeker's capacity. His capacity is reality, his reality is divinity and his divinity is Immortality.

Concentration is the connecting link between man's aspiration and God's Compassion, between earth's excruciating pangs and Heaven's liberating Smile.

Concentration is at once the power of rejection and the power of acceptance. A seeker, on the strength of his concentration, rejects the superficial body-substance. On the strength of his concentration, the seeker accepts the inner soul-essence. Concentration is the seeker's unfailing companion. It is the seeker's commanding captain and his illumining liberator.

In the morning, when we concentrate on God, we come to realise where God is: God is in the inmost recesses of our hearts. In the afternoon, when we concentrate on God, we come to learn why God exists: He exists precisely for our satisfaction. In the evening, when we concentrate on God, we come to learn who God actually is: God is our unrealised depth; God is our unmanifested height.

Concentration is at once the evolving man's triumphant success and the manifesting God's continuous progress here on earth and there in Heaven.

Man concentrates on God. He fights against his teeming doubts and brooding ignorance; therefore, he is a divine hero-warrior. God concentrates on man. In spite of knowing man's weaknesses, imperfections, limitations and ignorance-night, God concentrates on man with His infinite Love, eternal Compassion and immortal Life; therefore, God is the Supreme Lover.

When we concentrate on the past, the past awakens our sympathy, our concern, our love for our old life. But a seeker of the highest Truth says that the past is dust. He says so precisely because he sees that the past has not given him God-realisation, so he feels that the past is of no avail. But again, the seeker feels that he needs a solid foundation. If the past had something special to offer him and if he still carries that momentous, precious wealth, then that wealth adds to his present capacity.

When this same seeker concentrates on the present, if he has a free access to his heart and soul, then his spiritual journey is safe. But if he still remains most of the time in his mind — his doubting, suspicious mind, his earth-bound physical mind — then this seeker is suspected by the present itself. The present questions his motives for meditating on the present. The present examines his sincerity to see if he really wants to see the face of Reality in the heart of the present.

Finally, the seeker concentrates on the golden future. This future is in the immediacy of today's aspiration and tomorrow's realisation. The future tells the seeker that in today's heart God is his Dream-boat, and in tomorrow's heart God will be his Reality-shore.

Concentration has two brothers: meditation and contemplation. Concentration paves the way for the seeker to walk along the path. This path is sunlit, for concentration does not permit any shadow of doubt, any iota of thought to enter in as we proceed to our transcendental Goal. Meditation makes our mind calm and quiet and empties our heart so that the Inner Pilot can have free access to His Throne. Contemplation tells the seeker to play the cosmic Game together with the Supreme Pilot. Concentration is the first rung on the ladder of highest realisation. Meditation is the second rung on the ladder of highest realisation. Contemplation is the last rung on the ladder of highest, supreme realisation.

Each seeker has a specific way to concentrate. Each seeker has a specific thing to concentrate on. Each seeker has a specific way to offer his concentration-power to the world at large, to aspiring humanity. Each seeker has the power of concentration to give constant, dedicated, devoted and unconditional service to God.

161. What has life taught me?

Dear seekers, dear sisters and brothers, I wish to give a short talk on the subject "What has life taught me?" Life has taught me that there are many people on earth who see God in everybody and everything. In God's creation they see nothing but God. Therefore, they exist only for God. Each living breath of theirs they offer to the loving God.

There are some people who live on earth only for others.

They are not fully aware of God's existence in others; but they feel that if they can live for others, then their life of selfishness, narrowness and meanness will disappear. They live for others, not because they see God in others, but because they feel that they will derive satisfaction in life only by offering their service to others. Service, dedicated service, is for them satisfaction in its purest form.

Then, there are others who live only for themselves. For them there is no God, there are no other human beings, save and except themselves.

As an individual, I can live for God, I can live for others, I can live for myself. When I live for God, only for God — God the Creator and God the creation — then I feel that I am doing absolutely the right thing. Therefore, I am perfect.

When I live for others, that is to say, when I expand and extend my consciousness, then I feel that I am doing a divine thing that will elevate the consciousness, illumine the minds and fulfil the needs of others. Therefore, I am divine.

But when I live only for myself, to aggrandise my ego and fulfil my teeming desires, and when I ignore my countless imperfections, limitations and bondage, at that time I am nothing short of imperfection, limitation, bondage and death. I feel that I am of myself and for myself. I sing the song of ego, the song of my own self-centred consciousness. Each second, consciously and deliberately I dig my own grave. At that time, divinity and perfection remain a far cry.

There are various places for us to live. We can live in the body, we can live in the vital, we can live in the mind, we can live in the heart, we can live in the soul. When we live in the body, the gross physical body, we enjoy nothing but sleep, inertia, sloth and fun — life's continuous fun. When we live in the physical, a life of pleasure, we feel, is the life of reality for us.

When we live in the vital, the unaspiring vital, we feel that aggression is what we want and need. Unfortunately, what looms large in aggression is destruction, and before we destroy others we see that we are totally destroyed. Before we try to realise what we have actually done, we feel that our days are numbered, as a matter of fact, that we are already dead. The unaspiring vital identifies us with Julius Caesar, who said, *Veni, vidi, vici,* "I came, I saw, I conquered." But what have we conquered? We have conquered the very things that have to be utilised for God: love, faith, sincerity, humility. These divine things we have conquered in order to lord it over others. Our unaspiring vital conquers others' good qualities and tries to dominate others.

When we live in the mind, the reasoning mind, we feel there is nothing but reason and doubt. We feel that by using the reasoning mind, one day we shall arrive at the truth. But that is impossible. Truth is far beyond the reasoning mind. We feel that if we doubt others and if we doubt the existence of God, that means we are in a position to judge God's creation. But the sincere seeker in us knows that doubt is slow poison. If we doubt others, we gain nothing. If we doubt God, we gain nothing. And the moment we doubt ourselves, which we do quite often, we ruin all our possibilities and destroy the divine potentiality within us.

When we live in the heart, the aspiring heart, we get constant confidence, we feel that we have a Source. This Source is Light infinite, Delight eternal. We can sing with the Indian sages, the seers of the hoary past: *Ānandādd hy eva khalv imāni bhutāni jāyante* ... "From Delight we came into existence. In Delight we grow. At the end of our journey's close, into Delight we retire." Because we feel that God the infinite Supreme is our Source, we feel that we also have the opportunity to become the Infinite and to spread the Light of Infinity throughout the length and breadth of the world.

Some are of the opinion that hands are hands, head is head and heart is heart, that they cannot be combined. But I wish to say that this is not true. Since the hands are God's creation, since the head is God's creation, since the heart is God's creation, they have to be combined. With the heart we shall feel God's transcendental Peace and infinite Bliss. With the mind we shall discover the world of the yet-unknown. And with the hands we shall serve what we know and what we can feel. What we know is God's constant message: "Do good; be good." What we can feel is that God is all Love. What we serve is God the Smile. God's Smile we serve here on earth and aspiring humanity accepts this service from us, from the seekers of the infinite, eternal Truth.

Here we are all seekers. In the life of a seeker, quality comes first, without fail; then comes quantity. Quality comes from God; quantity also comes from God. If a seeker has the inner cry and if God comes to him with His descending Light, if Grace comes from Heaven and aspiration comes from earth, when they meet together quality can be multiplied into quantity. Again, quantity can also be transformed into quality.

Here on earth our life is a constant battle; we are always in the battlefield of life. Even unaspiring human beings are constantly struggling for survival. They are trying to satisfy their animal needs and their human needs. When they are struggling, that means they are fighting against something in order to achieve what they need or want. Aspiring seekers also constantly fight. Fight against whom? Against their own nature, against their doubt and fear, against anxiety, worry and imperfection. At the end of their journey they will be crowned with triumphant success.

Life is acceptance and life is rejection. The human in us rejects the divine, but the divine accepts the human. The finite in us is afraid of the Infinite. It feels that if it enters into the ocean of Infinity, then Infinity will devour its existence. It is ready to stand forever on the shore. But the divine in us knows well that life is meant for acceptance. The finite in us has to be accepted and then it has to be transformed into Infinity. If we have an iota of a good thought, an iota of a loving thought, then we have to increase it into Infinity. The divine in us tells us that it is in the finite that we will have to hear the song of Infinity. As we hear the song of Infinity in Eternity, Immortality and Infinity itself, even so we shall have to hear and finally sing the song of Infinity in the finite here on earth.

Life has taught me to go ahead. This is the aspiring life. The moment we have covered one step, we see that our loving Father runs towards us ninety-nine steps. This is an experience that a sincere seeker of the ultimate Truth is bound to have. But if one is not a seeker, then the undivine forces, the hostile forces will tempt him to dine with ignorance. And ignorance means unconscious or conscious destruction.

Life has taught me how to forget, how to forgive and how to unlearn. There are many things that I have to forget. If I don't forget, then my life becomes a sea of excruciating pangs. Again, there are many things that I have to forgive. If I don't forgive, then I feel the load of my whole body right on my head; I feel a heavy load of world-imperfection, which I am part and parcel of. The moment I forgive, I unload the heavy load. Then, I have to unlearn. There are many things the mind has taught me which are fruitless, useless, futile. When I just keep them, not to speak of treasuring them, then I feel that I am extremely heavy and I cannot run the fastest towards the Golden Shore. If I unlearn, I become light. And if I become light, I can run like a deer.

Life has taught me something else most significant: that self-importance must be cast aside. Let me try to think and feel sincerely that I am not at all indispensable. Who is indispensable? God. When I feel that I am not indispensable, at that time out of His infinite bounty God inundates my inner being with Joy, Love and Bliss. If I need Peace, if I need Love, if I need anything worth achieving, then I can have it only when I serve God lovingly, devotedly, unconditionally and with the feeling of humility, with the feeling that I am not at all indispensable. Today God is using me as a seeker. Tomorrow He can utilise somebody else as a seeker of the highest Truth. As long as He uses me as a seeker, I have to seek the highest Truth. As long as He uses me as a servitor, I shall serve mankind. But I am in no way indispensable, either on earth or in Heaven. When I have that kind of realisation, God can utilise me in His own inimitable Way. At that time I become His perfect, chosen instrument, a faithful, devoted, soulful and unconditional instrument of the Absolute Supreme.

162. Humanity's teachers

Dear seekers of the highest Truth, dear sisters and brothers, just because we are all seekers, we are all sailing in the boat of aspiration. At God's choice Hour we shall reach our destination: the Golden Shore.

Each human being has two teachers — desire and aspiration. Desire tells man to bind the world. It says, "You want joy; you want satisfaction. In order to achieve joy and satisfaction, you must possess the world." But alas, while you are trying to possess and bind the world, you see that the world has already bound you. Man's other teacher is aspiration. Aspiration lovingly and soulfully tells him, "My son, do not bind the world; do not try to attach it to you. Just try to free yourself and liberate the world." How can you liberate the world? You can liberate the world on the strength of the expansion of your own consciousness. When you expand your physical consciousness, vital consciousness, mental consciousness and psychic consciousness, lo and behold, the world within you is expanded and the world outside you is expanded.

The teacher aspiration tells man that when he liberates the world on the strength of his own inner expansion, God offers him His transcendental Smile. God makes him His divine instrument. God makes him His direct representative here on earth.

A human being has two other teachers: doubt and faith. Doubt tells him that there is nothing real enough. It says, "Where is the proof that God exists? It is all mental hallucination; therefore, you should doubt! Doubt God, doubt yourself, doubt all human beings!" While doubting God, while doubting himself, while doubting mankind, the human being becomes one with the physical mind. First the physical mind doubts God and humanity, then it starts doubting its own capacity. If we doubt God, no harm. God does not lose His Infinity, Eternity and Immortality. If we doubt others, they also lose nothing; they maintain their capacity. But when we doubt our own existence, our own capacity, our own possibility, at that moment we dig our own grave.

The teacher faith tells the seeker in each individual, "Have faith in God, have faith in yourself." Now what is this faith? Faith is the inner light that conquers ignorance-night. Faith is the light within us that constantly reminds us of our Source. Our Source is Delight. Thousands of years ago, the Vedic seers of the hoary past offered a sublime message which I would like to share with you: *Ānandādd hy eva khalv imāni bhutāni jāyante...* "From Delight we came into existence. In Delight we grow. At the end of our journey's close, into Delight we retire."

Man has two more teachers: Heaven and earth. Heaven teaches us how to dream the transcendental Dream and earth teaches us how to embody, reveal and manifest the divine Reality. Heaven is the Dream-boat and earth is the Reality-Shore. Our inner cry is the connecting link between Heaven's Dream and earth's Reality. The inner cry is our spontaneous personal effort. Earth offers its excruciating pangs to Heaven and Heaven offers its transcendental Smile to earth. When Heaven's Smile and earth's cry meet, our imperfection becomes perfect Perfection.

We have still two other teachers: love and surrender, love divine and surrender divine. Love tells the seeker, "Love the world because the world is the real reality; the Creator and His creation cannot be separated. If you love the creation, you are loving the Creator, and if you love the Creator, you must love His creation at the same time. Love mankind and love the Inner Pilot inside mankind. When you love man in God, I will show you the Body of God. When you love God in man, I will show you the Face of God." The seeker soulfully listens to the advice of love the teacher offers and sees both the Body and the Face of God. Then surrender comes and says, "I don't want you to be satisfied with what you have already seen. I want you to see something more. I want you to see God's Heart and God's Soul. You have seen the Body and the Face; now you will see the Heart and the Soul. Then you will have seen everything. You can see God's Heart and Soul on the strength of your self-giving, on the strength of your unconditional surrender." The seeker listens to this advice and he sees the Heart and Soul of God. At that time he becomes the Heart of God and he becomes the Soul of God. Then the divine lover and the supreme Beloved are forever united.

163. Realisation

Dear sisters and brothers, we are all seekers, seekers of the transcendental Truth; therefore, we are sailing in the same boat. In the spiritual life realisation is our first goal, revelation is our second goal and manifestation is our third goal. Today I wish to give a short talk on realisation.

To ordinary human beings, realisation is an ideal and nothing more. To unaspiring human beings, realisation is something useless and harmful. They consider it useless because they can remain on earth without it. They feel it is a mental hallucination. They consider it harmful because it is something strange. Now they are enjoying ignorance and they have become part and parcel of ignorance. They feel their earth-bound consciousness will burst into pieces when the realisation-sun dawns. They are afraid that the realisation-light will expose them. But a sincere seeker, a lover of Truth transcendental, knows that the spiritual life will never expose his imperfections. It will only illumine and perfect him.

Realisation is a slow and steady process: It is like going up a hill. We cannot achieve realisation in the twinkling of an eye. Getting realisation is not like getting instant coffee. We have to pray for realisation every day, every hour, every second. The mind that indulges in relaxation is not meant for realisation. The heart that indulges in vacation is not meant for realisation. Our mind needs vigilance and discipline. Our heart needs regularity and enthusiasm.

Realisation is like a tree. One individual can come right up to the tree and touch the bottom branches. Another can climb part way up the tree. Someone else can climb up to the top of the tree, if his aspiration is most intense. Naturally, the realisation of the person who climbs to the top of the tree surpasses the realisation of the others.

In order to realise God, we need aspiration, the inner mounting cry. This world is governed by two mighty powers: desire and aspiration. Desire-power binds us. Aspiration-power expands us. Desire-power makes us feel that we are of the finite. Aspiration-power makes us feel we are of the Infinite. Our aspiration has to be intense. When we aspire unconditionally and soulfully, we minimise our earthly needs and increase our capacity to receive the infinite Peace and Bliss.

A real seeker every day feels the necessity of aspiration. He feels that his realisation will one day loom large in his aspiration. But his aspiration depends on God's Grace, God's unconditional Grace. This Grace eventually enables the seeker to dive deep within to discover Peace, Light and Bliss in infinite measure. Before realisation the seeker thought that his personal effort was ninety-nine per cent responsible for his achievement and God's Compassion was one per cent responsible. After his realisation he sees that the reverse is true: his personal effort was only one per cent responsible and God's Compassion was ninety-nine per cent responsible. Then he looks around and sees his dear ones, his relatives, his acquaintances still wallowing in the pleasures of ignorance. How is it, he asks himself, that he was chosen? Who made him cry for the inner Light? It was his Inner Pilot. Who wanted him to wake up and run along the sunlit path to realise his eternal Beloved, the Supreme? It was the Supreme Himself. Finally, when he starts assimilating his realisation, in the process of his assimilation he comes to realise in an unmistakable way that even his one per cent personal effort was nothing short of God's Grace. He realises that it was God's boundless Compassion which was fully responsible for his God-realisation.

There are three brothers who help us considerably in our life of aspiration: concentration, meditation and contemplation. It is their help that eventually leads us to God-realisation.

What is concentration? Concentration is our one-pointed attention or focus on a particular subject or object.

What is meditation? Meditation is the act of emptying our inner vessel and filling it with God's Light and Delight.

What is contemplation? Contemplation is the inseparable union of lover and Beloved.

When we concentrate we try to put an end to our thought-waves. When we concentrate we try to minimise our earthly needs and to extinguish the desire-flame in us.

When we meditate we try to grow in silence; we try to become receptive so that the Lord Supreme can place His divine Throne in the inmost recesses of our heart. When we contemplate we try to become one with our Inner Pilot and surrender our tiny "i" to the universal "I".

Concentration tells us, "Run, run towards the Goal!" Meditation tells us, "The Goal is inside you. In perfect silence you will discover your Goal." Contemplation tells us, "Go on, dive deeper, fly higher. You will realise that the Goal is none other than your own highest part, your own most illumined existence."

In our life of aspiration we feel the necessity of devoted service and surrendered oneness: devoted service to the Inner Pilot and surrendered oneness with our Inner Pilot. Our devoted service is not an act of outer compulsion. No! It is an inner urge that compels us to be one with the Inner Pilot and to serve

Him soulfully and devotedly.

Right now the Goal is ahead of us. We have to reach the Goal soulfully, devotedly and unconditionally. But our road can be shortened if we have divine love, divine devotion and divine surrender. Our road can be sunlit if we cheerfully offer to God what we have and what we are. What we have is a constant and conscious inner cry. And what we are right now is a sea of ignorance. So if we can give to God what we have and what we are, then our road becomes sunlit and short.

Time is a great factor in our journey to realisation. There are people who say that since God is living in His eternal Time and we are His children, then we can also live in eternal Time. So why do we have to worry about God-realisation? God-realisation can take place in its own time. But if we love God, if we love mankind, then we feel the necessity of devoted, dedicated and unconditional service. If we are not awakened, how can we awaken others? If we are not realised, how can we help others in their realisation? A sincere seeker feels that he can be God's chosen child, His perfect instrument, only after he has realised God. God will grant us realisation, true. But we can expedite His offering, His gift to us. His blessingful gift we can achieve sooner if we sincerely and soulfully aspire. The sooner we achieve God-realisation, the sooner we can prepare ourselves for God-revelation and finally for God-manifestation.

God-realisation is our preparation for God revelation and God-revelation is our preparation for God-manifestation. What is preparation? Preparation is our self-giving and God's Self-giving. Our self-giving is all ignorance, limitation, bondage. God's Self-giving is all Compassion.

A seeker knows and feels that he can live without food, without water, without air, without everything on earth, but he cannot live without God's Compassion. God's Compassion is the seeker's Immortality. When he starts drinking the nectar of this Immortality, then he realises himself. When he realises himself, he feels that in and through him God is manifesting His highest Reality, that God is singing His Song of Eternity and dancing His Dance of Immortality. When a seeker drinks Ambrosia, he feels that Heaven is not somewhere else. Heaven is in his consciousness. We do not have to go to a particular state or country or kingdom called Heaven. No! Heaven, which is perpetual Life, the infinite Life within us, is a state of consciousness. This consciousness an aspiring seeker is bound to attain when he drinks Nectar. And this Nectar he gets on the strength of his self-giving, his unconditional self-giving. Today's self-giving is tomorrow's God-becoming.

164. Wisdom-Light

Dear sisters and brothers, dear seekers of the infinite Truth and Light, I wish to give a short talk on wisdom-light.

Wisdom-light is life-loving. Wisdom-light is self-giving. Wisdom-light is God-becoming.

He who loves life is beautiful. He who gives himself to others is fruitful. He who becomes God — like the Christ, Lord Buddha and Sri Krishna — is complete, perfect and supreme.

Why does one love? One loves because he knows that loving is self-expansion. Why does one give himself to others? He gives himself to others because he knows that in self-giving is the real satisfaction. Why does one want to become God? He wants to become God because he knows that God-becoming is perfect Perfection.

Our heart embodies the message of self-expansion. Our life embodies the message of satisfaction. Our soul embodies the message of perfection. In Heaven the message is the light of Divinity. On earth the message is the night of Eternity. In God the message is the delight of Immortality.

When we pray, Divinity blesses us. When we meditate, Eternity blesses us. When we surrender our earth-bound life to the adamantine Will of the Absolute Supreme, we become the delight of Immortality.

Divinity, Eternity and Immortality. Divinity we already had. Eternity we already have. Immortality we are in the process of becoming.

God's Vision and God's Reality we embody together. Our earthly existence is the transformed Vision of God manifested in living reality. Each vision is a seed of the reality-tree. Each form of reality is the tree which is embodied in the vision-seed. Silence-cry is the soul of the vision-seed. Sound-smile is the body of the reality-tree.

Each human being has a seeker and a lover in the inmost recesses of his heart. The seeker in him wants to reach the Highest, the transcendental Height, and then wants to come down to transform the teeming ignorance of earthly life and make of earth a Kingdom of Heaven. The lover in him wants to spread his universal wings and satisfy the inner hunger of millennia the hunger that can be fulfilled only by God's infinite Love, Compassion and Light.

The seeker in each human being is the collector and the receiver of God's Light. The lover in him is the distributor of God's Light to the world at large.

Wisdom-light is the awareness of God's Presence all-where, the awareness that God is omnipresent. This reality we can be aware of only when we see God within and without. There is an Indian parable about a spiritual teacher who offered a fruit to each of his disciples. He said to them, "Children, go and eat your fruit unseen by anybody at all. You must eat your fruit in complete privacy." Each went and ate his respective fruit except one. That one came back to the Master with his fruit. The Master asked him, "How is it that you have not eaten your fruit?" The disciple answered, "Master, how can I eat? You have asked me to eat the fruit only when there is nobody observing me. But God is all around me, so I have not eaten. If I eat, I will be caught red-handed." The Master was exceedingly pleased with this disciple.

From this parable we learn that a sincere seeker of the transcendental Truth sees and feels God both within and without. There also dawns in him a higher and deeper vision. He comes to realise that he is expected to say and do to the world at large only those things that can be said and done before God. Today's world of imperfection can easily be transformed into a world of perfect Perfection when the seeker in us sees God everywhere.

The motto of the State of Florida is, "In God we trust." For an ordinary seeker this loftiest message may seem redundant, for since we are all lovers of the highest Truth and Light, it goes without saying that we trust in God. But from the spiritual point of view I wish to say that there is a significant hidden truth inside this motto. This freedom-loving country has something significant to offer to the world at large. When we live an ordinary life, we place our trust in ourselves. When we have faith in ourselves, we sing the song of separativity and individuality, the song of "I". At that time the question of "we" never arises. But when we say, "In God we trust," our individuality merges into the sea of universality. On the strength of our inner cry we are trying to grow into God's Universality. When a seeker says, "In God we trust," he feels that his individuality has left him. He has now embraced God's entire creation as his own, very own.

A seeker trusts God and God trusts him. A seeker trusts God in order to reach the highest pinnacle of Light, Truth and Bliss, and God trusts him in order to reveal Himself and manifest Himself on earth. They enjoy a reciprocal need. The seeker needs God for his self-discovery and life-mastery and God needs the seeker for His perfect manifestation and complete satisfaction on earth.

Part XXXVIII — Questions and answers — University of Wyoming

165. Question: In learning to concentrate, what forms of self-discipline do you use? Sometimes it seems that learning self-discipline is selfish.

Sri Chinmoy: Not at all! Self-discipline is not at all selfish. If I do not discipline myself, if I do not pray and meditate, then how am I going to be of any use to the world or to God? If I pray and meditate, it does not mean that I am neglecting humanity. That is wrong. But there are various ways to offer our dedicated service to humanity. When we pray and meditate, we enter into the root of the life-tree. The root of the life-tree is God, and the branches are all the human beings. If we do not water the root, then how are we going to nourish the leaves on the branches? If we do not start at the foot of the tree, how are we going to climb up the tree and reach all the branches? When I pray and meditate, I feel that I am radiating something that I have just received from God: Peace, Light and Bliss. These are the very things that my colleagues, my friends, my relatives, my dear ones desperately need. I am meditating in one corner of the room, but while I am meditating, I am giving inwardly to others what

I am receiving from above. If this is not a form of service, then what else is service?

You may think that service is only outer help, but this is not true. Outer help is necessary, but inner help is more important. If somebody is poor, I may give him a dollar because I have money and I am generous. But tomorrow, again he will need money and he will have to go to someone else, and also the day after tomorrow. But if light enters into me during my meditation, then I will be able to inspire him and help him permanently. I will inwardly say to him, "Why are you wallowing in the pleasures of lethargy-ignorance? You are strong. Go and work!" Or God will listen to my prayer and in some way or other He will remove that person's poverty, if it is His Will.

There are many ways to be of service to mankind. The outer way is one way, but the inner way is also most effective. And sometimes, the inner way is more effective than the outer way, for if we help someone in an outer way, again and again he will have the same problem. But if we can go to the core of the problem and help the person who is suffering in an inner way, then his problem will be illumined for good, and he will not have to suffer from it again.

166. Question: What does it mean to please God in His own Way?

Sri Chinmoy: We love God because we feel that He is all Love. Just because we love God, we feel that it is our bounden duty to devote ourselves to Him and please Him. But we see that our love and service are not enough; surrender is also necessary. If we do not surrender our individual will to His Will, we will make many mistakes when we try to love Him and serve Him in the way He has chosen for us, which is the right way.

I am a spiritual teacher. If a student of mine happened to be here, he might notice that there are no flowers near me. He might think, "The best thing is for me to bring him some flowers." Now, this student wants to please me by bringing me flowers, because he knows that a spiritual Master always appreciates flowers. But suppose I am thirsty, and right now I need water more than I need flowers. If my student tries to please me by bringing me flowers, he will be pleasing me in his own way, because what I actually wanted from him was something else. In God's case also, unless we surrender to God's Will, we will try to please Him in our way. We may think that if we do this, then God will be extremely pleased with us. But how do we know that God wants us to do that thing? He may want something else from us.

In the spiritual life, when we please God in His own Way, unconditionally, then we will feel really satisfied, for in His satisfaction is our satisfaction. Many people try to derive satisfaction from the fulfilment of their desires. But when one desire is fulfilled, another desire looms large. In the fulfilment of desire there is no satisfaction, only constant greed, constant need. But if we enter into the life of aspiration, we want to reach the Highest to fulfil and manifest God. But how can we reach the Highest unless and until the Highest pulls us towards Itself? It is the Compassion-Light of the Supreme that elevates our consciousness and lifts us up. This takes place only when our surrender is complete.

Our surrender to God has to be unconditional. We will give God what we have and what we are, which is ignorance. If we can give our ignorance to God unconditionally and permanently, then God can fulfil Himself in and through us. Unfortunately, one day we want to get rid of our ignorance and the next day, when our aspiration is not strong, we cherish and treasure our ignorance. But if we can totally and unconditionally surrender our ignorance, which is our coveted possession, to God, then it will not come back. At that time, we will get total satisfaction from our life, and we will truly be pleasing God in His own Way.

167. Question: Do you see any way one could assimilate the way of living you are speaking about into the American culture?

Sri Chinmoy: Certainly. I have about eight hundred disciples. They are assimilating my thoughts, my ideas, my experiences. They are following our path — the path of love, devotion and surrender — and while walking along this path, they are assimilating what I am offering to them. Our path is the path of acceptance. It is not the path of rejection or renunciation. We accept life as such, and then we try to transform the face of ignorance into the face of light. We do not neglect, we do not negate anything. We accept, but while accepting, we know the limitations of the thing that we are accepting. Again, these limitations we must not take as somebody else's limitations. We take them as our own limitations, as our own shortcomings. Then we pray and meditate. When we pray and meditate, the light descends and, with our inner light, we transform the ignorance that we see within and without.

Part XXXIX — Questions and answers — University of Utah

168. Question: Sometimes when I talk to others, my mind sees a duality. In the act of trying to see the good in others, I feel a separation. What do you recommend?

Sri Chinmoy: The difficulty is that if you try to see good in others with your mind, you will see good for only one minute. Then the next minute you will try to see bad in them as well. And even when you do see good in others, you will doubt whether you have seen good; you will not know whether what you have seen is really good or bad. You want to see goodness in your friend and you do see it. But the next moment doubt will come and make you say, "Is it really good? Perhaps I am fooling myself."

But if you want to *feel* goodness in others, then please use your heart. The heart immediately identifies with the consciousness, with the essence of a person or thing. Our philosophy is the philosophy of identification. From identification we enter into oneness, inseparable oneness. First we identify ourselves with the Reality; then we feel that we are constantly, inseparably one with the Reality. In the case of the mind, the mind may see the Reality, but then the mind doubts the Reality.

If you use the mind you may say, "Today's lecturer is a good man." Then you start doubting. Before you leave the church you may say, "No, he is a very bad man." Then, after going a few steps, you may say, "Am I right? Was I right in judging him?" First I am good, then I am bad. But whatever I am, whether I am good or bad, your judgement does not affect me in any way. If I am good, I am good; if I am bad, I am bad. I do not lose anything when you doubt me. But the moment you doubt yourself, you have lost everything. By doubting others and by doubting yourself, you never get any sense of satisfaction. But by becoming one with the thing that you love, you get real satisfaction. Now, if you use your heart and if your heart says I am good, at that time you become one with me. And if you feel that I am a bad man, then immediately you will reject me. Then you will use the capacity of your heart to establish your identification and oneness with someone else.

In our path we always try to give importance to the heart first. Then we give importance to the mind. What has the light? The soul has the light. And where is the soul? The soul is inside the heart. Right now the heart has more light than the mind. This is what we feel and what we know. But the mind will not remain always unlit, obscure. Eventually we have to bring the same light into the mind. Otherwise, the doubting mind, the suspecting mind will never leave us.

Right now let us use the heart-room and remain in the heart-room as much as we can. And once our inner being is surcharged with light, then let us enter into the mind-room. At that time, the mind-room will be illumined. We have to illumine the mind-room, we have to illumine the vital-room, we have to illumine the physical-room. But let us do the first thing first. Let the light descend from above into the heart and from the heart into the mind. Let us not try to reverse the course. If we try to deal first with the mind, then no matter how many hours or how many years we stay in the unlit mind-room, the mind-room is not going to be illumined.

169. Question: What is the power that brings down God's Presence in all our actions and allows us to feel our oneness with God?

Sri Chinmoy: There are two powers that bring down God into all our actions and multifarious activities. One power is our gratitude-power. Always we have to offer our gratitude to God for everything that we do, for everything that we have become. The other power is the power of seeing God in others. If we don't see God in others, if we only see God in ourselves, then we will not be successful. We have to see divinity inside everybody, even inside our worst enemy. As a matter of fact, a spiritual person should not have any enemies. But suppose we have not yet become totally spiritual and we still say we have an enemy. Now let us say our enemy is doubt, our enemy is fear, our enemy is anxiety, our enemy is bondage. Let us see inside our enemy the Presence of God. Let us go deep within and from there bring out our capacity of identification with God. Let us try to see also in our enemy God's Presence. God's Presence is everywhere. But if we deny His Presence inside a particular thing, then that thing will eventually attack.

Right now God's Presence is not sufficiently operating in the mind, whereas inside the heart it is operating most powerfully. So from where it is operating most powerfully we have to carry it elsewhere. Everyone and everything has a soul. Even a bench has a soul. If we can feel the presence of the soul inside the bench, then we will never feel that we are without God. Now we have to know whose soul is more developed: our soul or the soul of the bench. Since our soul is more developed, we can enter into the consciousness of the bench.

So there are two powers that can keep us always one, inseparably one with God's Reality. One is our constant offering of gratitude. We feel that if He had not given us the capacity of receptivity, then we could not have become what we are now. The other power is the power to see in others the things that we see inside ourselves. If we see and feel that we are God's instrument, then we have to feel that he and she are equally God's instruments. In this way we can feel that God is constantly operating in and through us. Then we remain in the same highest level of consciousness while participating in God's cosmic Game.

You are all most sincere seekers. Nothing gives me greater joy than to be of dedicated service to the sincere seekers. I came into the world to be of dedicated service to mankind. I am God's child and I am serving Him in my capacity. You are also God's children in the cosmic Play. According to his capacity each individual will serve God. My capacity is to be of dedicated service to the sincere seekers who need inspiration. From inspiration one can get aspiration, and aspiration is the harbinger of realisation in our inner life.

170. Question: Will you accept me as your student?

Sri Chinmoy: May I tell you what our path is, so that you can be more convinced of what you are jumping into. Our path is the path of love, devotion and surrender. We love God, we devote ourselves to God and we surrender our will to God's Will.

This is the approach that we follow in our path. This is the realisation that I have had and am trying to share with my students. We have about fifty Centres all over the world and my students and I are trying to share with the aspiring souls the experience of love divine, devotion divine and surrender divine.

We feel that love, devotion and surrender are the three rungs in our ladder of evolution. We start with divine love. In human love we notice that we try to possess others; but before we possess, we are possessed. There is no sense of satisfaction either in possessing or in being possessed. While we are possessing we are only limiting our capacity; we are binding our reality. But in the divine love we constantly expand our reality. From the finite we try to enter into the Infinite. Constant expansion is the message of divine love.

In the ordinary life, if we love someone we spend time with that person and devote ourselves to him. But since we love God, it is to God that we have to devote ourselves, to God alone. We feel that there is nothing on earth which can be as sweet or as fulfilling as devoted service to God in seeking to devote ourselves to God, we come to realise that at times we serve Him according to our own understanding, according to our own light. We feel that if we do *this,* then God will be pleased with us; if we do *that,* then God will not be pleased with us. Finally, we come to realise that we know next to nothing about God's operation in and through us. At that time we surrender our will to God's Will. We tell God, "Lord, You guide our will. You manifest Yourself in and through us. We want only to be receptive." So we sing the song of receptivity. Our heart becomes full of receptivity and God offers His Capacity — which is Infinity, Eternity and Immortality — to our devoted, loving receptivity.

This surrender is not forced upon us. A slave surrenders to his master out of compulsion. He is at the beck and call of his master; he is at the very mercy of his master. But in God's case, He does not treat us in that way. He shows us His infinite Compassion. He is eternally kind. It is we who have the hunger for His Nectar, His Ambrosia, and we feel that if we can surrender our will to His Will, then we can accelerate our progress.

We have quite a few things to do on earth. We have not one goal, but three successive goals on earth. Our first goal is to realise God. Our second goal is to reveal Him in our action, in our dedicated service. And our third goal is to manifest Him in our life here on earth. It takes such a long time to reach even our first goal, God-realisation. Therefore, we feel that if there is a sunlit path, a shorter path, we want to walk along it. This sunlit path is the path of the heart. When the heart accepts something or someone, it accepts on the strength of its identification. And this identification eventually is transformed into inseparable oneness. When we become one with our Inner Pilot, His Will is executed in and through us. At that time, we feel real satisfaction. There is no other way of achieving real satisfaction other than by fulfilling Him in His own Way. Here on earth and there in Heaven, we exist only for one thing: satisfaction. And our satisfaction comes only from God's satisfaction.

This is our path: love, devotion and surrender. If you wish to follow our path, I will wholeheartedly welcome you to our little spiritual family.

171. Question: I've found in my search for God that He is all around me and within me. The unity with Him is becoming very understandable. What is puzzling me is the separation. What is the sense of separation?

Sri Chinmoy: If you see and feel Him around you and within you, then how can you have a sense of separation? Inside me is the heart; inside me is the soul. If something is outside my body, then I can have a feeling of separation. But I cannot separate my heart from my body or from myself. Because body and heart are part and parcel of each other and of my life, if I separate the one from the other, then I don't exist at all. If you really feel God within you, then I wish to say that there can be no sense of separation.

What actually happens, let us say, is that this moment you

are living in your heart and you feel God's Presence within you and His Presence looms large. But the next moment, perhaps you are living in the physical mind. At that time you doubt your own existence and you doubt the reality that you have just experienced. When you start doubting, the sense of separativity comes into existence. At that time you feel that you are losing something, that you are separated from something. But you don't lose anything. Once you have got something, it is there within you. But if you don't know how to utilise it all the time at your sweet will, then you feel that you have lost it.

When you pray early in the morning, at that time you feel God's Presence within you and around you. Then, when you enter into the hustle and bustle of life, perhaps you forget God's existence. The moment you forget, you feel a sense of separation. But I wish to say that the sense of separation is not actually caused by the absence of God within you. His Presence is there, but ignorance enters into you and veils your consciousness, which a few hours ago early in the morning helped you identify with God and feel your inseparable oneness with Him.

That is why inwardly we try to remain in constant prayer or meditation. Outwardly it is impossible. We have to stay on earth; we have to go to the office, we have to go to school, we have to enter into multifarious activities. But inside our mind, inside our heart, we can do whatever we want. Outwardly we may talk to our friends, and do everything that is necessary in our day-to-day life, but inside we can keep the living Presence of God. Since we have the soul within us, we feel we are divine; since we have the aspiring heart within us, we feel that we are divine. So also, when we go outside and mix with our friends, we have to remember — not out of pride or vanity, but out of sheer necessity — that we are of the Divine and we are for the Divine.

We have to feel not only the divinity in ourselves, but also the divinity in others. For in this way we can feel our oneness with the Supreme in mankind. One way to feel our oneness with others is to feel that we are everything. But then we may come to think that we are superior to everyone, and that will only ruin our purpose. If we feel that only we are divine, that only we possess divinity whereas others possess undivine forces, then immediately there will be a clash. But if we feel, while we are mixing with others, that we are of the Source, then we shall try also to see the Divine in others. If we feel that we are divine and, while talking and mixing with others, if we can see the Divine in them, then our divinity and their divinity will not quarrel or clash. When we feel that we are divine, it is absolutely true. But at the same time we have to feel that others are also divine, equally divine.

Our difficulty is that most of the time we don't have that kind of feeling. While we are praying at home, we see and feel God; God is ours. But the moment we come out of our house and look around at others, we don't try to see God inside them. What we try to see in them is imperfection, something unlike ourselves. After our meditation, we come out of the heart and enter into the mind, or we enter into the vital. Then we try to separate ourselves from others and we see others as undivine. But when we come out into the world, if we can bring with us the divinity that we saw and felt during our meditation at home, and if we try to see the same divinity in others, then there is no feeling of separation. And if we see the same thing in others which we feel inside ourselves, then we shall never miss God's Presence. We shall never lose our feeling of oneness with God.

Part XL — Questions and answers — Loyola University

172. Question: Do you believe in the cycle of rebirth?

Sri Chinmoy: Yes, I do believe in rebirth, in reincarnation. In the world of aspiration, we know that in one short span of life we cannot realise the Highest, the Absolute. But we also know that God will not allow us to remain unsatisfied. He will give us many opportunities to fulfil ourselves. Whatever we gain in one incarnation, whatever progress we make towards our Goal, will remain inside our soul after we leave the body. Then, after a short rest, our soul will come back with a new body, new vital, new mind to continue our journey and again try to realise and manifest divinity on earth. It is like a candle that goes from one room of the house to another.

Reincarnation is an undeniable fact even within a single life. In one life we see how we can leave the life of desire and be reborn into the life of aspiration. Then comes the life of realisation, then the life of revelation, and then the life of manifestation. So, even in one body we can go through many lives until we have achieved our highest Goal.

173. Question: When we achieve complete oneness with God, do we still see a polarity between good and evil?

Sri Chinmoy: When we are in a state of oneness with God, we cannot say that this is evil and that is good. When we become one with God, everything is a manifestation of the divine Will. But when we are not one with God, then one second we are with God, in God, and for the next hour we are in ourselves — in our own vital, in our own physical consciousness. Then there will always be both undivine and divine forces within and around us. But when we have the deepest type of meditation — the highest, most sublime meditation — at that time we do not see the polarities of good and evil. For then we are one with the transcendental Reality, and this transcends all human notions of good, evil, divine and undivine.

174. Question: Would you explain how we can get one-pointedness and stillness of mind when we have chaos in our thoughts.

Sri Chinmoy: In order to get a vacant mind, a calm mind, you have to focus your concentrated power on a particular subject or object. We feel that the heart is the safest spot. So if you can concentrate on your heart, if you can focus all your concentrated power on your heart, then you will be able to enjoy the calmness, the quietude and the tranquillity of the mind.

175. Question: If we are trying to go beyond the mind, is it only possible with Grace or is there something we can do?

Sri Chinmoy: You have to know that Grace is something we can never understand and will never understand unless and until we have realised God. Personal effort is also God's Grace. I have told you many, many stories about how seekers think it is all personal effort and later come to realise that it was all God's Grace. As long as we are not aware of God's Grace, His constant Grace, we have to use our personal effort as our own creation, own achievement. The best thing is to feel personal effort as our own achievement and then try to go one step higher or deeper.

But if we don't accept it at the very beginning, if we don't make the effort, then we will not enter into any activities at all.

God has been crying for us as individuals to come out of the sea of ignorance. I wish to tell you that God's Grace is responsible for everything, but before we can feel it, it is always advisable to have conscious personal effort. If we don't consciously make a personal effort, then we will never be able to know what God's Grace is. Again, what conscious, personal effort is, we shall know only after we have realised the highest Truth. At that time we shall see that personal effort is nothing but God's hidden Grace. God's hidden Grace is our personal effort.

176. Question: How can we bring intensity into our meditation without bringing it into the physical at the same time?

Sri Chinmoy: In your case, when you meditate you immediately think of a tug-of-war. There is tremendous tension in your forehead, as if your whole body were seated in firmness. But you have to know that the fastest runner runs the fastest on the strength of his co-ordination. The limbs of the body have to be in perfect co-ordination. If he exerts himself beyond necessity, then he loses his balance and he will slow down on the track. When you are meditating, you have to feel that your entire body is slowly, steadily and unerringly climbing up. But in your case, a portion of your mind and a portion of your vital are greedy. Each wants to reach the Highest, leaving aside the other members of the being. In a family there are five members, but one member feels if he can go all by himself before the rest, then he can eat the most. But it is not like that in the spiritual life. In the spiritual life, when all the members go together, only then does God give you the proper feast. Otherwise, He says, "How did you dare to leave the members of your family on the way?" So when you meditate, try to feel that your whole existence is going up. Each time you breathe in, feel a new member of the family is entering into you and when you breathe out, feel that you are lifting up that new member along with your aspiration. Then there can't be tension. Your tension comes because you neglect parts of your being when you meditate. That is wrong. Don't neglect anything. If you do, they will automatically revolt. You will try to pull them in a tug-of-war, but they outnumber you. Take them with you: then there will be no tension at all.

177. Question: In meditation, is it more important to aspire upwards or to become receptive?

Sri Chinmoy: It entirely depends on the seeker. When one is going up, one has to feel that it is the intensity of the prayer that is going up. When it goes up, usually it is the hidden prayer of the seeker that is going up. You may be repeating "Supreme," "Supreme," or something else. No words are necessary, but in a subtle way prayer is going up. This is a subtle form of prayer. Most of the time, it is the prayer aspect hidden in our meditation that takes us up. Meditation, however, is expansion. Meditation receives from above. True, God's Consciousness is everywhere, but when we meditate we feel that God's Consciousness is descending into us; and when we pray, we feel we are climbing up and entering into God's Consciousness. So when we meditate, if we are going up we have to see if there is a subtle prayer inside our meditation. Otherwise, if there is no prayer, we are like a bird spreading his wings. At that time we try to cover the length and breadth of the Universal Consciousness. That is receptivity. Only we have to know what gives us greater joy. If it is climbing, then we will do that, and if it is spreading the wings of our being, we have to try to do that. Both are equally important, but it is a matter of inner joy. If you get more joy in going up, do that; if you get more joy in expanding, then please do that.

Part XLI — Questions and answers — University of New Mexico

178. Question: Do you always sleep at night as you did before you reached cosmic consciousness?

Sri Chinmoy: Yes. Cosmic consciousness and sleep are two different things. Once one has achieved cosmic consciousness he does not lose his cosmic consciousness even in his sleep. It becomes part and parcel of his own existence. Suppose you have an object in your hand. Even while you are fast asleep you can still keep that object in your hand. Similarly, when you have become one with the cosmic consciousness, with Divinity itself, it is within you. But when one achieves the cosmic consciousness or realises God, he does not have to sleep seven or eight hours every night. One or two hours is more than enough for the realised soul. And this rest he takes because he feels sorry for the body, which every day enters into the battlefield of life. If he has students or disciples, he has to enter into their problems consciously and devotedly. Then, his body-consciousness needs and deserves some rest. If he does not sleep, it will not tell upon his health; but he may feel sorry for the physical body. So he will give the body some rest.

Many people sleep out of habit or lethargy. Some people

sleep eight hours, ten hours, eleven hours, twelve hours. But we have to know how much sleep the body actually *needs*, not how much the body *demands*. I wish to say that more than seven hours is not necessary for any individual. In the beginning, if somebody is weak, if he has some physical ailment, then naturally he will take more sleep. But if his health is sound, then seven hours is more than enough for any seeker to start with. If a sincere seeker sleeps more than seven hours, that means he is making friends with ignorance.

Now, in my case, I take a few hours' rest a night — sometimes two hours, sometimes three hours. But sometimes for many nights in a row I will not sleep — not because of my personal problems, but because of the problems of my disciples. I have to solve their problems before the day dawns. Of course these are also my problems, since I have accepted my spiritual students as my own.

The sleep of a God-realised soul is not like the sleep of ordinary people. When ordinary people are sleeping, at that time they are totally oblivious of the world around them. But when a real spiritual Master sleeps for two hours or so, even then he is inseparably one with the soul and the soul's light. The body takes rest, but his meditation is extremely profound. You may stand in front of him and see him snoring, but afterwards he will be able to tell you where he has been and what he has been doing. He will also be able to tell you what has been happening on the physical plane. Even during his sleep he is one with the soul, he is observing and meditating and bringing down Light for the earth-consciousness and for his dear ones, his spiritual children. In the case of a real spiritual Master who has attained the universal consciousness, his sleep is perfectly conscious.

179. Question: How does the Master recognise when one of his disciples is reaching a state of higher consciousness?

Sri Chinmoy: The Master's soul will recognise a higher consciousness in the disciples. If the Master does not know who, else will know? If you are a teacher, then you will know from your own knowledge whether the student is doing well or not. If you are a teacher, that means that you have already acquired some knowledge. You will compare your student's knowledge with your own knowledge, and if his knowledge is near yours, then you will know that he is doing extremely well. But if he is nowhere near you, then you will simply say that he is a beginning student.

180. Question: What do your disciples meditate on?

Sri Chinmoy: My disciples meditate on a picture of me taken in my transcendental consciousness. This picture embodies my highest consciousness.

When I tell my disciples to meditate on my picture, what I actually mean is for them to go deep within and discover the Supreme, who is more active in me than in them. Again, I tell them that when they are concentrating on my picture, they are not concentrating on the physical, not on me as Sri Chinmoy, but on the Supreme in me. The Supreme in me is my Guru, your Guru, everybody's Guru. No human being can be a real Guru. We are all representatives of the Supreme. But the spiritual Master is more conscious of the real Guru, who is the Supreme, than the beginner-seekers.

My disciples feel that I have realised something and that "something" for them is the highest. They feel that I have achieved something, that I am something. I tell them that I am only the elder brother in the family. In a family the elder brother is supposed to know a little more than the younger brothers. That is why his Father has asked him to bring the younger ones to Him. He shows the younger brothers where their Father is and he brings the younger brothers to the Father. Our Father is the Supreme. Once he shows his younger brothers the Father, then his role is over.

Again, I wish to say that one can concentrate and meditate on anything that inspires him. If a flower inspires someone, then let him concentrate on the flower. If a candle flame inspires him, then let him concentrate on it. If burning incense inspires him, let him then concentrate on it. But just because some individuals are my students, they love me most sincerely and devotedly. If you love me more than a flower, more than a candle, then meditate on me — but not on my personality or my individuality, no! The divinity in me is more than eager to be of service to the divinity in my disciples. So when I tell them to concentrate on my picture, it is not my ego-centred "I" that is speaking. It is only my loving oneness with them that tells them, "If you love me, then here is the easiest process for you to approach the One who is all Love. Concentrate on the Supreme within me. And when you discover the Supreme within yourself, you can concentrate and meditate there also." My Supreme and my disciples' Supreme are one. Just because they love me, they meditate on me. I have hundreds of pictures. I don't tell them to meditate on pictures in which I am running or jumping or in my ordinary consciousness. I have no right to ask them to concentrate on these pictures. But there are a few significant pictures taken of me in a very high consciousness. And there is a special picture, my transcendental picture, on which my students concentrate. When they do this, I assure them that they are bound to feel Peace, Light, Bliss or whatever divine qualities they need. They have hundreds of experiences while meditating on my transcendental picture.

181. Question: What is the source of man's suffering?

Sri Chinmoy: If we go deep within, we see that it is the limited "I", the ego, that suffers; the unlimited "I" does not suffer. He who wants to bind reality suffers. But he who wants to free and liberate the reality within himself will not suffer.

Again, we have to know that what we call suffering is not at all suffering in God's Eye. It is an experience that He has in and through us. If we do not remain in God's Consciousness, then naturally if we get a headache we will suffer. But if we live in God's Consciousness, then no matter what kind of disease we have, even if it is a fatal disease, we get tremendous joy because we are one with God's Will. In surrender to His Will there is constant joy. But when we are separated from His Will, no matter what we have, the sense of separativity is suffering itself.

Suffering is not only the feeling that something is wrong or that we have lost something or experienced something unpleasant in our life. No! Real suffering lies in our conscious feeling of separation from God. A seeker's suffering is his feeling of separation from God, from Light. If a seeker has surrendered to God's Will and has established oneness with God, then he does not suffer. No matter what happens in his life, he feels that His Beloved is having an experience in and through him.

182. Question: Is there any difference in your philosophy between a man and a woman?

Sri Chinmoy: No! In my philosophy, man and woman are one. Man and woman are both God's own creation, so there can be no difference. God is manifesting Himself in and through both man and woman. They are like children and God is their divine Father. He offers His children equal Love, equal Concern, equal Compassion, equal Blessings and equal Pride. To my dear ones, to my own men and women disciples, I always give the same opportunity, the same concern. I feel that they are equal; they are one. They are like two eyes. I need both eyes, left and right, if I want to see well. Similarly, if God wants to manifest Himself fully on earth, then He needs the dedicated service and surrendered oneness of both men and women.

183. Question: Is it necessary to come into contact with an enlightened person in order to realise God?

Sri Chinmoy: It is not necessary or obligatory to have a living Master. But if we have a living Master, it may help us considerably. The first person who realised God did it without the help of any human being. God Himself gave him God-realisation. But if we have a living Master, then we have more confidence in ourselves. We are more convinced.

Suppose we had a Master in a previous life. We have to know whether our previous Master was really great and also we have to know what kind of connection we established with the Master during our past incarnation. Each Master has first-class, second-class, third-class, fourth-class, fifth-class, sixth-class and seventh-class disciples. The first-class disciple naturally has a well established inner connection with his Master. This inner connection remains even after the Master leaves the earth-scene. If the Master is really great and if the disciple's inner oneness with the Master is extremely powerful, then it is more than enough for him. He does not need any other Master in this incarnation. But the situation will be different if he happened to be a seventh-class disciple, a very bad student. Let us say he had a Master, but still he used to wallow in the pleasures of ignorance. Did he listen to this Master? Did he practice meditation? No. But he was able to say that he *had* a very striking spiritual figure as a Master and that gave him a tremendous sense of satisfaction. So if one is a disciple that belongs to this category, I wish to say that if his Master is not in the physical, then for him it is better to have another Master. This Master may be far inferior to the previous Master, but he will be more than enough to inspire and guide this seeker. Suppose my father was an eminent doctor, but now he is in the other world. If I get a headache or a stomach upset, what can my father do? I have to go to another doctor who may be far inferior to my father. He may be just an ordinary doctor. But I go to that doctor to be cured. So everything depends on what kind of disciple one is and how deep his connection is with his Master who has left the body. If he feels his Master's constant and conscious presence, then he does not need any other Master.

184. Question: Is there a character to be found in the Yoga tradition, such as Christ, who will arise at some time with the purpose of ridding mankind of suffering?

Sri Chinmoy: Let us not think of individuals. If you speak about Jesus, the carpenter's son, then you have to know that he stayed on earth for only thirty-three years. If you take the Christ Consciousness as divine Consciousness, infinite Consciousness, universal Consciousness, eternal Reality, then I wish to say that he is eternal, he is immortal, he is infinite, he is everything. But if you say that the Christ as a person came to save the world, then immediately I will say, "What about Sri Krishna? Didn't he also come? Didn't the Lord Buddha come? Didn't Sri Ramakrishna come?" These are all individual figures who revealed the divine Consciousness. If we deal with the eternal Consciousness in the Christ, then we can say that this same Consciousness is in Sri Krishna, is in all the spiritual giants.

A few hours ago, in Phoenix, someone asked me, "When will Jesus come back?" I said, "Somebody comes back only when he has left. Has the Christ left us that he has to come back?" The Christ has not left us, so how can he come back? The Christ-Consciousness is within us; it is for all humanity. In the physical if we want to see something, if we want to bind the physical reality, then we are totally lost. It is the spirit that is eternal, immortal. Christ-Consciousness is one, inseparably one with God-Consciousness. According to our limited capacity, we say "He has come, she has come to save us." We can say that the Christ was the best instrument or the most perfect instrument of God. We are also instruments of God, imperfect instruments, let us say. Each individual is an instrument of God. But the conscious and liberated souls, the most chosen instruments of God for mankind are the Christ, Sri Krishna, Lord Buddha and the other great spiritual figures.

Is anybody going to come? If you mean a human figure, then the answer is "no". Many have come, many have gone. But if you mean a divine figure, I will say that there is a divine figure already within us, within you, within me, within everybody.

SRI CHINMOY

NOTES TO FIFTY FREEDOM-BOATS TO ONE GOLDEN SHORE, BOOK 5

160. University of Wyoming, Laramie, Wyoming, 23 April 1974 — 10:30 pm.
161. University of Utah, Salt Lake City, Utah, 24 April 1974 — 10:00 am.
162. University of Arizona, Tempe, Arizona, 24 April 1974 — 4:00 pm.
163. University of New Mexico, Albuquerque, New Mexico, 24 April 1974 — 8:30 pm.
164. University of Miami, Miami, Florida, 30 September 1974.
165-167. University of Wyoming, Laramie, Wyoming, 23 April 1974 — 10:30 pm.
168-171. University of Utah, Salt Lake City, Utah, 24 April 1974 — 10:00 am.
172-177. Originally printed Loyala University, venue and date cannot yet be tracked.
178-184. University of New Mexico, Albuquerque, New Mexico, 24 April 1974 — 8:30 pm.

FIFTY FREEDOM-BOATS TO
ONE GOLDEN SHORE

BOOK 6

Part XLII — Lectures

185. True spirituality and inner life

There are people who say that spirituality is not meant for this world or this outer life. There are people who say that spirituality should be practised only in the evening of one's life — that is to say, after having had all the experiences that the outer world can give, one should enter into the inner life. But these opinions are not true. Spirituality can and should be practised irrespective of place and time. Anybody on earth can practise spiritual life. Spiritual life can never be an artificial life. Spiritual life is something which is natural and spontaneous.

In our outer life we need energy to sustain our life, to fulfil our life. In our spiritual life, our inner life, we need illumination. If we don't have illumination, we shall remain in ignorance. In order to enter into the inner life we must have inspiration. When we have this inspiration, aspiration comes to the fore. When we have aspiration, we can go one step farther to what we call Yoga. Yoga means union with God.

If we accept spiritual life in the true sense of the term, we do not negate the world, we do not renounce the world. We accept the world, we embrace the world, we try to fulfil the world in a divine way, in the way the Supreme wants. We do not see eye to eye with those who say that God is only in Heaven and not elsewhere. God is in Heaven, and God is also on earth. The Creator can never be separated from His creation. This world of ours is His creation. He is here. He abides within all things. In order to fulfil Himself it is here that God has to remain.

We have in this world of ours a true friend, and that friend is the spiritual life. Spiritual life tells us that we have come from the Divine, we live in the Divine and we shall return to the Divine. Within us we have everything. Now we have to reveal what we have within. At the same time we have an enemy, an uncompromising enemy. It is our ignorance. Ignorance tells us that we are nothing and that we will never be able to amount to anything. Ignorance says, "O man, look down and see that you are nothing, you are useless." But spirituality tells us, "My child, look up, look deep within. You will see that you are everything. You are God's child, God's chosen child. To Him you are everything. God dreams. To materialise, to fulfil, to transform God's Dream into reality you have come into the world." That is what spirituality tells each individual here on earth the moment he enters sincerely into the inner and deeper life. Spiritual life also teaches us something momentous. It tells us that we need not be bound by the life of frustration, fear and anxiety. It tells us that if it is true that our present life is full of misery, frustration, defeat and limitation, it is equally true that we have an ideal life which is all harmony, all perfection, all fulfilment, all virtue. The inner life most gladly, most cheerfully, most devotedly wants to be the living bridge between our present life and the ideal life, the life that we want to have.

There are two kinds of hope: ordinary earthly hope and spiritual hope. Ordinary earthly hope is nothing but building castles in the air. We do nothing for God, nothing to improve ourselves, we just hope that we shall one day become great, famous, powerful. But the spiritual hope that we can cherish comes from our inner conviction of truth, the truth that abides within us and in which we live. This hope is surcharged with aspiration whether we are consciously aware of it or not. This hope is the harbinger of reality. This hope sees the reality and, while seeing, becomes the reality. This hope also takes us into the realm of faith, the faith that sustains our inner and outer lives. This faith comes to the fore and tells us that the moment we look to God with our eyes of aspiration God looks at us with His Eyes of Compassion. Our aspiration and His Compassion go together. We need His Compassion and He needs our aspiration. We fulfil God and God fulfils us. The moment we fulfil Him we are fulfilled.

There are people on earth who tell us that spirituality is no longer alive, it is long dead. Our forefathers were spiritual and divine. They communed with God. Not we! We are all worse than useless. Those days of spiritual achievement, of spiritual glory are long buried, they say. Now we are in a world of materialism. There is no God and no spiritual life, no inner experience and realisation. Spirituality is dead for good. But let us not subscribe to their proud opinion, for their opinion is utterly baseless. Spirituality can never, never die because spirituality is the necessity of God. It is also the necessity of human beings; but this necessity is more real to God than to humanity because it is God who created this spiritual necessity both for Himself and for humanity. This spirituality can never die, for God never dies. God has created spirituality to unite man with God; therefore, so long as God is on earth or in Heaven or anywhere in His creation, spirituality must exist in order to unite God and man.

Spirituality is the flame of aspiration. We have always to kindle this flame so that it can rise high, higher and highest until finally it reaches the acme of perfection, absolute fulfilment. It is only the spiritual life, the cry of the heart, the surge of the soul, that can fulfil us both in our inner and outer lives. It will be a deplorable mistake if we ever say or feel that the spiritual life will take us away from the life of the material world. On the contrary, it is the spiritual life that will open our eyes to show us how we can cope with the material physical world, how we can have mastery over the physical world, how we can use the material world to help us. Right now we are living in the material world. The material world at every moment is killing us with frustration and disappointment. We want from the material world what the material world cannot give us, and the material world wants something from us which we are unable to give. If we want to be the master of the material world, if we want to say that the material world is ours, not that we belong to the material world, then we have to have perfect control of the material world. How can we have that? Only on the strength of our inner light, inner awakening, inner experiences, inner fulfilment.

If we want only to enjoy the world, we are taking a simply absurd attitude towards life. When we go deep within, one day we will see that in order to have an iota of enjoyment we have to kill our very life. We are trying to enjoy but for this enjoyment we are killing the senses that we need for a divine purpose. If we are wise, then we will enter into the inner life and know what spiritual joy and delight are. Then we will be able to enter into the outer world with the strength of our inner joy. When we enter into the outer world with inner joy, we shall see that the wonder of wonders has been accomplished by us — that the inner life can easily be lived and practised in the outer life. The life of reality, the life of fulfilment, the life of victory, the life of oneness with God which we get in our inner life can easily, effectively, gloriously and divinely come forward in the outer life. That is to say, the outer life should be a perfect manifestation of the inner life.

Let us not divide the two lives, inner and outer. Let us unite them. Let us not make a compromise; it is not a compromise that we seek. Let us try to see the outer life through the inner life. Let us try to fulfil the outer life through the inner life.

Then alone, God's infinite Blessings will shower on us on earth. Then alone we shall not only see, feel and reach God, but finally we shall all become God Himself. So let each of us present here enter into the world of spirituality. Let us breathe in the breath of spirituality, and success is ours, perfection is ours, fulfilment is ours. God in His infinite Bounty, infinite Peace, Bliss, Light and Power is ours, eternally ours.

186. Sound-life and silence-life

Dear seekers, dear sisters and brothers, we are all sailing in our respective boats, but our destination is the same: the Golden Shore. We are all destined to reach our goal: the Goal of goals. I wish to give a talk as part of my devoted, dedicated service to the Divine Being, the Supreme Pilot in all of us. I wish to speak on sound and silence from the spiritual point of view.

In our outer life we notice that sound is quite often destructive; it embodies the message of destruction. In our outer life we also notice a kind of silence which is nothing short of isolation. The sound-life wants to destroy the world around us; this silence-life wants to destroy us. But destruction can never be the answer to our quest for the truth, light and bliss which our inner being needs in abundant measure. Nor is the isolation the answer to our life's divine needs.

But there is also inner silence and inner sound. Inner silence is God-preparation in us. Inner sound is God-manifestation in and through us.

Outer sound-life is often uncontrollable. Modern technology, modern machinery, modern nuclear weapons sometimes threaten us. Although we have created them, these creations of ours threaten and frighten us; our own creations are beyond our control. This is the outer sound-life. When we are in a position to bring this outer sound-life under our control, we create a new life, a new promise, a new illumination, a new perfection within us. At that time we grow into a new dawn at every second of our life of aspiration.

Silence which advocates isolation can never be our choice divine. Isolation is the result of false renunciation. We try to renounce our friends, our relatives, our dear ones. We try to renounce society. But if we go on renouncing each and every person that we know, finally there will come a time when we will try to renounce ourselves. Today we renounce our parents, tomorrow we shall renounce our own existence. This kind of renunciation is not the answer to the world's problems or to our individual problems. If we renounce the world, then we can never manifest the divinity within us. Acceptance is the answer, but not the ultimate answer. First we have to accept the world as it is and then we have to transform it. Today's world of imperfection must be transformed into tomorrow's world of perfect Perfection. This is our ultimate goal.

In the spiritual life we do have to renounce, but we have to be very careful about what we renounce. We have to renounce our undivine attitudes, our undivine earthly, unaspiring thoughts. And where do these things abide? They abide in our mind. We may enter into the Himalayan caves in the hope of totally forgetting about the outer world, but we carry with us our mind, the mind that unfortunately treasures undivine thoughts or, let us say, the mind that is an unfortunate victim to teeming undivine, unhealthy thoughts. No matter where we go, we cannot escape from the mind. Whether we are at home or elsewhere, the mind has to be transformed. And once the mind is transformed, a major problem in our life is solved.

In order to change or transform the mind, we have to take

shelter in the heart. The heart is more than ready to shelter us. The heart has divine light. The heart is not the light, but it *has* light. Why? Because inside the heart is the living presence of the soul. The quality, the capacity, the beauty, the divinity of the soul permeate the entire body, but there is a specific place where the soul abides, and that is in the heart. So the heart receives more illumination from the soul. Of course, I am speaking of the spiritual heart, the divine heart within us, and not the emotional or physical heart.

The heart identifies. The mind separates. When the mind sings the song of separativity and division, naturally the mind cannot achieve satisfaction. But the heart has the capacity to identify itself with the universal Reality, and it always tries to do so. On the strength of its identification, it achieves satisfaction in boundless measure.

The sound-life and the silence-life prepare us to enter into the world of art. There are two types of art: the outer art and the inner art. The outer art is satisfied when it observes and discovers imperfection in others. The inner art is satisfied only when it sees perfection in others and perfection in itself — perfection within and perfection without.

There is a saying: "art for art's sake." But this phrase does not satisfy a God-lover. If we say, "art for God's sake," then immediately God comes into the matter. Suppose I draw a chair. I have to know that the capacity, the beauty, the reality, the soul that the drawing embodies will be very limited. But if I try to see God inside the chair and I try to bring to the fore God the Reality from the chair, then there is infinite scope for my own inner experience, inner realisation and God-manifestation in this work of art.

We have to know that life itself is the supreme art. How do we regulate our life-art? We regulate and discover our life-art through prayer and meditation. When we pray, we come to realise that there is someone who is listening to us and who is showering His choicest Blessings upon our devoted head. While He is blessing us, He is descending into our prayer and moulding our lives into His very Image. When we meditate, we realise that God is constantly offering us His divine Message. While we were praying, we were talking and God was listening and doing the needful. Now, when we are meditating, we are just receiving. God is the talker and we are the listener. He is giving us constantly the message of what to do, how to do it, when to do it and why to do it. We are just preparing ourselves so that He can act in and through us in His own inimitable and supreme Way.

The ordinary sound-life is the desire-life. With the desire-life there is always a sense of incompleteness, insufficiency. No matter how much we achieve, there is always something lacking, something missing. But in the silence-life there is always a sense of satisfaction, inner satisfaction. Even if we have only an iota of peace, light and bliss, we feel that we are satisfied. Today we are a tiny drop but we know that this tiny drop has every opportunity and possibility of entering into the mighty ocean and becoming the mighty ocean itself.

The sound-life and the silence-life prepare us for joy, unlimited joy. Unfortunately, the human in us quite often makes a deplorable mistake when it notices joy in others or in us. It comes to the conclusion that this joy is self-indulgence. When we notice that somebody is cheerful and happy, immediately we come to the conclusion that he is indulging himself. But this is totally false. Indulgence and happiness are two different things, like north pole and south pole. Indulgence comes from the undivine part in us. When we indulge in something, we have to know that the undivine in us is cherishing something

— the small in us, not the vast, is cherishing something. When we are really happy, we have to know that the divine in us, the infinite in us, is treasuring something and enjoying something.

We enjoy. God enjoys. We enjoy our emotional vital life. God, the supreme Enjoyer, enjoys His Infinity, Eternity and Immortality. Enjoyment in the physical and the vital is the precursor of destruction. But enjoyment in the heart or in the soul is divine, perfect and supreme. Enjoyment in the physical is the pleasure-life. The pleasure-life and the happiness-life are totally different things. In pleasure, what immediately looms large is frustration, and frustration is the harbinger of destruction, whereas happiness is a gradual movement, a gradual progress in us. It is like a river flowing towards its source, the sea, and this source is within us, not without.

In order to enter into the source we have to be satisfied with what we have and what we are, but not in a complacent manner. Dissatisfaction with what we have and what we are does not mean that we are ready for a higher and more fulfilling life. No. If we are satisfied with what we have and, at the same time, if we know that there is a higher goal, a more fulfilling reality, then we can eventually reach our highest destination.

Life's ladder is right in front of us. It has quite a few rungs. After we step on the first rung, if we have confidence enough, then we can step to a higher rung. In this way we move from joy to greater joy to greatest joy. But if we are dissatisfied with where we are, then there is every possibility that the higher rungs also will not give us satisfaction. We have to know that life's process is just like progress through school. From kindergarten, we go to primary school, high school, college, university and so forth. At every moment we have to be satisfied with our present course of study, otherwise we will not study well and we will not progress to a higher level. But inside our satisfaction we should always be aiming at a higher goal. Divine satisfaction is not a complacent feeling. If we become complacent, then we are doomed to disappointment, for we will have no higher goal before us. We will not make any progress at all. We must be satisfied with what we have and, at the same time, we must feel that this is not the highest, the ultimate achievement. Today's goal can never be the ultimate goal. Today's goal has to be tomorrow's starting point, and tomorrow's goal has to be the starting point for the day after tomorrow.

In human life we notice two specific movements. From freedom, we have entered into the world of bondage. And from the world of bondage we are trying to enter into the world of freedom. If we try to live in the inner silence-world, then we feel that we have come into this world from a world of freedom, but that we have misused our freedom in the outer sound-world; therefore, we have been compelled to live in bondage. If we live in the inner sound-world, then we feel that from darkness we are entering into light. The inner sound-life tells us that we are in ignorance but that there is every possibility that we can enter into the world of light and delight and bring it into the earth-plane.

Right now the world of ignorance is our only reality. But when we meditate and light enters into us, we see that we have entered into the realm of darkness for a special purpose. We have to transform everything that is within us into something divine. Each and every part of our being has to be transformed. There is no other reason why we have entered into the world of ignorance. To be perfect in only one part of the being is not sufficient. Perfection must be found on every plane of our consciousness. That is why the light from above must enter into the world.

Service-life is the life of our soul. When we say "myself", or

"I", we should be referring to the soul and not the body or the body-consciousness. If I know myself as the soul, then I feel that I am the conscious representative of God. Him to manifest, Him to reveal: this is my purpose on earth. If I am of God and for God, then I must dive deep within. I must have a free access to the real reality within myself. When I feel at one with my inner reality, then I see around and within me the world of perfection.

The ultimate goal of the sound-life and the silence life is perfection, and this perfection can be founded only upon self-dedication. The message of self-dedication we give through our constant inner cry. The mounting cry wants to reach the transcendental height of perfect joy, with all its infinite Light and Delight, for earth's transformation and nature's perfection. Here we are all seekers. This is our supreme task.

187. Ego and emotion

Ego is emotion and emotion is ego. Ego and emotion are the obverse and the reverse of the same coin. There are two types of ego. One ego is self-binding, self-centred. The other ego is self-transcending and all-embracing. The self-centred ego has to be transformed into the self-transcending, all-embracing and God-fulfilling ego. This self-transcending ego is the knowledge of oneness, inseparable oneness with the Infinite, the Eternal, the Absolute and the Immortal.

In this world man has two significant possessions: intelligence and emotion. These two possessions govern our day-to-day life. But very often we see that emotion gets the upper hand in our life. We know that even if someone is extremely intelligent, when his emotion comes to the fore, it will devour him. He is compelled to do what his emotion asks him to do.

The human consciousness deals with emotion in its two different aspects. One type of emotion is impure, unlit and obscure. The other is pure, divine and all-fulfilling. The result of impure emotion is fear. But the divine, pure emotion brings us closest to God.

At times emotion is satisfactory and at times it is not. Human emotion binds us; divine emotion frees us. With human emotion we want to remain in the finite and for the finite. With divine emotion we want to remain in the Infinite, for the Absolute.

There are two ways to approach God. One way is through human emotion, through fear. We can feel, "God is omnipotent. If we do things wrong, then He is going to punish us. We had better try to please Him now, since we have committed Himalayan blunders countless times. The best thing is to please Him." This is the way we approach God through fear. The other way, a far better way, is to feel our oneness with God through divine emotion. At that time we say, "God is Light. I came from Him; I exist on earth only for Him." Human emotion is based on impurity, obscurity, imperfection, limitation, bondage and death. Divine emotion is founded on purity, real closeness to God, a divine feeling of oneness and the certainty that God-realisation is our birthright.

In our day-to-day life we express emotion through devotion. We are devoted to some cause or to someone or to something. When we offer our emotion in the form of devotion to ordinary human beings, it is all attachment. But when we offer our emotion in the form of devotion to God or to our spiritual Master who has realised God, then this is pure divine devotion. At that time we feel our oneness with the highest Reality.

In our daily life we express emotion, or ego, to each individual in a different way. We offer our emotion to our father in one way, to our sister in another way, to our friend in a totally different way. We offer our emotion according to our capacity and others receive our emotion according to their receptivity. Each individual has to offer emotion. To others it may be immaterial whether they receive our emotion or not. What is the human father? He is an individual. What is the human mother? She is an individual. What is the human brother? He is an individual. We have to express our emotion to an individual in a particular way. But when we deal with God it is totally different. God is our father, mother, sister, brother, friend; He is everything. All relationships we can have with God. With Him there is no bondage. When we deal with God, we can offer Him our divine emotion, pure emotion. Again, if we offer Him our impure, limited emotion, God accepts it. He illumines our limited, earthbound, unlit, obscure, impure emotion and transforms it into divine, pure, illumined emotion.

To make the most significant progress we should approach God through purity, sincerity, humility and the feeling of inner oneness. The other approach, through fear, very often leads to frustration, for at every moment we have an inner feeling that we are going to make more mistakes, more blunders. Then we hesitate to approach God at all. And when we do make a mistake, we ask God to forgive us. Then, the moment we feel that God has forgiven us we get a sense of relief, we relax, and again we make mistakes. In the human life we are constantly making mistakes, and we are constantly afraid that God is going to punish us. But God does not want to punish us. Just because you have done something wrong, God need not necessarily punish you. No, He will see how sincerely you want the inner life, the spiritual life, and how fast you want to run towards your Goal.

God is at once our father and our mother, our divine father and our divine mother. In the West, God the Father is prominent, while in the East, in India especially, God the Mother comes first. Jesus the Son of God always used the term "Father". He said, "I and my Father are One." Here in the West, the Father comes first. But God is our mother as well. In India the feeling for God the Mother is very strong. For the great spiritual Master Sri Ramakrishna, God was Mother Kali. And when India's first Avatar, or direct descendent of God, Sri Ramachandra, had to fight the great antidivine force, he invoked Durga, the Mother Divine. Most of the spiritual Masters of India have invoked God the Mother, while in the West we invoke God the Father. Both East and West are perfectly right. When we realise God the Father, we are bound to see God the Mother within Him. When we realise God the Mother, we will unmistakably see God the Father within Her.

We want to realise God the Father and God the Mother. How can we do this? There are two significant ways. One way is through prayer, soulful prayer, inner prayer, constant prayer. The other way is through determined will, adamantine will. In the East we use will-power, but before will-power we use something else. We feel that we get will-power from concentration and meditation. We concentrate, meditate and contemplate to attain will-power.

Prayer is of paramount importance in the West, and prayer does lead us to God. But while we pray we have to be extremely careful. Very often we do not offer soulful prayer to God. There is a tendency towards conscious desire in our prayer. When we pray with folded hands we often say, "God, please give me this, please do this." There is a feeling of desire in our prayer. Now, when we desire something we have to know that we are acting like a beggar. On the one hand we say that we are God's son, God's child, and on the other hand we are begging like an orphan. This is why it often happens that in the West we do not offer soulful prayer to God with a feeling of oneness. What we do is beg from God. This act of begging takes us away from our dearest, sweetest Father. But if we can pray soulfully, unconditionally, unreservedly, then we will definitely realise the Highest, the Absolute.

As I said before, from concentration, meditation and contemplation we derive divine will-power. Will-power makes us like a prince, whereas prayer, when it is not soulful, makes us like a beggar. Of course, if we use will-power in the wrong way, then we will act like a mad elephant. In that case there will not be divine dynamism in our will-power; it will be all aggression. But when we use will-power properly, divinely, then we will act like a divine prince. A divine prince knows that the divinity, the real reality within him is at his command. He also feels that his inner divinity is eager to meet him and come to his aid. On the strength of his aspiration he is eagerly entering deep within, and his inner divinity is constantly trying to come to the fore. This is what happens when we exercise our divine will-power.

Will-power also has the capacity to make us feel that God has already given us abundant inspiration and aspiration to realise Him. He will come and stand right in front of us, provided we accept Him in His own Way. But when we pray we tend to seek God in our own way, the way that suits us. We say, "God, I need You, I need You. Early in the morning I shall pray to You. Please come and stand before me." But with divine will-power we won't do that. The divine will-power says, "I am exercising my inner will to bring my divinity to the fore. Here my role ends. My divinity has to come in its own way, at its own choice hour." Here there is no begging. Here we say, "I am offering my capacity, my light, let the divinity within me fulfil itself in its own way.

When we approach God the Father, we feel His Wisdom, His inner Light, His Vastness. When we approach God the Mother, we feel infinite Love, infinite Compassion, infinite Concern. It is not that God the Father does not have Compassion. He also has it. But God expresses Love, Compassion and Concern through the feminine form more than through the masculine form. In the masculine form He offers Wisdom, Light, Vastness. Each of these divine qualities — Love, Compassion, Concern, Vastness, Light and Wisdom — is of paramount importance in the life of each aspiring soul. When we feel in the inmost recesses of our heart God's Love, Concern and Compassion and His Wisdom, Light and Vastness, we know that today's unfulfilled man will soon turn into tomorrow's realised, fulfilled and manifested God.

188. Yoga and spirituality

Dear sisters and brothers, dear seekers, I wish to give a short talk on spirituality. But before I give the talk, with your soul's permission I wish to say something.

At the beginning of the year I had the wish, or you can say desire, to be of dedicated service to all the states and give a talk in each state. In this way, my disciples and I found that we could be of service to aspiring humanity. This evening in Hawaii I am giving my forty-ninth talk. Tomorrow, my final talk will be in Alaska, and then the journey will be over. If we live in the physical consciousness, we will say that this is a self-imposed task. If we live in the soul, we know that it is a God-ordained task.

I have come here to be of service to the seekers of the highest Truth. There are many seekers here. Some are beginners, others have started walking, others are a little advanced and running along the spiritual path. Spirituality is a vast field. You can regard spirituality as a body. Inside the body is the heart. Yoga is the heart of the spiritual body.

Yoga is a Sanskrit word. It means union with God. This union is a conscious union. We are all united with God but we are not aware of it. When we practise Yoga, we become conscious of our union with God.

Why practise Yoga? There are millions and billions of people who are not practising Yoga. We want to practise Yoga in order to be satisfied. If we are sincere to ourselves, we know that we have everything except satisfaction. Some seekers feel that everything in life has meaning only when God comes first. They feel that God is the root. When they become one with the root, the source, then everything has meaning and everything is satisfaction. The practice of Yoga can lead us to this goal.

When we enter into the field of Yoga, a few significant questions arise. Is Yoga something normal? Is Yoga something natural? Is Yoga something practical? Is Yoga something attainable? Yoga deals with God. What can be more natural and normal than dealing with God, our very creator? Yoga is something practical. Yoga is inevitable, for God will not allow any human being to remain unrealised forever.

We are all seekers. Some of us are at the foot of the tree, some of us are climbing, some have already reached a great height. But we all have to climb up to the Highest, and from there we can bring down the fruit to the world at large. If we eat and do not offer the fruit to others, then God will not be satisfied. Some seekers want God only for themselves, but this is not the highest attitude. After we have realised God, we have to do something more. We have to reveal God to the world at large. Then God wants us to do something even more significant. He wants us to manifest Him. God-realisation, God-revelation and God-manifestation: these are the three goals that each seeker must eventually reach. Today God-realisation, tomorrow God-revelation, the day after tomorrow God-manifestation.

Again, God-realisation has no end, God-revelation has no end, God-manifestation has no end. We are aspiring to realise the highest Absolute, but the Absolute can never be bound by anything. The Absolute Supreme is always transcending His own highest transcendental Height. When we go deep within, we see that He is not satisfied with His transcendental Height. It is in self-transcendence only that He gets real satisfaction. In our case also, it is in self-transcendence that we will achieve satisfaction.

Yoga is a subject, an inner subject. This subject has to be taught and loved. In this subject, an inner cry is of paramount importance. With our outer cry we try to possess earthly material objects. With our inner cry we try to transcend the earth-bound consciousness and enter into the Heaven-free consciousness.

Yoga is a subject that has to be studied. When we study, there is a student and a teacher. There are many sincere seekers who are reluctant to have a teacher. They say that God is inside the heart, so it is not necessary to have a teacher. The Master says, "True, God is inside you. He is inside everything. God is also inside the books that you can read in the library. Why, then, do you go to the university and study under the guidance of a teacher? You study with the help of a teacher because you feel that when you study with him you will learn faster and you will be sure that what you learn is correct, whereas if you study alone, you will go slowly and doubt may assail you and make you think that you are not learning the right thing."

In the spiritual life also, a teacher is necessary. The spiritual teacher is not like an ordinary teacher who gives examinations and passes or fails the student. Rather, he is like a private tutor. The spiritual teacher expedites our journey and increases our thirst for Truth, Light and Bliss. In the spiritual life, the teacher and the student have a relationship founded upon mutual faith and trust. The student feels that the teacher has the capacity to illumine him. The teacher feels that the student is sincere and aspiring.

No human being can be the real Master. The real Master, the real spiritual teacher, the real Guru is not a human being at all. The real Guru is the Absolute Supreme. The human being who is a spiritual teacher is like the elder member of the family. The Father has taught the eldest son a few things about inner height and inner power. The Father has told the eldest son, "I have taught you. Now it is your duty to be of service to Me, to help your younger brothers come to Me so that I can also share with them My infinite Wisdom and Light." The eldest son listens to the dictates of the Father and takes the younger brothers who are meant to listen to him to their common Father, the real Guru, who is God Himself.

There are sincere teachers and false teachers, just as there are real coins and false coins. How can we recognise a false teacher? If a teacher says he will give God-realisation or a spiritual experience in the twinkling of an eye, then rest assured that he is a false teacher. The teacher who says that he will give you God-realisation if you give him a large amount of money is a false teacher.

Creator and creation. We are fond of the creation but not of the Creator. But inside the creation is the Creator. Again, if we are afraid of the creation and run towards the Creator, that is also a mistake. If we feel that the creation does not have anything to offer, we are making a mistake. Real Yoga will never ask us to renounce the world. We have to accept, transform and divinise the world and bring perfect Perfection onto this earth.

The world has everything except peace of mind. We get peace of mind when we feel that the world can go on without us, but that we cannot go on without the world. We have to know that we are not indispensable; only God is indispensable. When we come to this realisation, only then can we have peace of mind. When we have peace of mind, we love humanity, we expand and spread our wings. When we love humanity, we are satisfied because we have satisfied God.

Dear seekers, let us try to bring down the Highest and become the Highest. What we have seen is God's Light; what we have felt is God's Love. Now, let us grow into God-Delight.

189. Belief and faith

Dear seekers, dear sisters and brothers, with your soul's permission, I wish to say a few words before I give my talk. At the beginning of this year it was the fervent wish of myself and my students to be of dedicated, soulful service to seekers all over the country. In each state we decided to give a talk and offer our dedicated service. Today marks the end of this series. Today, I shall be offering my last talk.

I am most grateful to Mr and Mrs Addison, who have been extremely kind and hospitable to me. Their son, John Addison, is a devoted, energetic and dynamic student of mine. Here his parents have offered a similar kind of service to the Supreme in me and for that, to both Mr and Mrs Addison, I offer my heart's deepest gratitude. I also offer my loving joy to all the seekers who are present here this evening.

I wish to give a talk on belief and faith from the spiritual point of view. Belief and faith: these are of paramount importance in our spiritual life. They play a significant role in our ordinary life as well.

Belief is usually in the mind, whereas faith is in the heart. Belief, unfortunately, has doubt as its immediate neighbour. What is doubt? Doubt is nothing short of poison. In the spiritual life, when doubt enters into our mind, we can make no progress. Even in the ordinary life when we doubt someone, in no way do we gain anything from our doubt. Today we doubt someone, tomorrow we try to cultivate some faith in that person, and the day after tomorrow we doubt our own capacity to make any judgement. When we doubt someone, we may not lose our faith all at once. But when we doubt ourselves, that marks the end of our inner progress. Doubt is a dangerous road that leads to destruction.

Faith has conviction as its immediate neighbour. We can be very happy and very cheerful when faith abides in our heart. What is conviction? Conviction is the precursor of God-discovery and Self-discovery. Self-discovery and God-discovery are one and the same. When we discover ourselves, we come to know that God-realisation was always our birthright, but we had forgotten to exercise that birthright.

Belief does not discriminate. Very often mental belief accepts both good and bad, divine and undivine, the fleeting and the eternal, the finite and the infinite, the mortal and the immortal. But we have to be very careful when we are dealing with something finite and transitory, something undivine and hostile, for we may be totally ruined when we play with the undivine forces that are within us or outside us.

Faith is very careful. It always discriminates. It accepts only the real, the divine, the eternal, the infinite, the immortal. If we accept the real in us and not the unreal, then we grow into the transcendental Reality. If we accept Infinity and Immortality, then naturally in the course of time, in the process of our evolution, we will grow into Infinity and Immortality. If we accept the divine in us, then we will eventually grow into divinity.

Human belief has two good friends: imagination and inspiration. Very often we are told that imagination is sheer mental hallucination, but this is absolutely absurd. Imagination is the harbinger of realisation. If there is no imagination, there can be no creation. All the great discoveries of science were founded on the inner, illumined imagination. What we call imagination today, tomorrow will become realisation. Inspiration is always significant, both in the ordinary life and in the spiritual life. When we are inspired, we enter into the field of creativity. If our goal is a far cry, on the strength of our inspiration we can cover half the distance almost sooner than at once.

Belief has rational values. Faith has constructive and creative values. When we cultivate our inner faith we see that the Inner Pilot is experiencing His own Silence-Height in and through His earth-sound. What He was in silence is being manifested in sound as a divinising and immortalising force on earth. The supreme Artist is the Inner Pilot. When we have constructive and creative values, life itself becomes a supreme art.

Belief, in the human mind, quite often has to convince itself. Also, it dares to convince others, even though very often it is wanting in conviction itself. Belief can be shattered by the buffets of life, but it can be strengthened when opportunity continuously knocks at our mind's door. But faith is always conviction itself. In faith there looms large man's inseparable oneness with the universal Consciousness, with the transcendental Height.

Faith is always giving and becoming. Faith is self-giving and faith is God-becoming. Faith has the inner, indomitable strength to transcend its own height of light and delight and enter into the ocean of infinite Light and Delight. Belief is just a tiny drop in the ocean of Consciousness, while faith is the ocean itself.

From the spiritual point of view, in the inner or psychic plane, belief and faith have two distinct and different roles. Belief tries to free us from the earth-bound time. Time is binding us; therefore, we wallow in the meshes of ignorance and treasure consciously or unconsciously our existence there. But when belief looms large and comes to the fore we try to go far beyond the domains of earth-bound time. Then, when faith starts playing its role, we see that Heaven-free time, eternal Time, becomes our friend and encourages and inspires us to live in the everlasting Reality of universal Truth and transcendental Bliss.

Belief has; faith is. Belief has God-vision, God the cosmic Vision. Faith is God-reality, God the transcendental Reality. Belief and faith are like the obverse and the reverse of the same coin. They are like complementary souls. Belief carries us to the highest realm of consciousness. Faith brings us down from the highest transcendental Consciousness so that we can distribute Peace, Light and Bliss to the world at large.

In order to cultivate belief and faith in ourselves, we need two intimate and constant friends. These friends are prayer and meditation. Prayer helps us realise the highest Height. In prayer we climb high, higher, highest and see the Face of God. We cry and He listens to our fervent cry, our inmost cry. When we meditate, the Supreme Lord, our Eternal Beloved, comes down and dictates to us what to do, how to transform our nature, how to immortalise our life and how to derive satisfaction from our day-to-day, multifarious activities. If we listen to God's dictates, we feel that our life on earth is not a tissue of unrealities, but that a supreme Reality is operating in and through us. We feel that we are the chosen instruments of

God. He utilises us in His inimitable, supreme Way. We consciously take part in His cosmic Journey. Him to embody, Him to reveal, Him to manifest, we come to earth again and again. This realisation dawns in our devoted heads and surrendered hearts when we give due value to our ever-mounting belief and to our ever-descending and all-illumining faith.

Part XLIII — Questions and answers — Northern State College, South Dakota

190. Question: Sri Chinmoy, what do you consider to be the greatest obstacle on the spiritual path?

Sri Chinmoy: The greatest obstacle on the spiritual path is doubt, self-doubt. There is no obstacle as dangerous as doubt. If you doubt God, that is one thing. There is no harm in it in the sense that God will not lose any of His infinite capacities because of your doubt. But if you start doubting yourself, then you are totally lost. All your inner capacities will be washed away in the torrent of your self-doubt.

You should not doubt God and you should not doubt yourself. But if you have to doubt one of the two, then the best thing is to doubt God. Each moment you use the words "I" and "mine". Although you claim that you doubt yourself, at the same time you say, "*I* am eating, *I* am breathing, *my* friend, *my* house." Here is the proof of your own existence. God's existence you do not see and you cannot prove right now. But your own existence you can prove because you are experiencing it. If you use the terms "I", "mine" and "my" and then say that you don't exist, people will laugh at you. You will be caught; you will not be able to doubt your existence. But God's existence you can doubt if you want to, because He is not standing right in front of you; you do not see Him or consciously feel Him. In season and out of season, you can doubt Him.

Now, you may have absolute faith in God's existence, but you may doubt God's Compassion. You may say, "Is God so compassionate? I have done so many things wrong in my life. Will He give me His Knowledge-Light? Why should He show me His unconditional Compassion?" This is another kind of doubt. Right now you do not disbelieve God's existence or your own existence, but you doubt God's Compassion and God's Concern for you. Once upon a time you were a soul in the soul's world. Who brought your soul into this world? It was God who did it. Before you were consciously aware of spirituality, divinity and reality, God gave you life. God gave you the message of divinity. Already you can see how much God has given you for which you have never asked consciously. It has all come to you through your soul. And who created your soul? God. Who offered it to you? God. Who is going to fulfil you through your soul? Again, it is God. So you can easily stop doubting God's Concern.

Then you may feel that with your own capacity you cannot realise God. This is still another kind of doubt. But if somebody else has realised God, why should you not be able to do the same? God, the same God that exists in him, also exists in you, only you are not aspiring enough to see Him. All souls have come from God, not from anywhere else. So if one person has realised God through the aspiration of his soul, anyone can do it. You can also realise God. Your doubt is baseless. You have to feel only that your aspiration is not yet as intense as the other person's aspiration was. Finally you have to feel that God can never be fulfilled until you have realised Him. God's existence needs fulfilment in and through you. He will never be totally fulfilled as long as you remain unrealised. If your friend has realised God but you still remain unrealised, then rest assured that God remains unfulfilled. He will be fulfilled only on the day when all human beings have realised Him.

God's business is to fulfil Himself and manifest Himself on earth. If you consciously aspire, then it becomes easier for Him to fulfil and manifest Himself. You can rest assured that God needs your conscious co-operation for His fulfilment. If you offer Him your sincerity and your aspiration, and take one step towards Him, He will take ninety-nine steps towards you. You give what you can, and God will give you not only what He has but also what He is. What He has is infinite Concern and what He is is infinite Light.

So the worst obstacle in the spiritual life is doubt. If you can conquer all doubt, then you will be much closer to God-realisation. There are many other obstacles, of course, but these obstacles are not as dangerous as doubt. Doubt is a slow poison. If we cherish doubt every day, this slow poison will gradually kill us. We must throw doubt from our inner life and from our entire existence.

191. Question: Would you say something about feeling your body in a spiritual way? Is feeling a kind of electric force or wave a spiritual experience?

Sri Chinmoy: Certainly. An electric shock or thrill is a kind of spiritual experience. You have brought down some dynamic light into your system, and this dynamic light is operating inside you. But this is not a form of meditation; it is the result or after-effect of a meditation.

192. Question: Can you take the senses as an object of meditation?

Sri Chinmoy: Certainly, you can take the senses as an object of meditation. If you want to concentrate on one of your eyes, you can easily do it. But instead of concentrating on these physical eyes, if you can concentrate on your third eye, between and a little above your eyebrows, naturally you will one day be able to open up your third eye. This will give you the capacity to see the past, present and future. Furthermore, when the third eye is open, the mistakes, shortcomings, imperfections and limitations of millennia can be rectified and all obscurities in your life can be destroyed. If you concentrate properly on your third eye, you will get this result.

If you want to meditate only on the physical senses, you are welcome to do so, but you have to know that if you concentrate or meditate on something more significant, you are bound to get better results. If you meditate on a pencil or carrot or a cucumber, God is also there. But if you meditate on the sun early in the morning, or if you meditate on the vast sky, you will receive some of their power and vastness. If you meditate on a picture of your spiritual Master, immediately you will feel his oneness with God, his divine consciousness and his liberation, which you are striving for.

You have to know what is worthy of your meditation and concentration. If you concentrate on one finger, you will get a limited amount of will-power. If you concentrate on a flower, you will get abundant purity, and this purity is of the greatest necessity in the spiritual life. But if you concentrate on something supremely spiritual, then you will get more satisfaction, more attainment and more fulfilment. If you want to meditate on the senses, you can certainly do so, but this will not help you very much in your spiritual life. There are other things to meditate on which will offer you more satisfactory and abiding truth.

193. Question: Is it necessary to follow a life of renunciation?

Sri Chinmoy: Renunciation is a complicated term. We have to know what we are planning to renounce. If we mean that we are going to renounce our imperfection, limitation and ignorance, then I will say, yes, we do have to follow a life of renunciation. We have to renounce the things that are binding us. But if we mean that we are going to renounce the world and retire into a cave to try to realise God, then I will say, no, that kind of renunciation we do not need. Leading a very care-free life will not offer us God-realisation. We must renounce imperfection, obscurity and limitation. But if we say that we have to renounce our family, our jobs and all our responsibilities, then we are making a terrible mistake. God is in our near and dear ones, too.

We may think, "By praying to the God who is inside my dear ones, how am I going to realise the God who is all-pervading?" So today we may renounce our parents and the members of our family, and tomorrow we may enter into the Himalayan caves. But there we shall have to try to renounce our stupid mind. We have left our home, our parents and children, our jobs, the world, but our mind is still thinking of them: "What are they eating? Are they thinking of me? I was so cruel to leave them, I wonder if they are suffering." Geographically we can easily get away from these things, but mentally and emotionally we are still caught. We are bound to them as closely as ever. In the spiritual life when we renounce, we renounce our ignorance. But there comes a time when we realise that even ignorance we do not actually renounce, we transform it. Right now we are caught by ignorance; we are victims of ignorance. Ignorance is kicking us like a football, and sometimes, while we are being kicked, we are consciously cherishing ignorance. But eventually we shall catch ignorance. A day will come when knowledge will dawn in us and we will feel that ignorance is like a thief stealing away all our inner wealth. Then we will try to catch ignorance and threaten it. And soon we will come to feel that, rather than threatening ignorance, if we can flood it with light, it will no longer want to commit any mischief. Then our physical consciousness, our earth-bound consciousness, will not make any more mistakes.

To come back to your question, we have to know what we are renouncing. If we want to renounce ignorance, that is absolutely necessary. But we need not renounce our near and dear ones and enter into the Himalayan caves to realise God. That is absurd. Again, when real renunciation takes place, we have to feel that we do not renounce, we just transform. We transform night into day, impurity into purity, ignorance into wisdom, death into Immortality. We do not renounce; we just transform everything through our conscious, inseparable oneness with God's Light.

194. Question: Would you tell me what suffering is and what it means?

Sri Chinmoy: Suffering is an experience that God has in and through us. It is the result of our limited consciousness. When unlimited consciousness operates, we see the result in the form of joy and delight. God's unlimited Consciousness is all-pervading. But right now we are in the finite. When we accomplish something in the finite we are not satisfied. In the Infinite when we accomplish something we are satisfied. When an individual has five dollars he wants to make ten dollars. His five dollars does not satisfy him; he suffers, he is limited. He sees that his friend has ten dollars and he has only five dollars. He has inner suffering because he wants to have ten dollars. Then when he makes ten dollars, he sees that somebody else has twenty dollars. Again, he has inner suffering, and he enters into turmoil thinking about how to make twenty dollars.

In the finite there will always be suffering because we try to compete, to grasp, to possess. But in the Infinite there is no suffering because we enter into the universal Consciousness. There our will and the universal Will are the same. Our own will becomes totally and inseparably one with what the universal Will demands from the earth, and there is no suffering. But right now we are trying to satisfy the world with our limited consciousness, and the world also wants to satisfy us with its limited consciousness. We are limiting others and we ourselves are limited. Our main experience in this world is the experience of limitation, and that is why we suffer.

From the highest point of view, God embodies both the limited and the unlimited consciousness. He is the tiniest insect and at the same time He is the measureless cosmos. He is smaller than the smallest and larger than the largest. *Anor aniyan mahato mahiyan...* He is farther than the farthest and nearer than the nearest. He is nearer than the nearest for whom? For the seeker. He is farther than the farthest for whom? For the non-seeker. For those who are wallowing in the pleasures of ignorance, God is farther than the farthest. Naturally those individuals suffer. But God is nearer than the nearest for the seekers. When a seeker prays to God and meditates on God, he feels that he is God's dearest child. When he prays to God, he feels that God the Omniscient is there, listening to him. When he meditates on God he feels that God is talking to him and he is listening to God. If he is listening to God and God is listening to him, there can be no suffering. This truth is what the seeker learns from his spiritual life. But if one does not aspire, he has to stay all the time in a limited consciousness. Naturally, in the limited consciousness, there is much suffering.

195. Question: Would you speak about music, God and meditation?

Sri Chinmoy: I have written a book called *God the Supreme Musician* which I would like to send to you so that you can read it. In that book I have spoken at length about my views on God and music. God and music are inseparable. If you say that each musician is not God, I may agree with you, but if you say that soulful music is not God, then I will totally disagree with you. You may say that each individual is not God because you see many imperfections and undivine things in his life. You find it difficult to call him God, or to feel that he is God. But if you say that his creation — soulful music — is not representing God, then I totally disagree with you.

The earthly creator we misunderstand because of his shortcomings. But he is bringing down his creation from another world, especially if he is a musician. He brings down reality from a higher world on the strength of his intense aspiration, and for half an hour or an hour he remains high, very high. The music he writes or plays at that time comes from that high realm. But after half an hour or an hour he may enter into his ordinary consciousness again. That is why people appreciate a musician while they listen to his music and later look down upon him for his human failings. Everything he has brought down from the very high worlds to illumine and fulfil the earth consciousness is undoubtedly the representative and the reality of the life-breath of God coming down from the higher worlds. This is why I say that music is God, even though a musician may not always be God-like.

Part XLIV — Questions and answers — University of Minnesota

196. Question: There are so many spiritual paths and so many spiritual teachers. How does one figure out which is the right one?

Sri Chinmoy: It is a matter of one's inner feeling and inner affinity. In our outer life there are many schools, but an individual goes to only one school. Here in Minnesota and the neighbouring states there are hundreds of universities. But some people who live here go to New York to study, and vice versa. Why does someone prefer a New York university to a Minnesota university? For some reason he likes it better. There are various schools and various teachers, but an individual is bound to like one particular university better than another. He has read about that university, or he has an inner feeling that it is better. The choice is up to him.

In the inner life there is an easy way, a convincing way, to know who your Master is. Just take a piece of paper and write down the names of the spiritual Masters whom you have seen or whom you have read about or merely heard of. They may be here in America or somewhere else. As you write down the name of a particular Master, repeat his name aloud seven times most soulfully, placing your right palm on your heart. Try to feel the vibration you get from him. Now you become the teacher yourself. If you feel no vibration, give him zero. Repeat this procedure, giving a grade for each Master. If you get some vibration, give him the mark you feel he deserves.

You are the judge. It is you who are going to offer your life to someone, and you cannot be a fool. When you are going to dedicate your whole life to someone, you do not want to become that Master's disciple just because some person you know has accepted him as his Master, or just because he has thousands of disciples. On the other hand, if a Master has only a few disciples, you should not go to him solely for that reason either. It is all God's play. God has given to some Masters thousands and thousands of disciples, and to others He has given very few. God tells one Master that he has to be very selective, and God tells another Master to accept anyone who comes to him.

God has given you the opportunity to make a selection. Continue to write down the names of the Masters and repeat their names out loud. If you get an intense vibration and a real inner thrill, a feeling of ecstasy from one name, then give that Master eighty or ninety or even more. But if you get only a good vibration and not an inner thrill, then give him forty or fifty. If none of the Masters you know of is meant to be your Master, then you will not get that inner thrill from any of them. Perhaps you are not yet familiar with your Master's name. But in India we say, "When the disciple is ready, the Master is bound to come." If you are really ready for a Master, then I wish to say that your Master is available. He may be in the farthest corner of the globe, in India or somewhere else. But you are bound to find him.

If you accept a Master, his path becomes yours. You cannot be in two boats at once. If you keep one foot in one boat and the other foot in another boat, you are going to break your legs. Each Master is right in his own way. Each boatman will take you to the destined Goal. You have to know that the Goal is the same, but the roads may not and cannot be of the same length. There are many roads that lead to Rome, but you will see that one particular road will lead you there sooner than the others. In the spiritual life, that road, that path, is the path of Love. The road of knowledge, wisdom and intellect will lead you to your Goal, undoubtedly, but it will be a long, slow process.

Now I beg to be excused. I answered your question and then entered into other details. To come back to your question, I wish to say that the very name of your spiritual Master will immediately give you boundless joy. I have quite a few disciples who just heard my name on the phone or somewhere else and then came to me. God knows what their needs are and sends them to the right Master if they are sincere in their inner cry. The name of the person who is going to be your Master will give you a divine vibration, an inner thrill, because you will have a strong inner affinity for him. Perhaps you have not read any book by him, perhaps you know next to nothing about his outer or inner life, but his name will have a mantric effect on you, because sooner or later he is going to be your inner Pilot. Your inner cry has already reached the heart of your Master. In the outer life, the moment his name comes to you, you will feel a magic inner thrill and your heart will be touched.

197. Question: In the Bible there is a part that explains about Moses' revelation from God. Can you tell us a little bit about Moses?

Sri Chinmoy: I can answer this question, but it will not help you at all in your spiritual life. If you ask me questions about your own aspiration or about your own inner experiences then you will make the fastest progress. If I say something about Moses, about his inner connection with God, this will be only mental information to feed your curiosity. But it will not increase your aspiration. Please ask me another question that will be of real help to you.

198. Question: How does a person overcome doubt about himself?

Sri Chinmoy: We must treat doubt very seriously. As soon as a doubt comes we have to feel that it is someone standing in front of us with a knife, ready to stab us. Sometimes when we have doubt we cherish it, while at the same time wishing that this doubt could be conquered. But we will never be able to conquer doubt by mere wishful thinking. If we identify ourselves with the mind, we will not have the power to conquer all doubt because the mind itself unconsciously or consciously cherishes doubt. But the soul has more power than the mind. We should try to save ourselves with the light of the soul. Every day before doubt has the opportunity to enter into our mind, we should try to feel the light of the soul inside us. Each time doubt comes we should feel that the soul is not only protecting us, but is giving us a new life, a life of aspiration, a life of realisation, which is what we really want.

We can conquer doubt just by meditating on the soul or thinking always of the soul. The soul is infinitely more powerful than our mental doubt. We can and we should take the positive side. We come from the soul, inside us is the soul, we are the soul, we are for the soul. Always we can try to identify our physical being, our physical consciousness, with the soul which is all light and delight. When we feel that at every moment we are growing into the soul's light and delight then doubt can easily be transformed into divine confidence. At that time we will say, "I am God's son. If I cannot do it, who can do it? I can and I shall realise God. I can and I must manifest God." We can cherish that kind of divine awareness — that oneness with God each of us can and will establish. Then doubt is bound to leave us.

199. Question: How can I make my inner cry more sincere?

Sri Chinmoy: You can make your inner cry more sincere by feeling at every second that you are helpless, absolutely helpless and hopeless without God. With God, with God's Love, Concern and Guidance, you become omnipotent, but without God you are impotent. When you feel that kind of helpless feeling, then your inner cry will come to the fore spontaneously. When you feel that you are helpless without God, your inner cry comes to the fore with utmost sincerity. Why do you cry? You cry because you feel that you do not have something which you badly need. You cry for your conscious oneness with Infinity, Eternity and Immortality. These three divine blessings are your own, only you have to rediscover them. They are your own inner wealth which you have lost or misplaced. But you have every right to search for them and cry to the Supreme for them. In order to have that inner cry, always try to feel that you are absolutely helpless. When you feel helpless, automatically your aspiration grows. When you feel helpless, you will feel that the right thing is to pray and meditate. You will not try to make yourself miserable and helpless so that you can have a good meditation, but when pride or jealousy or lethargy or lack of aspiration come, cry inwardly to regain your own inner treasure. You have every right to cry for your own lost treasure.

200. Question: Sometimes during my meditation something shows me some imperfection in my human nature. Some event that occurred portrays this imperfection and I have this in my mind during my meditation. I am confused about what to do with it then. Should I hold it and destroy it or push it aside and try to concentrate on something divine?

Sri Chinmoy: When your mind brings to the fore some imperfection in your nature, in your outer life, immediately try to throw that imperfection into the universal Consciousness. Do not try to fight it, do not try to exercise your will-power and destroy it. Just throw it into the infinite ocean of consciousness from where you will not be able to get it back. But do not try to fight it during your meditation. You can't do two things properly at the same time. If you have to fight against something during your meditation, it will not be possible for you to maintain your highest meditation at the same time. Just empty yourself. Once you empty yourself, it becomes the duty of the Supreme to fill you with light and perfection.

201. Question: What is the best way to keep a spiritual consciousness during the day?

Sri Chinmoy: When you pray and meditate, try to feel that you have gained something real: light, bliss, peace, power. When you earn money, you can keep it in your pocket and use it whenever you want to. Similarly, when you meditate in the morning, you have to feel that you have gained some inner wealth, and this wealth you have to keep inside your heart. Then while you are mixing with your friends, working in the office or studying in the school, when you are thrown into multifarious activities, you can use this inner wealth whenever you need it. Just meditate for a minute and enter into the heart where you have kept your inner wealth safe. Then you can distribute it wherever you feel the need. In the morning you save your money, because you know you will need it later on during the day.

Part XLV — Questions and answers — University of Honolulu

202. Question: What is aspiration?

Sri Chinmoy: Aspiration is our inner cry. Deep within all of us we have this aspiration, this mounting inner cry. We start our journey with aspiration. In the beginning when we aspire, deep within us we feel that we have to realise God. When we realise God, we have to feel the necessity of revealing God to mankind. This again is aspiration, on a higher level. There is no end to our aspiration. After we have revealed God we have to manifest God. This is the third step. Manifestation is the flowering of real aspiration. But there is no end to our manifestation, just as there is no end to our realisation and no end to our revelation. Each realisation of today is tomorrow's starting point, tomorrow's new dawn. Today's realisation is the stepping-stone for the higher realisation of tomorrow.

To come back to your question, aspiration is the inner flame that is burning constantly, rising towards the highest ultimate Goal. It has no end. Constantly it is illumining our consciousness and the people who are around us. It is illumining within and without. And in the process of this illumination, we see that today we will realise God, tomorrow we will try to reveal God and the day after tomorrow we will try to manifest God. But there is no end to our realisation, revelation and manifestation, precisely because aspiration itself is an eternal inner flame.

203. Question: What is the difference between desire and aspiration?

Sri Chinmoy: Aspiration is our inner cry. The outer cry is the cry for name, fame, power and material prosperity. This is called desire. When we cry for peace, light, bliss and other divine things, this is aspiration. When we do not care for things that bind us, we have aspiration. With desire we try to bind others, but soon we discover that we ourselves are already bound. This is what desire does. When we aspire, we come to realise that we have to free ourselves and we have to free others. The more we free ourselves from the meshes of ignorance, the clearer becomes our vision. We feel that it is only through the expansion of our consciousness that we can have abiding peace within us. Aspiration is the inner cry that carries us to the Highest and also offers the message of total divine fulfilment here on earth. Aspiration deals with Eternity, Infinity and Immortality, whereas desire deals with a dollar, a house, a car or some other worldly thing. Aspiration deals with infinite Peace, Light and Bliss. Unless and until we have achieved this Peace, Light and Bliss we shall not be satisfied, no matter what we get from the material world. For everlasting Peace, Bliss and the sense of fulfilment, the thing that we need, the thing that is of paramount importance in our life, is aspiration, the inner flame which each of us has.

204. Question: Is there a difference between prayer and meditation?

Sri Chinmoy: Yes, there is a difference between prayer and meditation, although we can get the same result from both. With prayer we can realise God, and with meditation we can realise God. Usually when we pray, we say, "O God, give me this or give me that," and we always feel that God is listening to our prayer. But when we meditate, we feel that God is talking and we are listening. When we pray, God becomes the listener; when we meditate, we become the listener. When we meditate, God is talking to us, communing with us, and we are listening to Him. We are obeying whatever message He is bringing to us in our meditation.

When we pray, we try to raise our consciousness to the Highest. One-pointedly we try to go up. At that time we don't look forward, backward or sideways. Our intention is only to go up. When we meditate, however, we cover the length and breadth of the world with our consciousness. At that time we are like a bird spreading its wings and flying in the sky. When we meditate, we spread our widened and widening consciousness and reach the Highest. But prayer is not like that. It is one-pointed, like an arrow going up. There is one-pointed attention in our prayer, whereas when we spread our wings in deep meditation, we are entering into the reality with a broad heart.

Fulfilment has to take place not only in the individual but also in the collectivity. Very often we pray for our own salvation. But when we meditate, we do not do that. When we meditate, our consciousness is widened. Unconsciously or consciously we try to home the entire world deep within our meditation. Then, when we reach the Highest, we feel that we have carried the entire world along with us. Our meditation is like an ocean liner that can accommodate many people. But we can also go to the Goal in a tiny boat with our prayer. With prayer most of the time we see that only the individual can go one-pointedly to his destination. With meditation the collectivity can go. Prayer basically involves "me" and "mine". But when we meditate, our consciousness is expanded and it embraces the entire world.

205. Question: Does illumination come all at once?

Sri Chinmoy: No, illumination does not come all at once. It is a series of experiences. When we get the fullest, the highest illumination, at that time we feel, "This is the hour." But illumination is actually like a muscle which we develop. We cannot develop very strong muscles overnight. We have to exercise for a few months or a few years before we develop very powerful muscles. In Buddha's case, he meditated under the Bodhi Tree for six months. Before that he had meditated in various other places. There are many spiritual Masters who say that on one particular day they got realisation. But it did not happen all at once. There was long preparation behind it. They meditated for fifteen or twenty years.

On a specific day you get a diploma, but before that you study for twenty years. Every year adds to your higher illumination, higher knowledge. In the case of Buddha, he had meditated for many, many years in previous incarnations before he realised the highest Truth. It was a long preparation. Nobody gets illumination all at once. Illumination is the development of inner will, of inner consciousness. We can say that in the outer life it is a series of experiences. First we get an iota of light, and gradually it increases until we have abundant light. Then we enter into boundless Light, infinite Light. This is how illumination or realisation gradually takes place.

206. Question: I am having telepathic experiences with people who call themselves magicians. I talk with them while they are in other places. I can enter this realm at will. I'm curious about how you would respond to these experiences?

Sri Chinmoy: From the highest spiritual point of view I wish to answer your question. Will these experiences help you go faster towards your goal? No, they will not. These experiences are fascinating, undoubtedly, but they will never take you to reality. On the contrary, they are temptations on your way to God-realisation, the highest Truth. In our spiritual life very often we get fascinating experiences and then we don't want to aspire any more. It is true that experiences can give us encouragement, but very often when we get too many experiences we enter into the vital world. We see a kaleidoscope; we see all kinds of beautiful things, but these things are only temptations. Suppose you are walking along a street towards your goal. If you see beautiful trees, ponds and flowers alongside the street, what happens? The scenery is so beautiful that you take a rest. You say, "Let me stay here and enjoy this," and then you stop and enjoy it. But your destination remains a far cry.

A sincere seeker knows what his goal is: the highest Truth. He will not delay his journey. But in your case I can see that you enjoy these experiences; you give them your conscious attention. This is very wrong. In the spiritual life we aspire for the highest Truth, for God, and for nothing else. These experiences are real temptations for you. You should feel, "Once I realise God I will have infinitely more beautiful, meaningful and fruitful experiences." With that idea you have to cast these telepathic experiences aside. If you feel that by entering into these experiences or allowing them to enter into you, by cherishing them, you will get higher experiences, you are mistaken.

You will not go any farther. If you dwell on them all the time, if you are constantly fascinated by them and feel that you are part of them, you will be caught by them. Many people have made this mistake, and for them God-realisation has remained a far cry.

Sincere seekers take these experiences as obstructions on their way. Please pay no attention to these kinds of experiences. They are fascinating, but they are not fulfilling in your life of dedication, realisation and manifestation. Early in the morning try to silence your mind. If you can silence your mind, you will not have these experiences. They are coming to you from the vital world. You are cherishing these creations of the vital world and trying to possess them as your very own. But they cannot take you to the highest Goal. If your aim is the Highest, then these things have to be consciously discarded. I wish you to go to someone who will inspire you to enter into the realm of pure aspiration. Then you will be able to bring to the fore your soul's light and run the fastest towards the highest Goal.

207. Question: Can mantra meditation take you all the way to the Goal?

Sri Chinmoy: Certainly a mantra can take you to the Goal. A mantra has power. The mantric power can easily take one to the Highest, as prayer and meditation do. Chanting a mantra is also a form of approaching God. It has its own efficacy and its own approach towards the Highest. There are many people who have realised God only by repeating a mantra. Many, many Indians have realised God by repeating the mother of all mantras, the *Gayatri Mantra:*

*Aum bhūr bhuvaḥ svaḥ
Tat savitur vareṇyam
Bhargo devasya dhīmahi
Dhiyo yo naḥ pracodayāt.*

Other mantras are also quite helpful, but if you can chant this one every day most soulfully, it will definitely take you to the Highest. It is for the highest illumination that seekers chant this mantra.

If a spiritual Master gives you a specific mantra, he will offer his own spiritual power inside that mantra. If you repeat the mantra soulfully, you are bound to get fulfilling experiences, and eventually you will be able to realise God. But if you practise a mantra, it should come directly from a spiritual Master who is a God-realised soul. He has to give it to you personally. There cannot be a third person involved. If someone in India tells one of his unrealised disciples, "Since you are representing me in America, you can give mantras," then the mantra you get from that person will never, never illumine you. An ordinary person who has merely studied the scriptures will not be able to offer you illumination through a mantra. If a spiritual Master, a realised soul, gives you a mantra, then only will the mantra offer you measureless power.

208. Question: Practically speaking, how does one go about learning how to meditate?

Sri Chinmoy: To begin with, if one does not have a teacher or does not care for a teacher, one has to read a few spiritual books written by spiritual Masters who have realised God, not by professors and scholars. If you read books written by real spiritual Masters, you will get inspiration. When you read the books written by various Masters, their writings will be surcharged with their divine consciousness and light. That consciousness will enter into you and inspire you. But there will come a time when you will feel the necessity of learning directly from someone who already knows how to meditate. At that time you will have to take help from a spiritual guide.

If you want to aspire intensely and meditate regularly, you need more inspiration and more aspiration. This has to come from a spiritual Master in whom you have implicit faith. His very presence will give you abundant inspiration and aspiration. You can speak to him or, if he has accepted you on his path, then inwardly and silently he can teach you how to meditate. He himself will meditate on you. If he meditates on you for a minute or two daily, then he will offer you the capacity to meditate for half an hour or an hour a day. It is the Master who increases the power of meditation and aspiration in the seeker.

But to start off in the field of meditation, I advise you to read books. When you feel that you don't get enough inspiration from the books, although they are written by spiritual Masters, you should go to seekers who have already found some spiritual path. Their presence we call satsang — the companionship of a sincere seeker. If you are with them, if you talk with them, mix with them, then from their inspiration and aspiration you will get your own inner strength to meditate. Eventually, when you get your own Master, you will see how fast you will be able to progress.

209. Question: Is it necessary to have a Guru or can you reach enlightenment on your own?

Sri Chinmoy: One can reach enlightenment on the strength of his own aspiration. We know that the first person who realised God did not have a human Guru. But again, we know that there is something called speed. If one gets help from a qualified person, then he can make the fastest progress. Why do you attend this university? So many people are studying here. They could have studied at home instead. But they knew that they could not make the fastest progress by themselves, so they came here to study. Books are available for the students to read, but they also need a teacher who will be able to show them how to study the field they have chosen and how to interpret the meaning of what they learn. In this way they learn their lessons faster.

For everything we need a teacher. The mother is the first teacher. She teaches the child the alphabet for a few months. Then he has a kindergarten teacher, primary and high school teachers and college and university professors. Then this human study, earthly study, ends, and he himself becomes a teacher. But the mother played her role for a few months. She taught him the alphabet. If I want to learn how to sing, I need a teacher. If I want to learn how to sprint, I need a teacher. If I want to do anything on earth, I need a teacher to show me the best possible way. Then how is it that I do not want or need a teacher in the spiritual life? Spirituality is also a kind of knowledge. You will say, "God is within us. Why have we to take any help from anybody?" But I will say, "God is in this book also. Why do we ask a teacher to explain the book?" God is in everything, but we know that there is always someone who is more advanced in a particular subject than we are. A professor of English has more knowledge than a student. In the spiritual life also, a God-realised man, a spiritual Master, has much more God-Knowledge than a seeker. But when a seeker realises God, he is like a student who has received his Master's degree. He no longer needs a teacher.

We have to know how fast we want to go. In the spiritual life we can stumble, we can walk or we can run the fastest. When we have a Master, we can run the fastest because he offers us his own inner strength, his protection, his concern, his compassion and God's Light. He offers, and the disciple receives from him. A Guru is not indispensable, but again, one can be wise in this matter. If one can reach the Goal much faster by taking help from someone on the way, what is wrong with that? America is the land of speed. Everything here is faster than the fastest. If you want to realise God as fast as possible, then take the help of someone. After you have reached your Goal, you no longer need to take his help. I came to San Francisco from New York by jet. The jet pilot was my guide. As soon as I landed here, I no longer needed the jet or the pilot; I had reached my destination. In the spiritual life also, when you reach your destination you don't need anyone. But while you are travelling you have to know how fast you want to go. I could have come to San Francisco from New York by some other means, but it would have taken me a longer time. The seeker has to know whether he prefers to travel at the speed of a bullock cart or at the speed of a jet plane. If one wants to realise God on his own, he will proceed at the speed of a bullock cart; but if one wants to realise God with the help of a Master, he will complete his journey at jet speed.

210. Question: What is the greatest stumbling block for most seekers and how can it be overcome?

Sri Chinmoy: In the spiritual life there are quite a few obstacles: fear, anxiety, impurity, jealousy and the feeling of unworthiness, but the greatest obstacle is doubt. In comparison with doubt, all other obstacles pale into insignificance. We doubt the existence of God or we doubt ourselves. We may say, "Oh, I have prayed and meditated for so many years. If God existed, if there really were a God, by this time He would have come and stood in front of me." When we feel that it is high time for us to realise God, but still God-realisation does not dawn, we immediately say, "No, there is no such thing as God." We doubt God. Or we may feel that we don't have the capacity to realise God. We say to ourselves, "I have done so many things wrong in my life. Why should God come to me?" If we do not pray or cannot pray, we simply say, "It is impossible for me to realise God, so let me give up all hope." This is our self-doubt. But if we have wisdom, we will say, "There are others who have realised God. If they have realised God, how is it that I have not realised God? They eat and breathe just the same as I do. They do practically all the same things that I do. They also have two eyes and one nose and two arms. If they have realised God, how is it that I cannot realise God?" By saying this we can conquer our self-doubt. Doubting is like taking slow poison daily. Today we doubt God, tomorrow we will doubt ourselves, the day after tomorrow we will doubt the existence of everything. Then we will not be able to do anything. We need faith in ourselves and in God. In faith we build ourselves, and in doubt we destroy ourselves. God is all faith. God is all joy. When we meditate on God, we challenge doubt; and in the sea of peace and self-assurance, our doubt dissolves.

NOTES TO FIFTY FREEDOM-BOATS TO ONE GOLDEN SHORE, BOOK 6

185. North Dakota State University, Fargo, North Dakota, 25 October 1974 — 1:00 pm.
186. Northern State College, Aberdeen, South Dakota, 25 October 1974 — 8:30 pm.
187. University of Minnesota, Minneapolis, Minnesota, 26 October 1974.
188. University of Honolulu, Honolulu, Hawaii, 28 October 1974 — 7:00 pm.
189. Alaska Methodist University, Anchorage, Alaska, 29 October 1974 — 7:00 pm.
190-195. Northern State College, Aberdeen, South Dakota, 2 5 October 1974 — 8:30 pm.
196-201. University of Minnesota, Minneapolis, Minnesota, 26 October 1974.
202-210. University of Honolulu, Honolulu, Hawaii, 28 October 1974 — 7:00 pm.

APPENDIX

FOREWORDS TO FIRST EDITIONS

Foreword to first edition of My Rose Petals, part 1

Sri Chinmoy's European tour began on 8 November 1970. Twenty-six days later he returned to the United States, having delivered sixteen lectures and establishing Sri Chinmoy Centres in London, Glasgow, Scotland and Dublin, Ireland. All but one of those lectures are printed in this volume.

Foreword to first edition of My Rose Petals, part 3

This book is a collection of the first ten university lectures Sri Chinmoy delivered during his third European lecture tour in the summer of 1974. The remaining eleven talks of that tour will make up the fourth volume in this series. The Master's earlier European lectures are collected in *My Rose Petals* (part 1: 1970 talks and part 2: 1973 talks).

Foreword to first edition of My Rose Petals, part 4

This book is a collection of the last eleven university lectures Sri Chinmoy delivered during his third European lecture tour in the summer of 1974. The first ten talks of that tour make up the third volume in this series. The Master's earlier European lectures are collected in *My Rose Petals* (part 1: 1970 talks, part 2: 1973 talks and part 3: 1974 talks).

Foreword to first edition of My Rose Petals, parts 5-7

During the summer of 1976, Sri Chinmoy embarked on his fourth European lecture tour. The talks that he delivered, and his answers to selected questions, have been collected into a three-part series, *My Rose Petals*, parts 5-7.

Lectures from Sri Chinmoy's earlier European tours have been published in *My Rose Petals*, parts 1-4.

Fifty Freedom-Boats to one Golden Shore

Foreword to first edition of Fifty Freedom-Boats to one Golden Shore, part 1

The ten lectures in this book are part of a fifty-state lecture tour Sri Chinmoy was invited to give in 1974. The talks in this first series were delivered in January of 1974. The questions in this book were put to Sri Chinmoy by students at the universities where he spoke.

Foreword to first edition of Fifty Freedom-Boats to one Golden Shore, part 2

The ten lectures in this book are part of a fifty-state lecture tour Sri Chinmoy was invited to give in 1974. The talks in this second series were delivered in January and February of 1974. The questions in this book were put to Sri Chinmoy by students at the universities where he spoke.

Foreword to first edition of Fifty Freedom-Boats to one Golden Shore, part 3

The ten lectures in this book are part of a fifty-state lecture tour Sri Chinmoy was invited to give in 1974. The talks in this third series were delivered in February and March of 1974. The questions in this book were put to Sri Chinmoy by students at the universities where he spoke.

Foreword to first edition of Fifty Freedom-Boats to one Golden Shore, part 4

The ten lectures in this book are part of a fifty-state lecture tour Sri Chinmoy was invited to give in 1974. The talks in this fourth series were delivered in March and April of 1974. The questions in this book were put to Sri Chinmoy by students at the universities where he spoke.

Foreword to first edition of Fifty Freedom-Boats to one Golden Shore, part 5

The five lectures in this book are part of a fifty-state lecture tour Sri Chinmoy was invited to give in 1974. The talks in this fifth series were delivered on 23 and 24 April, and 30 September 1974. The questions in this book were put to Sri Chinmoy by students at the universities where he spoke.

Foreword to first edition of Fifty Freedom-Boats to one Golden Shore, part 6

The five lectures in this book are part of a fifty-state lecture tour Sri Chinmoy was invited to give in 1974. The talks in this sixth series were delivered between 25 and 29 October 1974. The questions in this book were put to Sri Chinmoy by students at the universities where he spoke.

BIBLIOGRAPHY

SRI CHINMOY:

My Rose Petals

- My Rose Petals, part 1, New York, Agni Press, 1971
- My Rose Petals, part 2, New York, Agni Press, 1974
- My Rose Petals, part 3, New York, Agni Press, 1974
- My Rose Petals, part 4, New York, Agni Press, 1974
- My Rose Petals, part 5, New York, Agni Press, 1976
- My Rose Petals, part 6, New York, Agni Press, 1976
- My Rose Petals, part 7, New York, Agni Press, 1976

[Suggested cite-key: MRP]

Fifty Freedom-Boats to one Golden Shore

- Fifty Freedom-Boats to one Golden Shore, part 1, New York, Agni Press, 1974
- Fifty Freedom-Boats to one Golden Shore, part 2, New York, Agni Press, 1974
- Fifty Freedom-Boats to one Golden Shore, part 3, New York, Agni Press, 1974
- Fifty Freedom-Boats to one Golden Shore, part 4, New York, Agni Press, 1974
- Fifty Freedom-Boats to one Golden Shore, part 5, New York, Agni Press, 1975
- Fifty Freedom-Boats to one Golden Shore, part 6, New York, Agni Press, 1975

[Suggested cite-key: FFB]

POSTFACE

Publishing principles

This edition of The works of Sri Chinmoy aims to obey the Author's wish: scrupulous fidelity to his original words, use of typographical style by him selected, specific spelling choices, end placement of any editorial content (i.e. not written by Sri Chinmoy himself), particular treatment of some personal nouns in special cases, etc.

Textual accuracy

The series has been checked to ensure faithful accuracy to the originals. Although much effort has been put in proofreading and comparing different versions of the text, this print may still present lingering errors. The publisher would be grateful to be apprised of any mistypes, possibly with a scan of the original page where the text is different. Please use original books only, specifying the year of publication.

Ongoing reprints will include any revised text from these errata.

Acknowledgements

The Publisher is very grateful to the late Professor Lambert and his équipe for his invaluable advice. For many decades Prof. Lambert conducted a small publishing house specialising in hand-made prints of philological edition of the classics. The standard of this edition would not have been the same without his scholarly advice.

The Publisher is also grateful to the international team of collaborators that spent countless hours proofreading and checking the current text against the originals.

Our deepest gratitude to Sri Chinmoy. His living presence can be felt breathing throughout his writings. It is a privilege to be involved with his works, in any form.

Sri Chinmoy Canon

We could not use better words than Professor Lambert's, who kindly offered the name Sri Chinmoy Canon:

> «By defining Sri Chinmoy's first editions as editio princeps we chose to follow classical scholarship criteria, not because we consider Sri Chinmoy's work antique, but because we believe it is among the few post ‹classical antiquity› works to rightly deserve to be considered a classicus, designating by that term superiority, authority and perfection.»

> «The monumental work Sri Chinmoy is offering to mankind is awe-inspiring and supremely pre-eminent in proportions and quality. It is manifest that Sri Chinmoy's work — which we feel right to call The Sri Chinmoy Canon — will be of profound help and source of enlightenment to anyone seeking a higher wisdom, truth and reality supreme.»

[Translated from French by M. G.S.]

TABLE OF CONTENTS

PART 1 - MY ROSE PETALS	13
PART 2 - FIFTY FREEDOM-BOATS TO ONE GOLDEN SHORE	365
APPENDIX	728
FOREWORDS TO FIRST EDITIONS	731
BIBLIOGRAPHY	737
POSTFACE	741
TABLE OF CONTENTS	743

www.ingramcontent.com/pod-product-compliance
Lightning Source LLC
Chambersburg PA
CBHW030110240426
43661CB00031B/1354/J